microeconomics

thirteenth canadian edition

Campbell R. McConnell
University of Nebraska—Emeritus

Stanley L. Brue
Pacific Lutheran University

Sean M. Flynn
Scripps College

Thomas P. Barbiero
Ryerson University

McGraw-Hill Ryerson
Connect. Learn. Succeed.

The McGraw·Hill Companies

McGraw-Hill Ryerson
Connect. Learn. Succeed.

Microeconomics
Thirteenth Canadian Edition

ISBN-13: 978-0-07-105201-6
ISBN-10: 0-07-105201-1

1 2 3 4 5 6 7 8 9 10   DOW   1 9 8 7 6 5 4 3

Printed and bound in the United States of America.

EDITORIAL DIRECTOR: Rhondda McNabb
SENIOR SPONSORING EDITOR: James Booty
MARKETING MANAGER: Jeremy Guimond
DEVELOPMENTAL EDITOR: Daphne Scriabin
SENIOR EDITORIAL ASSOCIATE: Stephanie Giles
SUPERVISING EDITOR: Stephanie Gay
PHOTO/PERMISSIONS RESEARCH: Alison Lloyd Baker
COPY EDITOR: Laurel Sparrow/ Kimberleigh Sparrow
PROOFREADER: Judy Sturrup
PRODUCTION COORDINATOR: Lena Keating
COVER DESIGN: Valid Design and Layout / Dave Murphy
COVER IMAGE: © Adam Gault/Getty Images
INTERIOR DESIGN: Valid Design and Layout / Dave Murphy
PAGE LAYOUT: Aptara®, Inc.
PRINTER: R.R. Donnelly / Willard

Library and Archives Canada Cataloguing in Publication

Microeconomics / Campbell R. McConnell ... [et al.]. — 13th Cdn. ed.
    Includes index.

ISBN 978-0-07-105201-6

    1. Microeconomics—Textbooks.   I. McConnell, Campbell R.

HB172.M115 2013   338.5   C2012-905759-2

Dedication

To Elsa, Marta, Emilia, Robert, and past instructors.

About the Authors

Campbell R. McConnell earned his Ph.D. from the University of Iowa after receiving degrees from Cornell College and the University of Illinois. He taught at the University of Nebraska–Lincoln from 1953 until his retirement in 1990. He is also coauthor of *Contemporary Labor Economics,* ninth edition; *Essentials of Economics,* second edition; *Macroeconomics: Brief Edition;* and *Microeconomics: Brief Edition* (all The McGraw-Hill Companies), and has edited readers for principles and labour economics courses. He is a recipient of both the University of Nebraska Distinguished Teaching Award and the James A. Lake Academic Freedom Award and is past president of the Midwest Economics Association. Professor McConnell was awarded an honorary Doctor of Laws degree from Cornell College in 1973 and received its Distinguished Achievement Award in 1994. His primary areas of interest are labour economics and economic education. He has an extensive collection of jazz recordings and enjoys reading jazz history.

Stanley L. Brue carried out his undergraduate work at Augustana College (South Dakota) and received its Distinguished Achievement Award in 1991. He received his Ph.D. from the University of Nebraska–Lincoln. He is retired from a long career at Pacific Lutheran University, where he was honoured as a recipient of the Burlington Northern Faculty Achievement Award. Professor Brue has also received the national Leavey Award for excellence in economic education. He has served as national president and chair of the Board of Trustees of Omicron Delta Epsilon International Economics Honorary. He is coauthor of *Economic Scenes,* fifth edition (Prentice-Hall); *Contemporary Labor Economics,* ninth edition; *Essentials of Economics,* second edition; *Macroeconomics: Brief Edition; Microeconomics: Brief Edition* (all The McGraw-Hill Companies); and *The Evolution of Economic Thought,* seventh edition (South-Western). For relaxation, he enjoys international travel, attending sporting events, and skiing with family and friends.

Sean M. Flynn carried out his undergraduate work at the University of Southern California before completing his Ph.D. at U.C. Berkeley, where he served as the Head Graduate Student Instructor for the Department of Economics after receiving the Outstanding Graduate Student Instructor Award. He teaches at Scripps College (of the Claremont Colleges) and is the author of *Economics for Dummies* (Wiley) and coauthor of *Essentials of Economics,* second edition; *Macroeconomics: Brief Edition;* and *Microeconomics: Brief Edition* (all The McGraw-Hill Companies). His research interests include finance and behavioural economics. An accomplished martial artist, he has represented the United States in international aikido tournaments and is the author of *Understanding Shodokan Aikido* (Shodokan Press). Other hobbies include running, travelling, and enjoying ethnic food.

Thomas P. Barbiero received his Ph.D. from the University of Toronto after completing undergraduate studies at the same university. He is a professor in the Department of Economics at Ryerson University in Toronto. His research interests include the economic history of Canada and modern Italy, and international institutions. He is an avid traveller whose father's family immigrated to Canada in the mid-20th century while his mother's family immigrated to Argentina. In a recent visit to Buenos Aires, Professor Barbiero met his first cousins in a family get-together that brought home to him the importance of economic growth. He spends his summers in Fontanarosa, a small town in his native region of Campania in southern Italy. It is situated in the vineyards of the Taurasi wine growing region, where he indulges in his favourite pastime: consuming good food and wine.

Brief Contents

Web Site Bonus Chapters available on Connect

Contents

Contents

Preface

Welcome to the thirteenth Canadian edition of *Microeconomics*. Thousands of Canadian students have studied economics from the Canadian editions of *Microeconomics* and *Macroeconomics*, and an estimated 14 million students worldwide have now used a version of the McConnell textbooks, making them the world's best-selling economic principles textbooks.

A Note about the Cover

We chose the cover for the thirteenth edition to reference the current debt crisis.

Fundamental Objectives

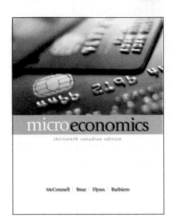

We have three main goals for *Microeconomics*:

- To help the beginning student master the principles essential for understanding economic problems, specific economic issues, and the policy alternatives.

- To help the student understand and apply the economic perspective, and reason accurately and objectively about economic matters.

- To promote a lasting student interest in economics and the economy.

What's New and Improved?

One of the benefits of writing a successful text is the opportunity to revise—to delete outdated content and disseminate up-to-date information, to clarify ambiguous statements, to introduce relevant and interesting illustrations, to improve the organizational structure, and to enhance the learning aids. The more significant changes include the following:

Restructured Introductory Chapters

The five-chapter grouping of introductory chapters contains Part 1 (An Introduction to Economics and the Economy), consisting of Chapter 1 (Limits, Alternatives, and Choices) and Chapter 2 (The Market System and the Circular Flow), and Part 2 (Price, Quantity, and Efficiency) which includes Chapter 3 (Demand, Supply, and Market Equilibrium), Chapter 4 (Elasticity), and Chapter 5 (Market Failures: Public Goods and Externalities).

Chapters 4 and 5 are much more concept oriented and analytical than general and descriptive as in the previous edition. Chapter 5 is new to this edition. Our new approach responds to suggestions by reviewers made over the years to locate the elasticity chapter immediately after the supply and demand chapter, and boost the analysis of market failures (public goods and externalities) in the introductory sections to complement and balance the strong but highly stylized introduction to the market system discussed in Chapter 2. Our new approach embraces these suggestions. The new ordering provides a clear supply-and-demand path to the chapters on consumer and producer behaviour.

New "Consider This" and "Last Word" Pieces

Our "Consider This" boxes are used to provide analogies, examples, or stories that help drive home central economic ideas in a student-oriented, real-world manner. For instance, how businesses exploit price discrimination is driven home in a "Consider This" box that explains why ballparks charge different admission prices for adults and children but only one set of prices at their concession stands. These brief vignettes, each accompanied by a photo, illustrate key points

in a lively, colourful, and easy-to-remember way. We have added four new "Consider This" boxes in this edition.

Our "Last Word" pieces are lengthier applications or case studies that are placed near the end of each chapter. For example, the "Last Word" section for Chapter 1 (Limits, Alternatives, and Choices) examines pitfalls to sound economic reasoning, while the "Last Word" section for Chapter 5 (Market Failures: Public Goods and Externalities) examines cap-and-trade versus carbon taxes as policy responses to excessive carbon dioxide emissions. There are four new "Last Word" sections in this edition.

If you are unfamiliar with *Microeconomics*, we encourage you to thumb through the chapters to take a quick look at these highly visible features.

New Content on Behavioural Economics

We have added new material covering the consumer-choice aspects of behavioural economics to the end of our chapter on consumer choice (Chapter 6). The new material on behavioural economics covers prospect theory, framing effects, loss aversion, anchoring effects, mental accounting, and the endowment effect. The behavioural economics theory and examples are tightly focused on consumer-choice applications so as to flow smoothly from, and build upon, the standard utility maximization theory and applications developed earlier in the chapter. The new material is intentionally at the end of the chapter, not only to show that behavioural economics extends standard theory (rather than replacing or refuting it) but also so that the new material is modular and thus can be skipped by instructors without loss of continuity. A new "Consider This" box on the "hedonic treadmill" and a new "Last Word" section on "nudges" bolster our overall coverage of behavioural economics.

Divided Perfect Competition Chapter

We have divided the very long perfect competition chapter (Chapter 7 of the twelfth Canadian edition) into two logically distinct chapters, one on perfect competition in the short run (Chapter 8) and the other on perfect competition in the long run (Chapter 9). These more "bite-sized" chapters should improve student retention of the material. Students will first master the logic behind the MC = MR rule for setting output as well as the short-run shutdown condition. Students will then be able to pause to test their understanding of this content through end-of-chapter questions and problems and other supporting materials before moving on to the next chapter's coverage of perfect competition in the long run. We have also used background highlights on equilibrium numbers in the tables to enable students to move back and forth more easily from references in the body to equilibrium numbers in the tables.

Reworked End-of-Chapter Questions and Problems

We have extensively reworked the end-of-chapter Study Questions, splitting them into Questions and Problems and adding many new Problems. The Questions are analytical and often ask for free responses, whereas the Problems are mainly quantitative. We have aligned the Questions and Problems with the Learning Objectives presented at the beginning of the chapters. All of the Questions and Problems are assignable through McGraw-Hill's Connect Economics; all of the Problems also contain additional algorithmic variations and can be automatically graded within the system. The new lists of Questions and Problems were very well received by reviewers, many of whom are long-time users of the book.

Chapter-by-Chapter Changes

Each chapter *of Microeconomics,* thirteenth Canadian edition, contains updated data reflecting the current economy, streamlined Learning Objectives, and reorganized end-of-chapter content. In addition to these changes, each chapter contains the following updates:

Chapter 1: Limits, Alternatives, and Choices features a new Learning Objective on consumption possibilities and a revised definition of "entrepreneur" that clarifies why risk taking is socially beneficial and, thus, why entrepreneurial ability is a valuable economic resource.

Chapter 2: The Market System and the Circular Flow features a revised explanation of property rights, a clarified discussion of firms' motives for choosing the lowest-cost production methods, and a revised discussion of the circular flow model.

Chapter 3: Demand, Supply, and Market Equilibrium features streamlined discussions that clarify the main concepts.

Chapter 4: Elasticity is a new chapter that focuses solely on elasticity. The material on consumer and producer surplus has been moved to Chapter 5.

Chapter 5: Market Failures: Public Goods and Externalities is a new chapter that includes the following topics: consumer and producer surplus from Chapter 4, twelfth Canadian edition; public goods and externalities from Chapter 16, twelfth Canadian edition; and the government's role in the economy. The chapter also features a new "Last Word" section that discusses the pros and cons of cap-and-trade emissions-control policies, a revised discussion of market failures related to public goods and externalities, and a new "Consider This" box that condenses the material on the Coase Theorem.

Chapter 6: Consumer Choice and Utility Maximization features additional coverage and discussion on the consumer-choice aspects of behavioural economics, including prospect theory, framing effects, loss aversion, anchoring effects, mental accounting, and the endowment effect; a new "Consider This" box that discusses the hedonic treadmill; and a new "Last Word" section discussing the ways in which governments and firms may utilize the insights of behavioural economics to encourage better outcomes.

Chapter 7: The Firm and the Costs of Production features a revised section on economic costs, explicit costs, implicit costs, accounting profit, normal profit, and economic profit; a new section on the rising price of gasoline that replaces the previous section on the doubling of the price of corn; and a rewritten example on daily newspapers.

Chapter 8: Perfect Competition in the Short Run is a new chapter that contains information on perfect competition in the short run from Chapter 7 of the twelfth Canadian edition. This chapter features revised table and figure pairs that improve pedagogy and a new "Last Word" on the short-run shutdown condition.

Chapter 9: Perfect Competition in the Long Run is a new chapter that contains information on perfect competition in the long run from Chapter 7 of the twelfth Canadian edition. This chapter features a new overview introductory section, a new figure clarifying the discussion of decreasing-cost industries, and a revised discussion of why long-run equilibrium in perfect competition yields allocative efficiency.

Chapter 10: Monopoly features a revised discussion of rate regulation for a natural monopoly and a streamlined section on the income transfers of monopoly.

Chapter 11: Monopolistic Competition and Oligopoly features a revised Figure 11.2 with labels at key points, and an updated discussion of OPEC emphasizing its difficulty with its members over whether they will obey their quotas or not.

Chapter 12: Competition Policy and Regulation features an expanded discussion emphasizing that monopoly pricing transfers surplus from consumers to producers.

Chapter 13: The Demand for Factors of Production features improved discussions to clarify the main concepts.

Chapter 14: Wage Determination features a clarified introduction of monopsony.

Chapter 15: Rent, Interest, and Profit features a new section on the interest rate on money loans; an expanded explanation of the differences between insurable and non-insurable risks; an additional source of non-insurable risk (new products or production methods pioneered by rivals); and a new "Consider This" piece on Steve Jobs as an entrepreneur.

Chapter 16: Natural Resource and Energy Economics features a new "Consider This" piece that deals with the high risk associated with commercializing alternative fuel sources.

Chapter 17: Asymmetric Information and Public Choice Theory adds new material to topics that were located in several other chapters in the twelfth Canadian edition, including: asymmetric information from Chapter 16, government failures and voting inefficiencies and paradoxes from Chapter 17, and the principal–agent problem from Chapter 4. This chapter features a section on insurance and health care, a new discussion of political corruption, a new "Global Perspective" piece comparing bribery in various countries, and a new Last Word on Singapore's health care system.

Integrated Text and Website

connect
WORKED PROBLEM 12.1
Single Bank Accounting

We continue to integrate the book and our website by including icons in the text margin that direct readers to additional content. **Worked Problems** are now available at on Connect and provide students with a step-by-step illustration of how to solve a problem. These pieces consist of side-by-side computational questions and the computational procedures used to derive the answers. In essence, they extend the textbook's explanations involving computations—for example, of real GDP, real GDP per capita, the unemployment rate, the inflation rate, per-unit production costs, and more. At relevant points in the text, the worked problem icon directs the student to the website for additional support.

connect
MATH 1.1
Ceteris Paribus

For those students who want to explore the mathematical details of the theoretical concepts covered in the text, **Math** icons direct the students to Connect.

connect
ORIGIN OF THE IDEA 6.1
Growth Theory

Also on Connect are **Origin of the Idea** articles. These brief histories examine the origins of 70 major ideas identified in the book. Students will be interested in learning about economists who first developed such ideas as opportunity cost, equilibrium price, the multiplier, and comparative advantage and elasticity. The **Origin of the Idea** icon directs students to Connect for this extension material.

connect

Selected **interactive graphs** are available on Connect/Developed under the supervision of Norris Peterson of Pacific Lutheran University, this interactive feature depicts major graphs and instructs students to shift the curves, observe the outcomes, and derive relevant generalizations.

Web Chapters

Bonus web chapters are available in PDF format for easy download at **mcgrawhillconnect.ca**. They are Chapter 16W (Income Inequality, Poverty, and Discrimination), Chapter 17W (International Trade), and Chapter 18W (Canadian Agriculture: Economics and Policy).

Organizational Alternatives

Although instructors generally agree as to the content of principles of economics courses, they sometimes differ as to how to arrange the material. *Microeconomics* includes five parts, and that provides considerable organizational flexibility. Some instructors will prefer to intersperse the microeconomics of Parts 2 and 3 with the chapters of Parts 4 and 5. Chapter 18W on agriculture may follow Chapters 8 and 9 on perfect competition; Chapter 10 on competition policy and regulation may follow either Chapter 8 or 9 on imperfect competition models; Chapter 16W on income inequality may follow Chapter 15 on rent, interest, and profit. Finally, as noted before, Chapter 17W on international trade can easily be moved up to immediately after Chapter 3 on supply and demand for instructors who want an early discussion of international trade.

Pedagogical Aids

Microeconomics has always been student oriented. Economics is concerned with efficiency—accomplishing goals using the best methods. Therefore, we offer the students some brief introductory comments on how to improve their efficiency and hence their grades.

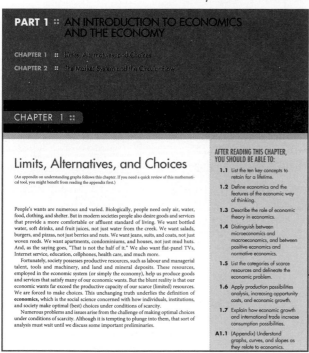

- *"After Reading This Chapter, You Should be Able to:"* We set out the Learning Objectives at the start of each chapter so the chapter's main concepts can be easily recognized. We have also tied the Learning Objectives to each of the numbered sections in each chapter and the Questions and Problems at the end of each chapter.

- *Terminology* A significant portion of any introductory course is terminology. Key terms are highlighted in bold type the first time they appear in the text. Key terms are defined in the margin and a comprehensive list appears at the end of each chapter. A glossary of definitions can also be found at the end of the book and on the website.

- *Ten Key Concepts* Ten Key Concepts have been identified to help students organize the main principles. The Ten Key Concepts are introduced in Chapter 1 and each one is reinforced throughout the textbook by an icon.

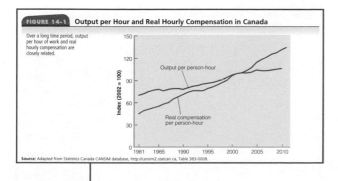

FIGURE 14-1 Output per Hour and Real Hourly Compensation in Canada

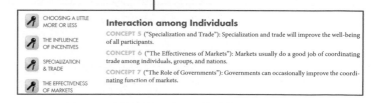

- *Data Updates* Data updates for selected graphs and tables can be found on Connect.

FIGURE 3-1   An Individual Buyer's Demand for Corn

Because price and quantity demanded are inversely related, an individual's demand schedule graphs as a downsloping curve such as *D*. Specifically, the law of demand says that, other things equal, consumers will buy more of a product as its price declines. Here, and in later figures, *P* stands for price, and *Q* stands for quantity (either demanded or supplied).

Price per bushel	Quantity demanded (bushels per week)
$5	10
4	20
3	35
2	55
1	80

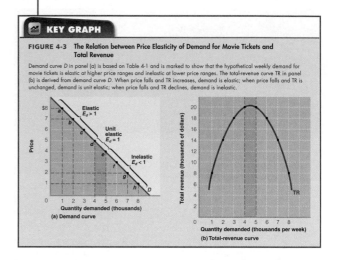

- **Graphics with Supporting Data** Where possible, we have provided data to support our graphs. In such cases a data table now appears in the same figure with the graph.

- **Key Graphs** We have labelled graphs having special relevance as Key Graphs. There is a quick quiz of four questions related to each Key Graph, with answers provided at the bottom of the graph.

- **Reviewing the Chapter** Important things should be said more than once. You will find a Chapter Summary at the conclusion of every chapter as well as two or three Quick Reviews within each chapter. The summary at the end of each chapter is presented by numbered chapter section. These review statements will help students to focus on the essential ideas of each chapter and also to study for exams.

KEY GRAPH

FIGURE 4-3   The Relation between Price Elasticity of Demand for Movie Tickets and Total Revenue

Demand curve *D* in panel (a) is based on Table 4-1 and is marked to show that the hypothetical weekly demand for movie tickets is elastic at higher price ranges and inelastic at lower price ranges. The total-revenue curve TR in panel (b) is derived from demand curve *D*. When price falls and TR increases, demand is elastic; when price falls and TR is unchanged, demand is unit elastic; when price falls and TR declines, demand is inelastic.

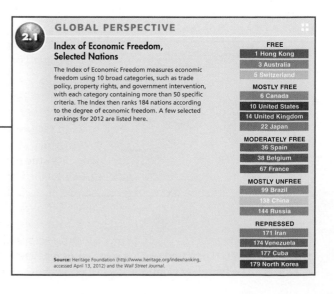

QUICK REVIEW

- The price elasticity of demand coefficient E_d is the ratio of the percentage change in quantity demanded to the percentage change in price. The averages of the two prices and two quantities are used as the base references in calculating the percentage changes.

- When E_d is greater than 1, demand is elastic; when E_d is less than 1, demand is inelastic; when E_d is equal to 1, demand is unit elastic.

- When price changes, total revenue will change in the opposite direction if demand is price elastic, in the same direction if demand is price inelastic, and not at all if demand is unit elastic.

- Demand is typically elastic in the high-price (low-quantity) range of the demand curve and inelastic in the low-price (high-quantity) range of the demand curve.

- Price elasticity of demand is greater (a) the larger the number of substitutes available; (b) the higher the price of a product relative to one's income; (c) the greater the extent to which the product is a luxury; and (d) the longer the time period involved.

- **Global Perspective Boxes** Each nation functions increasingly in a global economy. To help the students gain appreciation of this wider economic environment, we provide Global Perspective features, which compare Canada to other nations.

GLOBAL PERSPECTIVE

2.1

Index of Economic Freedom, Selected Nations

The Index of Economic Freedom measures economic freedom using 10 broad categories, such as trade policy, property rights, and government intervention, with each category containing more than 50 specific criteria. The Index then ranks 184 nations according to the degree of economic freedom. A few selected rankings for 2012 are listed here.

FREE
1 Hong Kong
3 Australia
5 Switzerland

MOSTLY FREE
6 Canada
10 United States
14 United Kingdom
22 Japan

MODERATELY FREE
36 Spain
38 Belgium
67 France

MOSTLY UNFREE
99 Brazil
138 China
144 Russia

REPRESSED
171 Iran
174 Venezuela
177 Cuba
179 North Korea

Source: Heritage Foundation (http://www.heritage.org/index/ranking, accessed April 13, 2012) and the *Wall Street Journal*.

• *Appendix on Graphs* Being comfortable with graphical analysis and a few related quantitative concepts will be a big advantage to students in understanding the principles of economics. The appendix to Chapter 1, which reviews graphing, line slopes, and linear equations, should not be skipped.

Appendix to Chapter 1

A1.1 Graphs and their Meanings

If you glance quickly through this text, you will find many graphs. Some seem simple, while others are more complicated. All are included to help you visualize and understand economic relationships. Physicists and chemists sometimes illustrate their theories by building arrangements of multi-coloured wooden balls, representing protons, neutrons, and electrons, which are held in proper relation to one another by wires or sticks. Economists use graphs to illustrate their models. By understanding these "pictures," you can more readily make sense of economic relationships. Most of our principles or models explain relationships between just two sets of economic facts, which can be conveniently represented with two-dimensional graphs.

Construction of a Graph

A *graph* is a visual representation of the relationship between two variables. Figure A1-1 is a hypothetical illustration showing the relationship between income and consumption for the economy as a whole. Without even studying economics, we would logically expect that people would buy more goods and services when their incomes go up. Thus it is not surprising to find in Figure A1-1 that total consumption in the economy increases as total income increases.

The information in Figure A1-1 is expressed both graphically and in table form. Here is how it is done: We want to show graphically how consumption changes as income changes. We therefore represent income on the **horizontal axis** of the graph and consumption on the **vertical axis**.

Now we arrange the vertical and horizontal scales of the graph to reflect the ranges of values of consumption and income, and mark the scales in convenient increments. As you can see in Figure A1-1, the values marked on the scales cover all the values in the table. The increments on both scales are $100 for approximately each centimetre.

Because the graph has two dimensions, each point within it represents an income value and its associated consumption value. To find a point that represents one of the five income–consumption combinations in the table, we draw straight lines from the appropriate values on the vertical and horizontal axes. For example, to plot point *c* ($200 income, $150 consumption), draw straight lines up from the horizontal (income) axis at $200 and across from the vertical (consumption) axis at $150. These straight lines intersect at point *c*, which represents this particular income–consumption combination. You should verify that the other income–consumption combinations shown in the table are properly located in the graph. Finally, by assuming that the same general relationship between income and

QUESTIONS

1. Explain the two causes of market failures. Given their definitions, could a market be affected by both types of market failures simultaneously? **[LO5.1]**

2. Draw a supply and demand graph and identify the areas of consumer surplus and producer surplus. Given the demand curve, what impact will an increase in supply have on the amount of consumer surplus shown in your diagram? Explain why. **[LO5.2]**

3. Use the ideas of consumer surplus and producer surplus to explain why economists say competitive markets are efficient. Why are below- or above-equilibrium levels of output inefficient, according to these two sets of ideas? **[LO5.2]**

4. What are the two characteristics of public goods? Explain the significance of each for public provision as opposed to private provision. What is the free-rider problem as it relates to public goods? Is Canadian border patrol a public good or a private good? Why? How about satellite TV? Explain. **[LO5.3]**

5. Draw a production possibilities curve with public goods on the vertical axis and private goods on the horizontal axis. Assuming the economy is initially operating on the curve, indicate how the production of public goods might be increased. How might the output of public goods be increased if the economy is initially operating at a point inside the curve? **[LO5.3]**

6. Use the distinction between the characteristics of private and public goods to determine whether the following should be produced through the market system or pro-

8. Why are spillover costs and spillover benefits also called negative and positive externalities? Show graphically how a tax can correct for a negative externality and how a subsidy to producers can correct for a positive externality. How does a subsidy to consumers differ from a subsidy to producers in correcting for a positive externality? **[LO5.4]**

9. An apple grower's orchard provides nectar to a neighbour's bees, while the beekeeper's bees help the apple grower by pollinating his apple blossoms. Use Figure 5-6b to explain why this situation of dual positive externalities might lead to an underallocation of resources to both apple growing and beekeeping. How might this underallocation get resolved via the means suggested by the Coase theorem? **[LO5.4]**

10. The Lojack car recovery system allows the police to track stolen cars. As a result, they not only recover 90% of Lojack-equipped stolen cars but also arrest many auto thieves and shut down many "chop shops" that dismantle stolen vehicles to get at their used parts. Thus, Lojack provides both private benefits and positive externalities. Should the government consider subsidizing Lojack purchases? **[LO5.4]**

11. Explain the following statement, using the MB curve in Figure 5-9 to illustrate: "The optimal amount of pollution abatement for some substances, say, dirty water from storm drains, is very low; the optimal amount of abatement for other substances, say, cyanide poison, is close to 100 percent." **[LO5.4]**

• *Questions and Problems* The Study Questions have been split into Questions and Problems, better aligning them with Learning Objectives, and adding new auto-gradable (through Connect) quantitative questions.

PROBLEMS

1. Refer to Table 5-1. If the six people listed in the table are the only consumers in the market and the equilibrium price is $11 (not the $8 shown), how much consumer surplus will the market generate? **[LO5.2]**

2. Refer to Table 5-2. If the six people listed in the table are the only producers in the market and the equilibrium

price is $6 (not the $8 shown), how much producer surplus will the market generate? **[LO5.2]**

3. Look at Tables 5-1 and 5-2 together. What is the total surplus if Bob buys a unit from Carlos? If Beata buys a unit from Courtney? If Bob buys a unit from Chad? If you match up pairs of buyers and sellers so as to maximize the

Comprehensive Learning and Teaching Package ::

The thirteenth Canadian edition is also accompanied by a variety of high-quality supplements that help students master the subject and help instructors implement customized courses.

connect Connect

McGraw-Hill Connect™ is a web-based assignment and assessment platform that gives students the means to better connect with their coursework, with their instructors, and with the important concepts that they will need to know for success now and in the future.

With Connect, instructors can deliver assignments, quizzes, and tests online. Nearly all the questions from the text are presented in an auto-gradable format and tied to the text's Learning Objectives. Instructors can edit existing questions and author entirely new problems. They can track individual student performance—by question, by assignment, or in relation to the class overall—with detailed grade reports. They can integrate grade reports easily with Learning Management Systems (LMS) such as WebCT and Blackboard, and much more.

By choosing Connect, instructors are providing their students with a powerful tool for improving academic performance and truly mastering course material. Connect allows students to practise important skills at their own pace and on their own schedule. Importantly, students' assessment results and instructors' feedback are all saved online—so students can continually review their progress and plot their course to success.

Connect also provides 24/7 online access to an eBook—an online edition of the text—to aid students in successfully completing their work, wherever and whenever they choose.

Key Features

Simple Assignment Management With Connect, creating assignments is easier than ever, so you can spend more time teaching and less time managing.

- Create and deliver assignments easily with new banks of homework questions and test bank material to assign online

- Streamline lesson planning, student progress reporting, and assignment grading to make classroom management more efficient than ever

- Go paperless with the eBook and online submission and grading of student assignments

Smart Grading When it comes to studying, time is precious. Connect helps students learn more efficiently by providing feedback and practice material when they need it, where they need it.

- Automatically score assignments, giving students immediate feedback on their work and side-by-side comparisons with correct answers

- Access and review each response; manually change grades or leave comments for students to review

- Reinforce classroom concepts with practice tests and instant quizzes

Instructor Library The Connect Instructor Library is your course creation hub. It provides all the critical resources you'll need to build your course, just how you want to teach it.

- Assign eBook readings and draw from a rich collection of textbook-specific assignments

- Access instructor resources, including ready-made PowerPoint presentations and media to use in your lectures

- View assignments and resources created for past sections

- Post your own resources for students to use

eBook Connect reinvents the textbook learning experience for the modern student. Every Connect subject area is seamlessly integrated with Connect eBooks, which are designed to keep students focused on the concepts key to their success.

- Provide students with a Connect eBook, allowing for anytime, anywhere access to the textbook

- Merge media, animation, and assessments with the text's narrative to engage students and improve learning and retention

- Pinpoint and connect key concepts in a snap using the powerful eBook search engine

- Manage notes, highlights, and bookmarks in one place for simple, comprehensive review

- **Graphing tools** enable you to draw graphs from the ground up and perform in-depth analysis of an existing graph.

- **Critical thinking activities** and **logic cases** explore the key chapter concepts with helpful explanations along the way.

- **Video Cases**—a series of videos illustrate key economic concepts. These were created specifically for the Principles course by leading economic authority Michael Mandel.

- Current **news articles** pulled from live news sources are organized according to your book for easy access.

LearnSmart

This adaptive learning system is designed to help students learn faster, study more efficiently, and retain more knowledge for greater success. LearnSmart adaptively assesses students' skill levels to determine which topics students have mastered and which require further practice. Then, LearnSmart delivers customized learning content based on their strengths and weaknesses.

LearnSmart is like a personal tutor guiding students to spend less time on what they already know and more on what they don't. Students learn faster and more efficiently because they get the help they need, right when they need it.

Instructor Resources

- *Instructor's Manual* The Instructor's Manual is prepared by Thomas Barbiero of Ryerson University, and Shawn D. Knabb of Western Washington University. Available again in this edition as a Microsoft® Office Word document, the manual includes: Chapter Overview, What's New, Instructional Objectives, Comments and Teaching Suggestions, Student Stumbling Blocks, Lecture Notes, Last Words, and answers to end-of-chapter questions and problems. Approximately 300 new multiple choice questions (8 to 10 per chapter) have been included in the IM.

- *Microsoft® PowerPoint® Presentation Software* Prepared by Amy Peng, Ryerson University, this presentation system is found on the Instructor's Site of Connect. It offers visual presentations that may be edited and manipulated to fit a particular course format.

- *Computerized Test Banks* Prepared by Bruno Fullone of George Brown College, the Computerized Test Bank contains about 6000 multiple-choice and true/false questions. Chandan Shirvaikar, of Athabasca University, has updated 30 short-answer questions with suggested answers for each chapter.

 Superior Learning Solutions and Support

The McGraw-Hill Ryerson team is ready to help you assess and integrate any of our products, technology, and services into your course for optimal teaching and learning performance. Whether it's helping your students improve their grades, or putting your entire course online, the McGraw-Hill Ryerson team is here to help you do it. Contact your iLearning Sales Specialist today to learn how to maximize all of McGraw-Hill Ryerson's resources!

For more information on the latest technology and Learning Solutions offered by McGraw-Hill Ryerson and its partners, please visit us online: **www.mcgrawhill.ca/he/solutions.**

Solutions that make a difference.
Technology that fits.

MH-Campus
LMS
Integration

Connect
Course
Management

LearnSmart
Adaptive
Learning

Tegrity
Lecture
Capture

Custom
Print &
Digital

Acknowledgements

The thirteenth Canadian edition of *Microeconomics* has benefitted from a number of perceptive reviewers, who were a rich source of suggestions for this revision. To each of you, and others we may have inadvertently overlooked, thank you for your considerable help in improving *Microeconomics*. Reviewers include:

Khyati Antani, Humber College

Aurelia Best, Centennial College

Ramesh Bhardwaj, George Brown College

Bruno Fullone, George Brown College

Paul Furzecott, Georgian College

Sandra Hadersbeck, Okanagan College

Hannah Holmes, McMaster University

Shahidul Islam, Grant MacEwan College

Rosmy Jean Louis, Vancouver Island University

Cheryl Jenkins, John Abbott College

Paul Pieper, Humber College

Krishnakali SenGupta, McMaster University

R.P. Seth, Mount St. Vincent University

Chandan Shirvaikar, Red Deer College

Brian VanBlarcom, Acadia University

We are greatly indebted to an all-star group of professionals at McGraw-Hill Ryerson—in particular James Booty, Senior Sponsoring Editor; Daphne Scriabin, Developmental Editor; Jeremy Guimond, Marketing Manager; Stephanie Giles, Senior Editorial Associate; and Stephanie Gay, Supervising Editor—for their publishing and marketing expertise. We thank Laurel Sparrow, Kimberleigh Sparrow, and Judy Sturrup for their thorough and sensitive editing and proofreading, Jacques Cournoyer for his vivid Last Word illustrations, Dave Murphy for the cover and interior design, Gianluigi Pelloni of the University of Bologna (Rimini Campus) and Jose Luis Alvarez Arce of the University of Navarra in Pamplona, Spain for their helpful suggestions and insights

We also strongly acknowledge the McGraw-Hill Ryerson sales staff, who greeted this edition with wholehearted enthusiasm.

Campbell R. McConnell
Stanley L. Brue
Sean M. Flynn
Thomas P. Barbiero

CHAPTER 1 ::

Limits, Alternatives, and Choices

(An appendix on understanding graphs follows this chapter. If you need a quick review of this mathematical tool, you might benefit from reading the appendix first.)

People's wants are numerous and varied. Biologically, people need only air, water, food, clothing, and shelter. But in modern societies people also desire goods and services that provide a more comfortable or affluent standard of living. We want bottled water, soft drinks, and fruit juices, not just water from the creek. We want salads, burgers, and pizzas, not just berries and nuts. We want jeans, suits, and coats, not just woven reeds. We want apartments, condominiums, and houses, not just mud huts. And, as the saying goes, "That is not the half of it." We also want flat-panel TVs, Internet service, education, cellphones, health care, and much more.

Fortunately, society possesses productive resources, such as labour and managerial talent, tools and machinery, and land and mineral deposits. These resources, employed in the economic system (or simply the economy), help us produce goods and services that satisfy many of our economic wants. But the blunt reality is that our economic wants far exceed the productive capacity of our scarce (limited) resources. We are forced to make choices. This unchanging truth underlies the definition of **economics,** which is the social science concerned with how individuals, institutions, and society make optimal (best) choices under conditions of scarcity.

Numerous problems and issues arise from the challenge of making optimal choices under conditions of scarcity. Although it is tempting to plunge into them, that sort of analysis must wait until we discuss some important preliminaries.

AFTER READING THIS CHAPTER, YOU SHOULD BE ABLE TO:

1.1 List the ten key concepts to retain for a lifetime.

1.2 Define economics and the features of the economic way of thinking.

1.3 Describe the role of economic theory in economics.

1.4 Distinguish between microeconomics and macroeconomics, and between positive economics and normative economics.

1.5 List the categories of scarce resources and delineate the economic problem.

1.6 Apply production possibilities analysis, increasing opportunity costs, and economic growth.

1.7 Explain how economic growth and international trade increase consumption possibilities.

A1.1 (Appendix) Understand graphs, curves, and slopes as they relate to economics.

connect
ORIGIN OF THE IDEA 1.1
Economics

economics
The social science concerned with how individuals, institutions, and society make optimal (best) choices under conditions of scarcity.

Economics is concerned with the efficient use of scarce resources to obtain the maximum satisfaction of society's unlimited wants.

 FACING TRADEOFFS

 OPPORTUNITY COSTS

 CHOOSING A LITTLE MORE OR LESS

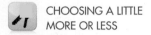 THE INFLUENCE OF INCENTIVES

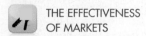 SPECIALIZATION & TRADE

 THE EFFECTIVENESS OF MARKETS

 THE ROLE OF GOVERNMENTS

 PRODUCTION & THE STANDARD OF LIVING

MONEY & INFLATION

INFLATION–UNEMPLOYMENT TRADEOFF

1.1 Ten Key Concepts to Retain for a Lifetime

Suppose you unexpectedly meet your introductory economics professor on the street five or ten years after you complete this course. What will you be able to tell her you retained from the course? More than likely you will not be able to remember very much. To help you retain the main ideas that economics has to offer, we have come up with *10 key concepts* that we believe are essential to understanding the world around you and will help you in your chosen career. These key concepts will be reinforced throughout the textbook so that you will, we hope, retain them long after the course is over. When a key concept is about to be discussed you will be alerted with an icon and the concept description.

The 10 key concepts are simply listed here; you will find elaboration on each key concept as we progress through the textbook. At the end of the course you should review these 10 key concepts. They will help you to organize and better understand the materials you have studied. We have divided the 10 key concepts into three categories: (a) concepts that pertain to the individual; (b) concepts that explain the interaction among individuals; and (c) concepts that deal with the economy as a whole and the standard of living.

The Individual

CONCEPT 1 ("Facing Tradeoffs"): Scarcity in relation to wants means you face *tradeoffs*; therefore, you have to make choices.

CONCEPT 2 ("Opportunity Costs"): The cost of the choice you make is what you give up for it, or the *opportunity cost*.

CONCEPT 3 ("Choosing a Little More or Less"): Choices are usually made at the margin; we choose a "little" more or a "little" less of something.

CONCEPT 4 ("The Influence of Incentives"): The choices you make are influenced by incentives.

Interaction among Individuals

CONCEPT 5 ("Specialization and Trade"): Specialization and trade will improve the well-being of all participants.

CONCEPT 6 ("The Effectiveness of Markets"): Markets usually do a good job of coordinating trade among individuals, groups, and nations.

CONCEPT 7 ("The Role of Governments"): Governments can occasionally improve the coordinating function of markets.

The Economy as a Whole and the Standard of Living

CONCEPT 8 ("Production and the Standard of Living"): The standard of living of the average person in a particular country is dependent on its production of goods and services. A rise in the standard of living requires a rise in the output of goods and services.

CONCEPT 9 ("Money and Inflation"): If the monetary authorities of a country annually print money in excess of the growth of output of goods and services, this practice will eventually lead to inflation.

CONCEPT 10 ("Inflation–Unemployment Tradeoff"): In the short run, society faces a short-run *tradeoff* between *inflation* and its level of *unemployment*.

As you read the text, be on the lookout for the icon that alerts you that one of these concepts is being discussed. We now turn to our first topic, the economic way of thinking.

1.2 The Economic Way of Thinking

Close your eyes for a minute and pretend you are in paradise, a place where you can have anything you want whenever you desire it. On a particular day you might decide you want a new pair of jeans, a new notebook computer, a cellphone, tickets to see a hockey game in which Sydney Crosby is playing, and a new red Ferrari sports car to cruise around in. Your friends might have a completely different list of wants, but in paradise all of their desires also will be satisfied. Indeed, everyone's desires are satisfied. The following day you can start all over and have any request fulfilled. And so it will continue, forever. Your body will never get old or sick, you will have all the friends and love you want, etc., etc.

Of course, paradise may be waiting for us in the afterlife, but in this world our wants greatly outstrip our ability to satisfy them. Whenever our wants are greater than the resources to meet those desires, we have an economic problem. It is this reality that gives economists their unique perspective. This **economic perspective** or *economic way of thinking* has several critical and closely interrelated features.

Scarcity and Choice

Scarcity limits our options and necessitates that we make choices. Because we "can't have it all," we must decide what we will have, and what we must forgo.

At the core of economics is the idea that "there is no free lunch." You may get treated to lunch, making it "free" to you, but there is a cost to someone—ultimately, society (see the Consider This … Free for All? box). Scarce inputs of land, equipment, farmers' labour, cooks' and waiters' labour, and managers' talent are required. Because these resources could be used in other production activities, they and the other goods and services they could have produced are sacrificed in making the lunch available. Economists call these sacrifices **opportunity costs.** To get more of one thing, you forgo the opportunity to get the next best thing. That sacrifice is the opportunity cost of the choice. For example, you have $100 that you can spend on a pair of jeans or shoes. The opportunity cost of buying the shoes is the jeans you could have purchased, and vice versa.

Purposeful Behaviour

Economics assumes that human behaviour reflects "rational self-interest." Individuals look for and pursue opportunities to increase their **utility**—the pleasure, happiness, or satisfaction

economic perspective
A viewpoint that envisions individuals and institutions making rational decisions by comparing the marginal benefits and marginal costs associated with their actions.

 OPPORTUNITY COSTS

opportunity cost
The amount of other products that must be forgone or sacrificed to produce a unit of a product.

connect
ORIGIN OF THE IDEA 1.2
Utility

utility
The satisfaction a person gets from consuming a good or service.

CONSIDER THIS :: Free for All?

Free products are seemingly everywhere. Sellers from time to time offer free software, free cellphones, and no-fee chequing accounts. Dentists give out free toothbrushes. At provincial visitors' centres, there are free brochures and maps.

Does the presence of so many free products contradict the economist's assertion that "there is no free lunch"? No! Scarce resources are used to produce each of these products, and because those resources have alternative uses, society gives up something else to get the "free" good. Where resources are used to produce goods and services, there is no free lunch.

So why are these goods offered for free? In a word: marketing. Firms sometimes offer free products to entice people

to try them and perhaps subsequently purchase them. The free version of software may eventually entice you to buy the next upgraded version; in other instances free brochures contain advertising for shops and restaurants, and free access to the Internet is filled with ads. In still other cases, the product is free only in conjunction with a purchase. To get the soft drink, you must buy the large pizza. To get the free cellphone, you need to sign up for a year (or more) of cellphone service.

So while "free" products may come at no cost to the individuals receiving them, they are never free to society.

obtained from consuming a good or service. They allocate their time, energy, and money to maximize their satisfaction. Because they weigh costs and benefits, their decisions are purposeful or rational, not random or chaotic.

Consumers are purposeful in deciding what goods and services to buy. Business firms are purposeful in deciding what products to produce and how to produce them. Government entities are purposeful in deciding what public services to provide and how to finance them.

"Purposeful behaviour" does not assume that people and institutions are immune from faulty logic and therefore are perfect decision makers. They sometimes make mistakes. Nor does it mean that people's decisions are unaffected by emotion or the decisions of those around them. Indeed, economists acknowledge that people are sometimes impulsive or emulate what others do. "Purposeful behaviour" simply means that people make decisions with some desired outcome in mind.

Rational self-interest is not the same as selfishness. In the economy, increasing one's own wage, rent, interest, or profit normally requires identifying and satisfying *somebody else's* wants! Also, people make personal sacrifices for others. They contribute time and money to charities because they derive pleasure from doing so. Parents help pay for their children's education for the same reason. These self-interested, but unselfish, acts help maximize the giver's satisfaction as much as any personal purchase of goods or services. Self-interested behaviour is simply behaviour designed to increase personal satisfaction, however it may be derived.

ⓜ connect
ORIGIN OF THE IDEA 1.3
Marginal Analysis

marginal analysis
The comparison of marginal ("extra" or "additional") benefits and marginal costs, usually for decision making.

Marginal Analysis: Comparing Benefits and Costs

The economic perspective focuses largely on **marginal analysis**—comparisons of *marginal benefits* and *marginal costs*. To economists, "marginal" means "extra," "additional," or "a change in." Most choices or decisions involve changes in the status quo (the existing state of affairs). Should you attend school for another year or not? Should you study an extra hour for an exam?

CONSIDER THIS :: Fast Food Lines

The economic perspective is useful in analyzing all sorts of behaviours. Consider an everyday example: the behaviour of customers at a fast-food restaurant. When customers enter the restaurant, they go to the shortest line, believing that line will minimize their time cost of obtaining food. They are acting purposefully; time is limited, and people prefer using it in some way other than standing in line.

If one fast-food line is temporarily shorter than other lines, some people will move to that line. These movers apparently view the time saving from the shorter line (marginal benefit) as exceeding the cost of moving from their present line (marginal cost). The line switching tends to equalize line lengths. No further movement of customers between lines occurs once all lines are about equal.

Fast-food customers face another cost–benefit decision when a clerk opens a new station at the counter: Should they move to the new station or stay put? Those who shift to the new line decide that the time saving from the move exceeds the extra cost of physically moving. In so deciding, customers must also consider just how quickly they can get to the new

station compared with others who may be contemplating the same move. (Those who hesitate in this situation are lost!)

Customers at the fast-food establishment do not have perfect information when they select lines. Thus, not all decisions turn out as expected. For example, you might enter a short line and find that the person in front of you is ordering hamburgers and fries for 40 people in the Greyhound bus parked out back (and that the employee is a trainee!). Nevertheless, at the time you made your decision, you thought it to be optimal.

Finally, customers must decide what food to order when they arrive at the counter. In making their choices, they again compare marginal costs and marginal benefits in attempting to obtain the greatest personal satisfaction for their expenditure.

Economists believe that what is true for the behaviour of customers at fast-food restaurants is true for economic behaviour in general. Faced with an array of choices, consumers, workers, and businesses rationally compare marginal costs and marginal benefits in making decisions.

CHOOSING A LITTLE MORE OR LESS

Should you add fries to your fast-food order? Similarly, should a business expand or reduce its output? Should government increase or decrease health care funding?

Each option will have marginal benefits and marginal costs. In making choices, the decision maker will compare those two amounts. Example: You and your fiancé are shopping for an engagement ring. Should you buy a ¼-carat diamond, a ½-carat diamond, a ¾-carat diamond, or a larger one? The marginal cost of the larger diamond is the added expense beyond the smaller diamond. The marginal benefit is the greater lifetime pleasure (utility) from the larger stone. If the marginal benefit of the larger diamond exceeds its marginal cost, you buy the larger stone. But if the marginal cost is more than the marginal benefit, buy the smaller diamond instead, even if you can afford the larger stone.

In a world of scarcity, the marginal benefit associated with some specific option always includes the marginal cost of forgoing something else. Spending money on the larger diamond may mean forgoing a honeymoon to an exotic location. Opportunity costs—the value of the next best thing forgone—are always present whenever a choice is made.

1.3 Theories, Principles, and Models

scientific method
The systematic pursuit of knowledge through observing a problem, collecting data, and formulating and testing hypotheses to obtain theories, principles, and laws.

Like the physical and life sciences, as well as other social sciences, economics relies on the **scientific method.** That procedure consists of several elements:

- Observing real-world behaviour and outcomes.

- Formulating a possible explanation of cause and effect (hypothesis), based on those observations.

- Testing this explanation by comparing the outcomes of specific events to the outcome predicted by the hypothesis.

- Accepting, rejecting, or modifying the hypothesis based on these comparisons.

- Continuing to test the hypothesis against the facts. If favourable results accumulate, the hypothesis evolves into a theory. A very well tested and widely accepted theory is referred to as an economic law or an **economic principle**—a statement about economic behaviour or the economy that enables prediction of the probable effects of certain actions. Combinations of such laws or principles are incorporated into models, which are simplified representations of how parts of the economy work, such as a market or segment of the economy.

economic principle
A statement about economic behaviour or the economy that makes it possible to predict the probable effects of certain actions.

Economists develop theories of the behaviour of individuals (consumers, workers) and institutions (businesses, governments) engaged in the production, exchange, and consumption of goods and services. Theories, principles, and models are "purposeful simplifications." The full scope of economic reality itself is too complex and bewildering to be understood as a whole. In developing theories, principles, and models, economists remove the clutter and simplify.

Economic principles and models are highly useful in analyzing economic behaviour and understanding how the economy operates. They are the tools for ascertaining cause and effect (or action and outcome) within the economic system. Good theories do a good job of explaining and predicting. They are supported by facts concerning how individuals and institutions actually behave in producing, exchanging, and consuming goods and services.

There are some other things you should know about economic principles.

generalizations
Statements of the nature of the relation between two or more sets of facts.

- *Generalizations* Economic principles are **generalizations** relating to economic behaviour or to the economy itself. Economic principles are expressed as the tendencies of typical or average consumers, workers, or business firms. For example, economists say that consumers buy more of a particular product when its price falls. Economists recognize that some consumers may increase their purchases by a large amount, others by a small amount, and a few not at all. This "price–quantity" principle holds both for the typical consumer and for consumers as a group.

ORIGIN OF THE IDEA 1.4
Ceteris Paribus

other-things-equal assumption
The assumption that factors other than those being considered are held constant.

MATH 1.1
Ceteris Paribus

economic model
A simplified picture of economic reality; an abstract generalization.

- *Other-Things-Equal Assumption* In constructing their theories, economists use the *ceteris paribus* or **other-things-equal assumption**—the assumption that factors other than those being considered do not change. They assume that all variables except those under immediate consideration are held constant for a particular analysis. For example, consider the relationship between the price of Pepsi and the amount of it purchased. Assume that of all the factors that might influence the amount of Pepsi purchased (for example, the price of Pepsi, the price of Coca-Cola, and consumer incomes and preferences), only the price of Pepsi varies. This is helpful because the economist can then focus on the relationship between the price of Pepsi and purchases of Pepsi in isolation without being confused by changes in other variables.

- *Graphical Expression* Many **economic models** are expressed graphically. Be sure to read the appendix at the end of this chapter as a review of graphs.

1.4 Microeconomics and Macroeconomics

Economists develop economic principles and models at two levels, microeconomics and macroeconomics.

Microeconomics

microeconomics
The part of economics concerned with such individual units as industries, firms, and households.

Microeconomics is the part of economics concerned with decision making by individual customers, workers, households, and business firms. At this level of analysis, we observe the details of their behaviour under a figurative microscope. We measure the price of a specific product, the number of workers employed by a single firm, the revenue or income of a particular firm or household, or the expenditures of a specific firm, government entity, or family. In microeconomics, we examine the grains of sand, the rocks, and the shells, not the beach.

Macroeconomics

macroeconomics
The part of economics concerned with the economy as a whole.

aggregate
A collection of specific economic units treated as if they were one unit.

Macroeconomics examines either the economy as a whole or its basic subdivisions or aggregates, such as the government, household, and business sectors. An **aggregate** is a collection of specific economic units treated as if they were one unit. Therefore, we might lump together the millions of consumers in the Canadian economy and treat them as if they were one huge unit called "consumers."

In using aggregates, macroeconomics seeks to obtain an overview, or general outline, of the structure of the economy and the relationships of its major aggregates. Macroeconomics speaks of such economic measures as total output, total employment, total income, aggregate expenditures, and the general level of prices in analyzing various economic problems. Very little attention is given to specific units making up the various aggregates. Figuratively, macroeconomics looks at the beach, not the grains of sand, the rocks, and the shells.

The micro–macro distinction does not mean that economics is so highly compartmentalized that every topic can be readily labelled as either macro or micro; many topics and subdivisions of economics are rooted in both. For example, while the problem of unemployment is usually treated as a macroeconomic topic (because unemployment relates to aggregate production), economists recognize that the decisions made by *individual* workers on how long to search for jobs and the way *specific* labour markets encourage or impede hiring are also critical in determining the unemployment rate.

Positive and Normative Economics

positive economics
The analysis of facts to establish cause-and-effect relationships.

Both microeconomics and macroeconomics contain elements of positive economics and normative economics. **Positive economics** focuses on facts and cause-and-effect relationships. It includes description, theory development, and theory testing. Positive economics avoids value judgments. It tries to establish scientific statements about economic behaviour, and deals with what the economy is actually like. Such scientifically based analysis is critical to good policy analysis.

Economic policy, on the other hand, involves **normative economics,** which incorporates value judgments about what the economy *should* be like or what particular policy actions *should* be recommended to achieve a desirable goal. Normative economics looks at the desirability of certain aspects of the economy. It underlies expressions of support for particular economic policies.

Positive economics concerns *what is,* while normative economics embodies subjective feelings about *what ought to be.* Examples: Positive statement: "The unemployment rate in France is higher than that in Canada." Normative statement: "France ought to undertake policies to make its labour market more flexible to reduce unemployment rates." When you see words such as "ought" or "should" in a sentence, you are likely encountering a normative statement.

Most of the disagreement among economists involves normative, value-based policy questions. Of course, there is often some disagreement about which theories or models best represent the economy and its parts. But economists agree on a full range of economic principles. Most economic controversy thus reflects differing opinions or value judgments about what society should be like.

normative economics
The part of economics involving value judgments about what the economy should be like.

QUICK REVIEW

- Economics examines how individuals, institutions, and society make choices under conditions of scarcity.

- The economic way of thinking stresses (a) resource scarcity and the necessity of making choices, (b) the assumption of purposeful (or rational) behaviour, and (c) comparisons of marginal benefit and marginal cost. In choosing among alternatives, people incur opportunity costs.

- In choosing the best option, people incur opportunity costs—the value of the next-best option.

- Economists use the scientific method to establish economic theories, cause–effect generalizations about the economic behaviour of individuals and institutions.

- Microeconomics focuses on specific units of the economy; macroeconomics examines the economy as a whole.

- Positive economics deals with factual statements ("what is"); normative economics involves value judgments ("what ought to be").

1.5 The Economic Problem

Both individuals and society face an **economic problem,** which is the need to make choices because economic wants are virtually unlimited but the means (income, time, resources) for satisfying those wants are limited. We will construct a simple microeconomic model to look at the general economic problem faced by an individual.

economic problem
The need to make choices because society's material wants for goods and services are unlimited but the resources available to satisfy these wants are limited (scarce).

Limited Income

We all have a finite amount of income, even the wealthiest among us. Even members of the Thomson and Weston families—Canada's richest—have to decide how to spend their money! And the majority of us have much more limited means. Our income comes to us in the form of wages, interest, rent, and profit, although we may also receive money from government programs

GLOBAL PERSPECTIVE

Average Income, Selected Nations

Average income (total income/ population) and therefore typical individual budget constraints vary greatly among nations.

Country	Per Capita Income, 2010 (U.S. dollars, based on exchange rates)
Switzerland	70,350
United States	47,140
France	42,390
Japan	42,150
Canada	41,950
South Korea	19,890
Brazil	9,390
Mexico	9,330
China	7,560
Pakistan	2,780
Nigeria	2,160
Rwanda	1,180
Liberia	330

Source: World Bank, www.worldbank.org.

or from family members. As Global Perspective 1.1 shows, the average income of Canadians in 2010 was $41,950 ($US). In the poorest nations, it was less than $500.

Unlimited Wants

For better or worse, most people have virtually unlimited wants. We desire various goods and services that provide utility. Our wants extend over a wide range of products, from *necessities* (food, shelter, and clothing) to *luxuries* (perfumes, yachts, and sports cars). Some wants such as basic food, shelter, and clothing have biological roots. Other wants—for example, specific kinds of food, shelter, and clothing—arise from the conventions and customs of society.

Over time, as new and improved products are introduced, economic wants tend to change and multiply, fuelled by new products. Only recently have people wanted iPods, Internet service, digital cameras, or camera phones, because those products did not exist a few decades ago. Also, the satisfaction of certain wants may trigger others: the acquisition of a Ford Focus or a Honda Civic has been known to whet the appetite for a Lexus or a Mercedes.

Services, as well as goods, satisfy our wants. Car repair work, the removal of an inflamed appendix, legal and accounting advice, and haircuts all satisfy human wants. Actually, we buy many goods, such as automobiles and washing machines, for the services they render. The differences between goods and services are often smaller than they appear to be.

For most people, the desires for goods and services cannot be fully satisfied. Bill Gates may have all that he wants for himself but it is clear from his massive charitable giving that he keenly wants better health care for the world's poor. Our desires for a particular good or service can be satisfied; over a short period of time we can surely get enough toothpaste or pasta. And one appendectomy is plenty. But our broader desire for more goods and services and higher-quality goods and services seems to be another story.

Because we have only limited income (usually through our work) but seemingly insatiable wants, it is in our self-interest to pick and choose goods and services that maximize our satisfaction given the limitations we face. It should be noted that while we are stressing limited income, there is rarely enough of all the other things people desire, such as health, time, physical/mental abilities, and much, much more.

FIGURE 1-1   A Consumer's Budget Line

The budget line (or budget constraint) shows all the combinations of any two products that can be purchased, given the prices of the products and the consumer's money income.

THE BUDGET LINE: WHOLE-UNIT COMBINATIONS OF DVDS AND PAPERBACK BOOKS ATTAINABLE WITH AN INCOME OF $120		
Units of DVDs (Price = $20)	Units of Books (Price = $10)	Total Expenditure
6	0	($120 = $120 + $0)
5	2	($120 = $100 + $20)
4	4	($120 = $80 + $40)
3	6	($120 = $60 + $60)
2	8	($120 = $40 + $80)
1	10	($120 = $20 + $100)
0	12	($120 = $0 + $120)

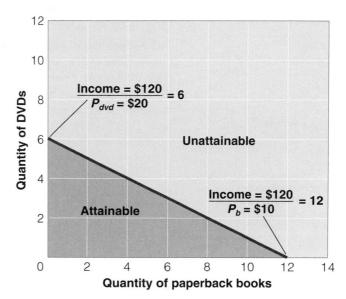

The Budget Line

budget line
A schedule or curve that shows various combinations of two products a consumer can purchase with a specific money income.

We can depict the economic problem facing individuals using a **budget line** (or, more technically, *budget constraint*). It is a schedule or curve that shows various combinations of two products a consumer can purchase with a specific money income. Although we assume two products, the analysis generalizes to the full range of products available to consumers.

To understand this idea, suppose that you received a bookstore gift card as a birthday present. The $120 card is soon to expire. You take the card to the store and confine your purchase decisions to two alternatives: DVDs and paperback books. DVDs are $20 each and paperback books are $10 each. Your purchase options are shown in the table in Figure 1-1.

At one extreme, you might spend all of your $120 "income" on 6 DVDs at $20 each and have nothing left to spend on books. Or, by giving up 2 DVDs and thereby gaining $40, you can have 4 DVDs at $20 each and 4 books at $10 each. And so on to the other extreme, at which you could buy 12 books at $10 each, spending your entire gift card on books with nothing left to spend on DVDs.

The graph in Figure 1-1 shows the budget line. Note that the graph is not restricted to whole units of DVDs and books as is the table. Every point on the graph represents a possible combination of DVDs and books, including fractional quantities. The slope of the graphed budget line measures the ratio of the price of books (P_b) to the price of DVDs (P_{dvd}); more precisely, the slope is $P_b/P_{dvd} = \$(-10)/\$(+20) = -\frac{1}{2}$. So you must forgo 1 DVD (measured on the vertical axis) to buy 2 books (measured on the horizontal axis). This yields a slope of $-\frac{1}{2}$ or -0.5.

The budget line illustrates several ideas.

ATTAINABLE AND UNATTAINABLE COMBINATIONS

All of the combinations of DVDs and books on or inside the budget line are *attainable* from the $120 of money income. You can afford to buy, for example, 3 DVDs at $20 each and 6 books at $10 each. You obviously can also afford to buy 2 DVDs and 5 books, thereby using up only $90 of the $120 available on your gift card. But, to achieve maximum utility you will want to spend the full $120. The budget line shows all combinations that cost exactly the full $120.

connect
ORIGIN OF THE IDEA 1.5
Opportunity Costs

tradeoff
The sacrifice of some or all of one economic goal, good, or service to achieve some other goal, good, or service.

constant opportunity cost
An opportunity cost that remains the same for each additional unit as a consumer (or society) shifts purchases (production) from one product to another along a straight-line budget line (production possibilities curve).

connect
WORKED PROBLEM 1.1
Budget Line

economic resources
The land, labour, capital, and entrepreneurial ability that are used in the production of goods and services.

land
Natural resources used to produce goods and services.

In contrast, all combinations beyond the budget line are *unattainable*. The $120 limit simply does not allow you to purchase, for example, 5 DVDs at $20 each and 5 books at $10 each. That $150 expenditure would clearly exceed the $120 limit. In Figure 1-1 the attainable combinations are on and within the budget line; the unattainable combinations are beyond the budget line.

TRADEOFFS AND OPPORTUNITY COSTS

The budget line in Figure 1-1 illustrates the idea of **tradeoffs** arising from limited income. To obtain more DVDs, you have to give up some books. For example, to obtain the first DVD you trade off 2 books. So the opportunity cost of the first DVD is 2 books. To obtain the second DVD the opportunity cost is also 2 books. The straight-line budget constraint, with its constant slope, indicates **constant opportunity cost.** That is, the opportunity cost of 1 extra DVD remains the same (= 2 books) as more DVDs are purchased. And, in reverse, the opportunity cost of 1 extra book does not change (= ½ DVD) as more books are bought.

CHOICE

Limited income forces people to choose what to buy and what to forgo to fulfill wants. You will select the combination of DVDs and paperback books that you think is "best." That is, you will evaluate your marginal benefits and marginal costs (here, product price) to make choices that maximize your satisfaction. Other people, with the same $120 gift card, would undoubtedly make different choices.

INCOME CHANGES

The location of the budget line varies with money income. An increase in money income shifts the budget line to the right; a decrease in money income shifts it to the left. To verify this, recalculate the table in Figure 1-1, assuming the card value (income) is (a) $240 and (b) $60, and plot the new budget lines in the graph. No wonder people like to have more income: Having more money shifts their budget lines outward and enables them to buy more goods and services. But even with more income, people will still face spending tradeoffs, opportunity costs, and choices.

Society's Economic Problem

It is not only the individual or household that faces the economic problem. Society must also make choices under conditions of scarcity. It, too, faces the economic problem. Should it devote more of its limited resources to the criminal justice system (police, courts, and prisons) or to education (teachers, books, and schools)? If it decides to devote more resources to both, what other goods and services does it forgo? Health care? Energy development?

Scarce Resources

Society has limited or scarce **economic resources,** meaning all natural, human, and manufactured resources that go into the production of goods and services. That includes the entire set of factory and farm buildings and all the equipment, tools, and machinery used to produce manufactured goods and agricultural products; all transportation and communication facilities; all types of labour; and land and mineral resources.

Resource Categories

Economists classify economic resources into four general categories.

LAND

Land means much more to the economist than it does to most people. To the economist, **land** includes all natural resources ("gifts of nature") used in the production process. These include forests, mineral and oil deposits, water resources, wind power, sunlight, and arable land.

LABOUR

labour
The physical and mental talents of individuals used in producing goods and services.

The resource **labour** consists of the physical actions and mental activities that people contribute to the production of goods and services. The work-related activities of a logger, retail clerk, machinist, teacher, professional hockey player, and nuclear physicist all fall under the general heading "labour."

CAPITAL

capital
Human-made resources (buildings, machinery, and equipment) used to produce goods and services.

For economists, **capital** (or capital goods) includes all manufactured aids used in producing consumer goods and services: tools and machinery, as well as all factory, storage, transportation, and distribution facilities. Note that the term "capital" does not refer to money; because money produces nothing, economists do not include it as an economic resource. Money (or money capital or financial capital) is simply a means for purchasing capital goods.

consumer goods
Products and services that satisfy human wants directly.

Capital goods differ from consumer goods because **consumer goods** satisfy wants directly, while **capital goods** do so indirectly by aiding the production of consumer goods. For example, large commercial baking ovens (capital goods) help make loaves of bread (consumer goods).

capital goods
Goods that do not directly satisfy human wants.

Economists refer to the purchase of capital goods as **investment.** The amount of training and education that a person acquires through his or her lifetime is referred to as *human capital,* since it is similar to an investment in capital goods in that it can enhance output. But you should note that human capital is normally categorized under labour resources.

investment
Spending for the production and accumulation of capital.

ENTREPRENEURIAL ABILITY

entrepreneurial ability
The human talents that combine the other resources to produce a product, make non-routine decisions, innovate, and bear risks.

Finally, there is the special human resource, distinct from labour, called **entrepreneurial ability.** The entrepreneur performs several functions:

- The entrepreneur takes the initiative in combining the resources of land, labour, and capital to produce a good or a service. Both a sparkplug and a catalyst, the entrepreneur is the driving force behind production and the agent who combines the other resources in what is hoped will be a successful business venture.

- The entrepreneur makes the strategic business decisions that set the course of an enterprise.

- The entrepreneur innovates. He or she commercializes new products, new production techniques, or even new forms of business organization.

innovation
The first successful commercial introduction of a new product, the first use of a new method of production, or the creation of a new form of business organization.

- The entrepreneur bears risk. **Innovation** is risky, as nearly all new products and ideas are subject to the possibility of failure as well as success. Progress would cease without entrepreneurs who are willing to take on risk by devoting their time, effort, and ability—as well as their own money and the money of others—to commercializing new products and ideas that may enhance society's standard of living.

factors of production
Economic resources: land, labour, capital, and entrepreneurial ability.

Because land, labour, capital, and entrepreneurial ability are combined to produce goods and services, they are called the **factors of production,** or simply "inputs."

1.6 Production Possibilities Model and Increasing Opportunity Costs

Society uses its scarce resources to produce goods and services. The alternatives and choices it faces can best be understood through a macroeconomic model of production possibilities. To keep things simple, let's initially assume:

- *Full Employment* The economy is employing all its available resources.
- *Fixed Resources* The quantity and quality of the factors of production are fixed.
- *Fixed Technology* The state of technology (the methods used to produce output) is constant.
- *Two Goods* The economy is producing only two goods: pizzas and industrial robots. Pizzas symbolize consumer goods, products that satisfy our wants directly; industrial robots (for example, the kind used to weld automobile frames) symbolize capital goods, products that satisfy our wants indirectly by making possible more efficient production of consumer goods.

Production Possibilities Table

production possibilities table
A table showing the different combinations of two products that can be produced with a specific set of resources in a full-employment, full-production economy.

A **production possibilities table** lists the different combinations of two products that can be produced with a specific set of resources, assuming full employment. Table 1-1 contains such a simple economy that is producing pizzas and industrial robots; the data are, of course, hypothetical. At alternative A, this economy would be devoting all its available resources to the production of industrial robots (capital goods); at alternative E, all resources would go to pizza production (consumer goods). Those alternatives are unrealistic extremes; an economy typically produces both capital goods and consumer goods, as in B, C, and D. As we move from alternative A to E, we increase the production of pizzas at the expense of the production of industrial robots.

Because consumer goods satisfy our wants directly, any movement toward E looks tempting. In producing more pizzas, society increases the satisfaction of its current wants. But there is a cost: More pizzas mean fewer industrial robots. This shift of resources to consumer goods catches up with society over time because the stock of capital expands more slowly, thereby reducing potential future production. By moving toward alternative E, society chooses "more now" at the expense of "much later."

By moving toward A, society chooses to forgo current consumption, thereby freeing up resources that can be used to increase the production of capital goods. By building up its stock of capital this way, society will have greater future production and, therefore, greater future consumption. By moving toward A, society is choosing "more later" at the cost of "less now."

Generalization: At any point in time, a fully employed economy must sacrifice some of one good to obtain more of another good. Scarce resources prohibit such an economy from having more of both goods. Society must choose among alternatives. There is no such thing as a free pizza, or a free industrial robot. Having more of one thing means having less of something else.

TABLE 1-1

Production Possibilities of Pizzas and Robots with Full Employment and Productive Efficiency

Type of Product	PRODUCTION ALTERNATIVES				
	A	**B**	**C**	**D**	**E**
Pizzas (in hundred thousands)	0	1	2	3	4
Robots (in thousands)	10	9	7	4	0

For example, if Canadians want more spending on health care, they will have to be satisfied with less spending on education.

Production Possibilities Curve

production possibilities curve
A curve showing the different combinations of goods or services that can be produced in a full-employment, full-production economy where the available supplies of resources and technology are fixed.

The data presented in a production possibilities table are shown graphically as a **production possibilities curve.** Such a curve displays the different combinations of goods and services that society can produce in a fully employed economy, assuming a fixed availability of supplies of resources and fixed technology. We arbitrarily represent the economy's output of capital goods (here, industrial robots) on the vertical axis and the output of consumer goods (here, pizzas) on the horizontal axis, as shown in Figure 1-2 **(Key Graph).**

Each point on the production possibilities curve represents some maximum output of the two products. The curve is a "constraint" because it shows the limit of attainable outputs. Points on the curve are attainable as long as the economy uses all of its available resources. Points lying inside the curve are also attainable but they reflect less total output and therefore are not as desirable as points on the curve. Points inside the curve imply that the economy could have more of both industrial robots and pizzas if it achieved full employment. Points lying beyond the production possibilities curve, like *W,* would represent a greater output than the output at any point on the curve. Such points are, however, unattainable with the current availability of resources and technology.

Law of Increasing Opportunity Costs

Figure 1-2 clearly shows that more pizzas mean fewer industrial robots. The number of units of industrial robots that must be given up to obtain another unit of pizzas is, of course, the opportunity cost of that unit of pizzas.

In moving from alternative A to alternative B in Table 1-1, the cost of 1 additional unit of pizzas is 1 unit fewer of industrial robots. But when additional units are considered—B to C, C to D, and D to E—an important economic principle is revealed: For society, the opportunity cost of each additional unit of pizzas is greater than the opportunity cost of the preceding one. When we move from A to B, just 1 unit of industrial robots is sacrificed for 1 more unit of pizzas; but in going from B to C we sacrifice 2 additional units of industrial robots for 1 more unit of pizzas; then 3 more of industrial robots for 1 more of pizzas; and finally 4 for 1. Conversely, confirm that as we move from E to A, the cost of an additional unit of industrial robots (on average) is ¼, ⅓, ½, and 1 unit of pizzas, respectively, for the four successive moves.

law of increasing opportunity costs
As the production of a good increases, the opportunity cost of producing an additional unit rises.

Our example illustrates the **law of increasing opportunity costs**: As the production of a particular good increases, the opportunity cost of producing an additional unit rises.

SHAPE OF THE CURVE

The law of increasing opportunity costs is reflected in the shape of the production possibilities curve: The curve is bowed out from the origin of the graph. Figure 1-2 shows that when the economy moves from *A* to *E,* it must give up successively larger amounts of industrial robots (1, 2, 3, and 4) to acquire equal increments of pizzas (1, 1, 1, and 1). This is shown in the slope of the production possibilities curve, which becomes steeper as we move from *A* to *E.*

ECONOMIC EXPLANATION

The economic explanation for the law of increasing opportunity costs is that *economic resources are not completely adaptable to alternative uses.* Many resources are better at producing one type of good than at producing others. Consider land. Some land is highly suited to growing the ingredients necessary for pizza production. But, as pizza production expands, society has to start using land that is less bountiful for farming. Other land is rich in mineral deposits and therefore well-suited to producing the materials needed to make industrial robots. That land will be the

 **KEY GRAPH**

FIGURE 1-2   The Production Possibilities Curve

Each point on the production possibilities curve represents some maximum combination of two products that can be produced if full employment and **full production** are achieved. When operating on the curve, more robots mean fewer pizzas, and vice versa. Limited resources and a fixed technology make any combination of robots and pizzas lying outside the curve (such as at *W*) unattainable. Points inside the curve are attainable, but they indicate that full employment and productive efficiency are not being realized.

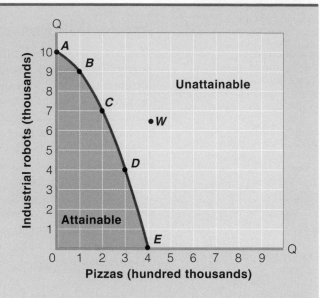

PRODUCTION ALTERNATIVES

Type of Product	A	B	C	D	E
Pizzas (in hundred thousands)	0	1	2	3	4
Robots (in thousands)	10	9	7	4	0

Quick Quiz

1. Production possibilities curve *ABCDE* is bowed out from the origin because:
   a. the marginal benefit of pizzas declines as more pizzas are consumed.
   b. the curve gets steeper as we move from *E* to *A*.
   c. it reflects the law of increasing opportunity costs.
   d. resources are scarce.

2. The marginal opportunity cost of the second unit of pizzas is:
   a. 2 units of robots.
   b. 3 units of robots.
   c. 7 units of robots.
   d. 9 units of robots.

3. The total opportunity cost of 7 units of robots is:
   a. 1 unit of pizzas.
   b. 2 units of pizzas.
   c. 3 units of pizzas.
   d. 4 units of pizzas.

4. All points on this production possibilities curve necessarily represent:
   a. society's optimal choice.
   b. less than full use of resources.
   c. unattainable levels of output.
   d. full employment.

Answers: 1. c; 2. a; 3. b; 4. d

full production
Employment of available resources so that the maximum amount of (or total value of) goods and services is produced; occurs when both productive efficiency and allocative efficiency are realized.

connect
WORKED PROBLEM 1.2
Production Possibilities

first land devoted to the production of industrial robots. But as society steps up the production of robots, it must use land that is less and less suited to making their components.

If we start at *A* and move to *B* in Figure 1-2, we can shift resources whose productivity is relatively high in pizza production and low in industrial robots. But as we move from *B* to *C, C* to *D,* and so on, resources highly productive in pizzas become increasingly scarce. To get more pizzas, resources will be needed whose productivity in industrial robots is relatively great. It will take increasingly more of such resources, and hence greater sacrifices of industrial robots, to achieve each 1-unit increase in pizzas. This lack of perfect flexibility, or interchangeability, on the part of resources is the cause of increasing opportunity costs for society.

Optimal Allocation

Of all the attainable combinations of pizzas and industrial robots on the curve in Figure 1-2, which is optimal (best)? That is, what specific quantities of resources should be allocated to pizzas and what specific quantities to industrial robots in order to maximize satisfaction?

Recall that economic decisions centre on comparisons of marginal benefit (MB) and marginal cost (MC). Any economic activity should be expanded as long as marginal benefit exceeds marginal cost and should be reduced if marginal cost exceeds marginal benefit. The optimal amount of the activity occurs where MB = MC. Society needs to make a similar assessment about its production decision.

Consider pizzas. We already know from the law of increasing opportunity costs that the marginal cost of additional units of pizzas will rise as more units are produced. At the same time, we need to recognize that the extra or marginal benefits that come from producing and consuming pizza decline with each successive unit of pizza. Consequently, each successive unit of pizza brings with it both increasing marginal costs and decreasing marginal benefits.

The optimal quantity of pizza production is indicated by point *e* at the intersection of the MB and MC curves: 200,000 units in Figure 1-3. Why is this amount the optimal quantity? If only 100,000 units of pizzas were produced, the marginal benefit of an extra unit of them (point *a*) would exceed its marginal cost (point *b*). In money terms, MB is $15, while MC is only $5. When society gains something worth $15 at a marginal cost of only $5, it is better off. In Figure 1-3, net gains can continue to be realized until pizza production has been increased to 200,000.

FIGURE 1-3 **Optimal Allocation: MB = MC**

Optimal allocation requires the expansion of a good's output until its marginal benefit (MB) and marginal cost (MC) are equal. No resources beyond that point should get allocated to the product. Here, allocative efficiency occurs when 200,000 pizzas are produced.

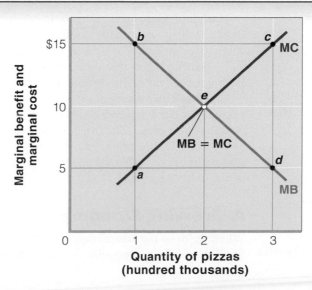

In contrast, the production of 300,000 units of pizzas is excessive. There the MC of an added unit is $15 (point *c*) and its MB is only $5 (point *d*). This means that 1 unit of pizzas is worth only $5 to society but costs society $15 to obtain. This is a losing proposition for society!

So resources are being efficiently allocated to any product when the marginal benefit and marginal cost of its output are equal (MB = MC). Suppose that by applying the above analysis to industrial robots, we find that their optimal (MB = MC) quantity is 7000. This would mean that alternative *C* (200,000 units of pizzas and 7000 units of industrial robots) on the production possibilities curve in Figure 1-2 would be optimal for this economy.

QUICK REVIEW

- The production possibilities curve illustrates (a) scarcity of resources, implied by the area of unattainable combinations of output lying outside the production possibilities curve; (b) choice among outputs, reflected in the variety of attainable combinations of goods lying along the curve; (c) opportunity cost, illustrated by the downward slope of the curve; and

(d) the law of increasing opportunity costs, reflected in the bowed-outward shape of the curve.

- A comparison of marginal benefits and marginal costs is needed to determine the best or optimal output mix on a production possibilities curve.

1.7 Economic Growth, Present Choices, and Future Possibilities

In the depths of the Great Depression of the 1930s, almost 20 percent of workers were unemployed and one-quarter of Canadian production capacity was idle. Subsequent downturns have been much less severe. During the relatively deep 2008–2009 recession, for instance, production fell by a comparably smaller 2.8 percent and the unemployment rate peaked at 8.7 percent. Almost all nations have experienced widespread unemployment and unused production capacity from business downturns at one time or another. Since 2000, for example, several nations—including Argentina, Japan, Mexico, Germany, and South Korea—have had economic downturns and unemployment.

How do these realities relate to the production possibilities model? Our analysis and conclusions change if we relax the assumption that all available resources are fully employed. The five alternatives in Table 1-1 represent maximum outputs; they illustrate the combinations of pizzas and industrial robots that can be produced when the economy is operating at full employment. With unemployment, this economy would produce less than each alternative shown in the table.

Graphically, we represent situations of unemployment by points inside the original production possibilities curve (reproduced here in Figure 1-4). Point *U* is one such point. Here the economy is falling short of the various maximum combinations of pizzas and industrial robots represented by the points on the production possibilities curve. The arrows in Figure 1-4 indicate three possible paths back to full employment. A move toward full employment would yield a greater output of one or both products.

A Growing Economy

When we drop the assumptions that the quantity and quality of resources and technology are fixed, the production possibilities curve shifts position and the potential maximum output of the economy changes.

FIGURE 1-4 | Unemployment, Productive Inefficiency, and the Production Possibilities Curve

Any point inside the production possibilities curve, such as *U*, represents unemployment or a failure to achieve productive efficiency. The arrows indicate that, by realizing full employment and productive efficiency, the economy could operate on the curve. This means it could produce more of one or both products than it is producing at point *U*.

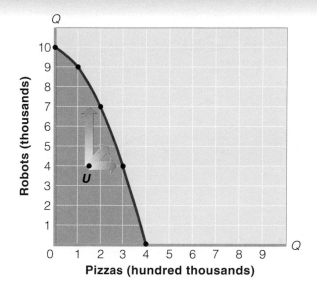

INCREASES IN FACTOR SUPPLIES

Although factor supplies are fixed at any specific moment, they change over time via more education and training. Historically, the economy's stock of capital has increased at a significant, though unsteady, rate. And although some of our energy and mineral resources are being depleted, new sources are also being discovered. The development of irrigation systems, for example, adds to the supply of arable land.

The net result of these increased supplies of the factors of production is the ability to produce more of both consumer goods and capital goods. Thus, 20 years from now the production possibilities may supersede those shown in Table 1-1. The new production possibilities might look like those in the table in Figure 1-5. The greater abundance of resources will result in a greater potential output of one or both products at each alternative. The economy will have achieved economic growth in the form of expanded potential output. Thus, when an increase in the quantity or quality of resources occurs, the production possibilities curve shifts outward and to the right, as illustrated by the move from the inner curve to curve A'B'C'D'E' in Figure 1-5. This sort of shift represents growth of economic capacity, which when used means **economic growth**: a larger total output.

economic growth
An outward shift in the production possibilities curve that results from an increase in factor supplies or quality, or an improvement in technology.

ADVANCES IN TECHNOLOGY

An advancing technology brings both new and better goods and improved ways of producing them. For now, let's think of technological advance as being only improvements in the methods of production; for example, the introduction of computerized systems to manage inventories and schedule production. These advances alter our previous discussion of the economizing problem by allowing society to produce more goods with available resources. As with increases in resource supplies, technological advances make possible the production of more industrial robots *and* more pizzas.

A real-world example of improved technology is the recent surge of new innovations relating to computers, communications, and biotechnology. Technological advances have dropped the prices of computers and greatly increased their speed. Improved software has greatly increased the everyday usefulness of computers. Cellphones and the Internet have increased communications capacity, enhancing production and improving the efficiency of markets. Advances in biotechnology have resulted in important agricultural and medical discoveries. These and other

FIGURE 1-5   **Economic Growth and the Production Possibilities Curve**

The increase in supplies of resources, the improvements in resource quality, and the technological advances that occur in a dynamic economy move the production possibilities curve outward and to the right, allowing the economy to have larger quantities of both types of goods.

PRODUCTION ALTERNATIVES					
Type of Product	A′	B′	C′	D′	E′
Pizzas (in hundred thousands)	0	2	4	6	8
Robots (in thousands)	14	12	9	5	0

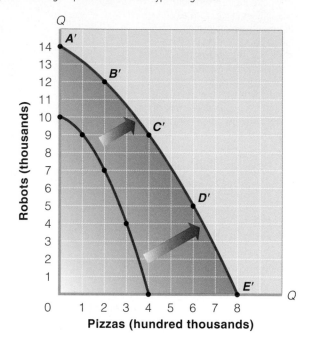

new and improved technologies have contributed to both global and Canadian economic growth (outward shifts of the nation's production possibilities curve).

Conclusion: Economic growth is the result of (1) increases in supplies of factors of production, (2) improvements in factor quality, and (3) technological advances. The consequence of growth is that a full-employment economy can enjoy a greater output of both consumption goods and capital goods. While static, no-growth economies must sacrifice some of one good to obtain more of another, dynamic, growing economies can have larger quantities of both goods.

Present Choices and Future Possibilities

An economy's current chosen position on its production possibilities curve helps determine the future location of that curve. Let's designate the two axes of the production possibilities curve as "goods for the future" and "goods for the present," as in Figure 1-6. Goods for the future are such things as capital goods, research and education, and preventive medicine. They increase the quantity and quality of property resources, enlarge the stock of technological information, and improve the quality of human resources. As we have already seen, goods for the future, such as capital goods, are the ingredients of economic growth. Goods for the present are consumer goods, such as food, clothing, and entertainment.

Now suppose there are two hypothetical economies, Presentville and Futureville, which are initially identical in every respect except one: Presentville's current chosen position on its production possibilities curve strongly favours present goods over future goods. Point P in Figure 1-6a indicates that choice. It is located quite far down the curve to the right, indicating a high priority for goods for the present, at the expense of fewer goods for the future. Futureville, in contrast, makes a current choice that stresses larger amounts of future goods and smaller amounts of present goods, as shown by point F in Figure 1-6b.

KEY GRAPH

FIGURE 1-6 **Present Choices and Future Locations of a Production Possibilities Curve**

A nation's current choice favouring "present goods," as made by Presentville in part (a), will cause a modest outward shift of the curve in the future. A nation's current choice favouring "future goods," as made by Futureville in part (b), will result in a greater outward shift of the curve in the future.

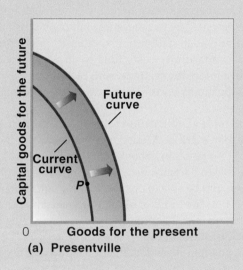

(a) Presentville

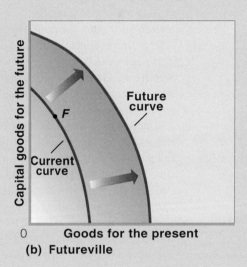

(b) Futureville

Now, other things equal, we can expect Futureville's future production possibilities curve to be farther to the right than Presentville's future production possibilities curve. By currently choosing an output more favourable to technological advances and to increases in the quantity and quality of resources, Futureville will achieve greater economic growth than Presentville. In terms of capital goods, Futureville is choosing to make larger current additions to its "national factory" by devoting more of its current output to capital than Presentville. The payoff from this choice for Futureville is greater future production capacity and economic growth. The opportunity cost is fewer consumer goods in the present for Futureville to enjoy.

CONSIDER THIS :: Women, the Workforce, and Production Possibilities

We have seen that more and better-quality factors of production and improved technology shift a nation's production possibilities curve outward. An example of more resources is the large increase in the number of employed women in Canada within the past five decades. 62 percent of adult Canadian women work full-time or part-time in paid jobs today, compared to only 40 percent in 1965.

Over recent decades, women have greatly increased their productivity in the workplace, mostly by becoming better educated and professionally trained. As a result, they can earn higher wages. Because those higher wages have increased the opportunity cost—the forgone wage earnings—of staying at home, women have substituted employment in the labour market for the now more "expensive" traditional home activities. This substitution has been particularly pronounced among married women. Along with other factors such as changing attitudes and expanded job access, the rising earnings of women have produced a substantial increase in the number of women workers in Canada. This increase in the quantity of available resources has helped push the Canadian production possibilities curve outward.

Is Futureville's choice thus necessarily "better" than Presentville's? That, we cannot say. The different outcomes simply reflect different preferences and priorities in the two countries. But each country will have to live with the economic consequences of its choice.

A Qualification: International Trade

Production possibilities analysis implies that an individual nation is limited to the combinations of output indicated by its production possibilities curve. But we must modify this principle when international specialization and trade exist.

You will see in later chapters that an economy can circumvent, through international specialization and trade, the output limits imposed by its domestic production possibilities curve. Under international specialization and trade, each nation first specializes in the production of those items for which it has the lowest opportunity costs (due to an abundance of the necessary resources). Countries then engage in international trade, with each country exchanging the items that it can produce at the lowest opportunity costs for the items that other countries can produce at the lowest opportunity costs.

International specialization and trade allow a nation to get more of a desired good at less sacrifice of some other good. Rather than sacrifice 3 units of domestically produced robots to get a third unit of domestically produced pizzas, as in Table 1-1, a nation that engages in international specialization and trade might be able to do much better. If it specializes in robots while another country specializes in pizzas, then it may be able to obtain the third unit of pizzas by trading only 2 units of domestically produced robots for 1 unit of foreign-produced pizzas. Specialization and trade have the same effect as having more and better resources or discovering improved production techniques; both increase the quantities of capital and consumer goods available to society. Expansion of domestic production possibilities and international trade are two separate routes for obtaining greater output.

post hoc, ergo propter hoc fallacy
Incorrectly reasoning that when one event precedes another the first event must have caused the second event.

QUICK REVIEW

- Unemployment causes an economy to operate at a point inside its production possibilities curve.

- Increases in resource supplies, improvements in resource quality, and technological advances cause economic growth, which is depicted as an outward shift of the production possibilities curve.

- An economy's present choice of capital and consumer goods helps determine the future location of its production possibilities curve.

- International specialization and trade enable a nation to obtain more goods than its production possibilities curve would indicate.

The **LAST WORD**   Pitfalls to Sound Economic Reasoning

Because they affect us so personally, we often have difficulty thinking accurately and objectively about economic issues.

Here are some common pitfalls to avoid in successfully applying the economic perspective.

Biases Most people bring a bundle of biases and preconceptions to the field of economics. For example, some might think that corporate profits are excessive or that lending money is always superior to borrowing money. Others might believe that government is necessarily less efficient than businesses, or that more government regulation is always better than less. Biases cloud thinking and interfere with objective analysis. All of us must be willing to shed biases and preconceptions that are not supported by facts.

Loaded Terminology The economic terminology used in newspapers and broadcast media is sometimes emotionally biased, or loaded. The writer or spokesperson may have a cause to promote or an axe to grind and may slant comments accordingly. High profits may be labelled "obscene," low wages may be called "exploitive," or self-interested behaviour may be identified as "greed." Government workers may be referred to as "mindless bureaucrats" and those favouring stronger government regulations may be called "socialists." To analyze economic issues objectively, you must be prepared to reject or discount such terminology.

Fallacy of Composition Another pitfall in economic thinking is the assumption that what is true for one individual or part of a whole is necessarily true for a group of individuals or the whole. This is a logical fallacy called the *fallacy of composition;* the assumption is not correct. A statement that is valid for an individual or part is not necessarily valid for the larger group or whole. As an example, you may see the action better if you leap to your feet to see an outstanding play at a football game. But if everyone leaps to their feet at the same time, nobody—including you—will have a better view than when all remained seated.

Here are two economic examples: An individual shareholder can sell shares of, say, Research In Motion (RIM, the maker of the BlackBerry) stock without affecting the price of the stock. The individual's sale will not noticeably reduce the share price because the sale is a negligible fraction of the total shares of RIM being bought and sold.

But if all the RIM shareholders decide to sell their shares on the same day, the market will be flooded with shares and the stock price will fall precipitously. Similarly, a single cattle ranch can increase its revenue by expanding the size of its livestock herd. The extra cattle will not affect the price of cattle when they are brought to market. But if all ranchers as a group expand their herds, the total output of cattle will increase so much that the price of cattle will decline when the cattle are sold. If the price reduction is relatively large, ranchers as a group might find that their income has fallen despite their having sold a greater number of cattle because the fall in price overwhelms the increase in quantity.

Post Hoc Fallacy You must think very carefully before concluding that because event A precedes event B, A is the cause of B. This kind of faulty reasoning is known as the *post hoc, ergo propter hoc,* or "after this, therefore because of this" fallacy. To give a non-economic example: The Calgary Flames team hires a new coach and the team's record improves. Is the new coach the cause? Maybe. Perhaps the presence of more experienced and talented players or an easier schedule is the true cause. Another example is that the rooster crows before dawn, but does not cause the sunrise.

Correlation But Not Causation Do not confuse correlation, or connection, with causation. Correlation between two events or two sets of data indicates only that they are associated in some systematic and dependable way. For example, we may find that when variable X increases, Y also increases. But this correlation does not necessarily mean that there is causation—that increases in X cause increases in Y. The relationship could be purely coincidental or dependent on some other factor, Z, not included in the analysis.

Here is an example: Economists have found a positive correlation between education and income. In general, people with more education earn higher incomes than those with less education. Common sense suggests that education is the cause and higher incomes are the effect; more education implies a more knowledgeable and productive worker, and such workers receive larger salaries.

But causation could also partly run the other way. People with higher incomes could buy more education, just as they buy more furniture and steaks. Or is part of the relationship explainable in still other ways? Are education and income correlated because the characteristics required for succeeding in education—ability and motivation—are the same ones required to be a productive and highly paid worker? If so, then people with those traits will probably both obtain more education and earn higher incomes. But greater education will not be the sole cause of the higher income.

Studies indicate that married men on average earn more income than unmarried men of the same age and education level. Why must we be cautious in concluding that marriage is the cause and higher income is the effect?

:: CHAPTER SUMMARY

1.1 :: TEN KEY CONCEPTS TO RETAIN FOR A LIFETIME

- We have divided the 10 key concepts into three categories: (a) concepts that pertain to the individual ("Facing Trade-offs," "Opportunity Costs," "Choosing a Little More or Less," and "The Influence of Incentives"); (b) concepts that explain the interaction among individuals ("Specialization and Trade," "The Effectiveness of Markets," and "The Role of Governments"); and (c) concepts that deal with the economy as a whole and the standard of living ("Production and the Standard of Living," "Money and Inflation," and "Inflation–Unemployment Tradeoff.")

1.2 :: THE ECONOMIC WAY OF THINKING

- Economics is the social science that examines how individuals, institutions, and society make choices under conditions of scarcity. Central to economics is the idea of opportunity cost: the value of the next-best good or service forgone to obtain something.

- The economic perspective includes three elements: scarcity and choice, purposeful behaviour, and marginal analysis. It sees individuals and institutions making rational decisions based on comparisons of marginal benefits and marginal costs.

1.3 :: THEORIES, PRINCIPLES, AND MODELS

- Economists employ the scientific method, in which they form and test hypotheses of cause-and-effect relationships to generate theories, principles, and laws. Economists often combine principles and laws into representations called models.

1.4 :: MICROECONOMICS AND MACROECONOMICS

- Microeconomics examines specific economic units or institutions. Macroeconomics looks at the economy as a whole or its major aggregates.

- Positive economics deals with facts; normative economics reflects value judgments.

1.5 :: THE ECONOMIC PROBLEM

- Individuals face an economic problem. Because their wants exceed their incomes, they must decide what to purchase and what to forgo. Society also faces the economic problem. Societal wants exceed the available resources necessary to fulfill them. Society therefore must decide what to produce and what to forgo.

- Graphically, a budget line (or budget constraint) illustrates the economic problem for individuals. The line shows the various combinations of two products that a consumer can purchase with a specific money income, given the prices of the two products.

- Economic resources are inputs into the production process and can be classified as land, labour, capital, and entrepreneurial ability. Economic resources are also known as factors of production or inputs.

1.6 :: PRODUCTION POSSIBILITIES MODEL AND INCREASING OPPORTUNITY COSTS

- Economists illustrate society's economic problem through production possibilities analysis. Production possibilities tables and curves show the different combinations of goods and services that can be produced in a fully employed economy, assuming that resource quantity, resource quality, and technology are fixed.

- An economy that is fully employed and thus operating on its production possibilities curve must sacrifice the output of some types of goods and services to increase the production of others. The gain in one type of good or service is always accompanied by an opportunity cost in the form of the loss in some of the other type.

- Because resources are not equally productive in all possible uses, shifting resources from one use to another creates increasing opportunity costs. The production of additional units of one product requires the sacrifice of increasing amounts of the other product.

- The optimal (best) point on the production possibilities curve represents the most desirable mix of goods and is determined by expanding the production of each good until its marginal benefit (MB) equals its marginal cost (MC).

1.7 :: ECONOMIC GROWTH, PRESENT CHOICES, AND FUTURE POSSIBILITIES

- Over time, technological advances and increases in the quantity and quality of resources enable the economy to produce more of all goods and services; that is, to experience economic growth. Society's choice as to the mix of consumer goods and capital goods in current output is a major determinant of the future location of the production possibilities curve and thus of the extent of economic growth. International trade enables nations to obtain more goods from their limited resources than their production possibilities curve indicates.

- International trade enables a nation to obtain more goods from its limited resources than its production possibilities curve would indicate.

∷ TERMS AND CONCEPTS

economics, p. 2
economic perspective, p. 3
opportunity cost, p. 3
utility, p. 3
marginal analysis, p. 4
scientific method, p. 5
economic principle, p. 5
generalization, p. 5
other-things-equal assumption, p. 6
economic model, p. 6
microeconomics, p. 6
macroeconomics, p. 6
aggregate, p. 6

positive economics, p. 6
normative economics, p. 7
economic problem, p. 7
budget line, p. 9
tradeoff, p. 10
constant opportunity cost, p. 10
economic resources, p. 10
land, p. 10
labour, p. 11
capital, p. 11
consumer goods, p. 11
capital goods, p. 11
investment, p. 11

entrepreneurial ability, p. 11
innovation, p. 11
factors of production, p. 11
production possibilities table, p. 12
production possibilities
    curve, p. 13
law of increasing opportunity
    costs, p. 13
full production, p. 15
economic growth, p. 17
post hoc, ergo propter hoc
    fallacy, p. 20

∷ QUESTIONS

1. What is an opportunity cost? How does the idea relate to the definition of economics? Which of the following decisions would entail the greater opportunity cost: allocating a square block in the heart of Toronto for a surface parking lot or allocating a square block at the edge of a typical suburb for such a lot? Explain.   **[LO1.2]**

2. Cite three examples of recent decisions that you made in which you (at least implicitly) weighed marginal cost and marginal benefit.   **[LO1.2]**

3. What is meant by the term "utility" and how does the idea relate to purposeful behaviour?   **[LO1.2]**

4. What are the key elements of the scientific method and how does this method relate to economic principles and laws?   **[LO1.3]**

5. Indicate whether each of the following statements applies to microeconomics or macroeconomics: **[LO1.4]**

   a. The unemployment rate in Canada was 7.4 percent in November 2011.

   b. A Canadian software firm discharged 15 workers last month and transferred the work to India.

   c. An unexpected freeze in central Florida reduced the citrus crop and caused the price of oranges to rise.

   d. Canadian output, adjusted for inflation, grew by 3.3 percent in 2010.

   e. Last week, Scotiabank lowered its interest rate on business loans by one-half of 1 percentage point.

   f. The Consumer Price Index rose by 1.8 percent in 2010.

6. State (a) a positive economic statement of your choice, and then (b) a normative economic statement relating to your first statement.   **[LO1.4]**

7. What are economic resources? What categories do economists use to classify them? Why are resources also called factors of production? Why are they called inputs?   **[LO1.5]**

8. Why is money not considered to be a capital resource in economics? Why is entrepreneurial ability considered a category of economic resource, distinct from labour? What are the major functions of the entrepreneur?   **[LO1.5]**

9. Specify and explain the typical shapes of marginal benefit and marginal cost curves. How are these curves used to determine the optimal allocation of resources to a particular product? If current output is such that marginal cost exceeds marginal benefit, should more or fewer resources be allocated to this product? Explain.   **[LO1.6]**

10. Explain if and how each of the following events affects the location of a country's production possibilities curve: **[LO1.6]**

    a. The quality of education increases.

    b. The number of unemployed workers increases.

    c. A new technique improves the efficiency of extracting iron from ore.

    d. A devastating earthquake destroys numerous production facilities.

11. Suppose that, on the basis of a nation's production possibilities curve, an economy must sacrifice 10,000 pizzas domestically to get the 1 additional industrial robot it desires, but that it can get the robot from another country in exchange for 9000 pizzas. Relate this information to the following statement: "Through international specialization and trade, a nation can reduce its opportunity cost of obtaining goods and thus move outside its production possibilities curve."   **[LO1.7]**

:: PROBLEMS

1. Potatoes cost Janice $1.00 per kilogram, and she has $5.00 that she could possibly spend on potatoes or other items. If she feels that the first kilogram of potatoes is worth $1.50, the second kilogram is worth $1.14, the third kilogram is worth $1.05, and all subsequent kilograms are worth $0.30, how many kilograms of potatoes will she purchase? What if she only had $2.00 to spend? [LO1.2]

2. Pham can work as many or as few hours as she wants at the university bookstore for $9 per hour. But due to her hectic schedule, she has just 15 hours per week that she can spend working at either the bookstore or at other potential jobs. One potential job, at a café, will pay her $12 per hour for up to 6 hours per week. She has another job offer at a garage that will pay her $10 an hour for up to 5 hours per week. And she has a potential job at a daycare centre that will pay her $8.50 per hour for as many hours as she can work. If her goal is to maximize the amount of money she can make each week, how many hours will she work at the bookstore? [LO1.5]

3. Suppose you won $15 on a Lotto Canada ticket at the local 7-Eleven and decided to spend all the winnings on candy bars and bags of peanuts. The price of a candy bar is $0.75 and the price of peanuts is $1.50. [LO1.5]

    a. Construct a table showing the alternative combinations of the two products that are available.

    b. Plot the data in your table as a budget line in a graph. What is the slope of the budget line? What is the opportunity cost of one more candy bar? Of one more bag of peanuts? Do these opportunity costs rise, fall, or remain constant as each additional unit of the product is purchased?

    c. Does the budget line tell you which of the available combinations of candy bars and bags of peanuts to buy?

    d. Suppose that you had won $30 on your ticket, not $15. Show the $30 budget line in your diagram. Has the number of available combinations increased or decreased?

4. Suppose that you are on a desert island and possess exactly 20 coconuts. Your neighbour, Friday, is a fisherman, and he is willing to trade 2 fish for every 1 coconut that you are willing to give him. Another neighbour, Kwame, is also a fisherman, and he is willing to trade 3 fish for every 1 coconut. [LO1.5]

    a. On a single figure, draw budget lines for trading with Friday and for trading with Kwame. (Put coconuts on the vertical axis.)

    b. What is the slope of the budget line from trading with Friday?

    c. What is the slope of the budget line from trading with Kwame?

    d. Which budget line features a larger set of attainable combinations of coconuts and fish?

    e. If you are going to trade coconuts for fish, would you rather trade with Friday or Kwame?

5. Below is a production possibilities table for consumer goods (automobiles) and capital goods (forklifts): [LO1.6]

    a. Show these data graphically. Upon what specific assumptions is this production possibilities curve based?

    b. If the economy is at point C, what is the cost of one more automobile? Of one more forklift? Which characteristic of the production possibilities curve reflects the law of increasing opportunity costs: its shape or its length?

    c. If the economy characterized by this production possibilities table and curve were producing 3 automobiles and 20 forklifts, what could you conclude about its use of its available resources?

    d. Is production at a point outside the production possibilities curve currently possible? Could a future advance in technology allow production beyond the current production possibilities curve? What about international trade?

PRODUCTION ALTERNATIVES

Type of Production	A	B	C	D	E
Automobiles	0	2	4	6	8
Forklifts	30	27	21	12	0

6. Look at Figure 1-3. Suppose that the cost of cheese falls, so that the marginal cost of producing pizza decreases. Will the MC curve shift up or down? Will the optimal amount of pizza increase or decrease? [LO1.6]

7. Referring to the table in Problem 5, suppose improvement occurs in the technology of producing forklifts but not in the technology of producing automobiles. Draw the new production possibilities curve. Now assume that a technological advance occurs in producing automobiles but not in producing forklifts. Draw the new production possibilities curve. Now draw a production possibilities curve that reflects technological improvement in the production of both goods. [LO1.7]

8. On average, households in China save 40 percent of their annual income each year, whereas households in Canada save less than 5 percent. Production possibilities are growing at roughly 9 percent annually in China and 3.5 percent in Canada. Use graphical analysis of "present goods" versus "future goods" to explain the differences in growth rates. [LO1.7]

Mc Graw Hill connect™ Practice and Learn Online with Connect

Connect allows you to practice important concepts at your own pace and on your own schedule, with 24/7 online access to an eBook, algorithmic questions and problems from the textbook, video and logic cases, graphing tutorials, flashcards, Internet exercises, key graphs, and more.

Appendix to Chapter 1

A1.1 Graphs and their Meanings

If you glance quickly through this text, you will find many graphs. Some seem simple, while others are more complicated. All are included to help you visualize and understand economic relationships. Physicists and chemists sometimes illustrate their theories by building arrangements of multi-coloured wooden balls, representing protons, neutrons, and electrons, which are held in proper relation to one another by wires or sticks. Economists use graphs to illustrate their models. By understanding these "pictures," you can more readily make sense of economic relationships. Most of our principles or models explain relationships between just two sets of economic facts, which can be conveniently represented with two-dimensional graphs.

Construction of a Graph

A *graph* is a visual representation of the relationship between two variables. Figure A1-1 is a hypothetical illustration showing the relationship between income and consumption for the economy as a whole. Without even studying economics, we would logically expect that people would buy more goods and services when their incomes go up. Thus it is not surprising to find in Figure A1-1 that total consumption in the economy increases as total income increases.

The information in Figure A1-1 is expressed both graphically and in table form. Here is how it is done: We want to show graphically how consumption changes as income changes. We therefore represent income on the **horizontal axis** of the graph and consumption on the **vertical axis.**

Now we arrange the vertical and horizontal scales of the graph to reflect the ranges of values of consumption and income, and mark the scales in convenient increments. As you can see in Figure A1-1, the values marked on the scales cover all the values in the table. The increments on both scales are $100 for approximately each centimetre.

Because the graph has two dimensions, each point within it represents an income value and its associated consumption value. To find a point that represents one of the five income–consumption combinations in the table, we draw straight lines from the appropriate values on the vertical and horizontal axes. For example, to plot point *c* ($200 income, $150 consumption), draw straight lines up from the horizontal (income) axis at $200 and across from the vertical (consumption) axis at $150. These straight lines intersect at point *c*, which represents this particular income–consumption combination. You should verify that the other income–consumption combinations shown in the table are properly located in the graph. Finally, by assuming that the same general relationship between income and

---

FIGURE A1-1   The Relationship between Income and Consumption

Two sets of data that are positively or directly related, such as consumption and income, graph as an upsloping line.

Income per week	Consumption per week	Point
$ 0	$ 50	a
100	100	b
200	150	c
300	200	d
400	250	e

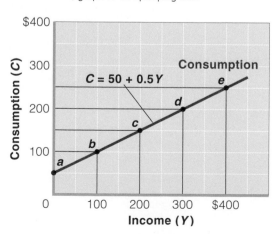

consumption prevails for all other incomes, we draw a line or smooth curve to connect these points. That line or curve represents the income–consumption relationship.

If the curve is a straight line, as in Figure A1-1, we say that the relationship is *linear*. (It is permissible, and even customary, to call straight lines in graphs "curves.")

Direct and Inverse Relationships

The line in Figure A1-1 slopes upward to the right, depicting a direct relationship between income and consumption. By a **direct relationship** (or positive relationship) we mean that two variables—in this case, consumption and income—change in the *same* direction. An increase in consumption is associated with an increase in income; a decrease in consumption accompanies a decrease in income. When two sets of data are positively or directly related, they always graph as an *upsloping* line, as in Figure A1-1.

In contrast, two sets of data may be inversely related. Consider Figure A1-2, which shows the relationship between the price of basketball tickets and game attendance at Informed University (IU). Here we have an **inverse relationship** (or negative relationship) because the two variables change in *opposite* directions. When ticket prices decrease, attendance increases. When ticket prices increase, attendance decreases. The six data points in the table are plotted in the graph. Observe that an inverse relationship always graphs as a *downsloping* line.

Dependent and Independent Variables

Although it is not always easy, economists seek to determine which variable is the "cause" and which is the "effect." Or, more formally, they seek the independent variable and the dependent variable. The **independent variable** is the cause or source; it is the variable that changes first. The **dependent variable** is the effect or outcome; it is the variable that changes because of the change in the independent variable. As in our income–consumption example, income generally is the independent variable and consumption the dependent variable. Income causes consumption to be what it is rather than the other way around. Similarly, ticket prices (set in advance of the season and printed on the ticket) determine attendance at Informed University basketball games; attendance at games does not determine the printed ticket prices for those games. Ticket price is the independent variable, and the quantity of tickets purchased is the dependent variable.

You may recall from your high school courses that mathematicians put the independent variable (cause) on the horizontal axis and the dependent variable (effect) on the vertical axis. Economists are less tidy; their graphing of independent and dependent variables is more arbitrary. Their conventional graphing of the income–consumption relationship is consistent with mathematical convention but economists put price and cost data on the vertical axis. Hence, economists' graphing

---

FIGURE A1-2   **The Relationship between Ticket Prices and Attendance**

Two sets of data that are negatively or inversely related, such as ticket price and the attendance at basketball games, graph as a downsloping line.

Ticket price	Attendance, thousands	Point
$50	0	a
40	4	b
30	8	c
20	12	d
10	16	e
0	20	f

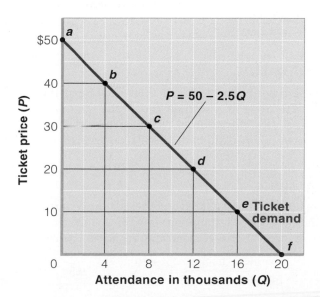

of IU's ticket price–attendance data differs from the normal mathematical procedure. This does not present a problem, but we want you to be aware of this fact to avoid any possible confusion.

Other Things Equal

Our simple two-variable graphs purposely ignore many other factors that might affect the amount of consumption occurring at each income level or the number of people who attend IU basketball games at each possible ticket price. When economists plot the relationship between any two variables, they employ the *ceteris paribus* (other-things-equal) assumption. Thus, in Figure A1-1 all factors other than income that might affect the amount of consumption are held constant. Similarly, in Figure A1-2 all factors other than ticket price that might influence attendance at IU basketball games are assumed constant. In reality, "other things" are not equal; they often change and when they do, the relationship represented in our two tables and graphs will change. Specifically, the lines we have plotted will *shift* to new locations.

Consider a stock market "crash." The dramatic drop in the value of stocks might cause people to feel less wealthy and therefore less willing to consume at each level of income. The result might be a downward shift of the consumption line. To see this, you should plot a new consumption line in Figure A1-1, assuming that consumption is, say, $20 less at each income level. Note that the relationship remains direct; the line merely shifts downward to reflect less consumption spending at each income level.

Similarly, factors other than ticket prices might affect IU game attendance. If IU loses most of its games, attendance at IU games might fall at each ticket price. To see this, redraw the graph in Figure A1-2, assuming that 2000 fewer fans attend IU games at each ticket price.

Slope of a Line

Lines can be described in terms of their slopes and their intercepts. The **slope of a straight line** is the ratio of the vertical change (the rise or drop) to the horizontal change (the run) between any two points of the line, or "rise" over "run."

POSITIVE SLOPE

Between point *c* and point *d* in Figure A1-1 the rise or vertical change (the change in consumption) is +$50 and the run or horizontal change (the change in income) is +$100. Therefore

$$\text{Slope} = \frac{\text{vertical change}}{\text{horizontal change}} = \frac{+50}{+100} = \frac{1}{2} = 0.5$$

Note that our slope of ½ or 0.5 is positive because consumption and income change in the same direction; that is, consumption and income are directly or positively related.

The slope of 0.5 tells us that there will be a $1 increase in consumption for every $2 increase in income. Similarly, it indicates that for every $2 decrease in income there will be a $1 decrease in consumption.

NEGATIVE SLOPE

Between any two of the identified points in Figure A1-2—say, point *c* and point *d*—the vertical change is −10 (the drop) and the horizontal change is +4 (the run). Therefore

$$\text{Slope} = \frac{\text{vertical change}}{\text{horizontal change}} = \frac{-10}{+4} = -2\frac{1}{2} = -2.5$$

This slope is negative because ticket price and attendance have an inverse or negative relationship.

Note that on the horizontal axis attendance is stated in thousands of people. So the slope of −10/+4 or −2.5 means that lowering the price by $10 will increase attendance by 4000 people. This is the same as saying that a $2.50 price reduction will increase attendance by 1000 people.

SLOPES AND MEASUREMENT UNITS

The slope of a line will be affected by the choice of units for either variable. If, in our ticket-price illustration, we had chosen to measure attendance in individual people, our horizontal change would have been 4000 and the slope would have been

$$\text{Slope} = \frac{-10}{+4000} = \frac{-1}{+400} = -0.0025$$

The slope depends on the units by which variables are measured.

SLOPES AND MARGINAL ANALYSIS

Recall that economics largely deals with changes from the status quo. The concept of slope is important in economics because it reflects marginal changes—those involving one more (or one fewer) unit. For example, in Figure A1-1 the 0.5 slope shows that $0.50 of extra or marginal consumption is associated with each $1 change in income. In this example, people collectively will consume $0.50 of any $1 increase in their incomes and reduce their consumption by $0.50 for each $1 decline in income.

INFINITE AND ZERO SLOPES

Many variables are unrelated or independent of one another. For example, the quantity of digital cameras purchased is not related to the price of bananas. In Figure A1-3a we represent the price of bananas on the vertical axis and the quantity of digital cameras demanded on the horizontal axis. The graph of their relationship is the line parallel to the vertical axis, indicating that

FIGURE A1-3   Infinite and Zero Slopes

(a) A line parallel to the vertical axis has an infinite slope. Here, purchases of digital cameras remain the same no matter what happens to the price of bananas.

(b) A line parallel to the horizontal axis has a slope of zero. In this case, consumption remains the same no matter what happens to the divorce rate. In both parts (a) and (b), the two variables are totally unrelated to one another.

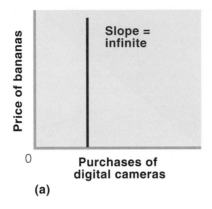

(a)

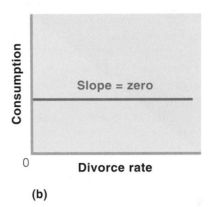

(b)

the same quantity of cameras is purchased no matter what the price of bananas. The slope of such a line is *infinite*.

Similarly, aggregate consumption is completely unrelated to the nation's divorce rate. In Figure A1-3b we put consumption on the vertical axis and the divorce rate on the horizontal axis. The line parallel to the horizontal axis represents this lack of relatedness. This line has a slope of *zero*.

Vertical Intercept

A line can be located on a graph (without plotting points) if we know its slope and its vertical intercept. We have already discussed the slope. The **vertical intercept** of a line is the point where the line meets the vertical axis. In Figure A1-1 the intercept is $50. This intercept means that if current income were zero, consumers would still spend $50. They might do this through borrowing or by selling some of their assets. Similarly, the $50 vertical intercept in Figure A1-2 shows that at a $50 ticket price, IU's basketball team would be playing in an empty arena.

Equation of a Linear Relationship

If we know the vertical intercept and slope, we can describe a line succinctly in equation form. In its general form the equation of a straight line is

$$y = a + bx$$

where y = dependent variable

a = vertical intercept

b = slope of line

x = independent variable

For our income–consumption example, if C represents consumption (the dependent variable) and Y represents income (the independent variable), we can write $C = a + bY$. By substituting the known values of the intercept and the slope, we get

$$C = 50 + 0.5Y$$

This equation also allows us to determine the amount of consumption C at any specific level of income. You should use it to confirm that at the $250 income level, consumption is $175.

When economists reverse mathematical convention by putting the independent variable on the vertical axis and the dependent variable on the horizontal axis, then y stands for the independent variable, rather than the dependent variable in the general form. We noted previously that this case is relevant for our IU ticket price–attendance data. If P represents the ticket price (independent variable) and Q represents attendance (dependent variable), their relationship is given by

$$P = 50 - 2.5Q$$

where the vertical intercept is 50 and the negative slope is $-2\frac{1}{2}$ or -2.5. Knowing the value of P lets us solve for Q, our dependent variable. You should use this equation to predict IU ticket sales when the ticket price is $15.

Slope of a Non-linear Curve

We now move from the simple world of linear relationships (straight lines) to the more complex world of non-linear relationships. The slope of a straight line is the same at all its

KEY GRAPH

FIGURE A1-4   Determining the Slopes of Curves

The slope of a non-linear curve changes from point to point on the curve. The slope at any point (say, *B*) can be determined by drawing a straight line that is tangent to that point (line *bb′*) and calculating the slope of that line.

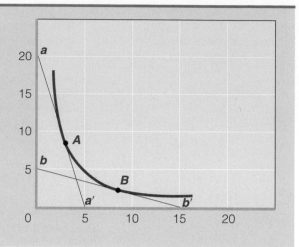

points. The slope of a line representing a non-linear relationship changes from one point to another. Such lines are always referred to as *curves*.

Consider the downsloping curve in Figure A1-4. Its slope is negative throughout, but the curve flattens as we move down along it. Thus, its slope constantly changes; the curve has a different slope at each point.

To measure the slope at a specific point, we draw a straight line tangent to the curve at that point. A straight line is *tangent* at a point if it touches, but does not intersect, the curve at that

point. Thus line *aa′* is tangent to the curve in Figure A1-4 at point *A*. The slope of the curve at that point is equal to the slope of the tangent line. Specifically, the total vertical change (drop) in the tangent line *aa′* is −20 and the total horizontal change (run) is +5. Because the slope of the tangent line *aa′* is −20/+5, or −4, the slope of the curve at point *A* is also −4.

Line *bb′* in Figure A1-4 is tangent to the curve at point *B*. Following the same procedure, we find the slope at *B* to be −5/+15, or −⅓. Thus, in this flatter part of the curve, the slope is less negative.

APPENDIX Summary

A1.1 GRAPHS AND THEIR MEANINGS

- Graphs are a convenient and revealing means of representing economic relationships.

- Two variables are positively or directly related when their values change in the same direction. The line (curve) representing two directly related variables slopes upward.

- Two variables are negatively or inversely related when their values change in opposite directions. The line (curve) representing two inversely related variables slopes downward.

- The value of the dependent variable (the "effect") is determined by the value of the independent variable (the "cause").

- When the "other factors" that might affect a two-variable relationship are allowed to change, the graph of the relationship will likely shift to a new location.

- The slope of a straight line is the ratio of the vertical change to the horizontal change between any two points. The slope of an upsloping line is positive; the slope of a downsloping line is negative.

- The slope of a line or curve depends on the units used in measuring the variables. It is especially relevant for economics because it measures marginal changes.

- The slope of a horizontal line is zero; the slope of a vertical line is infinite.

- Together, the vertical intercept and slope of a line determine its location; they are used in expressing the line—and the relationship between the two variables—as an equation.

- The slope of a curve at any point is determined by calculating the slope of a straight line tangent to the curve at that point.

APPENDIX Terms and Concepts

horizontal axis   The "left–right" or "west–east" axis on a graph or grid. (p. 26)

vertical axis   The "up–down" or "north–south" axis on a graph or grid. (p. 26)

direct relationship   The (positive) relationship between two variables that change in the same direction, for example, product price and quantity supplied. (p. 27)

inverse relationship   The (negative) relationship between two variables that change in opposite directions, for example, product price and quantity demanded. (p. 27)

independent variable   The variable causing a change in some other (dependent) variable. (p. 27)

dependent variable   A variable that changes as a consequence of a change in some other (independent) variable; the "effect" or outcome. (p. 27)

slope of a straight line   The ratio of the vertical change (the rise or fall) to the horizontal change (the run) between any two points on a line. The slope of an upsloping line is positive, reflecting a direct relationship between two variables; the slope of a downsloping line is negative, reflecting an inverse relationship between two variables. (p. 28)

vertical intercept   The point at which a line meets the vertical axis of a graph. (p. 29)

APPENDIX Questions

1. Briefly explain the use of graphs as a means of representing economic relationships. What is an inverse relationship? How does it graph? What is a direct relationship? How does it graph? [**LOA1.1**]

2. Describe the graphical relationship between ticket prices and the number of people choosing to visit amusement parks. Is that relationship consistent with the fact that, historically, park attendance and ticket prices have both risen? Explain.   [**LOA1.1**]

3. Look back at Figure A1-2, which shows the inverse relationship between ticket prices and game attendance at Informed University.   [**LOA1.1**]

   a. Interpret the meaning of both the slope and the intercept.

   b. If the slope of the line were steeper, what would that say about the amount by which ticket sales respond to increases in ticket prices?

   c. If the slope of the line stayed the same but the intercept increased, what could you say about the amount by which ticket sales respond to increases in ticket prices?

APPENDIX Problems

1. Graph and label as either direct or indirect the relationships you would expect to find between the following: [**LOA1.1**]

   a. the number of centimetres of rainfall per month and the sale of umbrellas.

   b. the amount of tuition and the level of enrolment at a college or university.

   c. the popularity of a music artist and the price of her concert tickets.

2. Indicate how each of the following might affect the data shown in Figure A1-2 of this appendix: [**LOA1.1**]

   a. IU's athletic director schedules higher-quality opponents.

   b. A National Basketball Association (NBA) team locates in the city where IU also plays.

   c. IU signs a contract to have all of its home games televised.

3. The following table contains data on the relationship between saving and income. Rearrange these data into a meaningful order and graph them on the accompanying grid. What is the slope of the line? What is the vertical intercept? Write the equation that represents this line.

What would you predict saving to be at the $12,500 level of income? [**LOA1.1**]

Income (per year)	Saving (per year)
$15,000	$1,000
0	−500
10,000	500
5,000	0
20,000	1,500

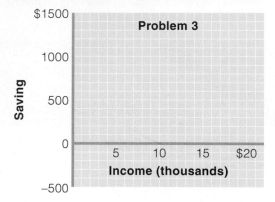

4. Construct a table from the data shown on the graph below. Which is the dependent variable and which the independent variable? Summarize the data in equation form. [**LOA1.1**]

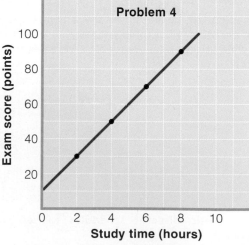

5. Suppose that when the interest rate on loans is 16 percent, businesses find it unprofitable to invest in machinery and equipment. However, when the interest rate is 14 percent, $5 billion worth of investment is profitable. At 12 percent interest, a total of $10 billion of investment is profitable. Similarly, total investment increases by $5 billion for each successive 2-percentage-point decline in the interest rate. [**LOA1.1**]

Describe the relevant relationship between the interest rate and investment, in a table, graphically, and as an equation. Put the interest rate on the vertical axis and

investment on the horizontal axis. In your equation use the form $i = a - bI$, where i is the interest rate, a is the vertical intercept, $-b$ is the slope of the line (which is negative), and I is the level of investment.

6. Suppose that $C = a + bY$, where C = consumption, a = consumption at zero income, b = slope, and Y = income. [**LOA1.1**]

   a. Are C and Y positively related or are they negatively related?

   b. If graphed, would the curve for this equation slope upward or slope downward?

   c. Are the variables C and Y inversely related or directly related?

   d. What is the value of C if $a = 10$, $b = 0.50$, and $Y = 200$?

   e. What is the value of Y if $C = 100$, $a = 10$, and $b = 0.25$?

7. The accompanying graph shows curve XX' and tangents at points A, B, and C. Calculate the slope of the curve at these three points. [**LOA1.1**]

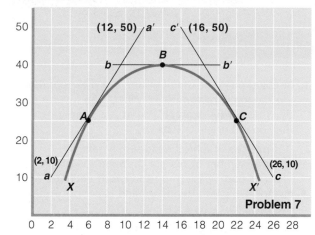

8. In the accompanying graph, is the slope of curve AA' positive or negative? Does the slope increase or decrease as we move along the curve from A to A'? Answer the same two questions for curve BB'. [**LOA1.1**]

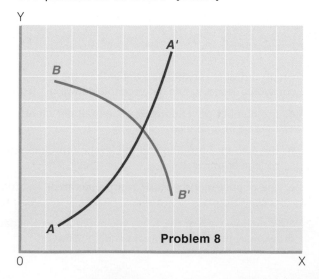

The Market System and the Circular Flow

AFTER READING THIS CHAPTER, YOU SHOULD BE ABLE TO:

2.1 Differentiate between a command system and a market system.

2.2 List the main characteristics of the market system.

2.3 Explain how the market system decides what to produce, how to produce it, and who obtains it. Discuss how the market system adjusts to change and promotes progress.

2.4 Explain the demise of the command system.

2.5 Describe the mechanics of the circular flow model.

Imagine you are at a mall in Halifax. Suppose you are assigned to compile a list of all the individual goods and services there, including the different brands and variations of each type of product. That task would be daunting and the list would be long! And even though a single shopping mall in Vancouver contains a remarkable quantity and variety of goods, it is only a tiny part of the Canadian economy.

Who decided that the particular goods and services available at the mall and in the broader Canadian economy should be produced? How did the producers determine which technology and types of factors to use in producing these particular goods? Who will obtain these products? What accounts for the new and improved products among these goods? This chapter will answer these and related questions.

2.1 Economic Systems ::

Every society needs to develop an **economic system**—a particular set of institutional arrangements and a coordinating mechanism—to respond to the economic problem. The economic system determines what goods are produced, how they are produced, who gets them, how to accommodate change, and how to promote technological progress.

economic system
A particular set of institutional arrangements and a coordinating mechanism for producing goods and services.

Economic systems differ as to (1) who owns the factors of production and (2) the method used to motivate, coordinate, and direct economic activity. There are two general types of economic systems: the command system and the market system.

The Command System

command system
An economic system in which most property resources are owned by the government and economic decisions are made by a central government body.

The **command system** is also known as *socialism* or *communism*. In a command system, government owns most property resources and economic decision making occurs through a central economic plan. A central planning board appointed by the government makes nearly all the major decisions concerning the use of resources, the composition and distribution of output, and the organization of production. The government owns most of the business firms, which produce according to government directives. The central planning board determines production goals for each enterprise and specifies the amount of resources to be allocated to each enterprise so that it can reach its production goals. The division of output between capital and consumer goods is centrally decided, and capital goods are allocated among industries on the basis of the central planning board's long-term priorities.

A pure command economy would rely exclusively on a central plan to allocate the government-owned property resources. But, in reality, even the pre-eminent command economy—the Soviet Union—tolerated some private ownership and incorporated some markets before its collapse in 1992. Recent reforms in Russia and most of the eastern European nations have to one degree or another transformed their command economies to market-oriented systems. China's reforms have not gone as far, but they have greatly reduced the reliance on central planning. Although there is still extensive government ownership of resources and capital in China, the nation has increasingly relied on free markets to organize and coordinate its economy. North Korea and Cuba are the last remaining examples of largely centrally planned economies although there are slow changes in Cuba that lead some observers to speculate that it will move toward a market economy. For example, in late 2011, the Cuban government declared that citizens would be able to buy and sell cars. Later in this chapter, we will explore the main reasons for the general demise of the command systems.

The Market System

market system
An economic system in which property resources are privately owned, and markets and prices are used to direct and coordinate economic activities.

The opposite of the command system is the **market system,** or *capitalism*. The system is characterized by the private ownership of resources and the use of markets and prices to coordinate and direct economic activity. Participants act in their own self-interest. Individuals and businesses seek to achieve their economic goals through their own decisions regarding work, consumption, or production. The system allows for the private ownership of capital, communicates through prices, and coordinates economic activity through *markets*—places where buyers and sellers come together to buy and sell goods, services, and resources. Goods and services are produced and resources are supplied by whoever is willing and able to do so at the prevailing prices. The result is competition among independently acting buyers and sellers of each product and resource. Thus, economic decision making is widely dispersed. Also, the high potential for monetary rewards creates powerful incentives for existing firms to innovate and entrepreneurs to pioneer new products and processes.

In *pure* capitalism—or *laissez-faire* capitalism—government's role is limited to protecting private property and establishing an environment appropriate to the operation of the market system. The term "laissez-faire" means "let it be"; that is, keep the government from interfering with the economy. The idea is that such interference will inhibit the efficient working of the market system.

But, in the capitalism practised in Canada and most other countries, government plays a significant role in the economy. It not only provides the rules for economic activity but also attempts

connect
ORIGIN OF THE IDEA 2.1
Laissez-faire

to promote economic stability and growth, provides certain goods and services that would otherwise be underproduced or not produced at all, and modifies the distribution of income. The government, however, is not the dominant economic force in deciding what to produce, how to produce it, and who will get it. That force is the market.

2.2 Characteristics of the Market System

An examination of some of the key features of the market system in detail will be instructive.

Private Property

private property
The right of private persons and firms to obtain, own, control, employ, dispose of, and bequeath land, capital, and other property.

In a market system, private individuals and firms, not the government, own most of the property resources (land and capital). It is this extensive private ownership of capital that gives capitalism its name. This right of **private property**, coupled with the freedom to negotiate binding legal contracts, enables individuals and businesses to obtain, use, and dispose of property resources as they see fit. The right of property owners to designate who will receive their property when they die sustains the institution of private property.

Property rights encourage investment, innovation, exchange, maintenance of property, and economic growth. No one would stock a store, build a factory, or clear land for farming if someone else, or the government itself, could take that property for his or her own benefit.

The most important consequence of property rights is that they encourage people to cooperate by helping to ensure that only *mutually agreeable* economic transactions take place. To consider why this is true, imagine a world without legally enforceable property rights. In such a world, the strong could simply take whatever they wanted from the weak without giving them any compensation. But in a world of legally enforceable property rights, any person wanting something from you has to get you to agree to give it to them. And you can say no. The result is that if they really want what you have, they must offer you something that you value more highly in return. That is, they must offer you a mutually agreeable economic transaction—one that benefits you as well as them.

Property rights also extend to intellectual property through patents, copyrights, and trademarks. Such long-term protection encourages people to write books, music, and computer programs and to invent new products and production processes without fear that others will steal them and the rewards they may bring.

Moreover, property rights facilitate exchange. The title to an automobile or the deed to a cattle ranch assures the buyer that the seller is the legitimate owner. Also, property rights encourage owners to maintain or improve their property so as to preserve or increase its value. Finally, property rights enable people to use their time and resources to produce more goods and services, rather than using them to protect and retain the property they have already produced or acquired.

Freedom of Enterprise and Choice

freedom of enterprise
The freedom of firms to obtain economic resources, to use these resources to produce products of the firm's own choosing, and to sell their products in markets of their choice.

Closely related to private ownership of property is freedom of enterprise and choice. The market system requires that various economic units make certain choices, which are expressed and implemented in the economy's markets:

- **Freedom of enterprise** ensures that entrepreneurs and private businesses are free to obtain and use economic resources to produce their choice of goods and services and to sell them in their chosen markets.

GLOBAL PERSPECTIVE

2.1

Index of Economic Freedom, Selected Nations

The Index of Economic Freedom measures economic freedom using 10 broad categories, such as trade policy, property rights, and government intervention, with each category containing more than 50 specific criteria. The Index then ranks 184 nations according to the degree of economic freedom. A few selected rankings for 2012 are listed here.

FREE
1 Hong Kong
3 Australia
5 Switzerland

MOSTLY FREE
6 Canada
10 United States
14 United Kingdom
22 Japan

MODERATELY FREE
36 Spain
38 Belgium
67 France

MOSTLY UNFREE
99 Brazil
138 China
144 Russia

REPRESSED
171 Iran
174 Venezuela
177 Cuba
179 North Korea

Source: Heritage Foundation (http://www.heritage.org/index/ranking, accessed April 13, 2012) and the *Wall Street Journal*.

freedom of choice
The freedom of owners of property resources to employ or dispose of them as they see fit, and of consumers to spend their incomes in a manner that they think is appropriate.

• **Freedom of choice** enables owners to employ or dispose of their property and money as they see fit. It also allows workers to enter any line of work for which they are qualified. Finally, it ensures that consumers are free to buy the goods and services that best satisfy their wants.

These choices are free only within broad legal limitations, of course. Illegal choices—such as selling human organs or buying illicit drugs—are punished through fines and imprisonment. (Global Perspective 2.1 reveals that the degree of economic freedom varies greatly from economy to economy.)

connect
ORIGIN OF THE IDEA 2.2
Self-Interest

self-interest
That which each firm, property owner, worker, and consumer believes is best for itself.

Self-Interest

In the market system, **self-interest** is the motivating force of the various economic units as they express their free choices. Self-interest simply means that each economic unit tries to achieve its own particular goal, which usually requires delivering something of value to others. Entrepreneurs try to maximize profit or minimize loss. Property owners try to get the highest price for selling or renting their resources. Workers try to maximize their utility (satisfaction) by finding jobs that offer the best combination of wages, hours, fringe benefits, and working conditions. Consumers try to obtain the products they want at the lowest possible price and apportion their expenditures to maximize their utility. The motive of self-interest gives direction and consistency to what might otherwise be a chaotic economy.

Competition

competition
The presence in a market of a large number of independent buyers and sellers competing with one another, and the freedom of buyers and sellers to enter and leave the market.

The market system depends on **competition** among economic units. The basis of this competition is freedom of choice exercised in pursuit of a monetary return. Very broadly defined, competition requires:

- independently acting sellers and buyers operating in a particular product or factor market
- freedom of sellers and buyers to enter or leave markets, on the basis of their economic self-interest

Competition among buyers and sellers diffuses economic power within the businesses and households that make up the economy. When there are independently acting sellers and buyers in a market, no single buyer or seller is able to dictate the price of the product or factor because others can undercut that price.

Competition also implies that producers can enter or leave an industry; there are no insurmountable barriers to an industry's expanding or contracting. This freedom of an industry to expand or contract provides the economy with the flexibility needed to remain efficient over time. Freedom of entry and exit enables the economy to adjust to changes in consumer tastes, technology, and factor availability.

The diffusion of economic power inherent in competition limits the potential abuse of that power. A producer that charges more than the competitive market price will lose sales to other producers. An employer who pays less than the competitive market wage rate will lose workers to other employers. A firm that fails to exploit new technology will lose profits to firms that do. A firm that produces shoddy products will be punished as customers switch to higher-quality items made by rival firms. Competition is the basic regulatory force in the market system.

Markets and Prices

We may wonder why an economy based on self-interest does not collapse in chaos. If consumers want breakfast cereal but businesses choose to produce running shoes and resource suppliers decide to make computer software, production would seem to be deadlocked by the apparent inconsistencies of free choices.

market
Any institution or mechanism that brings together buyers and sellers of particular goods, services, or resources for the purpose of exchange.

In reality, the millions of decisions made by households and businesses are highly coordinated with one another. Markets and prices are key components of the market system. They give the system its ability to coordinate millions of daily economic decisions. A **market** is an institution or mechanism that brings buyers ("demanders") and sellers ("suppliers") into contact. A market system conveys the decisions made by buyers and sellers of products and factors. The decisions made on each side of the market determine a set of product and factor prices that guide resource owners, entrepreneurs, and consumers as they make and revise their choices and pursue their self-interest.

Just as competition is the regulatory mechanism of the market system, the market system itself is the organizing and coordinating mechanism. It is an elaborate communication network through which innumerable individual free choices on the part of consumers and producers are recorded, summarized, and balanced. Those who respond to market signals and heed market dictates are rewarded with greater profit and income; those who do not respond to those signals and choose to ignore market dictates are penalized. Through this mechanism society decides what the economy should produce, how production can be organized efficiently, and how the fruits of production are to be distributed among the various units that make up the economy.

Technology and Capital Goods

In the market system, competition, freedom of choice, self-interest, and personal reward provide the opportunity and motivation for technological advance. The monetary rewards for new products or production techniques accrue directly to the innovator. The market system therefore encourages extensive use and rapid development of complex capital goods: tools, machinery, large-scale factories, and facilities for storage, communication, transportation, and marketing.

Advanced technology and capital goods are important because the most direct methods of production are often the least efficient. The only way to avoid that inefficiency is to rely on capital goods. It would be ridiculous for a farmer to go at production with bare hands. There are huge benefits to be derived from creating and using such capital equipment as plows, tractors, storage bins, and so on. More efficient production means much more abundant output.

Specialization

specialization
The use of the resources of an individual, a firm, a region, or a nation to produce one or a few goods and services.

The extent to which market economies rely on **specialization** is astonishing. Specialization is using the resources of an individual, region, or nation to produce one or a few goods or services rather than the entire range of goods and services. Those goods and services are then exchanged for a full range of desired products. The majority of consumers produce virtually none of the goods and services they consume, and they consume little or nothing of the items they produce. The person working nine-to-five installing windows in commercial aircraft may rarely fly. Many farmers sell their milk to the local dairy and then buy butter at the local grocery store. Society learned long ago that self-sufficiency breeds inefficiency. The jack-of-all-trades may be a very colourful individual but is certainly not an efficient producer.

DIVISION OF LABOUR

division of labour
Dividing the work required to produce a product into a number of different tasks that are performed by different workers.

connect
ORIGIN OF THE IDEA 2.3
Specialization: Division of Labour

Human specialization—called the **division of labour**—contributes to a society's output in several ways:

- *Specialization Makes Use of Differences in Ability* Specialization enables individuals to take advantage of existing differences in their abilities and skills. If Peyton is strong, athletic, and good at throwing a football and Beyoncé is beautiful, is agile, and can sing, their distribution of talents can be most efficiently used if Peyton plays professional football and Beyoncé records songs and gives concerts.

- *Specialization Fosters Learning by Doing* Even if the abilities of two people are identical, specialization may still be advantageous. By devoting time to a single task, a person is more likely to develop the skills required and to improve techniques than by working at a number of different tasks. You learn to be a good lawyer by studying and practising law.

- ***Specialization Saves Time*** By devoting time to a single task, a person avoids the loss of time incurred in shifting from one job to another. Also, time is saved by not "fumbling around" with tasks that one is not trained to do.

For all these reasons, specialization increases the total output society derives from limited resources.

GEOGRAPHIC SPECIALIZATION

Specialization also works on a regional and international basis. It is conceivable that apples could be grown in Saskatchewan, but because of the unsuitability of the land, rainfall, and temperature, the costs would be very high. And it is conceivable that wheat could be grown in British Columbia, but such production would be costly for similar geographical reasons. So, Saskatchewan farmers produce products—wheat in particular—for which their resources are best suited, and British Columbians (especially in the Okanagan Valley) do the same, producing apples and other fruits. By specializing, both regional economies produce more than is needed locally. Then, very sensibly, Saskatchewan and British Columbia exchange some of their surpluses—wheat for apples, apples for wheat.

Similarly, on an international scale, Canada specializes in producing such items as commercial aircraft (Bombardier) and communication equipment (Research In Motion), which it sells abroad in exchange for digital video cameras from Japan, bananas from Honduras, and woven baskets from Thailand. Both human specialization and geographic specialization are needed to achieve efficiency in the use of limited resources.

Use of Money

medium of exchange
Items sellers generally accept and buyers generally use to pay for a good or service.

barter
The exchange of one good or service for another good or service.

money
Any item that is generally acceptable to sellers in exchange for goods and services.

A rather obvious characteristic of any economic system is the extensive use of money. Money performs several functions, but first and foremost it is a **medium of exchange.** It makes trade easier.

Specialization requires exchange. Exchange can, and sometimes does, occur through **barter**—swapping goods for goods; say, exchanging wheat for apples. But barter poses serious problems because it requires a *coincidence of wants* between the buyer and the seller. In our example, we assumed that Saskatchewan had excess wheat to trade and wanted apples. And we assumed that British Columbia had excess apples to trade and wanted wheat. So an exchange occurred. But if such a coincidence of wants is missing, trade will not occur.

Suppose that Saskatchewan has no interest in British Columbia's apples but wants potatoes from Prince Edward Island. And suppose that Prince Edward Island wants British Columbia's apples but not Saskatchewan's wheat. And, to complicate matters, suppose that British Columbia wants some of Saskatchewan's wheat but none of Prince Edward Island's potatoes. We summarize the situation in Figure 2-1.

In none of the cases shown in the figure is there a coincidence of wants. Trade by barter would obviously be difficult. Instead, people in each province use **money,** which is simply a convenient social invention to facilitate exchanges of goods and services. Historically, people have used cattle, cigarettes, shells, stones, pieces of metal, and many other commodities, with varying degrees of success, as money. To serve as money, an item needs to pass only one test: It must be generally acceptable to sellers in exchange for their goods and services. Money is socially defined: whatever society accepts as a medium of exchange *is* money.

Today, most economies use pieces of paper as money. The use of paper dollars (currency) as a medium of exchange is what enables Saskatchewan, British Columbia, and Prince Edward Island to overcome their trade stalemate, as demonstrated in Figure 2-1.

FIGURE 2-1   **Money Facilitates Trade When Wants Do Not Coincide**

The use of money as a medium of exchange permits trade to be accomplished despite a non–coincidence of wants. (1) Saskatchewan trades the wheat that British Columbia wants for money; (2) Saskatchewan trades the money it receives from British Columbia for the potatoes it wants from Prince Edward Island; (3) Prince Edward Island trades the money it receives from Saskatchewan for the apples it wants from British Columbia.

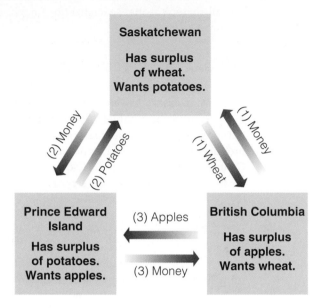

On a global basis, specialization and exchange are complicated by the fact that different nations have different currencies. But swapping dollars, yen, euros, pounds, and pesos for one another in markets in which currencies are bought and sold makes it possible for people living in different countries to exchange goods and services without resorting to barter.

Active, But Limited, Government

An active, but limited, government is the final characteristic of market systems in modern advanced industrial economies. Although a market system promotes a high degree of efficiency in the use of its resources, it has certain inherent shortcomings called "market failures." We will discover in subsequent chapters that government can increase the overall efficiency of the market system in several ways.

QUICK REVIEW

- The market systems of modern industrial economies are characterized by extensive use of technologically advanced capital goods. Such goods help these economies achieve greater efficiency in production.

- Specialization is extensive in market systems; it enhances efficiency and output

by enabling individuals, regions, and nations to produce the goods and services for which their resources are best suited.

- The use of money in market systems facilitates the exchange of goods and services that specialization requires.

2.3 Five Fundamental Questions

The key features of the market system help explain how market economies respond to five fundamental questions:

- What goods and services will be produced?
- How will the goods and services be produced?
- Who will get the goods and services?
- How will the system accommodate change?
- How will the system promote progress?

These five questions highlight the economic choices underlying the production possibilities curve discussed in Chapter 1. They reflect the reality of scarce resources in a world of unlimited wants. All economies, whether market or command, must address these five questions.

What Will Be Produced?

How will a market system decide on the specific types and quantities of goods and services to be produced? The simple answer is this: The goods and services that can be produced at a continuing profit will be produced while those whose production generates a continuing loss will be discontinued. Profits and losses are the difference between the total revenue (TR) a firm receives from the sale of its products and the total cost (TC) of producing those products. (For economists, total costs include not only wage and salary payments to labour, and interest and rental payments for capital and land, but also payments to the entrepreneur for organizing and combining the other resources to produce a product.)

Continuing economic profit (TR > TC) in an industry results in expanded production and the movement of resources toward that industry. Existing firms grow and new firms enter. The industry expands. Continuing losses (TC > TR) in an industry lead to reduced production and the departure of resources from that industry. Some existing firms shrink in size; others go out of business. The industry contracts.

consumer sovereignty
Determination by consumers of the types and quantities of goods and services that will be produced with the scarce resources of the economy.

In the market system, consumers are sovereign (in command). **Consumer sovereignty** is crucial in determining the types and quantities of goods produced. Consumers spend their income on the goods they are most willing and able to buy. Through these "**dollar votes**" they register their wants in the market. If the dollar votes for a certain product are large enough to create a profit, businesses will produce that product and offer it for sale. In contrast, if the dollar votes do not create sufficient revenues to cover costs, businesses will not produce the product. So the consumers are sovereign. Through their dollar votes they collectively direct resources to industries that are meeting consumer wants and away from industries that are not meeting consumer wants.

dollar votes
The "votes" that consumers and entrepreneurs cast for the production of consumer and capital goods, respectively, when they purchase them in product and resource markets.

The dollar votes of consumers determine not only which industries will continue to exist but also which products will survive or fail. Only profitable industries, firms, and products survive, so firms are not really free to produce whatever products they want. Consumers' buying decisions make the production of some products profitable and the production of other products unprofitable, thus restricting the choice of businesses in deciding what to produce. Businesses must match their production choices with consumer choices or else face losses and eventual bankruptcy.

The same holds true for resource (factor) suppliers. The employment of resources derives from the sale of the goods and services that the resources help produce. Autoworkers are employed because automobiles are sold. There are few remaining professors of early Latin because there are few people who want to learn the Latin language. Resource suppliers that want to earn income are not truly free to allocate their resources to the production of goods or services that consumers do not value highly. Consumers register their preferences in the market; producers and resource suppliers, prompted by their own self-interest, try to satisfy those preferences.

How Will the Goods and Services Be Produced?

What combinations of resources and technologies will be used to produce goods and services? How will the production be organized? The answer: in combinations and ways that minimize the cost per unit of output. This is true because inefficiency drives up costs and lowers profits. As a result, any firm wishing to maximize its profits will make great efforts to minimize production costs. These efforts will include using the right mix of labour and capital, given the prices and productivity of those factors of production. They also mean locating production facilities optimally to minimize production and transportation expenses.

Those efforts will be intensified if the firm faces competition, as consumers strongly prefer low prices and will shift their purchases over to the firms that can produce a quality product at the lowest possible price. Any firm foolish enough to use higher-cost production methods will go bankrupt as it is undersold by its more efficient competitors who can still make a profit when selling at a lower price. Simply stated: Competition eliminates high-cost producers.

Least-cost production means that firms must employ the most economically efficient technique of production in producing their output. The most efficient production technique depends on:

- the available technology; that is, the available body of knowledge and techniques that can be used to combine economic resources to produce the desired results.

- the prices of the needed resources.

A technique that requires just a few inputs of resources to produce a specific output may be highly inefficient economically if those resources are valued very highly in the market. Economic efficiency requires obtaining a particular output of product with the least input of scarce resources, when both output and resource inputs are measured in dollars and cents.

Mc Graw Hill connect
WORKED PROBLEM 2.1
Least Cost Production

Who Will Get the Output?

The market system enters the picture in two ways when determining the distribution of total output. Generally, any product will be distributed to consumers on the basis of their ability and willingness to pay its existing market price. If the price of some product—say, a small sailboat—is $3000, then buyers who are willing and able to pay that price will get it; those unwilling or unable to pay the price will not.

The ability to pay the prices for sailboats and other products depends on the amount of income that consumers have, along with the prices of, and preferences for, various goods. If consumers have sufficient income and want to spend their money on a particular good, they can have it. The amount of income they have depends on (1) the quantities of the property and human resources they supply and (2) the prices those resources command in the factor market. Factor prices (wages, interest, rent, profit) are crucial in determining the size of each person's income and therefore each person's ability to buy part of the economy's output. If a lawyer earning $300 an hour and a janitor earning $10 an hour both work the same number of hours each year, then each year the lawyer will be able to purchase 30 times more of society's output than the janitor.

How Will the System Accommodate Change?

Market systems are dynamic: consumer preferences, technology, and supplies of resources can all change at the same time. This means that the particular allocation of resources that is now the most efficient for a specific pattern of consumer tastes, range of technological alternatives, and amount of available resources will become obsolete and inefficient as consumer preferences change, new techniques of production are discovered, and resource supplies change over time. Can the market economy adjust to such changes?

Suppose consumer tastes change. For instance, assume that consumers decide they want more fruit juice and less milk than the economy currently provides. Those changes in consumer tastes will be communicated to producers through an increase in spending on fruit juice and a decline in spending on milk. Other things equal, prices and profits in the fruit juice industry will rise and those in the milk industry will fall. Self-interest will induce existing competitors to expand output and entice new competitors to enter the prosperous fruit juice industry and will in time force firms to scale down—or even exit—the depressed milk industry.

The higher prices and greater economic profit in the fruit juice industry will not only induce that industry to expand but will give it the revenue needed to obtain the resources necessary to its growth. Higher prices and profits will permit fruit juice producers to draw more resources from less urgent alternative employment. The reverse occurs in the milk industry, where fewer workers and other resources are employed. These adjustments in the economy are automatic responses to the changes in consumer tastes. This is consumer sovereignty at work.

The market system is a gigantic communications system. Through changes in prices and profits it communicates changes in consumer demand and elicits appropriate responses from businesses and resource suppliers. By affecting price and profits, changes in consumer demand direct the expansion of some industries and the contraction of others. Those adjustments are conveyed to the factor market. As expanding industries employ more factors of production and contracting industries employ fewer, the resulting changes in factor prices (wages and salaries, for example) and income flows steer resources from the contracting industries to the expanding industries.

guiding function of prices
The ability of prices to bring about changes in the quantities of products and resources demanded and supplied.

This *directing* or **guiding function of prices** and profits is a core element of the market system. Without such a system, a government planning board or some other administrative agency would have to direct businesses and resources into the appropriate industries. A similar analysis shows that the system can and does adjust to other fundamental changes—for example, to changes in technology and in the prices of various resources.

How Will the System Promote Progress?

Society desires economic growth (greater output) and higher standards of living (greater output *per person*). How does the market system promote technological improvements and capital accumulation, both of which contribute to a higher standard of living for society?

TECHNOLOGICAL ADVANCE

The market system provides a strong incentive for technological advance and enables better products and processes to supplant inferior ones. An entrepreneur or firm that introduces a popular new product will gain revenue and economic profit at the expense of rivals.

technological advance
New and better goods and services, and new and better ways of producing or distributing them.

Technological advance also includes new and improved methods that reduce production or distribution costs. By passing on part of its cost reduction to the consumer through a lower product price, the firm can increase sales and obtain economic profit at the expense of rival firms.

Moreover, the market system promotes the *rapid spread* of technological advance throughout an industry. Rival firms must follow the lead of the most innovative firm or else suffer immediate losses and eventual failure. In some cases, the result is **creative destruction:** the creation of new products and production methods completely destroys the market positions of firms that are wedded to existing products and older ways of doing business. For example, the advent of compact discs largely demolished long-play vinyl records, and iPods and other digital technologies are now supplanting CDs.

creative destruction
The hypothesis that the creation of new products and production methods simultaneously destroys the market power of firms that are wedded to existing products and older ways of doing business.

CAPITAL ACCUMULATION

Most technological advances require additional capital goods. The market system provides the resources necessary to produce additional capital goods through increased dollar votes for those goods.

But who will count the dollar votes for capital goods? Answer: entrepreneurs and business owners. As receivers of profit income, they often use part of that income to purchase capital goods. Doing so yields even greater profit income in the future if the technological innovation that required the additional capital good is successful. Also, by paying interest or selling ownership shares, the entrepreneur and firm can attract some of the income of households to cast dollar votes for the production of more capital goods.

- The output mix of the market system is determined by profits, which in turn depend heavily on consumer preferences. Economic profits cause industries to expand; losses cause industries to contract.

- Competition forces industries to use the least costly production methods.

- In a market economy, consumer income and product prices determine how output will be distributed.

- Competitive markets reallocate resources in response to changes in consumer tastes, technological advances, and changes in availability of resources.

- Competitive markets create incentives for technological advance and capital accumulation, both of which contribute to increases in standards of living.

The "Invisible Hand"

In his 1776 book *The Wealth of Nations,* Adam Smith first noted that the operation of a market system creates a curious unity between private interests and social interests. Firms and resource suppliers, seeking to further their own self-interest and operating within the framework of a highly competitive market system, will simultaneously, as though guided by an **"invisible hand,"** promote the public or social interest. For example, we have seen that in a competitive environment, businesses seek to build new and improved products to increase profits. Those enhanced products increase society's well-being. Businesses also use the least costly combination of resources to produce a specific output because it is in their self-interest to do so. To act otherwise would be to forgo profit or even to risk business failure. But, at the same time, to use scarce resources in the least costly way is clearly in the social interest as well. It "frees up" resources to produce something else that society desires.

Self-interest, awakened and guided by the competitive market system, is what induces responses appropriate to the changes in society's wants. Businesses seeking to make higher profits and to avoid losses, and resource suppliers pursuing greater monetary rewards, negotiate changes in the allocation of resources and end up with the output that society wants. Competition guides self-interest such that self-interest automatically and quite unintentionally furthers the best interest of society. The invisible hand ensures that when firms maximize their profits and resource suppliers maximize their incomes, these groups also help maximize society's output and income.

Of the various virtues of the market system, three merit re-emphasis:

- *Efficiency* The market system promotes the efficient use of resources, by guiding them into the production of the goods and services most wanted by society. It forces the use of the most efficient techniques in organizing resources for production, and it encourages the development and adoption of new and more efficient production techniques.

- *Incentives* The market system encourages skill acquisition, hard work, and innovation. Greater work skills and effort mean greater production and higher incomes, which usually translate into a higher standard of living. Similarly, the assumption of risks by entrepreneurs can result in substantial profit incomes. Successful innovations generate economic rewards.

- *Freedom* The major noneconomic argument for the market system is its emphasis on personal freedom. In contrast to central planning, the market system coordinates economic activity without coercion. The market system permits—indeed, it thrives on—freedom of enterprise and choice. Entrepreneurs and workers are free to further their own self-interest, subject to the rewards and penalties imposed by the market system itself.

Of course, no economic system, including the market system, is flawless. The global financial crisis that gripped most economies in 2008–2009 highlighted some of the shortcomings of

invisible hand
The tendency of firms and resource suppliers seeking to further their own self-interests in competitive markets to also promote the interest of society as a whole.

unfettered financial markets. In Chapter 5 we will explain two well-known shortcomings of the market system and examine the government policies that try to remedy them.

2.4 The Demise of the Command System

Our discussion of how a market system answers the five fundamental questions provides insights into why the command systems of the Soviet Union, Eastern Europe, and China (prior to its market reforms) failed. Those systems encountered two insurmountable problems.

The Coordination Problem

The first difficulty was the coordination problem. The central planners had to coordinate the millions of individual decisions by consumers, resource suppliers, and businesses. Consider the setting up of a factory to produce tractors. The central planners had to establish a realistic annual production target; for example, 1000 tractors. They then had to make available all the necessary inputs—labour, machinery, electric power, steel, tires, glass, paint, and transportation—for the production and delivery of those 1000 tractors.

Because the outputs of many industries serve as inputs to other industries, the failure of any single industry to achieve its output target caused a chain reaction of repercussions. For example, if iron mines, for want of machinery or labour or transportation, did not supply the steel industry with the required inputs of iron ore, the steel mills were unable to fulfill the input needs of the many industries that depended on steel. Steel-using industries that produced capital goods (such as factory equipment and modes of transportation) were unable to fulfill their planned production goals. Eventually the chain reaction spread to all firms that used steel as an input and from there to other input buyers or final consumers.

The coordination problem became more difficult as the economies expanded. Products and production processes grew more complex, and the number of industries requiring planning increased. Planning techniques that worked for the simpler economy proved highly inadequate and inefficient for the larger economy. Bottlenecks and production stoppages became the norm, not the exception. In trying to cope, planners further suppressed product variety, focusing on one or two products in each product category.

A lack of a reliable success indicator added to the coordination problem in the Soviet Union and China prior to its market reforms. We have seen that market economies rely on profit as a success indicator. Profit depends on consumer demand, production efficiency, and product quality. In contrast, the major success indicator for the command economies usually was a quantitative

CONSIDER THIS :: The Two Koreas

North Korea is one of the few command economies still standing. After the Second World War, Korea was divided into North Korea and South Korea. North Korea, under the influence of the Soviet Union, established a command economy that emphasized government ownership and central government planning. South Korea established a market economy based upon private ownership and the profit motive. Today, the differences in the economic outcomes of the two systems are striking.

	North Korea	South Korea
GDP	$40 billion*	$1.5 trillion*
GDP per capita	$1,800*	$30,000*
Exports	$2.0 billion	$464 billion
Imports	$3.1 billion	$422 billion
Agriculture as % of GDP	20.7%	2.6%

*Based on purchasing power equivalencies to the U.S. dollar.

Source: *CIA World Fact Book*, 2011, www.cia.gov.

production target that the central planners assigned. Production costs, product quality, and product mix were secondary considerations. Managers and workers often sacrificed product quality because they were being awarded bonuses for meeting quantitative, not qualitative, targets. If meeting production goals meant sloppy assembly work, so be it.

It was difficult at best for planners to assign quantitative production targets without unintentionally producing distortions in output. If the plan specified a production target for producing nails in terms of *weight* (tons of nails), the enterprise made only large nails. But if it specified the target as a *quantity* (thousands of nails), the firm made all small nails, and lots of them! That is precisely what happens in centrally planned economies.

The Incentive Problem

The command economies also faced an incentive problem. Central planners determined the output mix. When they misjudged how many automobiles, shoes, shirts, and chickens were wanted at the government-determined prices, persistent shortages and surpluses of those products often arose. But as long as the managers who oversaw the production of those goods were rewarded for meeting their assigned production goals, they had no incentive to adjust production in response to the shortages and surpluses. And there were no fluctuations in prices and profitability to signal that more or less of certain products was desired. Thus, many products were unavailable or in short supply, while other products were overproduced and sat for months or years in warehouses.

The command systems of the former Soviet Union and China before its market reforms also lacked entrepreneurship. Central planning did not trigger the profit motive, nor did it reward innovation and enterprise. The route for getting ahead was through participation in the political hierarchy of the Communist Party. Moving up the hierarchy meant better housing, better access to health care, and the right to shop in special stores. Meeting production targets and manoeuvring through the minefields of party politics were measures of success in "business." But a definition of business success based solely on political savvy is not conducive to technological advance, which is often disruptive to existing products, production methods, and organizational structures.

2.5 The Circular Flow Model

连 connect
ORIGIN OF THE IDEA 2.4
Circular Flow Diagram

circular flow diagram
The flow of resources from households to firms and of products from firms to households. These flows are accompanied by reverse flows of money from firms to households and from households to firms.

household
One or more persons occupying a housing unit, who buy businesses' goods and services in the product market using income derived from selling resources in the factor market.

The dynamic market economy creates continuous, repetitive flows of goods and services, resources, and money. The **circular flow diagram,** shown in **Figure 2-2 (Key Graph)**, illustrates those flows for a simplified economy in which there is no government. Observe that in the diagram we group this economy's decision makers into *businesses* and *households*. Additionally, we divide this economy's markets into the *factor market* and the *product market*.

Households

The cream coloured rectangle on the right side of the circular flow diagram in Figure 2-2 represents households, A **household** is defined as one or more persons occupying a housing unit. Households buy the goods and services that businesses make available in the product market. Households obtain the income needed to buy those products by selling resources in the factor market. There are currently about 9 million households in the Canadian economy.

All the resources in our no-government economy are ultimately owned or provided by households. For instance, the members of one household or another directly provide all of the labour and entrepreneurial ability in the economy. Households also own all of the land and all of the capital in the economy either directly, as personal property, or indirectly, as a consequence of owning all of the businesses in the economy (and thereby controlling all of the land and capital owned by businesses). Thus, all of the income in the economy—all wages, rents, interest, and profits—flows to households because they provide the economy's labour, land, capital, and entrepreneurial ability.

KEY GRAPH

FIGURE 2-2
The Circular Flow Diagram

Factors of production flow from households to businesses through the factor market and products flow from businesses to households through the product market. Opposite these real flows are monetary flows. Households receive income from businesses (their costs) through the factor market and businesses receive revenue from households (their expenditures) through the product market.

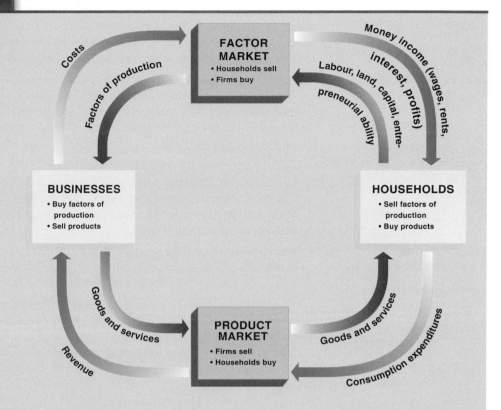

Quick Quiz

1. **The factor market is where:**
   a. households sell products and businesses buy products.
   b. businesses sell factors of production and households sell products.
   c. households sell factors of production and businesses buy factors of production (or the services of factors).
   d. businesses sell factors of production and households buy factors of production (or the services of factors).

2. **Which of the following would be determined in the product market?**
   a. a manager's salary.
   b. the price of equipment used in a bottling plant.
   c. the price of 80 hectares of farmland.
   d. the price of a new pair of athletic shoes.

3. **In this circular flow diagram:**
   a. money flows counterclockwise.
   b. resources flow counterclockwise.
   c. goods and services flow clockwise.
   d. households are on the selling side of the product market.

4. **In this circular flow diagram:**
   a. households spend income in the product market.
   b. firms sell resources to households.
   c. households receive income through the product market.
   d. households produce goods.

Answers: 1. c; 2. d; 3. b; 4. a

Businesses

businesses
Economic entities (firms) that purchase factors of production and provide goods and services to the economy.

sole proprietorship
An unincorporated firm owned and operated by one person.

partnership
An unincorporated firm owned and operated by two or more people.

corporation
A legal entity chartered by the federal or provincial government that operates as a body distinct and separate from the individuals who own it.

The cream coloured rectangle on the left side of the circular flow diagram represents **businesses,** which are economic entities (firms) that purchase factors of production and provide goods and services to the economy. These commercial establishments attempt to earn profits for their owners by offering goods and services for sale. Businesses fall into three main categories.

- A **sole proprietorship** is an unincorporated business owned and operated by a single person. The proprietor (the owner) provides all of the labour and produces all of the output. Examples include a woman who runs her own tree cutting business and an independent accountant who helps his clients with their taxes.

- The **partnership** form of business organization is a natural outgrowth of the sole proprietorship. In a partnership, two or more individuals (the partners) agree to own and operate an unincorporated business together. They pool their financial resources and business skills to operate the business, and they share any profits or losses that the business may generate. Many law firms and dental practices are organized as partnerships, as are a wide variety of firms in many other industries.

- A **corporation** is an independent legal entity that can—on its own behalf—acquire resources, own assets, produce and sell products, incur debts, extend credit, sue and be sued, and otherwise engage in any legal business activities.

The fact that a corporation is an independent legal entity means that its owners bear no personal financial responsibility for the fulfillment of the corporation's debts and obligations. For instance, if a corporation has failed to repay a loan to a bank, the bank can sue the corporation but not its owners. Professional managers run most corporations. They are hired and supervised by a board of directors that is elected annually by the corporation's owners. Research In Motion, Bombardier, Ford, and Air Canada are examples of large corporations, but corporations come in all sizes and operate in every type of industry.

There currently are about 1.1 million businesses in Canada, ranging from enormous corporations like the Royal Bank of Canada, with 2010 revenues of about $36 billion and 80,000 employees, to single-person sole proprietorships with sales of less than $100 per day.

Businesses sell goods and services in the product market in order to obtain revenue, and they incur costs in the resource market when they purchase the labour, land, capital, and entrepreneurial ability that they need to produce their respective goods and services.

Product Market

product market
A market in which products are sold by firms and bought by households.

The purple rectangle at the bottom of Figure 2-2 represents the **product market,** the place where the goods and services produced by businesses are bought and sold. Households use the income they receive from the sale of resources to buy goods and services. The money that they spend on goods and services flows to businesses as revenue.

Factor Market

factor market
A market in which households sell and firms buy factors of production.

Finally, the purple rectangle at the top of the circular flow diagram in Figure 2-2 represents the **factor market,** or resource market, in which households sell resources to businesses. The households sell resources to generate income, and the businesses buy resources to produce goods and services. Productive resources flow from households to businesses while money flows from businesses to households in the form of wages, rents, interest, and profits.

To summarize, the circular flow model depicts a complex web of economic activity in which businesses and households are both buyers and sellers. Businesses buy resources and sell products. Households buy products and sell resources. The counterclockwise flow of economic resources and finished products in Figure 2-2 is paid for by the clockwise flow of money income and consumption expenditures.

The **LAST WORD** | Shuffling the Deck

Economist Donald Boudreaux Marvels at the Way the Market System Systematically and Purposefully Arranges the World's Tens of Billions of Individual Resources.

In *The Future and Its Enemies,* Virginia Postrel notes the astonishing fact that if you thoroughly shuffle an ordinary deck of 52 playing cards, chances are practically 100 percent that the resulting arrangement of cards has never before existed. Never. Every time you shuffle a deck, you produce an arrangement of cards that exists for the first time in history.

The arithmetic works out that way. For a very small number of items, the number of possible arrangements is small. Three items, for example, can be arranged only six different ways. But the number of possible arrangements grows very quickly. The number of different ways to arrange five items is 120...for ten items it's 3,628,800...for fifteen items it's 1,307,674,368,000.

The number of different ways to arrange 52 items is 8.066×10^{67}. This is a big number. No human can comprehend its enormousness. By way of comparison, the number of possible ways to arrange a mere 20 items is 2,432,902,008,176,640,000—a number larger than the total number of seconds that have elapsed since the beginning of time ten billion years ago—and this number is Lilliputian compared to 8.066×10^{67}.

What's the significance of these facts about numbers? Consider the number of different resources available in the world—my labour, your labour, your land, oil, tungsten, cedar, coffee beans, chickens, rivers, the Empire State Building, [Microsoft]

Windows, the wharves at Houston, the classrooms at Oxford, the airport at Miami, and on and on and on. No one can possibly count all of the different, productive resources available for our use. But we can be sure that this number is at least in the tens of billions.

When you reflect on how incomprehensibly large is the number of ways to arrange a deck containing a mere 52 cards, the mind boggles at the number of different ways to arrange all the world's resources.

If our world were random—if resources combined together haphazardly, as if a giant took them all into his hands and tossed them down like so many [cards]—it's a virtual certainty that the resulting combination of resources would be useless. Unless this chance arrangement were quickly rearranged according to some productive logic, nothing worthwhile would be produced. We would all starve to

death. Because only a tiny fraction of possible arrangements serves human ends, any arrangement will be useless if it is chosen randomly or with inadequate knowledge of how each and every resource might be productively combined with each other.

And yet, we witness all around us an arrangement of resources that's productive and serves human goals. Today's arrangement of resources might not be perfect, but it is vastly superior to most of the trillions upon trillions of other possible arrangements.

How have we managed to get one of the minuscule number of arrangements that works? The answer is private property—a social institution that encourages mutual accommodation.

Private property eliminates the possibility that resource arrangements will be random, for each resource owner chooses a course of action only if it promises rewards to the owner that exceed the rewards promised by all other available courses.

[The result] is a breathtakingly complex and productive arrangement of countless resources. This arrangement emerged over time (and is still emerging) as the result of billions upon billions of individual, daily, small decisions made by people seeking to better employ their resources and labour in ways that other people find helpful.

Source: Abridged from Donald J. Boudreaux, "Mutual Accommodation," *Ideas on Liberty,* May 2000, pp. 4–5. Reprinted with permission.

Question

What explains why millions of economic resources tend to get arranged logically and productively rather than haphazardly and unproductively?

CHAPTER SUMMARY

2.1 :: ECONOMIC SYSTEMS

- The command system and the market system are the two broad types of economic systems used to address the economic problem. In the command system (or socialism or communism), government owns most resources, and central planners coordinate most economic activity. In the market system (or capitalism), private individuals own most resources, and markets coordinate most economic activity.

2.2 :: CHARACTERISTICS OF THE MARKET SYSTEM

- The market system is characterized by the private ownership of resources, including capital, and the freedom of individuals to engage in economic activities of their choice to advance their material well-being. Self-interest is the driving force of such an economy, and competition functions as a regulatory or control mechanism.

- In the market system, markets, prices, and profits organize and make effective the many millions of individual economic decisions that occur daily.

- The use of advanced technology, specialization, and the extensive use of capital goods are common features of market systems. Functioning as a medium of exchange, money eliminates the problems of bartering and permits easy trade and greater specialization, both domestically and internationally.

2.3 :: FIVE FUNDAMENTAL QUESTIONS

- Every economy faces five fundamental questions: (1) What goods and services will be produced? (2) How will the goods and services be produced? (3) Who will get the goods and services? (4) How will the system accommodate change? (5) How will the system promote progress?

- The market system produces products whose production and sale yield total revenue sufficient to cover total cost. It does not produce products for which total revenue continuously falls short of total cost. Competition forces firms to use the lowest-cost production techniques.

- Positive economic profit (total revenue minus total cost) indicates that an industry is prosperous and promotes its expansion. Losses signify that an industry is not prosperous and hasten its contraction.

- Consumer sovereignty means that both businesses and resource suppliers are subject to the wants of consumers. Through their dollar votes, consumers decide on the composition of output.

- The prices that a household receives for the resources it supplies to the economy determine that household's income. This income determines the household's claim on the economy's output. Those who have income to spend get the products produced in the market system.

- By communicating changes in consumer tastes to entrepreneurs and resource suppliers, the market system prompts appropriate adjustments in the allocation of the economy's resources. The market system also encourages technological advance and capital accumulation, both of which raise a nation's standard of living.

- Competition, the primary mechanism of control in the market economy, promotes a unity of self-interest and social interests. As if directed by an invisible hand, competition harnesses the self-interest motives of businesses and resource suppliers to further the social interest.

2.4 :: THE DEMISE OF THE COMMAND SYSTEM

- The command systems of the former Soviet Union and pre-reform China met their demise because of coordination difficulties caused by central planning and the lack of profit incentives that encourage product improvement, produce new products, and give rise to entrepreneurship.

2.5 :: THE CIRCULAR FLOW MODEL

- The circular flow model illustrates the flows of resources and products from households to businesses and from businesses to households, along with the corresponding monetary flows. Businesses are on the buying side of the resource market and the selling side of the product market. Households are on the selling side of the resource market and the buying side of the product market.

TERMS AND CONCEPTS

economic system, p. 34
command system, p. 34
market system, p. 34
private property, p. 35
freedom of enterprise, p. 35
freedom of choice, p. 36
self-interest, p. 36
competition, p. 37
market, p. 37
specialization, p. 38

division of labour, p. 38
medium of exchange, p. 39
barter, p. 39
money, p. 39
consumer sovereignty, p. 41
dollar votes, p. 41
guiding function of prices, p. 43
technological advance, p. 43
creative destruction, p. 43

invisible hand, p. 44
circular flow diagram, p. 46
households, p. 46
businesses, p. 48
sole proprietorship, p. 48
partnership, p. 48
corporation, p. 48
product market, p. 48
factor market, p. 48

QUESTIONS

1. Contrast how a market system and a command economy try to cope with economic scarcity. **[LO2.1]**

2. How does self-interest help achieve society's economic goals? Why is there such a wide variety of desired goods and services in a market system? In what way are entrepreneurs and businesses at the helm of the economy but commanded by consumers? **[LO2.2]**

3. Why is private property, and the protection of property rights, so critical to the success of the market system? How do property rights encourage cooperation? **[LO2.2]**

4. What are the advantages of using capital goods in the production process? What is meant by the term "division of labour"? What are the advantages of specialization in the use of human and material resources? Explain why exchange is the necessary consequence of specialization. **[LO2.2]**

5. What problem does barter entail? Indicate the economic significance of money as a medium of exchange. What is meant by the statement, "We want money only to part with it"? **[LO2.2]**

6. Evaluate and explain the following statements. **[LO2.2]**

   a. The market system is a profit-and-loss system.

   b. Competition is the disciplinarian of the market economy.

7. Some large hardware stores such as Canadian Tire boast of carrying as many as 20,000 different products in each store. What motivated the producers of those individual products to make them and offer them for sale? How did the producers decide on the best combinations of factors to use? Who made those factors available, and why? Who decides whether these particular hardware products should continue to be produced and offered for sale? **[LO2.3]**

8. What is meant by the term "creative destruction"? How does the emergence of MP3 (or iPod) technology relate to this idea? **[LO2.3]**

9. In a sentence, describe the meaning of the term "invisible hand." **[LO2.3]**

10. In market economies, firms rarely worry about the availability of inputs to produce their products, whereas in command economies input availability is a constant concern. Why is there a difference? **[LO2.4]**

11. Distinguish between the factor market and the product market in the circular flow model. In what way are businesses and households both sellers and buyers in this model? What are the flows in the circular flow model? **[LO2.5]**

PROBLEMS

1. Suppose Natasha currently makes $50,000 per year working as a manager at a cable TV company. She then develops two possible entrepreneurial business opportunities. In one, she will quit her job to start an organic soap company. In the other, she will try to develop an Internet-based competitor to the local cable company. For the soap-making opportunity, she anticipates annual revenue of $465,000 and costs for the necessary land, labour, and capital of $395,000 per year. For the Internet opportunity, she anticipates costs for land, labour, and capital of $3,250,000 per year as compared to revenues of $3,275,000 per year. **[LO2.3]**

   a. Should she quit her current job to become an entrepreneur?

   b. If she does quit her current job, which opportunity should she pursue?

2. With current technology, suppose a firm is producing 400 loaves of banana bread daily. Also assume that the least-cost combination of resources in producing those loaves is 5 units of labour, 7 units of land, 2 units of capital, and 1 unit of entrepreneurial ability, selling at prices of $40, $60, $60, and $20, respectively. If the firm can sell these 400 loaves at $2 per unit, what is its total revenue? Its total cost? Its profit or loss? Will it continue to produce banana bread? If this firm's situation is typical for the other makers of banana bread, will resources flow toward or away from this bakery good? **[LO2.3]**

3. Let's put dollar amounts on the flows in the circular flow diagram of Figure 2-2. **[LO2.5]**

   a. Suppose that businesses buy a total of $100 billion of the four resources (labour, land, capital, and entrepreneurial ability) from households. If households receive $60 billion in wages, $10 billion in rent, and $20 billion in interest, how much are households paid for providing entrepreneurial ability?

   b. If households spend $55 billion on goods and $45 billion on services, how much in revenues do businesses receive in the product market?

Mc Graw Hill **connect**™ **Practice and Learn Online with Connect**

Connect allows you to practice important concepts at your own pace and on your own schedule, with 24/7 online access to an eBook, algorithmic questions and problems from the textbook, video and logic cases, graphing tutorials, flashcards, Internet exercises, key graphs, and more.

CHAPTER 3 ::

Demand, Supply, and Market Equilibrium

AFTER READING THIS CHAPTER, YOU SHOULD BE ABLE TO:

3.1 Describe *demand* and explain how it can change.

3.2 Describe *supply* and explain how it can change.

3.3 Relate how supply and demand interact to determine market equilibrium.

3.4 Identify what government-set prices are and how they can cause surpluses and shortages.

A3.1 (Appendix) Illustrate how supply and demand analysis can provide insights into actual economy situations.

The model of supply and demand is the economics profession's greatest contribution to human understanding of markets because it explains their operation, on which we depend for nearly everything that we eat, drink, or consume. The model is so powerful and so widely used that, to many people, it *is* economics.

This chapter explains how the model works and how it can explain both the *quantities* that are bought and sold in markets and the *prices* at which they trade

Markets bring together buyers ("demanders") and sellers ("suppliers"). The corner gas station, an e-commerce website, the local music store, a farmer's roadside stand—all are familiar markets. The Toronto Stock Exchange and the Chicago Board of Trade are markets where buyers and sellers from all over the world communicate with one another to buy and sell stocks and bonds and commodities. Auctioneers bring together potential buyers and sellers of art, livestock, used farm equipment, and, sometimes, real estate. In labour markets, new college or university graduates "sell" and employers "buy" specific labour services.

Some markets are local, while others are national or international. Some are highly personal, involving face-to-face contact between demander and supplier; others are faceless, with buyer and seller never seeing or knowing each other.

To keep things simple, we will focus in this chapter on markets in which large numbers of independently acting buyers and sellers come together to buy and sell standardized products. Markets with these characteristics are the most highly competitive, and include the wheat market, the stock market, and the market for foreign currencies. All such markets involve demand, supply, price, and quantity. As you will soon see, the price is "discovered" through the interacting decisions of buyers and sellers.

■ connect™
ORIGIN OF THE IDEA 3.1
Demand and Supply

demand
A schedule or curve that shows the various amounts of a product that consumers are willing and able to purchase at each of a series of possible prices during a specified period of time.

As price falls, the quantity demanded rises, and as price rises, the quantity demanded falls.

3.1 Demand

A **demand** is a schedule or a curve that shows the various amounts of a product that consumers are willing and able to purchase at each of a series of possible prices during a specified period of time.[1] Demand shows the quantities of a product that will be purchased at various possible prices, other things equal. It is, in a sense, a planning curve for consumers. Demand can easily be shown in table form. Figure 3-1 shows a hypothetical demand schedule for a single consumer purchasing bushels of corn.

The table in Figure 3-1 reveals the relationship between the various prices of corn and the quantity of corn a particular consumer would be willing *and able* to purchase at each of these prices. We say willing *and able* because willingness alone is not effective in the market. You may be willing to buy a 3D television set, but if that willingness is not backed by the necessary dollars, it will not be effective and, therefore, will not be reflected in the market. If the price of corn were $5 per bushel, our consumer would be willing and able to buy 10 bushels per week; if it were $4, the consumer would be willing and able to buy 20 bushels per week, and so forth.

The table in Figure 3-1 does not tell us which of the five possible prices will actually exist in the corn market. That depends on the interaction between demand and supply. Demand is simply a statement of a buyer's plans, or intentions, with respect to the purchase of a product.

To be meaningful, the quantities demanded at each price must relate to a specific period—a day, a week, a month, etc. Saying, "A consumer will buy 10 bushels of corn at $5 per bushel" is meaningless. Saying "A consumer will buy 10 bushels of corn per week at $5 per bushel" is meaningful. Unless a specific time period is stated, we do not know whether the demand for a product is large or small.

FIGURE 3-1 **An Individual Buyer's Demand for Corn**

Because price and quantity demanded are inversely related, an individual's demand schedule graphs as a downsloping curve such as *D*. Specifically, the law of demand says that, other things equal, consumers will buy more of a product as its price declines. Here, and in later figures, *P* stands for price, and *Q* stands for quantity (either demanded or supplied).

Price per bushel	Quantity demanded (bushels per week)
$5	10
4	20
3	35
2	55
1	80

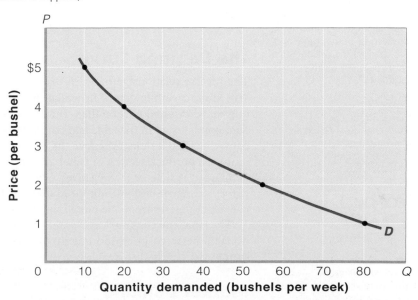

---

[1] This definition is obviously worded to apply to product markets. To adjust it to apply to factor markets, substitute the word *factor* for *product* and the word *businesses* for *consumers*.

■ connect™
ORIGIN OF THE IDEA 3.2
Law of Demand

law of demand
Other things equal, as price falls
the quantity demanded rises,
and vice versa.

■ connect™
ORIGIN OF THE IDEA 3.3
Diminishing Marginal
Utility

**diminishing marginal
utility**
As a consumer increases the
consumption of a good or
service, the marginal utility
obtained from each additional
unit of the good or service
decreases.

■ connect™
ORIGIN OF THE IDEA 3.4
Income and Substitution
Effects

substitution effect
A change in the price of a
product changes the relative
expensiveness of that good and
hence changes the willingness of
consumers to buy it rather than
other goods.

income effect
A change in the price of a
product changes a consumer's
real income (purchasing power)
and thus the quantity of the
product purchased.

■ connect™
MATH 3.1
The Demand Function

demand curve
A curve illustrating the inverse
(negative) relationship between
the quantity demanded of a
good or service and its price,
other things equal.

Law of Demand

A fundamental characteristic of demand is this: *Other things equal, as price falls the quantity demanded rises, and as price rises the quantity demanded falls.* There is a negative or *inverse* relationship between price and quantity demanded. This inverse relationship is called the **law of demand.**

The "other-things-equal" assumption is critical here (see Chapter 1). Many factors other than the price of the product being considered affect the amount purchased. The quantity of Nike shoes purchased will depend not only on the price of Nike shoes but also on the prices of substitutes such as Reebok, Adidas, and New Balance shoes. The law of demand in this case says that fewer Nikes will be purchased if the price of Nikes rises *and if the prices of Reebok, Adidas, and New Balance shoes all remain constant.* Another way of stating it is that if the *relative price* of Nikes rises, fewer Nikes will be bought.

Why is there an inverse relationship between price and quantity demanded? Let's look at two explanations:

- In any specific time period, each buyer of a product will derive less satisfaction (or benefit, or utility) from each successive unit of the product consumed. The second Big Mac will yield less additional satisfaction to the consumer than the first, and the third still less than the second. That is, consumption is subject to **diminishing marginal utility.** And because successive units of a particular product yield less and less marginal utility, consumers will buy additional units only if the price of those units is progressively reduced.

- We can also explain the law of demand in terms of *income* and *substitution* effects. The **income effect** indicates that a lower price increases the purchasing power of a buyer's money income, enabling the buyer to purchase more of the product than she or he could buy before. A higher price has the opposite effect. The **substitution effect** suggests that at a lower price, buyers have the incentive to substitute what is now a less expensive product for other products that are now *relatively* more expensive. The product whose price has fallen is now "a better deal" relative to the other products.

For example, a decline in the price of chicken will increase the purchasing power of consumer incomes, enabling them to buy more chicken (the **income effect**). At a lower price, chicken is relatively more attractive and consumers tend to substitute it for pork, beef, and fish (the substitution effect). The income and substitution effects combine to make consumers able and willing to buy more of a product at a low price than at a high price.

The Demand Curve

The inverse relationship between price and quantity demanded for any product can be represented on a simple graph, in which, by convention, we measure *quantity demanded* on the horizontal axis and *price* on the vertical axis. In Figure 3-1 we have plotted the five price–quantity data points listed in the table and connected the points with a smooth curve, labelled *D.* Such a curve is called a **demand curve.** Its downward slope reflects the law of demand—people buy more of a product, service, or factor as its price falls. The relationship between price and quantity demanded is inverse (or negative). We also refer to the demand curve as the *marginal benefit curve,* a concept first introduced in Chapter 1. The demand curve tells us the extra benefit the consumer derives from one more unit of a good or service.

The table and the graph in Figure 3-1 contain exactly the same data and reflect the same relationship between price and quantity demanded. But the graph shows that relationship more simply and clearly than a table or a description in words.

Market Demand

So far, we have concentrated on just one consumer. By adding the quantities demanded by all consumers at each of the various possible prices, we can get from *individual* demand to *market*

FIGURE 3-2 Market Demand for Corn, Three Buyers

The market demand curve D is the horizontal summation of the individual demand curves (D_1, D_2, and D_3) of all the consumers in the market. At the price of $3, for example, the three individual curves yield a total quantity demanded of 100 bushels.

Price per bushel	Joe		Jen		Jay		Total quantity demanded per week
$5	10	+	12	+	8	=	30
4	20	+	23	+	17	=	60
3	35	+	39	+	26	=	100
2	55	+	60	+	39	=	154
1	80	+	87	+	54	=	221

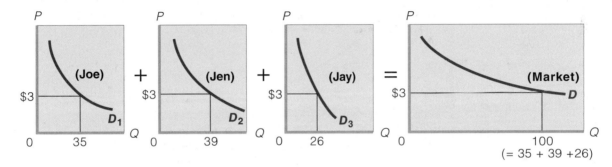

demand. If there are just three buyers in the market, as represented in Figure 3-2, it is relatively easy to determine the total quantity demanded at each price. Figure 3-2 shows the graphical summing procedure: At each price we sum horizontally the individual quantities demanded to obtain the total quantity demanded at that price; we then plot the price and the total quantity demanded as one point of the market demand curve.

Competition, of course, ordinarily entails many more than three buyers of a product. To avoid hundreds or thousands or millions of additions, we suppose that all the buyers in a market are willing and able to buy the same amounts at each of the possible prices. Then we just multiply those amounts by the number of buyers to obtain the market demand. This is how we arrived at the demand schedule and demand curve D_1, in Figure 3-3, for a market with 200 corn buyers. The table in Figure 3-3 shows the calculations for 200 corn buyers.

Determinants of Demand

determinants of demand
Factors other than price that determine the quantities demanded of a good or service.

In constructing a demand curve such as D_1 in Figure 3-3, we assume that price is the most important influence on the amount of any product purchased, even though other factors can and do affect purchases. These factors, called **determinants of demand,** are assumed to be constant when a demand curve such as D_1 is drawn. They are the "other things equal" in the relationship between price and quantity demanded. When any of these determinants changes, the demand curve will shift to the right or left.

The basic determinants of demand are (1) consumers' tastes (preferences), (2) the number of consumers in the market, (3) consumers' incomes, (4) the prices of related goods, and (5) consumers' expectations.

FIGURE 3-3   Changes in the Demand for Corn

A change in one or more of the determinants of demand causes a change in demand. An increase in demand is shown as a shift of the demand curve to the right, as from D_1 to D_2. A decrease in demand is shown as a shift of the demand curve to the left, as from D_1 to D_3. These changes in demand are to be distinguished from a change in quantity demanded, which is caused by a change in the price of the product, as shown by a movement from, say, point *a* to point *b* on fixed demand curve D_1.

Market demand for corn, 200 buyers, D_1	
(1) Price per bushel	(2) Total quantity demanded per week
$5	2,000
4	4,000
3	7,000
2	11,000
1	16,000

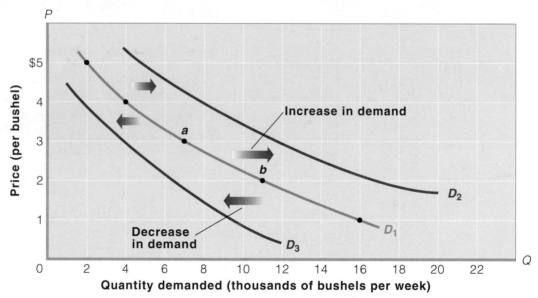

Changes in Demand

A change in one or more of the determinants of demand will change the demand data (the demand schedule) in the table accompanying Figure 3-3, and therefore the location of the demand curve there. A change in the demand schedule—or, graphically, a shift in the demand curve—is called a *change in demand.*

If consumers desire to buy more corn at each possible price than is reflected in column 2 of the table in Figure 3-3, that *increase in demand* is shown as a shift of the demand curve to the right— say, from D_1 to D_2. Conversely, a *decrease in demand* occurs when consumers buy less corn at each possible price than is indicated in column 2 of the table in Figure 3-3. The leftward shift of the demand curve from D_1 to D_3 in Figure 3-3 shows that situation.

Now let's see how changes in each determinant affect demand.

TASTES

A favourable change in consumer tastes (preferences) for a product—a change that makes the product more desirable—means that more of it will be demanded at each price. Demand will increase; the demand curve will shift rightward. An unfavourable change in consumer preferences will decrease demand, shifting the demand curve to the left.

New products may affect consumer tastes; for example, the introduction of digital cameras has greatly decreased demand for film cameras. Consumers' concern over the health hazards of cholesterol and obesity have increased the demand for broccoli, low-calorie sweeteners, and fresh fruit, while decreasing the demand for beef, veal, eggs, and whole milk. Over the past several years, the demand for coffee drinks and table wine has greatly increased, driven by changes in tastes. So, too, has the demand for touch-screen mobile phones and fuel-efficient hybrid vehicles.

NUMBER OF BUYERS

An increase in the number of buyers in a market increases demand; a decrease in the number of buyers decreases demand. For example, the rising number of older persons in Canada in recent years has increased the demand for motor homes, medical care, and retirement communities. Immigration to Canada from many parts of the world has greatly increased the demand for a whole range of ethnic goods and services, in southern Ontario and British Columbia in particular. Improvements in communications have given financial markets international range and have thus increased the demand for stocks and bonds. International trade agreements have reduced foreign trade barriers to Canadian farm commodities, increasing the number of buyers and the demand for those products. In contrast, the emigration (out-migration) from many small rural communities has reduced the population and thus the demand for housing, home appliances, and auto repair in those towns.

INCOME

How changes in income affect demand is more complex. For most products, a rise in income causes an increase in demand. Consumers typically buy more steaks, furniture, and electronic equipment as their incomes increase. Conversely, the demand for such products declines as income falls. Products for which demand varies directly with money income are called **normal goods.**

Although most products are normal goods, there are some exceptions. As incomes increase beyond some point, the demand for used clothing, retread tires, and third-hand automobiles may decrease, because the higher incomes enable consumers to buy new versions of those products. Similarly, rising incomes may cause the demand for charcoal grills to decline as wealthier consumers switch to gas grills. Goods for which demand varies *inversely* with money income are called **inferior goods.**

PRICES OF RELATED GOODS

A change in the price of a related good may either increase or decrease the demand for a product, depending on whether the related good is a substitute or a complement. Goods that can be used in place of another good are **substitute goods.** Goods that are used together with one or more other goods are **complementary goods.**

- *Substitutes* Häagen-Dazs ice cream and Ben & Jerry's ice cream are substitute goods or, simply, *substitutes*. When two products are substitutes, an increase in the price of one will increase the demand for the other. Conversely, a decrease in the price of one will decrease the demand for the other. For example, when the price of Häagen-Dazs ice cream rises, consumers will demand less of it and increase their demand for Ben & Jerry's ice cream. When the price of Colgate toothpaste declines, the demand for Crest declines. So it is with other product pairs such as Nike and Reebok shoes, Molson and Labatt beer, or Chevrolet and Ford pickup trucks. They are *substitutes in consumption*.

- *Complements* Because complementary goods (or, simply, *complements*) are used together, they are typically demanded jointly. Examples include computers and software, cellphones and cellular service, and snowboards and lift tickets. If the price of a complement (for example, lettuce) goes up, the demand for the related good (salad dressing) will decline. Conversely, if the price of a complement (for example, tuition) falls, the demand for a related good (textbooks) will increase.

normal goods
Goods or services whose consumption rises when income increases and falls when income decreases, price remaining constant.

inferior goods
Goods or services whose consumption falls when income increases and rises when income decreases, price remaining constant.

substitute goods
Products or services that can be used in place of each other.

complementary goods
Products and services that are used together.

- **Unrelated Goods** The vast majority of goods that are not related to one another are called *independent goods*. Examples are butter and golf balls, potatoes and automobiles, and bananas and wristwatches. A change in the price of one does not affect the demand for the other.

CONSUMER EXPECTATIONS

Changes in consumer expectations may shift demand. A newly formed expectation of higher future prices may cause consumers to buy now in order to "beat" the anticipated price rises, thus increasing current demand. That is often what happens in so-called hot real estate markets. Buyers rush in because they think the price of new homes will continue to escalate rapidly. Some buyers fear being "priced out of the market" and therefore not obtaining the home they desire. Other buyers—speculators—believe they will be able to sell the houses later at a higher price. Whichever their motivation, these buyers increase the demand for houses.

Similarly, a change in expectations concerning future income may prompt consumers to change their current spending. For example, first-round NHL draft choices may splurge on new luxury cars in anticipation of lucrative professional hockey contracts. Or workers who become fearful of losing their jobs may reduce their demand for, say, vacation travel.

In summary, an *increase* in demand—the decision by consumers to buy larger quantities of a product at each possible price—may be caused by:

- a favourable change in consumer tastes
- an increase in the number of buyers
- an increase in incomes if the product is a normal good
- a decrease in incomes if the product is an inferior good
- an increase in the price of a substitute good
- a decrease in the price of a complementary good
- a new consumer expectation that prices and income will be higher in the future

You should "reverse" these generalizations to explain a *decrease* in demand. Table 3-1 provides additional illustrations of the determinants of demand.

TABLE 3-1   Determinants of Demand Curve Shifts

Determinant	Examples
Change in buyer tastes	Physical fitness rises in popularity, increasing the demand for jogging shoes and bicycles; cellphone popularity rises, reducing the demand for land-line phones.
Change in number of buyers	A decline in the birth rate reduces the demand for children's toys.
Change in income	A rise in incomes increases the demand for such normal goods as restaurant meals, sports tickets, and MP3 players, while reducing the demand for such inferior goods as cabbage, turnips, and inexpensive wine.
Change in the prices of related goods	A reduction in airfares reduces the demand for bus transportation (substitute goods); a decline in the price of DVD players increases the demand for DVD movies (complementary goods).
Change in consumer expectations	Political instability in South America creates an expectation of higher future coffee bean prices, thereby increasing today's demand for coffee beans.

Changes in Quantity Demanded

change in demand
A change in the quantity demanded of a good or service at every price; a shift of the entire demand curve to the right (an increase in demand) or to the left (a decrease in demand).

change in quantity demanded
A movement from one point to another on a fixed demand curve.

A *change in demand* must not be confused with a *change in quantity demanded*. A **change in demand** is a shift of the entire demand curve to the right (an increase in demand) or to the left (a decrease in demand). It occurs because the consumer's state of mind about purchasing the product has been altered in response to a change in one or more of the determinants of demand. Recall that *demand* is a schedule or a curve; therefore, a *change in demand* means a change in the schedule and a shift of the curve.

In contrast, a **change in quantity demanded** is a movement from one point to another point—from one price–quantity combination to another—on a fixed demand curve. The cause of such a change is an increase or decrease in the price of the product under consideration. In Figure 3-3, for example, a decline in the price of corn from $5 to $4 will increase the quantity of corn demanded from 2000 to 4000 bushels.

In Figure 3-3, the shift of the demand curve D_1 to either D_2 or D_3 is a change in demand. But the movement from point *a* to point *b* on curve D_1 represents a change in quantity demanded: Demand has not changed; it is the entire curve, and it remains fixed in place.

QUICK REVIEW

- A market is any arrangement that facilitates the purchase and sale of goods, services, or resources.
- Demand is a schedule or a curve showing the amount of a product that buyers are willing and able to purchase at each possible price in a series of prices, in a particular time period.
- The law of demand states that, other things equal, the quantity of a good purchased varies inversely with its price.
- The demand curve shifts because of changes in (a) consumer tastes, (b) the number of buyers in the market, (c) consumer income, (d) the prices of substitute or complementary goods, and (e) consumer expectations.
- A change in demand is a shift of the demand curve; a change in quantity demanded is a movement from one point to another on a fixed demand curve.

3.2 Supply

supply
A schedule or curve that shows the amounts of a product that producers are willing and able to make available for sale at each of a series of possible prices during a specific period.

Supply is a schedule or curve that shows the amounts of a product that producers are willing and able to make available for sale at each of a series of possible prices during a specific period.[2] It is, in a sense, a planning curve for producers. Figure 3-4 is a hypothetical supply schedule for a single producer of corn. It shows the quantities of corn that will be supplied at various prices, other things equal.

Law of Supply

law of supply
The principle that, other things equal, an increase in the price of a product will increase the quantity of it supplied, and conversely for a price decrease.

The table in Figure 3-4 shows that a direct relationship prevails between price and quantity supplied. As price rises, the quantity supplied rises; as price falls, the quantity supplied falls. This relationship is called the **law of supply.** A supply schedule tells us that, other things equal, firms

[2] This definition is worded to apply to product markets. To adjust it to apply to factor markets, substitute the word *factor* for *product* and the word *owner* for *producer*.

FIGURE 3-4   An Individual Producer's Supply of Corn

Because price and quantity supplied are positively related, a firm's supply schedule is an upward-sloping curve such as *S*. Specifically, the law of supply says that, other things equal, firms will supply more of a product as its price rises.

Price per bushel	Quantity supplied (bushels per week)
$5	60
4	50
3	35
2	20
1	5

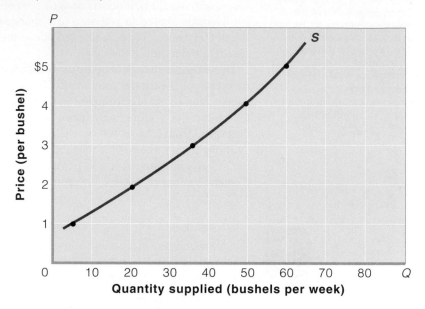

will produce and offer for sale more of their product at a high price than at a low price. The higher the price, the greater the incentive and the greater the quantity supplied.

Price is an obstacle from the standpoint of the consumer, who is on the paying end. The higher the price, the less the consumer will buy. But the supplier is on the receiving end of the product's price. To the supplier, price represents *revenue*, which serves as an incentive to produce and sell a product. The higher the price, the greater the incentive and the greater the quantity supplied.

Consider a farmer in Ontario who is deciding how much corn to plant. As corn prices rise, as shown in the table in Figure 3-4, the farmer finds it profitable to plant more. And the higher corn prices enable the Ontario farmer to cover the increased costs associated with more intensive cultivation and the use of more seed, fertilizer, and pesticide. The overall result is more corn.

Now consider a manufacturer. Beyond some quantity of production, manufacturers usually encounter increasing *marginal cost*—the added cost of producing one more unit of output. Certain productive resources—in particular, the firm's plant and machinery—cannot be expanded quickly, so the firm uses more of other resources, such as labour, to produce more output. But as labour becomes more abundant relative to the fixed plant and equipment, the additional workers have relatively less space and access to equipment. For example, the added workers may have to wait to gain access to machines. As a result, each added worker produces less added output, and the marginal cost of successive units of output rises accordingly. The firm will not produce the more costly units unless it receives a higher price for them. Again, price and quantity supplied are directly related.

The Supply Curve

supply curve
A curve illustrating the positive (direct) relationship between the quantity supplied of a good or service and its price, other things equal.

As with demand, it is convenient to represent individual supply graphically. In Figure 3-4, curve *S* is the **supply curve** that corresponds to the price–quantity data in the accompanying table. The upward slope of the curve reflects the law of supply—a producer will offer more of a good, service, or factor for sale as its price rises. The relationship between price and quantity supplied is positive or direct.

FIGURE 3-5 **Changes in the Supply of Corn**

A change in one or more of the determinants of supply causes a shift in supply. An increase in supply is shown as a rightward shift of the supply curve, as from S_1 to S_2. A decrease in supply is depicted as a leftward shift of the curve, as from S_1 to S_3. In contrast, a change in the quantity supplied is caused by a change in the product's price and is shown by a movement from one point to another, as from point *a* to point *b*, on a fixed supply curve.

Market supply of corn, 200 producers, S_1	
(1) **Price per bushel**	**(2) Total quantity** **supplied per week**
$5	12,000
4	10,000
3	7,000
2	4,000
1	1,000

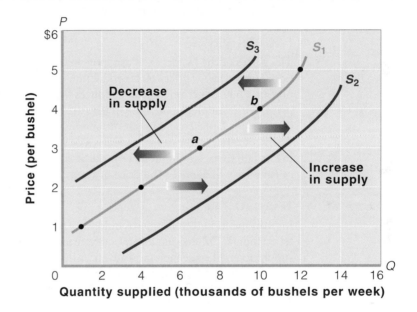

Market Supply

Market supply is derived from individual supply in exactly the same way that market demand is derived from individual demand. We sum the quantities supplied by each producer at each price. That is, we obtain the market supply curve by "horizontally adding" the supply curves of the individual producers. The price–quantity supplied data in the table in Figure 3-5 are for an assumed 200 identical producers in the market, each willing to supply corn according to the supply schedule shown in Figure 3-4. Curve S_1 in Figure 3-5 is a graph of the market supply data. Note that the axes in Figure 3-5 are the same as those used in our graph of market demand (Figure 3-2). The only difference is that we change the label on the horizontal axis from "quantity demanded" to "quantity supplied."

Determinants of Supply

In constructing a supply curve, we assume that price is the most significant influence on the quantity supplied of any product. But other factors (the "other things equal") can and do affect supply. The supply curve is drawn on the assumption that these other things are fixed and do not

connect

MATH 3.2
The Supply Function

change. If one of them does change, a *change in supply* will occur, meaning that the entire supply curve will shift.

The basic **determinants of supply** are (1) factor prices, (2) technology, (3) taxes and subsidies, (4) prices of other goods, (5) price expectations, and (6) the number of sellers in the market. A change in any one or more of these determinants of supply will move the supply curve for a product either to the right or to the left. A shift to the *right,* as from S_1 to S_2 in Figure 3-5, signifies an *increase* in supply: Producers supply larger quantities of the product at each possible price. A shift to the *left,* as from S_1 to S_3, indicates a *decrease* in supply.

Changes in Supply

Let's consider how changes in each of the determinants affect supply. The key idea is that costs are a major factor underlying supply curves; anything that affects costs (other than changes in output itself) usually shifts the supply curve.

FACTOR PRICES

The prices of the factors used as inputs in the production process determine the costs of production. Higher *factor* prices raise production costs and, assuming a particular *product* price, squeeze profits. That reduction in profits reduces the incentive for firms to supply output at each product price. For example, an increase in the price of iron ore and coke will increase the cost of producing steel for Dofasco and reduce its supply.

In contrast, lower *factor* prices reduce production costs and increase profits. So, when input prices fall, firms supply greater output at each product price. For example, a decrease in the price of iron ore will decrease the price of steel.

TECHNOLOGY

Improvements in technology (techniques of production) enable firms to produce units of output with fewer inputs. Because inputs are costly, using fewer of them lowers production costs and increases supply. Example: Technological advances in producing flat-panel LCD (liquid crystal display) computer monitors have greatly reduced their cost. The manufacturers will now offer more such monitors than previously at various prices: the supply of flat-panel LCD monitors has increased.

TAXES AND SUBSIDIES

Businesses treat most taxes as costs. An increase in sales or property taxes will increase production costs and reduce supply. In contrast, subsidies are "taxes in reverse." If the government subsidizes the production of a good, it in effect lowers the producers' costs and increases supply. Government subsidies will, for example, help increase the number of rural medical practitioners.

PRICES OF OTHER GOODS

Firms that produce a particular product (say, soccer balls) can sometimes use their plant and equipment to produce alternative goods (say, basketballs and volleyballs). The higher prices of these "other goods" may entice soccer ball producers to switch production to those other goods to increase profits. This substitution in production results in a decline in the supply of soccer balls. Alternatively, when the prices of basketballs and volleyballs decline relative to the price of soccer balls, producers of those goods may decide to produce more soccer balls instead, increasing their supply.

PRODUCER EXPECTATIONS

Changes in expectations about the future price of a product may affect the producer's current willingness to supply that product. Ontario farmers anticipating a higher corn price in the future

TABLE 3-2	Determinants of Supply Curve Shifts

Determinant	Examples
Change in factor prices	A decrease in the price of microchips increases the supply of computers; an increase in the price of crude oil reduces the supply of gasoline.
Change in technology	The development of more effective wireless technology increases the supply of cellphones.
Change in taxes and subsidies	An increase in the excise tax on cigarettes reduces the supply of cigarettes; a decline in subsidies to universities reduces the supply of higher education.
Change in prices of other goods	An increase in the price of cucumbers decreases the supply of watermelons.
Change in producer expectations	An expectation of a substantial rise in future log prices decreases the supply of logs today.
Change in number of suppliers	An increase in the number of tattoo parlours increases the supply of tattoos; the formation of women's professional basketball leagues increases the supply of women's professional basketball games.

might withhold some of their current corn harvest from the market, thereby causing a decrease in the current supply of corn. In contrast, in many types of manufacturing industries, newly formed expectations that price will increase may induce firms to add another shift of workers or to expand their production facilities, causing current supply to increase.

NUMBER OF SELLERS

Other things equal, the larger the number of suppliers, the greater the market supply. As more firms enter an industry, the supply curve shifts to the right. Conversely, the smaller the number of firms in the industry, the less the market supply. This means that as firms leave an industry, the supply curve shifts to the left. Example: Canada and the United States have imposed restrictions on haddock fishing to replenish dwindling stocks. As part of that policy, the federal government has bought the boats of some of the haddock fishers as a way of putting them out of business and decreasing the catch. The result has been a decline in the market supply of haddock.

Table 3-2 is a checklist of the determinants of supply, along with further illustrations.

Changes in Quantity Supplied

change in supply
A change in the quantity supplied of a good or service at every price; a shift of the supply curve to the left or right.

change in quantity supplied
A movement from one point to another on a fixed supply curve.

The distinction between a *change in supply* and a *change in quantity supplied* mirrors the distinction between a change in demand and a change in quantity demanded. Because supply is a schedule or curve, a **change in supply** means a change in the entire schedule and a shift of the entire curve. An increase in supply shifts the curve to the right; a decrease in supply shifts it to the left. The cause of a change in supply is a change in one or more of the determinants of supply.

In contrast, a **change in quantity supplied** is a movement from one point to another on a fixed supply curve. The cause of such a movement is a change in the price of the specific product being considered. Consider supply curve S_1 in Figure 3-5. A decline in the price of corn from $4 to $3 decreases the quantity of corn supplied per week from 10,000 to 7000 bushels. This movement from point *b* to point *a* along S_1 is a change in quantity supplied, not a change in supply. Supply is the full schedule of prices and quantities shown, and this schedule does not change when the price of corn changes.

3.3 Market Equilibrium

With our understanding of demand and supply, we can now show how the decisions of buyers of corn and sellers of corn interact to determine the price and quantity of corn. In the table in **Figure 3-6 (Key Graph),** columns 1 and 2 repeat the market supply of corn (from Figure 3-5), and columns 3 and 4 repeat the market demand for corn (from the table in Figure 3-3). We assume this is a competitive market, so that neither buyers nor sellers can set the price.

Equilibrium Price and Quantity

equilibrium price
The price in a competitive market at which the quantity demanded and the quantity supplied are equal.

equilibrium quantity
The quantity demanded and supplied at the equilibrium price in a competitive market.

connect
MATH 3.3
Equilibrium Price and Quantity

surplus
The amount by which the quantity supplied of a product exceeds the quantity demanded at a specific (above-equilibrium) price.

shortage
The amount by which the quantity demanded of a product exceeds the quantity supplied at a specific (below-equilibrium) price.

We are looking for the equilibrium price and equilibrium quantity. The **equilibrium price** (or "market-clearing price") is the price at which the intentions of buyers and sellers match. It is the price at which quantity demanded equals quantity supplied. The table in Figure 3-6 reveals that at $3, *and only at that price,* the number of bushels of corn that sellers wish to sell (7000) is identical to the number consumers want to buy (also 7000). At $3 and 7000 bushels of corn, there is neither a shortage nor a surplus of corn. So 7000 bushels of corn is the **equilibrium quantity:** the quantity at which the intentions of buyers and sellers match so that the quantity demanded and the quantity supplied are equal.

Graphically, the equilibrium price is indicated by the intersection of the supply curve and the demand curve in Figure 3-6. (The horizontal axis now measures both quantity demanded and quantity supplied.) With neither a shortage nor a surplus at $3, the market is *in equilibrium,* meaning "in balance" or "at rest."

Competition among buyers and among sellers drives the price to the equilibrium price, where it will remain unless it is subsequently disturbed by changes in demand or supply (shifts of the curves). To better understand the uniqueness of the equilibrium price, let's consider other prices. At any above-equilibrium price, quantity supplied exceeds quantity demanded. For example, at the $4 price, sellers will offer 10,000 bushels of corn, but buyers will purchase only 4000. The $4 price encourages sellers to offer lots of corn but discourages many consumers from buying it. The result is a **surplus** (or *excess supply*) of 6000 bushels. If corn sellers produced them all, they would find themselves with 6000 unsold bushels of corn.

Surpluses drive prices down. Even if the $4 price existed temporarily, it could not persist. The large surplus would prompt competing sellers to lower the price to encourage buyers to take the surplus off their hands. As the price fell, the incentive to produce corn would decline and the incentive for consumers to buy corn would increase. As shown in Figure 3-6, the market would move to its equilibrium at $3.

Any price below the $3 equilibrium price would create a shortage; quantity demanded would exceed quantity supplied. Consider a $2 price, for example. We see both from column 2 of the table and from the demand curve in Figure 3-6 that quantity demanded exceeds quantity supplied at that price. The result is a **shortage** (or *excess demand*) of 7000 bushels of corn. The $2 price

KEY GRAPH

FIGURE 3-6
Equilibrium Price and Quantity

The intersection of the downward-sloping demand curve *D* and the upward-sloping supply curve *S* indicates the equilibrium price and quantity, here $3 and 7000 bushels of corn. The shortages of corn at below-equilibrium prices (for example, 7000 bushels at $2) drive up price. These higher prices increase the quantity supplied and reduce the quantity demanded until equilibrium is achieved. The surpluses caused by above-equilibrium prices (for example, 6000 bushels at $4) push price down. As price drops, the quantity demanded rises and the quantity supplied falls until equilibrium is established. At the equilibrium price and quantity, there are neither shortages nor surpluses of corn.

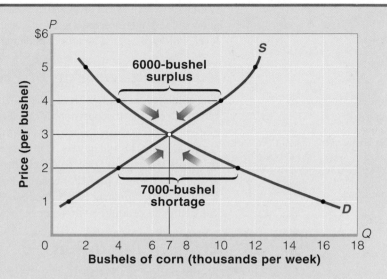

(1) Total quantity supplied per week	(2) Price per bushel	(3) Total quantity demanded per week	(4) Surplus (+) or shortage (−)
12,000	$5	2,000	+10,000↓
10,000	4	4,000	+ 6,000↓
7,000	3	7,000	0
4,000	2	11,000	− 7,000↑
1,000	1	16,000	−15,000↑

The arrows indicate the effect on price.

Quick Quiz

1. **Demand curve *D* in Figure 3-6 is downward sloping because:**
   a. producers offer less product for sale as the price of the product falls.
   b. lower prices of a product create income and substitution effects, which lead consumers to purchase more of it.
   c. the larger the number of buyers in a market, the lower the product price.
   d. price and quantity demanded are directly (positively) related.

2. **Supply curve *S*:**
   a. reflects an inverse (negative) relationship between price and quantity supplied.
   b. reflects a direct (positive) relationship between price and quantity supplied.
   c. depicts the collective behaviour of buyers in this market.
   d. shows that producers will offer more of a product for sale at a low product price than at a high product price.

3. **At the $3 price:**
   a. quantity supplied exceeds quantity demanded.
   b. quantity demanded exceeds quantity supplied.
   c. the product is abundant and a surplus exists.
   d. there is no pressure on price to rise or fall.

4. **At price $5 in this market:**
   a. there will be a shortage of 10,000 units.
   b. there will be a surplus of 10,000 units.
   c. quantity demanded will be 12,000 units.
   d. quantity demanded will equal quantity supplied.

Answers: 1. b; 2. b; 3. d; 4. b

discourages sellers from devoting resources to corn and encourages consumers to desire more bushels than are available. The $2 price cannot persist as the equilibrium price. Many consumers who want to buy corn at this price will not obtain it. They will express a willingness to pay more than $2 to get corn. Competition among these buyers will drive up the price, eventually to the $3 equilibrium level. Unless disrupted by supply or demand changes, this $3 price of corn will continue to prevail.

Rationing Function of Prices

rationing function of prices
The ability of the competitive forces of supply and demand to establish a price at which selling and buying decisions are consistent.

The ability of the competitive forces of supply and demand to establish a price at which selling and buying decisions are consistent is called the **rationing function of prices.** In our case, the equilibrium price of $3 clears the market, leaving no burdensome surplus for sellers and no inconvenient shortage for potential buyers. It is the combination of freely made individual decisions that sets this market-clearing price. In effect, the market outcome says that all buyers who are willing and able to pay $3 for a bushel of corn will obtain it; all buyers who cannot or will not pay $3 will go without corn. Similarly, all producers who are willing and able to offer corn for sale at $3 a bushel will sell it; all producers who cannot or will not sell for $3 per bushel will not sell their product.

Efficient Allocation

productive efficiency
The production of a good in the least costly way.

A competitive market such as we have described not only rations goods to consumers but also allocates society's resources efficiently to the particular product. Competition among corn producers forces them to use the best technology and right mix of productive resources. If they didn't, their costs would be too high relative to the market price, and they would be unprofitable. The result is **productive efficiency:** the production of any particular good in the least costly way. When society produces corn at the lowest achievable per-unit cost, it is expending the smallest amount of resources to produce that product and therefore is making available the largest amount of resources to produce other desired goods. Suppose society has only $100 worth of resources available. If it can produce a bushel of corn using $3 of those resources, then it will have $97 of available resources remaining to produce other goods. This is clearly better than producing the corn for $5 and having only $95 of resources available for the alternative uses.

allocative efficiency
The distribution of resources among firms and industries to produce the goods most wanted by society.

Competitive markets also produce **allocative efficiency:** the *particular mix* of goods and services most highly valued by society (minimum-cost production assumed). For example, society wants land suitable for growing corn to be used for that purpose, not to grow dandelions. It wants diamonds to be used for jewellery, not to be crushed up and used as an additive to give concrete more sparkle. It wants iPods and MP4 players, not cassette players and tapes. Moreover, society does not want to devote all its resources to corn, diamonds, and portable digital media players. It wants to assign some resources to wheat, gasoline, and cellphones. Competitive markets make those proper assignments.

MATH 3.4
Allocative Efficiency

The equilibrium price and quantity in competitive markets usually produce an assignment of resources that is "right" from an economic perspective. Demand essentially reflects the marginal benefit (MB) of the good (the extra benefit received from consuming one more unit of a good or service) and supply reflects the marginal cost (MC) of the good (the extra cost associated with producing one more unit of a good or service). The market ensures that firms produce all units of goods for which MB exceeds MC, and no units for which MC exceeds MB. At the intersection of the demand and supply curves, MB equals MC and allocative efficiency results. As economists say, there is neither an underallocation of resources nor an overallocation of resources to the product. We say more about productive and allocative efficiency in later chapters of *Microeconomics*.

Changes in Supply, Demand, and Equilibrium

We know that demand might change because of fluctuations in consumer tastes or incomes, changes in consumer expectations, or variations in the prices of related goods. Supply might change in response to changes in resource prices, technology, or taxes. What effects will such changes in supply and demand have on equilibrium price and quantity?

CONSIDER THIS :: Ticket Scalping: Unfair Criticism!

Ticket prices for athletic events and musical concerts are usually set far in advance of the events. Sometimes the original ticket price is too low to be the equilibrium price. Lines form at the ticket window, and a severe shortage of tickets occurs at the printed price. What happens next? Buyers who are willing to pay more than the original price bid up the ticket price in resale ticket markets.

Tickets sometimes get resold for much greater amounts than the original price—in a market transaction known as "scalping." For example, an original buyer of an NHL ticket to a Vancouver Canucks game may resell a $75 ticket to an important game for $200, $250, or more. The media sometimes denounce scalpers for "ripping off" buyers by charging "exorbitant" prices.

But is scalping really a rip-off? We must first recognize that such ticket resales are voluntary transactions. If both buyer and seller did not expect to gain from the exchange, it would not occur! The seller must value the $200 more than seeing the sporting event, and the buyer must value seeing

the sporting event at $200. So there are no losers or victims here: Both buyer and seller benefit from the transaction. The "scalping" market simply redistributes assets (game or concert tickets) from those who would rather have the money (and the other things money can buy) to those who would rather have the tickets.

Does scalping impose losses or injury on the sponsors of the event? If the sponsors are injured, it is because they initially priced tickets below the equilibrium level. Perhaps they did this to create a long waiting line and the attendant media publicity. Alternatively, they may have had a genuine desire to keep tickets affordable for lower-income, ardent fans. In either case, the event sponsors suffer an opportunity cost in the form of less ticket revenue than they might have otherwise received. But such losses are self-inflicted and quite separate and distinct from the fact that some tickets are later resold at a higher price.

So is ticket scalping undesirable? Not on economic grounds! It is an entirely voluntary activity that benefits both sellers and buyers.

CHANGES IN DEMAND

Suppose that the supply for some good (for example, potatoes) is constant and demand increases, as shown in Figure 3-7a. As a result, the new intersection of the supply and demand curves is at higher values on both the price and quantity axes. An increase in demand raises both equilibrium price and equilibrium quantity. Conversely, a decrease in demand, such as that shown in Figure 3-7b, reduces both equilibrium price and equilibrium quantity. (The value of graphical analysis is now apparent: We need not fumble with columns of figures to determine the outcomes; we need only compare the new and the old points of intersection on the graph.)

CHANGES IN SUPPLY

What happens if demand for some good (for example, flash drives) is constant but supply increases, as in Figure 3-7c? The new intersection of supply and demand is located at a lower equilibrium price but at a higher equilibrium quantity. An increase in supply reduces equilibrium price but increases equilibrium quantity. In contrast, if supply decreases, as in Figure 3-7d, equilibrium price rises while equilibrium quantity declines.

COMPLEX CASES

When both supply and demand change, the effect is a combination of the individual effects. As you study the following cases, keep in mind that each effect on the demand and supply curves has to be considered independently.

1. **Supply Increase; Demand Decrease** What effect will a supply increase and a demand decrease for some good (for example, apples) have on equilibrium price? Both changes decrease price, so the net result is a price drop greater than that resulting from either change alone.

   What about equilibrium quantity? Here the effects of the changes in supply and demand are opposed: The increase in supply increases equilibrium quantity, but the decrease in demand reduces it. The direction of the change in equilibrium quantity depends on the relative

| FIGURE 3-7 | Changes in Demand and Supply and the Effects on Price and Quantity |

The increase in demand from D_1 to D_2 in panel (a) increases both equilibrium price and quantity. The decrease in demand from D_1 to D_2 in panel (b) decreases both equilibrium price and quantity. The increase in supply from S_1 to S_2 in panel (c) decreases equilibrium price and increases equilibrium quantity. The decline in supply from S_1 to S_2 in panel (d) increases equilibrium price and decreases equilibrium quantity. The boxes in the top right corners summarize the respective changes and outcomes. The upward arrows in those boxes signify increases in demand (D), supply (S), equilibrium price (P), and equilibrium quantity (Q); the downward arrows signify decreases in these items.

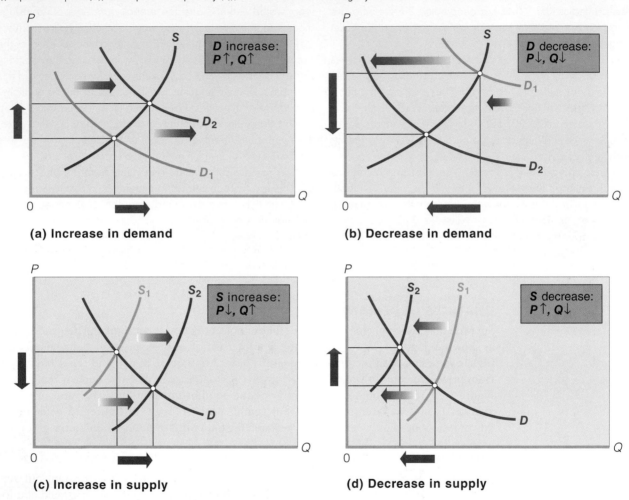

(a) Increase in demand

(b) Decrease in demand

(c) Increase in supply

(d) Decrease in supply

sizes of the changes in supply and demand. If the increase in supply is larger than the decrease in demand, the equilibrium quantity will increase. But if the decrease in demand is greater than the increase in supply, the equilibrium quantity will decrease.

2. **Supply Decrease; Demand Increase** A decrease in supply and an increase in demand for some good (for example, gasoline) both increase price. Their combined effect is an increase in equilibrium price greater than that caused by either change separately. But their effect on the equilibrium quantity is again indeterminate, depending on the relative sizes of the changes in supply and demand. If the decrease in supply is larger than the increase in demand, the equilibrium quantity will decrease. In contrast, if the increase in demand is greater than the decrease in supply, the equilibrium quantity will increase.

3. **Supply Increase; Demand Increase** What if supply and demand both increase for some good (for example, cellphones)? A supply increase drops equilibrium price, while a demand

CONSIDER THIS :: Salsa and Coffee Beans

If you forget the other-things-equal assumption, you can encounter situations that seem to be in conflict with the laws of demand and supply. For example, suppose salsa manufacturers sell 1 million bottles of salsa at $4 a bottle in one year; 2 million bottles at $5 in the next year; and 3 million at $6 in the year thereafter. Price and quantity purchased vary directly, and these data seem to be at odds with the law of demand.

But there is no conflict here; the data do not refute the law of demand. The catch is that the law of demand's other-things-equal assumption has been violated over the three years in the example. Specifically, because of changing tastes and rising incomes, the demand for salsa has increased sharply, as in Figure 3-7a. The result is higher prices and larger quantities purchased.

Another example: The price of coffee beans occasionally has shot upward at the same time that the quantity of coffee beans harvested has declined. These events seemingly contradict the direct relationship between price and quantity denoted by supply. The other-things-equal assumption underlying the upward-sloping supply curve was violated. Poor coffee harvests decreased supply, as in Figure 3-7d, increasing the equilibrium price of coffee and reducing the equilibrium quantity.

The laws of demand and supply are not refuted by observations of price and quantity made over periods of time in which either demand or supply changes.

increase boosts it. If the increase in supply is greater than the increase in demand, the equilibrium price will fall. If the opposite holds, the equilibrium price will rise.

The effect on equilibrium quantity is certain: The increases in supply and demand both raise the equilibrium quantity. Therefore, the equilibrium quantity will increase by an amount greater than that caused by either change alone.

MATH 3.5
Changes in Supply, Demand, and Equilibrium

4. *Supply Decrease; Demand Decrease* What about decreases in both supply and demand? If the decrease in supply is greater than the decrease in demand, equilibrium price will rise. If the reverse is true, equilibrium price will fall. Because the decreases in supply and demand each reduce equilibrium quantity, we can be sure that equilibrium quantity will fall.

Table 3-3 summarizes these four cases. To understand them fully you should draw supply and demand diagrams for each case to confirm the effects listed in Table 3-3.

Special cases arise when a decrease in demand and a decrease in supply, or an increase in demand and an increase in supply, exactly cancel out. In both cases, the net effect on equilibrium price will be zero; price will not change.

The optional appendix accompanying this chapter provides additional examples of situations in which both supply and demand change at the same time.

TABLE 3-3 **Effects of Changes in Both Supply and Demand**

	Change in supply	Change in demand	Effect on equilibrium price	Effect on equilibrium quantity
1	Increase	Decrease	Decrease	Indeterminate
2	Decrease	Increase	Increase	Indeterminate
3	Increase	Increase	Indeterminate	Increase
4	Decrease	Decrease	Indeterminate	Decrease

3.4 Application: Government-Set Prices

Prices in most markets are free to rise or fall to their equilibrium levels, no matter how high or low that might be. However, government sometimes concludes that supply and demand will produce prices that are unfairly high for buyers or unfairly low for sellers. So government may place legal limits on how high or low a price or prices may go. Is that a good idea?

Price Ceilings

price ceiling
A legally established maximum price for a good or service.

A **price ceiling** is the maximum legal price a seller may charge for a product or service. A price at or below the ceiling is legal; a price above it is not. The rationale for establishing price ceilings (or ceiling prices) on specific products is that they purportedly enable consumers to obtain some essential good or service that they could not afford at the equilibrium price. Examples are rent controls and usury laws, which specify maximum prices in the forms of rent and interest that can be charged to borrowers.

To be effective, a price ceiling on gasoline must be below the equilibrium price.

GRAPHICAL ANALYSIS

We can easily demonstrate the effects of price ceilings graphically using the example of gasoline. Let's suppose that rapidly rising world income boosts the purchase of automobiles and shifts the demand for gasoline to the right so that the equilibrium or market price reaches $1.25 per litre, shown as P_0 in Figure 3-8. The rapidly rising price of gasoline greatly burdens low-income and moderate-income households, who pressure the federal government to "do something." To keep gasoline prices down, the government imposes a ceiling price, P_c, of $0.75 per litre. To be effective, a price ceiling must be below the equilibrium price. A ceiling price of $1.50, for example, would have no effect on the price of gasoline in the current situation.

What are the effects of this $0.75 ceiling price? The rationing ability of the free market is rendered ineffective. Because the ceiling price, P_c, is below the market-clearing price, P_0, there is a shortage of gasoline. The quantity of gasoline demanded at P_c is Q_d and the quantity supplied is only Q_s; an excess demand or shortage of amount $Q_d - Q_s$ occurs.

The price ceiling, P_c, prevents the usual market adjustment in which competition among buyers bids up price, inducing more production and rationing some buyers out of the market. That process would normally continue until the shortage disappeared at the equilibrium price and quantity, P_0 and Q_0.

FIGURE 3-8   **A Price Ceiling Results in a Shortage**

A price ceiling is a maximum legal price, such as P_c. When the ceiling price is below the equilibrium price, a persistent product shortage results. Here that shortage is shown by the horizontal distance between Q_d and Q_s.

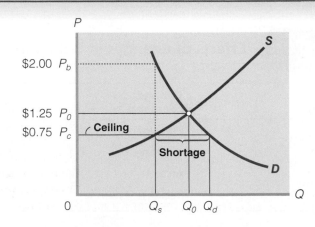

RATIONING PROBLEM

How will the government apportion the available supply, Q_s, among buyers who want the greater amount Q_d? Should gasoline be distributed on a first-come, first-served basis—that is, to those willing and able to get in line the soonest or stay in line the longest? Or should gas stations distribute it on the basis of favouritism? Since an unregulated shortage does not lead to an equitable distribution of gasoline, the federal government must establish some formal system for rationing it to consumers. One option is to issue ration coupons, which allow coupon-holders to purchase a fixed amount of gasoline per month. The rationing system might require the printing of coupons for Q_s litres of gasoline and then the equal distribution of the coupons among consumers so that the wealthy family of four and the poor family of four both receive the same number of coupons.

BLACK MARKETS

Ration coupons would not prevent a second problem from arising. The demand curve in Figure 3-8 tells us that many buyers are willing to pay more than the ceiling price P_c, and, of course, it is more profitable for gasoline stations to sell at prices above the ceiling. For example, at Q_s in Figure 3-8, some consumers would be willing to pay a price of up to $2.00 ($P_b$) to acquire some gasoline. Thus, despite the sizable enforcement bureaucracy that will accompany the price controls, *black markets* in which gasoline is illegally bought and sold at prices above the legal limits will flourish. Counterfeiting of ration coupons will also be a problem, and since the price of gasoline is now set by the federal government, there would be political pressure to set the price even lower.

CREDIT CARD INTEREST CEILINGS

Over the years there have been many calls in Canada for interest-rate ceilings on credit card accounts. The usual rationale for interest-rate ceilings is that the chartered banks and retail stores issuing such cards are presumably taking unfair advantage of users—and, in particular, lower-income users—by charging interest rates that average about 18 percent per year.

What might be the response if the Canadian government imposed a below-equilibrium interest rate on credit cards? The lower interest income associated with a legal interest ceiling would require the issuers of cards to reduce their costs or enhance their revenues:

- Card issuers might tighten credit standards to reduce losses due to non-payment and collection costs. Then, low-income and young Canadians who have not yet established their creditworthiness would find it more difficult to obtain credit cards.

- The annual fee charged to cardholders might be increased, as might the fee charged to merchants for processing credit card sales. Similarly, card users might be charged a fee for every transaction.

- Card users now have a post-purchase grace period during which the credit provided is interest-free. That period might be shortened or eliminated.

- Certain "enhancements" that accompany some credit cards (for example, extended warranties on products bought with a card) might be eliminated.

- Oil companies such as Petro-Canada, that issue their own cards to consumers who buy from their gasoline stations, might increase their prices to help offset the decline of interest income; customers who pay cash would in effect be subsidizing customers who use credit cards.

Price Floors

price floor
A legally established minimum price.

A **price floor** is a minimum price fixed by the government. A price at or above the price floor is legal; a price below it is not. Price floors above equilibrium prices are usually invoked when society believes that the free functioning of the market system has not provided a sufficient income for certain groups of resource suppliers or producers. Supported prices for some agricultural products and current minimum wages are two examples of price (or wage) floors. Let's analyze the results of imposing a price floor on wheat.

FIGURE 3-9   **A Price Floor Results in a Surplus**

A price floor is a minimum legal price, such as P_f. When the price floor is above the equilibrium price, a persistent product surplus results. Here that surplus is shown by the horizontal distance between Q_s and Q_d.

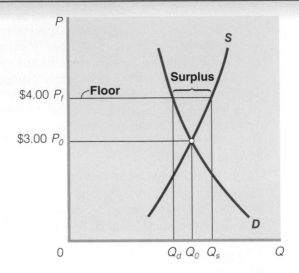

Supported prices for some agricultural products are an example of price floors.

Suppose that many farmers have extremely low incomes when the price of wheat is at its equilibrium value of $3 per bushel. The federal government decides to help by establishing a legal price floor or price support of $4 per bushel.

What will be the effects? At any price above the equilibrium price, quantity supplied will exceed quantity demanded—that is, there will be an excess supply or surplus of the product. Prairie farmers will be willing to produce and offer for sale more than private buyers are willing to purchase at the price floor. As we saw with a price ceiling, an imposed legal price disrupts the rationing ability of the free market.

GRAPHICAL ANALYSIS

Figure 3-9 illustrates the effect of a price floor on wheat. Suppose that S and D are the supply and demand curves for wheat. Equilibrium price and quantity are P_0 and Q_0, respectively. If the federal government imposes a price floor of P_f, farmers will produce Q_s, but private buyers will purchase only Q_d. The surplus is the excess of Q_s over Q_d.

The government can cope with the surplus resulting from a price floor in only two ways:

1. It can restrict supply (for example, by asking farmers in Alberta, Saskatchewan, and Manitoba to agree to take a certain amount of land out of production) or increase demand (for example, by researching new uses for the product involved). These actions may reduce the difference between the equilibrium price and the price floor and thereby reduce the size of the resulting surplus.

2. The federal government can purchase the surplus output at the $4 price (thereby subsidizing Prairie farmers) and store or otherwise dispose of it.

ADDITIONAL CONSEQUENCES

Price floors such as P_f in Figure 3-9 not only disrupt the rationing ability of prices but also distort resource allocation. Without the price floor, the $3 equilibrium price of wheat would cause financial losses and force high-cost wheat producers to plant other crops or abandon farming altogether. But the $4 price floor allows them to continue to grow wheat and remain farmers. So society devotes too many of its scarce resources to wheat production and too few to producing other, more valuable, goods and services. It fails to achieve allocative efficiency.

That's not all. Consumers of wheat-based products pay higher prices because of the price floor. Taxpayers pay higher taxes to finance the government's purchase of the surplus. Also, the price floor causes potential environmental damage by encouraging wheat farmers to bring "marginal land" into production. The higher price also prompts imports of wheat. But, since such imports would increase the quantity of wheat supplied and thus undermine the price floor, the government needs to erect tariffs (taxes on imports) to keep the foreign wheat out. Such tariffs usually prompt other countries to retaliate with their own tariffs against Canadian agricultural or manufacturing exports.

It is easy to see why economists "sound the alarm" when politicians advocate imposing price ceilings or price floors such as price controls, interest-rate caps, or agricultural price supports. In all these cases, good intentions lead to bad economic outcomes. Government-controlled prices cause shortages or surpluses, distort resource allocation, and produce negative side effects.

An interesting example of government involvement in influencing prices so as to ensure farmers higher prices was the Canadian Wheat Marketing Board (CWMB), a marketing board created in 1935 through which western wheat and barley producers in Alberta, Saskatchewan, Manitoba, and a small part of British Columbia were required to sell their output. No farmer was allowed to opt out of selling through the CWMB. When farmers delivered their wheat or barley, they received an initial payment per bushel from the CWMB that was 75 percent of the expected average selling price. This was in effect a floor price and set low enough that the Wheat Board was reasonably sure to sell the wheat or barley at least at that price. The producers subsequently would get the full average selling price the CWMB was able to get on the domestic and international markets, minus transportation costs, storage costs, and administrative expenses. Farmers would get the average price the CWMB was able to realize over the course of the year. There were many critics of the CWMB, who believed farmers should be allowed to opt out of the board. Indeed, the critics won out, and the CWMB ceased to exist as of August 2012.

QUICK REVIEW

- In competitive markets, prices adjust to the equilibrium level at which quantity demanded equals quantity supplied.

- The equilibrium price and quantity are those indicated by the intersection of the supply and demand curves for any product or resource.

- An increase in demand increases equilibrium price and quantity; a decrease in demand decreases equilibrium price and quantity.

- An increase in supply reduces equilibrium price but increases equilibrium quantity;

- a decrease in supply increases equilibrium price but reduces equilibrium quantity.

- Over time, equilibrium price and quantity may change in directions that seem at odds with the laws of demand and supply because the other-things-equal assumption is violated.

- Government-controlled prices in the form of ceilings and floors stifle the rationing functions of prices, distort resource allocations, and cause negative side effects.

The **LAST WORD** A Legal Market for Human Organs?

A legal market might eliminate the present shortage of human organs for transplant. But many serious objections exist to turning human body parts into commodities for purchase and sale.

It has become increasingly commonplace in medicine to transplant kidneys, lungs, livers, eye corneas, pancreases, and hearts from deceased individuals to those whose organs have failed or are failing. But surgeons and many of their patients face a growing problem: Too few donated organs are available for transplant. Not everyone who needs a transplant can get one. Indeed, an inadequate supply of donated organs causes an estimated 400 Canadian deaths per year.

Why Shortages? Seldom do we hear of shortages of desired goods in market economies. What is different about organs for transplant? One difference is that no legal market exists for human organs. To understand this situation, observe the demand curve D_1 and supply curve S_1 in the accompanying figure. The downward slope of the demand curve tells us that if there were a market for human organs, the quantity of organs demanded would be greater at lower prices than at higher prices. Vertical supply curve S_1 represents the fixed quantity of human organs now donated via consent before death. Because the price of these donated organs is in effect zero, quantity demanded, Q_3, exceeds quantity supplied, Q_1. The shortage of $Q_3 - Q_1$ is rationed through a waiting list of those in medical need of transplants. Many people die while still on the waiting list.

Use of a Market A market for human organs would increase the incentive to donate organs. Such a market might work like this: An individual might specify in a legal document a willingness to sell one or more usable human organs on death or brain death. The person could specify where the money from

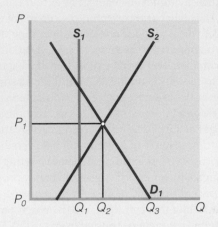

the sale would go, for example, to family, a church, an educational institution, or a charity. Firms would then emerge to purchase organs and resell them where needed for profit. Under such a system, the supply curve of usable organs would take on the normal upward slope of typical supply curves. The higher the expected price of an organ, the greater the number of people willing to have their organs sold at death. Suppose that the supply curve is S_2 in the figure. At the equilibrium price P_1, the number of organs made available for transplant (Q_2) would equal the number purchased for transplant (also Q_2). In this generalized case, the shortage of organs would be eliminated and, of particular importance, the number of organs available for transplanting would rise from Q_1 to Q_2. More lives

would be saved and enhanced than under the present donor system.

Objections In view of this positive outcome, why is there no such market for human organs? Critics of market-based solutions have two main objections. The first is a moral objection: Critics feel that turning human organs into commodities commercializes human beings and diminishes the special nature of human life. They say there is something unseemly about selling and buying body organs as if they were bushels of wheat or ounces of gold. Moreover, critics note that the market would ration the available organs (as represented by Q_2 in the figure) to people who either can afford them (at P_1) or have health insurance for transplants. Second, a health cost objection suggests that a market for body organs would greatly increase the cost of health care. Rather than obtaining freely donated (although too few) body organs, patients would have to pay market prices for them, increasing the cost of medical care.

Rebuttal Supporters of market-based solutions to organ shortages point out that the market is simply being driven underground. Worldwide, an illegal market in human organs worth an estimated $1 billion annually has emerged. As in other illegal markets, the unscrupulous tend to thrive.

Question

In some countries, such as France, every corpse is available for doctors to "harvest" for organs unless the deceased, while still alive, signed a form forbidding the organs to be harvested. In Canada and the USA, it is the opposite: No harvesting is allowed unless the deceased signed, while still alive, an organ donor form authorizing doctors to harvest any needed organs. Use supply and demand figures to show in which country organ shortages are likely to be less severe.

CHAPTER SUMMARY

3.1 :: DEMAND

- Demand is a schedule or curve representing the willingness of buyers in a specific period to purchase a particular product at each of various prices. The law of demand implies that consumers will buy more of a product at a low price than at a high price. Therefore, other things equal, the relationship between price and quantity demanded is negative or inverse and is graphed as a downward-sloping curve.

- Market demand curves are found by summing up (horizontally) the demand curves of the many individual consumers in the market.

- Changes in one or more of the determinants of demand (consumer tastes, the number of buyers in the market, the money incomes of consumers, the prices of related goods, and consumer expectations) shift the market demand curve. A shift to the right is an increase in demand; a shift to the left is a decrease in demand. A change in demand is different from a change in the quantity demanded, the latter being a movement from one point to another point on a fixed demand curve because of a change in the product's price.

3.2 :: SUPPLY

- Supply is a schedule or curve showing the amounts of a product that producers are willing to offer in the market at each possible price during a specific period. The law of supply states that, other things equal, producers will offer more of a product at a high price than at a low price. Thus, the relationship between price and quantity supplied is positive or direct, and supply is graphed as an upward-sloping curve.

- The market supply curve is the horizontal summation of the supply curves of the individual producers of the product.

- Changes in one or more of the determinants of supply (factor prices, technology, taxes and subsidies, price expectations, or the number of sellers in the market) shift the supply curve of a product. A shift to the right is an increase in supply; a shift to the left is a decrease in supply. In contrast, a change in the price of the product being considered causes a change in the quantity supplied, which is shown as a movement from one point to another point on a fixed supply curve.

3.3 :: MARKET EQUILIBRIUM

- The equilibrium price and quantity are established at the intersection of the supply and demand curves. The interaction of market demand and market supply adjusts the price to the point at which the quantity demanded and quantity supplied are equal. This is the equilibrium price. The corresponding quantity is the equilibrium quantity.

- The ability of market forces to synchronize selling and buying decisions to eliminate potential surpluses and shortages is known as the rationing function of prices. The equilibrium quantity in competitive markets reflects both productive efficiency (least-cost production) and allocative efficiency (producing the right amount of the product relative to other products).

- A change in either demand or supply changes the equilibrium price and quantity. Increases in demand raise both equilibrium price and equilibrium quantity; decreases in demand lower both equilibrium price and equilibrium quantity. Increases in supply lower equilibrium price and raise equilibrium quantity; decreases in supply raise equilibrium price and lower equilibrium quantity.

- Simultaneous changes in demand and supply affect equilibrium price and quantity in various ways, depending on their direction and relative magnitudes.

3.4 :: APPLICATION: GOVERNMENT-SET PRICES

- A price ceiling is a maximum price set by government and is designed to help consumers.

- A price floor is a minimum price set by government and is designed to aid producers.

- Government-set prices stifle the rationing function of prices and distort the allocation of resources.

TERMS AND CONCEPTS

demand, p. 53
law of demand, p. 54
diminishing marginal utility, p. 54
income effect, p. 54
substitution effect, p. 54
demand curve, p. 54
determinants of demand, p. 55
normal goods, p. 57
inferior goods, p. 57
substitute goods, p. 57

complementary goods, p. 57
change in demand, p. 59
change in quantity demanded, p. 59
supply, p. 59
law of supply, p. 59
supply curve, p. 59
determinants of supply, p. 62
change in supply, p. 63
change in quantity supplied, p. 63
equilibrium price, p. 64

equilibrium quantity, p. 64
surplus, p. 64
shortage, p. 64
rationing function of prices, p. 66
productive efficiency, p. 66
allocative efficiency, p. 66
price ceiling, p. 70
price floor, p. 71

:: QUESTIONS

1. Explain the law of demand. Why does a demand curve slope downward? How is a market demand curve derived from individual demand curves?   [**LO3.1**]

2. What are the determinants of demand? What happens to the demand curve when any of these determinants changes? Distinguish between a change in demand and a change in the quantity demanded, noting the cause(s) of each.   [**LO3.1**]

3. What effect will each of the following have on the demand for small automobiles such as the MINI Cooper and Smart Car?   [**LO3.1**]

   a. Small automobiles become more fashionable.

   b. The price of large automobiles rises (with the price of small autos remaining the same).

   c. Income declines and small autos are an inferior good.

   d. Consumers anticipate that the price of small autos will greatly come down in the near future.

   e. The price of gasoline substantially drops.

4. Explain the law of supply. Why does the supply curve slope upward? How is the market supply curve derived from the supply curves of individual producers?   [**LO3.2**]

5. What are the determinants of supply? What happens to the supply curve when any of these determinants changes? Distinguish between a change in supply and a change in the quantity supplied, noting the cause(s) of each.   [**LO3.2**]

6. What effect will each of the following have on the supply of auto tires?   [**LO3.2**]

   a. A technological advance in the methods of producing tires.

   b. A decline in the number of firms in the tire industry.

   c. An increase in the price of rubber used in the production of tires.

   d. The expectation that the equilibrium price of auto tires will be lower in the future than currently.

   e. A decline in the price of the large tires used for semi-trailers and earth-hauling rigs (with no change in the price of auto tires).

   f. The levying of a per-unit tax on each auto tire sold.

   g. The granting of a subsidy of 50 cents per unit for each auto tire produced.

7. "In the corn market, demand often exceeds supply and supply sometimes exceeds demand." "The price of corn rises and falls in response to changes in supply and demand." In which of these two statements are the terms "supply" and "demand" used correctly? Explain.   [**LO3.3**]

8. In 2001, an outbreak of foot-and-mouth disease in Europe led to the burning of millions of cattle carcasses. What impact do you think this had on the supply of cattle hides, hide prices, the supply of leather goods, and the price of leather goods?   [**LO3.3**]

9. Critically evaluate the following statement: "In comparing the two equilibrium positions in Figure 3-7b, I note that a smaller amount is actually demanded at a lower price. This refutes the law of demand."   [**LO3.3**]

10. For each stock in the stock market, the number of shares sold daily equals the number of shares purchased. That is, the quantity of each firm's shares demanded equals the quantity supplied. So, if this equality always occurs, why do the prices of stocks ever change?   [**LO3.3**]

11. Suppose the total demand for wheat and the total supply of wheat per month in the Winnipeg grain market are as follows: [**LO3.3**]

Thousands of bushels demanded	Price per bushel	Thousands of bushels supplied
85	$3.40	72
80	3.70	73
75	4.00	75
70	4.30	77
65	4.60	79
60	4.90	81

   a. Suppose that the government establishes a price ceiling of $3.70 for wheat. What might prompt the government to establish this price ceiling? Carefully explain the main effects. Demonstrate your answer graphically.

   b. Next, suppose that the government establishes a price floor of $4.60 for wheat. What will be the main effects of this price floor? Demonstrate your answer graphically.

12. What do economists mean when they say that "price floors and ceilings stifle the rationing function of prices and distort resource allocation"?   [**LO3.4**]

PROBLEMS

1. Suppose there are three buyers of candy in a market: Tex, Dex, and Rex. The market demand and the individual demands of Tex, Dex, and Rex for candy are given in the table below.   [LO3.1]

   a. Fill in the table for the missing values.

   b. Which buyer demands the least at a price of $5? The most at a price of $7?

   c. Which buyer's quantity demanded increases the most when the price is lowered from $7 to $6?

   d. In which direction would the market demand curve shift if Tex withdrew from the market? What if Dex doubled his purchases at each possible price?

   e. Suppose that at a price of $6, the total quantity demanded increases from 19 to 38. Is this a "change in the quantity demanded" or a "change in demand"?

Price per candy	Individual quantities demanded						Total quantity demanded
	Tex		Dex		Rex		
$8	3	+	1	+	0	=	—
7	8	+	2	+	—	=	12
6	—	+	3	+	4	=	19
5	17	+	—	+	6	=	27
4	23	+	5	+	8	=	—

2. The figure below shows the supply curve for tennis balls, S_1, for Drop Volley tennis, a producer of tennis equipment. Use the figure and the table below to give your answers to the following questions.   [LO3.2]

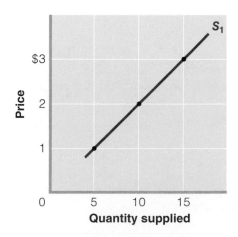

a. Use the figure to fill in the quantity supplied on supply curve S_1 for each price in the table below.

Price	S_1 Quantity supplied	S_2 Quantity supplied	Change in quantity supplied
$3	_____	4	_____
2	_____	2	_____
1	_____	0	_____

b. If production costs were to increase, the quantities supplied at each price would be as shown by the third column of the table ("S_2 Quantity supplied"). Use that data to draw supply curve S_2 on the same graph as supply curve S_1.

c. In the fourth column of the table, enter the amount by which the quantity supplied at each price changes due to the increase in product costs. (Use positive numbers for increases and negative numbers for decreases.)

d. Did the increase in production costs cause a "decrease in supply" or a "decrease in quantity supplied"?

3. Refer to the expanded table below from Question 11. [LO3.3]

Thousands of bushels demanded	Price per bushel	Thousands of bushels supplied	Surplus (+) or shortage (−)
85	$3.40	72	_____
80	3.70	73	_____
75	4.00	75	_____
70	4.30	77	_____
65	4.60	79	_____
60	4.90	81	_____

a. What is the equilibrium price? At what price is there neither a shortage nor a surplus? Fill in the surplus–shortage column and use it to confirm your answers.

b. Graph the demand for wheat and the supply of wheat. Be sure to label the axes of your graph correctly. Label equilibrium price *P* and equilibrium quantity *Q*.

c. How big is the surplus or shortage at $3.40? At $4.90? How big a surplus or shortage results if the price is 60 cents higher than the equilibrium price? 30 cents lower than the equilibrium price?

4. How will each of the following changes in demand and/or supply affect equilibrium price and equilibrium quantity in a competitive market? That is, do price and quantity rise, fall, or remain unchanged, or are the answers indeterminate because they depend on the magnitudes of the shifts? Use supply and demand to verify your answers.   [LO3.3]

   a. Supply decreases and demand is constant.

   b. Demand decreases and supply is constant.

   c. Supply increases and demand is constant.

   d. Demand increases and supply increases.

   e. Demand increases and supply is constant.

   f. Supply increases and demand decreases.

   g. Demand increases and supply decreases.

   h. Demand decreases and supply decreases.

5. **Advanced analysis** Assume that demand for a commodity is represented by the equation $P = 10 - 0.2Q_d$ and supply by the equation $P = 2 + 0.2Q_s$, where Q_d and Q_s are quantity demanded and quantity supplied, respectively, and P is price. Using the equilibrium condition $Q_s = Q_d$, solve the equations to determine equilibrium price. Now determine equilibrium quantity.   [LO3.3]

6. Suppose that the demand and supply schedules for rental apartments in the city of Gotham are as given in the table below.   [LO3.4]

Monthly rent	Apartments demanded	Apartments supplied
$2,500	10,000	15,000
2,000	12,500	12,500
1,500	15,000	10,000
1,000	17,500	7,500
500	20,000	5,000

   a. What is the market equilibrium rental price per month and the market equilibrium number of apartments demanded and supplied?

   b. If the municipal government can enforce a rent-control law that sets the maximum monthly rent at $1500, will there be a surplus or a shortage? Of how many units? How many units will actually be rented each month?

   c. Suppose that a new government is elected that wants to keep out the poor. It declares that the minimum allowable rent is $2500 per month. If the government can enforce that price floor, will there be a surplus or a shortage? Of how many units? And how many units will actually be rented each month?

   d. Suppose that the government wishes to decrease the market equilibrium monthly rent by increasing the supply of housing. Assuming that demand remains unchanged, by how many units of housing would the government have to increase the supply of housing in order to get the market equilibrium rental price to fall to $1500 per month? To $1000 per month? To $500 per month?

Mc Graw Hill connect™ Practice and Learn Online with Connect

Connect allows you to practice important concepts at your own pace and on your own schedule, with 24/7 online access to an eBook, algorithmic questions and problems from the textbook, video and logic cases, graphing tutorials, flashcards, Internet exercises, key graphs, and more.

Appendix to Chapter 3

Additional Examples of Supply and Demand

Our discussion has clearly demonstrated that supply and demand analysis is a powerful tool for understanding equilibrium prices and quantities. The information provided in the main body of this chapter is fully sufficient for moving forward in the book, but you may find that additional examples of supply and demand are helpful. This optional appendix provides several concrete illustrations of changes in supply and demand. It also applies supply and demand analysis to non-priced goods (goods owned in common and not bought and sold in markets).

Your instructor may assign all, some, or none of this appendix, depending on time availability and personal preference.

Changes in Supply and Demand

As Figure 3-6 demonstrates, changes in supply and demand cause changes in price, quantity, or both. The following applications illustrate this fact in several real-world markets. The simplest situations are those in which either supply changes while demand remains constant, or demand changes while supply remains constant. Let's consider two such simple cases first, before looking at more complex applications.

LETTUCE

Every now and then, the media report that extreme weather has severely reduced the size of some crop. Suppose, for example, that a severe freeze destroys a sizable portion of the lettuce crop. This unfortunate situation implies a significant decline in supply, which we represent in Figure A3-1 as a leftward shift of the supply curve from S_1 to S_2. At each price, consumers desire as much lettuce as before, so the freeze does not affect the demand for lettuce. That is, demand curve D_1 does not shift.

What are the consequences of the reduced supply of lettuce for equilibrium price and quantity? As shown in Figure A3-1, the leftward shift of the supply curve disrupts the previous equilibrium in the market for lettuce and drives the equilibrium price up from P_1 to P_2.

Consumers respond to that price hike by reducing the quantity of lettuce demanded from Q_1 to Q_2. Equilibrium in the market is restored at P_2 and Q_2. Consumers who are willing and able to pay price P_2 obtain lettuce; consumers unwilling or unable to pay that price do not. Some consumers continue to buy as much lettuce as before, even at the higher price. Others buy some lettuce but not as much as before, and still others forgo

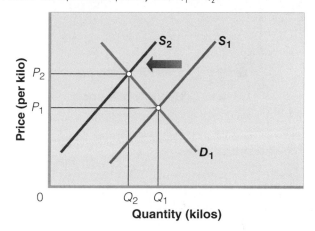

FIGURE A3-1   The Market for Lettuce

The decrease in the supply of lettuce, shown here by the shift from S_1 to S_2, increases the equilibrium price of lettuce from P_1 to P_2 and reduces the equilibrium quantity from Q_1 to Q_2.

lettuce altogether. The latter two groups use the money they would have spent on lettuce to obtain other products, say, carrots. (Because of our other-things-equal assumption, the prices of other products have not changed.)

EXCHANGE RATES

Exchange rates are the prices at which one currency can be traded (exchanged) for another. Exchange rates are normally determined in **foreign exchange markets.** One exchange market is the euro–Canadian dollar market in which the currency used in most of Europe, the *euro*, is exchanged for Canadian dollars. In Canada, this market is set up so that euros are priced in dollars—that is, the "product" being traded is the euro and the "price" to buy that product is quoted in dollars. Thus, the market equilibrium price one day might be $1.25 to buy one euro, while on another day it might be $1.50 to buy one euro.

Foreign exchange markets are used by individuals and companies that need to make purchases or payments in a different currency. Canadian companies exporting goods to Germany, for instance, wish to be paid in Canadian dollars. Thus, their German customers will need to convert euros into dollars. The euros that they bring to the euro–dollar market will become part of the overall market supply of euros.

FIGURE A3-2 **The Market for Euros**

The increase in the demand for euros, shown here by the shift from D_1 to D_2, increases the equilibrium price of a euro from \$1.25 to \$1.50 and increases the equilibrium quantity of euros from Q_1 to Q_2. The Canadian dollar has depreciated.

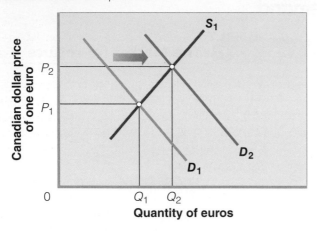

FIGURE A3-3 **The Market for Pink Salmon**

In the last two decades, the supply of pink salmon has increased and the demand for pink salmon has decreased. As a result, the price of pink salmon has declined, as from P_1 to P_2. Because supply has increased more than demand has decreased, the equilibrium quantity of pink salmon has increased, as from Q_1 to Q_2.

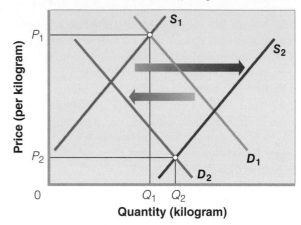

Conversely, a Canadian mutual fund may wish to purchase some real estate in France. But to purchase that real estate, it will need to pay in euros since the property's current French owners will accept payment only in euros. Thus, the Canadian mutual fund has a demand to purchase euros that will form part of the overall market demand for euros. The mutual fund will bring dollars to the euro–dollar foreign exchange market in order to purchase the euros it desires.

Sometimes, the demand for euros increases. This might be because a European product surges in popularity in foreign countries. For example, if a new German-made automobile is a big hit in Canada, car dealers here will demand more euros with which to pay for more units of that new model. This will shift the demand curve for euros to the right, as from D_1 to D_2 in Figure A3-2. Given the fixed euro supply curve S_1, the increase in demand raises the equilibrium exchange rate (the equilibrium number of dollars needed to purchase one euro) from \$1.25 to \$1.50. The equilibrium quantity of euros purchased increases from Q_1 to Q_2. Because a higher dollar amount is now needed to purchase one euro, economists say that the dollar has *depreciated*—gone down in value—relative to the euro. Alternatively, the euro has *appreciated*—gone up in value—relative to the Canadian dollar because one euro now buys \$1.50 rather than \$1.25.

PINK SALMON

Now let's see what happens when both supply and demand change at the same time. Several decades ago, people who caught salmon earned as much as \$2 for each kilogram of pink salmon—the type used mainly for canning—brought to

the buyer. In Figure A3-3 that price is represented as P_1, at the intersection of supply curve S_1 and demand curve D_1. The corresponding quantity of pink salmon is shown as Q_1 kilograms. As time passed, supply and demand changed in the market for pink salmon. On the supply side, improved technology in the form of larger, more efficient fishing boats greatly increased the catch and lowered the cost of obtaining it. Also, high profits at price P_1 encouraged many new fishers to enter the industry. As a result of these changes, the supply of pink salmon greatly increased and the supply curve shifted to the right, as from S_1 to S_2 in Figure A3-3.

Over the same years, the demand for pink salmon declined, as represented by the leftward shift from D_1 to D_2 in Figure A3-3. That decrease resulted from increases in consumer income and reductions of the price of substitute products. As buyers' incomes rose, consumers shifted demand away from canned fish and toward higher-quality fresh or frozen fish, including more-valued Atlantic, Chinook, Sockeye, and Coho salmon. Moreover, the emergence of fish farming, in which salmon are raised in ocean net pens, lowered the prices of these substitute species. That, too, reduced the demand for pink salmon.

The altered supply and demand reduced the price of pink salmon to as low as \$0.20 per kilogram, as represented by the drop in price from P_1 to P_2 in Figure A3-3. Both the supply increase and the demand decrease helped reduce the equilibrium price. However, in this particular case the equilibrium quantity of pink salmon increased, as represented by the move from Q_1 to Q_2. Both shifts of the curves reduced the equilibrium price, but equilibrium quantity increased because the increase in supply exceeded the decrease in demand.

GASOLINE

The price of gasoline has increased rapidly in Canada over the past several years. For example, the average price of a litre of gasoline rose from around $0.60 in 2004 to about $1.40 in 2011. What caused the price of gasoline to more than double? How would we diagram this increase?

We begin in Figure A3-4 with the price of a litre of gasoline at P_1, representing the $0.60 price. Simultaneous supply and demand factors disturbed this equilibrium. On the supply side, supply uncertainties relating to Middle East politics and warfare and expanded demand for oil by fast-growing countries such as China pushed up the price of a barrel of oil from $37 in 2004 to over $100 in 2011. Oil is the main input for producing gasoline, so any sustained rise in its price boosts the per-unit cost of producing gasoline. Such cost rises decrease the supply of gasoline, as represented by the leftward shift of the supply curve from S_1 to S_2 in Figure A3-4. At times, refinery breakdowns in North America also contributed to this reduced supply.

While the supply of gasoline declined between 2004 and 2011, the demand for gasoline increased, as depicted by the rightward shift of the demand curve from D_1 to D_2. Incomes in general were rising over these years because the Canadian economy was rapidly expanding. Rising incomes raise demand for all normal goods, including gasoline. An increased number of low-gas-mileage SUVs and light trucks on the road also contributed to growing gas demand.

The combined decrease in gasoline supply and increase in gasoline demand boosted the price of gasoline from $0.60 to $1.40, as represented by the rise from P_1 to P_2 in Figure A3-4. Because the demand increase outweighed the supply decrease, the equilibrium quantity expanded here, from Q_1 to Q_2.

In other periods the price of gasoline has *declined* as the demand for gasoline has increased. Test your understanding of the analysis by explaining how such a price decrease could occur.

SUSHI

Sushi bars are springing up at a rapid rate in Canadian cities. Consumption of sushi—the raw-fish delicacy from Japan—has soared in Canada in recent years. Nevertheless, the price of sushi has remained relatively constant.

Supply and demand analysis helps explain this circumstance of increased quantity and constant price. A change in tastes has increased the Canadian demand for sushi. Many first-time consumers of sushi find it highly tasty. And, as implied by the growing number of sushi bars in Canada, the supply of sushi has also expanded.

We represent these supply and demand changes in Figure A3-5 as the rightward shift of the demand curve from D_1 to D_2 and the rightward shift of the supply curve from S_1 to S_2. Observe that the equilibrium quantity of sushi increases from Q_1 to Q_2 and the equilibrium price remains constant at P_1. The increase in supply, which taken alone would reduce the price, has perfectly offset the increase in demand, which taken alone would raise the price. The price of sushi does not change but the equilibrium quantity greatly increases because both the increase in demand and the increase in supply act to expand purchases and sales.

Simultaneous increases in demand and supply can cause the price to rise, fall, or remain constant, depending on the relative magnitudes of the supply and demand increases. In this case, the price remained constant.

FIGURE A3-4 **The Market for Gasoline**

An increase in the demand for gasoline, as shown by the shift from D_1 to D_2, coupled with a decrease in supply, as shown by the shift from S_1 to S_2, boosts equilibrium price (here, from P_1 to P_2). In this case, equilibrium quantity increases from Q_1 to Q_2 because the increase in demand outweighs the decrease in supply.

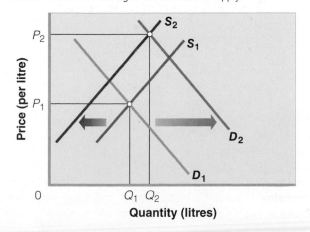

FIGURE A3-5 **The Market for Sushi**

Equal increases in the demand for sushi, as from D_1 to D_2, and in the supply of sushi, as from S_1 to S_2, expand the equilibrium quantity of sushi (here from Q_1 to Q_2), while leaving the price of sushi unchanged at P_1.

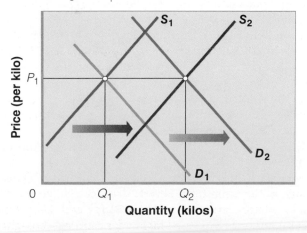

Preset Prices

In the body of this chapter we saw that an effective government-imposed price ceiling (legal maximum price) causes quantity demanded to exceed quantity supplied—a shortage. An effective government-imposed price floor (legal minimum price) causes quantity supplied to exceed quantity demanded—a surplus. Put simply: Shortages result when prices are set below equilibrium prices, and surpluses result when prices are set above equilibrium prices. We now want to establish that shortages and surpluses can occur in markets other than those in which government imposes price floors and ceilings. Such market imbalances happen when the seller or sellers set prices in advance of sales and the prices selected turn out to be below or above equilibrium prices. Consider the following two examples.

OLYMPIC FIGURE SKATING FINALS

Tickets for the women's figure skating championship at the Olympics are among the world's hottest tickets. The popularity of this event and the high incomes of buyers translate into tremendous ticket demand. Olympic officials set the price for the tickets in advance. Invariably, the price, although high, is considerably below the equilibrium price that would equate quantity demanded and quantity supplied. A severe shortage of tickets therefore occurs in this *primary market*—the market involving the official ticket office. The shortage, in turn, creates a *secondary market* in which buyers bid for tickets held by initial purchasers rather than the original seller. Scalping tickets—selling them above the original ticket price—may be legal or illegal, depending on local laws. Figure A3-6 shows

how the shortage in the primary ticket market looks in terms of supply and demand analysis. Demand curve D represents the strong demand for tickets, and supply curve S represents the supply of tickets. The supply curve is vertical because a fixed number of tickets are printed to match the capacity of the arena. At the printed ticket price of P_1, the quantity of tickets demanded, Q_2, exceeds the quantity supplied, Q_1. The result is a shortage of ab—the horizontal distance between Q_2 and Q_1 in the primary market. If the printed ticket price had been the higher equilibrium price P_2, no shortage of tickets would have occurred. But at the lower price P_1, a shortage and secondary ticket market will emerge among those buyers willing to pay more than the original price and those sellers willing to sell their purchased tickets for more than the printed price. Wherever there are shortages and secondary markets, we can safely assume that the original price was set below the equilibrium price.

OLYMPIC CURLING PRELIMINARIES

Contrast the shortage of tickets for the women's figure skating finals at the Olympics to the surplus of tickets for one of the preliminary curling matches. Curling is a sport in which participants slide a heavy round object called a stone down the ice toward a target while people called sweepers use brooms to alter the course of the stone when desired. Curling is a popular spectator sport in a few nations such as Canada, but it does not draw many fans in most countries. So the demand for tickets to most of the preliminary curling events is not very strong. We demonstrate this weak demand as D in Figure A3-7. As in our previous example, the supply of tickets is fixed by the size of the arena and is shown as vertical line S.

FIGURE A3-6   The Market for Tickets to Olympic Women's Figure Skating Finals

The demand curve D and the supply curve S produce an equilibrium price above the P_1 price printed on the ticket. At price P_1 the quantity of tickets demanded, Q_2, greatly exceeds the quantity of tickets available (Q_1). The resulting shortage of ab (= Q_2Q_1) gives rise to a legal or illegal secondary market.

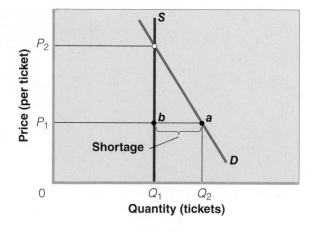

FIGURE A3-7 **The Market for Tickets to the Olympic Curling Preliminaries**

The demand curve D and the supply curve S produce an equilibrium price below the P_1 price printed on the ticket. At price P_1 the quantity of tickets demanded is less than the quantity of tickets available. The resulting surplus of ba $(= Q_1Q_2)$ means the event is not sold out.

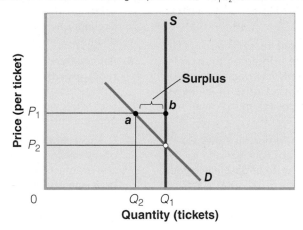

We represent the printed ticket price as P_1 in Figure A3-7. In this case the printed price is much higher than the equilibrium price of P_2. At the printed ticket price, quantity supplied is Q_1 and quantity demanded is Q_2. So a surplus of tickets of ba $(= Q_1 - Q_2)$ occurs. No ticket scalping occurs and there are numerous empty seats. Only if Olympic officials had priced the tickets at the lower price P_2 would the event have been a sell-out. (Actually, Olympic officials try to adjust to demand realities for curling contests by holding them in smaller arenas and by charging less for tickets. Nevertheless, the stands are rarely full for the preliminary contests, which compete against final events in other winter Olympic sports.)

APPENDIX Summary

- A decrease in the supply of a product increases its equilibrium price and reduces its equilibrium quantity. In contrast, an increase in the demand for a product boosts both its equilibrium price and its equilibrium quantity.

- Simultaneous changes in supply and demand affect equilibrium price and quantity in various ways, depending on the relative magnitudes of the changes in supply and demand. Equal increases in supply and demand, for example, leave equilibrium price unchanged.

- Sellers set prices of some items such as tickets in advance of the event. These items are sold in the primary market that involves the original seller and buyers. If preset prices turn out to be below the equilibrium prices, shortages occur and scalping in legal or illegal secondary markets arises. The prices in the secondary market then rise above the preset prices. In contrast, surpluses occur when the preset prices happen to exceed the equilibrium prices.

- Non-priced goods, such as fish in public waters and game on public lands, are owned in common and therefore not bought and sold in markets. A surplus of a non-priced good occurs when the sustainable quantity of the good exceeds the quantity demanded. A shortage of a non-priced good occurs when the quantity demanded exceeds the sustainable quantity. In this latter case, the good tends to be overconsumed and, without protection, may eventually be exhausted.

APPENDIX Terms and Concepts

exchange rate The rate of exchange of one nation's currency for another nation's currency. (p. 79)

foreign exchange market A market in which the money (currency) of one nation can be used to purchase (can be exchanged for) the money of another nation. (p. 79)

APPENDIX Questions

1. Why are shortages or surpluses more likely with preset prices, such as for tickets, than with flexible prices, such as for gasoline? [LOA3.1]

2. Most scalping laws make it illegal to sell—but not to buy—tickets at prices above those printed on the tickets. Assuming that is the case, use supply and demand analysis to explain why the equilibrium ticket price in an illegal secondary market tends to be higher than in a legal secondary market. [LOA3.1]

3. How high (or how low) are gasoline prices now? Go to Gasticker.com or www.garnetknight.com/gas and follow the links to find the current retail price of gasoline in your area. How does the current price of regular gasoline compare with the price a year ago? What must have happened to either supply, demand, or both to explain the observed price change? [LOA3.1]

4. Suppose the supply of apples sharply increases because of perfect weather conditions throughout the growing season. Assuming no change in demand, explain the effect on the equilibrium price and quantity of apples. Explain why quantity demanded increases even though demand does not change. [LOA3.1]

5. Assume the demand for lumber suddenly rises because of a rapid growth of demand for new housing. Assume no change in supply. Why does the equilibrium price of lumber rise? What would happen if the price did not rise under the demand and supply circumstances described? [LOA3.1]

6. Suppose both the demand for olives and the supply of olives decline by equal amounts over some time period. Use graphical analysis to show the effect on equilibrium price and quantity. [LOA3.1]

7. Assume that both the supply of bottled water and the demand for bottled water rise during the summer but that supply increases more rapidly than demand. What can you conclude about the directions of the impacts on equilibrium price and equilibrium quantity? [LOA3.1]

APPENDIX Problems

1. Demand and supply often shift in the retail market for gasoline. Here are two demand curves and two supply curves for litres of gasoline in the month of May in a small town in New Brunswick. Some of the data are missing. [LOA3.1]

Price	Quantities demanded D_1	D_2	Quantities supplied S_1	S_2
$4.00	5000	7500	9000	9500
___	6000	8000	8000	9000
2.00	___	8500	___	8500
___	___	9000	5000	___

a. Use the following facts to fill in the missing data in the table. If demand is D_1 and supply is S_1, the equilibrium quantity is 7000 litres per month. When demand is D_2 and supply is S_1, the equilibrium price is $3.00 per litre. When demand is D_2 and supply is S_1, there is an excess demand of 4000 litres per month at a price of $1.00 per litre. If demand is D_1 and supply is S_2, the equilibrium quantity is 8000 litres per month.

b. Compare two equilibriums. In the first, demand is D_1 and supply is S_1. In the second, demand is D_1 and supply is S_2. By how much does the equilibrium quantity change? By how much does the equilibrium price change?

c. If supply falls from S_2 to S_1 while demand declines from D_2 to D_1, does the equilibrium price rise or fall or stay the same? What if only supply falls? What if only demand falls?

d. Suppose that supply is fixed at S_1 and that demand starts at D_1. By how many litres per month would demand have to increase at each price level such that the equilibrium price per litre would be $3.00? $4.00?

2. The table below shows two demand schedules for a given style of men's shoes—that is, how many pairs per month will be demanded at various prices at a men's clothing store in Winnipeg called Stromnord. [LOA3.1]

Price	D_1 Quantity demanded	D_2 Quantity demanded
$75	53	13
70	60	15
65	68	18
60	77	22
55	87	27

Suppose that Stromnord has exactly 65 pairs of this style of shoe in inventory at the start of the month of July and will not receive any more pairs of this style until at least August 1.

a. If demand is D_1, what is the lowest price that Stromnord can charge so that it will not run out of this model of shoe in the month of July? What if demand is D_2?

b. If the price of shoes is set at $75 for both July and August and demand will be D_2 in July and D_1 in August, how many pairs of shoes should Stromnord order for August if it wants to end the month of August with exactly zero pairs of shoes in its inventory? What if the price is set at $55 for both months and demand is D_1 in July and D_2 in August?

3. Use the table below to answer the questions that follow: [**LOA3.1**]

Quantity demanded, thousands	Price	Quantity supplied, thousands
80	$25	60
75	35	60
70	45	60
65	55	60
60	65	60
55	75	60
50	85	60

a. If this table reflects the supply of and demand for tickets to a particular World Cup soccer game, what is the stadium capacity?

b. If the preset ticket price is $45, would we expect to see a secondary market for tickets? Would the price of a ticket in the secondary market be higher than, the same as, or lower than the price in the primary (original) market?

c. Suppose for some other World Cup game that the quantities of tickets demanded are 20,000 lower at each ticket price than shown in the table. If the ticket price remains $45, would the event be a sell-out?

Math Appendix to Chapter 3

A3.1 The Mathematics of Market Equilibrium

A market equilibrium is the price and the quantity, denoted as the pair (Q^*, P^*), of a commodity bought or sold at price P^*. The following mathematical note provides an introduction to how a market equilibrium (Q^*, P^*) is derived.

The market equilibrium is found by using the market demand (buyers' behaviour), the market supply (sellers' behaviour), and the negotiating process (to find the agreed upon price and quantity, namely P^* and Q^*, on which to transact). The market equilibrium is identified by the condition reached at the end of the negotiating process that at the price they negotiated, P^*, the quantity of the commodity that buyers are willing to buy, denoted as Q_d, and the quantity sellers are willing to sell, denoted as Q_s, match exactly.

The Demand Curve

The equation describing the downward-sloping demand when the demand curve is a straight line, in which Q_d represents the quantity demanded by buyers and P the price, is

$$P = a - bQ_d$$

The demand equation and curve below tell us that if the price is higher than a, the buyers will not buy; thus, for a transaction to occur the price must be lower. The demand equation and curve also tell us that at a price lower than a the quantity demanded by the buyers increases. Buyers' behaviour, as described by the demand equation, is that at lower prices buyers buy more quantity.

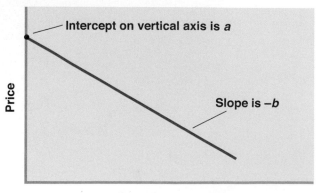

Intercept on vertical axis is *a*

Price

Slope is −*b*

Quantity demanded

The Supply Curve

The equation describing the upward-sloping market supply function when the supply curve is a straight line, in which Q_s represents the quantity supplied by sellers and P the price, is

$$P = c + dQ_s$$

If the price is lower than c, the sellers will sell nothing, as the figure below shows. If the price is c or higher, then the supply equation states that sellers facing higher prices sell more quantity. Sellers' behaviour, as described by the supply curve and equation, is that at higher prices sellers make more quantity available.

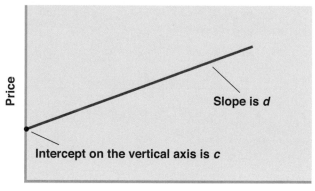

Price

Slope is *d*

Intercept on the vertical axis is *c*

Quantity supplied

The Market Equilibrium

The negotiating process (in which price or quantity or both adjust) provides the mechanism by which, eventually, buyers and sellers agree upon a price, P^*, and a quantity, Q^*, at which they can buy and sell and thus complete the transaction. At the end of the negotiating process, the quantity demanded by the buyers, Q_d, is equal to the quantity supplied by the sellers, Q_s (at the agreed-upon price), and thus the market is in equilibrium. The mathematical representation of such a negotiating process is described as follows.

At the agreed price, P^*, the equilibrium condition of the negotiating process—the equality in the quantity demanded and supplied—is

$$Q_d = Q_s$$

Having denoted Q^* as the equilibrium quantity, then it must be that $Q^* = Q_d = Q_s$. To solve for the equilibrium quantity Q^* and the equilibrium price P^*, the demand and supply functions are used. With Q^* the equilibrium quantity, for the buyers

$$P^* = a - bQ^*,$$

and for the sellers

$$P^* = c + dQ^*.$$

Now, since P^* is the same agreed-upon price by both buyer and seller, then

$$a - bQ^* = c + dQ^*,$$

giving the equilibrium quantity, Q^*, as

$$Q^* = \frac{(a - c)}{(b + d)}$$

To find P^*, substitute $\dfrac{(a - c)}{(b + d)}$ in the supply (or demand) function.

$$P^* = c + d \times \frac{(a - c)}{(b + d)}, \text{ thus}$$

$$P^* = \frac{(ad + bc)}{(b + d)}$$

The equilibrium is $(Q^*, P^*) = \left[\dfrac{(a - c)}{(b + d)}, \dfrac{(ad + bc)}{(b + d)} \right]$.

The market equilibrium may also be represented diagrammatically, as shown below.

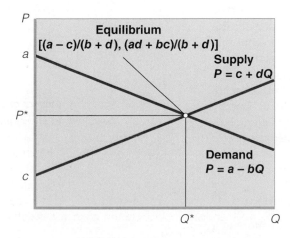

Example

Assume the demand for a pair of jeans is represented by the equation:

$$P = 100 - 0.2Q_d$$

Assume the supply of a pair of jeans is represented by the equation:

$$P = 20 + 0.2Q_s$$

Assume quantities are expressed in pairs of jeans per day, and the price in dollars.

To find the equilibrium price, P^*, and equilibrium quantity, Q^*, substitute Q^* for Q_d and Q_s and P^* for P in the demand and supply equations. To solve for Q^*:

$$100 - 0.2Q^* = 20 + 0.2Q^*$$
$$0.4Q^* = 80$$
$$Q^* = 200$$

To solve for P^*:

$$P^* = 100 - 0.2(200)$$
$$= 60$$

The equilibrium quantity of pairs of jeans is 200 per day, and the equilibrium price is $60 per pair of jeans.

CHAPTER 4

Elasticity

4.1 Discuss price elasticity of demand and how it can be applied.

4.2 Explain the usefulness of the total-revenue test for price elasticity of demand.

4.3 Describe price elasticity of supply and how it can be applied.

4.4 Apply cross elasticity of demand and income elasticity of demand.

4.5 Apply the concept of elasticity to real-world situations.

In this chapter we extend Chapter 3's discussion of demand and supply by explaining *elasticity*, an extremely important concept that will help us answer such questions as: Why do buyers of some products (for example, ocean cruises) respond to price increases by substantially reducing their purchases, while buyers of other products (say, gasoline) respond by only slightly cutting back? Why do higher market prices for some products (for example, chicken) cause producers to greatly increase their output, while price rises for other products (say, gold) cause only limited increases in output? Why does the demand for some products (for example, books) rise a great deal when household income increases, while the demand for other products (say, green beans) rises just a little? Elasticity extends our understanding of markets by letting us know the degree to which changes in prices and incomes affect supply and demand. Sometimes the responses are substantial; at other times, the responses are minimal or even non-existent. But, by knowing what to expect, businesses and the government can do a much better job in deciding what to produce, how much to charge, and, surprisingly, what items to tax.

4.1 Price Elasticity of Demand ::

The law of demand tells us that, other things equal, consumers will buy more of a product when its price declines and less when its price increases. But *how much* more or less will they buy?

The responsiveness (or sensitivity) of consumers to a price change is measured by a product's **price elasticity of demand.** For some products—for example, restaurant meals—consumers are highly responsive to price changes. Modest price changes cause very large changes in the quantity purchased. Economists say that the demand for such products is *relatively elastic* or simply *elastic*.

For other products—for example, toothpaste—consumers are less responsive to price changes. Substantial price changes cause only small changes in the amount purchased. The demand for such products is *relatively inelastic* or simply *inelastic*.

The Price Elasticity Coefficient and Formula

We measure the degree to which demand is elastic or inelastic with the coefficient E_d, defined as

$$E_d = \frac{\text{percentage change in quantity demanded of product X}}{\text{percentage change in price of product X}}$$

Let's look at a specific example from Table 4-1, rows 1 to 3, to see how the price elasticity of demand is calculated (don't worry about columns 4 and 5 for now; they will be discussed later). This table shows the number of movie tickets demanded (in thousands) per week at each specified price. Let's calculate E_d for, say, the $5 to $4 price range. But before we do so, let's look at how we calculate a percentage.

CALCULATING A PERCENTAGE

To calculate the percentage change in quantity demanded between two points, we divide the change in quantity demanded (ΔQ_d) by the original quantity demanded (Q_0) that we are considering. (Note that the Greek letter delta (Δ) signifies "change in.")

$$\%\Delta Q_d = \frac{\text{change in quantity demanded of product X}}{\text{original price of product X}} \times 100\%$$

For example, if the quantity demanded increases from 4 to 5 units, the percentage change in quantity demanded is calculated as follows:

$$\%\Delta Q_d = \frac{\Delta Q_d}{Q_0} = \frac{1}{4} \times 100\% = 25\%$$

TABLE 4-1

Price Elasticity of Demand for Movie Tickets as Measured by the Elasticity Coefficient and the Total-Revenue Test

(1) Total quantity demanded per week (thousands)	(2) Price per unit	(3) Elasticity coefficient, E_d	(4) Total revenue (1) × (2)	(5) Total-revenue test
1	$8		$ 8,000	
		5.00		Elastic
2	7		14,000	
		2.60		Elastic
3	6		18,000	
		1.57		Elastic
4	5		20,000	
		1.00		Unit elastic
5	4		20,000	
		0.64		Inelastic
6	3		18,000	
		0.38		Inelastic
7	2		14,000	
		0.20		Inelastic
8	1		8,000	

To calculate the percentage change in price between two points, we divide the change in price (ΔP) by the original price (P_0):

$$\% \Delta P = \frac{\text{change in price of product X}}{\text{original price of product X}} \times 100\%$$

For example, if the price dropped from $5 to $4, the percentage change in price is calculated as follows:

$$\% \Delta P = \frac{\Delta P}{P_0} = \frac{1}{5} \times 100\% = 20\%$$

USING AVERAGES

Unfortunately, an annoying problem arises in computing the price elasticity coefficient. A price change, say, from $4 to $5 is a 25 percent (= $1/$4) increase; the quantity change from 5 to 4 units is a 20 percent (= 1/5) decrease in quantity, resulting in a price elasticity of 0.8 (= 20/25). But a price change from $5 to $4 is a 20 percent (= $1/$5) decrease; the quantity change from 4 to 5 units is a 25 percent increase, resulting in a price elasticity of 1.25 (= 25/20). Which percentage change in price should we use in the denominator to compute the price elasticity coefficient? Elasticity should be the same whether price rises or falls!

The simplest solution to the problem is to use the **midpoint formula** for calculating elasticity. This formula simply averages the two prices and the two quantities as the reference points for computing the percentages. That is:

$$E_d = \frac{\text{change in quantity}}{\text{sum of quantities}/2} \div \frac{\text{change in price}}{\text{sum of prices}/2}$$

In symbols, the formula becomes:

$$E_d = \frac{\Delta Q}{(Q_0 + Q_1)/2} \div \frac{\Delta P}{(P_0 + P_1)/2}$$

midpoint formula
A method for calculating price elasticity of demand or price elasticity of supply that averages the two prices and two quantities as the reference points for competing percentages.

connect
WORKED PROBLEM 4.1
Elasticity of Demand

For the same $5 to $4 price range, the price reference is $4.50 [= ($5 + $4)/2], and for the 4 to 5 quantity range the quantity reference is 4.5 units [= (4 + 5)/2]. The percentage change in price is now $1/$4.50, or about 22 percent, and the percentage change in quantity is 1/4.5, or also about 22 percent. So E_d is 1. This solution eliminates the "up versus down" problem. All the price elasticity coefficients that follow are calculated using this midpoint formula. *We emphasize that the midpoint formula should be used in all cases, unless you are provided with the actual price and quantity percentage changes.*

USING PERCENTAGES

Note that we use percentages rather than absolute amounts in measuring consumer responsiveness. If we use absolute changes, the choice of units will arbitrarily affect our impression of buyer responsiveness. To illustrate, if the price of a bag of popcorn at the local hockey game is reduced from $3 to $2, and consumers increase their purchases from 60 to 100 bags, it appears that consumers are quite sensitive to price changes and, therefore, that demand is elastic. After all, a price change of one unit has caused a change of 40 units in the amount demanded. But by changing the monetary unit from dollars to pennies (why not?), we find that a price change of 100 units (pennies) causes a quantity change of 40 units. This result may falsely lead us to believe that demand is inelastic. We avoid this problem by using percentage changes. This particular price decline is the same whether we measure in dollars or pennies.

Also, by using percentages, we can correctly compare consumer responsiveness to changes in the prices of different products. It makes little sense to compare the effects on quantity demanded of a $1 increase in the price of a $10,000 used car with a $1 increase in the price of a $1 soft drink.

Here the price of the used car increased by 0.01 percent, while the price of the soft drink increased by 100 percent.

ELIMINATING THE MINUS SIGN

We know from the downsloping demand curve shown in Chapter 3 that price and quantity demanded are inversely related. Thus, the price elasticity coefficient of demand E_d will always be a negative number. We usually ignore the minus sign and simply present the absolute value of the elasticity coefficient to avoid an ambiguity that might otherwise arise. It can be confusing to say that an E_d of -4 is greater than an E_d of -2. This possible confusion is avoided when we say that an E_d of 4 reveals greater elasticity than an E_d of 2. Incidentally, the ambiguity does not arise with supply because price and quantity supplied are positively related. All elasticity of supply coefficients therefore are positive numbers.

Interpretation of E_d

We interpret the coefficient of price elasticity of demand (E_d) as follows.

ELASTIC DEMAND

elastic demand
Product or resource demand with a price elasticity coefficient that is greater than 1.

Demand is elastic (**elastic demand**) if a specific percentage change in price results in a larger percentage change in quantity demanded. In such cases, E_d will be greater than 1. For example, suppose that a 2 percent decline in the price of cut flowers results in a 4 percent increase in quantity demanded. Because $E_d = 0.04/0.02 = 2$, the demand for cut flowers is elastic.

INELASTIC DEMAND

inelastic demand
Product or resource demand with a price elasticity coefficient that is less than 1.

If a specific percentage change in price produces a smaller percentage change in quantity demanded, demand is inelastic (**inelastic demand**). In such cases, E_d will be less than 1. For example, suppose that a 2 percent decline in the price of coffee leads to only a 1 percent increase in quantity demanded. Because $E_d = 0.01/0.02 = 0.5$, demand for coffee is inelastic.

UNIT ELASTICITY

unit elasticity
Demand or supply with a price elasticity coefficient that is equal to 1.

The case separating elastic and inelastic demands occurs when a percentage change in price and the resulting percentage change in quantity demanded are the same. For example, suppose that a 2 percent drop in the price of chocolate causes a 2 percent increase in quantity demanded. This special case is termed **unit elasticity** because E_d is exactly 1, or unity. In this example, $E_d = 0.02/0.02 = 1$.

EXTREME CASES

perfectly inelastic demand
Quantity demanded does not respond to a change in price.

When we say demand is *inelastic,* we do not mean that consumers are completely unresponsive to a price change. In that extreme situation, when a price change results in no change whatsoever in the quantity demanded, economists call it **perfectly inelastic demand.** The price elasticity coefficient is zero because there is no response to a change in price. Approximate examples include a diabetic's demand for insulin or an addict's demand for heroin. A line parallel to the vertical axis, such as D_1 in Figure 4-1a, shows perfectly inelastic demand graphically.

perfectly elastic demand
Quantity demanded can be any amount at a particular price.

Conversely, when we say that demand is *elastic,* we do not mean that consumers are fully responsive to a price change. In that extreme situation, when a small price reduction causes buyers to increase their purchases from zero to all they can obtain, the elasticity coefficient is infinite $(= \infty)$, and economists say it is a **perfectly elastic demand.** A line parallel to the horizontal axis, such as D_2 in Figure 4-1b, shows perfectly elastic demand. You will see in Chapter 8 that such a demand applies to a firm—say, a mining firm—that is selling in a perfectly competitive market.

CONSIDER THIS :: A Bit of a Stretch

The following analogy might help you remember the distinction between "elastic" and "inelastic." Imagine two objects—one an Ace elastic bandage used to wrap injured joints and the other a relatively firm Bungee cord (rubber strap) used for securing items for transport. The Ace bandage stretches a great deal when pulled with a particular force; the Bungee cord stretches some, but not a lot.

Similar differences occur for the quantity demanded of various products when their prices change. For some products, a price change causes a substantial "stretch" of quantity demanded. When this stretch in percentage terms exceeds the percentage change in price, demand is elastic. For other products, quantity demanded stretches very little in response to the price change. When this stretch in percentage terms is less than the percentage change in price, demand is inelastic.

In summary:

- Elastic demand displays considerable "quantity stretch" (as with the Ace bandage).

- Inelastic demand displays relatively little "quantity stretch" (as with the Bungee cord).

And by extension:

- Perfectly elastic demand has infinite quantity stretch.

- Perfectly inelastic demand has zero quantity stretch.

FIGURE 4-1   **Perfectly Inelastic and Perfectly Elastic Demand**

Demand curve D_1 in panel (a) represents perfectly inelastic demand ($E_d = 0$). A price increase does not change the quantity demanded. Demand curve D_2 in panel (b) represents perfectly elastic demand. A price increase causes quantity demanded to decline from an infinite amount to zero ($E_d = \infty$).

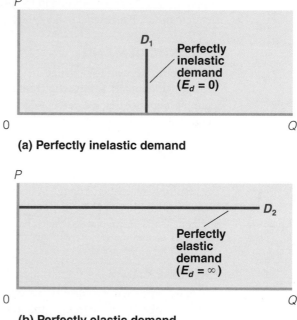

(a) Perfectly inelastic demand

(b) Perfectly elastic demand

4.2   The Total-Revenue Test

total revenue (TR)
The total amount a seller receives from the sale of a product in a particular time period.

The importance of elasticity for firms is due to the effect of price changes on **total revenue (TR)** and thus on profits (= total revenue minus total costs).

Total revenue (TR) is the total amount the seller receives from the sale of a product (or service) in a particular time period; it is calculated by multiplying the product price (P) by the quantity demanded and sold (Q). In equation form:

$$TR = P \times Q$$

FIGURE 4-2   **The Total-Revenue Test for Price Elasticity**

(a) Price declines from $2 to $1, and total revenue increases from $20 to $40. So demand is elastic. The gain in revenue (green area) exceeds the loss of revenue (blue area). (b) Price declines from $4 to $1, and total revenue falls from $40 to $20. So demand is inelastic. The gain in revenue (green area) is less than the loss of revenue (blue area). (c) Price declines from $3 to $1, and total revenue does not change. Demand is unit elastic. The gain in revenue (green area) equals the loss of revenue (blue area).

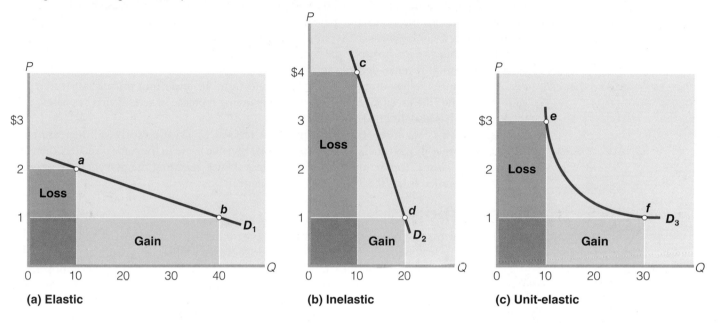

(a) Elastic   (b) Inelastic   (c) Unit-elastic

:: connect

MATH 4.2
The Total Revenue Test

total-revenue test
A test to determine elasticity of demand between any two prices, by noting what happens to total revenue when price changes.

Graphically, total revenue is represented by the $P \times Q$ rectangle lying below a point on a demand curve. At point *a* in Figure 4-2a, for example, price is $2 and quantity demanded is 10 units. So total revenue is $20 (= $2 \times 10), shown by the rectangle composed of the blue and purple areas under the demand curve. We know from basic geometry that the area of a rectangle is found by multiplying one side by the other. Here, one side is "price" ($2) and the other is "quantity demanded" (10 units).

Total revenue and the price elasticity of demand are related. In fact, the easiest way to determine whether demand is elastic or inelastic is to employ the **total-revenue test:** Note what happens to total revenue when price changes. If total revenue changes in the opposite direction from price, demand is elastic. If total revenue changes in the same direction as price, demand is inelastic. If total revenue does not change when price changes, demand is unit elastic.

Elastic Demand

If demand is elastic, a decrease in price will increase total revenue. Even though a lesser price is received per unit, enough additional units are sold to more than make up for the lower price. For example, look at demand curve D_1 in Figure 4-2a. We have already established that at point *a*, total revenue is $20 (= $2 \times 10), shown as the purple plus blue area. If the price declines from $2 to $1 (point *b*), the quantity demanded becomes 40 units and total revenue is $40 (= $1 \times 40). As a result of the price decline, total revenue has increased from $20 to $40. Total revenue has increased in this case because the $1 decline in price applies to 10 units, with a consequent revenue loss of $10 (the blue area). But 30 more units are sold at $1 each, resulting in a revenue gain of $30 (the green area). Visually, it is apparent that the gain of the green area exceeds the loss of the blue area. As indicated, the overall result is a net increase in total revenue of $20 (= $30 − $10).

The analysis is reversible: If demand is elastic, a price increase will reduce total revenue. The revenue gained on the higher-priced units will be more than offset by the revenue lost from the lower quantity sold. Bottom line: Other things equal, when price and total revenue move in opposite directions, demand is elastic. *Elastic demand* occurs when E_d is greater than 1, meaning the percentage change in quantity demanded is greater than the percentage change in price.

connect
WORKED PROBLEM 4.2
Total-Revenue Test

Inelastic Demand

If demand is inelastic, a price decrease will reduce total revenue. The increase in sales will not fully offset the decline in revenue per unit, and total revenue will decline. To see this, look at demand curve D_2 in Figure 4-2b. At point c on the curve, price is $4 and quantity demanded is 10. So, total revenue is $40, shown by the combined purple and blue rectangles. If the price drops to $1 (point d), total revenue declines to $20, which obviously is less than $40. Total revenue has declined because the loss of revenue (the blue area) from the lower unit price is larger than the gain in revenue (the green area) from the accompanying increase in sales. Price has fallen, and total revenue has also declined.

The analysis is again reversible: If demand is inelastic, a price increase will increase total revenue. So, other things equal, when price and total revenue move in the same direction, demand is inelastic. *Inelastic demand* occurs when E_d is less than 1, meaning the percentage change in quantity demanded is less than the percentage change in price.

Unit Elasticity

In the special case of unit elasticity, an increase or a decrease in price leaves total revenue unchanged. The loss in revenue from a lower unit price is exactly offset by the gain in revenue from the accompanying increase in sales. Conversely, the gain in revenue from a higher unit price is exactly offset by the revenue loss associated with the accompanying decline in the amount demanded.

In Figure 4-2c (demand curve D_3) we find that at the price of $3, 10 units will be sold, yielding total revenue of $30. At the lower $1 price, a total of 30 units will be sold, again resulting in $30 of total revenue. The $2 price reduction causes the loss of revenue shown by the blue area, but this is exactly offset by the revenue gain shown by the green area. Total revenue does not change. In fact, that would be true for all price changes along this particular curve. Other things equal, when price changes and total revenue remains constant, demand is unit elastic (or unitary). *Unit elasticity* occurs when E_d is 1, meaning the percentage change in quantity demanded equals the percentage change in price.

Price Elasticity along a Linear Demand Curve

Although the demand curves depicted in Figure 4-2 nicely illustrate the total-revenue test for elasticity, two of the graphs involve specific movements along linear (straight-line) demand curves. That presents no problem for explaining the total-revenue test. However, you need to know that elasticity typically varies over different price ranges of the same demand curve. (The exception is the curve in Figure 4-2c, where elasticity is 1 along the entire curve.)

Table 4-1 and Figure 4-3 demonstrate that elasticity typically varies over the different price ranges of the same demand curve. Plotting the hypothetical data for movie tickets shown in columns 1 and 2 of Table 4-1 yields demand curve D in Figure 4-3. Observe that the demand curve is linear. But we see from column 3 of the table that the price elasticity coefficient for this demand curve declines as we move from higher to lower prices. For all downsloping, straight-line, and most other demand curves, demand is more price elastic toward the upper left (here, the $5 to $8 price range of D) than toward the lower right (here, the $4 to $1 price range of D).

This difference is the consequence of arithmetic properties of the elasticity measure. Specifically, in the upper left segment of the demand curve, the percentage change in quantity is large because the original reference quantity is small. Similarly, the percentage change in price is small in that segment because the original reference price is large. The relatively large percentage change in quantity divided by the relatively small change in price yields a large E_d—an elastic demand.

KEY GRAPH

FIGURE 4-3   The Relation between Price Elasticity of Demand for Movie Tickets and Total Revenue

Demand curve *D* in panel (a) is based on Table 4-1 and is marked to show that the hypothetical weekly demand for movie tickets is elastic at higher price ranges and inelastic at lower price ranges. The total-revenue curve TR in panel (b) is derived from demand curve *D*. When price falls and TR increases, demand is elastic; when price falls and TR is unchanged, demand is unit elastic; when price falls and TR declines, demand is inelastic.

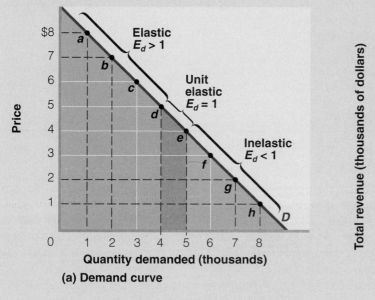

(a) Demand curve

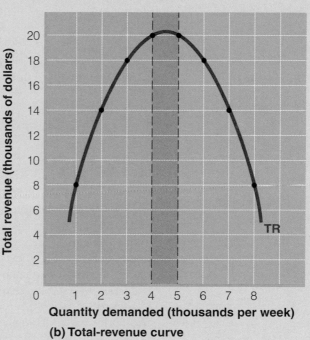

(b) Total-revenue curve

The reverse holds true for the lower right segment of the demand curve. Here the percentage change in quantity is small because the original reference quantity is large; similarly, the percentage change in price is large because the original reference price is small. The relatively small percentage change in quantity divided by the relatively large percentage change in price results in a small E_d—an inelastic demand.

The demand curve in Figure 4-3a also illustrates that the slope of a demand curve—its flatness or steepness—is not a sound basis for judging elasticity. The catch is that the slope of the curve is computed from *absolute* changes in price and quantity, while elasticity involves *relative* or *percentage* changes in price and quantity. The demand curve in Figure 4-3a is linear, which by definition means that the slope is constant throughout, but we have demonstrated that such a curve is elastic in its high-price ($8 to $5) range and inelastic in its low-price ($4 to $1) range.

Price Elasticity and the Total-Revenue Curve

In Figure 4-3b we plot the total revenue per week to the theatre owner that corresponds to each price–quantity combination indicated along demand curve *D* in Figure 4-3a. Comparison of curves *D* and TR sharply focuses the relationship between elasticity and total revenue. Lowering the ticket price in the elastic range of demand—for example, from $8 to $5—increases total

TABLE 4-2	Price Elasticity of Demand: A Summary			
			Impact on total revenue of a	
Absolute value of elasticity coefficient	Demand is	Description	Price increase	Price decrease
Greater than 1 ($E_d > 1$)	Elastic or relatively elastic	Quantity demanded changes by a larger percentage than does price	Total revenue decreases	Total revenue increases
Equal to 1 ($E_d = 1$)	Unit or unitary elastic	Quantity demanded changes by the same percentage as does price	Total revenue is unchanged	Total revenue is unchanged
Less than 1 ($E_d < 1$)	Inelastic or relatively inelastic	Quantity demanded changes by a smaller percentage than does price	Total revenue increases	Total revenue decreases

revenue. Conversely, increasing the ticket price in that range reduces total revenue. In both cases, price and total revenue change in opposite directions, confirming that demand is elastic.

The $5 to $4 price range of demand curve D reflects unit elasticity. When price either decreases from $5 to $4 or increases from $4 to $5, total revenue remains $20,000. In both cases, price has changed and total revenue has remained constant, confirming that demand is unit elastic when we consider these particular price changes.

In the inelastic range of demand curve D, lowering the price—for example, from $4 to $1—decreases total revenue, as shown in Figure 4-3b. Raising the price boosts total revenue. In both cases, price and total revenue move in the same direction, confirming that demand is inelastic.

Table 4-2 summarizes the characteristics of price elasticity of demand. You should review it carefully.

Determinants of Price Elasticity of Demand

We cannot say just what will determine the price elasticity of demand in each individual situation. However, the following generalizations are often helpful. Table 4-3 shows the estimated price elasticity coefficients for several products. Each coefficient reflects some combination of the elasticity determinants we will now discuss.

SUBSTITUTABILITY

Generally, the larger the number of substitute goods that are available, the greater the price elasticity of demand. Various brands of candy bars are usually substitutable for one another, making the demand for one brand of candy bar, say, Snickers, highly elastic. Toward the other extreme, the demand for corrective lenses (glasses or contacts) is highly inelastic because there simply are no close substitutes.

The elasticity of demand for a product depends on how narrowly the product is defined. Demand for Reebok sneakers is more elastic than is the overall demand for shoes. Many other brands are readily substitutable for Reebok sneakers, but there are few, if any, good substitutes for shoes.

PROPORTION OF INCOME

Other things equal, the greater the proportion of income spent on a good, the greater the price elasticity of demand for it. A 10 percent increase in the price of relatively low-priced pencils or

TABLE 4-3		Selected Price Elasticities of Demand	
Product or service	**Coefficient of price elasticity of demand, E_d**	**Product or service**	**Coefficient of price elasticity of demand, E_d**
Newspapers	0.10	Household appliances	0.63
Electricity (household)	0.13	Movies	0.87
Bread	0.15	Beer	0.90
Major league baseball tickets	0.23	Shoes	0.91
Telephone service	0.26	Motor vehicles	1.14
Sugar	0.30	Beef	1.27
Eggs	0.32	China, glassware, tableware	1.54
Legal services	0.37	Residential land	1.60
Automobile repair	0.40	Restaurant meals	2.27
Clothing	0.49	Lamb and mutton	2.65
Gasoline	0.60	Fresh peas	2.83
Milk	0.63		

Source: Compiled from numerous studies and sources reporting price elasticity of demand.

chewing gum amounts to a very small proportion of a consumer's income, and quantity demanded will probably decline only slightly. Thus, price elasticity for such items tends to be low. But a 10 percent increase in the price of relatively high-priced automobiles or houses means additional expenditures of perhaps $3000 or $20,000, respectively. These price increases are significant fractions of the annual incomes and budgets of most families, and quantities demanded will likely diminish significantly. The price elasticities for such items tend to be high.

LUXURIES VERSUS NECESSITIES

In general, the more that a good is considered a luxury rather than a necessity, the greater is the price elasticity of demand. Electricity is generally regarded as a necessity; a price increase will not significantly reduce the amount of lighting and power used in a household. (Note the very low price elasticity coefficient of electricity in Table 4-3.) In an extreme example, a person does not decline an operation for acute appendicitis because the surgeon has found a way to increase the cost.

However, vacation travel and jewellery are luxuries, which, by definition, can easily be forgone. If the prices of vacation travel or jewellery rise, a consumer need not buy them and will suffer no greater hardship without them. What about the demand for a common product like salt? It is highly inelastic on three counts: few good substitutes are available, salt is a negligible item in the family budget, and it is a "necessity" rather than a luxury.

TIME

Generally, product demand is more elastic the longer the period under consideration. Consumers often need time to adjust to changes in prices. When the price of a product rises, it takes time to find and experiment with other products to see whether they are acceptable. Consumers may not immediately reduce their purchases very much when the price of beef rises by 10 percent, but in time they may switch to chicken, pork, or fish.

Another consideration is product durability. Studies show that short-run demand for gasoline is more inelastic ($E_d = 0.2$) than long-run demand ($E_d = 0.7$). In the short run, people are stuck

In general, the more a good is considered a luxury rather than a necessity, the greater is the price elasticity of demand.

with their present cars and trucks, but with rising gasoline prices they will eventually replace them with smaller, more fuel-efficient vehicles, or switch to mass transit.

Applications of Price Elasticity of Demand

The concept of price elasticity of demand has great practical significance, as the following examples suggest.

LARGE CROP YIELDS

The demand for most farm products is highly inelastic; E_d is perhaps 0.20 or 0.25. As a result, increases in the supply of farm products arising from a good growing season or from increased productivity tend to depress both the prices of farm products and the total revenues (incomes) of farmers. For farmers as a group, the inelastic demand for their product means that a large crop may be undesirable. For policymakers it means that achieving the goal of higher total farm income requires that farm output be restricted.

SALES TAXES

Both federal and provincial governments pay attention to elasticity of demand when selecting goods and services on which to levy sales taxes. If a $1 tax is levied on a product and 10,000 units are sold, tax revenue will be $10,000 (= $1 × 10,000 units sold). If the government raises the tax to $1.50 but the higher price reduces sales to 5000 because of elastic demand, tax revenue will decline to $7500 (= $1.50 × 5000 units sold). Because a higher tax on a product with elastic demand will bring in less tax revenue, legislatures seek out products that have inelastic demand—such as liquor, gasoline, and cigarettes—when levying sales tax.

DECRIMINALIZATION OF ILLEGAL DRUGS

In recent years proposals to legalize drugs have been widely debated. Proponents contend that drugs should be treated like alcohol: made legal for adults and regulated for purity and potency. Efforts to reduce consumption of illegal drugs by cracking down on users, it is argued, have been unsuccessful and the associated costs—including enlarged police forces, the construction of more prisons, an overburdened court system, and untold human costs—have increased markedly. Some contend that legalization would reduce drug trafficking significantly by taking the profit out of it. Cocaine and heroin, for example, are cheap to produce and could be sold at low prices in legal markets. Because the demand of addicts is highly inelastic, the amounts consumed at the lower prices would increase only modestly. Addicts' total expenditures for cocaine and heroin would decline and so would the street crime that finances those expenditures.

Opponents of legalization say that the overall demand for cocaine and heroin is far more elastic than proponents think. In addition to the inelastic demand of addicts, there is the relatively elastic demand of another market segment consisting of occasional users, who use hard drugs when the prices are low but who abstain or substitute, say, alcohol when the prices are high. Thus, the lower prices associated with the legalization of hard drugs would increase consumption by occasional users. Also, removal of the legal prohibitions against using drugs might make drug use more socially acceptable, increasing the demand for cocaine and heroin.

Many economists predict that the legalization of cocaine and heroin would reduce street prices by up to 60 percent, depending on whether and how much it was taxed. According to an important study, price declines of that size would increase the number of occasional users of heroin by 54 percent and the number of occasional users of cocaine by 33 percent. The total quantity of heroin demanded would rise by an estimated 100 percent and the quantity of cocaine demanded would rise by 50 percent.[1] Assuming street prices for both heroin and cocaine rose by 60 percent, such changes in quantity demanded imply price elasticity of demand of 1.66 for heroin and 0.83 for cocaine. Many

[1] Henry Saffer and Frank Chaloupka, "The Demand for Illegal Drugs," *Economic Inquiry*, July 1999, pp. 401–411.

existing and first-time users might eventually become addicts. The overall result, say the opponents of legalization, would be higher social costs, possibly including an increase in street crime.

QUICK REVIEW

- The price elasticity of demand coefficient E_d is the ratio of the percentage change in quantity demanded to the percentage change in price. The averages of the two prices and two quantities are used as the base references in calculating the percentage changes.

- When E_d is greater than 1, demand is elastic; when E_d is less than 1, demand is inelastic; when E_d is equal to 1, demand is unit elastic.

- When price changes, total revenue will change in the opposite direction if demand is price elastic, in the same direction if demand is price inelastic, and not at all if demand is unit elastic.

- Demand is typically elastic in the high-price (low-quantity) range of the demand curve and inelastic in the low-price (high-quantity) range of the demand curve.

- Price elasticity of demand is greater (a) the larger the number of substitutes available; (b) the higher the price of a product relative to one's income; (c) the greater the extent to which the product is a luxury; and (d) the longer the time period involved.

4.3 Price Elasticity of Supply

connect

ORIGIN OF THE IDEA 4.2
Price Elasticity of Supply

price elasticity of supply
The ratio of the percentage change in quantity supplied of a product to the percentage change in its price.

The concept of price elasticity also applies to supply. If producers are relatively responsive to price changes, supply is elastic. If they are relatively insensitive to price changes, supply is inelastic.

We measure the degree of **price elasticity of supply** with the coefficient E_s, defined almost like E_d except that we substitute "percentage change in quantity supplied" for "percentage change in quantity demanded":

$$E_s = \frac{\text{percentage change in quantity supplied of product X}}{\text{percentage change in price of product X}}$$

For reasons explained earlier in the chapter, the averages, or midpoints, of the before and after quantities supplied and the before and after prices are used as reference points for the percentage changes. Suppose an increase in the price of a good from \$4 to \$6 increases the quantity supplied from 10 units to 14 units. The percentage change in price would be 2/5, or 40 percent, and the percentage change in quantity would be 4/12, or 33 percent. Consequently:

$$E_s = 0.33/0.40 = 0.83$$

In this case, supply is inelastic because the price elasticity coefficient is less than 1. If E_s is greater than 1, supply is elastic. If it is equal to 1, supply is unit elastic. Also, E_s is never negative, since price and quantity supplied are directly related. Thus, there are no minus signs to drop, as was necessary with elasticity of demand.

The degree of price elasticity of supply depends on how easily—and therefore quickly—producers can shift resources between alternative uses. The more easily and quickly producers can shift resources, the greater the price elasticity of supply. A firm's response to, say, an increase in the price of Christmas trees depends on its ability to shift resources from the production of other products (whose prices we assume remain constant) to the production of trees. And shifting resources takes time: the longer the time available, the greater the resource "shiftability." So, we can expect a greater response, and therefore greater elasticity of supply, the longer a firm has to adjust to a price change.

In analyzing the impact of time on elasticity, we distinguish among the immediate market period, the short run, and the long run.

The Market Period

market period
A period in which producers are unable to change the quantity of a product they produce in response to a change in its price.

The **market period** occurs when the time immediately after a change in market price is too short for producers to respond with a change in quantity supplied. Suppose the owner of a small farm in southwestern Ontario brings to market one truckload of tomatoes, which is the entire season's output. The supply curve for the tomatoes is perfectly inelastic (vertical): the farmer will sell the truckload whether the price is high or low. Why? Because the farmer can offer only one truckload of tomatoes even if the price of tomatoes is much higher than anticipated. The farmer would like to offer more tomatoes, but tomatoes cannot be produced overnight. Another full growing season is needed to respond to a higher-than-expected price by producing more than one truckload. Similarly, because the product is perishable, the farmer cannot withhold it from the market. If the price is lower than anticipated, the farmer will still sell the entire truckload.

The farmer's costs of production, incidentally, will not enter into this decision to sell. Though the price of tomatoes may fall far short of production costs, the farmer will nevertheless sell everything he brought to market to avoid a total loss through spoilage. In the market period, both the supply of tomatoes and the quantity of tomatoes supplied are fixed. The farmer offers only one truckload no matter how high or low the price. Figure 4-4a shows the farmer's vertical supply curve during the market period. Supply is perfectly inelastic because the farmer does not have time to respond to a change in demand, say, from D_1 to D_2. The resulting price increase from P_0 to P_m simply determines which buyers get the fixed quantity supplied; it elicits no increase in output.

However, not all supply curves are perfectly inelastic immediately after a price change. If the product is not perishable and the price rises, producers may choose to increase quantity supplied by drawing down their inventories of unsold, stored goods, causing the market supply curve to attain some positive slope. For our tomato farmer, the market period may be a full growing season; for producers of goods that can be inexpensively stored, there may be no market period at all.

The Short Run

short run
A period of time in which producers are able to change the quantities of some but not all of the resources they employ.

The **short run** in microeconomics is a period of time too short to change plant capacity but long enough to use the fixed plant capacity more or less intensively. In the short run, our farmer's plant (land and farm machinery) is fixed, but time is available to cultivate tomatoes more intensively by applying more labour and more fertilizer and pesticides to the crop. The result is a greater output in response to an increase in demand; this greater output is reflected in a more elastic supply of

---

FIGURE 4-4   **Time and Elasticity of Supply**

The greater the amount of time producers have to adjust to a change in demand, here from D_1 to D_2, the greater will be their output response. In the immediate market period in panel (a), producers have insufficient time to change output, and so supply is perfectly inelastic. In the short run in panel (b), plant capacity is fixed, but changing the intensity of its use can alter output; supply is therefore more elastic. In the long run in panel (c), all desired adjustments, including changes in plant capacity, can be made, and supply becomes still more elastic.

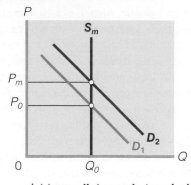

(a) Immediate market period

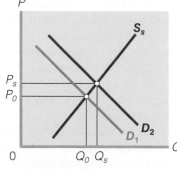

(b) Short run

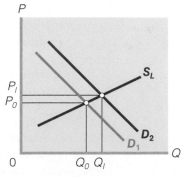

(c) Long run

tomatoes, as shown by S_s in Figure 4-4b. Note that the increase in demand from D_1 to D_2 is met by an increase in quantity (from Q_0 to Q_s), so there is a smaller price adjustment (from P_0 to P_s) than in the market period. The equilibrium price is, therefore, lower in the short run than in the market period (for an explanation of equilibrium price, refer to Chapter 3).

The Long Run

The **long run** is a period long enough for firms to adjust their plant sizes and for new firms to enter (or existing firms to leave) the industry. In the tomato industry, for example, our farmer has time to acquire additional land and buy more machinery and equipment. Furthermore, other farmers may, over time, be attracted to tomato farming by the increased demand and higher price. Such adjustments create a larger supply response, as represented by the more elastic supply curve S_L in Figure 4-4c. The outcome is a smaller price rise (P_0 to P_l) and a larger output increase (Q_0 to Q_l) in response to the increase in demand from D_1 to D_2.

There is no total-revenue test for elasticity of supply. Supply shows a positive or direct relationship between price and amount supplied; the supply curve is upsloping. Regardless of the degree of elasticity or inelasticity, price and total revenue always move together.

Applications of Price Elasticity of Supply

The idea of price elasticity of supply has widespread applicability, as suggested by the following examples.

ANTIQUES AND REPRODUCTIONS

In several places across Canada, people take antiques to a central location for appraisal by experts. Some people are pleased to learn that their old piece of furniture or funky folk art is worth a large amount, say, $30,000 or more. The high price of an antique results from strong demand and limited, highly inelastic supply. Because a genuine antique can no longer be reproduced, the quantity supplied either does not rise or rises only slightly as its price goes up. The higher price might prompt the discovery of a few more of the remaining originals and thus add to the quantity available for sale, but this quantity response is usually quite small. So the supply of antiques and other collectibles tends to be inelastic. For one-of-a-kind antiques, the supply is perfectly inelastic.

Factors such as increased population, higher income, and greater enthusiasm for collecting antiques have increased the demand for antiques over time. Because the supply of antiques is limited and inelastic, those increases in demand have greatly boosted the prices of antiques.

Contrast the inelastic supply of original antiques with the elastic supply of modern "made-to-look-old" reproductions. Such faux antiques are quite popular and widely available. When the demand for reproductions increases, the firms making them simply boost production. Because the supply of reproductions is highly elastic, increased demand raises their price only slightly.

VOLATILE GOLD PRICES

The price of gold is quite volatile, sometimes shooting upward one period and plummeting downward the next. The main sources of these fluctuations are shifts in demand interacting with highly inelastic supply. Gold production is a costly and time-consuming process of exploration, mining, and refining. Moreover, the physical availability of gold is highly limited. For both reasons, increases in gold prices do not bring forth substantial increases in quantity supplied. Conversely, gold mining is costly to shut down and existing gold bars are expensive to store. Price decreases therefore do not produce large drops in the quantity of gold supplied. In short, the supply of gold is inelastic.

The demand for gold is partly derived from the demand for its uses in jewellery, dental fillings, and coins. But people also demand gold as a speculative financial investment, increasing their demand when they fear general inflation or domestic or international turmoil that might undermine the value of currency and more traditional investments, and reducing their demand when events settle down. Because of the inelastic supply of gold, even relatively small changes in demand produce relatively large changes in price.

4.4 Cross Elasticity and Income Elasticity of Demand

Price elasticities measure the responsiveness of the quantity of a product demanded or supplied when its price changes. The consumption of a good is also affected by a change in the price of a related product or by a change in income.

Cross Elasticity of Demand

The **cross elasticity of demand** measures how responsive consumer purchases of one product (say, X) are to a change in the price of some other product (say, Y). We calculate the coefficient of cross elasticity of demand E_{xy} just as we do the coefficient of simple price elasticity, except that we relate the percentage change in the consumption of X to the percentage change in the price of Y:

$$E_{xy} = \frac{\text{percentage change in quantity demanded of product X}}{\text{percentage change in price of product Y}}$$

The concept of cross elasticity (or cross price elasticity) allows us to quantify and more fully understand substitute and complementary goods, introduced in Chapter 3. Unlike price elasticity, we allow the coefficient of cross elasticity of demand to be either positive or negative.

SUBSTITUTE GOODS

If cross elasticity of demand is positive, meaning that sales of X move in the same direction as a change in the price of Y, then X and Y are substitute goods. An example is Evian water (X) and Dasani water (Y). An increase in the price of Evian causes consumers to buy more Dasani, resulting in a positive cross elasticity. The larger the positive cross elasticity coefficient, the greater the substitutability between the two products.

COMPLEMENTARY GOODS

When cross elasticity is negative, we know that X and Y "go together." An increase in the price of one decreases the demand for the other, so the two are complementary goods. For example, a decrease in the price of digital cameras will increase the amount of photo paper purchased. The larger the negative cross elasticity coefficient, the greater the complementarity between the two goods.

INDEPENDENT GOODS

A zero or near-zero cross elasticity indicates that the two products being considered are unrelated or independent goods. An example is walnuts and photo paper; we would not expect a change in the price of walnuts to have any effect on purchases of photo paper, and vice versa.

APPLICATIONS

The degree of product substitutability, measured by the cross elasticity coefficient, is important to businesses and government. Suppose Coca-Cola is considering whether to lower the price of its Sprite brand. It will want to know not only the price elasticity of demand for Sprite (will the price cut increase or decrease total revenue?), but also whether the increased sale of Sprite will come at the expense of its Coke brand. How sensitive are the sales of one of its products (Coke) to a change in the price of another of its products (Sprite)? By how much will the increased sales of Sprite reduce the sales of Coke? A low cross elasticity would indicate that Coke and

Sprite are weak substitutes for each other and that a lower price for Sprite would have little effect on Coke sales.

Government also implicitly uses the concept of cross elasticity of demand in assessing whether a proposed merger between two large firms will substantially reduce competition and violate the anticombines laws. For example, the cross elasticity between Coke and Pepsi is high, making them strong substitutes for each other. In addition, Coke and Pepsi together sell about 75 percent of all carbonated cola drinks consumed in Canada. Taken together, the high cross elasticities and the large market shares suggest that the government would likely block a merger between Coke and Pepsi because it would substantially lessen competition. In contrast, the cross elasticity between photo paper and gasoline is low or zero. A merger between Coke and Petro-Canada oil company would have a minimal effect on competition, so government would be more likely to allow it.

Income Elasticity of Demand

income elasticity of demand
Measures the responsiveness of consumer purchases to income changes.

To measure the degree to which consumers respond to a change in their income by buying more or less of a particular good we use the **income elasticity of demand.** The coefficient of income elasticity of demand, E_i, is determined with the formula

$$E_i = \frac{\text{percentage change in quantity demanded}}{\text{percentage change in income}}$$

NORMAL GOODS

For most goods, the income elasticity coefficient E_i is positive, meaning that more of them are demanded as incomes rise. Such goods are called normal goods (and were first described in Chapter 3). But the value of E_i varies greatly among normal goods. For example, income elasticity of demand for automobiles is about $+3.00$, while income elasticity for most farm products is only about $+0.20$.

INFERIOR GOODS

A negative income elasticity coefficient designates an inferior good. Retread tires, cabbage, long-distance bus tickets, and used clothing are likely candidates. Consumers decrease their purchases of inferior goods as incomes rise.

INSIGHTS TO THE ECONOMY

Coefficients of income elasticity of demand provide insights into the Canadian economy. For example, income elasticity helps to explain the expansion and contraction of industries. On average, total income in the economy has grown by 2–3 percent annually. As income has expanded, industries producing products for which demand is quite income elastic have expanded their outputs. Thus, automobiles ($E_i = +3.0$), housing ($E_i = +1.5$), books ($E_i = +1.4$), and restaurant meals ($E_i = +1.4$) have all experienced strong growth of output. Also, studies show that the demand for health services is income elastic. The implication of this is that the demand on the Canadian health care system will continue to outpace income growth. Meanwhile, industries producing products for which income elasticity is low or negative have tended to either grow slowly or to decline. For example, agriculture ($E_i = +0.20$) has grown far more slowly than has the economy's total output. We do not eat twice as much when our income doubles.

As another example, when recessions occur and incomes decline, grocery stores fare relatively better than stores selling electronic equipment. People do not substantially cut back on their purchases of food when their incomes fall; income elasticity of demand for food is relatively low. But they do substantially cut back on their purchases of electronic equipment; income elasticity on such equipment is relatively high.

Table 4-4 provides a convenient synopsis of the cross elasticity and income elasticity concepts.

TABLE 4-4	Cross Elasticity and Income Elasticity of Demand	
Value of coefficient	**Description**	**Type of good(s)**
Cross elasticity: Positive ($E_{wz} > 0$)	Quantity demanded of W changes in same direction as change in price of Z	Substitutes
Negative ($E_{xy} < 0$)	Quantity demanded of X changes in opposite direction from change in price of Y	Complements
Income elasticity: Positive ($E_i > 0$)	Quantity demanded of the product changes in same direction as change in income	Normal
Negative ($E_i < 0$)	Quantity demanded of the product changes in opposite direction from change in income	Inferior

4.5   Elasticity and Real-World Applications

Demand and supply analysis and the elasticity concept are applied repeatedly in the remainder of this book. Let's strengthen our understanding of these analytical tools and their importance by examining elasticity and tax incidence. In recent years many of Canada's provinces (Ontario, New Brunswick, Nova Scotia, and Newfoundland and Labrador) have moved to a *harmonized sales tax* (HST), which combines the federal goods and services tax (GST) and provincial sales tax (PST). The HST varies across provinces because each sets its own sales tax rate. In general, the HST extends provincial taxes on services as well as goods, whereas the PST was only levied on goods. Despite the extension of the HST to many services previously not covered, the introduction of the HST is expected to be revenue neutral once all the exemptions are included. Quebec is also scheduled to harmonize its PST with the GST in the next few years.

Elasticity and Tax Incidence

In Figure 4-5, S and D represent the pre-tax market for a certain domestic wine from the Niagara Peninsula. The no-tax equilibrium price and quantity are $8 per bottle and 15 million bottles. If the Ontario government levies a tax of $2 per bottle directly on the winery for every bottle sold, who actually pays it?

DIVISION OF BURDEN

Since the provincial government places the tax on the sellers (suppliers), the tax can be viewed as an addition to the cost of the product. Now sellers must get $2 more for each bottle to receive the same per-unit profit they were getting before the tax. While sellers are willing to offer, for example, 5 million bottles of untaxed wine at $4 per bottle, they must now receive $6 per bottle—$4 plus the $2 tax—to offer the same 5 million bottles. The tax shifts the supply curve upward (leftward) as shown in Figure 4-5, where S_t is the after-tax supply curve.

The after-tax equilibrium price is $9 per bottle, whereas the before-tax price was $8. So, in this case, half the $2 tax is paid by consumers as a higher price; the other half must be paid by producers in a lower after-tax per-unit revenue. That is, after paying the $2 tax per unit to the provincial

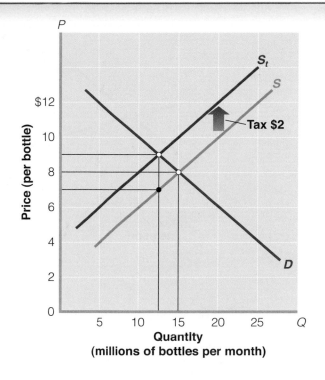

FIGURE 4-5   The Incidence of a Tax

A tax of a specified amount per unit levied on producers—here, $2 per unit—shifts the supply curve upward by the amount of the tax per unit: the vertical distance between S and S_t. This shift results in a higher price (here, $9) to the consumer and a lower after-tax price (here, $7) to the producer. Thus, consumers and producers share the burden of the tax in some proportion (here, equally at $2 per unit).

government, producers receive $7, or $1 less than the $8 before-tax price. In this instance, consumers and producers share the burden of this tax equally; producers shift half the tax to consumers in a higher price and bear the other half themselves.

Note also that the equilibrium quantity decreases as a result of the tax levy and the higher price it imposes on consumers. In Figure 4-5 that decline in quantity is from 15 million bottles per month to 12.5 million bottles per month.

ELASTICITIES

If the elasticities of demand and supply were different from those shown in Figure 4-5, the incidence of tax would also be different. Two generalizations are relevant.

1. *With a specific supply, the more inelastic the demand for the product, the larger the portion of the tax shifted to consumers.* To verify this, sketch graphically the extreme cases where demand is perfectly elastic or perfectly inelastic. In the first case, the incidence of the tax is entirely on sellers; in the second, the tax is shifted entirely to consumers.

   Figure 4-6 contrasts the more usual cases where demand is either relatively elastic or relatively inelastic in the relevant price range. With elastic demand, shown in Figure 4-6a, a small portion of the tax ($P_e - P_1$) is shifted to consumers and most of the tax ($P_1 - P_a$) is paid by producers. With inelastic demand, shown in Figure 4-6b, most of the tax ($P_i - P_1$) is shifted to consumers and only a small amount ($P_1 - P_b$) is paid by producers. In both graphs the per-unit tax is represented by the vertical distance between S_t and S.

   Note also that the decline in equilibrium quantity ($Q_2 - Q_1$) is smaller when demand is more inelastic, which is the basis of our previous applications of the elasticity concept: Revenue-seeking legislatures place heavy sales taxes on liquor, cigarettes, and other products whose demands are thought to be inelastic. Since demand for these products is relatively inelastic, the tax does not reduce sales much, so the tax revenue stays high.

FIGURE 4-6   Demand Elasticity and the Incidence of a Tax

Panel (a): If demand is elastic in the relevant price range, price rises modestly (P_1 to P_e) when a tax is levied. Hence, the producer bears most of the tax burden. Panel (b): If demand is inelastic, the price to the buyer will increase substantially (P_1 to P_i) and most of the tax will be shifted to consumers.

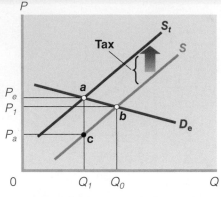

(a) Tax incidence and elastic demand

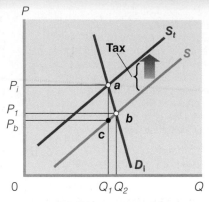

(b) Tax incidence and inelastic demand

2. *With a specific demand, the more inelastic the supply, the larger the portion of the tax paid by producers.* When supply is elastic, as in Figure 4-7a, most of the tax ($P_e - P_1$) is shifted to consumers, and only a small portion ($P_1 - P_a$) is paid by sellers. But when supply is inelastic, as in Figure 4-7b, the reverse is true: the major portion of the tax ($P_1 - P_b$) falls on sellers, and a relatively small amount ($P_i - P_1$) is shifted to buyers. The equilibrium quantity also declines less with an inelastic supply than it does with an elastic supply.

Gold is an example of a product with an inelastic supply, one where the burden of a tax would mainly fall on producers. Conversely, because the supply of baseballs is elastic, producers would pass on to consumers much of a tax on baseballs. You may want to reverse the analysis and assume that the government levies a (sales) tax on consumers.

FIGURE 4-7   Supply Elasticity and the Incidence of a Tax

Panel (a): With an elastic supply, the sales tax results in a large price increase (P_1 to P_e), and the tax is therefore paid mainly by consumers. Panel (b): If supply is inelastic, the price rise is small (P_1 to P_i), and sellers will have to bear most of the tax.

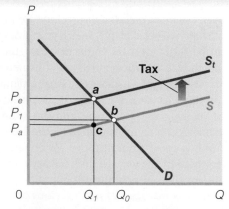

(a) Tax incidence and elastic supply

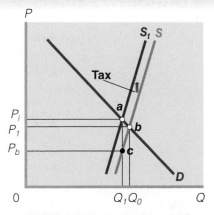

(b) Tax incidence and inelastic supply

QUICK REVIEW

- Price elasticity of supply measures the sensitivity of suppliers to changes in the price of a product. The price elasticity of supply coefficient E_s is the ratio of the percentage change in quantity supplied to the percentage change in price. The elasticity of supply varies directly with the amount of time producers have to respond to the price change.

- The cross elasticity of demand coefficient E_{xy} is computed as the percentage change in the quantity demanded of product X divided by the percentage change in the price of product Y. If the cross elasticity coefficient is positive, the two products are substitutes; if negative, they are complements.

- The income elasticity coefficient E_i is computed as the percentage change in quantity demanded divided by the percentage change in income. A positive coefficient indicates a normal or superior good. The coefficient is negative for an inferior good.

The LAST WORD   Elasticity and Pricing Power: Why Different Consumers Pay Different Prices

Firms and nonprofit institutions often recognize and exploit differences in price elasticity of demand.

All the buyers of a product traded in a highly competitive market pay the same market price for the product, regardless of their individual price elasticities of demand. If the price rises, Jones may have an elastic demand and greatly reduce her purchases. Green may have a unit-elastic demand and reduce his purchases less than Jones. Lopez may have an inelastic demand and hardly curtail his purchases at all. But all three consumers will pay the single higher price regardless of their demand elasticities.

In later chapters we will find that not all sellers must passively accept a "one-for-all" price. Some firms have "market power" or "pricing power" that allows them to set their product prices in their best interests. For some goods and services, firms may find it advantageous to determine differ-ences in price elasticity of demand and then charge different prices to different buyers.

It is extremely difficult to tailor prices for each customer on the basis of elasticity of demand, but it is rela-tively easy to observe differences in group elasticities. Consider airline tickets. Business travellers generally have inelastic demand for air travel. Because their time is highly valuable, they do not see slower modes of transportation as realistic substitutes. Also, their employers pay for their tickets as part of their business ex-penses. In contrast, leisure travellers tend to have elastic demand. They have the option to drive rather than fly, or simply not to travel at all. They also pay for their tickets out of their own pockets and thus are more sensi-tive to price.

Airlines recognize the difference be-tween the groups in terms of price elasticity of demand and charge busi-ness travellers more than leisure travellers. To accomplish that, they have to dissuade business travellers from buying the less expensive round-trip tickets aimed at leisure travellers. One way to do this is by placing restric-tions on the lower-priced tickets. For example, airlines make the tickets non-refundable, require at least two-week advance purchase, and require Saturday-night stays. These restrictions chase off most business travellers who engage in last-minute travel and want to be home for the weekend. As a result, a business traveller often pays hundreds of dollars more for a ticket than a leisure traveller on the same plane.

Discounts for children are another example of pricing based on group differences in price elasticity of demand. For many products, children have more elastic demands than adults because children have low budgets, often financed by their parents. Sellers recognize the elasticity difference and price accordingly. The barber spends as much time cutting a child's hair as an adult's but charges the child much less. A child takes up a full seat at the baseball game but pays a lower price than an adult. A child snowboarder occupies the same space on a chairlift as an adult snowboarder but qualifies for a discounted lift ticket.

Finally, consider pricing by colleges and universities. Price elasticities of demand for higher education are greater for prospective students from low-income families, who generally have more elastic demands for higher education than similar students from high-income families. This makes sense because tuition is a much larger

proportion of household income for a low-income student or family than for his or her high-income counterpart. Desiring a diverse student body, universities charge different *net* prices (= tuition *minus* financial aid) to the two groups on the basis of elasticity of demand. High-income students pay full tuition, unless they receive merit-based scholarships. Low-income students receive considerable financial aid in addition to merit-based

scholarships and, in effect, pay a lower net price.

It is common for schools to announce a large tuition increase and immediately cushion the news by emphasizing that they are also increasing financial aid. In effect, the school is increasing the tuition for students who have inelastic demand by the full amount and raising the net tuition of those with elastic demand by some lesser amount or not at all. Through this strategy, colleges and universities boost revenue to cover rising costs while maintaining affordability for a wide range of students.

There are a number of other examples of dual or multiple pricing. All relate directly to price elasticity of demand. We will revisit this topic in Chapter 10 when we discuss what economists call *price discrimination*—charging different prices to different customers for the same product.

Question

What is the purpose of charging different groups of customers different prices? Supplement the three broad examples in this Last Word with two additional examples of your own. Hint: Think of price discounts based on group characteristics or time of purchase.

:: CHAPTER SUMMARY

4.1 :: PRICE ELASTICITY OF DEMAND

- Price elasticity of demand measures consumer response to price changes. If consumers are relatively sensitive to price changes, demand is elastic. If they are relatively unresponsive to price changes, demand is inelastic.

- The price elasticity coefficient E_d measures the degree of elasticity or inelasticity of demand. The coefficient is found by the formula

$$E_d = \frac{\text{percentage change in quantity demanded of product X}}{\text{percentage change in price of product X}}$$

The averages of prices and quantities under consideration are used as reference points in determining percentage

changes in price and quantity. If E_d is greater than 1, demand is elastic. If E_d is less than 1, demand is inelastic. Unit elasticity is the special case in which E_d equals 1.

- Perfectly inelastic demand is graphed as a line parallel to the vertical axis; perfectly elastic demand is shown by a line above and parallel to the horizontal axis.

4.2 :: THE TOTAL-REVENUE TEST

- Elasticity varies at different price ranges on a demand curve, tending to be elastic in the upper left segment and inelastic in the lower right segment. Elasticity cannot be judged by the steepness or flatness of a demand curve.

- If total revenue changes in the opposite direction from prices, demand is elastic. If price and total revenue change in the same direction, demand is inelastic. Where demand is of unit elasticity, a change in prices leaves total revenue unchanged.

- The number of available substitutes, the size of an item's price relative to one's income, whether the product is a luxury or a necessity, and the time given to adjust are all determinants of elasticity of demand.

4.3 :: PRICE ELASTICITY OF SUPPLY

- The elasticity concept also applies to supply. The coefficient of price elasticity of supply is found by the formula

$$E_s = \frac{\text{percentage change in quantity supplied of product X}}{\text{percentage change in price of product X}}$$

The averages of the price and quantities under consideration are used as reference points for computing percentage changes. Elasticity of supply depends on the ease of shifting resources between alternative uses, which in turn varies directly with the time producers have to adjust to a particular price change.

4.4 :: CROSS ELASTICITY AND INCOME ELASTICITY OF DEMAND

- Cross elasticity of demand indicates how sensitive the purchase of one product is to changes in the price of another product. The coefficient of cross elasticity of demand is found by the formula

$$E_{xy} = \frac{\text{percentage change in quantity demanded of product X}}{\text{percentage change in price of product Y}}$$

Positive cross elasticity of demand identifies substitute goods; negative cross elasticity identifies complementary goods.

- Income elasticity of demand indicates the responsiveness of consumer purchases to a change in income. The coefficient of income elasticity of demand is found by the formula

$$E_i = \frac{\text{percentage change in quantity demanded of product X}}{\text{percentage change in income}}$$

The coefficient is positive for normal goods and negative for inferior goods.

- Industries that sell products which have high-income elasticity of demand coefficients are particularly hard hit by recessions. Those with products that have low or negative income elasticity of demand coefficients fare much better.

4.5 :: ELASTICITY AND REAL-WORLD APPLICATIONS

- Sales taxes affect supply and, therefore, equilibrium price and quantity. The more inelastic the demand for a product, the greater is the proportion of a sales tax that is shifted to consumers. The greater the inelasticity of supply, the larger the proportion of the tax that is paid by the seller.

TERMS AND CONCEPTS

price elasticity of demand, p. 89
midpoint formula, p. 90
elastic demand, p. 91
inelastic demand, p. 91
unit elasticity, p. 91
perfectly inelastic demand, p. 91

perfectly elastic demand, p. 91
total revenue (TR), p. 92
total-revenue test, p. 93
price elasticity of supply, p. 99
market period, p. 100
short run, p. 100

long run, p. 101
cross elasticity of demand, p. 102
income elasticity of demand, p. 103

QUESTIONS

1. Explain why the choice between 1, 2, 3, 4, 5, 6, 7, and 8 units or 1000, 2000, 3000, 4000, 5000, 6000, 7000, and 8000 movie tickets makes no difference in determining elasticity in Table 4-1. [LO4.1]

2. Graph the accompanying demand data and then use the midpoint formula for E_d to determine price elasticity of demand for each of the four possible $1 price changes. What can you conclude about the relationship between the slope of a curve and its elasticity? Explain in a non-technical way why demand is elastic in the upper left segment of the demand curve and inelastic in the lower right segment. [LO4.1]

Product price	Quantity demanded
$5	1
4	2
3	3
2	4
1	5

3. What are the major determinants of price elasticity of demand? Use those determinants and your own reasoning

in judging whether demand for each of the following products is probably elastic or inelastic: [**LO4.2**]

a. bottled water

b. toothpaste

c. Crest toothpaste

d. ketchup

e. diamond bracelets

f. Microsoft's Windows operating system.

4. What effect would a rule stating that university students must live in university dormitories have on the price elasticity of demand for dormitory space? What impact might this in turn have on room rates?   [**LO4.2**]

5. Calculate total-revenue data from the demand schedule in Question 2. Graph total revenue below your demand curve. Generalize about the relationship between price elasticity and total revenue.   [**LO4.2**]

6. How would the following changes in price affect total revenue? That is, would total revenue increase, decrease, or remain unchanged?   [**LO4.2**]

a. Price falls and demand is inelastic.

b. Price rises and demand is elastic.

c. Price rises and supply is elastic.

d. Price rises and supply is inelastic.

e. Price rises and demand is inelastic.

f. Price falls and demand is elastic.

g. Price falls and demand is of unit elasticity.

7. In 2006, Willem De Kooning's abstract painting *Woman III* sold for $137.5 million. Portray this sale in a demand and supply diagram and comment on the elasticity of supply. Comedian George Carlin once mused, "If a painting can be forged well enough to fool some experts, why is the original so valuable?" Provide an answer.   [**LO4.3**]

8. Suppose the cross elasticity of demand for products A and B is +3.6 and for products C and D is −5.4. What can you conclude about how products A and B are related? Products C and D?   [**LO4.4**]

9. The income elasticities of demand for movies, dental services, and clothing have been estimated to be +3.4, +1.0, and +0.5, respectively. Interpret these coefficients. What does it mean if an income elasticity coefficient is negative?   [**LO4.4**]

10. Research has found that an increase in the price of beer would reduce the amount of marijuana consumed. Is cross elasticity of demand between the two products positive or negative? Are these products substitutes or complements? What might be the logic behind this relationship?   [**LO4.4**]

11. What is the incidence of a tax when demand is highly inelastic? Highly elastic? What effect does the elasticity of supply have on the incidence of a tax?   [**LO4.5**]

12. **ADVANCED ANALYSIS** Suppose the equation for the demand curve for some product X is $P = 8 − 0.6Q$ and the supply curve is $P = 2 + 0.4Q$. What are the equilibrium price and quantity? Now suppose an excise tax is imposed on X such that the new supply equation is $P = 4 + 0.4Q$. How much tax revenue will this excise tax yield the government?   [**LO4.5**]

:: PROBLEMS

1. Look at the demand curve in Figure 4-2a. Use the midpoint formula and points *a* and *b* to calculate the elasticity of demand for that range of the demand curve. Do the same for the demand curves in Figures 4-2b and 4-2c using, respectively, points *c* and *d* for Figure 4-2b and points *e* and *f* for Figure 4-2c.   [**LO4.1**]

2. Investigate how demand elasticities are affected by increases in demand. Shift each of the demand curves in Figures 4-2a, 4-2b, and 4-2c to the right by 10 units. For example, point *a* in Figure 4-2a would shift to the right from location (10 units, $2) to (20 units, $2) while point *b* would shift to the right from location (40 units, $1) to (50 units, $1). After making these shifts, apply the midpoint formula to calculate the demand elasticities for the shifted points. Are they larger or smaller than the elasticities you calculated in Problem 1 for the original points? In terms of the midpoint formula, what explains the change in elasticities?   [**LO4.1**]

3. Suppose that the total revenue received by a company selling basketballs is $600 when the price is set at $30 per basketball and $600 when the price is set at $20 per basketball. Without using the midpoint formula, can you tell whether demand is elastic, inelastic, or unit-elastic over this price range?   [**LO4.2**]

4. Danny "Dimes" Donahue is a neighbourhood's nine-year-old entrepreneur. His most recent venture is selling homemade brownies that he bakes himself. At a price of $1.50 each, he sells 100. At a price of $1.00 each, he sells 300. Is demand elastic or inelastic over this price range? If demand had the same elasticity for a price decline from $1.00 to $0.50 as it does for the decline from $1.50 to $1.00, would cutting the price from $1.00 to $0.50 increase or decrease Danny's total revenue?   [**LO4.2**]

5. What is the formula for measuring the price elasticity of supply? Suppose the price of apples goes up from $20 to $22 a box. In direct response, Goldsboro Farms supplies 1200 boxes of apples instead of 1000 boxes. Compute the coefficient of price elasticity (midpoints approach) for Goldsboro's supply. Is its supply elastic, or is it inelastic?   [**LO4.3**]

6. **ADVANCED ANALYSIS** Currently, at a price of $1 each, 100 popsicles are sold per day in the perpetually hot town of Rostin. Consider the elasticity of supply. In the short run, a price increase from $1 to $2 is unit elastic ($E_s = 1.0$). How many popsicles will be sold each day in the short run if the price rises to $2 each? In the long run, a price increase from $1 to $2 has an elasticity of supply of 1.50. How many popsicles will be sold per day in the long run if the price rises to $2 each? (Hint: Apply the midpoints approach to the elasticity of supply.) [LO4.3]

7. Lorena likes to play golf. How many times per year she plays depends on two things: (1) the price of playing a round of golf, and (2) Lorena's income and the cost of other types of entertainment—in particular, how much it costs to see a movie instead of playing golf. The three demand schedules in the table below show how many rounds of golf per year Lorena will demand at each price in three different scenarios. In scenario D_1, Lorena's income is $50,000 per year and movies cost $9 each. In scenario D_2, Lorena's income is also $50,000 per year, but the price of seeing a movie rises to $11. And in scenario D_3, Lorena's income goes up to $70,000 per year while movies cost $11. [LO4.4]

Price	Quantity demanded		
	D_1	D_2	D_3
$50	15	10	15
35	25	15	30
20	40	20	50

a. Using the data under D_1 and D_2, calculate the cross elasticity of Lorena's demand for golf at all three prices. (To do this, apply the midpoints approach to the cross elasticity of demand.) Is the cross elasticity the same at all three prices? Are movies and golf substitute goods, complementary goods, or independent goods?

b. Using the data under D_2 and D_3, calculate the income elasticity of Lorena's demand for golf at all three prices. (To do this, apply the midpoints approach to the income elasticity of demand.) Is the income elasticity the same at all three prices? Is golf an inferior good?

Mc Graw Hill connect™ **Practice and Learn Online with Connect**

Connect allows you to practice important concepts at your own pace and on your own schedule, with 24/7 online access to an eBook, algorithmic questions and problems from the textbook, video and logic cases, graphing tutorials, flashcards, Internet exercises, key graphs, and more.

CHAPTER 5

Market Failures: Public Goods and Externalities

Competitive markets usually do a remarkably effective job of allocating society's scarce resources to their most highly valued uses. Thus, we begin this chapter by demonstrating how properly functioning markets efficiently allocate resources. We then explore what happens when markets don't function properly. In some circumstances, economically desirable goods are not produced at all. In other situations, they are either overproduced or underproduced. This chapter focuses on these situations, which economists refer to as **market failures.**

In such situations, an economic role for government may arise. We will examine that role as it relates to public goods and so-called externalities—situations where market failures lead to sub-optimal outcomes that the government may be able to improve upon by using its powers to tax, spend, and regulate. The government may, for instance, pay for the production of goods that the private sector fails to produce. It may also act to reduce the production of goods and services that the private sector overproduces. Implementing such policies can, however, be both costly and complicated. Thus, we conclude the chapter by noting the government inefficiencies that can potentially hinder government's efforts to improve economic outcomes.

AFTER READING THIS CHAPTER, YOU SHOULD BE ABLE TO:

5.1 Differentiate between demand-side market failures and supply-side market failures.

5.2 Explain the origin of both consumer surplus and producer surplus, and explain how properly functioning markets maximize their sum, economic surplus, while optimally allocating resources.

5.3 Describe free riding and public goods, and illustrate why private firms cannot normally produce public goods.

5.4 Explain how positive and negative externalities cause underallocations and overallocations of resources.

5.1 Market Failures in Competitive Markets[1]

market failures
When markets fail to function properly, whether by overproducing, underproducing, or failing to produce economically desirable goods.

In Chapter 3 we asserted that, "Competitive markets usually produce an assignment of resources that is 'right' from an economic perspective." We now want to focus on the word "usually" and discuss exceptions. We must do this because unfortunately the presence of robust competition involving many buyers and many sellers may not, by itself, be enough to guarantee that a market will allocate resources correctly. Market failures sometimes happen in competitive markets. The focus of this chapter is to explain how and why such market failures can arise.

Fortunately, the broad picture is simple. Market failures in competitive markets fall into just two categories:

demand-side market failure
When demand curves fail to reflect consumers' full willingness to pay for goods or services.

- A **demand-side market failure** happens when demand curves do not reflect consumers' full willingness to pay for a good or service.

- A **supply-side market failure** occurs when supply curves do not reflect the full cost of producing a good or service.

Demand-Side Market Failures

supply-side market failure
When supply curves fail to reflect the full cost of producing a good or service.

Demand-side market failures arise because it is impossible in certain cases to charge consumers what they are willing to pay for a product. Consider outdoor fireworks displays. People enjoy fireworks and would therefore be *willing* to pay to see them if the only way to see them was to have to pay for the right to do so. But because such displays are outdoors and in public, people don't actually *have* to pay to see them because there is no way to exclude those who haven't paid from also enjoying the show. Private firms will therefore be unwilling to produce outdoor fireworks displays, as it will be nearly impossible for them to raise enough revenue to cover production costs.

Supply-Side Market Failures

Supply-side market failures arise in situations in which a firm does not have to pay the full cost of producing its output. Consider a coal-burning power plant. The firm running the plant will have to pay for all of the land, labour, capital, and entrepreneurship that it uses to generate electricity by burning coal. But if the firm is not charged for the smoke that it releases into the atmosphere, it will fail to pay another set of costs—the costs that its pollution imposes on other people. These include future harm from global warming, toxins that affect wildlife, and possible damage to agricultural crops downwind.

A market failure arises because it is not possible for the market to correctly weigh costs and benefits in a situation in which some of the costs are completely unaccounted for. The coal-burning power plant produces more electricity and generates more pollution than it would if it had to pay for each tonne of smoke that it released into the atmosphere. The extra units that are produced are units of output for which the costs are *greater than* the benefits. Obviously, these units should not be produced.

5.2 Efficiently Functioning Markets

The best way to understand market failure is to understand how properly functioning competitive markets achieve economic efficiency. We touched on this subject in Chapter 3, but we now want to expand and deepen that analysis, both for its own sake and to set up our discussion of

---

[1] Other market failures arise when there are not enough buyers or sellers to ensure competition. In those situations, the lack of competition allows either buyers or sellers to restrict purchases or sales below optimal levels for their own benefit. As an example, a monopoly—a firm that is the only producer in its industry—can restrict the amount of output that it supplies in order to drive up the market price and thereby increase its own profit.

public goods and externalities. Two conditions must hold if a competitive market is to produce efficient outcomes: (1) the demand curve in the market must reflect consumers' full willingness to pay, and (2) the supply curve in the market must reflect all the costs of production. If these conditions hold, then the market will produce only units for which benefits are at least equal to costs. It will also maximize the amount of "benefits surpluses" that are shared between consumers and producers.

Consumer Surplus

The benefit surplus received by a consumer or consumers in a market is called **consumer surplus.** It is defined as the difference between the maximum price a consumer is (or consumers are) willing to pay for a product and the actual price that they do pay.

The maximum price that a person is willing to pay for a unit of a product depends on the opportunity cost of his consumption alternatives. Suppose that Ted is offered the chance to purchase an apple. He would of course like to have it for free, but the maximum amount he would be willing to pay depends on the alternative uses to which he can put his money. If his maximum willingness to pay for that particular apple is $1.25, then we know that he is willing to forgo up to—but not more than—$1.25 of other goods and services. Paying even one cent more would entail having to give up too much of other goods and services.

It also means that if Ted is charged any market price less than $1.25, he will receive a consumer surplus equal to the difference between the $1.25 maximum price that he would have been willing to pay and the lower market price. For instance, if the market price is $0.50 per apple, Ted will receive a consumer surplus of $0.75 per apple (= $1.25 – $0.50). In nearly all markets, consumers individually and collectively gain greater total utility or satisfaction in dollar terms from their purchases than the amount of their expenditures (= product price × quantity). This utility surplus arises because each consumer who buys the product only has to pay the equilibrium price even though many of them would have been willing to pay more than the equilibrium price to obtain the product.

The concept of maximum willingness to pay also gives us another way to understand demand curves. Consider Table 5-1, where the first two columns show the maximum amounts that six consumers would each be willing to pay for a bag of oranges. Bob, for instance, would be willing to pay a maximum of $13 for a bag of oranges. Betty, by contrast, would only be willing to pay a maximum of $8 for a bag of oranges.

Notice that the maximum prices these individuals are willing to pay represent points on a demand curve because the lower the market price, the more bags of oranges will be demanded. At a

TABLE 5-1   Consumer Surplus

(1) Person	(2) Maximum price willing to pay	(3) Actual price (equilibrium price)	(4) Consumer surplus
Bob	$13	$8	$5 (= $13 − $8)
Beata	12	8	4 (= $12 − $8)
Bill	11	8	3 (= $11 − $8)
Bella	10	8	2 (= $10 − $8)
Brent	9	8	1 (= $9 − $8)
Betty	8	8	0 (= $8 − $8)

price of $12.50, for instance, Bob will be the only person listed in the table who will purchase a bag. But at a price of $11.50, both Bob and Beata will want to purchase a bag. And at a price of $10.50, Bob, Beata, and Bill will each purchase a bag. The lower the price, the greater the total quantity demanded as the market price falls below the maximum prices of more and more consumers.

Lower prices also imply larger consumer surpluses. When the price is $12.50, Bob only gets $0.50 in consumer surplus because his maximum willingness to pay of $13 is only $0.50 higher than the market price of $12.50. But if the market price were to fall to $8, then his consumer surplus would be $5 (= $13 − $8). The third and fourth columns of Table 5-1 show how much consumer surplus each of our six consumers will receive if the market price of a bag of oranges is $8. Only Betty receives no consumer surplus because her maximum willingness to pay exactly matches the $8 equilibrium price.

It is easy to show on a graph both the individual consumer surplus received by each particular buyer in a market and the collective consumer surplus received by all buyers. Consider Figure 5-1, which shows the market equilibrium price $P_1 = \$8$ as well as the downsloping demand curve D for bags of oranges. Demand curve D includes not only the six consumers named in Table 5-1 but also every other consumer of oranges in the market. The individual consumer surplus of each particular person who is willing to buy at the $8 market price is simply the vertical distance from the horizontal line that marks the $8 market price up to that particular buyer's maximum willingness to pay. The collective consumer surplus obtained by all of our named and unnamed buyers is found by adding together each of their individual consumer surpluses.

To obtain the Q_1 bags of oranges represented, consumers collectively are willing to pay the total amount shown by the sum of the green triangle and blue rectangle under the demand curve and to the left of Q_1. But consumers need to pay only the amount represented by the blue rectangle (= $P_1 \times Q_1$). So the green triangle is the consumer surplus in this market. It is the sum of the vertical distances between the demand curve and the $8 equilibrium price at each quantity up to Q_1. Alternatively, it is the sum of the gaps between maximum willingness to pay and actual price, such as those we calculated in Table 5-1. Thus, consumer surplus can also be defined as the area that lies below the demand curve and above the price line that extends horizontally from P_1.

Consumer surplus and price are inversely (negatively) related. Given the demand curve, higher prices reduce consumer surplus; lower prices increase it. To test this generalization, draw in an equilibrium price above $8 in Figure 5-1 and observe the reduced size of the triangle representing

---

FIGURE 5-1 **Consumer Surplus**

Consumer surplus—shown as the green triangle—is the difference between the maximum price consumers are willing to pay for a product and the lower equilibrium price, here assumed to be $8. For quantity Q_1, consumers are willing to pay the sum of the amounts represented by the green triangle and the blue rectangle. Because they need to pay only the amount shown as the blue rectangle, the green triangle shows consumer surplus.

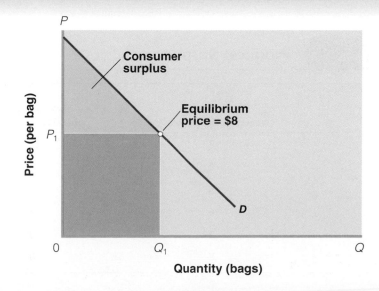

consumer surplus. When price goes up, the gap narrows between the maximum willingness to pay and the actual price. Next, draw in an equilibrium price below $8 and see that consumer surplus increases. When the price declines, the gap widens between maximum willingness to pay and actual price.

Producer Surplus

producer surplus
The difference between the actual price producers receive for a product and the minimum acceptable price.

Like consumers, producers also receive a benefit surplus in markets. This **producer surplus** is the difference between the actual price a producer receives (or producers receive) and the minimum acceptable price that you would have to pay the producer to make a particular unit of his or her product.

A producer's minimum acceptable price for a particular unit will equal the producer's marginal cost of producing that particular unit. That marginal cost will be the sum of the rent, wages, interest, and profit that the producer will need to pay in order to obtain the land, labour, capital, and entrepreneurship required to produce that particular unit. In this section, we are assuming that the marginal cost of producing a unit will include *all* of the costs of production. Unlike the coal-burning power plant mentioned above, the producer must pay for all of her costs, including the cost of pollution. In later sections, we will explore the market failures that arise in situations where firms do not have to pay all of their costs.

In addition to equalling marginal cost, a producer's minimum acceptable price can also be interpreted as the opportunity cost of bidding resources away from the production of other products. To see why this is true, suppose that Leah is an apple grower. The resources necessary for her to produce one apple could be used to produce other things. To get them directed toward producing an apple, it is necessary to pay Leah what it will cost her to bid the necessary resources away from other entrepreneurs who would like to use them to produce other products. Leah would, naturally, like to get paid as much as possible to produce the apple for you. But her minimum acceptable price is the lowest price you could pay her such that she can just break even after bidding away from other uses the land, labour, capital, and entrepreneurship necessary to produce the apple.

connect
WORKED PROBLEM 5.1
Consumer and Producer Surplus

The size of the producer surplus earned on any particular unit will be the difference between the market price that the producer actually receives and the producer's minimum acceptable price. Consider Table 5-2, which shows the minimum acceptable prices of six different orange growers. With a market price of $8, Carlos—for instance—has a producer surplus of $5, which is equal to the market price of $8 minus his minimum acceptable price of $3. Chad, by contrast, receives no producer surplus because his minimum acceptable price of $8 just equals the market equilibrium price of $8.

TABLE 5-2	Producer Surplus		
(1) **Person**	**(2)** **Minimum** **acceptable price**	**(3)** **Actual price** **(equilibrium price)**	**(4)** **Producer** **surplus**
Carlos	$3	$8	$5 (= $8 − $3)
Courtney	4	8	4 (= $8 − $4)
Carla	5	8	3 (= $8 − $5)
Cindy	6	8	2 (= $8 − $6)
Carmela	7	8	1 (= $8 − $7)
Chad	8	8	0 (= $8 − $8)

Carlos's minimum acceptable price is lower than Chad's minimum acceptable price because Carlos is a more efficient producer than Chad, by which we mean that Carlos produces oranges using a less-costly combination of resources than Chad uses. The differences in efficiency between Carlos and Chad are likely due to differences in the type and quality of resources available to them. Carlos, for instance, may own land perfectly suited to growing oranges, while Chad has land in the desert that requires costly irrigation if it is to be used to grow oranges. Thus, Chad has a higher marginal cost of producing oranges.

The minimum acceptable prices that producers are willing to accept form points on a supply curve because the higher the price, the more bags of oranges will be supplied. At a price of $3.50, for instance, only Carlos would be willing to supply a bag of oranges. But at a price of $5.50, Carlos, Courtney, and Carla would all be willing to supply a bag of oranges. The higher the market price, the more oranges will be supplied as the market price surpasses the marginal costs and minimum acceptable prices of more and more producers. Thus, supply curves shown in this competitive market are both marginal-cost curves and minimum-acceptable-price curves.

The supply curve in Figure 5-2 includes not only the six producers named in Table 5-2 but also every other producer of oranges in the market. At the market price of $8 per bag, Q_1 bags are produced because only those producers whose minimum acceptable prices are less than $8 per bag will choose to produce oranges with their resources. Those lower acceptable prices for each of the units up to Q_1 are shown by the portion of the supply curve lying to the left of and below the assumed $8 market price.

The individual producer surplus of each of these sellers is thus the vertical distance from each seller's respective minimum acceptable price on the supply curve up to the $8 market price. Their collective producer surplus is shown by the blue triangle in Figure 5-2. In that figure, producers collect revenues of $P_1 \times Q_1$, which is the sum of the blue and green triangles. As shown by the supply curve, however, revenues of only those illustrated by the green triangle would be required to entice producers to offer Q_1 bags of oranges for sale. The sellers therefore receive a producer surplus shown by the blue triangle. That surplus is the sum of the vertical distances between the supply curve and the $8 equilibrium price at each of the quantities to the left of Q_1.

There is a direct (positive) relationship between equilibrium price and the amount of producer surplus. Given the supply curve, lower prices reduce producer surplus; higher prices increase it. If you pencil in a lower equilibrium price than $8, you will see that the producer surplus triangle

---

FIGURE 5-2   Producer Surplus

Producer surplus—shown as the blue triangle—reflects the difference between the equilibrium price producers receive for a product (here, $8) and the lower minimum payments they are willing to accept. For quantity Q_1, producers receive the sum of the amounts represented by the blue triangle plus the green triangle. Because they need to receive only the amount shown by the green triangle to produce Q_1, the blue triangle represents producer surplus.

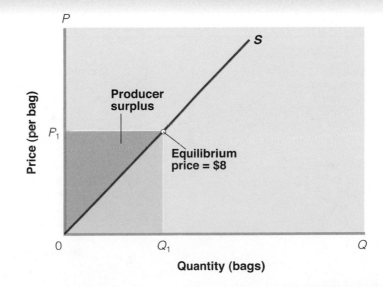

gets smaller. The gaps between the minimum acceptable payments and the actual prices narrow when the price falls. If you pencil in an equilibrium price above $8, the size of the producer surplus triangle increases. The gaps between minimum acceptable payments and actual prices widen when the price increases.

Efficiency Revisited

In Figure 5-3 we bring together the demand and supply curves of Figures 5-1 and 5-2 to show the equilibrium price and quantity and the previously described regions of consumer and producer surplus. All markets that have downsloping demand curves and upsloping supply curves yield consumer and producer surplus.

Because we are assuming in Figure 5-3 that the demand curve reflects buyers' full willingness to pay and the supply curve reflects all the costs facing sellers, the equilibrium quantity in Figure 5-3 reflects economic efficiency, which consists of productive efficiency and allocative efficiency. In **productive efficiency,** competition forces orange growers to use the best technologies and combinations of resources available. Doing so minimizes the per-unit cost of the output produced. In **allocative efficiency,** the correct quantity of oranges—Q_1—is produced relative to other goods and services.

productive efficiency
The production of a good in the least costly way.

allocative efficiency
The apportionment of resources among firms and industries to produce the goods most wanted by society.

There are two ways to understand why Q_1 is the correct quantity of oranges. Both involve realizing that any resources directed toward the production of oranges are resources that could have been used to produce other products. Thus, the only way to justify taking any amount of any resource (land, labour, capital, entrepreneurship, etc.) away from the production of other products is if it brings more utility or satisfaction when devoted to the production of oranges than it would if it were used to produce other products.

The first way to see why Q_1 is the allocatively efficient quantity of oranges is to note that demand and supply curves can be interpreted as measuring marginal benefit (MB) and marginal cost (MC). Recall from the discussion relating to Figure 1-3 that optimal allocation is achieved at the output level where MB = MC. We have already seen that supply curves are marginal cost curves. As it turns out, demand curves are marginal benefit curves. This is true because the maximum price that a consumer would be willing to pay for any particular unit is equal to the benefit that she would get if she were to consume that unit. Thus, each point on a demand

---

FIGURE 5-3 | **Efficiency: Maximum Combined Consumer and Producer Goods**

At quantity Q_1 the combined amount of consumer surplus, shown as the blue triangle, and producer surplus, shown as the green triangle, is maximized. Efficiency occurs because, at Q_1, maximum willingness to pay, indicated by the points on the demand curve, equals minimum acceptable price, shown by the points on the supply curve.

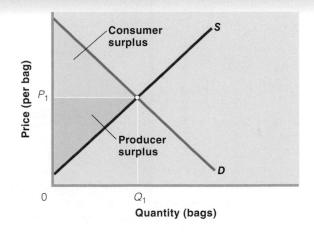

curve represents both some consumer's maximum willingness to pay and the marginal benefit that he or she would get from consuming the particular unit in question.

Thus, combining the fact that supply curves are MC curves with the fact that demand curves are MB curves, we see that points on the demand curve in Figure 5-3 measure the marginal benefit of oranges at each level of output, while points on the supply curve measure the marginal cost of oranges at each level of output. As a result, MB = MC where the demand and supply curves intersect—which means that the equilibrium quantity Q_1 must be allocatively efficient.

To gain a deeper understanding of why Q_1 is allocatively efficient, notice that for every unit up to Q_1 it is the case that marginal benefit exceeds marginal cost (MB > MC). And because marginal cost includes the opportunity cost of not making other things with the resources needed to make these units, we know that people are better off when the resources necessary to make these units are allocated to producing oranges rather than to producing anything else.

The second way to see why Q_1 is the correct quantity of oranges is based on our analysis of consumer and producer surplus and the fact that we can interpret demand and supply curves in terms of maximum willingness to pay and minimum acceptable price. In Figure 5-3, the maximum willingness to pay on the demand curve for each bag of oranges up to Q_1 exceeds the corresponding minimum acceptable price on the supply curve. Thus, each of these bags adds a positive amount (= maximum willingness to pay *minus* minimum acceptable price) to the *total* of consumer and producer surplus.

The fact that maximum willingness to pay exceeds minimum acceptable price for every unit up to Q_1 means that people gain more utility from producing and consuming those units than they would if they produced and consumed anything else that could be made with the resources that went into making those units. This is true because both the maximum willingness to pay and the minimum acceptable price take opportunity costs into account. As long as the maximum willingness to pay exceeds the minimum acceptable price, people are willing to pay more to consume a unit of the good in question (here, bags of oranges) than they would pay to consume anything else that could be made with the same resources. Only at the equilibrium quantity Q_1—where the maximum willingness to pay exactly equals the minimum acceptable price—does society exhaust all opportunities to produce units for which benefits exceed costs (including opportunity costs). Producing Q_1 units therefore achieves allocative efficiency because the market is producing and distributing only those units that make people happier with bags of oranges than they would be with anything else that could be produced with the same resources.

Geometrically, producing Q_1 units maximizes the combined area of consumer and producer surplus in Figure 5-3. In this context, the combined area is referred to as **total surplus.** Thus, when Q_1 units are produced, total surplus is equal to the large triangle formed by the green consumer surplus triangle and the blue producer surplus triangle.

When demand curves reflect buyers' full willingness to pay and when supply curves reflect all the costs facing sellers, competitive markets produce equilibrium quantities that maximize the sum of consumer and producer surplus. Allocative efficiency occurs at the market equilibrium quantity, where three conditions exist simultaneously:

1. MB = MC (Figure 1-3).

2. Maximum willingness to pay = minimum acceptable price.

3. Total surplus (= sum of consumer and producer surplus) is at a maximum.

Economists are enamoured of markets because properly functioning markets automatically achieve allocative efficiency. Other methods of allocating resources—such as government central planning—do exist. But since they cannot do any better than properly functioning markets—and may in many cases do much worse—economists usually prefer that resources be allocated through markets whenever properly functioning markets are available.

Figures 5-4a and 5-4b demonstrate that **efficiency losses (or deadweight losses)**—reductions of combined consumer and producer surplus—result from both underproduction and overproduction.

total surplus
The surplus created by combining the consumer and producer surpluses.

efficiency losses (or deadweight losses)
Reductions of combined consumer and producer surplus associated with underproduction or overproduction of a product.

FIGURE 5-4   **Efficiency Losses (or Deadweight Losses)**

Quantity levels less than or greater than the efficient quantity Q_1 create efficiency losses. In panel (a), triangle *dbe* shows the efficiency loss associated with underproduction at output Q_2. Triangle *bfg* in panel (b) illustrates the efficiency loss associated with overproduction at output level Q_3.

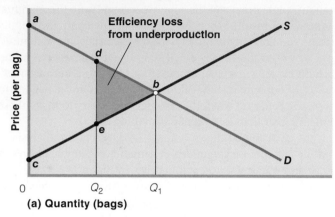

(a) Quantity (bags)

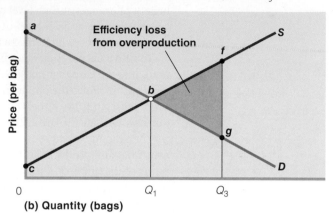

(b) Quantity (bags)

First, consider Figure 5-4a, which analyzes the case of underproduction by considering what happens if output falls from the efficient level Q_1 to the smaller amount Q_2. When that happens, the sum of consumer and producer surplus, previously *abc*, falls to *adec*. So the combined consumer and producer surplus declines by the amount of the blue triangle to the left of Q_1. That triangle represents an efficiency loss to buyers and sellers. And because buyers and sellers are members of society, it represents an efficiency loss to society.

For output levels from Q_2 to Q_1, the maximum willingness to pay by consumers (as reflected by points on the demand curve) exceeds the minimum acceptable price of sellers (as reflected by points on the supply curve). By failing to produce units of this product for which a consumer is willing to pay more than a producer is willing to accept, society suffers a loss of net benefits. As a concrete example, consider a particular unit for which a consumer is willing to pay $10 and a producer is willing to accept $6. The $4 difference between those values is a net benefit that will not be realized if this unit is not produced. In addition, the resources that should have gone to producing this unit will go instead to producing other products that will not generate as much utility as if those resources had been used here to produce this unit of this product. The triangle *dbe* in Figure 5-4a shows the total loss of net benefits that results from failing to produce the units from Q_2 to Q_1.

In contrast, consider the case of overproduction shown in Figure 5-4b, in which the number of oranges produced is Q_3 rather than the efficient level Q_1. In Figure 5-4b the combined consumer and producer surplus therefore declines by *bfg*—the blue triangle to the right of Q_1. This triangle subtracts from the total consumer and producer surplus of *abc* that would occur if the quantity had been Q_1. That is, for all units from zero to Q_1, benefits exceed costs, so that those units generate the economic surplus shown by triangle *abc*. But the units from Q_1 to Q_3 are such that costs exceed benefits. Thus, they generate an economic loss shown by triangle *bfg*. The total economic surplus for all units from zero to Q_3 is therefore the economic surplus given by *abc* for the units from 0 to Q_1 *minus* the economic loss given by *bfg* for the units from Q_1 to Q_3.

Producing any unit beyond Q_1 generates an economic loss because the willingness to pay for such units on the part of consumers is less than the minimum acceptable price to produce such units on the part of producers. As a concrete example, note that producing an item for which the maximum willingness to pay is, say, $7 and the minimum acceptable price is, say, $10 subtracts $3 from society's net benefits. Such production is uneconomical and creates an efficiency loss (or deadweight loss) for society. Because the net benefit of each bag of oranges from Q_1 to Q_3 is negative, we know that the benefits from these units are smaller than the opportunity costs of the other products that could have been produced with the resources that were used to produce these bags of oranges. The resources used to produce the bags from Q_1 to Q_3 could have generated net benefits instead of net losses if they had been directed toward producing other products. The brown triangle *bfg* to the right of Q_1 in Figure 5-4b shows the total efficiency loss from overproduction at Q_3.

The magic of markets is that when demand reflects consumers' full willingness to pay and when supply reflects all costs, the market equilibrium quantity will automatically equal the allocatively efficient output level. Under these conditions, the market equilibrium quantity will ensure that there are neither efficiency losses from underproduction nor efficiency losses from overproduction. As we are about to see, however, such losses do happen when either demand does not reflect consumers' full willingness to pay or supply does not reflect all costs.

QUICK REVIEW

- Market failures in competitive markets have two possible causes: demand curves that do not reflect consumers' full willingness to pay, and supply curves that do not reflect producers' full cost of production.

- Consumer surplus is the difference between the maximum price a consumer is willing to pay for a product and the lower price actually paid.

- Producer surplus is the difference between the minimum price a producer is willing to accept for a product and the higher price actually received.

- At the equilibrium price and quantity in competitive markets, marginal benefit equals marginal cost, maximum willingness to pay equals minimum acceptable price, and the total of consumer surplus and producer surplus is maximized. These individual conditions each define allocative efficiency.

- Quantities less than or greater than the allocatively efficient level of output create efficiency losses, also called deadweight losses.

5.3 Public Goods

As you have learned, demand-side market failures arise in competitive markets when demand curves fail to reflect consumers' full willingness to pay for a good or service. In such situations, markets fail to produce all of the units for which there are net benefits because demand curves underreport how much consumers are willing and able to pay. This underreporting problem reaches its most extreme form in the case of a public good: Markets may fail to produce *any* of the public good because its demand curve may reflect *none* of its consumers' willingness to pay.

Private Goods Characteristics

private goods
Goods or services that are individually consumed and that can be profitably provided by privately owned firms because they can exclude nonpayers from receiving the benefits.

rivalry
A situation in which when one person buys and consumes a product, it is not available for another person to buy and consume.

excludability
A situation in which sellers can keep people who do not pay for a product from obtaining its benefits.

We have seen that a full range of **private goods** are produced through the competitive market system. These are the goods offered for sale in stores, in shops, and on the Internet. Examples include automobiles, clothing, personal computers, household appliances, and sporting goods. Private goods have two characteristics: rivalry and excludability.

- A **rivalry** (in consumption) means that when one person buys and consumes a product, it is not available for another person to buy and consume. When Adams purchases and drinks a bottle of mineral water, it is not available for Benson to purchase and consume.

- When sellers can keep people who do not pay for a product from obtaining its benefits, this is called **excludability.** Only people who are willing and able to pay the market price for bottles of mineral water can obtain these drinks and the benefits they confer.

Consumers fully express their personal demands for private goods in the market. If Adams likes bottled mineral water, that fact will be known by her desire to purchase the product. Other things equal, the higher the price of bottled water, the fewer bottles she will buy. So Adams's demand for bottled water will reflect an inverse relationship between the price of bottled water and the quantity of it demanded. This is simply *individual* demand, as described in Chapter 3.

The *market* demand for a private good is the horizontal summation of the individual demand schedules (review Figure 3-2). Suppose there are just two consumers in the market for bottled water and the price is $1 per bottle. If Adams will purchase 3 bottles and Benson will buy 2, the market demand will reflect that consumers demand 5 bottles at the $1 price. Similar summations of quantities demanded at other prices will generate the market demand schedule and curve.

Suppose the equilibrium price of bottled water is $1. Adams and Benson will buy a total of 5 bottles, and the sellers will obtain total revenue of $5 (= $1 × 5). If the sellers' cost per bottle is $0.80, their total cost will be $4 (= $0.80 × 5). So sellers charging $1 per bottle will obtain $5 of total revenue, incur $4 of total cost, and earn $1 of profits for the 5 bottles sold.

Because firms can profitably tap market demand for private goods, they will produce and offer them for sale. Consumers demand private goods, and profit-seeking suppliers produce goods that satisfy the demand. Consumers willing to pay the market price obtain the goods; nonpayers go without.

A competitive market not only makes private goods available to consumers but also allocates society's resources efficiently to the particular product. There is neither underproduction nor overproduction of the product.

Public Goods Characteristics

public goods
Goods or services that can be simultaneously consumed by everyone, and from which no one can be excluded, even if they don't pay for them.

nonrivalry
When the consumption of a good by one person does not preclude consumption of the good by others.

non-excludability
When there is no effective way of excluding individuals from the benefit of the good once it has been created.

free-rider problem
The inability of potential providers of an economically desirable but indivisible good or service to obtain payment from those who benefit, because the exclusion principle is not applicable.

Goods that have the opposite characteristics of private goods are called **public goods.** Public goods are distinguished by nonrivalry and non-excludability.

- If one person's consumption of a good does not preclude consumption of the good by others, the good has a characteristic known as **nonrivalry** (in consumption). Everyone can simultaneously obtain the benefit from a public good such as a global positioning system, national defence, street lighting, and environmental protection.

- When there is no effective way of excluding individuals from the benefit of the good once it comes into existence, the good has the characteristic of **non-excludability.**

These two characteristics create a **free-rider problem.** Once a producer has provided a public good, everyone—including nonpayers—can obtain the benefit. Because most people do not voluntarily pay for something that they can obtain for free, most people become free riders. These free riders like the public good and would be willing to pay for it if producers could somehow force them to pay—but non-excludability means that there is no way for producers to withhold the good from the free riders without also denying it to the few who do pay. As a result, free riding means that the free riders' willingness to pay is not expressed in the market. From the viewpoint of producers, free riding reduces demand. The more free riding, the less demand. And if all consumers free ride, demand will collapse all the way to zero.

The low or even zero demand caused by free riding makes it virtually impossible for private firms to profitably provide public goods. With little or no demand, firms have no potential to "tap market demand" for revenues and profits. As a result, they will not produce public goods. Society will therefore suffer efficiency losses because goods for which marginal benefits exceed marginal costs are not produced. Thus, if society wants a public good to be produced, it will have to direct government to provide it. Because the public good will still feature non-excludability, the government won't have any better luck preventing free riding or charging people for it. But because the government can finance the provision of the public good through the taxation of other things, the government does not have to worry about profitability. It can therefore provide the public good even when private firms can't.

Examples of public goods include national defence, outdoor fireworks displays, the light beams thrown out by lighthouses, public art displays, public music concerts, MP3 music files posted to file-sharing websites, and ideas and inventions that are not protected by patents or copyrights. Each of these goods or services shows both nonrivalry and non-excludability.

In a few special cases, private firms can provide public goods because the production costs of these public goods can be covered by the profits generated by closely related private goods. For instance, private companies can make a profit providing broadcast TV—which is a nonrival, non-excludable public good—because they control who gets to air TV commercials, which are rival and excludable private goods. The money that broadcasters make from selling airtime for ads allows them to turn a profit despite having to give their main product, broadcast TV, away for free.

Unfortunately, only a few public goods can be subsidized in this way by closely related private goods. For the large majority of public goods, private provision is unprofitable. As a result, there are only two remaining ways for a public good to be provided: private philanthropy or government provision. For many less expensive or less important public goods like fireworks displays or public art, society may feel comfortable relying on private philanthropy. But when it comes to public goods like national defence, people normally look to the government.

This leads to an important question: Once a government decides to produce a particular public good, how can it determine the optimal amount that it should produce? How can it avoid either underallocating or overallocating society's scarce resources to the production of the public good?

One person's consumption of a public good does not preclude consumption of the same good by others.

connect

MATH 5.1
The Optimal Amount of a Public Good

Optimal Quantity of a Public Good

If consumers need not reveal their true demand for a public good in the marketplace, how can society determine the optimal amount of that good? The answer is that the government has to try to estimate the demand for a public good through surveys or public votes. It can then compare the marginal benefit (MB) of an added unit of the good against the government's marginal cost (MC) of providing it. Adhering to the MB = MC rule, government can provide the "right"— meaning "efficient"—amount of the public good.

Demand for Public Goods

The demand for a public good is somewhat unusual. Suppose Adams and Benson are the only two people in the society, and their marginal willingness to pay for a public good—this time, national defence—is as shown in columns 1, 2, and 3 in Table 5-3.

Notice that the schedules in Table 5-3 are demand schedules. Rather than depicting demand in the usual way—the quantity of a product someone is willing to buy at each possible price—these schedules show the price someone is willing to pay for the marginal unit of each possible quantity.

TABLE 5-3	Demand for a Public Good, Two Individuals					
(1) Quantity of public good	(2) Adams's willingness to pay (price)		(3) Benson's willingness to pay (price)		(4) Collective willingness to pay (price)	
1	$4	+	$5	=	$9	
2	3	+	4	=	7	
3	2	+	3	=	5	
4	1	+	2	=	3	
5	0	+	1	=	1	

That is, Adams is willing to pay $4 for the first unit of the public good, $3 for the second, $2 for the third, and so on.

Suppose the government produces one unit of this public good. Because of the non-excludability characteristic of a public good, Adams's consumption of the good does not preclude Benson from also consuming it, and vice versa. So both consume the good, and neither volunteers to pay for it. But from Table 5-3, column 4, we can find the amount these two people would be willing to pay, together. Columns 1 and 2 show that Adams would be willing to pay $4 for the first unit of the public good; columns 1 and 3 show that Benson would be willing to pay $5 for it. So the two people are jointly willing to pay $9 (= $4 + $5) for this unit.

For the second unit of the public good, the collective price they are willing to pay is $7 (= $3 from Adams plus $4 from Benson); for the third unit they will pay $5 (= $2 plus $3); and so on. By finding the collective willingness to pay for each additional unit (column 4), we can construct a collective demand schedule (a willingness-to-pay schedule) for the public good. Here, we are not adding the quantities demanded at each possible price as when we determine the market demand for a private good. Instead, we are adding *the prices that people are willing to pay for the last unit of the public good at each possible quantity demanded.*

Figure 5-5 shows the same adding procedure graphically, using the data from Table 5-3. Note that we sum Adams's and Benson's willingness-to-pay curves *vertically* to derive the collective willingness-to-pay curve (demand curve). The summing procedure is upward from the lower graph to the middle graph to the top (total) graph. For example, the height of the collective demand curve D_c at two units of output in the top graph is $7, the sum of the amounts that Adams and Benson are each willing to pay for the second unit (= $3 + $4). Likewise, the height of the collective demand curve at four units of the public good is $3 (= $1 + $2).

What does it mean in Figure 5-5a that, for example, Adams is willing to pay $3 for the second unit of the public good? It means that Adams expects to receive $3 of extra benefit or utility from that unit. And we know from the law of diminishing marginal utility that successive units of any good yield less and less added benefit. This is also true for public goods, explaining the downward slope of the willingness-to-pay curves of both Adams and Benson, and of the collective demand curve. These curves, in essence, are marginal benefit curves.

Comparing MB and MC

We can now determine the optimal quantity of the public good. The collective demand curve D_c in Figure 5-5c measures society's marginal benefit of each unit of this particular good. The supply curve S in that figure measures society's marginal cost of each unit. The optimal quantity of this public good occurs where marginal benefit equals marginal cost, or where the two curves intersect. In Figure 5-5c that point is three units of the public good, where the collective willingness to pay for the last (third) unit—the marginal benefit—just matches that unit's marginal cost ($5 = $5). As we saw in Chapter 1, equating marginal benefit and marginal cost efficiently allocates society's scarce resources.

Cost–Benefit Analysis

cost–benefit analysis
Comparing the marginal costs with the marginal benefits to decide whether to employ more or less resources in that project.

The above example suggests a practical means, called **cost–benefit analysis,** for deciding whether to provide a particular public good and how much of it to provide. Like our example, cost–benefit analysis (or marginal benefit–marginal cost analysis) involves a comparison of marginal costs and marginal benefits.

CONCEPT

Suppose the federal government is contemplating a highway construction plan. Because the economy's resources are limited, any decision to use more resources in the public sector will mean fewer resources for the private sector. There will be both a cost and a benefit. The cost is the loss of satisfaction resulting from the accompanying decline in the production of private

FIGURE 5-5   **The Optimal Amount of a Public Good**

The collective demand curve for a public good, as shown by D_c in panel (c), is found by summing vertically the individual willingness-to-pay curves D_1 in panel (a) and D_2 in panel (b) of Adams and Benson, the only two people in the economy. The supply curve of the public good represented in panel (c) slopes upward and to the right, reflecting rising marginal costs. The optimal amount of the public good is three units, determined by the intersection of D_c and S. At that output, marginal benefit (reflected in the collective demand curve D_c) equals marginal cost (reflected in the supply curve S).

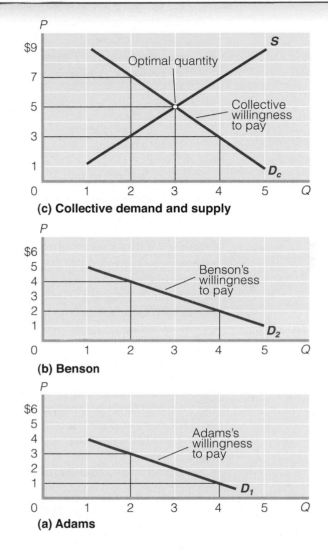

(c) Collective demand and supply

(b) Benson

(a) Adams

goods; the benefit is the extra satisfaction resulting from the output of more public goods. Should the needed resources be shifted from the private to the public sector? The answer is yes if the benefit from the extra public goods exceeds the cost that results from having fewer private goods. The answer is no if the cost of the forgone private goods is greater than the benefit associated with the extra public goods.

ILLUSTRATION

Roads and highways can be run privately, as excludability is possible with toll gates. However, the federal highway system is almost entirely non-exclusive because anyone with a car can get on and off most federal highways without restriction anytime they want. Federal highways therefore satisfy one characteristic of a public good, non-excludability. The other characteristic, nonrivalry, is also satisfied by the fact that unless a highway is already extremely crowded, one person's driving on the highway does not preclude another person's driving on the highway. Thus, the federal highway system is effectively a public good. This leads us to ask: Should the federal government expand the national highway system? If so, what is the proper size or scope for the overall project?

TABLE 5-4

Cost–Benefit Analysis for a National Highway Construction Project, billions of dollars

(1) Plan	(2) Total cost of project	(3) Marginal cost	(4) Total benefit	(5) Marginal benefit	(6) Net benefit (4) − (2)
No new construction	$ 0		$ 0		$0
		$ 4		$ 5	
A: Widen existing highways	4		5		1
		6		8	
B: Two-lane highways	10		13		3
		8		10	
C: Four-lane highways	18		23		5
		10		3	
D: Six-lane highways	28		26		−2

Table 5-4 lists a series of increasingly costly highway projects: widening existing two-lane highways; building new two-lane highways; building new four-lane highways; and building new six-lane highways. The extent to which government should undertake highway construction depends on the costs and benefits. The costs are largely the costs of constructing and maintaining the highways; the benefit is an improved flow of people and goods throughout the country.[2]

The table shows that total benefit (column 4) exceeds total cost (column 2) for plans A, B, and C, indicating that some highway construction is economically justifiable. We see this directly in column 6, where total costs (column 2) are subtracted from total annual benefits (column 4). Net benefits are positive for plans A, B, and C. Plan D is not justifiable because net benefits are negative.

But the question of optimal size or scope for this project remains. Comparing the marginal cost (the change in total cost) and the marginal benefit (the change in total benefit) relating to each plan determines the answer. In this case, plan C (building new four-lane highways) is the best plan. For plans A and B, the marginal benefits exceed the marginal costs. Plan D's marginal cost ($10 billion) exceeds the marginal benefit ($3 billion) and therefore cannot be justified; it overallocates resources to the project. Plan C is closest to the optimum because its marginal benefit ($10 billion) still exceeds marginal cost ($8 billion) but approaches the MB = MC (or MC = MB) ideal.

This **marginal cost = marginal benefit rule** actually tells us which plan provides society with the maximum net benefit. You can confirm directly in column 6 that the maximum net benefit (= $5 billion) is associated with plan C.

Cost–benefit analysis shatters the myth that "economy in government" and "reduced government spending" are synonymous. "Economy" is concerned with using scarce resources efficiently. If the costs of a proposed government program exceed its benefits, then the proposed public program should not be undertaken, but if the benefits exceed the costs, then it would be uneconomical or "wasteful" not to spend on that government program. Economy in government does not mean minimization of public spending; it means allocating resources between the private and public sectors and among public goods to achieve maximum net benefit.

QUASI-PUBLIC GOODS

The government provides many goods that fit the economist's definition of a public good. However, it also provides other goods and services that could be produced and delivered in such a way that exclusion would be possible. Such goods, called **quasi-public goods,** include education, streets and highways, police and fire protection, libraries and museums, preventive medicine,

marginal cost = marginal benefit rule
For a government project, marginal benefit should equal marginal cost to produce maximum benefit to society.

quasi-public goods
Goods provided by the government that fit the economist's definition of a public good but can be produced in such a way that exclusion would be possible.

---

[2] Because the costs of public goods typically are immediate while the benefits often accrue over longer time periods, economists convert both costs and benefits to present values for comparison. Using present value properly accounts for the time value of money, discussed in Chapter 14.

CONSIDER THIS :: Street Entertainers

Street entertainers are often found in tourist areas of major cities. These entertainers illuminate the concepts of free riders and public goods. Most street entertainers have a hard time earning a living from their activities (unless event organizers pay them) because they have no way of excluding nonpayers from the benefits of their entertainment. They essentially are providing public, not private, goods and must rely on voluntary payments. The result is a significant free-rider problem. Only a few in the audience put money in the container or instrument case, and many who do so contribute only token amounts. The rest are free riders who obtain the benefits of the street entertainment and retain their money for purchases that *they* initiate.

Street entertainers are acutely aware of the free-rider problem, and some have found creative ways to lessen it. For example, some entertainers involve the audience directly in the act. This usually creates a greater sense of audience willingness (or obligation) to contribute money at the end of the performance. "Pay for performance" is another creative approach to lessening the free-rider problem. A good example is the street entertainer painted up to look like a statue. When people drop coins into the container, the "statue" makes a slight movement. The greater the contributions, the greater the movement. But these human "statues" still face a free-rider problem: Nonpayers also get to enjoy the acts.

and sewage disposal. They could all be priced and provided by private firms through the market system. But, as we noted earlier, because they all have substantial positive externalities, they would be underproduced by the market system. Therefore, government often provides them to avoid the underallocation of resources that would otherwise occur.

THE REALLOCATION PROCESS

How are resources reallocated from the production of private goods to the production of public and quasi-public goods? If the resources of the economy are fully employed, government must free up resources from the production of private goods and make them available for producing public and quasi-public goods. It does so by reducing private demand for them. And it does that by levying taxes on households and businesses, taking some of their income out of the circular flow. With lower incomes and hence less purchasing power, households and businesses must curtail their consumption and investment spending. As a result, the private demand for goods and services declines, as does the private demand for resources. So by diverting purchasing power from private spenders to government, taxes remove resources from private use.

Government then spends the tax proceeds to provide public and quasi-public goods and services. Taxation releases resources from the production of private consumer goods (food, clothing, television sets) and private investment goods (printing presses, boxcars, warehouses). Government shifts those resources to the production of public and quasi-public goods (post offices, submarines, parks), changing the composition of the economy's total output.

QUICK REVIEW

- Public goods are characterized by non-rivalry and non-excludability.

- The demand (marginal benefit) curve for a public good is found by vertically adding the prices all the members of society are willing to pay for the last unit of output at various output levels.

- The socially optimal amount of a public good is the amount at which the marginal cost and marginal benefit of the good are equal.

- Cost–benefit analysis is the method of evaluating alternative projects by comparing the marginal cost and marginal benefit and applying the MC = MB rule.

- The government uses taxes to allocate resources from the production of private goods to the production of public and quasi-public goods.

5.4   Externalities

externality
Benefits or costs from production or consumption accruing without compensation to nonbuyers and nonsellers of the product.

In addition to providing public goods, governments can also improve the allocation of resources in the economy by correcting for market failures caused by externalities. An **externality** occurs when some of the costs or the benefits of a good or service are passed on to or "spill over to" someone other than the immediate buyer or seller. Such spillovers are called externalities because they are benefits or costs that accrue to some third party that is external to the market transaction.

There are both positive and negative externalities. An example of a spillover cost or a *negative externality* is the cost of breathing polluted air; an example of a spillover benefit or a *positive externality* is the benefit of having everyone else inoculated against some communicable disease. When there are negative externalities, there is an overproduction of the product and an overallocation of resources to this product. Conversely, positive externalities result in underproduction of the product and an underallocation of resources. We can demonstrate both graphically.

connect

ORIGIN OF THE IDEA 5.2
Externalities

An example of a negative externality is the cost of breathing polluted air.

negative externality
A cost imposed without compensation on third parties by the production or consumption of sellers or buyers (e.g., a manufacturer dumps toxic chemicals into a river, killing the fish sought by sport fishers). An external cost or spillover cost.

Negative Externalities

Negative externalities cause supply-side market failures. These failures happen because producers do not take into account the costs that their negative externalities impose on others. This failure to account for all production costs causes firms' supply curves to shift to the right of (or below) where they would be if firms properly accounted for all costs. Consider the costs of breathing polluted air that are imposed on third parties living downwind of smoke-spewing factories. Because polluting firms do not take account of such costs, they oversupply the products they make, producing units for which total costs (including those that fall on third parties) exceed total benefits. The same is true when airlines fail to account for the costs that noisy jet engines impose on people living near airports and when biodiesel factories that convert dead animal parts into fuel release foul smelling gases that disgust those living nearby.

Figure 5-6a illustrates how negative externalities affect the allocation of resources. When producers shift some of their costs onto the community as externality costs, producers' marginal costs are lower than they would be if they had to pay for these costs. So their supply curves do not include or capture all the costs associated with the production of their goods. A polluting producer's supply curve such as S in Figure 5-6a, therefore, understates the total cost of production. The firm's supply curve lies to the right of the full-cost supply curve S_t, which would include the spillover cost. Through polluting and thus transferring cost to others in society, the firm enjoys lower production costs and has the supply curve S.

The outcome is shown in Figure 5-6a, where equilibrium output Q_e is larger than the optimal output Q_o. This means that resources are overallocated to the production of this commodity; too

---

FIGURE 5-6   Negative Externalities and Positive Externalities

Panel (a): With negative externalities borne by society, the producers' supply curve S is to the right of (below) the full-cost curve S_t. Consequently, the equilibrium output Q_e is greater than the optimal output Q_o and the efficiency loss is *abc*. Panel (b): When positive externalities accrue to society, the market demand curve D is to the left of (below) the full-benefit demand curve D_t. As a result, the equilibrium output Q_e is less than the optimal output Q_o and the efficiency loss is *xyz*.

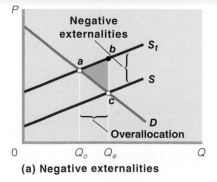

(a) Negative externalities

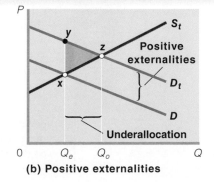

(b) Positive externalities

many units of it are produced. In fact, there is a net loss to society for every unit from Q_o to Q_e because, for those units, the supply curve that accounts for all costs, S_t, lies above the demand curve. Therefore, MC exceeds MB for those units. The resources that went into producing those units should have been used elsewhere in the economy to produce other things.

In terms of our previous analysis, the negative externality results in an efficiency loss represented by triangle *abc*.

Positive Externalities

positive externality
A benefit obtained without compensation by third parties from the production or consumption of sellers or buyers (e.g., a beekeeper benefits when a neighbouring farmer plants clover). An external benefit or spillover benefit.

Positive externalities cause demand-side market failures. These failures happen because market demand curves in such cases fail to include the willingness to pay of the third parties who receive the external benefits caused by the positive externality. This failure to account for all benefits shifts market demand curves to the left of (or below) where they would be if they included all benefits and the willingness to pay of both the third parties and the primary beneficiaries. Because demand curves fail to take into account all benefits when there are positive externalities, markets in such cases fail to produce all units for which benefits (including those that are received by third parties) exceed costs. As a result, products featuring positive externalities are underproduced.

Vaccinations are a good example of how positive externalities reduce demand and shift demand curves down and to the left. When John gets vaccinated against a disease, he benefits not only himself (because he can no longer contract the disease) but also everyone else around him (because they know that in the future he will never be able to infect them). These other people would presumably be willing to pay some positive amount of money for the benefits they receive when John is vaccinated. But because his vaccination is a public good, there is no way to make them pay.

To see why his vaccination is a public good, note that the vaccination benefits that John provides to others feature nonrivalry and non-excludability. There is nonrivalry because the protection his vaccination provides to one person does not lessen the protection that it provides to other people. There is non-excludability because once he is vaccinated, there is no way to exclude anyone in particular from benefiting from his vaccination. Thus, the market demand for vaccinations will only include John's personal willingness to pay for the benefits that he personally receives from the vaccination. The market demand will fail to include the benefits that others receive. As a result, demand will be too low and vaccinations will be underproduced.

Figure 5-6b shows the impact of positive externalities on resource allocation. When external benefits occur, the market demand curve D lies to the left of the full-benefits demand curve, D_t. That is, D does not include the external benefits of the product, whereas D_t does. The outcome is that the equilibrium output, Q_e, is less than the optimal output, Q_o. The market fails to produce enough vaccinations and resources are underallocated to this product. The underproduction implies that society is missing out on a significant amount of potential net benefits. For every unit from Q_e to Q_o, the demand curve that accounts for all benefits, D_t, lies above the supply curve that accounts for all costs—including the opportunity cost of producing other items with the resources that would be needed to produce these units. Therefore, MB exceeds MC for each of these units and we know that society should redeploy some of its resources away from the production of other things in order to produce these units that generate net benefits.

In terms of our previous analysis, the positive externality results in an efficiency loss represented by triangle *xyz*.

Government Intervention

Government intervention may be called upon to achieve economic efficiency when externalities affect large numbers of people or when community interests are at stake. Government can use direct controls and taxes to counter negative externalities; it may provide subsidies or public goods to deal with positive externalities.

CONSIDER THIS :: The Fable of the Bees

Economist Ronald Coase received the Nobel Prize for his so-called **Coase theorem,** which pointed out that under the right conditions, private individuals can often negotiate their own mutually agreeable solutions to externality problems through *individual bargaining* without the need for government interventions like pollution taxes.

This is a very important insight because it means that we shouldn't automatically call for government intervention every time we see a potential externality problem. Consider the positive externalities that bees provide by pollinating farmers' crops. Should we assume that beekeeping will be under-provided unless the government intervenes with, for instance, subsidies to encourage more hives and hence more pollination?

As it turns out, no. Research has shown that farmers and beekeepers long ago used individual bargaining to develop

customs and payment systems that avoid free riding by farmers and which encourage beekeepers to keep the optimal number of hives. Free riding is avoided by the custom that all farmers in an area simultaneously hire beekeepers to provide bees to pollinate their crops. And farmers always pay the beekeepers for their pollination services because if they didn't, no beekeeper would ever work with them in the future—a situation that would lead to massively reduced crop yields due to a lack of pollination.

The "Fable of the Bees" is a good reminder that it is a fallacy to assume that the government must always get involved to remedy externalities. In many cases, the private sector can solve both positive and negative externality problems on its own.

Coase theorem
Under the right conditions, private individuals can often negotiate their own mutually agreeable solutions to externality problems through individual bargaining with no need of government intervention.

ORIGIN OF THE IDEA 5.3
Coase Theorem

DIRECT CONTROLS

The direct way to reduce negative externalities from a certain activity is to pass legislation limiting that activity. Such direct controls force the offending firms to incur the actual costs of the offending activity. To date, this approach has dominated public policy in Canada. Historically, direct controls in the form of uniform emissions standards—limits on allowable pollution—have dominated Canadian air pollution policy. Clean air legislation forces factories, cars, and businesses to install "maximum achievable control technology" to reduce emissions. Clean-water legislation limits the amount of heavy metals, detergents, and other pollutants firms can discharge into rivers and bays. Toxic-waste laws mandate special procedures and dump sites for disposing of contaminated soil and solvents. Violating these laws means fines and, in some cases, imprisonment.

Direct controls raise the marginal cost of production because the firms must operate and maintain pollution-control equipment. The supply curve S in Figure 5-7b, which does not reflect the external costs, shifts leftward (upward) to the full-cost supply curve, S_t. Product price increases, equilibrium output falls from Q_e to Q_o, and the initial overallocation of resources shown in Figure 5-7a is corrected. Observe that the efficiency loss shown by triangle *abc* in Figure 5-7a disappears after the overallocation is corrected in Figure 5-7b.

SPECIFIC TAXES

A second policy approach to negative externalities is for government to levy taxes or charges specifically on the related good. For example, the government has placed a manufacturing tax on CFCs, which deplete the stratospheric ozone layer protecting the Earth from excessive solar ultraviolet radiation. Facing such a tax, manufacturers must decide whether to pay the tax or expend additional funds to purchase or develop substitute products. In either case, the tax raises the marginal cost of producing CFCs, shifting the private supply curve for this product leftward.

In Figure 5-7b, a tax equal to T per unit increases the firm's marginal cost, shifting the supply curve from S to S_t. The equilibrium price rises and the equilibrium output declines from Q_e to the economically efficient level Q_o. The tax thus eliminates the initial overallocation of resources and therefore the efficiency loss.

FIGURE 5-7   Correcting for Negative Externalities

Panel (a): Negative externalities result in an overallocation of resources. Panel (b): Government can correct this overallocation in two ways: (1) using direct controls, which would shift the supply curve from S to S_t and reduce output from Q_e to Q_o, or (2) imposing a specific tax T, which would also shift the supply curve from S to S_t, eliminating the overallocation of resources and thus the efficiency loss.

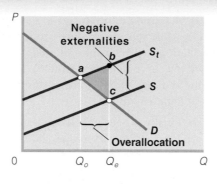

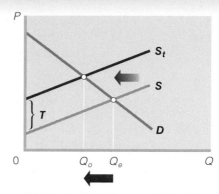

(a) Negative externalities

(b) Correcting the overallocation of resources via direct controls or via a tax

SUBSIDIES AND GOVERNMENT PROVISION

Where positive externalities are large and diffuse, as in our earlier example of vaccinations, government has three options for correcting the underallocation of resources:

1. **Subsidies to Buyers** Figure 5-8a shows the supply–demand situation for positive externalities. Government could correct the underallocation of resources—for example, to inoculations—by subsidizing consumers of the product; it could give each new mother a discount coupon to be used to obtain a series of vaccinations for her child. The coupon would reduce the price to the mother by, say, 50 percent. As shown in Figure 5-8b, this program would shift the demand curve for inoculations from too-low D to the appropriate D_t. The number of vaccinations

FIGURE 5-8   Correcting for Positive Externalities

Panel (a): Positive externalities result in an underallocation of resources. Panel (b): This underallocation can be corrected by a subsidy to consumers, which shifts market demand from D to D_t and increases output from Q_e to Q_o. Panel (c): Alternatively, the underallocation can be eliminated by providing producers with a subsidy of U, which shifts their supply curve from S_t to S'_t, increasing output from Q_e to Q_o and eliminating the underallocation and thus the efficiency loss shown in panel (a).

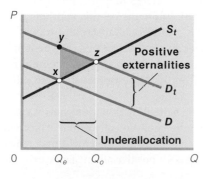

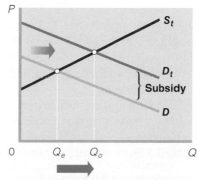

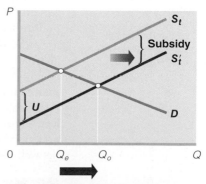

(a) Positive externalities

(b) Correcting the underallocation of resources via a subsidy to consumers

(c) Correcting the underallocation of resources via a subsidy to producers

would rise from Q_e to the optimal Q_o, eliminating the underallocation of resources and efficiency loss shown in Figure 5-8a.

2. **Subsidies to Producers**   A subsidy to producers is a specific tax in reverse. Taxes impose an extra cost on producers, while subsidies reduce producers' costs. As shown in Figure 5-8c, a subsidy of U per inoculation to physicians and medical clinics would reduce their marginal costs and shift their supply curve rightward from S_t to S'_t. The output of inoculations would increase from Q_e to the optimal level Q_o, correcting the underallocation of resources and efficiency loss shown in Figure 5-8a.

3. **Government Provision**   Finally, where positive externalities are large, the government may decide to provide the product for free to everyone. The Canadian government largely eradicated the crippling disease polio by administering free vaccines to all children. India ended smallpox by paying people in rural areas to come to public clinics to have their children vaccinated.

Society's Optimal Amount of Externality Reduction

CHOOSING A LITTLE
MORE OR LESS

Negative externalities such as pollution reduce the utility of those affected. These spillovers are not economic goods but economic "bads." If something is bad, shouldn't society eliminate it? Why should society allow firms or municipalities to discharge *any* impure waste into public waterways or to emit *any* pollution into the air?

Economists answer these questions by pointing out that reducing pollution and negative externalities is not free. There are costs as well as benefits to reducing pollution. As a result, the correct question to ask when it comes to cleaning up negative externalities is not, "Do we pollute a lot or pollute zero?" That is an all-or-nothing question that ignores marginal costs and marginal benefits. Instead, the correct question is, "What is the optimal amount to clean up—the amount that equalizes the marginal cost of cleaning up with the marginal benefit of a cleaner environment?"

If we ask that question, we see that reducing a negative externality has a price. Society must decide how much of a reduction it wants to buy. High costs may mean that totally eliminating pollution entirely might not be desirable, even if it is technologically feasible. Because of the law of diminishing returns, cleaning up the last 10 percent of pollutants from an industrial smokestack is normally far more costly than cleaning up the prior 10 percent.

The marginal cost (MC) to the firm and hence to society—the opportunity cost of the extra resources used—rises as pollution is reduced further. At some point MC may rise so high that it exceeds society's marginal benefit (MB) of further pollution abatement (reduction). Additional actions to reduce pollution will therefore lower society's well-being; total cost will rise more than total benefit, as the more pollution reduction society accomplishes, the lower the utility (and benefit) of the next unit of pollution reduction.

optimal reduction of an externality
The point at which society's marginal cost and marginal benefit of reducing that externality are equal.

The **optimal reduction of an externality** occurs when society's marginal cost and marginal benefit of reducing that externality are equal (MC = MB). In Figure 5-9 this optimal amount of pollution abatement is Q_1 units. When MB exceeds MC, additional abatement moves society toward economic efficiency; the added benefit of cleaner air or water exceeds the benefit of any alternative use of the required resources. When MC exceeds MB, additional abatement reduces economic efficiency; there would be greater benefits from using resources in some other way than to further reduce pollution.

In reality, it is difficult to measure the marginal costs and benefits of pollution control. Nevertheless, Figure 5-9 demonstrates that some pollution may be economically efficient not because pollution is desirable but because beyond some level of control, further abatement may reduce our net well-being. Table 5-5 lists some methods for managing both positive and negative externalities.

MC, MB, AND EQUILIBRIUM QUANTITY

Figure 5-9 shows both the rising marginal cost curve, MC, for pollution reduction and the downward-sloping marginal benefit curve, MB, for this outcome. MB slopes downward because of the law of diminishing marginal utility.

FIGURE 5-9   Money Facilitates Trade when Wants Do Not Coincide

The optimal amount of externality reduction—in this case, pollution abatement—occurs at Q_1, where society's marginal cost MC and marginal benefit MB of reducing the spillover are equal.

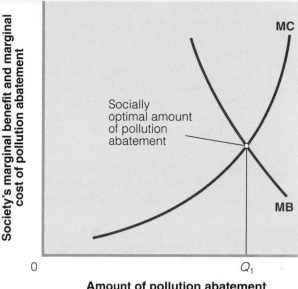

Government's Role in the Economy

As we have just discussed, market failures can be used to justify government interventions in the economy. The inability of private-sector firms to break even when attempting to provide public goods and the overproduction and underproduction problems caused by positive and negative externalities mean that government can have an important role to play if society's resources are to be efficiently allocated to the goods and services that people most highly desire.

Correcting for market failures is not, however, an easy task. To begin with, government officials must correctly identify the existence and the cause of any given market failure. That by itself

TABLE 5-5   Methods for Dealing with Externalities

Problem	Resource allocation outcome	Ways to correct
Negative externalities (spillover costs)	Overproduction of output and therefore overallocation of resources	1. Private bargaining 2. Liability rules and lawsuits 3. Tax on producers 4. Direct controls 5. Market for externality rights
Positive externalities (spillover benefits)	Underproduction of output and therefore underallocation of resources	1. Private bargaining 2. Subsidy to consumers 3. Subsidy to producers 4. Government provision

FIGURE 6-2   Deriving an Individual Demand Curve

At a price of $2 the consumer represented by the data in the table maximizes utility by purchasing four oranges. The decline in the price of oranges to $1 upsets the consumer's initial utility-maximizing equilibrium. The consumer restores equilibrium by purchasing six rather than four oranges. Thus, a simple price–quantity schedule emerges, which locates two points on a downward-sloping demand curve.

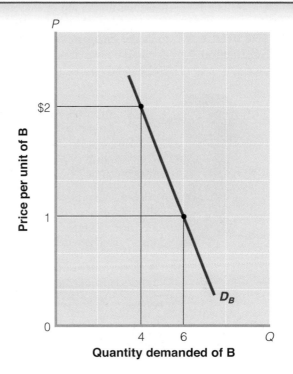

Price per unit of B	Quantity demanded
$2	4
1	6

Income and Substitution Effects

income effect
A change in the price of a product changes a consumer's real income (purchasing power) and thus the quantity of the product purchased.

substitution effect
A change in the price of a product changes the relative expensiveness of that product and hence changes the consumer's willingness to buy it rather than other goods.

Recall from Chapter 3 that the **income effect** is the impact that a change in the price of a product has on a consumer's real income and consequently on the quantity demanded of that good. In contrast, the **substitution effect** is the impact that a change in a product's price has on its relative expensiveness and consequently on the quantity demanded. Both effects help explain why a demand curve such as that in Figure 6-2 is downward sloping.

Let's first look at the substitution effect. Recall that before the price of oranges declined, Holly was in equilibrium when purchasing two apples and four oranges because

$$\frac{\text{MU of apples of 8}}{\text{price of apples of \$1}} = \frac{\text{MU of oranges of 16}}{\text{price of oranges of \$2}}$$

But after the price of oranges declines from $2 to $1,

$$\frac{\text{MU of apples of 8}}{\text{price of apples of \$1}} < \frac{\text{MU of oranges of 16}}{\text{price of oranges of \$1}}$$

More simply, the last dollar spent on oranges now yields more utility (16 utils) than does the last dollar spent on apples (8 utils). This will lead Holly to switch, or substitute, purchases away from apples and toward oranges so as to restore consumer equilibrium. This substitution effect contributes to the inverse relationship between price and quantity that is found along her demand curve for oranges: when the price of oranges declines, the substitution effect causes Holly to buy more oranges.

What about the income effect? The decline in the price of oranges from $2 to $1 increases Holly's real income. Before the price decline, she wanted two apples and four oranges. But at the lower $1 price for oranges, Holly would have to spend only $6 rather than $10 on the same combination of goods. That means the lower price of oranges has freed up $4 Holly can spend on buying more apples, more oranges, or more of both. How many more will be determined by applying the utility-maximizing rule to the new situation. But it is quite likely that the increase in real income caused by the reduction in the price of oranges will cause Holly to end up buying more oranges than before the price reduction. Any such increase in orange purchases is referred to as the income effect of the reduction in the price of oranges and it, too, helps to explain why demand curves are downward sloping: when the price of oranges falls, the income effect causes Holly to buy more oranges.

connect
ORIGIN OF THE IDEA 6.2
Income and Substitution Effects

QUICK REVIEW

- The theory of consumer choice assumes that, with limited income and a set of product prices, consumers make rational choices on the basis of well-defined preferences.

- A consumer maximizes utility by allocating income so that the marginal utility per dollar spent is the same for every good purchased.

- A downward-sloping demand curve can be derived by changing the price of one product in the consumer-choice model and noting the change in the utility-maximizing quantity of that product demanded.

- By providing insights on the income effect and substitution effect of a price decline, the utility-maximization model helps explain why demand curves are downward sloping.

6.4 Applications and Extensions

Many real-world phenomena can be explained by applying the theory of consumer choice.

iPods

Every so often a new product totally captures consumers' imaginations. One such product is Apple's iPod, which debuted in November 2001. Less than six years later, Apple sold its 100 millionth unit—units that in turn enabled Apple to sell more than 2.5 billion songs through its online iTunes store.

The swift ascendancy of the iPod resulted mainly from a leap in technology. The iPod is much more compact than the portable CD player it replaced, and it can store and play back several thousand songs—whereas a single CD only has a 74-minute recording capacity. The improved portability and storage—the enhanced consumer satisfaction—caused a major shift in consumer demand away from the portable CD player and toward the iPod.

In the language of our analysis, Apple's introduction of the iPod severely disrupted consumer equilibrium. Consumers concluded en masse that iPods had a higher marginal-utility-to-price ratio ($= MU/P$) than the ratios for alternative products. Therefore, they shifted spending away from those other products and toward iPods as a way to increase total utility. Of course, for most people the marginal utility of a second or third iPod relative to price is quite low, so most consumers purchased only a single unit. But Apple continued to enhance the iPod, enticing some of the buyers of older models to buy new models. Apple's introduction of the iPad in 2010 may have an impact on notebook computers similar to the iPod's effect on CD players.

This example demonstrates a simple but important point: New products succeed by enhancing consumers' total utility. This "delivery of value" generates a revenue stream that, if greater than the costs of production, produces a profit.

The Diamond–Water Paradox

Early economists such as Adam Smith were puzzled that some essential goods had much lower prices than some unimportant goods. Why would water, essential to life, be priced below diamonds, which have much less usefulness? The paradox is resolved when we consider that water is in great supply relative to demand and thus has a very low price per litre. Diamonds, in contrast, are rare. Their supply is small relative to demand and, as a result, they have a very high price per carat.

Moreover, the marginal utility of the last unit of water consumed is very low. The reason follows from our utility-maximizing rule. Consumers (and producers) respond to the very low price of water by using a great deal of it for generating electricity, irrigating crops, heating buildings, watering lawns, quenching thirst, and so on. Consumption is expanded until marginal utility, which declines as more water is consumed, equals its low price. Conversely, relatively few diamonds are purchased because of their prohibitively high price, meaning that their marginal utility remains high. In equilibrium,

$$\frac{\text{MU of water (low)}}{\text{price of water (low)}} = \frac{\text{MU of diamonds (high)}}{\text{price of diamonds (high)}}$$

Although the marginal utility of the last unit of water consumed is low and the marginal utility of the last diamond purchased is high, the total utility of water is very high and the total utility of diamonds is quite low. The total utility derived from the consumption of water is large because of the enormous amounts of water consumed. Total utility is the sum of the marginal utilities of all the litres of water consumed, including the trillions of litres that have far higher marginal utilities than the last unit consumed. In contrast, the total utility derived from diamonds is low since their high price means relatively few are bought. Thus the diamond–water paradox is solved: water has much more total utility (roughly, usefulness) than diamonds even though the price of diamonds greatly exceeds the price of water. These relative prices relate to marginal utility, not total utility.

connect
ORIGIN OF THE IDEA 6.3
Diamond–Water Paradox

Opportunity Cost and the Value of Time

The theory of consumer choice can be generalized to account for the economic value of *time*. Both consumption and production take time. Time is a valuable economic commodity; by using an hour in productive work, a person can earn $6, $10, $50, or more, depending on education and skills. By using that hour for leisure or in consumption activities, the individual incurs the opportunity cost of forgone income and sacrifices the $6, $10, or $50 that could have been earned by working.

Imagine a self-employed consumer in Victoria named Linden who is considering buying a round of golf and a concert ticket. The market price of the golf game is $30 and that of the ticket is $40, but the golf game takes more time than the concert. Suppose Linden spends four hours on the golf course but only two hours at the concert. If Linden's time is worth $10 per hour as evidenced by the $10 wage obtained by working, then the full price of the golf game is $70 (the $30 market price plus $40 worth of time), while the full price of the concert is $60 (the $40 market price plus $20 worth of time). We find that, contrary to what market prices alone indicate, the full price of the concert is really less than the full price of the golf game.

If we now assume that the marginal utilities derived from successive golf games and concerts are identical, traditional theory would indicate that Linden should consume more golf games than concerts because the market price of golf games ($30) is lower than that of concerts ($40). But when time is taken into account, the situation is reversed and golf games ($70) are more expensive than concerts ($60). So it is rational for Linden to consume more concerts than golf games.

Another example is the consumption of health care services. In Canada, government-sponsored insurance pays the full amount of a doctor's visit. The price the consumer pays is zero. But if we consider the time and cost of travelling to the doctor's office, and the waiting time in the office, the full price is considerably more than zero.

By accounting for the opportunity cost of a consumer's time, we can explain certain phenomena that are otherwise quite puzzling. It may be rational for the unskilled worker or retiree whose time has little market value to ride a bus from Edmonton to Saskatoon, but the corporate executive, whose time is very valuable, will find it cheaper to fly, even though bus fare is only a fraction of plane fare. It is sensible for the retiree, living on a modest income and having ample time, to spend many hours shopping for bargains at the mall or taking long trips in a motor home. It is equally rational for the highly paid physician, working 55 hours per week, to buy a new personal computer over the Internet and take short vacations at expensive resorts.

People in poor nations often conclude that affluent Canadians are wasteful of food and other material goods but overly economical in their use of time. Canadians who visit developing countries may think that time is used casually or squandered, while material goods are very highly prized and carefully used. These differences are not a paradox or a case of radically different temperaments; the differences are primarily a rational reflection that the high productivity of labour in an industrially advanced society gives time a high market value, whereas the opposite is true in a low-income, developing country.

Cash and Noncash Gifts

Marginal utility analysis also helps us understand why people generally prefer cash gifts to non-cash gifts costing the same amount. The reason is simply that the noncash gifts may not match the recipient's preferences and thus may not add as much as cash to total utility. Thought of differently, consumers know their own preferences better than the gift giver does, and the $100 cash gift provides more choices.

Look back at Table 6-1. Suppose Holly has zero earned income but is given the choice of a $2 cash gift or a noncash gift of two apples. Because two apples can be bought with $2, these two gifts are of equal monetary value, but by spending the $2 cash gift on the first orange Holly could obtain 24 utils. The noncash gift of the first two apples would yield only 18 (= 10 + 8) units of utility. Conclusion: The noncash gift yields less utility to the beneficiary than the cash gift.

Since giving of noncash gifts is common, considerable value of those gifts is potentially lost because they do not match their recipients' tastes. For example, Aunt Flo may have paid $15 for the Avril Lavigne CD she gave you for your birthday, but you would pay only $7.50 for it. Thus, a $7.50, or 50 percent, value loss is involved. Multiplied by billions of gifts a year, the total potential loss of value is huge.

But some of that loss is avoided by the creative ways individuals handle the problem. For example, newlyweds set up gift registries for their weddings to help match their wants to the non-cash gifts received. Also, people obtain cash refunds or exchanges for gifts, so they can buy goods that provide more utility. And people have even been known to recycle gifts by giving them to someone else at a later time. All three actions support the proposition that individuals take actions to maximize their total utility.

6.5 Behavioural Economics and Prospect Theory ::

Up to this point, we have restricted ourselves to dealing with consumer-choice situations in which people only have to deal with "goods" as opposed to "bads." When deciding how to spend a budget, people only consider items that can bring them positive marginal utility—that is, "good" things. They then use the utility-maximizing rule to select how much of each of those good things they should consume to get as much utility as possible from their limited budgets.

Unfortunately, life often forces us to deal with bad things, too. Our houses may burn down. A potential investment may go bad. The money we lend out may not be repaid. How people deal with these negative possibilities is a central focus of **behavioural economics**—the branch of economics that combines insights from economics, psychology, and neuroscience to better understand those situations in which actual choice behaviour deviates from the predictions made by earlier theories, which incorrectly concluded that people were *always* rational, deliberate, and unswayed by emotions. By studying how people actually deal with the prospect of bad things as

behavioural economics
The branch of economics that combines insights from economics, psychology, and neuroscience to better understand those situations in which actual choice behaviour deviates from the predictions made by earlier theories.

well as good things, behavioural economists discovered three very interesting facts about how people react to goods and bads:

status quo
The current situation from which gains and losses are calculated.

- People judge good things and bad things in relative terms, as gains and losses relative to their current situation or **status quo.**

- People experience both diminishing marginal utility for gains (as you have already seen) as well as diminishing marginal disutility for losses (meaning that each successive unit of loss hurts, but less painfully than the previous unit).

loss averse
A characteristic that makes losses feel more intense than the pleasure generated by gains.

- People are **loss averse,** meaning that for losses and gains near the status quo, losses are felt *much* more intensely than gains—in fact, about 2.5 times more intensely. Thus, for instance, the pain experienced by an investor who loses one dollar from his current status quo level of wealth will be about 2.5 times more intense than the pleasure he would have felt if he had gained one dollar relative to his current level of wealth.

prospect theory
An explanation of how consumers plan for and deal with life's ups and downs, as well as of why they often appear narrow minded and fail to "see the big picture."

These three facts about how people deal with goods and bads form the basis of **prospect theory,** which sheds important light on how consumers plan for and deal with life's ups and downs, as well as on why they often appear narrow minded and fail to "see the big picture." To give you an idea of how powerful prospect theory is—and why its pioneer Daniel Kahneman was awarded the Nobel Prize in Economics—let's go through some examples of consumer behaviour that would be hard to explain without the insights provided by prospect theory.

Losses and Shrinking Packages

Because people see the world in terms of gains and losses relative to the status quo situations that they are used to, businesses have to be very careful about increasing the prices they charge for their products. Once consumers become used to a given price, they will view any increase in the price as a loss relative to the status quo price they were accustomed to.

The fact that consumers may view a price increase as a loss explains the otherwise very curious fact that many food producers react to rising input costs by shrinking the sizes of their products. The company most famous for doing this was Hershey's Chocolates, which during its first decades of operation about 100 years ago would always charge exactly 5 cents for one of its Hershey's Chocolate Bars. But the size of the bars would increase or decrease depending on the cost of the company's inputs. When the cost of raw materials rose, the company would keep the price fixed at 5 cents but decrease the size of the bar. When the cost of raw materials fell, it would again keep the price fixed at 5 cents but increase the size of the bar.

This seems rather bizarre when you consider that consumers were not in any way *actually* being shielded from the changes in input prices. That is because what should rationally matter to consumers is the price per ounce that they are paying for Hershey's Chocolate Bars. And that *does* go up and down when the price remains fixed but the size of the bars changes.

But people aren't being fully rational here. They mentally fixate on the product's price because that is the characteristic that they are used to focusing on when making their purchasing decisions. And because the 5-cent price had become the status quo, Hershey's understood that any price increase would be mentally categorized as a loss. Thus, Hershey's wisely chose to keep the price of its product fixed at 5 cents even when input prices were rising.

Other companies employ the same strategy today. In 2008, the prices of many raw materials including sugar, wheat, and corn rose substantially. Many major manufacturers reacted by reducing product sizes while keeping prices fixed. Kellogg's reduced the size of its Frosted Flakes and Rice Krispies cereal boxes. Frito-Lay also reduced Doritos bags and Dial Soap bars shrank slightly. And Proctor and Gamble reduced the size of Bounty paper towel rolls from 60 to 52 sheets.

Framing Effects and Advertising

Because people evaluate situations in terms of gains and losses, their decision-making can be very sensitive to the *mental frame* that they use to evaluate whether a possible outcome should be

CONSIDER THIS :: Rising Consumption and the Hedonic Treadmill

For many sensations, people's brains are wired to notice changes rather than states. For example, your brain can sense acceleration—your change in speed—but not speed itself. As a result, standing still feels the same as moving at a constant 50 kilometres per hour. And if you accelerate from one constant speed to another—say, from 50 kilometres per hour to 70 kilometres per hour—you will feel the acceleration only while it's happening. Once you settle down at the new higher speed, it will feel like you are standing still again.

Consumption appears to work in much the same way. If you are used to a given level of consumption—say, $50,000 per year—then you will get a lot of enjoyment for a while if your consumption accelerates to $100,000 per year. But, as time passes, you will get used to that higher level of consumption, so that $100,000 per year seems ordinary and doesn't bring you any more pleasure than $50,000 per year used to bring you when it was your status quo.

Economist Richard Easterlin coined the term *hedonic treadmill* (pleasure treadmill) to describe this phenomenon. Just as a person walking on a real treadmill gets nowhere, people trying to make themselves permanently happier by consuming more also get nowhere because they end up getting used to any higher level of consumption. Indeed, except for the extremely poor, people across the income spectrum report similar levels of happiness and satisfaction with their lives. This has led several economists including Robert Frank to argue that we should all stop trying to consume more since doing so doesn't make us any happier in the long run. What do you think? Should we all step off of the hedonic treadmill?

viewed as a gain or a loss. Here are a couple of examples in which differences in the context or "frame" change the perception of whether a situation should be treated as a gain or loss. See how you react to them.

- Would you be happy with a salary of $100,000 per year? You might say yes. But what if your salary last year had been $140,000? Are you still going to say yes? Now that you know you are taking a $40,000 pay cut, does that $100,000 salary seem as good as it did before?

- Similarly, suppose you have a part-time job. One day, your boss, Joe, walks in and says that he is going to give you a 10 percent raise. Would that please you? Now, what if he also mentioned that *everyone else* at your firm would be getting a 15 percent raise? Are you still going to be just as pleased? Or does your raise now seem like a loss compared to what everyone else will be getting?

framing effects
Changes in people's preferences that are caused by new information that alters the frame used to define whether situations are gains or losses.

Changes in people's preferences that are caused by new information that alters the frame used to define whether situations are gains or losses are referred to as **framing effects.** These are important to recognize because they can be manipulated by advertisers, lawyers, and politicians to try to alter people's decisions. For instance, would an advertising company be better off marketing a particular brand of hamburger as "20 percent fat" or as "80 percent lean"? Both phrases describe the same meat, but one frames the situation as a loss (20 percent fat) while the other frames it as a gain (80 percent lean).

And would you be more willing to take a particular medicine if you were told that 99.9 percent of the people who take it live, or if you were told that 0.1 percent of the people who take it die? Continuing to live is a gain, whereas dying is clearly a loss. Which frame sounds better to you?

Finally, note that framing effects have important consequences for the utility-maximizing rule that we studied earlier in this chapter. If a frame alters people's valuations of marginal utility, it *will* affect their consumption decisions!

Anchoring and Credit Card Bills

Before people can calculate their gains and losses, they must first define the status quo from which to measure those changes. But it turns out that irrelevant information can unconsciously influence people's feelings about the *status quo*. Here's a striking example. Find a group of people and ask each person to write down the last two digits of his or her Social Insurance Number. Then ask each person to write down his or her best estimate of the value of some object that you display to them—say, a nice cordless keyboard. What you will find is that the people whose Social Insurance Numbers end in higher numbers—say, 67 or 89—will give higher estimates for the value of the keyboard than people whose Social Insurance Numbers end in smaller numbers like 18 or 37. The effect can be huge, as shown by an experiment in the United States (where Social Security Numbers are the equivalent of the Canadian Social Insurance Number). Among students in one MBA class at the Massachusetts Institute of Technology, those with Social Security Numbers ending between 80 and 99 gave average estimates of $56 for a cordless keyboard while their classmates whose Social Security Numbers ended in numbers from 00 to 20 gave average estimates of just $16.

anchoring
The idea that irrelevant information can unconsciously influence people's feelings about the status quo.

Psychologists and behavioural economists refer to this phenomenon as **anchoring** because people's estimates about the value of the keyboard are influenced, or "anchored," by the recently considered information about the last two digits of their Social Insurance or Social Security Numbers. Why irrelevant information can anchor subsequent valuations is not fully understood. But the anchoring effect is real and can lead people to unconsciously alter how they evaluate different options.

Unfortunately, credit card companies have figured this out. They use anchoring to increase their profits by showing very small minimum-payment amounts on borrowers' monthly credit card statements. The companies could require larger minimum payments, but the minimum-payment numbers that they present are only typically about 2 percent of what a customer owes. Why such a small amount? Because it acts as an anchor that causes people to unconsciously make smaller payments each month. This can make a huge difference in how long it takes to pay off their bill and how much in total interest they will end up paying. For a customer who owes $1000 on a credit card that charges the typical interest rate of 19 percent per year, it will take 22 years and $3398.12 in total payments (including accumulated interest) to pay off the debt if he only makes 2 percent monthly payments. By showing such small minimum-payment amounts, credit card companies anchor many customers into the expensive habit of paying off their debts slowly rather than quickly.

Mental Accounting and Overpriced Warranties

The utility-maximizing rule assumes that people will look at all of their potential consumption options simultaneously when trying to maximize the total utility that they can get from spending their limited incomes. But economist Richard Thaler famously noted that people sometimes look at consumption options in isolation, thereby irrationally failing to look at all their options simultaneously. Thaler coined the term **mental accounting** to describe this behaviour because it was as if people arbitrarily put certain options into totally separate "mental accounts" that they dealt with without any thought to options outside of those accounts. An example of where this suboptimal tendency leads is the warranties that patrons of big electronics stores are offered when they purchase an expensive product, such as a plasma TV that costs $1000. These warranties are very much overpriced given that the products they insure hardly ever break down. Personal financial experts universally tell people not to buy them. Yet, many people do buy them because they engage in mental accounting.

mental accounting
The idea that people sometimes look at consumption options in isolation, thereby irrationally failing to look at all of their options simultaneously.

They do this by mentally labelling their purchase of the TV as an isolated, individual transaction, sticking it into a separate mental account in their brain that might have a title like, "Purchase of New TV." Viewing the purchase in isolation exaggerates the size of the potential loss that would come from a broken TV. Customers who view the transaction in isolation see the possibility of a $1000 loss on their $1000 purchase as a potential total loss—"Holy cow! I could lose $1000 on a

$1000 TV!" By contrast, people who see the big picture compare the potential loss with their entire future income stream—thereby seeing it correctly as a relatively minor loss. Because of this difference, mental accounting inclines people to pay for overpriced warranties.

The Endowment Effect and Market Transactions

endowment effect
The tendency that people have to put a higher valuation on anything that they currently possess (are endowed with) than on identical items that they do not.

Prospect theory also offers an explanation for the **endowment effect,** which is the tendency that people have to put a higher valuation on anything that they currently possess (are endowed with) than on identical items that they do not own but might purchase. For instance, if we show a person a new coffee mug and ask him what the maximum amount is that he would pay to buy it, he might say $10. But if we then give the mug to him so that he now owns it, and we then ask how much we would have to pay him to buy it back, he will very likely report a much higher value—say, $15.

The interesting thing is that he is not just bluffing or driving a hard bargain. Human brains appear wired to do this, to put a higher value on things we own than on things we don't. Economist John List has shown that this tendency can moderate if people are used to buying things for resale—that is buying them with the intention of getting rid of them—but without such experience the endowment effect can be quite strong. If it is, it can make market transactions between buyers and sellers harder because sellers will be demanding higher prices for the items they are selling ("Hey, *my* mug is worth $15 to me!") than the values put on those items by potential buyers ("Dude, *your* mug is only worth $10 to me").

Several researchers have pointed to the fact that human beings are loss averse as providing an explanation for the endowment effect. Once a person possesses something, the thought of parting with it seems like a potential loss. And because potential losses are felt so intensely (2.5 times more intensely than potential gains), the owners of items end up demanding a lot of money as compensation when asked to sell their property. The potential purchasers, on the other hand, do not own the property and thus do not feel any potential sense of loss. So they put lower valuations on the items in question than do the sellers.

The **LAST WORD**   Nudging People Toward Better Decisions

*Behavioural economists have recently found success in using people's behavioural quirks to "nudge" them toward making better decisions.**

Behavioural economics began as a descriptive science, meaning that its first goal was to develop theories that accurately described human economic behaviour. In particular, it sought to explain a number of behaviours that at first glance seemed irrational. Now that behavioural economics has made significant headway in explaining many of those behaviours, its insights are beginning to be put to use developing policies that can work with those tendencies to nudge people toward choices that are better for themselves and others.

A key feature of "nudges" is that they are subtle. This subtlety means that nudges can cause large changes in behaviour without making people feel bullied or coerced—and also without imposing stringent new rules or having to offer people big monetary incentives or disincentives to get them to do what you want.

Take retirement savings. As you may know, people tend to consume too much in the present and therefore undersave for retirement. But as it turns out, this unfortunate behavioural tendency can be very easily offset by

another behavioural tendency: the tendency people have to stick with default options. In terms of retirement savings, this comes down to designing corporate retirement programs in which each worker is "defaulted into" her company's retirement savings program.

Under those savings programs, money is automatically deducted each month from a worker's paycheque and

* The term "nudge" was popularized by Richard Thaler and Cass Sunstein in their book *Nudge: Improving Decisions about Health, Wealth, and Happiness,* Yale University Press, 2008.

deposited in her retirement savings account. It used to be the case that the default for such programs was for workers to start out *not* enrolled in them. To get enrolled, they would have to request to join the program. That is, they would have to choose to go against the default option of not being enrolled. And because people have the behavioural tendency of sticking with whatever option is presented to them as the default, relatively few workers would make the change and enroll in their company's savings program. That was disappointing. But instead of being deterred, behavioural economists saw an opportunity.

Why not change the default? Why not do just the opposite and have the default be automatic enrollment? By making that change, people's tendency to stick with default options would work in their own favour—they would stay enrolled and save money for retirement. When this strategy of switching the default was actually implemented, the number of workers participating in retirement savings programs skyrocketed—jumping from 60 percent to 98 percent. Those workers can now look forward to much more pleasant retirements thanks to this simple change that works *with* people's preference to stick with default options.

People's tendency to look around them for social cues as to what

constitutes good behaviour can also be exploited to modify their consumption behaviour. But you have to be careful about how you do it, as was discovered by a California power company that wanted to encourage its customers to conserve electricity. Its first attempt to use social cues involved sending each customer a bill that showed not only his or her own usage of electricity in kilowatt-hours, but also the average usage of nearby houses. The company hoped that by showing the average usage of neighbours, customers would receive a subtle hint about their own usage. In particular, it was hoped that customers who used more than their neighbours would feel that they were being wasteful and would thus cut back on their usage.

And that did indeed happen. *But,* their reduction in electricity usage ended up being completely swamped by an increase in electricity usage on the part of the customers who had previously been below-average users.

Those customers interpreted the new information that they were below-average electricity users to mean that they should feel free to consume more. After all, why should they use so little when their neighbours were using so much more?

The power company finally hit upon a solution that worked. Smilies. Yes, symbols like ☺ and ☹. In addition to printing people's own usage and the average usage of their neighbours, the company also started printing a ☺ on a customer's bill if his usage was below average and a ☹ on his bill if his usage was above average. The unhappy smilies embarrassed the heavy users into reducing their consumption even more while the happy smilies gave a pat on the back to the light users—a pat on the back that kept their usage low.

Bear in mind that both the electricity customers and the workers saving for retirement were being *manipulated* by the people who designed the nudges. This fact is perhaps even more disturbing when you consider that the changes in behaviour that were caused by the nudges were most likely *unconscious* on the part of those being manipulated. Keep this in mind as you consider for yourself when and if it is morally or ethically acceptable to use nudges to guide people's behaviour.

Question

What do you think of the ethics of using unconscious nudges to alter people's behaviour? Before you answer, consider the following argument made by economists Richard Thaler and Cass Sunstein, who favour the use of nudges. They argue that in most situations we couldn't avoid nudging even if we wanted to because whatever policy we choose will contain some set of unconscious nudges and incentives that will influence people. Thus, they say, we might as well choose the wisest set of nudges.

:: CHAPTER SUMMARY

6.1 :: THE LAW OF DIMINISHING MARGINAL UTILITY

- The law of diminishing marginal utility states that, beyond a certain quantity, additional units of a specific good will yield declining amounts of extra satisfaction to a consumer.

6.2 :: THE THEORY OF CONSUMER CHOICE

- The utility-maximizing model assumes that the typical consumer is rational and acts based on well-defined preferences. Because income is limited and goods have prices, consumers cannot purchase all the goods and services they might want. Consumers therefore select the attainable combination of goods that maximizes their utility or satisfaction.

- A consumer's utility is maximized when income is allocated so that the last dollar spent on each product purchased yields the same amount of extra satisfaction. Algebraically, the utility-maximizing rule is fulfilled when the consumer's total income is spent and

$$\frac{MU \text{ of product A}}{\text{price of A}} = \frac{Mu \text{ of product B}}{\text{price of B}}$$

6.3 :: UTILITY MAXIMIZATION AND THE DEMAND CURVE

- The utility-maximizing rule and the demand curve are logically consistent. Because marginal utility declines, a lower price is needed to induce the consumer to buy more of a particular product.

- The utility-maximization model illuminates the income and substitution effects of a price change. The income effect implies that a decline in the price of a product increases the consumer's real income and enables the consumer to buy more of that product with a fixed money income. The substitution effect implies that a lower price makes a product relatively more attractive and therefore increases the consumer's willingness to substitute it for other products.

6.4 :: APPLICATIONS AND EXTENSIONS

- The theory of consumer choice can be used to explain real-world phenomena. For example, consumers have switched from CD players to iPods because the new product succeeded in enhancing consumers' total utility. And the price of diamonds is high compared to the price of water because it is the marginal utility (MU) of diamonds that is high, and it is MU, not total utility, that determines what people are prepared to pay for an item.

6.5 :: BEHAVIOURAL ECONOMICS AND PROSPECT THEORY

- Behavioural economics explains many consumption behaviours including why irrelevant information can anchor valuations, how people value possibilities in terms of gains and losses relative to a status quo, and how framing effects can change people's decisions by affecting whether particular consumption possibilities seem like gains or losses.

:: TERMS AND CONCEPTS

law of diminishing marginal utility, p. 140
total utility, p. 140
marginal utility, p. 140
rational behaviour, p. 143
budget constraint, p. 143

utility-maximizing rule, p. 143
income effect, p. 147
substitution effect, p. 147
behavioural economics, 150
status quo, p. 151
loss averse, p. 151

prospect theory, p. 151
framing effects, p. 152
anchoring, p. 153
mental accounting, p. 153
endowment effect, p. 154

:: QUESTIONS

1. Complete the following table and answer the questions. [LO6.1]

   a. At which rate is total utility increasing: a constant rate, a decreasing rate, or an increasing rate? How do you know?

   b. "A rational consumer will purchase only one unit of the product represented by these data, since that amount maximizes marginal utility." Do you agree? Explain why or why not.

   c. "It is possible that a rational consumer will not purchase any units of the product represented by these data." Do you agree? Explain why or why not.

Units consumed	Total utility	Marginal utility
0	0	
1	10	10
2	—	8
3	25	—
4	30	—
5	—	3
6	34	—

2. Mrs. Simpson buys loaves of bread and litres of milk each week at prices of $1 and $0.80, respectively. At present she is buying these two products in amounts such that the marginal utilities from the last units purchased of the two products are 80 and 70 utils, respectively. Is she buying the utility-maximizing combination of bread and milk? If not, how should she reallocate her expenditures between the two goods? [**LO6.2**]

3. How can time be incorporated into the theory of consumer behaviour? Explain the following comment: "Want to make millions of dollars? Devise a product that saves Canadians lots of time." [**LO6.2, 6.4**]

4. Explain what is meant by the following statements: [**LO6.2**]

   a. Before economic growth, there were too few goods; after growth, there is too little time.

   b. It is irrational for an individual to take the time to be completely rational in economic decision making.

   c. Telling your spouse where you would like to go out to eat for your birthday makes sense in terms of utility maximization.

5. In the last decade or so there has been a dramatic expansion of small retail convenience stores (such as Mac's, 7-Eleven, Becker's, etc.) although their prices are generally much higher than prices in large supermarkets. What explains the success of the convenience stores? [**LO6.2**]

6. Many apartment-complex owners are installing water meters for each apartment and billing the occupants according to the amount of water they use, in contrast to the former procedure of having a central meter for the entire complex and dividing up the water expense as part of the rent. Where individual meters have been installed, water usage has declined 10–40 percent. Explain that drop, referring to price and marginal utility. [**LO6.3, 6.4**]

7. Using the utility-maximizing rule as your point of reference, explain the income and substitution effects of an increase in the price of product B with no change in the price of product A. [**LO6.3**]

8. **ADVANCED ANALYSIS** A mathematically "fair bet" is one in which a gambler bets, say, $100 for a 10 percent chance to win $1000 ($100 = 0.10 × $1000). Assuming diminishing marginal utility of dollars, explain why this is *not* a fair bet in terms of utility. Why is it an even less fair bet when the house takes a cut of each dollar bet? So is gambling irrational? [**LO6.3**]

9. Suppose that Ike is loss averse. In the morning, Ike's stock-broker calls to tell him that he has gained $1000 on his stock portfolio. In the evening, his accountant calls to tell him that he owes an extra $1000 in taxes. At the end of the day, does Ike feel emotionally neutral since the dollar value of the gain in his stock portfolio exactly offsets the amount of extra taxes he has to pay? Explain. [**LO6.5**]

10. You just accepted a job helping to raise money for your school's athletic program. You are told to draft a fund-raising letter. The bottom of the letter asks recipients to write down a donation amount. If you want to raise as much money as possible, would it be better to mention that your school is Number 3 in the nation in sports, or that you are better than 99 percent of other schools at sports? Explain. [**LO6.5**]

:: PROBLEMS

1. Miley's total utility from singing the same song over and over is 50 utils after one repetition, 90 utils after two repetitions, 70 utils after three repetitions, 20 utils after four repetitions, –50 utils after five repetitions, and –200 utils after six repetitions. Write down her marginal utility for each repetition. Once Miley's total utility begins to decrease, does each additional repetition of the song hurt more than the previous one or less than the previous one? [**LO6.1**]

2. John likes Coca-Cola. After consuming one Coke, John has a total utility of 10 utils. After two Cokes, he has a total utility of 25 utils. After three Cokes, he has a total utility of 50 utils. Does John show decreasing or increasing marginal utility for Coke? Suppose that John has $3 in his pocket. If Cokes cost $1 each and John is willing to spend one of his dollars on purchasing a first can of Coke, would he spend his second dollar on a Coke, too? What about the third dollar? If John's marginal utility for Coke keeps on increasing no matter how many Cokes he drinks, would it be fair to say that he is addicted to Coke? [**LO6.1**]

3. Suppose that Omar's marginal utility for cups of coffee is constant at 1.5 utils per cup no matter how many cups he drinks. On the other hand, his marginal utility per doughnut is 10 utils for the first doughnut he eats, 9 utils for the second, 8 utils for the third, and so on (that is, declining by 1 util per additional doughnut). In addition, suppose that coffee costs $1 per cup, doughnuts cost $1 each, and Omar has a budget that he can spend only on doughnuts, coffee, or both. How big would that budget have to be before he would spend a dollar buying a first cup of coffee? [**LO6.2**]

4. Columns 1 through 4 in the table on the following page the marginal utility, measured in utils, that Ricardo would get by purchasing various amounts of products A, B, C, and D. Column 5 shows the marginal utility Ricardo gets from saving. Assume that the prices of A, B, C, and D are $18, $6, $4, and $24, respectively, and that Ricardo has an income of $106. [**LO6.2**]

   a. What quantities of A, B, C, and D will Ricardo purchase in maximizing his utility?

   b. How many dollars will Ricardo choose to save?

Column 1		Column 2		Column 3		Column 4		Column 5	
Units of A	MU	Units of B	MU	Units of C	MU	Units of D	MU	Number of dollars saved	MU
1	72	1	24	1	15	1	36	1	5
2	54	2	15	2	12	2	30	2	4
3	45	3	12	3	8	3	24	3	3
4	36	4	9	4	7	4	18	4	2
5	27	5	7	5	5	5	13	5	1
6	18	6	5	6	4	6	7	6	½
7	15	7	2	7	3½	7	4	7	¼
8	12	8	1	8	3	8	2	8	⅛

c. Check your answers by substituting them into the algebraic statement of the utility-maximizing rule.

5. You are choosing between two goods, X and Y, and your marginal utility from each is as shown below. If your income is $9 and the prices of X and Y are $2 and $1, respectively, what quantities of each will you purchase to maximize utility? What total utility will you realize? Assume that, other things remaining unchanged, the price of X falls to $1. What quantities of X and Y will you now purchase? Using the two prices and quantities for X, derive a demand schedule (a table showing prices and quantities demanded) for X. [LO6.3]

Units of X	MU_X	Units of Y	MU_Y
1	10	1	8
2	8	2	7
3	6	3	6
4	4	4	5
5	3	5	4
6	2	6	3

6. **ADVANCED ANALYSIS** Let $MU_A = z = 10 - x$ and $MU_B = z = 21 - 2y$, where z is marginal utility per dollar measured in utils, x is the amount spent on product A, and y is the amount spent on product B. Assume that the consumer has $10 to spend on A and B—that is, $x + y = 10$. How is the $10 best allocated between A and B? How much utility will the marginal dollar yield? [LO6.3]

7. Suppose that with a budget of $100, Deborah spends $60 on sushi and $40 on bagels when sushi costs $2 per piece and bagels cost $2 per bagel. But then, after the price of bagels falls to $1 per bagel, she spends $50 on sushi and $50 on bagels. How many pieces of sushi and how many bagels did Deborah consume before the price change? At the new prices, how much money would it have cost Deborah to buy those same quantities (the ones that she consumed before the price change)? Given that it used to take Deborah's entire $100 to buy those quantities, how big is the income effect caused by the reduction in the price of bagels? [LO6.3]

connect **Practice and Learn Online with Connect**

Connect allows you to practice important concepts at your own pace and on your own schedule, with 24/7 online access to an eBook, algorithmic questions and problems from the textbook, video and logic cases, graphing tutorials, flashcards, Internet exercises, key graphs, and more.

Appendix to Chapter 6

A6.1 Indifference Curve Analysis

The utility-maximizing rule requires individuals to measure and compare utility, much as a business would measure and compare costs or revenues. Such *cardinal utility* is measured in units such as 1, 2, 3, 4, etc., and can be added, subtracted, multiplied, and divided, just like the cardinal numbers in mathematics. More importantly, cardinal utility allows us to precisely quantify the marginal utilities upon which the utility-maximizing rule depends. In fact, the marginal-utility theory of consumer demand that we explained in the body of this chapter rests squarely on the assumption that economists are able to measure cardinal utility. However, measuring cardinal utility in real people is nearly impossible. (Can you, for instance, state exactly how many utils you are getting from reading this book right now, or how many utils you would get from watching a sunset?) As a result, economists have developed an alternative explanation of consumer choice and equilibrium in which such measurement is not required. In this more advanced analysis, the consumer must simply *rank* various combinations of goods in terms of preference. For instance, Sally can simply report that she *prefers* four units of A to six units of B without having to put number values on how much she likes either option. The model of consumer choice that is based on such *ordinal utility* rankings is called indifference curve analysis. It has two main elements: budget lines and indifference curves.

The Budget Line: What Is Attainable

We know from Chapter 1 that a **budget line** (or, more technically, a *budget constraint*) is a schedule or curve showing various combinations of two products a consumer can purchase with a specific money income. If the price of product A is $1.50 and the price of product B is $1.00, a consumer could purchase all the combinations of A and B shown in the table of Figure A6-1 with $12 of money income. At one extreme, the consumer might spend all the income on eight units of A and have nothing left to spend on B. Or, by giving up two units of A and thereby freeing $3, the consumer could have six units of A and three of B. At the other extreme, the consumer could buy 12 units of B at $1.00 each, spending his or her entire money income on B with nothing left to spend on A.

Figure A6-1 also shows the budget line graphically. Note that the graph is not restricted to whole units of A and B as is the table. Every point on the graph represents a possible combination of A and B, including fractional quantities. The slope of the graphed budget line measures the ratio of the price of B

FIGURE A6-1 **A Consumer's Budget Line**

The budget line shows all the combinations of any two products that can be purchased given the prices of the products and the consumer's money income.

Units of A (price = $1.50)	Units of B (price = $1.00)	Total expenditure
8	0	$12 (= $12 + $0)
6	3	$12 (= $9 + $3)
4	6	$12 (= $6 + $6)
2	9	$12 (= $3 + $9)
0	12	$12 (= $0 + $12)

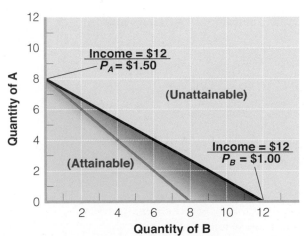

to the price of A; more precisely, the absolute value of the slope is P_B/P_A = $1.00/$1.50 = 2/3. This is the mathematical way of saying that the consumer must forgo two units of A (measured on the vertical axis) to buy three units of B (measured on the horizontal axis). In moving down the budget or price line, two units of A (at $1.50 each) must be given up to obtain three more units of B (at $1.00 each). This yields a slope of 2/3.

The budget line has two other significant characteristics:

1. *Income Changes* The location of the budget line varies with money income. An increase in money income shifts the budget line to the right; a decrease in money income shifts it to the left. To verify this, recalculate the table in Figure A6-1, assuming that money income is (a) $24 and (b) $6, and plot the new budget lines.

2. *Price Changes* A change in product prices also shifts the budget line. A decline in the prices of both products— the equivalent of an increase in real income—shifts the curve to the right. (You can verify this by recalculating the table in Figure A6-1 and replotting the graph, assuming that P_A = $0.75 and P_B = $0.50.) Conversely, an increase in the prices of A and B shifts the curve to the left. (Assume P_A = $3 and P_B = $2 and rework the table and the graph to substantiate this statement.)

Note what happens if P_B changes while P_A and money income remain constant. In particular, if P_B drops, say from $1.00 to $0.50, the lower end of the budget line fans outward to the right. Conversely, if P_B increases, say, from $1.00 to $1.50, the lower end of the line fans inward to the left as illustrated in Figure A6-1. In both instances the line remains anchored at eight units on the vertical axis because P_A has not changed.

Indifference Curves: What Is Preferred

Budget lines reflect objective market data, specifically income and prices. They reveal combinations of products A and B that can be purchased given current money income and prices.

Indifference curves, on the other hand, reflect subjective information about consumer preferences for A and B. An **indifference curve** shows all the combinations of two products A and B that will yield the same total satisfaction or total utility to a consumer. Figure A6-2 presents a hypothetical indifference curve for products A and B. The consumer's subjective preferences are such that he or she will realize the same total utility from each combination of A and B shown in the table or on the curve. The consumer will be indifferent (will not care) as to which combination is actually obtained.

Indifference curves have several important characteristics.

INDIFFERENCE CURVES SLOPE DOWNWARD

An indifference curve slopes downward because more of one product means less of the other if total utility is to remain unchanged. Suppose the consumer moves from one combination of A and B to another, say, from j to k in Figure A6-2. In so doing, the consumer obtains more of product B, increasing total utility. But because total utility is the same everywhere on the curve, the consumer must give up some of the other product, A, to reduce total utility by a precisely offsetting amount. Thus more of B necessitates less of A, and the quantities of A and B are inversely related. A curve that reflects inversely related variables is downsloping.

FIGURE A6-2   **A Consumer's Indifference Curve**

Every point on indifference curve I represents some combination of products A and B, and all those combinations are equally satisfactory to the consumer. That is, each combination of A and B on the curve yields the same total utility.

Combination	Units of A	Units of B
j	12	2
k	6	4
l	4	6
m	3	8

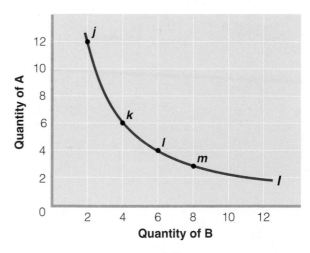

INDIFFERENCE CURVES ARE CONVEX TO THE ORIGIN

MATH A6.1
The Marginal Rate of Substitution

Recall from the appendix to Chapter 1 that the slope of a curve at a particular point is measured by drawing a straight line that is tangent to that point and then measuring the "rise over run" of the straight line. If you drew such straight lines for several points on the curve in Figure A6-2, you would find that their slopes decline (in absolute terms) as you move down the curve. Technically, the slope of the indifference curve at each point measures the **marginal rate of substitution (MRS)** of the combination represented by that point. The slope or MRS shows the rate at which the consumer who possesses that combination must substitute one good for the other (say, B for A) to remain equally satisfied. The diminishing slope of the indifference curve means that the willingness to substitute B for A diminishes as more of B is obtained.

The rationale for this convexity—that is, for a diminishing MRS—is that consumers' subjective willingness to substitute B for A (or A for B) will depend on the amounts of B and A they have to begin with. Consider Figure A6-2 again, beginning at point *j*. Here, in relative terms, the consumer has a substantial amount of A and very little of B. Within this combination, a unit of B is very valuable (that is, its marginal utility is high), while a unit of A is less valuable (its marginal utility is low). The consumer will then be willing to give up a substantial amount of A to get, say, 2 more units of B. In this case, the consumer is willing to forgo 6 units of A to get 2 more units of B; the MRS is 6/2, or 3, for the *j* segment of the curve.

But at point *k* the consumer has less A and more B. Here A is somewhat more valuable and B less valuable at the margin. In a move from point *k* to point *l*, the consumer is willing to give up only 2 units of A to get 2 more units of B, so the MRS is only 2/2, or 1. Having still less of A and more of B at point *l*, the consumer is willing to give up only 1 unit of A in return for 2 more units of B and the MRS falls to 1/2 between points *l* and *m*.[2]

In general, as the amount of B *increases*, the marginal utility of additional units of B *decreases*. Similarly, as the quantity of A *decreases*, its marginal utility *increases*. In Figure A6-2 we see that in moving down the curve, the consumer will be willing to give up smaller and smaller amounts of A to offset acquiring each additional unit of B. The result is a curve with a diminishing slope, a curve that is convex to the origin. The MRS declines as one moves southeast along the indifference curve.

[2] MRS declines continuously between *j* and *k*, *k* and *l*, and *l* and *m*. Our numerical values for MRS relate to the curve segments between points and are not the actual values of the MRS at each point. For example, the MRS *at* point *l* is 2/3.

FIGURE A6-3 An Indifference Map

An indifference map is a set of indifference curves. Curves farther from the origin indicate higher levels of total utility. Thus, any combination of products A and B represented by a point on I_4 has greater total utility than any combination of A and B represented by a point on I_3, I_2, and I_1.

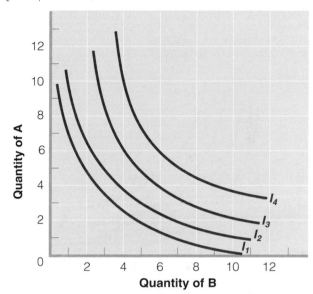

The Indifference Map

The single indifference curve of Figure A6-2 reflects some constant (but unspecified) level of total utility or satisfaction. It is possible and useful to sketch a whole series of indifference curves or an **indifference map**, as shown in Figure A6-3. Each curve reflects a different level of total utility and therefore never crosses another indifference curve. Specifically, each curve to the right of our original curve (labelled I_3 in Figure A6-3) reflects combinations of A and B that yield more utility than I_3. Each curve to the left of I_3 reflects less total utility than I_3. As we move out from the origin, each successive indifference curve represents a higher level of total utility. To demonstrate this fact, draw a line in a northeasterly direction from the origin; note that its points of intersection with successive curves entail larger amounts of both A and B and, therefore, higher levels of total utility.

Equilibrium at Tangency

Since the axes in Figures A6-1 and A6-3 are identical, we can superimpose a budget line on the consumer's indifference map, as shown in Figure A6-4. By definition, the budget line indicates all the combinations of A and B that the consumer can attain with his or her money income given the prices of A and B. Of these attainable combinations, the consumer will

The Consumer's Equilibrium Position

The consumer's equilibrium position is represented by point *X*, where the black budget line is tangent to indifference curve *I₃*. The consumer buys four units of A at $1.50 per unit and six of B at $1.00 per unit with a $12 money income. Points *Z* and *Y* represent attainable combinations of A and B that yield less total utility, as is evidenced by the fact that they are on lower indifference curves. Point *W* would entail more utility than *X*, but it requires a greater income than the $12 represented by the budget line.

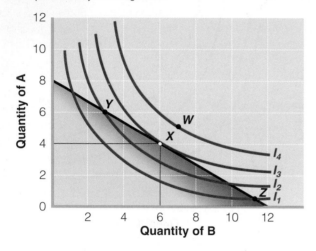

prefer that combination that yields the greatest satisfaction or utility. Specifically, the utility-maximizing combination will be the combination lying on the highest attainable indifference curve. It is called the consumer's **equilibrium position.**

In Figure A6-4 the consumer's equilibrium position is at point *X*, where the budget line is *tangent* to I_3. Why not point *Y*? Because *Y* is on a lower indifference curve, I_2. By moving down the budget line—by shifting dollars from purchases of A to purchases of B—the consumer can attain an indifference curve farther from the origin and thereby increase the total utility from the same income. Why not point *Z*? For the same reason as for *Y*: point *Z* is on a lower indifference curve, I_1. By moving up the budget line—by reallocating dollars from B to A—the consumer can get on the higher indifference curve I_3 and increase total utility.

How about point *W* on indifference curve I_4? While it is true that *W* would yield a greater total utility than *X*, point *W* is beyond (outside) the budget line and, hence, is *not* attainable by the consumer. Point *X* represents the optimal *attainable* combination of products A and B. Note that, according to the definition of tangency, the slope of the highest attainable indifference curve equals the slope of the budget line. Because the slope of the indifference curve reflects the MRS (marginal

rate of substitution) and the slope of the budget line is P_B/P_A, the consumer's optimal or equilibrium position is the point where

$$\text{MRS} = \frac{P_B}{P_A}$$

(You may benefit from trying to answer *Appendix Question 3* at this time.)

Equivalency at Equilibrium

As indicated at the beginning of this appendix, there is an important difference between the marginal utility theory of consumer demand and the indifference curve theory. The marginal utility theory assumes that utility is *numerically* measurable; that is, that the consumer can say how much extra utility he or she derives from each extra unit of A or B. The consumer needs that information to realize the utility-maximizing (equilibrium) position, as indicated by

$$\frac{\text{marginal utility of A}}{\text{price of A}} = \frac{\text{marginal utility of B}}{\text{price of B}}$$

The indifference curve approach imposes a less stringent requirement on the consumer, who need only specify whether a particular combination of A and B will yield more, less, or the same amount of utility than some other combination of A and B. The consumer need only say, for example, that six units of A and seven of B will yield more (or less) satisfaction than four of A and nine of B. Indifference curve theory does not require that the consumer specify *how much* more (or less) satisfaction will be realized.

That being said, it is a remarkable mathematical fact that both models of consumer behaviour will, in any given situation, point to exactly the same consumer equilibrium and, consequently, exactly the same demand behaviour. This fact allows us to combine the separate pieces of information that each theory gives us about equilibrium in order to deduce an interesting property about marginal utilities that must also hold true in equilibrium. To see this, note that when we compare the equilibrium situations in the two theories, we find that in the indifference curve analysis, the MRS equals P_B/P_A at equilibrium; however, in the marginal utility approach, the ratio of marginal utilities equals P_B/P_A. We therefore deduce that at equilibrium, the MRS is equivalent in the marginal utility approach to the ratio of the marginal utilities of the last purchased units of the two products.[3]

---

[3] If we begin with the utility-maximizing rule, $MU_A/P_A = MU_B/P_B$, and then multiply through by P_B and divide through by MU_A, we obtain $P_B/P_A = MU_B/MU_A$. In indifference curve analysis we know that at the equilibrium position MRS = P_B/P_A. Hence, at equilibrium, MRS also equals MU_B/MU_A.

The Derivation of the Demand Curve

We noted earlier that with a fixed price for A, an increase in the price of B will cause the bottom of the budget line to fan inward to the left. We can use that fact to derive a demand curve for product B. In Figure A6-5a we reproduce the part of Figure A6-4 that shows our initial consumer equilibrium at

point X. The budget line determining this equilibrium position assumes that money income is $12 and that $P_A = \$1.50$ and $P_B = \$1.00$. Let's see what happens to the equilibrium position when we increase P_B to $1.50 and hold constant both money income and the price of A.

The result is shown in Figure A6-5a. The budget line fans to the left, yielding a new equilibrium point X' where it is tangent to lower indifference curve I_2. At X' the consumer buys three units of B and five of A compared with four of A and six of B at X. Our interest is in B, and we now have sufficient information to locate two points on the demand curve for product B. We know that at equilibrium point X, the price of B is $1.00 and six units are purchased; at equilibrium point X', the price of B is $1.50 and three units are purchased.

These data are shown graphically in Figure A6-5b as points on the consumer's demand curve for B. Note that the horizontal axes of Figure A6-5a and A6-5b are identical; both measure the quantity demanded of B. We can therefore drop vertical reference lines from Figure A6-5a down to the horizontal axis of Figure A6-5b. On the vertical axis of Figure A6-5b we locate the two chosen prices of B. Knowing that these prices yield the relevant quantities demanded, we locate two points on the demand curve for B. By simple manipulation of the price of B in an indifference curve–budget line context, we have obtained a downsloping demand curve for B. We have thus again derived the law of demand assuming other things are equal, since only the price of B was changed (the price of A and the consumer's money income and tastes remained constant). In this case, we have derived the demand curve without resorting to the questionable assumption that consumers can measure utility in units called utils. In this indifference-curve approach, consumers simply compare combinations of products A and B and determine which combination they prefer given their incomes and the prices of the two products.

FIGURE A6-5 Deriving the Demand Curve

Panel (a): When the price of product B is increased from $1.00 to $1.50, the equilibrium position moves from X to X', decreasing the quantity of product B demanded from six to three units. Panel (b): The demand curve for product B is determined by plotting the $1.00–six-unit and $1.50–three-unit price–quantity combinations for product B.

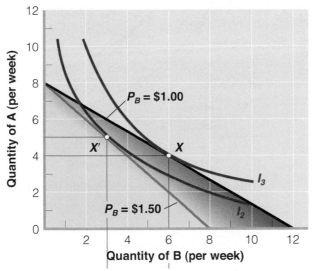

(a) Two equilibrium positions

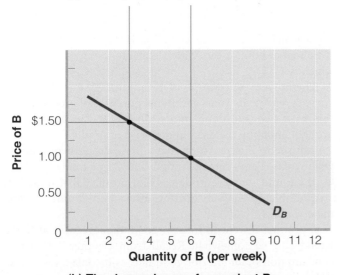

(b) The demand curve for product B

Income and Substitution Effects

In the body of this chapter we noted that a change in price is composed of two effects. The *income effect* is the impact that a change in the price of a product has on a consumer's real income and the consequent effect on the quantity demanded of that good. In contrast, the *substitution effect* is the impact that a change in a product's price has on its relative expensiveness and consequently on the quantity demanded.

We can measure the magnitude of the income and substitution effects with the help of indifference curve analysis. Let's assume we have consumer Pam with a budget of $20 and that she consumes two normal goods, A and B. Good A is priced at $2 and good B at $1. In Figure A6-6a we can see that Pam can purchase a maximum of 10 units of good A and a maximum of 20 units of good B. Given Pam's indifference curve and the relative prices of goods A and B, she is at

FIGURE A6-6   Income and Substitution Effects of a Fall in Price

When the price of product B falls, Pam demands more of product B and less of product A. In panel (a) the fall in price of product B leads Pam to move to point Z on a higher indifference curve. The move from X to Z in panel (a) represents the increased quantity demanded of product B due to both the substitution effect and income effect. In panel (b), if Pam's income is held constant (dashed line) the now lower price of B leads her to demand more of it and she moves to point Y on indifference curve I_3. This rise in quantity demanded is the substitution effect due to the lower price of product B. The move from Y on indifference curve I_3 to Z on indifference curve I_4 represents the increased demand of product B due to the income effect as a result of the lower price of product B. At point Y the MRS is equal to the new price ratio.

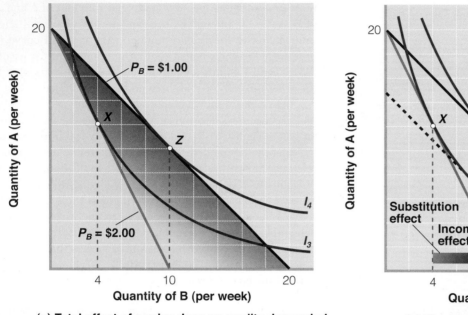

(a) Total effect of a price drop on quality demanded

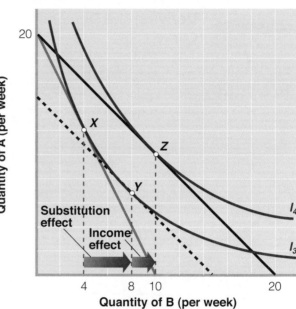

(b) The income and substitution effects

equilibrium at point X on indifference curve I_3, consuming 4 units of good B.

Now let's assume that the price of good B drops to $1. In Figure A6-6a you can see that when the price of good B drops from $2 to $1 Pam will be at a new equilibrium, at point Z, and on the higher indifference curve I_4. Pam now consumes more of good B (10 units, compared to 4 units previously) and less of good A.

The analysis so far has been similar to what we saw in Figure A6-5. But now we want to discover what part of Pam's increased purchase of good B from 4 units to 10 units was due to the substitution effect and what part was due to the income effect. To determine the substitution effect in Figure A6-6b we have added a dashed line parallel to the new budget constraint to see the extra amount Pam would consume of product B solely due to lower price. In reality the dashed line keeps Pam's real income constant. The slope of the dashed line is the same as the new budget constraint, meaning that the price ratio between product A and product B is 1, $(10/10 = 1)$. The initial price ratio between products A and B was 2, $(20/10 = 2)$. Thus, we are holding Pam's income constant and keeping her

on the original indifference curve to see how much of product B she will want at the lower price.

Holding Pam's income constant we find in Figure A6-6b that the drop in price of product B from $2 to $1 leads her to increase the purchase of product B by 4 units, moving her to point Y on indifference curve I_3. This is the substitution effect. Note that at point Y the MRS is equal to the new price ratio, which is 1.

The movement from point Y to point Z on indifference curve I_4 represents Pam's additional purchase of product B, in this case two additional units, due to the income effect brought about by the drop in the price of product B. So now we can see in Figure A6-6b that a price drop for product B will increase Pam's demand for product B by a total of 6 units. Of the 6 unit increase in demand of product B, 4 units are attributable to the substitution effect and 2 units to the income effect.

If product B were an inferior good, the foregoing analysis would change somewhat. Recall from Chapter 4 that the consumption of an inferior good falls as income rises. Thus, the income effect would be negative for an inferior good.

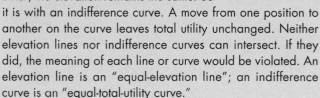

CONSIDER THIS :: Indifference Maps and Topographical Maps

The familiar topographical map may help you understand the idea of indifference curves and indifference maps. Each line on a topographical map represents a particular elevation above sea level, say, 1200 metres. Similarly, an indifference curve represents a particular level of total utility. When you move from one point on a specific elevation line to another, the elevation remains the same. So it is with an indifference curve. A move from one position to another on the curve leaves total utility unchanged. Neither elevation lines nor indifference curves can intersect. If they did, the meaning of each line or curve would be violated. An elevation line is an "equal-elevation line"; an indifference curve is an "equal-total-utility curve."

Maps a la carte, Inc.

Like the topographical map, an indifference map contains not just one line but a series of lines. That is, the topographical map may have elevation lines representing successively higher elevations of 500, 1000, 1500, 2000, and 2500 metres. Similarly, the indifference curves on the indifference map represent successively higher levels of total utility. The climber whose goal is to maximize elevation wants to get to the highest possible elevation line; the consumer desiring to maximize total utility wants to get to the highest possible indifference curve.

Finally, both topographical maps and indifference maps show only a few of the many such lines that could be drawn. The topographical map, for example, leaves out the elevation lines for 501 metres, 502 metres, 503 metres, and so on. The indifference map leaves out all the indifference curves that could be drawn between those that are displayed.

APPENDIX Summary

A6.1 INDIFFERENCE CURVE ANALYSIS

- The indifference curve approach to consumer behaviour is based on the consumer's budget line and indifference curves.

- The budget line shows all combinations of two products that the consumer can purchase given product prices and money income.

- A change in either product prices or money income moves the budget line.

- An indifference curve shows all combinations of two products that will yield the same total utility to a consumer. Indifference curves are downward sloping and convex from the origin.

- An indifference map consists of a number of indifference curves; the farther from the origin, the higher the total utility associated with a curve.

- The consumer is in equilibrium (utility is maximized) at the point on the budget line that lies on the highest attainable indifference curve. At that point the budget line and indifference curve are tangent.

- Changing the price of one product shifts the budget line and determines a new equilibrium point. A downsloping demand curve can be determined by plotting the price–quantity combinations associated with two or more equilibrium points.

- A price change causes a change in the quantity demanded. The change in the quantity demanded is due to the substitution and income effects.

APPENDIX Terms and Concepts

budget line A schedule or curve that shows various combinations of two products a consumer can purchase with a specific money income. (p. 159)

indifference curve A curve showing the different combinations of two products that yield the same satisfaction or utility to a consumer. (p. 160)

marginal rate of substitution (MRS) The rate at which a consumer is prepared to substitute one good for another

(from a given combination of goods) and remain equally satisfied (have the same total utility). (p. 161)

indifference map A series of indifference curves, each of which represents a different level of total utility and together show the preferences of the consumer. (p. 161)

equilibrium position The combination of products that yields the greatest satisfaction or utility. (p. 162)

APPENDIX Questions

1. What information is embodied in a budget line? What shifts occur in the budget line when money income (a) increases and (b) decreases? What shifts occur in the budget line when the price of the product shown on the vertical axis (a) increases and (b) decreases? **[LOA6.1]**

2. What information is contained in an indifference curve? Why are such curves (a) downsloping and (b) convex to the origin? Why does total utility increase as the consumer

moves to indifference curves farther from the origin? Why can't indifference curves intersect? **[LOA6.1]**

3. Using Figure A6-4, explain why the point of tangency of the budget line with an indifference curve is the consumer's equilibrium position. Explain why any point where the budget line intersects an indifference curve is not equilibrium. Also, explain the following statement: "The consumer is in equilibrium where MRS = P_B/P_A." **[LOA6.1]**

APPENDIX Problems

1. Assume that the data in the accompanying table give an indifference curve for Mr. Chen. Graph this curve, putting A on the vertical axis and B on the horizontal axis. Assuming that the prices of A and B are $1.50 and $1.00, respectively, and that Mr. Chen has $24 to spend, add his budget line to your graph. What combination of A and B will Mr. Chen purchase? Does your answer meet the MRS = P_B/P_A rule for equilibrium? **[LOA6.1]**

Units of A	Units of B
16	6
12	8
8	2
4	24

2. Explain graphically how indifference analysis can be used to derive a demand curve. **[LOA6.1]**

3. Show the substitution and income effects of a decrease in the price of gasoline. Assume gasoline is a normal good. How would your result change if gasoline were an inferior good? **[LOA6.1]**

4. **ADVANCED ANALYSIS** First, graphically illustrate a doubling of income without price changes in the indifference curve model. Next, on the same graph, show a situation in which the person whose indifference curves you are drawing buys considerably more of good B than A after the income increase. What can you conclude about the relative coefficients of income elasticity of demand for goods A and B (Chapter 4)? **[LOA6.1]**

The Firm and the Costs of Production

AFTER READING THIS CHAPTER, YOU SHOULD BE ABLE TO:

7.1 Explain why economic costs include both explicit (revealed and expressed) costs and implicit costs.

7.2 Relate the law of diminishing returns to a firm's short-run production costs.

7.3 Identify and classify a firm's short-run production costs as fixed or variable.

7.4 Use economies of scale to link a firm's size and production costs in the long run.

Our attention now turns from the behaviour of consumers to the behaviour of producers. In market economies, a wide variety of firms, from family-owned businesses to large corporations, produce an even wider variety of goods and services. Each business requires inputs to produce its products. To acquire the needed inputs, a firm makes monetary payments to factor owners (for example, workers) and incurs opportunity costs when using resources it already owns (for example, entrepreneurial talent). Those payments and opportunity costs together make up the firm's *costs of production,* which we discuss in this chapter. Then in the next several chapters we bring product demand, product prices, and revenue back into the analysis and explain how firms compare revenues and costs to determine how much to produce. Our ultimate purpose is to show how those comparisons relate to economic efficiency.

7.1 Economic Costs

Firms face costs because the resources they need to produce their products are scarce and have alternative uses. Because of scarcity, firms wanting a particular resource have to bid it away from other firms. That process is costly for firms because it requires a payment to the resource owner. This reality causes economists to define **economic (opportunity) cost** as the payment that must be made to obtain and retain the services of a resource. It is the income the firm must provide to resource suppliers to attract resources away from alternative uses.

 OPPORTUNITY
COSTS

economic cost
A value equal to the quantity of other products that cannot be produced when resources are instead used to make a particular product.

This section explains how firms incorporate opportunity costs to calculate economic costs. If necessary, review the section on opportunity costs in Chapter 1 before continuing with the rest of this section.

Explicit and Implicit Costs

To properly calculate a firm's economic costs, you must remember that *all* of the resources (factors of production) used by the firm have an opportunity cost. This is true for both the resources that a firm purchases from outsiders and the resources that it already owns.

As an example, consider a table-making firm that starts this month with $5000 in cash as well as ownership of a small oak forest from which it gets the oak that it turns into tables. Suppose that during the month it spends the $5000 paying its workers. Clearly, the $5000 the firm spends purchasing labour comes at the opportunity cost of forgoing the best alternatives that could have been bought with that money. Less obvious, however, is the opportunity cost of the oak that the firm grows itself and that it uses to make tables. Suppose that the oak has a market value of $1500, meaning that our table-making firm could sell it to outsiders for $1500. This implies that using the oak to make tables has an opportunity cost of $1500. Choosing to convert the oak into tables means giving up the best alternatives that the firm could have purchased with the $1500.

As a result, keep in mind that *all* of the resources that a firm uses—whether purchased from outside or already owned—have opportunity costs and thus economic costs. Economists refer to these two types of economic costs as *explicit costs* and *implicit costs*:

explicit costs
The monetary payments a firm must make to an outsider to obtain a resource.

- A firm's **explicit costs** are the monetary payments it makes to those from whom it must purchase resources that it does not own. Because these costs involve an obvious cash transaction, they are referred to as explicit costs. Be sure to remember that explicit costs are opportunity costs because every monetary payment used to purchase outside resources necessarily involves forgoing the best alternatives that could have been purchased with the money.

implicit costs
The monetary income a firm sacrifices when it uses a resource it owns rather than supplying the resource in the market; equals what the resource could have earned in the best-paying alternative employment (including a normal profit).

- A firm's **implicit costs** are the opportunity costs of using the resources that it already owns to make the firm's own product rather than selling those resources to outsiders for cash. Because these costs are present but not obvious, they are referred to as implicit costs.

A firm's economic costs are the sum of its explicit costs and its implicit costs:

Economic costs = explicit costs + implicit costs

The following example makes clear how both explicit costs and implicit costs affect firm profits and firm behaviour.

Accounting Profit and Normal Profit

Suppose that after many years working as a sales representative for a large T-shirt manufacturer, you decide to strike out on your own. After considering many potential business ventures, you decide to open a retail T-shirt shop. As we explained in Chapter 2, you will be providing two different economic resources to your new enterprise: labour and entrepreneurial ability. The part of your job that involves providing labour includes any of the routine tasks that are needed to help run the business—things like answering customer emails, taking inventory, and sweeping the floor. The part of your job that involves providing entrepreneurial ability includes any of the non-routine tasks involved with organizing the business and directing its strategy—such as deciding on whether to use Internet ads or in-person events to promote your business, whether to include children's clothing in your product mix, and how to decorate your store to maximize its appeal to potential customers.

You begin providing entrepreneurial ability to your new firm by making some initial organizational decisions. You decide to work full time at your new business, so you quit your old job that paid you $22,000 per year. You invest $20,000 of savings that have been earning $1000 per year. You decide that your new firm will occupy a small retail space that you own and which you had been previously renting out for $5000 per year. Finally, you decide to hire one clerk to help you in the store. She agrees to work for you for $18,000 per year.

After a year in business, you total up your accounts and find the following:

Total sales revenue		$120,000
Cost of T-shirts	$40,000	
Clerk's salary	18,000	
Utilities	5,000	
Total (explicit) costs		63,000
Accounting profit		57,000

accounting profit
The total revenue of a firm less its explicit costs.

Costs of production exist because resources are scarce and have alternative uses.

normal profit
The payment made by a firm to obtain and retain entrepreneurial ability.

These numbers look very good. In particular, you are happy with your $57,000 **accounting profit,** the profit number that accountants calculate by subtracting total explicit costs from total sales revenue. This is the profit (or net income) that would appear on your accounting statement and that you would report to the government for tax purposes.

But don't celebrate yet! Your $57,000 accounting profit overstates the economic success of your business because it ignores your implicit costs. Success is not defined as "having a total sales revenue that exceeds total explicit costs." Rather, the true measure of success is doing as well as you possibly can—that is, making more money in your new venture selling T-shirts than you could pursuing any other business venture. To figure out whether you are achieving that goal, you must take into account all of your opportunity costs—both your implicit costs and your explicit costs. Doing so will indicate whether your new business venture is earning more money than what you could have earned in any other business venture.

To see how these calculations are made, let's continue with our example. By providing your own financial capital, retail space, and labour, you incurred three different implicit costs during the year: $1000 of forgone interest, $5000 of forgone rent, and $22,000 of forgone wages. But don't forget that there is another implicit cost that you must also take into account—how much income you chose to forgo by applying your entrepreneurial abilities to your current retail T-shirt venture rather than applying them to other potential business ventures. But what dollar value should we place on the size of the profits that you might have made if you had provided your entrepreneurial ability to one of those other ventures? The answer is given by estimating a **normal profit,** the typical (or "normal") amount of accounting profit that you would most likely have earned in one of these other ventures. For the sake of argument, let us assume that with your particular set of skills and talents your entrepreneurial abilities would have on average yielded a normal profit of $5000 in one of the other potential ventures. Knowing that value, we can take all of your implicit costs properly into account by subtracting them from your accounting profit:

Accounting profit		$57,000
Forgone interest	$ 1,000	
Forgone rent	5,000	
Forgone wages	22,000	
Forgone entrepreneurial income	5,000	
Total implicit costs		33,000
Economic profit		24,000

Economic Profit

After subtracting your $33,000 of implicit costs from your accounting profit of $57,000, we are left with an *economic profit* of $24,000.

Please distinguish clearly between accounting profit and economic profit. Accounting profit is the result of subtracting only explicit costs from revenue:

Accounting profit = revenue − explicit costs

economic profit
A firm's total revenue less its economic costs (both explicit costs and implicit costs).

By contrast, **economic profit** is the result of subtracting all of your economic costs—both explicit costs and implicit costs—from revenue:

Economic profit = revenue − explicit costs − implicit costs

By subtracting all of your economic costs from your revenue, you determine how your current business venture compares with your best alternative business venture. In our example, the fact that you are generating an economic profit of $24,000 means that you are making $24,000 more than you could expect to make in your best alternative business venture. By contrast, suppose that you had instead done poorly in business, so that this year your firm generated an economic loss (a negative economic profit) of $8000. This would mean that you were doing worse in your current venture than you could have done in your best alternative venture. You would, as a result, wish to switch to that alternative.

Generalizing this point, we see that there is a very important behavioural threshold at $0 of economic profit. If a firm is breaking even (that is, earning exactly $0 of economic profit), then its entrepreneurs know that they are doing exactly as well as they could expect to do in their best alternative business venture. They are earning enough to cover all their explicit and implicit costs, including the normal profit that they could expect to earn in other business ventures. Thus, they have no incentive to change. By contrast, anyone earning a positive economic profit knows they are doing better than they could in alternative ventures and will want to continue doing what they are doing or maybe even expand their business. And anyone earning an economic loss (a negative economic profit) knows that they could do better by switching to something else.

It is for this reason that economists focus on economic profits rather than accounting profits. Simply put, economic profits direct how resources are allocated in the economy. Entrepreneurs running economic losses close their current businesses, thereby freeing up the land, labour, capital, and entrepreneurial ability that they had been using. These resources are freed up to be used by firms that are generating positive economic profits or are at least breaking even. Resources thus flow from producing goods and services with lower net benefits toward producing goods and services with higher net benefits. Allocative efficiency increases as firms are led by their profit signals to produce more of what consumers want the most.

Figure 7-1 shows the relationship among the various cost and profit concepts that we have just discussed. To test yourself, you might want to enter cost data from our example in the appropriate blocks.

Mc Graw Hill connect
WORKED PROBLEM 7.1
Economic Profit

FIGURE 7-1 **Economic Profit versus Accounting Profit**

Economic profit is equal to total revenue less economic costs. Economic costs are the sum of explicit and implicit costs and include a normal profit to the entrepreneur. Accounting profit is equal to total revenue less accounting (explicit) costs.

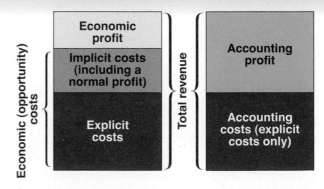

Short Run and Long Run

When the demand for a firm's product changes, the firm's profitability may depend on how quickly it can adjust the amounts of the various factors it employs. It can easily and quickly adjust the quantities employed of many resources such as hourly labour, raw materials, fuel, and power. It needs much more time, however, to adjust its *plant capacity*—the size of the factory building, the amount of machinery and equipment, and other capital resources. In some heavy industries, such as aircraft manufacturing, a firm such as Bombardier may need several years to alter plant capacity. Because of these differences in adjustment time, economists find it useful to distinguish between two conceptual periods: the *short run* and the *long run*. We will discover that costs differ in these two periods.

short run
A period of time in which producers are able to change the quantities of some but not all of the resources they employ.

long run
A period of time long enough to enable producers to change the quantities of all the resources they employ.

- *Short Run: Fixed Plant* In microeconomics, the **short run** is a period too brief for a firm to alter its plant capacity, yet long enough to permit a change in the degree to which the plant's current capacity is used. The firm's plant capacity is fixed in the short run. However, the firm can vary its output by applying larger or smaller amounts of labour, materials, and other inputs to that plant, using its existing plant capacity more or less intensively in the short run.

- *Long Run: Variable Plant* In microeconomics, the **long run** is a period long enough for it to adjust the quantities of all the factors that it employs, including plant capacity. For the industry, the long run also includes enough time for existing firms to dissolve and leave the industry or for new firms to be created and enter the industry. While the short run is a "fixed-plant" period, the long run is a "variable-plant" period.

ILLUSTRATION

If Bombardier hires 100 extra workers for one of its aircraft plants, or adds an entire shift of workers, we are speaking of the short run. If it adds a new production facility and installs more equipment, we are referring to the long run. The first situation is a short-run adjustment; the second is a long-run adjustment.

The short run and the long run are conceptual periods rather than calendar periods. In light-manufacturing industries, changes in plant capacity may be accomplished almost overnight. A small T-shirt manufacturer can increase its plant capacity in a matter of days by ordering and installing two or three new cutting tables and several extra sewing machines. But for heavy industry the long run is a different matter. Petro-Canada may require several years to construct a new oil refinery.

QUICK REVIEW

- Explicit costs are money payments a firm makes to outside suppliers of factors of production; implicit costs are the opportunity costs associated with a firm's use of inputs it owns.

- Normal profit is the implicit cost of entrepreneurship. Economic profit is total revenue less all explicit and implicit costs, including normal profit.

- In the short run, a firm's plant capacity is fixed; in the long run, a firm can vary its plant size and firms can enter or leave the industry.

7.2 Short-Run Production Relationships ::

A firm's costs of producing a specific output depend on the prices of the needed inputs and the quantities of inputs needed to produce that output. Factor supply and demand determine input prices. The technological aspects of production, specifically the relationships between inputs and output, determine the quantities of factors of production needed. Our focus will be on the *labour*–output relationship, given a fixed-plant capacity. But before examining that relationship, we need to define three terms:

total product (TP)
The total output of a particular good or service produced by a firm.

1. The **total product (TP)** is the total quantity, or total output, of a particular good or service produced.

marginal product (MP)
The extra output associated with adding a unit of a variable factor to the production process.

2. The **marginal product (MP)** is the extra output associated with adding a unit of variable input, in this case labour, to the production process. Thus,

$$\text{Marginal product} = \frac{\text{change in total product}}{\text{change in labour input}}$$

average product (AP)
The total output divided by the quantity of that employed resource.

3. The **average product (AP),** also called labour productivity, is output per unit of labour input:

$$\text{Average product} = \frac{\text{total product}}{\text{units of labour}}$$

Law of Diminishing Returns

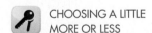
ORIGIN OF THE IDEA 7.1
Law of Diminishing Returns

law of diminishing returns
As successive increments of a variable factor are added to a fixed factor, the marginal product of the variable factor will eventually decrease.

In the short run, a firm can, for a time, increase its output by adding units of labour to its fixed plant. But by how much will output rise when a firm adds more labour? Why do we say "for a time"? The answers are provided in general terms by the **law of diminishing returns,** also called the *law of diminishing marginal product.* This law assumes that technology is fixed, so that the techniques of production do not change. It states that as successive units of a variable factor (say, labour) are added to a fixed factor (say, capital or land), beyond some point the extra, or marginal, product that can be attributed to each additional unit of the variable factor will decline. For example, if additional workers are hired to work with a constant amount of capital equipment, output will eventually rise by smaller and smaller amounts as more workers are hired. (See the *Consider This…Diminishing Returns from Study* box for a noneconomic example of diminishing returns.)

RATIONALE

Suppose a farmer in Ontario has a fixed supply of 80 hectares planted in corn. If the farmer does not cultivate the cornfields, the yield will be 40 bushels per hectare. If she cultivates the land once, output may rise to 50 bushels per hectare. A second cultivation may increase output to 57 bushels per hectare, a third to 61, and a fourth to 63. Succeeding cultivations would add less and less to the land's yield. If this were not so, the world's need for corn could be fulfilled by extremely intense cultivation of this single 80-hectare plot of land. Indeed, if diminishing returns did not occur, the world could be fed out of a flowerpot. Why not? Just keep adding more seed, fertilizer, and harvesters!

CHOOSING A LITTLE MORE OR LESS

The law of diminishing returns also holds true in nonagricultural industries. Assume a wood shop is manufacturing chairs. It has a specific amount of equipment such as lathes, planers, saws, and sanders. If this shop hired just one or two workers, total output and productivity (output per worker) would be low. (Note that we assume all units of labour are of equal quality.) The workers would have to perform many different jobs, and the advantages of specialization would not be realized. Time would be lost switching from one job to another, and machines would stand idle much of the time. In short, the plant would be understaffed, and production would be inefficient because there would be too much capital relative to the amount of labour.

The shop could eliminate those difficulties by hiring more workers. Then the equipment would be more fully used, and workers could specialize in doing a single job. Time would no longer be lost switching from job to job. As more workers were added, production would become more efficient and the marginal product of each succeeding worker would rise.

But the rise could not go on indefinitely. Beyond a certain point, adding more workers would cause overcrowding. Since workers would then have to wait in line to use the machinery, it would be underused. Total output would increase at a diminishing rate, because, given the fixed

CONSIDER THIS :: Diminishing Returns from Study

A noneconomic example of the relationship between "inputs" and "output" may help you better understand the idea of diminishing returns. Suppose for an individual that total course learning = f(intelligence, quality of course materials, instructor effectiveness, class time, and study time) where f means "function of" or "depends on." So this relationship supposes that total course learning depends on intelligence (however defined), the quality of course materials such as the textbook, the effectiveness of the instructor, the amount of class time, and the amount of personal study time outside the class.

Let's assume that one's intelligence, the quality of course materials, the effectiveness of the instructor, and the amount of class time are *fixed*—meaning they do not change over the length of the course. Now let's add units of study time per day over the length of the course to "produce" greater course learning. The first hour of study time per day increases total course learning. Will the second hour enhance course learning by as much as the first? By how much will the third, fourth, fifth, … fifteenth hour of study per day contribute to total course learning relative to the *immediately previous hour*?

We think you will agree that diminishing returns to course learning eventually will set in as successive hours of study are added each day. At some point the marginal product of an extra hour of study time will decline and, at some further point, become zero.

This is also true of production relationships within firms. As successive units of a variable input (say, labour) are added to a fixed input (say, capital), the marginal product of the variable input eventually declines. In short, diminishing returns will occur sooner or later. Total product eventually will rise at a diminishing rate, reach a maximum, and then decline.

---

size of the plant, each worker would have less capital equipment to work with as more and more labour was hired. The marginal product of additional workers would decline because there would be more labour in proportion to the fixed amount of capital. Eventually, adding still more workers would cause so much congestion that marginal product would become negative and total product would decline. At the extreme, the addition of more and more labour would exhaust all the standing room, and total product would fall to zero.

WORKED PROBLEM 7.2
Total, Marginal, and Average Product

TABULAR EXAMPLE

Table 7-1 is a numerical hypothetical illustration of the law of diminishing returns in a wood shop manufacturing chairs. Column 2 shows the total product, or total output, resulting from combining each level of a variable input (labour) in column 1 with a fixed amount of capital.

Column 3 shows the marginal product (MP), the change in total product associated with each additional unit of labour. Note that with no labour input, total product is zero; a plant with no workers will produce no output. The first three units of labour reflect increasing marginal returns, with marginal products of 10, 15, and 20 units, respectively. But beginning with the fourth unit of labour, marginal product diminishes continually, becoming zero with the seventh unit of labour and negative with the eighth.

Average product, or output per labour unit, is shown in column 4. It is calculated by dividing total product (column 2) by the number of labour units needed to produce it (column 1). At five units of labour, for example, AP is 14 (= 70/5).

GRAPHICAL PORTRAYAL

Figure 7-2 (Key Graph) shows the diminishing returns data in Table 7-1 graphically and further clarifies the relationships between total, marginal, and average products. (Marginal product in Figure 7-2b is plotted halfway between the units of labour, since it applies to the addition of each labour unit.)

TABLE 7-1   Total, Marginal, and Average Product: The Law of Diminishing Returns

(1) Units of the variable factor (workers per day)	(2) Total product (TP) (chairs per day)	(3) Marginal product (MP) (chairs per additional worker) change in (2)/change in (1)	(4) Average product (AP) (chairs per worker) (2)/(1)
0	0		—
1	10	10 ⎫ Increasing marginal returns	10.00
2	25	15 ⎬	12.50
3	45	20 ⎭	15.00
4	60	15 ⎫ Diminishing marginal returns	15.00
5	70	10 ⎬	14.00
6	75	5 ⎭	12.50
7	75	0 ⎫ Negative marginal returns	10.71
8	70	−5 ⎭	8.75

connect
MATH 7.1
Marginal Product and Average Product

Note first in Figure 7-2a that total product, TP, goes through three phases: it rises initially at an increasing rate; then it increases, but at a diminishing rate; finally, after reaching a maximum, it declines.

Geometrically, marginal product—shown by the MP curve in Figure 7-2b—is the slope of the total product curve. Marginal product measures the change in total output of chairs associated with each succeeding unit of labour. Thus, the three phases of total product are also reflected in marginal product. Where total product is increasing at an increasing rate, marginal product is rising. Here, extra units of labour are adding larger and larger amounts to total product. Similarly, where total product is increasing but at a decreasing rate, marginal product is positive but falling. Each additional unit of labour adds fewer chairs than did the previous unit. When total product is at a maximum, marginal product is zero. When total product declines, marginal product becomes negative.

Average product, AP in Figure 7-2b, displays the same tendencies as marginal product. It increases, reaches a maximum, and then decreases as more units of labour are added to the fixed plant. But note the relationship between marginal product and average product: Where marginal product exceeds average product, average product rises. And where marginal product is less than average product, average product declines. It follows that marginal product intersects average product where average product is at a maximum.

This relationship is a mathematical necessity. If you add to a total a number that is larger than the current average of that total, the average must rise; if you add to a total a number that is smaller than the current average of that total, the average must fall. You raise your average examination grade only when your score on an additional (marginal) examination is greater than the average of all your past scores. You lower your average when your grade on an additional exam is below your current average. In our production example, when the amount an extra worker adds to total product exceeds the average product of all workers currently employed, average product will rise. Conversely, when the amount an extra worker adds to total product is less than the current average product, then average product will decrease.

connect
ORIGIN OF THE IDEA 7.2
Production Relationships

The law of diminishing returns is reflected in the shapes of all three curves. But, as our definition of the law of diminishing returns indicates, we are most concerned with its effects on marginal product. The regions of increasing, diminishing, and negative marginal product (returns) are shown in Figure 7-2b.

KEY GRAPH

FIGURE 7-2   The Law of Diminishing Returns

Panel (a): As a variable resource (labour) is added to fixed amounts of other resources (land or capital), the total product that results will eventually increase by diminishing amounts, reach a maximum, and then decline. Panel (b): Marginal product is the change in total product associated with each new unit of labour. Average product is simply output per labour unit. Note that marginal product intersects average product at the maximum average product.

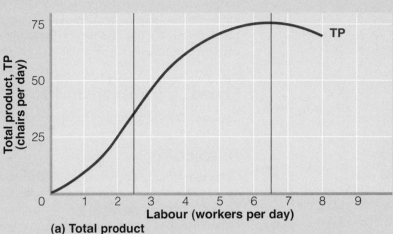

(a) Total product

(b) Marginal and average product

Quick Quiz

1. **Which of the following is an assumption underlying these figures?**
   a. Firms first hire highly skilled workers and then hire less skilled workers.
   b. Capital and labour are both variable, but labour increases more rapidly than capital.
   c. Consumers will buy all the output (total product) produced.
   d. Workers are of equal quality.

2. **Marginal product is**
   a. the change in total product divided by the change in the quantity of labour.
   b. total product divided by the quantity of labour.
   c. always positive.
   d. unrelated to total product.

3. **Marginal product in panel (b) is zero when**
   a. average product in panel (b) stops rising.
   b. the slope of the marginal-product curve in panel (b) is zero.
   c. total product in panel (a) begins to rise at a diminishing rate.
   d. the slope of the total-product curve in panel (a) is zero.

4. **Average product in panel (b)**
   a. rises when it is less than marginal product.
   b. is the change in total product divided by the change in the quantity of labour.
   c. can never exceed marginal product.
   d. falls whenever total product in panel (a) rises at a diminishing rate.

Answers: 1. d; 2. a; 3. d; 4. a

Short-Run Production Costs

Production information such as that provided in Table 7-1 and Figures 7-2a and 7-2b must be coupled with prices of factors of production to determine the total and per-unit costs of producing various levels of output. We know that, in the short run, resources associated with the firm's plant are fixed. Other resources, however, are variable in the short run. As a result, short-run costs can be either fixed or variable.

Fixed, Variable, and Total Costs

Let's see what distinguishes fixed costs, variable costs, and total costs from one another.

FIXED COSTS

fixed costs
Costs that in total do not change when the firm changes its output.

Costs that in total do not vary with changes in output are known as **fixed costs.** Fixed costs are associated with the very existence of a firm's plant and, therefore, must be paid even if its output is zero. Such costs as rental payments, interest on a firm's debts, and insurance premiums are generally fixed costs; they are fixed and do not change even if a firm produces more. In column 2 in Table 7-2 we assume that the firm's total fixed cost is $100. By definition, this fixed cost is incurred at all levels of output, including zero. The firm cannot avoid paying these costs in the short run.

| TABLE 7-2 | Total-Cost, Average-Cost, and Marginal-Cost Schedules for an Individual Firm in the Short Run |

	TOTAL-COST DATA			AVERAGE-COST DATA			MARGINAL COST
(1) Total product (Q)	(2) Total fixed cost (TFC)	(3) Total variable cost (TVC)	(4) Total cost (TC)	(5) Average fixed cost (AFC)	(6) Average variable cost (AVC)	(7) Average total cost (ATC)	(8) Marginal cost (MC)
(chairs per day)	(dollars per day)			(dollars per chair)			(dollars per additional chair)
0	$100	$ 0	$ 100				
							$ 90
1	100	90	190	$100.00	$90.00	$190.00	
							80
2	100	170	270	50.00	85.00	135.00	
							70
3	100	240	340	33.33	80.00	113.33	
							60
4	100	300	400	25.00	75.00	100.00	
							70
5	100	370	470	20.00	74.00	94.00	
							80
6	100	450	550	16.67	75.00	91.67	
							90
7	100	540	640	14.29	77.14	91.43	
							110
8	100	650	750	12.50	81.25	93.75	
							130
9	100	780	880	11.11	86.67	97.78	
							150
10	100	930	1,030	10.00	93.00	103.00	

VARIABLE COSTS

variable costs
Costs that increase or decrease with a firm's output.

Costs that change with the level of output—payments for materials, fuel, power, transportation services, most labour, and similar variable resources—are known as **variable costs.** In column 3 of Table 7-2 we find that the total of variable costs changes directly with output, but note that the increases in variable cost associated with succeeding one-unit increases in output are not equal. As production begins, variable cost will for a time increase by a decreasing amount; this is true through the fourth unit of output in Table 7-2. Beyond the fourth unit, however, variable cost rises by increasing amounts for succeeding units of output.

The reason lies in the shape of the marginal product curve. At first, as in Figure 7-2b, marginal product is increasing, so smaller and smaller increases in the amounts of variable inputs are needed to produce successive units of output. Thus, the variable cost of successive units of output decreases. But when, as diminishing returns are encountered, marginal product begins to decline, larger and larger additional amounts of variable inputs are needed to produce successive units of output. Total variable cost, therefore, increases by increasing amounts.

TOTAL COST

total cost
The sum of fixed cost and variable cost.

The **total cost** is the sum of the fixed costs and variable costs at each level of output:

$$TC = TFC + TVC$$

It is shown in column 4 in Table 7-2. At zero units of output, total cost is equal to the firm's fixed cost. Then for each unit of the 10 units of production, total cost increases by the same amount as variable cost.

Figure 7-3 shows graphically the fixed-cost, variable-cost, and total-cost data given in Table 7-2. Observe that total variable cost, TVC, is measured vertically from the horizontal axis at each level of output. The amount of fixed cost, shown as TFC, is added vertically to the total variable cost curve to obtain the points on the total-cost curve, TC.

The distinction between fixed and variable costs is significant to the business manager. Variable costs can be controlled or altered in the short run by changing production levels. Fixed costs

---

FIGURE 7-3   ## Total Cost Is the Sum of Fixed Cost and Variable Cost

Total variable cost (TVC) changes with output. Total fixed cost (TFC) is independent of the level of output. The total cost (TC) at any output is the vertical sum of the fixed cost and variable cost at that output.

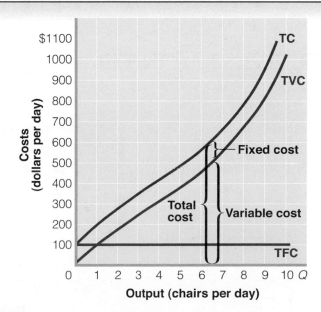

are beyond the business manager's current control; they are incurred in the short run and must be paid regardless of output level.

Per-Unit, or Average Costs

Producers are certainly interested in their total costs, but they are equally concerned with per-unit, or average costs. In particular, average-cost data are more meaningful for making comparisons with product price, which is always stated on a per-unit basis. Average fixed cost, average variable cost, and average total cost are shown in columns 5 to 7, Table 7-2.

AFC

average fixed cost (AFC)
A firm's total fixed cost divided by output.

The **average fixed cost (AFC)** for any output level is found by dividing total fixed cost (TFC) by that amount of output (Q). That is,

$$AFC = \frac{TFC}{Q}$$

Because the total fixed cost is, by definition, the same regardless of output, AFC must decline as output increases. As output rises, the total fixed cost is spread over a larger and larger output. When output is just one unit in Table 7-2, TFC and AFC are the same at $100. But at two units of output, the total fixed cost of $100 becomes $50 of AFC or fixed cost per unit; then it becomes $33.33 per unit as $100 is spread over three units, and $25 per unit when spread over four units. This process is sometimes referred to as "spreading the overhead." Figure 7-4 shows that AFC graphs as a continuously declining curve as total output is increased.

AVC

average variable cost (AVC)
A firm's total variable cost divided by output.

The **average variable cost (AVC)** for any output level is calculated by dividing total variable cost (TVC) by that amount of output (Q):

$$AVC = \frac{TVC}{Q}$$

Due to increasing and then diminishing returns, AVC declines initially, reaches a minimum, and then increases again. A graph of AVC is a U-shaped curve, as shown in Figure 7-4.

FIGURE 7-4 **The Average-Cost Curves**

AFC falls as a given amount of fixed costs is apportioned over a larger and larger output. AVC initially falls because of increasing marginal returns but then rises because of diminishing marginal returns. Average total cost (ATC) is the vertical sum of average variable cost (AVC) and average fixed cost (AFC).

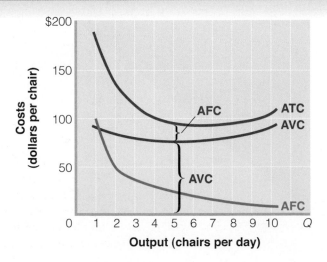

Because total variable cost reflects the law of diminishing returns, so must AVC, which is derived from total variable cost. Marginal returns increase initially because it takes fewer and fewer additional variable inputs to produce each of the first four units of output. As a result, variable cost per unit declines. AVC hits a minimum with the fifth unit of output, and beyond that point AVC rises as diminishing returns require more variable inputs to produce each additional unit of output.

You can verify the U shape of the AVC curve by returning to Table 7-1. Assume the price of labour is $10 per unit. By dividing average product (output per labour unit) into $10 (price per labour unit), we determine the labour cost per unit of output. Because we have assumed labour to be the only variable input, the labour cost per unit of output is the variable cost per unit of output or AVC. When average product is initially low, AVC is high. As workers are added, average product rises and AVC falls. When average product is at its maximum, AVC is at its minimum. Then, as still more workers are added and average product declines, AVC rises. The hump of the average product curve is reflected in the U shape of the AVC curve. As you will soon see, the two are mirror images.

ATC

average total cost (ATC)
A firm's total cost divided by output.

The **average total cost (ATC)** for any output level is found by dividing the total cost (TC) by that output (Q) or by adding AFC and AVC at that output:

$$ATC = \frac{TC}{Q} = \frac{TFC}{Q} + \frac{TVC}{Q}$$
$$= AFC + AVC$$

Graphically, ATC can be found by adding vertically the AFC and AVC curves, as in Figure 7-4. Thus, the vertical distance between the ATC and AVC curves measures AFC at any level of output.

Marginal Cost

marginal cost (MC)
The additional cost of producing one more unit of output.

One final and very crucial cost concept remains: The **marginal cost (MC)** is the extra, or additional, cost of producing one more unit of output. MC can be determined for each added unit of output by noting the change in total cost that that unit's production entails:

$$MC = \frac{change\ in\ TC}{change\ in\ Q}$$

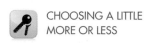
MATH 7.2
Marginal Cost as a
Change in Cost

CALCULATIONS

In column 4, Table 7-2, production of the first unit of output increases total cost from $100 to $190. Therefore, the additional, or marginal, cost of that first unit is $90 (column 8). The marginal cost of the second unit is $80 (= $270 − $190); the MC of the third is $70 (= $340 − $270); and so forth. The MC for each of the 10 units of output is shown in column 8. MC can also be calculated from the total-variable-cost column, because the only difference between total cost and total variable cost is the constant amount of fixed costs ($100). Thus, the change in total cost and the change in total variable cost associated with each additional unit of output are always the same.

MARGINAL DECISIONS

CHOOSING A LITTLE MORE OR LESS

Marginal costs are costs the firm can control directly and immediately. Specifically, MC designates all the additional cost incurred in producing the last unit of output. Thus, it also designates the cost that can be saved by not producing that last unit. Average-cost figures do not provide this information. For example, suppose the firm is undecided whether to produce three or four units of output. At four units, Table 7-2 indicates that ATC is $100. But the firm does not increase its total costs by $100 by producing the fourth unit, nor does it save $100 by not producing that unit. Rather, the change in costs is only $60, as the MC column in Table 7-2 reveals.

WORKED PROBLEM 7.3
Per-Unit Cost

A firm's decisions as to what output level to produce are typically decisions to produce a few more or a few less units. Marginal cost is the change in costs when one more or one less unit of

KEY GRAPH

FIGURE 7-5 **The Relationship of the Marginal-Cost Curve to the Average-Total-Cost and Average-Variable-Cost Curves**

The marginal-cost (MC) curve cuts through the average-total-cost (ATC) curve and the average-variable-cost (AVC) curve at their minimum points. When MC is below average total cost, ATC falls; when MC is above average total cost, ATC rises. Similarly, when MC is below average variable cost, AVC falls; when MC is above average variable cost, AVC rises.

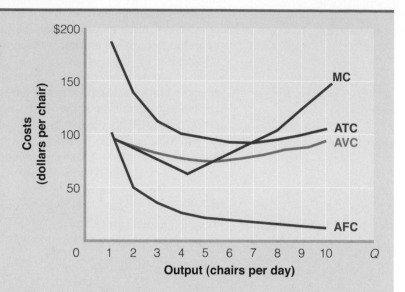

Quick Quiz

1. **The marginal-cost curve first declines and then increases because of**
   a. increasing, then diminishing, marginal utility.
   b. the decline in the gap between ATC and AVC as output expands.
   c. increasing, then diminishing, marginal returns.
   d. constant marginal revenue.

2. **The vertical distance between ATC and AVC measures**
   a. marginal cost.
   b. total fixed cost.
   c. average fixed cost.
   d. economic profit per unit.

3. **ATC is**
   a. AVC − AFC.
   b. MC + AVC.
   c. AFC + AVC.
   d. (AFC + AVC) × Q.

4. **When the marginal-cost curve lies**
   a. above the ATC curve, ATC rises.
   b. above the AVC curve, ATC rises.
   c. below the AVC curve, total fixed cost increases.
   d. below the ATC curve, total fixed cost falls.

Answers: 1. c; 2. c; 3. c; 4. a

output is produced. When coupled with marginal revenue, marginal cost allows a firm to determine whether it is profitable to expand or contract its production. The analysis in the next three chapters focuses on those marginal calculations.

GRAPHICAL PORTRAYAL
Marginal cost is shown graphically in **Figure 7-5 (Key Graph)**. Marginal cost at first declines sharply, reaches a minimum, and then rises rather abruptly. This pattern reflects the fact that the variable costs, and therefore total cost, increase at first by decreasing amounts and then by increasing amounts (see columns 3 and 4, Table 7-2).

connect
MATH 7.3
Marginal Cost and Marginal Product

MARGINAL COST AND MARGINAL PRODUCT
The shape of the marginal-cost curve is a consequence of the law of diminishing returns. Looking back at Table 7-1, we can see the relationship between marginal product and marginal cost. If all

units of a variable factor (here, labour) are hired at the same price, the marginal cost of each extra unit of output will fall as long as the marginal product of each additional worker is rising, because marginal cost is the (constant) cost of an extra worker divided by his or her marginal product. Therefore, in Table 7-1, suppose that each worker can be hired for $10. Because the first worker's marginal product is 10 units of output, and hiring this worker increases the firm's costs by $10, the marginal cost of each of these 10 extra units of output is $1 (= $10 ÷ 10 units). The second worker also increases costs by $10, but the marginal product is 15, so the marginal cost of each of these 15 extra units of output is $0.67 (= $10 ÷ 15 units). Similarly, the MC of each of the 20 extra units of output contributed by the third worker is $0.50 (= $10 ÷ 20 units). To generalize, as long as marginal product is rising, marginal cost will fall.

But with the fourth worker, diminishing returns set in and marginal cost begins to rise. For the fourth worker, marginal cost is $0.67 (= $10 ÷ 15 units); for the fifth worker, MC is $1.00 (= $10 ÷ 10 units); for the sixth, MC is $2.00 (= $10 ÷ 5 units), and so on. If the price (cost) of the variable resource remains constant, increasing marginal returns will be reflected in a declining marginal cost, and diminishing marginal returns in a rising marginal cost. The MC curve is a mirror reflection of the marginal-product curve. As you can see in Figure 7-6, when marginal product is rising, marginal cost is necessarily falling. When marginal product is at its maximum, marginal cost is at its minimum; when marginal product is falling, marginal cost is rising.

RELATION OF MC TO AVC AND ATC

Figure 7-5 shows that the marginal-cost curve MC intersects both the AVC and ATC curves at their minimum points. As noted earlier, this marginal-average relationship is a mathematical necessity, which a simple illustration will reveal. Suppose a Toronto Raptors basketball player

FIGURE 7-6 **The Relationship between Productivity Curves and Cost Curves**

The marginal-cost (MC) curve and the average-variable-cost (AVC) curve in panel (b) are mirror images of the marginal-product (MP) and average-product (AP) curves in panel (a). Assuming that labour is the only variable input and that its price (the wage rate) is constant, then when MP is rising, MC is falling, and when MP is falling, MC is rising. Under the same assumptions, when AP is rising, AVC is falling, and when AP is falling, AVC is rising.

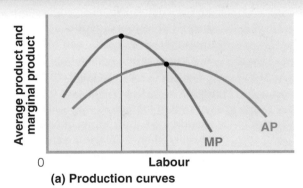
(a) Production curves

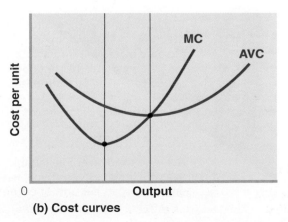
(b) Cost curves

scored an average of 20 points a game in the first three games he has played. Now, whether his average rises or falls as a result of playing a fourth (marginal) game will depend on whether the additional points he scores in that game are fewer or more than his current 20-point average. If in the fourth game he scores fewer than 20 points—for example, 16—his total points will rise from 60 to 76 and his average will fall from 20 to 19 (= 76/4). Conversely, if in the fourth (marginal) game he scores more than 20 points—say, 24—his total will increase from 60 to 84 and his average will rise from 20 to 21 (= 84/4).

So it is with costs. When the amount (the marginal cost) added to total cost is less than the current average total cost, ATC will fall. Conversely, when the marginal cost exceeds ATC, ATC will rise, which means that in Figure 7-5, as long as MC lies below ATC, ATC will fall, and whenever MC lies above ATC, ATC will rise. At the point of intersection, where MC equals ATC, ATC has just stopped falling but has not yet begun rising. This point, by definition, is the minimum point on the ATC curve. The marginal-cost curve intersects the average-total-cost curve at the ATC curve's minimum point.

Marginal cost can be defined as the addition either to total cost or to total variable cost resulting from one more unit of output; thus, this same rationale explains why the MC curve also crosses the AVC curve at the AVC curve's minimum point. No such relationship exists between the MC curve and the average-fixed-cost curve, because the two are not related; marginal cost includes only those costs that change with output, and fixed costs by definition are those that are independent of output.

Shifts of Cost Curves

Changes in either factors of production prices or technology will change costs, and therefore the cost curves will shift. If fixed costs were to double from $100 to $200, the AFC curve in Figure 7-5 would shift upward. At each level of output, fixed costs would be higher. The ATC curve would also move upward, because AFC is a component of ATC. The positions of the AVC and MC curves would be unchanged, because their locations are based on the prices of variable rather than fixed factors of production. However, if the price (wage) of labour or some other variable input rose, AVC, ATC, and MC would rise, and those cost curves would all shift upward. The AFC curve would remain in place because fixed costs have not changed.

The discovery of a more efficient technology would increase the productivity of all inputs, and the AVC, ATC, and MC cost figures in Table 7-2 would all be lower. To illustrate, if labour is the only variable input, if wages are $10 per hour, and if the average product is 10 units, then AVC would be $1. But if a technological improvement increases the average product of labour to 20 units, then AVC will decline to $0.50. More generally, an upward shift in the productivity curves shown in Figure 7-6a means a downward shift in the cost curves portrayed in Figure 7-6b.

connect
MATH 7.4
Relation of MC to AVC and ATC

QUICK REVIEW

- The law of diminishing returns indicates that, beyond some point, output will increase by diminishing amounts as more units of a variable factor (labour) are added to a fixed factor (capital).

- In the short run, the total cost of any level of output is the sum of fixed and variable costs (TC = TFC + TVC).

- Average fixed, average variable, and average total costs are fixed, variable, and total costs per unit of output;

marginal cost is the extra cost of producing one more unit of output.

- Average fixed cost declines continuously as output increases; the average-variable-cost and average-total-cost curves are U-shaped, reflecting increasing and then diminishing returns; the marginal-cost curve falls but then rises, intersecting both the average-variable-cost curve and the average-total-cost curve at their minimum points.

7.4 Long-Run Production Costs

In the long run firms can undertake all desired input adjustments. The firm can alter its plant capacity; it can build a larger plant or revert to a smaller plant than that assumed in Table 7-2. The industry also can change its plant size; the long run allows sufficient time for new firms to enter or for existing firms to leave an industry. We will discuss the impact of the entry and exit of firms to and from an industry in the next chapter; here we are concerned only with changes in plant capacity made by a single firm. Let's express our analysis in terms of average total cost (ATC), making no distinction between fixed and variable costs because all inputs, and therefore all costs, are variable in the long run.

Firm Size and Costs

Suppose a single-plant manufacturer begins on a small scale and, as the result of successful operations, expands to successively larger plant sizes with larger output capacities. What happens to average total cost as this occurs? For a time, successively larger plants will reduce average total cost. However, eventually the building of a still larger plant will cause ATC to rise.

Figure 7-7 illustrates this situation for five possible plant sizes. ATC-1 is the short-run average-total-cost curve for the smallest of the five plants, and ATC-5 is the curve for the largest. Constructing larger plants will lower the minimum average total costs through plant size 3, but then larger plants will mean higher minimum average total costs.

The Long-Run Cost Curve

The vertical lines perpendicular to the output axis in Figure 7-7 indicate those outputs at which the firm should change plant size to realize the lowest attainable average total costs of production. These are the outputs at which the per-unit costs for a larger plant drop below those for the current, smaller plant. For all outputs up to 20 units, the lowest average total costs are attainable with plant size 1. However, if the firm's volume of sales expands to between 20 and 30 units, it can achieve lower per-unit costs by constructing larger plant size 2. Although total cost will be higher at the expanded levels of production, the cost per unit of output will be less. For any output between 30 and 50 units, plant size 3 will yield the lowest average total costs. From 50 to 60 units of output, the firm must build plant size 4 to achieve the lowest unit costs. Lowest average total costs for any output over 60 units require construction of the still larger plant size 5.

FIGURE 7-7 **The Long-Run Average-Total-Cost Curve: Five Possible Plant Sizes**

The long-run average-total-cost curve is made up of segments of the short-run cost curves (ATC-1, ATC-2, etc.) of the various-size plants from which the firm might choose. Each point on the planning curve shows the least unit cost attainable for any output when the firm has had time to make all desired changes in its plant size.

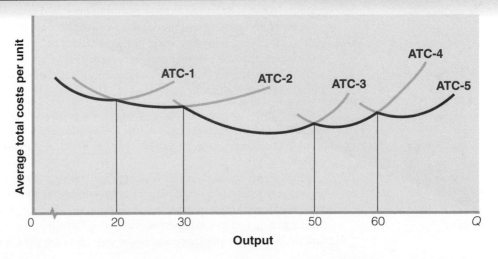

Tracing these adjustments, we find that the long-run ATC curve for the enterprise is made up of segments of the short-run ATC curves for the various plant sizes that can be constructed. The long-run ATC curve shows the lowest average total cost at which *any output level* can be produced after the firm has had time to make all appropriate adjustments in its plant size. In Figure 7-7 the dark blue, uneven curve is the firm's long-run ATC curve or, as it is often called, the firm's *planning curve.*

In most lines of production, the choice of plant size is much wider than in our illustration. In many industries the number of possible plant sizes is virtually unlimited, and in time quite small changes in the volume of output will lead to changes in plant size. Graphically, this implies an unlimited number of short-run ATC curves, one for each output level, as suggested by **Figure 7-8 (Key Graph).** Then, rather than consisting of segments of short-run ATC curves as in Figure 7-7, the long-run ATC curve is made up of all the points of tangency of the unlimited number of short-run ATC curves from which the long-run ATC curve is derived. Therefore, the planning curve is smooth rather than bumpy. Each point on it tells us the minimum ATC of producing the corresponding level of output.

Economies and Diseconomies of Scale

We have assumed that for a time increasing plant sizes will lead to lower unit costs but that beyond some point successively larger plants will mean higher average total costs. That is, we have assumed that the long-run ATC curve is U-shaped. But why should this be? It turns out that the U shape is caused by economies and diseconomies of large-scale production, as we explain in a moment. But before we do, please understand that the U shape of the long-run average-total-cost curve *cannot* be the result of rising factor prices or the law of diminishing returns. First, our discussion assumes that factor prices are constant. Second, the law of diminishing returns does not apply to production in the long run. This is true because the law of diminishing returns deals only with situations in which a productive input is held constant. Under our definition of "long run," all resources and inputs are variable.

ECONOMIES OF SCALE

economies of scale
Reductions in the average total cost of producing a product as the firm increases plant size (output) in the long run.

The downward-sloping part of the long-run ATC curve can be explained through **economies of scale,** or economies of mass production. As plant size increases, a number of factors will for a time lead to lower average costs of production.

Labour Specialization Increased specialization in the use of labour becomes more achievable as a plant increases in size. Hiring more workers means jobs can be divided and subdivided. Each worker may now have just one task to perform instead of five or six. Workers can work full-time on those tasks for which they have special skills. By contrast, skilled machinists in a small plant may spend half their time performing unskilled tasks, leading to higher production costs.

Further, by working at fewer tasks, workers become even more proficient at those tasks. The jack-of-all-trades doing five or six jobs is not likely to be efficient in any of them. By concentrating on one task, the same worker may become highly efficient.

Finally, greater labour specialization eliminates the loss of time that accompanies each shift of a worker from one task to another.

Managerial Specialization Large-scale production also means better use of, and greater specialization in, management. A supervisor who can handle 20 workers is underused in a small plant that employs only 10 people. The production staff could be doubled with no increase in supervisory costs.

Small firms cannot use management specialists to their best advantage. For example, a sales specialist working in a small plant may have to spend some time on functions outside her area of expertise, for example, marketing, personnel, and finance. A larger scale of operations means that the marketing expert can supervise marketing full-time, while specialists perform other managerial functions. Greater efficiency and lower unit costs are the net result.

KEY GRAPH

FIGURE 7-8
The Long-Run Average-Total-Cost Curve: Unlimited Number of Plant Sizes

If the number of possible plant sizes is very large, the long-run average-total-cost curve approximates a smooth curve. Economies of scale, followed by diseconomies of scale, cause the curve to be U-shaped.

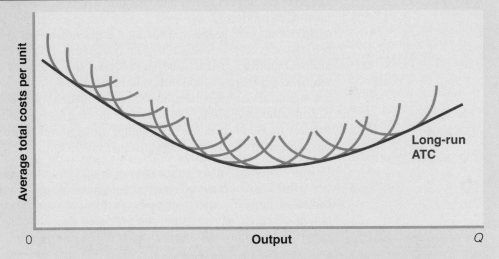

Quick Quiz

1. **The unlabelled light blue curves in this figure illustrate the**
   a. long-run average-total-cost curves of various firms constituting the industry.
   b. short-run average-total-cost curves of various firms constituting the industry.
   c. short-run average-total-cost curves of various plant sizes available to a particular firm.
   d. short-run marginal-cost curves of various plant sizes available to a particular firm.

2. **The unlabelled light blue curves in this figure derive their shapes from**
   a. decreasing, then increasing, short-run returns.
   b. increasing, then decreasing, short-run returns.
   c. economies, then diseconomies, of scale.
   d. diseconomies, then economies, of scale.

3. **The long-run ATC curve in this figure derives its shape from**
   a. decreasing, then increasing, short-run returns.
   b. increasing, then decreasing, short-run returns.
   c. economies, then diseconomies, of scale.
   d. diseconomies, then economies, of scale.

4. **The long-run ATC curve is often called the firm's**
   a. planning curve.
   b. capital-expansion path.
   c. total-product curve.
   d. production possibilities curve.

Answers: 1. c; 2. b; 3. c; 4. a

Efficient Capital   Small firms often cannot afford the most efficient equipment. In many lines of production such machinery is available only in very large and extremely expensive units. Effective use of such equipment demands a high volume of production, and that again requires large-scale producers.

In the automobile industry the most efficient fabrication method in North America employs robotics and elaborate assembly-line equipment. Effective use of this equipment demands an annual output of several hundred thousand automobiles. Only very large-scale producers can afford to purchase and use this equipment efficiently. The small-scale producer is faced with a dilemma. Fabricating automobiles using other equipment is inefficient and therefore more costly per unit. But so, too, is buying and underutilizing the equipment used by the large manufacturers. Because it cannot spread the high equipment cost over very many units of output, the small-scale producer will be stuck with high costs per unit of output.

Other Factors   Many products have design and development costs, as well as other startup costs, that must be incurred regardless of projected sales. These costs decline per unit as output is increased. Similarly, advertising costs decline per auto, per computer, per stereo system, and per box of detergent as more units are produced and sold. The firm's production and marketing expertise usually rises as it produces and sells more output. This learning by doing is a further source of economies of scale.

All these factors contribute to lower average total costs for the firm that is able to expand its scale of operations. Where economies of scale are possible, an increase in all inputs of, say, 10 percent will cause a more-than-proportionate increase in output of, say, 20 percent. The result will be a decline in ATC.

In many Canadian manufacturing industries, from automobile to aircraft production, economies of scale have been of great significance. Firms that have expanded their scale of operations to obtain economies of mass production have survived and flourished. Those unable to expand have become relatively high-cost producers, doomed to struggle to survive.

DISECONOMIES OF SCALE

diseconomies of scale
Increases in the average total cost of producing a product as the firm increases plant size (output) in the long run.

In time the expansion of a firm may lead to diseconomies and, therefore, higher average total costs. The main factor causing **diseconomies of scale** is the difficulty of efficiently controlling and coordinating a firm's operations as it becomes a large-scale producer. In a small plant a single key executive may make all the basic decisions for the plant's operation. Because of the firm's small size, the executive is close to the production line, understands the firm's operations, and can make efficient decisions because the small plant size requires only a relatively small amount of information to be examined and understood in optimizing production. This neat picture changes as a firm grows. One person cannot assemble, digest, and understand all the information essential to decision making on a large scale. Authority must be delegated to many vice presidents, second vice presidents, and so forth. This expansion of the management hierarchy leads to problems of communication and cooperation, bureaucratic red tape, and the possibility that decisions will not be coordinated. At the same time, each new manager must be paid a salary. Thus declining efficiency in making and executing decisions goes hand-in-hand with rising average total costs as bureaucracy expands beyond a certain point.

Also, in massive production facilities workers may feel alienated from their employers and care little about working efficiently. Opportunities to shirk responsibilities, by avoiding work in favour of on-the-job leisure, may be greater in large plants than in small ones. Countering worker alienation and shirking may require additional supervision, which increases costs.

Where diseconomies of scale are operative, an increase in all inputs of, say, 10 percent will cause a less-than-proportionate increase in output of, say, 5 percent. As a consequence, ATC will increase. The rising portion of the long-run cost curves in Figure 7-9a illustrates diseconomies of scale.

FIGURE 7-9 **Various Possible Long-Run Average-Total-Cost Curves**

In panel (a), economies of scale are rather rapidly obtained as plant size rises, and diseconomies of scale are not encountered until a considerably large scale of output has been achieved. Thus, long-run average total cost is constant over a wide range of output. In panel (b), economies of scale are extensive, and diseconomies of scale occur only at very large outputs. Average total cost, therefore, declines over a broad range of output. In panel (c), economies of scale are exhausted quickly, followed immediately by diseconomies of scale. Minimum ATC thus occurs at a relatively low output.

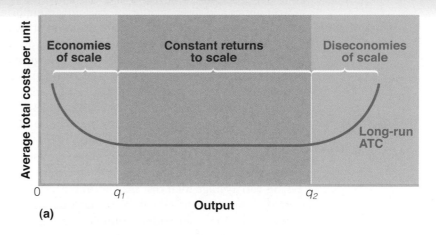

(a)

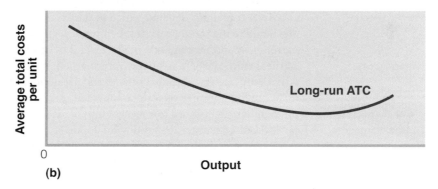

(b)

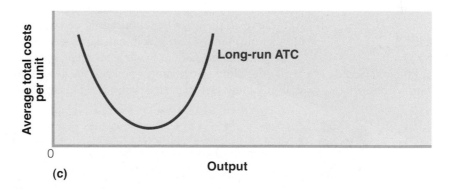

(c)

CONSTANT RETURNS TO SCALE

constant returns to scale
The range of output between the points where economies of scale end and diseconomies of scale begin.

In some industries a rather wide range of output may exist between the output at which economies of scale end and the output at which diseconomies of scale begin. That is, a range of **constant returns to scale** may exist over which long-run average cost does not change. The $q_1 q_2$ output range of Figure 7-9a is an example. Here a given percentage increase in all inputs of, say, 10 percent will cause a proportionate 10 percent increase in output. Thus, in this range ATC is constant.

Minimum Efficient Scale and Industry Structure

minimum efficient scale (MES)
The lowest level of output at which a firm can minimize long-run average costs.

Economies and diseconomies of scale are an important determinant of an industry's structure. We now introduce the concept of **minimum efficient scale (MES),** which is the lowest level of output at which a firm can minimize long-run average costs. In Figure 7-9a that level occurs at q_1 units of output. Because of the extended range of constant returns to scale, firms within the q_1 to q_2 range would be equally efficient, so we would not be surprised to find an industry with such cost conditions to be populated by firms of quite different sizes. The apparel, food processing, furniture, wood products, snowboard, and small-appliance industries are examples. With an extended range of constant returns to scale, relatively large and relatively small firms can coexist in an industry and be equally successful.

Compare this with Figure 7-9b, where economies of scale prevail over a wide range of output and diseconomies of scale appear only at very high levels of output. This pattern of declining long-run average total cost may occur over an extended range of output, as in the automobile, aluminum, steel, and other heavy industries. The same pattern holds in several of the new industries related to information technology, for example, computer microchips, operating system software, and Internet service provision.

Given consumer demand, efficient production will be achieved with a few large-scale producers. Small firms cannot realize the minimum efficient scale and will not be able to compete. In the extreme, economies of scale might extend beyond the market's size, resulting in what is termed **natural monopoly,** a relatively rare market situation in which average total cost is minimized when only one firm produces the particular good or service.

natural monopoly
An industry in which economies of scale are so great that a single firm can produce the product at a lower average total cost than if more than one firm produced the product.

Where economies of scale are few and diseconomies come into play quickly, the minimum efficient size occurs at a low level of output, as shown in Figure 7-9c. In such industries a particular level of consumer demand will support a large number of relatively small producers. Many retail trades and some types of farming fall into this category. So do certain kinds of light manufacturing, such as the baking, clothing, and shoe industries. Fairly small firms are as efficient as, or more efficient than, large-scale producers in such industries.

Our point here is that the shape of the long-run average-total-cost curve is determined by technology and the economies and diseconomies of scale that result. The shape of the long-run ATC curve, in turn, can be significant in determining whether an industry has a relatively large number of small firms or is dominated by a few large producers—or lies somewhere in between.

connect
ORIGIN 7.3
Minimum Efficient Scale and Natural Monopoly

But we must be cautious in our assessment, because industry structure does not depend on cost conditions alone. Government policies, the geographic size of markets, managerial strategy and skill, and other factors must be considered in explaining the structure of a particular industry.

QUICK REVIEW

- Most firms have U-shaped long-run average-total-cost curves, reflecting economies and then diseconomies of scale.

- Economies of scale are the consequence of greater specialization of labour and management, more efficient capital equipment, and spreading startup costs over more units of output.

- Diseconomies of scale are caused by the problems of coordination and communication that arise in large firms.

- Minimum efficient scale is the lowest level of output at which a firm's long-run average total cost is at a minimum.

Applications and Illustrations

The business world offers many examples relating to short-run costs, economies of scale, and minimum efficient scale (MES). Here are just a few.

RISING GASOLINE PRICES

As we discussed in the appendix to Chapter 3, changes in supply and demand often lead to rapid increases in the price of gasoline. Because gasoline is used to power nearly all motor vehicles, including those used by businesses, increases in the price of gasoline lead to increases in firms' short-run variable costs, marginal costs, and average total costs. In terms of our analysis, their AVC, MC, and ATC curves all shift upward when an increase in the price of gasoline increases their production costs.

The extent of these upward shifts depends upon the relative importance of gasoline as a variable input in the various firms' individual production processes. Package-delivery companies like FedEx that use a lot of gasoline-powered vehicles will see substantial upward shifts while software companies like Open Text (an enterprise software company based in Waterloo, Ontario) that mainly deliver their products through Internet downloads, may see only very small upward shifts.

SUCCESSFUL STARTUP FIRMS

The Canadian economy has greatly benefited over the past few decades from explosive growth of startup firms. Where economies of scale are significant, firms can enjoy years or even decades of growth accompanied by lower average total costs—examples include Second Cup (coffee), Research In Motion (wireless communication), Celestica (computer components), and JDS Uniphase (fibre optics).

A major source of lower average costs is the ability to spread huge product development and advertising costs over an increasing number of units of output. These firms also achieve economies of scale from learning by doing, through increased specialization of labour, management, and equipment. After starting up, such firms experience declining average total costs over the years or even decades it takes them to eventually reach their respective MES.

THE DAILY NEWSPAPER

Daily newspapers have been going bankrupt in rapid succession over the past several years as both advertising dollars and news readership have shifted to the Internet. The falling circulation numbers have caused average fixed costs to skyrocket as newspapers are forced to spread their substantial fixed costs over fewer and fewer papers. The spike in average fixed costs has, in turn, forced newspapers to sharply increase their prices. Between July 2007 and July 2009, for instance, the *New York Times* had to raise is cover price three times as advertising revenues tanked and fixed costs had to be spread over fewer and fewer papers. Starting at $1 per copy, the cover price had to be raised to $1.25, then $1.50, and then $2.00.

With readership continuing to fall, newspapers face an average-fixed-cost death spiral. The more they raise prices, the fewer the people who will buy their papers. But the fewer the people who buy their papers, the higher their AFCs and thus the more they need to raise prices. As a result, many economists expect printed newspapers to largely go the way of the dinosaurs, with both advertising and news delivery shifting almost entirely to the Internet.

THE VERSON STAMPING MACHINE

In 1996, Verson (a U.S. firm located in Chicago) introduced a 15-metre-tall metal-stamping machine that is the size of a house and weighs as much as 12 locomotives. This U.S.$30 million machine, which cuts and sculpts raw sheets of steel into automobile hoods and fenders, enables automakers to make new parts in just 5 minutes compared with 8 hours for older stamping presses. A single machine is designed to make 5 million auto parts per year. So, to achieve the cost saving from the machine, an auto manufacturer must have sufficient auto production to use all of these parts. By allowing the use of this cost-saving piece of equipment, large firm size achieves economies of scale.

AIRCRAFT AND CONCRETE PLANTS

Why are there only two plants in Canada (in Toronto and Montreal, both operated by Bombardier) that produce business and regional aircraft, but hundreds of plants that produce ready-mixed

Economies and diseconomies of scale are important determinants of an industry's market structure.

concrete? The simple answer is that MES is radically different in the two industries. Why is that? First, economies of scale are extensive in assembling business and regional aircraft and very modest in mixing concrete. Manufacturing airplanes is a complex process that requires huge facilities, thousands of workers, and very expensive, specialized machinery. Economies of scale extend to huge plant sizes. But mixing cement, sand, gravel, and water efficiently to produce concrete requires only a handful of workers and relatively inexpensive equipment. Economies of scale are exhausted at a relatively small size.

The differing minimum efficient scales also derive from the vastly different sizes of the geographic markets. The market for business and regional airplanes is global, and aircraft manufacturers can deliver new airplanes anywhere in the world by flying them there. In contrast, the geographic market for a concrete plant is roughly the 75-kilometre radius that enables the concrete to be delivered before it "sets up." So hundreds of small concrete plants locate close to their customers in small and large cities in Canada, or even temporarily, such as next to a highway under construction.

The LAST WORD | Don't Cry over Sunk Costs

Sunk costs are irrelevant in decision making.

There is an old saying: Don't cry over spilt milk. The message is that once you have spilled a glass of milk, there is nothing you can do to recover it, so you should forget about it and move on from there. This saying has great relevance to what economists call sunk costs. Such costs are like sunken ships on the ocean floor: once these costs are incurred, they cannot be recovered.

Let's gain an understanding of this idea by applying it first to consumers and then to businesses. Suppose you buy an expensive ticket to an upcoming Grey Cup football game between the Calgary Stampeders and the Hamilton Tiger Cats. But the morning of the game you wake up with a bad case of the flu. Feeling miserable, you step outside to find that the wind chill is about −20°C. You absolutely do not want to go to the game, but you remind yourself that you paid a steep price for the ticket. You call several people to try to sell the ticket, but you soon discover that no one is interested in it, even at a discounted price. You conclude that everyone who wants a ticket has one.

Should you go to the game? Economic analysis says that you should not take actions for which marginal cost exceeds marginal benefit. In this case, if the marginal cost of going to the game is greater than the marginal benefit, the best decision is to go back to bed. In correctly applying this rule, however, it is crucial that you recognize that the price you paid for the ticket is *not* a marginal cost. Even if the ticket was hideously expensive, it was purchased previously. Thus, its cost is not a marginal, extra cost that depends on whether or not you go to the game. The cost has already been incurred and must therefore be dealt with even if you decide not to attend!

With the cost of the ticket out of the picture, your cost–benefit analysis is going to be settled by your opinion that you absolutely do not want to go. With such a strongly negative opinion, the marginal cost obviously exceeds the marginal benefit, and you should not go.

Here is a second consumer example. Suppose a family is on vacation in B.C.'s Okanagan Valley and stops at a roadside stand to buy some apples. The kids get back into the car and bite into their apples, immediately pronouncing them "totally mushy" and unworthy of another bite. Both parents agree that the apples are terrible, but the father continues to eat his, because, as he says, "We paid a premium price for them." One of the older children replies, "Dad, that's irrelevant." Although not stated very diplomatically, the child is exactly right. In making a new decision, you should ignore all costs that are not affected by the decision. The prior bad decision (in retrospect) to buy the apples should not dictate a second decision for which marginal benefit is less than marginal cost.

Now let's apply the idea of sunk costs to firms. Some of a firm's costs not only are fixed (recurring, but unrelated to the level of output), but also are sunk (unrecoverable). For example, a non-refundable annual lease payment for the use of a store cannot be recouped once it has been paid. A firm's decision about whether to move from the store to a more profitable location does not depend on the amount of time remaining on the lease. If moving means greater profit, it makes sense to move whether there are 300 days, 30 days, or 3 days left on the lease.

Or, as another example, suppose a firm spends $1 million on R&D to bring out a new product, only to discover that the product sells very poorly. Should the firm continue to produce the product at a loss even when there is no realistic hope for future success? Obviously, it should not. In making this decision, the firm realizes that the amount it has spent in developing the product is irrelevant; it should stop production of the product and cut its losses. In fact, many firms have dropped products after spending millions of dollars on their development. A recent example is Pfizer's decision in 2007 to shelve its novel insulin inhaler because of poor sales and concerns about long-term side effects. The product withdrawal forced Pfizer to take a $2.8 billion pretax loss on this highly touted product.

Consider a final real-world example. Nortel Networks is one of the best-known Canadian telecommunications companies. It started business in 1895, when it began making equipment for traditional phone companies. It was originally part of Bell Telephone, before it became known as Northern Telecom, later shortened to Nortel. In the 1990s, especially under the leadership of John Roth beginning in 1997, Nortel experienced explosive growth as it transformed itself from a telephone equipment manufacturer to a provider of network gear and optical transmission lines for the Internet. By the late 1990s it was also heavily into wireless transmission gear. As the Internet quickly grew, Nortel could not keep up with the large number of orders flowing in. At its peak in early 2000, Nortel employed over 90,000 employees worldwide and the company's stock rose to over $100. The frenzied expansion came to an abrupt end as overextended telephone companies sharply reduced capital expenditures, especially on fibre optics equipment. By the end of 2008, Nortel had only 32,000 employees and was shedding part of its unprofitable lines. During this downsizing, in October 2002, Nortel sold its optical transmitter and receiver business and its pump laser and amplifiers business, which it had acquired during the heady days of rapid expansion, to a British company for a small fraction of the original purchase price. But at that point, the original acquisition cost was irrelevant because the telecommunication business had changed.

In short, if a cost has been incurred and cannot be partly or fully recouped by some other choice, a rational consumer or firm should ignore it. Sunk costs are irrelevant. Don't cry over sunk costs.

Question

What is a sunk cost? Provide an example of a sunk cost other than the one in the text. Why are such costs irrelevant in making decisions about future actions?

:: CHAPTER SUMMARY

7.1 :: ECONOMIC COSTS

- The economic cost of using a resource to produce a good or service is the value or worth that the resource would have had in its best alternative use. Economic costs include all payments that must be received by resource owners of factors of production to ensure a continued supply of needed inputs to a particular line of production.

- Explicit costs flow to factors of production owned and supplied by others; implicit costs are payments for the use of self-owned and self-employed factors of production. One implicit cost is a normal profit to the entrepreneur.

- Economic profit occurs when total revenue exceeds total cost (= explicit costs + implicit costs, including a normal profit).

7.2 :: SHORT-RUN PRODUCTION RELATIONSHIPS

- In the short run a firm's plant capacity is fixed. The firm can use its plant more or less intensively by adding or subtracting units of various factors of production, but it does not have sufficient time in the short run to alter plant size.

- The law of diminishing returns describes what happens to output as a fixed plant is used more intensively; as successive units of a variable factor such as labour are added to a fixed plant, beyond some point the marginal product associated with each additional worker declines.

7.3 :: SHORT-RUN PRODUCTION COSTS

- Because some factors of production are fixed and others are variable, costs can be classified as fixed or variable in the short run. Fixed costs are independent of the level of output; variable costs vary with output. The total cost of any output is the sum of fixed and variable costs at that output.

- Average fixed costs, average variable costs, and average total costs are fixed, variable, and total costs per unit of output. Average fixed cost declines continuously as output increases because a fixed sum is being spread over an increasing number of units of production. A graph of average variable cost is U-shaped, reflecting the law of diminishing returns. Average total cost is the sum of average fixed and average variable costs; its graph is also U-shaped.

- Marginal cost is the extra cost of producing one more unit of output. It is the amount by which total cost and total variable cost change when one more or one fewer unit of output is produced. Graphically, the marginal cost curve intersects the ATC and AVC curves at their minimum points.

- Lower input prices shift cost curves downward, as does technological progress. Higher input prices shift cost curves upward.

7.4 :: LONG-RUN PRODUCTION COSTS

- The long run is a period of time sufficiently long for a firm to vary the amounts of all inputs used, including plant size. In the long run all costs are variable. The long-run ATC, or planning, curve is composed of segments of the short-run ATC curves, and it represents the various plant sizes a firm can construct in the long run.

- The long-run ATC curve is generally U-shaped. Economies of scale are first encountered as a small firm expands. Greater specialization in the use of labour and management, the ability to use the most efficient equipment, and spreading startup costs among more units of output all contribute to economies of scale. As the firm continues to grow, it will encounter diseconomies of scale stemming from the managerial complexities that accompany large-scale production. The output ranges over which economies and diseconomies of scale occur in an industry are often an important determinant of the structure of that industry.

- A firm's minimum efficient scale (MES) is the lowest level of output at which it can minimize its long-run average cost. In some industries, MES occurs at such low levels of output that numerous firms can populate the industry. In other industries, MES occurs at such high output levels that only a few firms can exist in the long run.

:: TERMS AND CONCEPTS

economic cost, p. 168	total product (TP), p. 172	average variable cost (AVC), p. 178
explicit costs, p. 168	marginal product (MP), p. 172	average total cost (ATC), p. 179
implicit costs, p. 168	average product (AP), p. 172	marginal cost (MC), p. 179
accounting profit, p. 169	law of diminishing returns, p. 172	economies of scale, p. 184
normal profit, p. 169	fixed costs, p. 176	diseconomies of scale, p. 186
economic profit, p. 170	variable costs, p. 177	constant returns to scale, p. 187
short run, p. 171	total cost, p. 177	minimum efficient scale (MES), p. 188
long run, p. 171	average fixed cost (AFC), p. 178	natural monopoly, p. 188

:: QUESTIONS

1. Distinguish between explicit and implicit costs, giving examples of each. What are some explicit and implicit costs of attending college or university?   [**LO7.1**]

2. Distinguish between accounting profit, economic profit, and normal profit. Does accounting profit or economic profit determine how entrepreneurs allocate resources between different business ventures? Explain.   [**LO7.1**]

3. Which of the following are short-run and which are long-run adjustments?   [**LO7.1**]

   a. Wendy's builds a new restaurant.

   b. Scotiabank hires 200 more workers.

   c. A farmer increases the amount of fertilizer used on her corn crop.

   d. An Alcan aluminum plant adds a third shift of workers.

4. Complete the following table by calculating marginal product and average product from the data given. [**LO7.2**]

Inputs of labour	Total product	Marginal product	Average product
0	0	_____	_____
1	15	_____	_____
2	34	_____	_____
3	51	_____	_____
4	65	_____	_____
5	74	_____	_____
6	80	_____	_____
7	83	_____	_____
8	82	_____	_____

a. Plot the total, marginal, and average products and explain in detail the relationship between each pair of curves.

b. Explain why marginal product first rises, then declines, and ultimately becomes negative.

c. What bearing does the law of diminishing returns have on short-run costs? Be specific.

d. When marginal product is rising, marginal cost is falling. And when marginal product is diminishing, marginal cost is rising. Explain and illustrate graphically.

5. Why can the distinction between fixed costs and variable costs be made in the short run? Explain the following statement: "There are no fixed costs in the long run; all costs are variable." Classify the following as fixed or variable costs. **[LO7.3]**

a. Advertising expenditures

b. Fuel

c. Interest on company-issued bonds

d. Shipping charges

e. Payments for raw materials

f. Real estate taxes

g. Executive salaries

h. Insurance premiums

i. Wage payments

j. Depreciation and obsolescence charges

k. Sales taxes

l. Rental payments on leased office machinery

6. List several fixed and variable costs associated with owning and operating an automobile. Suppose you are considering whether to drive your car or fly 2000 kilometres for spring break. Which costs—fixed, variable, or both—would you take into account in making your decision? Would any implicit costs be relevant? Explain. **[LO7.3]**

7. A firm has $60 in fixed costs and variable costs as indicated in the table below. Complete the table; check your calculations by referring to Question 4 at the end of Chapter 8. **[LO7.3]**

a. Graph total fixed cost, total variable cost, and total cost. Explain how the law of diminishing returns influences the shapes of the variable-cost and total-cost curves.

b. Graph AFC, AVC, ATC, and MC. Explain the derivation and shape of each of these four curves and their relationships to one another. Specifically, explain in nontechnical terms why the MC curve intersects both the AVC and ATC curves at their minimum points.

c. Explain how the location of each curve graphed in question 7b would be altered if (1) total fixed cost had been $100 rather than $60 and (2) total variable cost had been $10 less at each level of output.

Total product	Total fixed cost	Total variable cost	Total cost	Average fixed cost	Average variable cost	Average total cost	Marginal cost
0	$_____	$ 0	$_____	$_____	$_____	$_____	$_____
1	_____	45	_____	_____	_____	_____	_____
2	_____	85	_____	_____	_____	_____	_____
3	_____	120	_____	_____	_____	_____	_____
4	_____	150	_____	_____	_____	_____	_____
5	_____	185	_____	_____	_____	_____	_____
6	_____	225	_____	_____	_____	_____	_____
7	_____	270	_____	_____	_____	_____	_____
8	_____	325	_____	_____	_____	_____	_____
9	_____	390	_____	_____	_____	_____	_____
10	_____	465	_____	_____	_____	_____	_____

8. Indicate how each of the following would shift the (1) marginal-cost curve, (2) average-variable-cost curve, (3) average-fixed-cost curve, and (4) average-total-cost curve of a manufacturing firm. In each case specify the direction of the shift. [**LO7.3**]

   a. A reduction in business property taxes

   b. An increase in the nominal wages of production workers

   c. A decrease in the price of electricity

   d. An increase in insurance rates on plant and equipment

   e. An increase in transportation costs

9. Suppose a firm has only three possible plant-size options, represented by the ATC curves shown in the accompanying figure. What plant size will the firm choose in producing (a) 50, (b) 130, (c) 160, and (d) 250 units of output? Draw the firm's long-run average-cost curve on the diagram and describe this curve. [**LO7.4**]

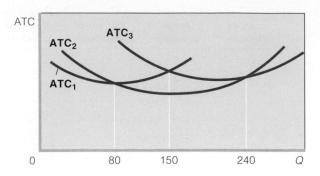

10. Use the concepts of economies and diseconomies of scale to explain the shape of a firm's long-run ATC curve. What is the concept of minimum efficient scale? What bearing can the shape of the long-run ATC curve have on the structure of an industry? [**LO7.4**]

:: PROBLEMS

1. Gomez runs a small pottery firm. He hires one helper at $12,000 per year, pays annual rent of $5000 for his shop, and spends $20,000 per year on materials. He has $40,000 of his own funds invested in equipment (pottery wheels, kilns, and so forth) that could earn him $4000 per year if alternatively invested. He has been offered $15,000 per year to work as a potter for a competitor. He estimates his entrepreneurial talents to be worth $3000 per year. Total annual revenue from pottery sales is $72,000. Calculate the accounting profit and the economic profit for Gomez's pottery firm. [**LO7.1**]

2. Imagine you have some workers and some hand-held computers that you can use to take inventory at a warehouse. There are diminishing returns to taking inventory. If one worker uses one computer, he can inventory 100 items per hour. Two workers can together inventory 150 items per hour. Three workers can together inventory 160 items per hour. And four or more workers can together inventory fewer than 160 items per hour. Computers cost $100 each and you must pay each worker $25 per hour. If you assign one worker per computer, what is the cost of inventorying a single item with one worker? What if you assign two workers per computer? Three? How many workers per computer should you assign if you wish to minimize the cost of inventorying a single item? [**LO7.2**]

3. You are a newspaper publisher. You are in the middle of a one-year rental contract for your factory that requires you to pay $500,000 per month, and you have contractual labour obligations of $1 million per month that you can't get out of. You also have a marginal printing cost of $0.25 per paper as well as a marginal delivery cost of $0.10 per paper. If sales fall by 20 percent from 1 million papers per month to 800,000 papers per month, what happens to the AFC per paper, to the MC per paper, and to the minimum amount that you must charge to break even on these costs? [**LO7.3**]

4. There are economies of scale in ranching, especially with regard to fencing land. Suppose that barbed-wire fencing costs $10,000 per kilometre to set up. How much would it cost to fence a single property whose area is one square kilometre if that property also happens to be perfectly square, with sides that are each one kilometre long? How much would it cost to fence exactly four such properties, which together would contain four square kilometres of area? Now, consider how much it would cost to fence in four square kilometres of ranch land if, instead, it comes as a single large square that is two kilometres long on each side. Which is more costly—fencing in the four, one-square-kilometre properties or the single four-square-kilometre property? [**LO7.4**]

CHAPTER 8 ::

Perfect Competition in the Short Run

In Chapter 4 we examined the relationship between product demand and total revenue, and in Chapter 7 we discussed production costs. Now we want to connect revenues and costs to see how a business decides what price to charge and how much output to produce. A firm's decisions concerning price and production depend greatly on the market structure of the industry in which it operates. No "average" or "typical" industry exists. At one extreme is an industry in which a single producer dominates the market; at the other extreme are industries in which thousands of firms each produce a minute fraction of market supply. Between these extremes are many other types of industries.

Since we cannot examine each industry individually, we will focus on four basic models of market structure. Together, these models will help you to understand how price and output are determined in the many product markets in the economy, and *to evaluate the efficiency or inefficiency of those markets*. These four models also provide a crucial background for assessing public policies (such as anticombines policy) relating to certain firms and industries, which we will explore in later chapters.

8.1 Four Market Structures ::

Economists group industries into four distinct market structures: perfect competition, monopoly, monopolistic competition, and oligopoly. These four market models differ in several respects: the number of firms in the industry, whether those firms

AFTER READING THIS CHAPTER, YOU SHOULD BE ABLE TO:

8.1 Name the four basic market structures and summarize their main characteristics.

8.2 List the conditions required for perfectly competitive markets.

8.3 Convey how firms in perfect competition maximize profits or minimize losses in the short run.

8.4 Explain why a competitive firm's marginal cost curve is the same as its supply curve.

TABLE 8-1	Characteristics of the Four Basic Market Models

MARKET MODEL

Characteristic	Perfect competition	Monopolistic competition	Oligopoly	Monopoly
Number of firms	A very large number	Many	Few	One
Type of product	Standardized	Differentiated	Standardized or differentiated	Unique; no close substitutes
Control over price	None	Some, but within rather narrow limits	Limited by mutual interdependence; considerable with collusion	Considerable
Conditions of entry	Very easy, no obstacles	Relatively easy	Significant obstacles	Blocked
Nonprice competition	None	Considerable emphasis on advertising, brand names, trademarks	Typically a great deal, particularly with product differentiation	Mostly public relations/ advertising
Examples	Agriculture	Retail trade, dresses, shoes	Steel, automobiles, farm implements, many household appliances	Local utilities

produce a standardized product or try to differentiate their products from those of other firms, and how easy or how difficult it is for firms to enter the industry.

Very briefly, the four models are as follows:

perfect competition
A market structure in which a very large number of firms produce a standardized product.

1. The **perfect competition** market structure is characterized by a very large number of firms producing a standardized product (that is, a product such as cotton for which each producer's output is virtually identical to that of every other producer). New firms can enter the industry very easily.

monopoly
A market structure in which one firm is the sole seller of a product or service.

2. In the **monopoly** market structure, one firm is the sole seller of a product or service (for example, a regional electrical power supplier). Since the entry of additional firms is blocked, one firm constitutes the entire industry. The monopolist produces a unique product, so product differentiation is not an issue.

monopolistic competition
A market structure in which a relatively large number of sellers produce differentiated products.

3. In **monopolistic competition,** a relatively large number of sellers produce differentiated products (clothing, furniture, books). Present in this model is widespread *nonprice competition,* a selling strategy in which a firm does not try to distinguish its product on the basis of price but instead on attributes like design and quality (an approach called *product differentiation*). Entry to monopolistically competitive industries is quite easy.

oligopoly
A market structure in which a few large firms produce homogeneous or differentiated products.

4. In **oligopoly,** there are only a few sellers of a homogeneous or differentiated product; consequently each firm is affected by the decisions of its rivals and must take those decisions into account when determining its own price and output.

imperfect competition
The market models of monopoly, monopolistic competition, and oligopoly considered as a group.

Table 8-1 summarizes the characteristics of the four models for easy comparison and later reference. In discussing these four market models, we occasionally distinguish the characteristics of *perfect competition* from those of the three other basic market structures, which together we designate as **imperfect competition.**

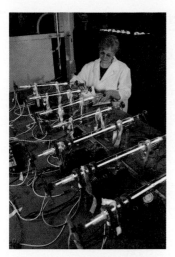

Firms in a perfectly competitive industry produce a standardized product.

Characteristics of Perfect Competition and the Firm's Demand Curve

Although perfect competition is relatively rare in the real world, this market model is highly relevant. A few industries more closely approximate perfect competition than any other market structure. In particular, we can learn much about markets for agricultural goods, fish products, foreign exchange, basic metals, and stock shares by studying the perfect competition model. Also, perfect competition is a meaningful starting point for any discussion of price and output determination. The operation of a competitive economy provides a standard, or norm, for evaluating the efficiency of the real-world economy. Let's take a fuller look at perfect competition, the focus of the remainder of this chapter. Perfect competition is characterized by:

- *Very Large Numbers* A basic feature of a perfectly competitive market is the presence of a large number of independently acting sellers offering their products in large national or international markets. None of the firms in a perfectly competitive market structure have market power Examples: the farm commodities market, the stock market, and the foreign exchange market.

- *Standardized Product* Firms in perfect competition produce a standardized (identical or homogeneous) product. As long as the price is the same, consumers will be indifferent about which seller to buy the product from. Buyers view the products of firms B, C, D, and E as perfect substitutes for the product of firm A. Because firms in a perfectly competitive industry sell standardized products, they make no attempt to differentiate their products and do not engage in other forms of nonprice competition. An example of a standardized product is organically grown apples.

price-taker
A firm in a purely competitive market that cannot change market price, but can only adjust to it.

- *Price-Takers* Individual firms in perfectly competitive markets do not exert control over product price. Each firm produces such a small fraction of total output that increasing or decreasing its output will not noticeably influence total supply or, therefore, product price. In short, the competitive firm is a **price-taker:** it cannot change the market price, but can only adjust to it. Asking a price higher than the market price would be futile; consumers will not buy from firm A at $2.05 per unit when its 9999 competitors are selling an identical product at $2 per unit. Conversely, because firm A can sell as much as it chooses at $2 per unit, it has no reason to charge a lower price, say, $1.95. Doing that would lower its profit. It should be noted that many firms in Canada exporting goods and services in the international market are, for all intents and purposes, price-takers.

- *Easy Entry and Exit* New firms can easily enter, and existing firms can easily leave perfectly competitive industries in the long run. No significant legal, technological, financial, or other obstacles prohibit new firms from selling their output in any competitive market.

Demand for a Firm in Perfect Competition

We begin by examining demand from a perfectly competitive seller's viewpoint to see how it affects revenue. This seller might be a wheat farmer, a strawberry grower, or a foreign currency broker. Each firm in a perfectly competitive industry offers only a negligible fraction of total market supply, so it must accept the price determined by the market; it is a price-taker, not a price-maker.

PERFECTLY ELASTIC DEMAND

The demand schedule faced by the *individual firm* in a purely competitive industry is perfectly elastic at the market price, as demonstrated in Figure 8-1. As shown in column 1 of the table in Figure 8-1, the market price is $131. The firm cannot obtain a higher price by restricting its output, nor does it need to lower its price to increase its sales volume. Columns 1 and 2 show that the firm can produce and sell as many or as few units as it likes at the market price of $131.

Although perfect competition is rare in the real world, by studying it we can learn much about markets such as the market for agricultural products.

| FIGURE 8-1 | The Demand and Revenue Curves for a Firm in Perfect Competition |

FIRM'S DEMAND SCHEDULE		FIRM'S REVENUE DATA	
(1) Product price (P) (average revenue)	(2) Quantity demanded (Q)	(3) Total revenue (TR) (1) × (2)	(4) Marginal revenue (MR)
$ 131	0	$ 0	
			$ 131
131	1	131	
			131
131	2	262	
			131
131	3	393	
			131
131	4	524	
			131
131	5	655	
			131
131	6	786	
			131
131	7	917	
			131
131	8	1048	
			131
131	9	1179	
			131
131	10	1310	

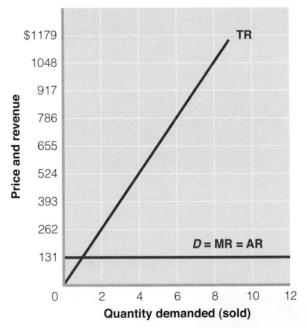

The demand curve (D) of a firm in a perfectly competitive industry is a horizontal line (perfectly elastic) because the firm can sell as much output as it wants at the market price (here, $131). Because each additional unit sold increases total revenue by the amount of the price, the firm's total-revenue curve (TR) is a straight upward-sloping line and its marginal-revenue curve (MR) coincides with the firm's demand curve. The average-revenue curve (AR) also coincides with the demand curve.

We are *not* saying that *market* demand is perfectly elastic in a competitive market. Rather, market demand graphs as a downward-sloping curve. An entire industry (all firms producing a particular product) can affect price by changing industry output. For example, all firms, acting independently but simultaneously, can increase price by reducing output. But the individual competitive firm cannot do that because its output represents such a small fraction of its industry's total output. For the individual competitive firm, the market price is therefore a fixed value at which it can sell as many or as few units as it cares to. Graphically, this implies that the individual competitive firm's demand curve will plot as a straight, horizontal line such as D in Figure 8-1.

Average, Total, and Marginal Revenue

average revenue
Total revenue from the sale of a product divided by the quantity of the product sold.

total revenue
The total number of dollars received by a firm from the sale of a product.

marginal revenue
The change in total revenue that results from selling one more unit of a firm's product.

The firm's demand schedule is also its average-revenue schedule. Price per unit to the purchaser is also revenue per unit, or average revenue, to the seller. To say that all buyers must pay $131 per unit is to say that the revenue per unit, or **average revenue** received by the seller, is $131. Price and average revenue are the same thing.

The **total revenue** for each sales level is found by multiplying price by the corresponding quantity the firm can sell (column 1 multiplied by column 2 in the table in Figure 8-1 yields column 3). In this case, total revenue increases by a constant amount, $131, for each additional unit of sales. Each unit sold adds exactly its constant price—no more and no less—to total revenue.

When a firm is pondering a change in its output, it considers how its total revenue will change as a result. **Marginal revenue** is the change in total revenue (or the extra revenue) that results from selling one more unit of output. In column 3 of the table in Figure 8-1, total revenue is zero when zero units are sold. The first unit of output sold increases total revenue from zero to $131, so marginal revenue for that unit is $131. The second unit sold increases total revenue from $131 to $262, and marginal revenue is again $131. Note in column 4 that marginal revenue is a constant $131, as is price. *In perfect competition, marginal revenue and price are equal.*

Figure 8-1 shows the perfectly competitive firm's total-revenue, demand, marginal-revenue, and average-revenue curves. Total revenue (TR) is a straight line that slopes upward to the right. Its slope is constant because each extra unit of sales increases TR by $131. The demand curve (*D*) is horizontal, indicating perfect price elasticity. The marginal-revenue curve (MR) coincides with the demand curve because the product price (and hence MR) is constant. The average revenue equals price and therefore also coincides with the demand curve.

QUICK REVIEW

- In a perfectly competitive industry a large number of firms produce a standardized product and no significant barriers to entry exist.

- The demand of a competitive firm is perfectly elastic—horizontal on a graph—at the market price.

- Marginal revenue and average revenue for a competitive firm coincide with the firm's demand curve; total revenue rises by the product price for each additional unit sold.

8.3 Profit Maximization in the Short Run

Since the firm in a perfectly competitive market structure is a price-taker, it cannot attempt to maximize its profit by raising or lowering the price it charges. With its price set by supply and demand in the overall market, the only variable that the firm can control is its output. As a result, the purely competitive firm attempts to maximize its economic profit (or minimize its economic loss) by adjusting its *output*. And in the short run, the firm has a fixed plant. Thus, it can adjust its output only through changes in the amount of variable inputs (materials, labour) it uses. It adjusts its variable inputs to achieve the output level that maximizes its profit.

There are two ways to determine the level of output at which a competitive firm will obtain maximum profit or minimum loss. One method is to compare total revenue and total cost; the other is to compare marginal revenue and marginal cost. Both approaches apply to all firms, whether they are perfectly competitive, monopolists, monopolistic competitors, or oligopolists.[1]

---

[1] To make sure you understand these two approaches, we will apply them both to output determination under perfect competition, but since we want to emphasize the marginal approach, we will limit our graphical application of the total-revenue approach to a situation where the firm maximizes profits. We will then use the marginal approach to examine three cases: profit maximization, loss minimization, and shutdown.

connect
WORKED PROBLEM 8.1
Profit Maximization:
TR−TC Approach

Total-Revenue–Total-Cost Approach

We begin by examining profit maximization using the total-revenue−total-cost approach. Confronted with the market price of its product, the competitive producer will ask: (1) Should we produce this product? (2) If so, in what amount? (3) What economic profit (or loss) will we realize?

Let's demonstrate how a firm in perfect competition answers these questions, given a particular set of cost data and a specific market price in Figure 8-2. Our cost data are total fixed-cost, total variable-cost, and total-cost data that reflect explicit and implicit costs, including a normal profit. Assuming that the market price is $131, the total revenue for each output level is found by multiplying output (total product) by price. Total revenue data are in column 5. Then in column 6 we find the profit or loss at each output level by subtracting total cost, TC (column 4), from total revenue, TR (column 5).

Should the firm produce? Definitely. It can make a profit by doing so. How much should it produce? Nine units. Column 6 tells us that this is the output at which total economic profit is at a maximum. What economic profit (or loss) will the firm realize? A $299 economic profit—the difference between total revenue ($1179) and total cost ($880).

Figure 8-2a compares total revenue and total cost graphically for this profit-maximizing case. Observe again that the total-revenue curve for a firm in a perfectly competitive industry is a straight line. Total cost increases with output because more production requires more factors of production, but the *rate* of increase in total cost varies with the efficiency of the firm, which in turn varies with the amount of variable inputs that are being combined with the firm's current amount of capital (which is fixed in the short run). Stated slightly differently, the cost data reflect Chapter 7's law of diminishing returns. From zero to four units of output, total cost increases at a decreasing rate as the firm temporarily experiences increasing returns. At higher levels of output, however, efficiency falls as crowding causes diminishing returns to set in. Once that happens, the firm's total cost increases at an increasing rate because each additional unit of input yields less output than the previous unit.

Total revenue and total cost are equal where the two curves in Figure 8-2a intersect (at roughly two units of output). Total revenue covers all costs (including a normal profit, which is included in the cost curve) but there is no economic profit. For this reason economists call this output a **break-even point:** an output at which a firm makes a *normal profit* but not an economic profit. If we extended the data beyond 10 units of output, another break-even point would occur where total cost would catch up with total revenue somewhere between 13 and 14 units of output in Figure 8-2a. Any output between the two break-even points identified in the figure will yield an economic profit. The firm achieves maximum profit, however, where the vertical distance between the total-revenue and total-cost curves is greatest. For our particular data, this is at nine units of output, where maximum profit is $299.

The profit-maximizing output is easier to see in Figure 8-2b, where total economic profit is graphed for each level of output. Where the total-revenue and total-cost curves intersect in Figure 8-2a, economic profit is zero, as shown by the total-profit line in Figure 8-2b. Where the vertical distance between TR and TC is greatest in the upper graph, economic profit is at its peak ($299), as shown in the lower graph. This firm will choose to produce nine units, since that output maximizes its profit.

Marginal-Revenue–Marginal-Cost Approach

In the second approach, the firm compares the amounts that each *additional* unit of output would add to total revenue and to total cost. In other words, the firm compares the *marginal revenue* (MR) and the *marginal cost* (MC) of each successive unit of output. Assuming that producing is preferable to shutting down, the firm will produce any unit of output whose marginal revenue exceeds its marginal cost because the firm would gain more in revenue from selling that unit than it would add to its costs by producing it. Conversely, if the marginal cost of a unit of output exceeds its marginal revenue, the firm will not produce that unit. Producing it would add more to costs than to revenue, and profit would decline or loss would increase.

break-even point
An output at which a firm makes a normal profit but not an economic profit.

CHOOSING A LITTLE
MORE OR LESS

FIGURE 8-2

Total-Revenue–Total-Cost Approach to Profit Maximization for a Firm in a Perfectly Competitive Industry

				PRICE: $131	
(1) Total product (output), Q	(2) Total fixed cost, TFC	(3) Total variable cost, TVC	(4) Total cost, TC	(5) Total revenue, TR	(6) Profit (+) or loss (−)
0	$ 100	$ 0	$ 100	$ 0	$−100
1	100	90	190	131	−59
2	100	170	270	262	−8
3	100	240	340	393	+53
4	100	300	400	524	+124
5	100	370	470	655	+185
6	100	450	550	786	+236
7	100	540	640	917	+277
8	100	650	750	1048	+298
9	100	780	880	1179	+299
10	100	930	1030	1310	+280

Panel (a): The firm's profit is maximized at that output (nine units) where total revenue, TR, exceeds total cost, TC, by the maximum amount. Panel (b): The vertical distance between TR and TC in panel (a) is plotted as a total-economic-profit curve. Maximum economic profit is $299 at nine units of output.

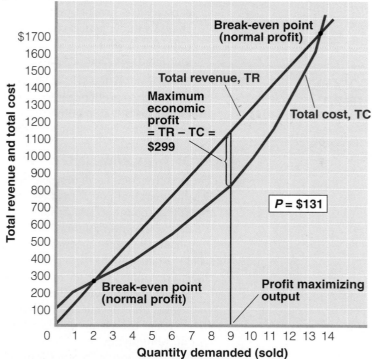

(a) Profit-maximizing case

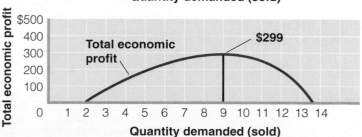

(b) Total economic profit

In the initial stages of production, where output is relatively low, marginal revenue will usually (but not always) exceed marginal cost. So it is profitable to produce through this range of output. But at later stages of production, where output is relatively high, rising marginal costs will exceed marginal revenue. Obviously, a profit-maximizing firm will want to avoid output levels in that range. Separating these two production ranges is a unique point at which marginal revenue equals marginal cost. This point is the key to the output-determining rule: *In the short run, the firm will maximize profit or minimize loss by producing the output at which marginal revenue equals marginal cost (as long as producing is preferable to shutting down)*. This profit-maximizing guide is known as the **MR = MC rule.**

MR = MC rule
A method of determining the total output at which economic profit is at a maximum (or losses are at a minimum).

Keep in mind these features of the MR = MC rule:

- For most sets of MR and MC data, MR and MC will be precisely equal at a fractional level of output. In such instances the firm should produce the last complete unit of output for which MR exceeds MC.

- The rule applies only if producing is preferable to shutting down. We will show shortly that if marginal revenue does not equal or exceed average variable cost, the firm will shut down rather than produce the MR = MC output.

- The rule is an accurate guide to profit maximization for all firms, whether they are perfectly competitive, monopolistic, monopolistically competitive, or oligopolistic.

- The rule can be restated as $P = $ MC when applied to a firm in a perfectly competitive industry. Because the demand schedule faced by a competitive seller is perfectly elastic at the going market price, product price and marginal revenue are equal. So under perfect competition (and only under perfect competition) we may substitute P for MR in the rule: *When producing is preferable to shutting down, the competitive firm should produce at that point where price equals marginal cost ($P = $ MC).*

MATH 8.1
MR = MC

Now let's apply the MR = MC rule, first using the same price as in our total-revenue–total-cost approach to profit maximization. Then, by considering other prices, we will demonstrate two additional cases: loss minimization and shutdown. It is crucial that you understand the MR = MC analysis that follows, since it reappears in Chapters 9, 10, and 11.

PROFIT-MAXIMIZING CASE

The first five columns of the table in **Figure 8-3 (Key Graph)** are AFC, AVC, ATC, and MC data. It is the marginal-cost data of column 6 that we will compare with price (equals marginal revenue) for each unit of output. Suppose first that the market price, and therefore marginal revenue, is $131, as shown in column 7.

What is the profit-maximizing output? Each of the first nine units adds to the firm's profit and will be produced. The tenth unit, however, will not be produced. It would add more to cost ($150) than to revenue ($131). So, nine units is the profit-maximizing output.

The economic profit realized by producing nine units can be calculated by subtracting total cost from total revenue. Multiplying price ($131) by output (9), we find that total revenue is $1179. From the average-total-cost data in column 4, we see that ATC is $97.78 at nine units of output. Multiplying $97.78 by 9 gives us total cost of $880.[2] The difference of $299 (= $1179 − $880) is the economic profit. Clearly, this firm will prefer to operate rather than shut down.

WORKED PROBLEM 8.2
Profit Maximization: MR = MC Approach

Perhaps an easier way to calculate the economic profit is to use this simple equation, in which A is average total cost:

$$\text{Profit} = (P - A) \times Q$$

[2] Most of the unit-cost data are rounded figures. Therefore, economic profits calculated from them will typically vary by a few cents from the profits determined in the total-revenue–total-cost approach. Here we simply ignore the few-cents differentials to make our answers consistent with the results of the total-revenue–total-cost approach.

KEY GRAPH

connect

FIGURE 8-3 Short-Run Profit-Maximizing for a Firm in a Perfectly Competitive Industry

The MR = MC output enables the firm in a perfectly competitive industry to maximize profits or to minimize losses. In this case MR (= P in pure competition) and MC are equal at an output Q of nine units. There, P exceeds the average total cost A = $97.78, so the firm realizes an economic profit of P − A per unit. The total economic profit is represented by the grey rectangle and is 9 × (P − A).

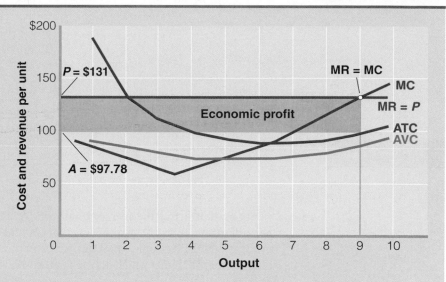

(1) Total product (output)	(2) Average fixed cost, AFC	(3) Average variable cost, AVC	(4) Average total cost, ATC	(5) Total cost, TC	(6) Marginal cost, MC	(7) Price = marginal revenue, MR	(8) Total economic profit (+) or loss (−)
0				$100			$−100
					$ 90		
1	$100.00	$ 90.00	$190.00	190		$ 131	−59
					80		
2	50.00	85.00	135.00	270		131	−8
					70		
3	33.33	80.00	113.33	340		131	+53
					60		
4	25.00	75.00	100.00	400		131	+124
					70		
5	20.00	74.00	94.00	470		131	+185
					80		
6	16.67	75.00	91.67	550		131	+236
					90		
7	14.29	77.14	91.43	640		131	+277
					110		
8	12.50	81.25	93.75	750		131	+298
					130		
9	11.11	86.67	97.78	880		131	+299
					150		
10	10.00	93.00	103.00	1030		131	+280

Quick Quiz

1. Curve MR is horizontal because
   a. product price falls as output increases.
   b. the law of diminishing marginal utility is at work.
   c. the market demand for this product is perfectly elastic.
   d. the firm is a price-taker.

2. At a price of $131 and seven units of output
   a. MR exceeds MC, and the firm should expand its output.
   b. total revenue is less than total cost.
   c. AVC exceeds ATC.
   d. the firm would earn only a normal profit.

3. **In maximizing profits at nine units of output, this firm is adhering to which of the following decision rules?**
   a. Produce where MR exceeds MC by the greatest amount.
   b. Produce where P exceeds ATC by the greatest amount.
   c. Produce where total revenue exceeds total cost by the greatest amount.
   d. Produce where average fixed costs are zero.

4. **Suppose price declined from $131 to $100. This firm's**
   a. marginal-cost curve would shift downward.
   b. economic profit would fall to zero.
   c. profit-maximizing output would decline.
   d. total cost would fall by more than its total revenue.

Answers: 1. d; 2. a; 3. c; 4. c

So, by subtracting the average total cost ($97.78) from the product price ($131), we obtain a per-unit profit of $33.22. Multiplying that amount by nine units of output, we determine that the profit is $299. Take some time now to verify the numbers in column 7. You will find that any output other than that which adheres to the MR = MC rule will mean either profits below $299 or losses.

The graph in Figure 8-3 shows price (= MR) and marginal cost graphically. Price equals marginal cost at the profit-maximizing output of nine units. There the per-unit economic profit is $P - A$, where P is the market price and A is the average total cost for an output of nine units. The total economic profit is $9 \times (P - A)$, shown by the grey rectangular area.

Note that the firm wants to maximize its total profit, not its per-unit profit. Per-unit profit is greatest at seven units of output, where price exceeds average total cost by $39.57 (= $131 − $91.43). But by producing only seven units, the firm would not produce two additional units of output that would clearly contribute to total profit. The firm is happy to accept lower per-unit profits for additional units of output because they nonetheless add to total profit.

LOSS-MINIMIZING CASE

Now let's assume that the market price is $81 rather than $131. Should the firm still produce? If so, how much? What will be the resulting profit or loss? The answers, respectively, are "yes," "six units," and "a loss of $64."

Column 6 of the table in Figure 8-4 shows the new price (equal to MR), $81. Comparing columns 5 and 6, we find that the first unit of output adds $90 to total cost but only $81 to total revenue. One might conclude: "Don't produce—close down!" But that would be hasty. For units two through six, price exceeds marginal cost. Each of these five units adds more to revenue than to cost and, as shown in column 7, they decrease the total loss. Together they more than compensate for the loss taken on the first unit. Beyond six units, however, MC exceeds MR (= P). The firm should therefore produce six units.

Will production be profitable? No, because at six units of output the average total cost of $91.67 exceeds the price of $81 by $10.67 per unit. If we multiply that by the six units of output, we find the firm's total loss is $64.

Then why produce? Because this loss is less than the firm's $100 of fixed costs, which is the $100 loss the firm would incur in the short run by closing down. The firm receives enough revenue per unit ($81) to cover its average variable costs of $75 and also provide $6 per unit, or a total of $36, to apply against fixed costs. Therefore, the firm's loss is only $64 (= $100 − $36), not $100.

This loss-minimizing case is also illustrated in the graph in Figure 8-4. Wherever price P exceeds average variable cost, AVC, the firm can pay part, but not all, of its fixed costs by producing. The loss is minimized by producing the output at which MC = MR (here, six units). At that output, each unit contributes $P - V$ to covering fixed cost, where V is the AVC at six units of output. The per-unit loss is $A - P = $10.67, and the total loss is $6 \times (A - P)$, or $64, as shown by the grey area.

The Short-Run Loss-Minimizing Position of a Firm in a Perfectly Competitive Industry

FIGURE 8-4

(1) Total product (output)	(2) Average fixed cost, AFC	(3) Average variable cost, AVC	(4) Average total cost, ATC	(5) Marginal cost, MC	(6) $81 price = marginal revenue, MR	(7) Profit (+) or loss (−), $81 price	(8) $71 price = marginal revenue, MR	(9) Profit (+) or loss (−), $71 price
0						$−100		$−100
1	$100.00	$90.00	$190.00	$ 90	$81	−109	$71	−119
2	50.00	85.00	135.00	80	81	−108	71	−128
3	33.33	80.00	113.33	70	81	−97	71	−127
4	25.00	75.00	100.00	60	81	−76	71	−116
5	20.00	74.00	94.00	70	81	−65	71	−115
6	16.67	75.00	91.67	80	81	−64	71	−124
7	14.29	77.14	91.43	90	81	−73	71	−143
8	12.50	81.25	93.75	110	81	−102	71	−182
9	11.11	86.67	97.78	130	81	−151	71	−241
10	10.00	93.00	103.00	150	81	−220	71	−320

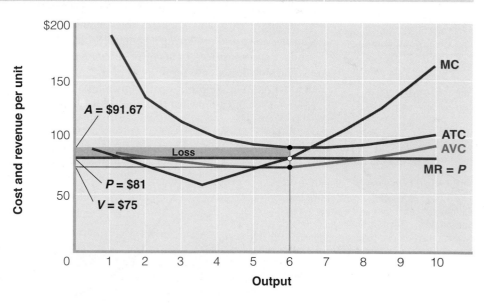

If price P exceeds the minimum AVC (here, $74 at $Q = 5$) but is less than ATC, the MR = MC output (here, six units) will permit the firm to minimize its losses. In this instance the loss is $A − P$ per unit, where A is the average total cost at six units of output. The total loss is shown by the grey area and is equal to $6 \times (A − P)$.

SHUTDOWN CASE

Suppose now that the market price is only $71. Should the firm produce? No, because at every output level the firm's average variable cost is greater than the price (compare columns 3 and 8 of the table in Figure 8-4). The smallest loss the firm can incur by producing is greater than the $100 fixed cost it will lose by shutting down (as shown by column 9). The best action is to shut down.

You can see this shutdown situation in Figure 8-5. Price comes closest to covering average variable costs at the MR (= P) = MC output of five units. But even here, price or revenue per unit would fall short of average variable cost by $3 (= $74 − $71). By producing at the MR (= P) = MC output, the

CONSIDER THIS :: The Still There Motel

Have you ever driven by a poorly maintained business facility and wondered why the owner doesn't either fix up the property or go out of business? The somewhat surprising answer is that it may be unprofitable to improve the facility, yet profitable to continue to operate it as it deteriorates. Seeing why will aid your understanding of fixed cost, variable cost, profit-maximization, and shutdown points.

Consider the story of the Still There Motel, a one-storey motel on Old Highway North, Any Town, Canada. The owner of Still There built the motel on the basis of traffic patterns and competition that existed several decades ago. As more highways were built, Still There found itself located on a relatively vacant stretch of road. Also, it faced greatly heightened competition from new "chain" motels located closer to the main highway that crossed the province.

As demand and revenue fell, Still There moved from profitability to loss. At first its room rates and annual revenue were sufficient to cover its total variable costs and contribute some to the payment of fixed costs such as insurance and property

taxes (or $P > $ AVC; $P < $ ATC). By staying open, Still There lost less than it would have if it had shut down. But since its total revenue did not cover its total costs (or $P < $ ATC), the owner realized that something must be done in the long run. The owner decided to lower costs by reducing annual maintenance. In effect, the owner opted to allow the motel to deteriorate as a way of regaining temporary profitability.

This renewed profitability of Still There cannot last because in time no further reduction of maintenance costs will be possible. The deterioration of the motel structure will produce even lower room rates, and therefore even less total revenue. The owner of Still There knows that sooner or later total revenue will again fall below total cost (or P will again fall below ATC), even with an annual maintenance expense of zero. When that occurs, the owner will close down the business, tear down the structure, and sell the vacant property. But, in the meantime, the motel is still there—open, deteriorating, and profitable.

shutdown case
The circumstance in which a firm would experience a loss greater than its total fixed cost if it were to produce any output greater than zero; alternatively, a situation in which a firm would cease to operate when the price at which it can sell its product is less than its average variable cost.

firm would lose its $100 worth of fixed cost plus $15 ($3 of variable cost on each of the five units), for a total loss of $115. This compares unfavourably with the $100 fixed-cost loss the firm would incur by shutting down and producing no output. So, it will make sense for the firm to shut down rather than produce at a $71 price—or at any price less than the minimum average variable cost of $74.

The **shutdown case** reminds us of the qualifier to our MR ($= P$) = MC rule. A competitive firm will maximize profit or minimize loss in the short run by producing that output at which MR ($= P$) = MC, *provided that market price exceeds minimum average variable cost.*

FIGURE 8-5   **The Short-Run Shutdown Position of a Firm in Perfect Competition**

If price P falls below the minimum AVC (here $74 at $Q = 5$), the competitive firm will minimize its losses in the short run by shutting down. There is no level of output at which the firm can produce and incur a loss smaller than its total fixed cost

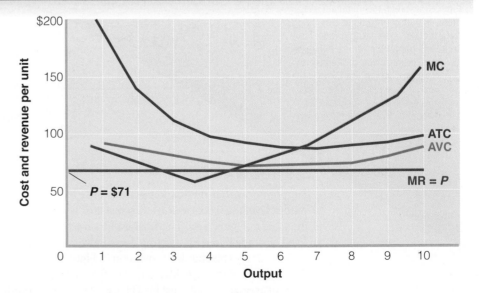

8.4 Marginal Cost and Short-Run Supply

In the preceding section we simply selected three different prices and asked what quantity the profit-seeking competitive firm, faced with certain costs, would choose to offer in the market at each price. This set of product prices and corresponding quantities supplied constitutes part of the supply schedule for the competitive firm.

Table 8-2 summarizes the supply schedule data for those three prices ($131, $81, and $71) and four others. This table confirms the direct relationship between product price and quantity supplied that we identified in Chapter 3. Note first that the firm will not produce at price $61 or $71, because both are less than the $74 minimum AVC. Then note that quantity supplied increases as price increases. Observe finally that economic profit is higher at higher prices.

Generalized Depiction

Figure 8-6 (Key Graph) generalizes the MR = MC rule and the relationship between short-run production costs and the firm's supply behaviour. The ATC, AVC, and MC curves are shown, along with several marginal-revenue lines drawn at possible market prices. Let's observe quantity supplied at each of these prices.

- Price P_1 is below the firm's minimum average variable cost, so at this price the firm won't operate at all. Quantity supplied will be zero, as it will be at all other prices below P_2.

- Price P_2 is just equal to the minimum average variable cost. The firm will supply Q_2 units of output (where $MR_2 = MC$) and just cover its total variable cost. Its loss will equal its total fixed cost. (Actually, the firm would be indifferent as to shutting down or supplying Q_2 units of output, but we assume it produces.)

TABLE 8-2

The Supply Schedule of a Competitive Firm with the Cost Data in Figure 8-3

Price	Quantity supplied	Maximum profit (+) or minimum loss (−)
$151	10	$+480
131	9	+299
111	8	+138
91	7	−3
81	6	−64
71	0	−100
61	0	−100

KEY GRAPH

FIGURE 8-6 The $P = MC$ Rule and the Competitive Firm's Short-Run Supply Curve

Application of the $P = MC$ rule, as modified by the shutdown case, reveals that the (solid) segment of the firm's MC curve that lies above AVC is the firm's short-run supply curve. More specifically, at price P_1, $P = MC$ at point a, but the firm will produce no output because P_1 is less than minimum AVC. At price P_2 the firm will operate at point b, where it produces Q_2 units and incurs a loss equal to its total fixed cost. At P_3 it operates at point c, where output is Q_3 and the loss is less than the total fixed cost. With the price of P_4, the firm operates at point d; in this case the firm earns a normal profit because at output Q_4 price equals ATC. At price P_5 the firm operates at point e and maximizes its economic profit by producing Q_5 units.

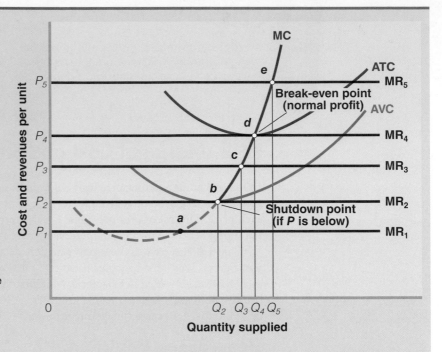

Quick Quiz

1. **Which of the following might increase product price from P_3 to P_5?**
   a. An improvement in production technology
   b. A decline in the price of a substitute good
   c. An increase in the price of a complementary good
   d. Rising incomes if the product is a normal good

2. **An increase in price from P_3 to P_5 would**
   a. shift this firm's MC curve to the right.
   b. mean that MR_5 exceeds MC at Q_3 units, inducing the firm to expand output to Q_5.
   c. decrease this firm's average variable costs.
   d. enable this firm to obtain a normal, but not an economic, profit.

3. **At P_4**
   a. this firm has no economic profit.
   b. this firm will earn only a normal profit and thus will shut down.
   c. MR_4 will be less than MC at the profit-maximizing output.
   d. the profit-maximizing output will be Q_5.

4. **Suppose P_4 is $10, P_5 is $15, Q_4 is 8 units, and Q_5 is 10 units. This firm's**
   a. supply curve is elastic over the Q_4–Q_5 range of output.
   b. supply curve is inelastic over the Q_4–Q_5 range of output.
   c. total revenue will decline if price rises from P_4 to P_5.
   d. marginal-cost curve will shift downward if price falls from P_5 to P_4.

Answers: 1. d; 2. b; 3. a; 4. b

- At price P_3 the firm will supply Q_3 units of output to minimize its short-run losses. At any of the other prices between P_2 and P_4 the firm will also minimize its losses by producing and supplying the quantity at which MR $(= P) =$ MC.

- The firm will just break even at price P_4, where it will supply Q_4 units of output (where $MR_4 =$ MC), earning a normal profit but not an economic profit. Total revenue will just cover total cost, including a normal profit, because the revenue per unit $(MR_4 = P_4)$ and the total cost per unit (ATC) are the same.

- At price P_5 the firm will earn an economic profit by producing and supplying Q_5 units of output. In fact, at any price above P_4 the firm will earn an economic profit by producing to the point where MR $(= P) =$ MC.

Note that each of the MR $(= P) =$ MC intersection points labelled *b, c, d,* and *e* in Figure 8-6 indicates a possible product price (on the vertical axis) and the corresponding quantity that the firm would supply at that price (on the horizontal axis). Thus, points such as these are on the upsloping supply curve of the competitive firm. Note, too, that quantity supplied would be zero at any price below the minimum average variable cost (AVC). *We can conclude that the portion of the firm's marginal-cost curve lying above its average-variable-cost curve is its short-run supply curve.* In Figure 8-6, the solid segment of the marginal-cost curve MC is this firm's **short-run supply curve.** It tells us the amount of output the firm will supply at each price in a series of prices. Table 8-3 summarizes the MR $=$ MC approach to determining the competitive firm's profit-maximizing output level. It also shows the equivalent analysis in terms of total revenue and total cost.

short-run supply curve
A curve that shows the quantities of the product a firm in a purely competitive industry will offer to sell at various prices in the short run.

Diminishing Returns, Production Costs, and Product Supply

We have now identified the links between the law of diminishing returns (Chapter 6), production costs, and product supply in the short run. Because of the law of diminishing returns, marginal cost eventually rises as more units of output are produced. And because marginal cost rises with output, a firm in a perfectly competitive industry must get successively higher prices to motivate it to produce additional units of output.

Changes in Supply

In Chapter 7 we saw that changes in such factors as the prices of variable inputs or in technology will shift the marginal-cost or short-run supply curve to a new location. All else equal, a wage increase, for example, would shift the supply curve in Figure 8-6 upward and to the left, which means a decrease in supply. Similarly, technological progress that increases the productivity of labour would shift the marginal-cost or supply curve downward to the right, representing an increase in supply.

Firm and Industry: Equilibrium Price

In the preceding section we established the competitive firm's short-run supply curve by applying the MR $(= P) =$ MC rule. But which of the various possible prices will actually be the market equilibrium price? From Chapter 3 we know that the market equilibrium price is the price at which the total quantity supplied of the product equals the total quantity demanded. So to determine equilibrium price, we first need to obtain a total supply schedule and a total demand schedule. We find the total supply schedule by assuming a particular number of firms in the industry and supposing that each firm has the same individual supply schedule as the firm represented in Figure 8-6. Then we sum the quantities supplied at each price level to obtain the total (or market) supply schedule. Columns 1 and 3 in Table 8-3 repeat the supply schedule for

TABLE 8-3   **Firm and Market Supply and Market Demand**

(1) Quantity supplied, single firm	(2) Total quantity supplied, 1,000 firms	(3) Product price	(4) Total quantity demanded
10	10,000	$151	4,000
9	9,000	131	6,000
8	8,000	111	8,000
7	7,000	91	9,000
6	6,000	81	11,000
0	0	71	13,000
0	0	61	16,000

the individual competitive firm, as derived in Table 8-2. Suppose 1000 firms compete in this industry, all having the same total and unit costs as the single firm we discussed. This assumption
allows us to calculate the market supply schedule (columns 2 and 3) by multiplying the quantity-
supplied figures of the single firm (column 1) by 1000.

MARKET PRICE AND PROFITS

To determine the equilibrium price and output, these total-supply data must be compared with
total-demand data. Let's assume that total demand is as shown in columns 3 and 4 in Table 8-3.
By comparing the total quantity supplied and the total quantity demanded at the seven possible
prices, we determine that the equilibrium price is $111 and the equilibrium quantity is 8000 units
for the industry—eight units for each of the 1000 identical firms.

Will these conditions of market supply and demand make this a profitable industry? Multiplying product price ($111) by output (8 units), we find that the total revenue of each firm is $888.
The total cost is $750, found by looking at column 4 of the table in Figure 8-2. The $138 difference is the economic profit of each firm. For the industry, total economic profit is $138,000. This,
then, is a profitable industry.

Another way of calculating economic profit is to determine per-unit profit by subtracting
average total cost ($93.75) from product price ($111) and multiplying the difference (per-unit
profit of $17.25) by the firm's equilibrium level of output (8). Again we obtain an economic profit
of $138 per firm and $138,000 for the industry.

Figure 8-7 shows this analysis graphically. The individual supply curves of each of the 1000
identical firms—one of which is shown as $s = $ MC in Figure 8-7a—are summed horizontally
to get the total-supply curve $S = \Sigma$MC of Figure 8-7b. Together with total-demand curve D, it
determines the equilibrium price $111 and equilibrium quantity (for the industry) 8000 units.
This equilibrium price is given and unalterable to the individual firm; that is, each firm's
demand curve is perfectly elastic at the equilibrium price, as indicated by d in Figure 8-7a.
Because the individual firm is a price-taker, the marginal-revenue curve coincides with the
firm's demand curve d. This $111 price exceeds the average total cost at the firm's equilibrium
MR = MC output of eight units, so the firm earns an economic profit represented by the grey
area in Figure 8-7a.

Assuming costs and market demand do not change, these diagrams reveal a genuine equilibrium in the short run. No shortages or surpluses occur in the market to cause price or total

FIGURE 8-7 Short-Run Competitive Equilibrium for a Firm (Panel A) and the Industry (Panel B)

The horizontal sum of the 1000 firms' individual supply curves (s) determines the industry supply curve (S). Given industry demand (D), the short-run equilibrium price and output for the industry are $111 and 8000 units. Taking the equilibrium price as given, the individual firm establishes its profit-maximizing output at eight units and, in this case, realizes the economic profit represented by the grey area.

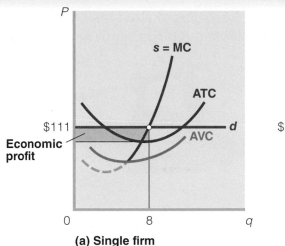

(a) Single firm

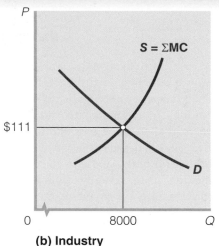

(b) Industry

quantity to change. Nor can any one firm in the industry increase its profit by changing its output. Note, too, that higher unit and marginal costs on the one hand, or weaker market demand on the other, could change the situation so that Figure 8-7a resembles Figure 8-4 or Figure 8-5.

Table 8-4 summarizes what we have discussed about output determination under perfect competition in the short run.

connect

WORKED PROBLEM 8.3
Short-Run Competitive
Equilibrium

FIRM VERSUS INDUSTRY

Figure 8-7 underscores a point made earlier: Product price is a given fact to the *individual* competitive firm, but the supply plans of all competitive producers *as a group* are a basic determinant of product price. If we recall the fallacy of composition (The Last Word, Chapter 1), we find there is no inconsistency here. Although one firm, supplying a negligible fraction of total supply, cannot affect price, the industry supply curve does have an important bearing on price.

TABLE 8-4 Output Determination in Perfect Competition in the Short Run

Question	Answer
Should this firm produce?	Yes, if price is equal to, or greater than, minimum average variable cost. This means that the firm is profitable or that its losses are less than its fixed cost.
What quantity should this firm produce?	Produce where MR (= P) = MC; there, profit is maximized (TR exceeds TC by a maximum amount) or loss is minimized.
Will production result in economic profit?	Yes, if price exceeds average total cost (so that TR exceeds TC). No, if average total cost exceeds price (so that TC exceeds TR).

The **LAST WORD** | Fixed Costs: Digging Yourself Out of a Hole

*For firms facing losses due to fixed costs, shutting down in
the short run does not mean shutting down forever.*

A firm with fixed costs starts each month standing at the bottom of a deep financial hole. The depth of that "money pit" is equal to the dollar value of all the payments that the firm is legally obligated to make even if it is producing nothing. These fixed costs include contractually guaranteed salaries, interest payments on loans, and equipment rental fees that are locked in by long-term contracts. As the firm stands at the bottom of this fixed-cost financial hole and stares upward looking for a way out, it has to ask itself the following question: Will producing output make the hole even deeper?

Naturally, the firm hopes that producing output will generate positive cash flows that will offset its fixed costs and start filling in the hole. If those positive flows are large enough, they may completely offset the firm's fixed costs, fill up the hole, and allow the firm to break even. And if they are just a bit larger, they will not only fill up the hole but also accumulate a nice little pile of profits above ground.

But those are just the firm's hopes. The firm's reality may be quite unpleasant. In particular, the firm may be facing a situation in which producing output would make its financial situation worse rather than better. As explained in this chapter, if the firm's price falls too low, then producing output will yield cash flows that are negative rather than positive because revenues will be less than variable costs. If that happens, producing output will lose money for the firm so that the firm would be better off shutting down production rather than producing output. By shutting down, it will

lose only its fixed costs. By shutting down, its financial hole won't get even deeper.

A crucial thing to understand, however, is that the low prices that cause firms to shut down production are often temporary—so that shutdowns are also often temporary. Just because a firm shuts down at a given moment to prevent its financial hole from getting any deeper does not mean that the firm will go out of business forever. On the contrary, many industries are characterized by firms that regularly switch production on and off depending upon the market price they can get for their output and, consequently, whether producing output will generate positive or negative cash flows.

Oil production is a good example. Different wells have different variable production costs. If the price of oil drops below a given well's variable costs, then it would be better to halt production on that well and just lose the value of its fixed costs rather than pumping oil whose variable costs exceed the revenue that it generates when sold.

Seasonal resorts are another good example of turning production on and off depending on the price. The demand for hotel rooms near ski resorts

in Quebec, for instance, is much higher during the winter ski season than it is during the summer. As a result, the market price of hotel rooms falls so low during the summer that many inns and resorts close during the warmer months. They have all sorts of fixed costs, but it makes more sense for them to shut down rather than remain open because operating in the summer would cost more in variable costs than it would generate in revenues. It is better to lose only their fixed costs.

Numerous other examples of temporary shutdowns occur during recessions, the occasional economy-wide economic slowdowns during which demand declines for nearly all goods and services. The 2008–2009 recession in Canada, for instance, saw many manufacturing companies temporarily shut down and "mothball" their production facilities. The recession witnessed the mothballing of electric generating plants, factories that make fibre optic cable, automobile factories, and chemical plants. Many other firms also shut down production to wait out the recession—so many, in fact, that there was a mini-boom for consulting firms that specialized in helping firms mothball their factories (the main problem being how to properly store idle machinery so that it will work again when it is eventually brought back into service).

Firms that mothball factories or equipment during a recession do so expecting to eventually turn them back on. But the lengths of recessions vary, as do the specific circumstances of individual firms. So while many firms shut down in the short run with the expectation of reopening as soon as their particular business conditions improve, sometimes their business conditions do not improve. Sometimes the only way to terminate fixed costs is to terminate the firm.

Question

If a firm's current revenues are less than its current variable costs, when should it shut down? If it decides to shut down, should we expect that decision to be final? Explain using an example that is not in the textbook.

:: CHAPTER SUMMARY

8.1 :: FOUR MARKET STRUCTURES

- Economists group industries into four models based on their market structures: (1) perfect competition, (2) monopoly, (3) monopolistic competition, and (4) oligopoly.

8.2 :: CHARACTERISTICS OF PERFECT COMPETITION AND THE FIRM'S DEMAND CURVE

- A perfectly competitive industry consists of a large number of independent firms producing a standardized product. Perfect competition assumes that firms and factors of production are mobile among different industries.

- In a competitive industry, no single firm can influence market price, which means that the firm's demand curve is perfectly elastic and price equals marginal revenue.

8.3 :: PROFIT MAXIMIZATION IN THE SHORT RUN

- We can analyze short-run profit maximization by a competitive firm by comparing total revenue and total cost or by applying marginal analysis. A firm maximizes its short-run profit by producing the output at which total revenue exceeds total cost by the greatest amount.

- Provided price exceeds minimum average variable cost, a competitive firm maximizes profit or minimizes loss in the short run by producing the output at which price or marginal revenue equals marginal cost.

- If price is less than average variable cost, the firm minimizes its loss by shutting down. If price is greater than average

variable cost but is less than average total cost, the firm minimizes its loss by producing the $P = MC$ output. If price also exceeds average total cost, the firm maximizes its economic profit at the $P = MC$ output.

8.4 :: MARGINAL COST AND SHORT-RUN SUPPLY

- Applying the MR ($= P$) $= MC$ rule at various possible market prices leads to the conclusion that the segment of the firm's short-run marginal-cost curve that lies above the firm's average-variable-cost curve is its short-run supply curve.

- A competitive firm shuts down production at least temporarily if price is less than minimum average variable cost because in those situations producing any amount of output will always result in variable costs exceeding revenues. Shutting down therefore results in a smaller loss because the firm will only lose its fixed cost whereas, if it operated, it would lose its fixed cost plus whatever money is lost due to variable costs exceeding revenues.

- Competitive firms choose to operate rather than shut down whenever price is greater than average variable cost but less than average total cost because in those situations revenues will always exceed variable costs. The amount by which revenues exceed variable costs can be used to help pay down some of the firm's fixed costs. Thus, the firm loses less money by operating (and paying down some of its fixed costs) than it would if it shut down (in which case it would suffer a loss equal to the full amount of its fixed costs).

:: TERMS AND CONCEPTS

perfect competition, p. 196
monopoly, p. 196
monopolistic competition, p. 196
oligopoly, p. 196
imperfect competition, p. 196

price-taker, p. 197
average revenue, p. 199
total revenue, p. 199
marginal revenue, p. 199
break-even point, p. 200

MR = MC rule, p. 202
shutdown case, p. 206
short-run supply curve, p. 209

⚏ QUESTIONS

1. Briefly state the basic characteristics of perfect competition, monopoly, monopolistic competition, and oligopoly. Under which of these market classifications does each of the following most accurately fit? (a) a supermarket in your home town; (b) the steel industry; (c) a Saskatchewan wheat farm; (d) the chartered bank in which you have or your family has an account; (e) the automobile industry. In each case, justify your classification.   [LO8.1]

2. Strictly speaking, perfect competition is relatively rare. Then why study it?   [LO8.2]

3. Use the following demand schedule to determine total revenue and marginal revenue for each possible level of sales: [LO8.3]

Product price	Quantity demanded	Total revenue	Marginal revenue
$2	0	$_____	$_____
2	1	_____	_____
2	2	_____	_____
2	3	_____	_____
2	4	_____	_____
2	5	_____	_____

a. What can you conclude about the structure of the industry in which this firm is operating? Explain.

b. Graph the demand, total-revenue, and marginal-revenue curves for this firm.

c. Why do the demand and marginal-revenue curves coincide?

d. "Marginal revenue is the change in total revenue associated with additional units of output." Explain in words and graphically, using the data in the table.

4. "Even if a firm is losing money, it may be better to stay in business in the short run." Is this statement ever true? Under what condition(s)?   [LO8.3]

5. Consider a firm that has no fixed costs and which is currently losing money. Are there any situations in which it would want to stay open for business in the short run? If a firm has no fixed costs, is it sensible to speak of the firm distinguishing between the short run and the long run?   [LO8.3]

6. Why is the equality of marginal revenue and marginal cost essential for profit maximization in all market structures? Explain why price can be substituted for marginal revenue in the MR = MC rule when an industry is perfectly competitive.   [LO8.4]

7. "That segment of a competitive firm's marginal-cost curve that lies above its average variable-cost curve constitutes the short-run supply curve for the firm." Explain using a graph and words.   [LO8.4]

⚏ PROBLEMS

1. A perfectly competitive firm finds that the market price for its product is $20. It has a fixed cost of $100 and a variable cost of $10 per unit for the first 50 units and then $25 per unit for all successive units. Does price exceed average variable cost for the first 50 units? What about for the first 100 units? What is the marginal cost per unit for the first 50 units? What about for units 51 and higher? For each of the first 50 units, does MR exceed MC? What about for units 51 and higher? What output level will yield the largest possible profit for this perfectly competitive firm? (Hint: Draw a graph similar to Figure 8-2 using data for this firm.)   [LO8.3]

2. A wheat farmer in a perfectly competitive industry can sell any wheat he grows for $10 per bushel. His five hectares of land show diminishing returns because some are better suited for wheat production than others. The first hectare can produce 1000 bushels of wheat, the second hectare 900, the third 800, and so on. Draw a table with multiple columns to help you answer the following questions.   [LO8.3]

a. How many bushels will each of the farmer's five hectares produce?

b. How much revenue will each hectare generate?

c. What are the TR and MR for each hectare?

d. If the marginal cost of planting and harvesting a hectare is $7000 per hectare for each of the five hectares, how many hectares should the farmer plant and harvest?

3. Karen runs a print shop that makes posters for large companies. It is a very competitive business. The market price is currently $1 per poster. She has fixed costs of $250. Her variable costs are $1000 for the first thousand posters, $800 for the second thousand, and then $750 for each additional thousand posters. What is her AFC per poster (not per thousand!) if she prints 1000 posters? 2000? 10,000? What is her ATC per poster if she prints 1000? 2000? 10,000? If the market price fell to 70 cents per poster, would there be any output level at which Karen would not shut down production immediately?   [LO8.3]

4. Assume the following cost data are for a firm in perfect competition: [**LO8.3**]

Total product	Average fixed cost	Average variable cost	Average total cost	Marginal cost
0				
				$45
1	$60.00	$45.00	$105.00	
				40
2	30.00	42.50	72.50	
				35
3	20.00	40.00	60.00	
				30
4	15.00	37.50	52.50	
				35
5	12.00	37.00	49.00	
				40
6	10.00	37.50	47.50	
				45
7	8.57	38.57	47.14	
				55
8	7.50	40.63	48.13	
				65
9	6.67	43.33	50.00	
				75
10	6.00	46.50	52.50	

a. At a product price of $56, will this firm produce in the short run? If it preferable to produce, what will be the profit-maximizing or loss-minimizing output? What economic profit or loss will the firm realize per unit of output?

b. Answer the questions in part (a) assuming product price is $41.

c. Answer the questions in part (a) assuming product price is $32.

d. In the table below, complete the short-run supply schedule for the firm (columns 1 and 2) and indicate the profit or loss incurred at each output (column 3).

(1) Price	(2) Quantity supplied, single firm	(3) Profit (+) or loss (−)	(4) Quantity supplied, 1500 firms
$26	_____	$_____	_____
32	_____	_____	_____
38	_____	_____	_____
41	_____	_____	_____
46	_____	_____	_____
56	_____	_____	_____
66	_____	_____	_____

e. Now assume that there are 1500 identical firms in this competitive industry; that is, there are 1500 firms, each of which has the cost data shown in the table. Complete the industry supply schedule (column 4).

f. Suppose the market demand data for the product are as follows:

Price	Total quantity demanded
$26	17,000
32	15,000
38	13,500
41	12,000
46	10,500
56	9,500
66	8,000

What will be the equilibrium price? What will be the equilibrium output for the industry? For each firm? What will profit or loss be per unit? Per firm? Will this industry expand or contract in the long run?

CHAPTER 9

Perfect Competition in the Long Run

The previous chapter discussed how pure competition operates in the short run, the time period during which the individual firms in an industry are stuck with their current plant sizes and fixed-cost commitments. As you know, firms in perfect competition shut down their operations if prices are too low, or if prices are high enough, produce where MR = MC to minimize their losses or maximize their profits. Whether they make a profit or a loss depends on how high the market price is relative to their costs.

But profits and losses clearly cannot be the end of the pure competition story because one of the key characteristics of perfect competition is the freedom of firms to enter or exit the industry. We know from Chapter 2 that profits attract entry and losses prompt exit.

In this chapter, we are keenly interested in how entry and exit relate to allocative and productive efficiency. We are also interested in how continuing competition leads to new products and new business methods replacing older products and older business methods through a process aptly referred to as *creative destruction*.

9.1 The Long Run Versus the Short Run in Perfect Competition ::

The entry and exit of firms in our market models can only take place in the long run. In the short run, the industry is composed of a specific number of firms, each with a plant size that is fixed and unalterable in the short run. Firms may shut down, in the

AFTER READING THIS CHAPTER, YOU SHOULD BE ABLE TO:

9.1 Explain how the long run differs from the short run in perfect competition.

9.2 Explain how the entry and exit of firms affects long-run equilibrium through resource flows and long-run profits and losses.

9.3 Explain the differences between constant-cost, increasing-cost, and decreasing-cost industries.

9.4 Discuss perfect competition and efficiency.

9.5 Discuss creative destruction and the profit incentives for technological innovation.

sense that they can produce zero units of output in the short run, but they do not have sufficient time to liquidate their assets and go out of business. In the long run, by contrast, the firms already in an industry have sufficient time to either expand or contract their capacities. More important, the number of firms in the industry may either increase or decrease as new firms enter or existing firms leave.

The length of time constituting the long run varies substantially by industry, however, so that you should not fix in your mind any specific number of years, months, or days. Instead, focus your attention on the incentives provided by profits and losses for the entry and exit of firms within any perfectly competitive industry and, later in the chapter, on how those incentives lead to productive and allocative efficiency. The time horizons are far less important than the process by which profits and losses guide business managers toward the efficient use of society's resources.

Profit Maximization in the Long Run

The first part of the perfect competition story (Chapter 8) was about profit, loss, and shut-down in the short run. The rest of the story (this chapter) is about entry and exit, and their impacts on industry size and allocative and productive efficiency in the long run.

To tell the rest of story well, we need to return to our graphical analysis and examine profit-maximization by firms in perfect competition in the long run. Three assumptions, none of which affect our conclusions, will keep things simple:

1. **Entry and Exit Only** The only long-run adjustment in our graphical analysis is caused by the entry or exit of firms. Moreover, we ignore all short-run adjustments to concentrate on the effects of the long-run adjustments.

2. **Identical Costs** All firms in the industry have identical cost curves. This assumption allows us to discuss a representative firm, knowing that all other firms in the industry are similarly affected by any long-run adjustments that occur. Using a representative firm allows us to simplify and better understand the perfectly competitive market structure.

3. **Constant-Cost Industry** The industry is a constant-cost industry, which means that the entry or exit of firms does not affect resource prices or, consequently, shift the average-total-cost or marginal-cost curves of individual firms.

The Goal of Our Analysis

The basic conclusion we want to explain is this: After all long-run adjustments in a perfectly competitive industry, product price will be exactly equal to, and production will occur at, each firm's minimum average total cost.

This conclusion follows from two basic facts: (1) firms seek profits and avoid losses, and (2) under perfect competition, firms are free to enter and leave an industry. If market price in the short run exceeds average total costs, the resulting economic profits will attract new firms to the industry, but this industry expansion will increase supply until price is brought back down to equality with minimum average total cost in the long run. Conversely, if price in the short run is less than average total cost, the resulting losses will cause firms to leave the industry in the long run. As they leave, total supply will decline, bringing the price back up to equality with minimum average total cost.

9.2 Long-Run Equilibrium

Consider the average firm in a perfectly competitive industry that is initially in long-run equilibrium. This firm is represented in Figure 9-1a, where MR = MC and price and minimum average total cost are equal at $50. Economic profit here is zero; the industry is in equilibrium and there is no tendency for firms to enter or to leave. The existing firms are earning normal profits, which means that their accounting profits are equal to those that the owners of these firms could expect to receive on average in other industries. It is because their current profits are the same as they

| FIGURE 9-1 |

Temporary Profits and the Re-establishment of Long-Run Equilibrium in a Representative Firm (Panel A) and the Industry (Panel B)

A favourable shift in demand (D_1 to D_2) will upset the original industry equilibrium and produce economic profits. But those profits will entice new firms to enter the industry, increasing supply (S_1 to S_2) and lowering product price until economic profits are once again zero.

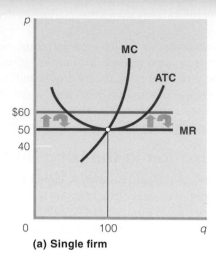

(a) Single firm

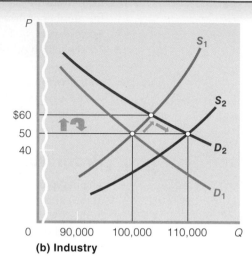

(b) Industry

could expect to earn elsewhere that there is no tendency for firms to enter or leave the industry. The $50 market price is determined in Figure 9-1b by market demand D_1 and supply S_1. (S_1 is a short-run supply curve; we will develop the long-run industry supply curve in our discussion.) And remember that normal profits earned by these firms are considered an opportunity cost and, therefore, are included in the firms' cost curves.

As shown on the quantity axes of the two graphs, equilibrium output in the industry is 100,000, while equilibrium output for the single firm is 100. If all firms in the industry are identical, there must be 1000 firms (= 100,000/100).

ENTRY ELIMINATES ECONOMIC PROFITS

Let's upset the long-run equilibrium in Figure 9-1 and see what happens. Suppose a change in consumer tastes increases product demand from D_1 to D_2. Price will rise to $60, as determined at the intersection of D_2 and S_1, and the firm's marginal-revenue curve will shift upward to $60. This $60 price exceeds the firm's average total cost of $50 at output 100, creating an economic profit of $10 per unit. This economic profit will lure new firms into the industry. Some entrants will be newly created firms; others will shift from less prosperous industries.

As firms enter, the market supply of the product increases, pushing the product price below $60. Economic profits persist, and entry continues until short-run supply increases to S_2. Market price falls to $50, as does marginal revenue for the firm. Price and minimum average total cost are again equal at $50. The economic profits caused by the boost in demand have disappeared because the firms that remain are earning only a normal profit (zero economic profit). Entry ceases and a new long-run equilibrium is reached. Observe in Figure 9-1 that total quantity supplied is now 110,000 units and each firm is producing 100 units. Now 1100 firms rather than the original 1000 populate the industry. Economic profits have attracted 100 more firms.

EXIT ELIMINATES LOSSES

Now let's consider a shift in the opposite direction. We begin in Figure 9-2b with curves S_1 and D_1 setting the same initial long-run equilibrium situation as in our previous analysis, including the $50 price.

Suppose consumer demand declines from D_1 to D_3. This decline forces the market price and marginal revenue down to $40, making production unprofitable at the minimum ATC of $50. In

FIGURE 9-2
Temporary Losses and the Re-establishment of Long-Run Equilibrium in a Representative Firm (Panel A) and the Industry (Panel B)

An unfavourable shift in demand (D_1 to D_3) will upset the original industry equilibrium and produce losses, but those losses will cause firms to leave the industry, decreasing supply (S_1 to S_3) and increasing product price until all losses have disappeared.

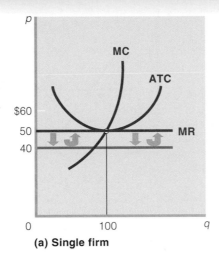

(a) Single firm

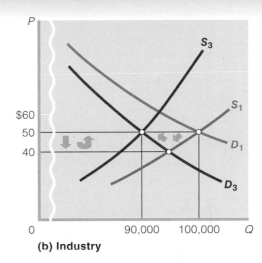

(b) Industry

time the resulting economic losses will induce firms to leave the industry. Their owners will seek a normal profit elsewhere rather than accept the below-normal profits (loss) now confronting them. Other firms will simply go out of business. As this exodus of firms proceeds, however, industry supply in the long run decreases, pushing the price up from $40 toward $50. Losses continue and more firms leave the industry until the supply curve shifts to S_3. Once this happens, price is again $50, just equal to the minimum average total cost. Losses have been eliminated so that the firms that remain are earning only a normal profit (zero economic profit). Since this is no better or worse than entrepreneurs could expect to earn in other business ventures, there is no longer any incentive to exit the industry. Long-run equilibrium is restored.

In Figure 9-2b, total quantity supplied is now 90,000 units and each firm is producing 10 units. Only 900 firms, not the original 1000, populate the industry. Losses have forced 100 firms out.

We have now reached an intermediate goal: Our analysis verifies that competition, reflected in the entry and exit of firms, eliminates economic profits or losses by adjusting price to equal minimum long-run average total cost. In addition, this competition forces firms to select output levels at which average total cost is minimized.

9.3 Long-Run Supply for Constant-Cost, Increasing-Cost, and Decreasing-Cost Industries

long-run supply curve
A curve that shows the prices at which a purely competitive industry will make various quantities of a product available in the long run.

constant-cost industry
An industry in which the entry of new firms has no effect on resource prices and thus no effect on production costs.

Although our analysis has dealt with the long run, we have noted that the market supply curves in Figures 9-1b and 9-2b are short-run curves. What then is the character of the **long-run supply curve** of a competitive industry? The analysis points us toward an answer. The crucial factor here is the effect, if any, that changes in the number of firms in the industry will have on costs of the individual firms in the industry.

In our analysis of long-run competitive equilibrium we assumed that the industry under discussion was a **constant-cost industry,** which means that industry expansion or contraction will not affect resource prices or production costs. Graphically, it means that the entry or exit of firms does not shift the long-run ATC curves of individual firms. This is the case when the industry's demand for factors of production is small in relation to the total demand for those resources; the industry can expand or contract without significantly affecting factor prices and costs.

FIGURE 9-3   The Long-Run Supply Curve for a Constant-Cost Industry Is Horizontal

In a constant-cost industry, the entry and exit of firms does not affect resource prices, or, therefore, unit costs. So an increase in demand (D_1 to D_2) raises industry output (Q_1 to Q_2) but not price ($50). Similarly, a decrease in demand (D_1 to D_3) reduces output (Q_1 to Q_3) but not price. Thus the long-run industry supply curve (S) is horizontal through points Z_1, Z_2, and Z_3.

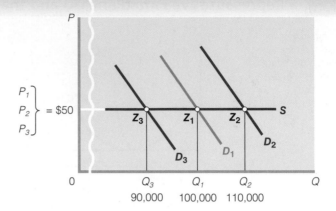

What does the long-run supply curve of a constant-cost industry look like? The answer is contained in our previous analysis. There we saw that the entry and exit of firms changes industry output but always brings the product price back to its original level, where it is just equal to the constant minimum ATC. Specifically, we discovered that the industry would supply 90,000, 100,000, or 110,000 units of output, all at a price of $50 per unit. In other words, the long-run supply of a constant-cost industry is perfectly elastic.

This is demonstrated graphically in Figure 9-3, which uses data from Figures 9-1 and 9-2. Suppose industry demand is originally D_1, industry output is Q_1 (100,000 units), and product price is P_1 ($50). This situation, from Figure 9-1, is one of long-run equilibrium. We saw that when demand increases to D_2, upsetting this equilibrium, the resulting economic profits attract new firms. Because this is a constant-cost industry, entry continues and industry output expands until the price is driven back down to the level of the unchanged minimum ATC, which is at price P_2 ($50) and output Q_2 (110,000).

From Figure 9-2, we saw that a decline in market demand from D_1 to D_3 causes an exit of firms and ultimately restores equilibrium at price P_3 ($50) and output Q_3 (90,000 units). The points Z_1, Z_2, and Z_3 in Figure 9-3 represent these three price–quantity combinations. A line or curve connecting all such points shows the various price–quantity combinations that firms would produce if they had enough time to make all desired adjustments to changes in demand. This line or curve is the industry's long-run supply curve. In a constant-cost industry this curve (straight line) is horizontal, as in Figure 9-3, thus representing perfectly elastic supply.

Long-Run Supply for an Increasing-Cost Industry

increasing-cost industry
An industry in which the entry of new firms raises resource prices and thus increases production costs.

Constant-cost industries are a special case. Most industries would fall into the **increasing-cost industry** category, in which firms' ATC curves shift upward as the industry expands and downward as the industry contracts. Usually, the entry of new firms will increase factor prices, particularly in industries using specialized inputs whose long-run supplies do not readily increase in response to increases in factor demand. Higher input prices result in higher long-run average total costs for all firms in the industry. These higher costs cause upward shifts in each firm's long-run ATC curve.

Thus, when an increase in product demand results in economic profits and attracts new firms to an increasing-cost industry, a two-way squeeze works to eliminate those profits. As before, the entry of new firms increases market supply and lowers the market price, but now the entire ATC curve shifts upward. The overall result is a higher-than-original equilibrium price. The industry produces a larger output at a higher product price because the industry expansion has increased factor prices and the minimum average total cost. Since greater output will be supplied at a higher

FIGURE 9-4 The Long-Run Supply Curve for an Increasing-Cost Industry Is Upsloping

In an increasing-cost industry, the entry of new firms in response to an increase in demand (D_3 to D_1 to D_2) will bid up resource prices and thereby increase unit costs. As a result, an increased industry output (Q_3 to Q_1 to Q_2) will be forthcoming only at higher prices ($55 > $50 > $45). The long-run industry supply curve (S) therefore slopes upward through points Y_3, Y_1, and, Y_2.

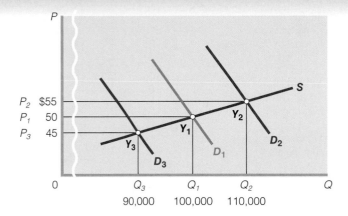

price, the long-run industry supply curve is upsloping. Instead of supplying 90,000, 100,000, or 110,000 units at the same price of $50, an increasing-cost industry might supply 90,000 units at $45; 100,000 units at $50; and 110,000 units at $55. A higher price is required to induce more production, because costs per unit of output increase as production rises.

Figure 9-4 nicely illustrates the situation. Original market demand is D_1 and industry price and output are P_1 ($50) and Q_1 (100,000 units), respectively, at equilibrium point Y_1. An increase in demand to D_2 upsets this equilibrium and leads to economic profits. New firms enter the industry, increasing both market supply and production costs of individual firms. A new price is established at point Y_2, where P_2 is $55 and Q_2 is 110,000 units.

Conversely, a decline in demand from D_1 to D_3 makes production unprofitable and causes firms to leave the industry. The resulting decline in factor prices reduces the minimum average total cost of production for firms that stay. A new equilibrium price is established at some level below the original price—say, at point Y_3, where P_3 is $45 and Q_3 is 90,000 units. Connecting these three equilibrium positions, we derive the upward-sloping long-run supply curve S in Figure 9-4.

Long-Run Supply for a Decreasing-Cost Industry

decreasing-cost industry
An industry in which the entry of firms lowers resource prices and thus decreases production costs.

In a **decreasing-cost industry,** a firm experiences lower costs as the industry expands. For example, as demand for personal computers increased, new manufacturers entered the personal computer industry and greatly increased the input demand for the components used to build them (memory chips, hard drives, monitors, and operating software). The expanded production of those components enabled the producers of those items to achieve substantial economies of scale. The decreased production costs of the components reduced their prices, which greatly lowered the computer manufacturers' average costs of production. The supply of personal computers increased by more than demand, and the price of personal computers declined.

Unfortunately, however, the industries that show decreasing costs when output expands also show increasing costs if output contracts. A good example is the Canadian shoe-manufacturing industry as it contracted due to foreign competition. Back when the industry was doing well and there were many shoemaking firms, the cost of specialized technicians who repair shoe-making machinery could be spread across many firms. This was because the repairmen worked as independent contractors going from one firm's factory to another firm's factory on a daily basis as various pieces of equipment at different factories needed repairs. But as the demand for Canadian-made footwear fell over time, there were fewer and fewer factories so that the cost of a repairman had to be spread over fewer and fewer firms. Thus, costs per firm and per unit of output increased.

FIGURE 9-5

The Long-Run Supply Curve for a Decreasing-Cost Industry Is Downsloping

In a decreasing-cost industry the entry of new firms in response to an increase in demand (D_3 to D_1 to D_2) will lead to decreased input prices and consequently decreased unit costs. As a result, an increase in industry output (Q_3 to Q_1 to Q_2) will be accompanied by lower prices ($\$55 > \$50 > \$45$). The long-run industry supply curve (S) therefore slopes downward through points X_3, X_1, and X_2.

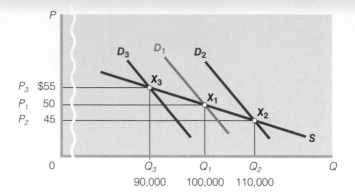

Figure 9-5 illustrates the situation. Original market demand is D_1 and industry price and output are P_1 ($\$50$) and Q_1 (100,000 units), respectively at equilibrium point X_1. An increase in demand to D_2 upsets this equilibrium and leads to economic profits. New firms enter the industry, increasing market supply but decreasing the production costs of individual firms. A new price is established at point X_2, where P_2 is $\$45$ and Q_2 is 110,000 units.

Conversely, a decline in demand from D_1 to D_3 makes production unprofitable and causes firms to leave the industry. The resulting increase in input prices increases the minimum average total cost of production for the firms that remain. A new equilibrium price is established at some level above the original price—say, at point X_3, where P_3 is $\$55$ and Q_3 is 90,000 units. Connecting these three equilibrium positions in Figure 9-5, we derive the downsloping long-run supply curve S for this decreasing-cost industry.

QUICK REVIEW

- In perfect competition, entrepreneurs remove resources from industries and firms that are generating economic losses in order to transfer them to industries and firms that are generating economic profits.

- In the long run, the entry of firms into an industry will compete away any economic profits, and the exit of firms will

eliminate economic losses, so price and minimum average total cost are equal. Entry and exit cease when the firms in the industry return to making a normal profit (zero economic profit).

- The long-run supply curves of constant-, increasing-, and decreasing-cost industries are horizontal, upsloping, and downsloping, respectively.

9.4 Perfect Competition and Efficiency

Figure 9-6 (Key Graph) demonstrates the efficiency characteristics of the individual firms (Figure 9-6a) and the market (Figure 9-6b) after long-run adjustments in perfect competition. Assuming a constant- or increasing-cost industry, the final long-run equilibrium positions of all firms have the same basic efficiency characteristics. As shown in Figure 9-6a, price (and marginal revenue) will settle where it is equal to minimum average total cost: P (and MR) = minimum ATC. Moreover, since the marginal-cost curve intersects the average-total-cost curve at its minimum point, marginal cost and average total cost are equal: MC = minimum ATC. So in long-run equilibrium a

KEY GRAPH

FIGURE 9-6 Long-Run Equilibrium: A Competitive Firm and Market

Panel (a): The equality of price (P), marginal cost (MC), and minimum average total cost (ATC) at output Q_f indicates that the firm is achieving productive efficiency and allocative efficiency. It is using the most efficient technology, charging the lowest price, and producing the greatest output consistent with its costs. It is receiving only a normal profit, which is incorporated into the ATC curve. The equality of price and marginal cost indicates that society is allocating its scarce resources in accordance with consumer preferences. Panel (b): In the perfectly competitive market, allocative efficiency occurs at the market equilibrium output Q_e. The sum of consumer surplus (green area) and producer surplus (blue area) is maximized.

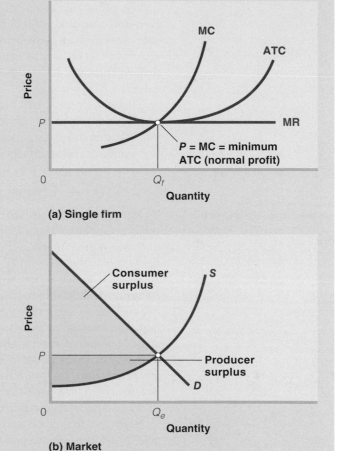

(a) Single firm

(b) Market

Quick Quiz

1. We know the firm is a price-taker because
   a. its MC curve slopes upward.
   b. its ATC curve is U-shaped.
   c. its MR curve is horizontal.
   d. MC and ATC are equal at the profit-maximizing output.

2. At this firm's profit-maximizing output,
   a. total revenue equals total cost.
   b. it is earning an economic profit.
   c. allocative, but not necessarily productive, efficiency is achieved.
   d. productive, but not necessarily allocative, efficiency is achieved.

3. The equality of P, MC, and minimum ATC
   a. occurs only in constant-cost industries.
   b. encourages entry of new firms.
   c. means that the "right goods" are being produced in the "right ways."
   d. results in a zero accounting profit.

4. When P = MC = lowest ATC for individual firms, in the market
   a. consumer surplus necessarily exceeds producer surplus.
   b. consumer surplus plus producer surplus is at a maximum.
   c. producer surplus necessarily exceeds consumer surplus.
   d. supply and demand are identical.

Answers: 1. d; 2. a; 3. c; 4. b

triple equality occurs: P (and MR) = MC = minimum ATC. Thus, in long-run equilibrium, each firm produces at the output level Q_f that is associated with this triple equality.[1]

The triple equality tells us two very important things about long-run equilibrium. First, it tells us that although a competitive firm may realize economic profit or loss in the short run, it will earn only a normal profit by producing in accordance with the MR (= P) = MC rule in the long run. Second, the triple equality tells us that in long-run equilibrium, the profit-maximizing decision rule that leads each firm to produce the quantity at which P = MR also implies that each firm will produce at the output level Q_f that is associated with the minimum point on each identical firm's ATC curve.

This is very important because it suggests that pure competition leads to the most efficient possible use of society's resources. Indeed, subject only to Chapter 5's qualifications relating to public goods and externalities, an idealized perfectly competitive economy composed of constant- or increasing-cost industries will generate both productive efficiency and allocative efficiency.

Productive Efficiency: P = Minimum ATC

To have **productive efficiency** goods must be produced in the least costly way. In the long run, perfect competition forces firms to produce at the minimum average total cost of production and to charge a price that is just consistent with that cost. This is true because firms that do not use the best available (least cost) production methods and combinations of inputs will not survive.

To see why that is true, let's suppose that Figure 9-6 has to do with perfect competition in the cucumber industry. In the final equilibrium position shown in Figure 9-6a, suppose each firm in the cucumber industry is producing 100 units (say, truckloads) of cucumbers by using $5000 (equal to average total cost of $50 × 100 units) of resources. If any firm produced that same amount of output at any higher total cost—say, $7000—it would be wasting resources because all of the other firms in the industry are able to produce that same amount of output using only $5000 of resources. Society would be faced with a net loss of $2000 worth of alternative products. But this cannot happen in perfect competition; this firm would incur a loss of $2000, requiring it either to reduce its costs or to go out of business.

Note, too, that consumers benefit from productive efficiency by paying the lowest product price possible under the prevailing technology and cost conditions. And the firm receives only a normal profit, which is part of its economic costs and thus incorporated in its ATC curve.

Allocative Efficiency: P = MC

Long-run equilibrium in pure competition guarantees productive efficiency, such that output will be produced in the least costly way. But productive efficiency by itself does not guarantee that anyone will want to buy the items that are being produced in the least-cost manner. For all we know, consumers might prefer that the resources used to produce those items be redirected toward producing other products instead.

Fortunately, long-run equilibrium in pure competition also guarantees **allocative efficiency** so that we can be certain that society's scarce resources are directed toward producing the goods and services that people most want to consume. Stated formally, allocative efficiency occurs when it is impossible to produce any net gains for society by altering the combination of goods and services that are produced from society's limited supply of resources.

To understand how pure competition leads to allocative efficiency, recall the concept of opportunity cost while looking at Figure 9-6b, where Q_e total units are being produced in equilibrium by the firms in a purely competitive industry. For every unit up to Q_e, market demand curve D

---

[1] This triple equality does not hold for decreasing-cost industries because MC always remains below ATC if average costs are decreasing. We will discuss this situation of "natural monopoly" in Chapter 10.

lies above market supply curve *S*. Recall from Chapter 5 what this means in terms of marginal benefits and marginal costs.

- For each unit of output on the horizontal axis, the point directly above it on demand curve *D* shows how many dollars' worth of other goods and services consumers are willing to give up to obtain that unit of output. Consequently, the demand curve shows the dollar value of the marginal benefit that consumers place on each unit.

- For each unit of output on the horizontal axis, the point directly above it on supply curve *S* shows how many dollars' worth of other products have to be sacrificed in order to direct the underlying resources toward producing each unit of this product. Consequently, the supply curve shows the dollar value of the marginal opportunity cost of each unit.

Keeping these definitions in mind, the fact that the demand curve lies above the supply curve for every unit up to Q_e means that marginal benefit exceeds marginal cost for every one of these units. Stated slightly differently, producing and consuming these units brings net benefits because consumers are willing to give up more of other goods to obtain these units than must actually be forgone to produce them. Furthermore, because the supply curve includes the opportunity cost of the other goods that must be given up when resources are directed to producing these units, we can be certain that consumers prefer to have the necessary resources directed toward producing these units rather than anything else. In other words, allocative efficiency has been achieved because redirecting the necessary resources toward producing anything else would make people less happy.

The fact that perfect competition yields allocative efficiency can also be understood by looking at the situation facing each individual firm in long-run equilibrium. To see this, take the market equilibrium price *P* that is determined in Figure 9-6b and sees how it affects the behaviour of the individual firm shown in Figure 9-6a. This profit-maximizing firm takes *P* as fixed and produces Q_f units, the output level at which $P = $ MC.

By comparing the horizontal line at *P* with the upsloping MC curve, it is clear that for every unit up to Q_f, the price at which each unit can be sold exceeds the marginal cost of producing it. That is equivalent to saying that these units are worth more to consumers than they cost to make. Why? Because consumers are willing to forgo *P* dollars' worth of other goods and services when they pay *P* dollars for these units, but at the same time the firm only has to use less than *P* dollars' worth of resources to produce them. Thus, if these units are produced and consumed, there are net benefits and society comes out ahead. And, as with our previous analysis, allocative efficiency is also achieved because by spending their *P* dollars per unit on these units rather than anything else, consumers are indicating that they would rather have the necessary resources directed toward producing these units rather than anything else.

Maximum Consumer and Producer Surplus

consumer surplus
The difference between the maximum price consumers are willing to pay and the actual price.

producer surplus
The difference between the actual price producers are willing to accept and the minimum acceptable price.

We confirm the existence of allocative efficiency in Figure 9-6b, where we see that perfect competition maximizes the sum of the "benefit surpluses" to consumers and producers. Recall from Chapter 5 that **consumer surplus** is the difference between the maximum prices that consumers are willing to pay for a product (as shown by the demand curve) and the market price of that product. In Figure 9-6b, consumer surplus is the green triangle, which is the sum of the vertical distances between the demand curve and equilibrium price. In contrast, **producer surplus** is the difference between the minimum prices that producers are willing to accept for a product (as shown by the supply curve) and the market price of the product. Producer surplus is the sum of the vertical distances between the equilibrium price and supply curve. Here producer surplus is the blue area.

At the equilibrium quantity Q_e, the combined amount of consumer surplus and producer surplus is maximized. Allocative efficiency occurs because, at Q_e, marginal benefit, reflected by points on the demand curve, equals marginal cost, reflected by the points on the supply curve.

Alternatively, the maximum willingness of consumers to pay for unit Q_e equals the minimum acceptable price of that unit to producers. At any output less than Q_e, the sum of consumer and producer surplus—the combined size of the green and blue areas—would be less than that shown. At any output greater than Q_e, an efficiency loss would subtract from the combined consumer and producer surplus shown by the green and blue areas.

After long-run adjustments, perfect competition produces allocative efficiency. It yields a level of output at which: $P = MC =$ lowest ATC; marginal benefit = marginal cost; maximum willingness to pay for the last unit = minimum acceptable price for that unit; and combined consumer and producer surplus are maximized.

Dynamic Adjustments

A further attribute of perfectly competitive markets is their ability to restore the efficiency just described when disrupted by changes in the economy. A change in consumer tastes, resource supplies, or technology will automatically set in motion the appropriate realignments of resources. For example, suppose that cucumbers and pickles become dramatically more popular. First, the demand for cucumbers will increase in the market, increasing the price of cucumbers. So, at current output, the price of cucumbers will exceed their marginal cost. At this point efficiency will be lost, but the higher price will create economic profits in the cucumber industry and stimulate its expansion. The profitability of cucumbers will permit the industry to bid resources away from now less pressing uses, say, watermelons. Expansion of the industry will end only when the supply of cucumbers has expanded such that the price of cucumbers and their marginal cost are equal—that is, when allocative efficiency has been restored.

Similarly, a change in the supply of a particular resource—for example, the field labourers who pick cucumbers—or in a production technique will upset an existing price–marginal cost equality by either raising or lowering marginal cost. The resulting inequality of MC and P will cause producers, in either pursuing profit or avoiding loss, to reallocate resources until product supply is such that price once again equals marginal cost. In so doing, they will correct any inefficiency in the allocation of resources that the original change may have temporarily imposed on the economy.

The "Invisible Hand" Revisited

Finally, the highly efficient allocation of resources that a perfectly competitive economy promotes comes about because businesses and resource suppliers seek to further their self-interest. For private goods with no externalities, the invisible hand is at work (Chapter 2). The competitive system not only maximizes profits for individual producers but at the same time creates a pattern of resource allocation that maximizes consumer satisfaction. The invisible hand thus organizes the private interests of producers in a way that is fully in sync with society's interest in using scarce resources efficiently. Striving to obtain profit (and avoid losses) produces highly desirable economic outcomes.

9.5 Technological Advance and Competition

In explaining the model of perfect competition, we assumed for simplicity that all the firms in an industry had the same cost curves. Competition, as a result, only involved entrepreneurs entering and exiting industries in response to changes in profits caused by changes in the market price. This form of competition is important, but it is just a game of copycat because firms entering an

CONSIDER THIS :: Running a Company Is Hard Business

The life expectancy of a Canadian business is just 10.2 years. About 9.5 percent of Canadian firms go out of business each year. In addition, 22 percent of new "startup" firms go bankrupt within two years, 53 percent within five years, and nearly 65 percent within ten years.

These numbers testify to the ability of competition to quickly dispose of firms that have high production costs or unpopular products. In a competitive environment, such firms quickly prove unprofitable and are shut down by their owners. For example, Research In Motion, once one of Canada's outstanding successes, has recently lost market share due to the relentless competition from Apple's iPhone and cellphones running Google's Android operating system.

Balancing out the bankrupt firms are startups that hope to use the resources freed up by the closed firms to deliver better products or lower costs. In a typical year, more than 65,000 new businesses are started in Canada. Most of these new firms will themselves eventually fall victim to creative destruction and the pressures of competition, but it's also possible that one of them will be the next Apple or Tim Hortons.

industry simply duplicate the production methods and cost curves of existing firms in order to duplicate their above-normal profits. In this type of competition, there is no dynamism and no innovation, just more of the same.

By contrast, the most dynamic and interesting parts of competition are the fights between firms over the creation of new production technologies and new products. Firms have a strong profit incentive to develop improved ways of making existing products as well as totally new products. To put that incentive in context, recall what you just learned about long-run equilibrium in perfect competition. When each firm in a perfectly competitive industry has the same productive technology and therefore the same cost structure for producing output, entry and exit assure that in the long run every firm will make the exact same normal profit.

Entrepreneurs, of course, would like to earn more than a normal profit. As a result, they are constantly attempting two different strategies for increasing their profits. The first involves attempting to lower the production costs of existing products through better technology or improved business organization. Because perfect competition implies that individual firms cannot affect the market price, anything that lowers an innovating firm's production costs will result in higher profits since the innovating firm's revenues per unit (which are equal to the market price per unit) will stay the same while its costs per unit fall due to its improved production technology.

The second strategy for earning a rate of return greater than a normal profit is to try to develop a totally new product that is popular with consumers. If a firm is first-to-market with a popular new product, it will face no competition, as it is the only producer. As long as the product remains popular and the firm remains the only producer, it will be able to charge prices that are higher than production costs, thereby allowing it to earn above-normal profits. (We say much more about this in Chapter 10, which covers monopoly.)

Notably, however, any advantages that innovative firms gain either by lowering the production costs of existing products or by introducing entirely new products will not normally persist. An innovative entrepreneur may put some of her current rivals out of business, but there are always other entrepreneurs with new ideas so that very soon it may be *her* firm that is going out of business due to innovations made by others. The *Consider This* box above shows just how rapid the destruction and creation of new firms is.

Creative Destruction

The innovations that firms achieve thanks to competition are considered by many economists to be the driving force behind economic growth and rising living standards. The transformative effects of competition are often referred to as **creative destruction** to capture the idea that the creation of new products and new production methods destroys the market positions of firms committed to existing products and old ways of doing business. In addition, just the *threat* that a rival may soon come out with a new technology or product can cause other firms to innovate and thereby replace or destroy their old ways of doing business. As argued many years ago by Harvard economist Joseph Schumpeter, the most important type of competition is:

connect
ORIGIN OF THE IDEA 9.2
Creative Destruction

> . . . competition from the new commodity, the new technology, the new source of supply, the new type of business organization—competition which commands a decisive cost or quality advantage and which strikes not at the margins of profits of the existing firms but at their foundation and their very lives. This kind of competition is . . . so . . . important that it becomes a matter of comparative indifference whether competition in the ordinary [short-run or long-run] sense functions more or less promptly. . . .
>
> . . . competition of the kind we now have in mind acts not only when in being but also when it is merely an ever-present threat. It disciplines before it attacks. The businessman feels himself to be in a competitive situation even if he is alone in his field.[2]

There are many examples of creative destruction: In the 1800s wagons, ships, and barges were the only means of transporting freight until the railroads broke up their monopoly; the dominant market position of the railroads was, in turn, undermined by trucks and, later, by airplanes. Movies brought new competition to live theatre, at one time the "only show in town." But movies were later challenged by broadcast television, which was then challenged by cable TV. Both are now challenged by Hulu, YouTube, and other online video-on-demand services. Cassettes replaced records before compact discs undermined cassettes. Now iPods, MP3 players, and Internet music downloads will soon make the compact disc obsolete. Electronic communications—including faxes and emails—have greatly impacted Canada Post. And online retailers like Amazon.com have stolen substantial business away from "bricks-and-mortar" retailers.

The "creative" part of "creative destruction" leads to new products and lower-cost production methods that are of great benefit to society because they allow for a more efficient use of society's scarce resources. Keep in mind, however, that the "destruction" part of "creative destruction" can be very hard on workers in the industries being displaced by new technologies. A worker at a CD-making factory may see her job eliminated as consumers switch to online music downloads. Canada Post cut hundreds of jobs in 2011 partly due to the impact that email has had on the demand for postal services. We need fewer and fewer postal workers each year thanks to email and texting. And many jobs in retail have been eliminated due to competition with Amazon.com and other online retailers.

Normally, the process of creative destruction goes slowly enough that workers at firms being downsized can transition smoothly to jobs in firms that are expanding. But sometimes the change is too swift for all of them to find new jobs easily. And in other instances, such as a town with only one major employer—like a rural coal-mining town or a small town with a large auto factory—the loss of that one major employer can be devastating because there are not enough other firms in the local area to employ the workers laid off by the major employer.

While the net effects of creative destruction are indisputably positive—including ongoing economic growth and rising living standards—creative destruction involves costs as well as benefits. And while the benefits are widespread, the costs tend to be borne almost entirely by the relatively few workers in declining industries who are not positioned to make easy transitions to new jobs.

[2] Joseph A. Schumpeter, *Capitalism, Socialism, and Democracy,* 3rd ed. (New York: Harper & Row, 1950, pp.84–85)

The LAST WORD   Efficiency Gains from Entry: The Case of Generic Drugs

When a generic drug becomes available, the price of the drug falls, consumer surplus rises, and society experiences an efficiency gain.

The competitive model predicts that entry will lower price, expand output, and increase efficiency. A good actual-economy test of this prediction occurs where new producers enter a formerly monopolized market, such as when prescription drugs lose their patent protection. A patent on a prescription drug gives the pharmaceutical company that developed it an exclusive right to produce and sell the medication for 20 years from the time of patent application. The purpose of drug patents is to encourage research and development (R&D), leading to new medications and the increased well-being they enable. With patent protection a firm can charge prices that exceed marginal cost and average total cost and earn economic profits on its popular brand-name medicines. Those economic profits provide a return on past development costs and help fund more R&D.

Although competitors often develop similar drugs, they cannot copy and sell the patented medication. Such drugs as Lipitor (for high cholesterol), Zoloft (for depression), and Nexium (for gastrointestinal disorders) are examples of best-selling, brand-name, patented drugs.

When a patent expires, any pharmaceutical company can produce and sell the drug under the generic name for the medication if it gets approval from Health Canada and if it can demonstrate that the production of a specific drug will not infringe any existing patents. Because such generic drugs have the same chemical composition as the

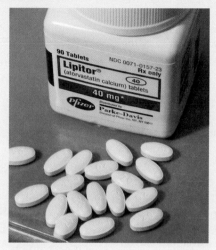

branded drug, they compete directly against it. The generic price is lower than the branded price, so the price of the drug (at least on average) drops as "generics" claim a share of the market. Studies indicate that the price drop is typically 30–40 percent. When generics become available, medical insurance plans either mandate that patients buy generics or provide financial incentives to encourage them to do so. Today,

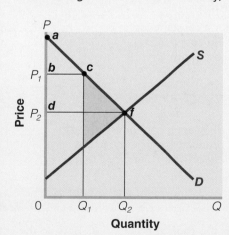

Quantity

generics make up about 65 percent of all prescriptions dispensed in Canada.

It is useful to see how patent expiration and the competition from generic drugs relate to consumer surplus and efficiency gains. Consider the accompanying figure, which is similar to Figure 9-6b. The patent gives the firm monopoly power that allows it to charge a higher-than-competitive price. Suppose that the sole seller's profit-maximizing price is P_1. (In Chapter 10 we explain how a monopolist chooses this price.)

The expiration of the patent creates competition from generics, which reduces the price of the medication from P_1 to, say, P_2. If you compare the consumer surplus triangles above the price lines, you can see that consumer surplus rises from *bac* to *daf* when the price falls. As the price of the medication drops from P_1 to P_2, output increases from Q_1 to Q_2. In this case, the efficiency gain from competition is shown by the addition of the blue triangle. At price P_2 and quantity Q_2, the combined amounts of consumer surplus and producer surplus are at a maximum. (In reality, the price might not drop all the way to P_2 because of continued loyalty to the branded drug by prescribing physicians.)

Patents aid consumers and society by encouraging the development of new medicines that might otherwise not be available. Entry of the generics at the time of patent expiration further helps consumers by lowering prices, increasing consumer surplus, and enhancing efficiency—just as the competitive model predicts.

Question

How does a generic drug differ from its brand-name, previously patented equivalent? Explain why the price of a brand-name drug typically declines when an equivalent generic drug becomes available. Explain how that drop in price affects allocative efficiency.

:: CHAPTER SUMMARY

9.1 :: THE LONG RUN VERSUS THE SHORT RUN IN PERFECT COMPETITION

- In the short run when plant and equipment are fixed, the firms in a perfectly competitive industry may earn profits or suffer losses. In the long run when plant and equipment are adjustable, profits will attract new entrants while losses will cause existing firms to leave the industry.

9.2 :: LONG-RUN EQUILIBRIUM

- The entry or exit of firms will change industry supply. Entry or exit will continue until the market price determined by industry supply interacting with market demand generates a normal profit for firms in the industry. With firms earning a normal profit, there will be no incentive to either enter or exit the industry. This situation constitutes long-run equilibrium in a purely competitive industry.

- Entry and exit help to improve resource allocation. Firms that exit an industry due to low profits release their resources to be used more profitably in other industries. Firms that enter an industry chasing higher profits bring with them resources that were less profitably used in other industries. Both processes increase allocative efficiency.

- In the long run, the market price of a product will equal the minimum average total cost of production. At a higher price, economic profits would cause firms to enter the industry until those profits had been competed away. At a lower price, losses would force the exit of firms from the industry until the product price rose to equal average total cost.

9.3 :: LONG-RUN SUPPLY FOR CONSTANT-COST, INCREASING-COST, AND DECREASING-COST INDUSTRIES

- The long-run supply curve is horizontal for a constant-cost industry, upward sloping for an increasing-cost industry, and downward sloping for a decreasing-cost industry.

9.4 :: PERFECT COMPETITION AND EFFICIENCY

- The long-run equality of price and minimum average total cost means that competitive firms will use the most efficient technology and charge the lowest price consistent with their production costs. That is, the firms will achieve productive efficiency.

- The long-run equality of price and marginal cost implies that resources will be allocated in accordance with consumer tastes. Allocative efficiency will occur. In the market, the combined amount of consumer surplus and producer surplus will be at a maximum.

- The competitive price system will reallocate resources in response to a change in consumer tastes, in technology, or in factor supplies and will thereby maintain allocative efficiency over time.

9.5 :: TECHNOLOGICAL ADVANCE AND COMPETITION

- Competition involves the never-ending attempts by entrepreneurs and managers to earn above-normal profits either by creating new products or by developing lower-cost production methods for existing products. These efforts cause creative destruction, the financial undoing of the market positions of firms committed to existing products and old ways of doing business by new firms with new products and innovative ways of doing business.

:: TERMS AND CONCEPTS

long-run supply curve, p. 219
constant-cost industry, p. 219
increasing-cost industry, p. 220

decreasing-cost industry, p. 221
productive efficiency, p. 224
allocative efficiency, p. 224

consumer surplus, p. 226
producer surplus, p. 226
creative destruction, p. 228

:: QUESTIONS

1. Explain how the long run differs from the short run in perfect competition. [LO9.1]

2. Relate opportunity costs to why profits encourage entry into perfectly competitive industries and how losses encourage exit from perfectly competitive industries. [LO9.2]

3. How do the entry and exit of firms in a perfectly competitive industry affect resource flows and long-run profits and losses? [LO9.2]

4. Using diagrams for both the industry and a representative firm, illustrate competitive long-run equilibrium. Assuming constant costs, employ these diagrams to show how

(a) an increase and (b) a decrease in market demand will upset that long-run equilibrium. Trace graphically and describe in words the adjustment processes by which long-run equilibrium is restored. Now rework your analysis for increasing-cost and decreasing-cost industries and compare the three long-run supply curves.   [**LO9.3**]

5. In long-run equilibrium, P = minimum ATC = MC. Of what significance for economic efficiency is the equality of P and minimum ATC? The equality of P and MC? Distinguish between productive efficiency and allocative efficiency in your answer.   [**LO9.4**]

6. Suppose that firms in a perfectly competitive industry producing cashews discover that P exceeds MC. Will their combined output of cashews be too little, too much, or just right to achieve allocative efficiency? In the long run,

what will happen to the supply of cashews and the price of cashews? Use a supply and demand diagram to show how that response will change the combined amount of consumer surplus and producer surplus in the market for cashews.   [**LO9.4**]

7. The basic model of perfect competition reviewed in this chapter finds that in the long run all firms in a perfectly competitive industry will earn normal profits. If all firms will only earn a normal profit in the long run, why would any firms bother to develop new products or lower-cost production methods? Explain.   [**LO9.5**]

8. "Ninety percent of new products fail within two years—so you shouldn't be so eager to innovate." Do you agree? Explain why or why not.   [**LO9.5**]

:: PROBLEMS

1. A firm in a perfectly competitive industry has a typical cost structure. The normal rate of profit in the economy is 5 percent. This firm is earning $5.50 on every $50 invested by its founders. What is its percentage rate of return? Is it earning an economic profit? If so, how large? Will this industry see entry or exit? What will be the rate of return earned by firms in this industry once the industry reaches long-run equilibrium?   [**LO9.2**]

2. A firm in a perfectly competitive industry is currently producing 1000 units per day at a total cost of $450. If it produced 800 units per day, its total cost would be $300, and if it produced 500 units per day, its total cost would be $275. What is the firm's ATC per unit at these three levels of production? If every firm in this industry has the same cost structure, is the industry in long run competitive equilibrium? From what you know about these firms' cost structures, what is the highest possible price per unit that could exist as the market price in long-run

equilibrium? If that price ends up being the market price and if the normal rate of profit is 10 percent, then how big will each firm's accounting profit per unit be?   [**LO9.4**]

3. There are 300 farms in the perfectly competitive local dairy market. Of the 300 dairy farms, 298 have a cost structure that generates profits of $24 for every $300 invested. What is their percentage rate of return? The other two dairies have a cost structure that generates profits of $22 for every $200 invested. What is their percentage rate of return? Assuming that the normal rate of profit in the economy is 10 percent, will there be entry or exit? Will the change in the number of farms affect the two farms that earn $22 for every $200 invested? What will be the rate of return earned by most farms in the industry in long-run equilibrium? If farms can copy each other's technology, what will be the rate of return eventually earned by all farms?   [**LO9.4**]

CHAPTER 10

Monopoly

We turn now from perfect competition to monopoly, which is at the opposite end of the spectrum of market structures listed in Table 8-1. You deal with monopolies more often than you might think. If you see the logo for Microsoft's Windows on your computer, you are dealing with a monopoly (or at least near-monopoly). When you purchase certain prescription drugs, you may be buying monopolized products. When you make a local telephone call, turn on your lights, or subscribe to cable TV, you may be patronizing a monopoly, depending on your location.

What precisely do we mean by monopoly and what conditions allow it to arise and survive? How does a monopolist determine its profit-maximizing price and output? Does a monopolist achieve the efficiencies associated with perfect competition? If not, what, if anything, should the government do about it? A simplified model of monopoly will help us answer these questions. It is the first of three models of imperfect competition; the other two are discussed in Chapter 11.

10.1 Characteristics of Monopoly ::

A **monopoly** exists when a single firm is the sole producer of a product or service for which there are no close substitutes. Here are the main characteristics of monopoly.

- **Single Seller** A monopoly is an industry in which a single firm is the sole producer or seller of a specific good or the sole supplier of a service.

- **No Close Substitutes** A monopoly's product is unique in that there are no close substitutes.

connect
**ORIGIN OF
THE IDEA 10.1**
Monopoly

A monopoly exists when a single firm is the sole producer of a product or service for which no close substitutes exist.

- *Price-Maker* The monopolist controls the total quantity supplied and thus has considerable control over price; it is a *price-maker*. The monopolist confronts the usual downward-sloping product demand curve. It can change its product price by changing the quantity of the product it produces. The monopolist will use this power whenever it is advantageous to do so.

- *Blocked Entry* A monopolist has no competitors because certain barriers keep potential competitors from entering the industry. Those barriers may be economic, technological, legal, or of some other type, but entry is totally blocked in monopoly.

- *Nonprice Competition* The product produced by a monopolist may be either standardized (as with natural gas and electricity) or differentiated (as with Microsoft's Windows software or Frisbees). Monopolists that have standardized products engage mainly in public relations advertising, whereas those with differentiated products sometimes advertise their products' attributes.

Examples of Monopoly

Examples of a single-price monopoly are relatively rare in Canada, but many examples of less pure forms exist. In many cities, government-owned or government-regulated public utilities—natural gas and electric companies, the water company, the cable TV company, and the local telephone company—may be monopolies or virtually so. For example, Toronto Hydro is the sole supplier of electricity in that urban market. In some Canadian markets, competition has been introduced for some of these traditional monopolies. Many urban areas now have more than one gas supplier to choose from, and rapid technological change has dramatically altered the delivery of communications services, effectively eliminating what was a virtual monopoly by Bell Canada. In some urban markets, such as Toronto and Montreal, Rogers Cable Communications now competes with Bell Canada in the local telephone market. Wireless telephone services by relative newcomers Telus and Rogers have further eroded Bell's monopoly position in local markets. The telecom industry has gone from a virtual monopoly to an oligopolistic market structure. Ontario and Alberta have moved toward deregulating their electricity markets, although the public furor that this has caused has delayed full deregulation.

Many "near-monopolies" also exist in which a single firm has the bulk of sales in a specific market. Intel, for example, produces 80 percent of the central microprocessors used in personal computers. Microsoft's Windows operating system is on some 90 percent of home and business computers; Wham-O, through its Frisbee brand, sells 90 percent of plastic throwing disks. The De Beers diamond syndicate effectively controls 55 percent of the world's supply of rough-cut diamonds (see this chapter's *The Last Word*).

Professional sports teams are, in a sense, monopolies because they are the sole suppliers of specific services in large geographic areas. With a few exceptions, a single major-league team in each sport serves each large Canadian city. If you want to see a live Major League Baseball game in Toronto, you must patronize the Blue Jays. Other geographic monopolies exist. For example, a small town may be served by only one airline or railroad. In a small, isolated community, the local barber shop, dry cleaner, or grocery store may approximate a monopoly.

Of course, some competition almost always exists. Satellite television is a substitute for cable, and amateur softball is a substitute for professional baseball. The Apple operating system can substitute for Windows, and so on. But such substitutes are typically either more costly or in some way less appealing.

Dual Objectives of the Study of Monopoly

Monopoly is worth studying both for its own sake and because it provides insights about the more common market structures of monopolistic competition and oligopoly (see Chapter 9). These two market structures combine, in differing degrees, characteristics of perfect competition and monopoly.

Barriers to Entry

The factors that prohibit firms from entering an industry are called **barriers to entry.** In monopoly, strong barriers to entry effectively block all potential competition. Somewhat weaker barriers may permit oligopoly, a market structure dominated by a few firms. Still weaker barriers may permit the entry of a fairly large number of competing firms, giving rise to monopolistic competition. The absence of any effective entry barriers permits the entry of a very large number of firms, which provides the basis of perfect competition. So, barriers to entry are pertinent not only to the extreme case of monopoly but also to other market structures in which there are monopoly-like characteristics or monopoly-like behaviours.

We now discuss the four most prominent barriers to entry.

barriers to entry
Anything that artificially prevents the entry of firms into an industry.

ECONOMIES OF SCALE

Modern technology in some industries is such that economies of scale—declining average total cost with added firm size—are extensive. In such cases, a firm's long-run average-cost schedule will decline over a wide range of output. Given market demand, only a few large firms or, in the extreme, only a single large firm can achieve low average total costs.

Figure 10-1 indicates economies of scale over a wide range of outputs. If total consumer demand is within that output range, then only a single producer can satisfy demand at least cost. Note, for example, that a monopolist can produce 200 units at a per-unit cost of $10 and a total cost of $2000. If there are two firms in the industry and each produces 100 units, the unit cost is $15 and total cost rises to $3000 (= 200 units × $15). A still more competitive situation with four firms each producing 50 units would boost unit and total cost to $20 and $4000, respectively. Conclusion: When long-run average total cost (ATC) is declining, only a single producer, a monopolist, can produce any particular output at minimum total cost.

If a monopoly exists in such an industry, economies of scale will serve as an entry barrier and will protect the monopolist from competition. New firms that try to enter the industry as small-scale producers cannot realize the cost economies of the monopolist and therefore cannot obtain the normal profits necessary for survival or growth. A new firm might try to enter the industry as a large-scale producer so as to achieve the necessary economies of scale, but the massive plant facilities needed would require huge amounts of financing, which a new and untried enterprise would find difficult to secure. In most cases the financial obstacles and risks to starting big are prohibitive, which explains why efforts to enter such industries as those manufacturing automobiles, computer operating software, commercial aircraft, and basic steel are rare.

FIGURE 10-1 **Economies of Scale: The Natural Monopoly Case**

A declining long-run average-total-cost curve over a wide range of output quantities indicates extensive economies of scale. A single monopoly firm can produce, say, 200 units of output at lower cost ($10 each) than could two or more firms that had a combined output of 200 units.

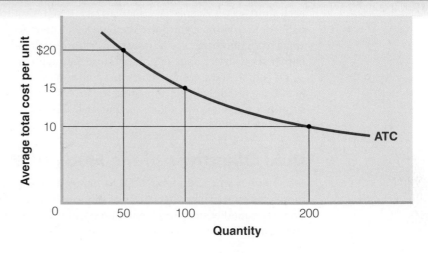

A monopoly firm is referred to as a *natural monopoly* if the market demand curve intersects the long-run ATC curve at any point where average total costs are declining. If a natural monopoly were to set its price where market demand intersects long-run ATC, its price would be lower than if the industry were more competitive. But it will probably set a higher price. A monopolist may, instead, set its price far above ATC and obtain substantial economic profit. In that event, the cost advantage of a natural monopolist would accrue to the monopolist as profit and not as lower prices to consumers. That is why the government regulates some natural monopolies, specifying the price they may charge. We will say more about that later.

LEGAL BARRIERS TO ENTRY: PATENTS AND LICENCES

Government also creates legal barriers to entry by awarding patents and licences.

- **Patents** A *patent* is the exclusive right of an inventor to use, or to allow another to use, her or his invention. Patent laws protect the inventor from rivals who would use the invention without having shared in the effort and expense of developing it. Patents thus provide the inventor with a monopoly position for the life of the patent. The world's nations have agreed on a uniform patent length of 20 years from the time of application. Patents have figured prominently in the growth of modern-day giants such as IBM, Microsoft, Pfizer, Xcrox, Bombardier, General Electric, and Research In Motion.

  Research and development (R&D) is what leads to most patentable inventions and products. Firms that gain monopoly power through their own research or by purchasing the patents of others can use patents to strengthen their market position. The profit from one patent can finance the research required to develop new patentable products. In the pharmaceutical industry, patents on prescription drugs have produced large monopoly profits that have helped finance the discovery of new patentable medicines. So, monopoly power achieved through patents may well be self-sustaining, even though patents eventually expire and generic drugs then compete with the original brand.

- **Licences** The government may also limit entry into an industry or occupation through *licensing*. At the national level, the Canadian Radio-television and Telecommunications Commission (CRTC) licenses a limited number of radio and television stations in each geographic area. In many large cities, one of a limited number of municipal licences is required to drive a taxicab. The restriction of the supply of cabs creates economic profit for cab owners and drivers. New cabs cannot enter the industry to force prices and profit lower. In a few instances the government might license itself to provide some product and thereby create a public monopoly. For example, in some provinces only province-owned retail outlets can sell liquor. Similarly, many provinces have licensed themselves to run lotteries.

OWNERSHIP OR CONTROL OF ESSENTIAL RESOURCES

A monopolist can use private property as an obstacle to potential rivals. For example, a firm that owns or controls a resource essential to the production process can prohibit the entry of rival firms. Governments can also control access to certain needed resources. The Canadian government has all the rights to distribute the use of airwaves by television and radio stations, for example. A municipal sand and gravel firm may own all the nearby deposits of sand and gravel. And it is very difficult for new professional sports leagues to be created because existing leagues have contracts with the best players and long-term leases on the major stadiums and arenas.

PRICING AND OTHER STRATEGIC BARRIERS TO ENTRY

Even if a firm is not protected from entry by, say, extensive economies of scale or ownership of essential resources, entry may effectively be blocked by the way the monopolist responds when rivals attempt to enter the industry. Confronted with a new entrant, the monopolist may create an entry barrier by slashing prices, stepping up advertising, or taking other strategic action to make it difficult for the entrant to succeed.

A prominent example of entry deterrence is the case of Microsoft, the software giant. In 2001 a U.S. court of appeals upheld a lower court's finding that Microsoft used a series of illegal actions to maintain its monopoly in Intel-compatible PC operating systems (95 percent market share). One such action was charging higher prices for its Windows operating system to computer manufacturers that featured Netscape's Navigator rather than Microsoft's Internet Explorer.

Monopoly Demand

Now that we have explained the sources of monopoly, we will build a model of monopoly so that we can analyze its price and output decisions. Let's start by making three assumptions:

1. Economies of scale, patents, or resource ownership secure the monopolist's status.

2. Government does not regulate the firm.

3. The firm is a single-price monopolist; it charges the same price for all units of output.

The crucial difference between a monopolist and a seller in perfect competition lies on the demand side of the market. The seller in a competitive market faces a perfectly elastic demand at the price determined by market supply and demand. It is a *price-taker* that can sell as much or as little as it wants at the going market price.

The demand curve for the monopolist (and for any imperfectly competitive seller) is quite different from that of a firm in perfect competition. Because the monopolist *is* the industry, its demand curve is *the market demand curve,* which is downsloping. Columns 1 and 2 in Table 10-1 illustrate this; note that quantity demanded increases as price decreases.

In Figure 8-7 we drew separate demand curves for the perfectly competitive industry and for a single firm in such an industry; only a single demand curve is needed in monopoly because the firm and the industry are one and the same. We have graphed part of the demand data in Table 10-1 as demand curve D in Figure 10-2. This is the monopolist's demand curve *and* the

---

TABLE 10-1   **Revenue and Cost Data of a Monopolist**

	REVENUE DATA				COST DATA		
(1) Quantity of output (Q)	(2) Price (average revenue) (P)	(3) Total revenue (TR = P × Q)	(4) Marginal revenue MR = $\frac{\Delta TR}{\Delta Q}$	(5) Average total cost (ATC)	(6) Total cost Q × ATC (TC)	(7) Marginal cost (MC)	(8) Profit (+) or loss (−)
0	$172	$ 0			$ 100		$−100
			$162			$ 90	
1	162	162		$190.00	190		−28
			142			80	
2	152	304		135.00	270		+34
			122			70	
3	142	426		113.33	340		+86
			102			60	
4	132	528		100.00	400		+128
			82			70	
5	122	610		94.00	470		+140
			62			80	
6	112	672		91.67	550		+122
			42			90	
7	102	714		91.43	640		+74
			22			110	
8	92	736		93.75	750		−14
			2			130	
9	82	738		97.78	880		−142
			−18			150	
10	72	720		103.00	1030		−310

FIGURE 10-2 Price and Marginal Revenue in Monopoly

A monopolist with a downward-sloping demand curve such as *D* must set a lower price to sell more output. Here, by charging $132 rather than $142, the monopolist sells an extra unit (the fourth unit) and gains $132 from that sale. But from this gain must be subtracted $30, which reflects the $10 less the monopolist charged for each of the first three units. Thus, the marginal revenue of the fourth unit is $102 (= $132 − $30), considerably less than its $132 price.

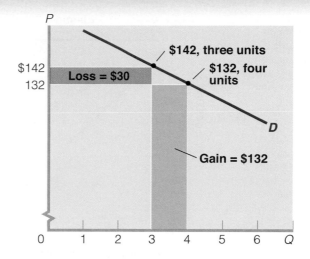

market demand curve. The downward-sloping demand curve has three implications that are essential to understanding the monopoly model.

1. MARGINAL REVENUE IS LESS THAN PRICE

With a fixed downward-sloping demand curve, the monopolist can increase sales only by charging a lower price. Consequently, marginal revenue is less than price (average revenue) for every level of output except the first. Why? The lower price of the extra unit of output also applies to all prior units of output. Each additional unit of output sold increases total revenue by an amount equal to its own price less the sum of the price cuts that apply to all prior units of output.

Figure 10-2 confirms this point. There, we have highlighted two price–quantity combinations from the monopolist's demand curve. The monopolist can sell one more unit at $132 than it can at $142 and that way get an additional $132 of revenue (the light blue area). But to sell that fourth unit for $132, the monopolist must also sell the first three units at $132 rather than $142. This $10 reduction in revenue on three units results in a $30 revenue loss (the pink area). Thus, the net difference in total revenue from selling a fourth unit is $102: the $132 gain from the fourth unit minus the $30 forgone on the first three units ($10 per unit × 3 units = $30). This net gain of $102—the marginal revenue of the fourth unit—is clearly less than the $132 price of the fourth unit.

Column 4 in Table 10-1 shows that marginal revenue is always less than the corresponding product price in column 2, except for the first unit of output. Because marginal revenue is the change in total revenue associated with each *additional* unit of output, the declining amounts of marginal revenue in column 4 mean that total revenue increases at a diminishing rate (as shown in column 3).

We show the relationship between the monopolist's marginal-revenue curve and total-revenue curve in Figure 10-3. For this figure, we extended the demand and revenue data of columns 1 through 4 in Table 10-1, assuming that successive $10 price cuts each increase sales by one unit. For example, the monopolist can sell 11 units at $62, 12 units at $52, and so on.

Note that the monopolist's MR curve lies below the demand curve, indicating that marginal revenue is less than price at every output quantity but the very first unit. Observe also the special relationship between total revenue (shown in the lower graph) and marginal revenue (shown in the top graph). Because marginal revenue is the change in total revenue, marginal revenue is positive while total revenue is increasing. When total revenue reaches its maximum, marginal revenue is zero. When total revenue is diminishing, marginal revenue is negative.

FIGURE 10-3   Demand, Marginal Revenue, and Total Revenue for a Monopolist

Panel (a): Because an imperfectly competitive firm must lower its price on all units sold in order to increase its sales, the marginal-revenue curve (MR) lies below its downward-sloping demand curve (*D*). The elastic and inelastic regions of demand are highlighted. Panel (b): Total revenue (TR) increases at a decreasing rate, reaches maximum, and then declines. Note that in the elastic region, TR is increasing and hence MR is positive. When TR reaches its maximum, MR is zero. In the inelastic region of demand, TR is declining, so MR is negative.

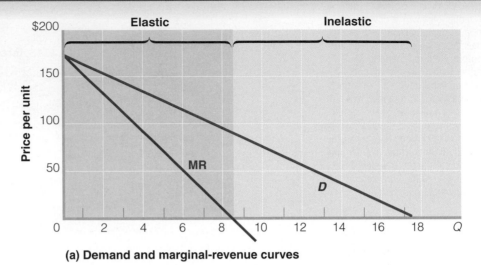

(a) Demand and marginal-revenue curves

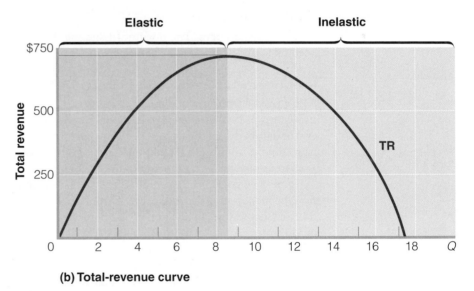

(b) Total-revenue curve

2. THE MONOPOLIST IS A PRICE-MAKER

All firms in imperfectly competitive market structures—whether monopoly, oligopoly, or monopolistic competition—face downsloping demand curves. As a result, any change in quantity produced causes a movement along their respective demand curves and a change in the price they can charge for their respective products. Economists summarize this fact by saying that firms with downsloping demand curves are *price-makers*.

This is most evident in monopoly, where an industry consists of a single monopoly firm so that total industry output is exactly equal to whatever the single monopoly firm chooses to produce. As we just mentioned, the monopolist faces a downward-sloping demand curve in which each amount of output is associated with some unique price. Thus, in deciding on the quantity of output to produce, the monopolist is also indirectly determining the price it will charge. Through control of output, it can make the price. From columns 1 and 2 in Table 10-1 we find that the monopolist can charge a price of $72 if it produces 10 units, a price of $82 if it produces 9 units, and so forth.

MATH 10.1
Monopoly and the
Elasticity of Demand

3. THE MONOPOLIST SETS PRICES IN THE ELASTIC REGION OF DEMAND

The total-revenue test for price elasticity of demand is the basis for our third implication. Recall from Chapter 4 that the total-revenue test reveals that when demand is elastic, a decline in price will increase total revenue. Similarly, when demand is inelastic, a decline in price will *reduce* total revenue. Beginning at the top of demand curve *D* in Figure 10-3a, observe that as the price declines from $172 to approximately $82, total revenue increases (and marginal revenue, therefore, is positive), which means that demand is elastic in this price range. Conversely, for price declines below $82, total revenue decreases (marginal revenue is negative), which indicates that demand is inelastic there.

The implication is that a profit-maximizing monopolist will always want to avoid the inelastic segment of its demand curve in favour of some price–quantity combination in the elastic region. Here's why: To get into the inelastic region, the monopolist must lower price and increase output. In the inelastic region a lower price means less total revenue. And increased output always means increased total cost. Less total revenue and higher total cost yield lower profit.

QUICK REVIEW

- A monopolist is the sole supplier of a product or service for which no close substitutes exist.

- A monopoly survives because of entry barriers such as economies of scale, patents and licences, the ownership of essential resources, and strategic actions to exclude rivals.

- The monopolist's demand curve is downsloping, and its marginal-revenue curve lies below its demand curve.

- The downsloping demand curve means that the monopolist is a price-maker.

- The monopolist will operate in the elastic region of demand since it can increase total revenue and reduce total cost by reducing output.

10.2   Output and Price Determination

At what specific price–quantity combination will a profit-maximizing monopolist choose to operate? To answer this question, we must add production costs to our analysis.

Cost Data

On the cost side, we will assume that, although the firm is a monopolist in the product market, it hires factors of production in competitive markets and employs the same technology and, therefore, has the same cost structure as the perfectly competitive firm that we studied in Chapters 8 and 9. By using the same cost data that we developed in Chapter 7, and applied to the competitive firm in Chapters 8 and 9, we will be able to directly compare the price and output decisions of a monopoly with those of a firm in perfect competition. This will help us demonstrate that the price and output differences between a monopolist and a firm in perfect competition are not the result of two different sets of costs. Columns 5 through 7 in Table 10-1 reproduce the relevant cost data from Table 7-2.

MR = MC Rule

A monopolist seeking to maximize total profit will employ the same rationale as a profit-seeking firm in a competitive industry. It will produce another unit of output as long as that unit adds more to total revenue than it adds to total cost. The firm will increase output up to the output at which marginal revenue equals marginal cost (MR = MC).

A comparison of columns 4 and 7 in Table 10-1 indicates that the profit-maximizing output is five units, because the fifth unit is the last unit of output whose marginal revenue exceeds its marginal cost. What price will the monopolist charge? The demand schedule shown as columns 1 and 2 in Table 10-1 indicates there is only one price at which five units can be sold: $122.

This analysis is shown in **Figure 10-4 (Key Graph),** where we have graphed the demand, marginal-revenue, average-total-cost, and marginal-cost data of Table 10-1. The profit-maximizing output occurs at five units of output (Q_m) where the marginal-revenue (MR) and marginal-cost (MC) curves intersect (MR = MC).

To find the price the monopolist will charge, we extend a vertical line from Q_m up to the demand curve D. The price P_m at which Q_m units can be sold is $122, which is in this case the profit-maximizing price. So the monopolist sets the quantity at Q_m to charge its profit-maximizing price of $122.

Columns 2 and 5 in Table 10-1 show that, at five units of output, the product price ($122) exceeds the average total cost ($94). The monopolist thus earns an economic profit of $28 per unit and the total economic profit is $140 (= 5 units × $28). In Figure 10-4, per-unit profit is $P_m - A$, where A is the average total cost of producing Q_m units. Total economic profit—the blue rectangle—is found by multiplying this per-unit profit by the profit-maximizing output Q_m.

Another way we can determine the profit-maximizing output is by comparing total revenue and total cost at each level of production and choosing the output with the greatest positive difference. Use columns 3 and 6 in Table 10-1 to verify our conclusion that five units is the profit-maximizing output. Graphing total revenue and total cost also shows the greatest difference (the maximum profit) at five units of output. Table 10-2 summarizes the process for determining the profit-maximizing output, the profit-maximizing price, and economic profit in monopoly.

No Monopoly Supply Curve

Recall that for firms in perfect competition MR equals P and the supply curve of a firm is determined by applying the MR (= P) = MC profit-maximizing rule. The supply curve for each firm is the portion of the firm's MC curve that lies above the average-variable-cost curve (see Figure 8-6).

connect

WORKED PROBLEM 10.1
Monopoly Price and
Output

TABLE 10-2

Steps for Graphically Determining the Profit-Maximizing Price and Economic Profit (if any) in Monopoly

Step 1	Determine the profit-maximizing output by finding where MR = MC.
Step 2	Determine the profit-maximizing price by extending a vertical line upward from the output determined in step 1 to the monopolist's demand curve.
Step 3	Determine the monopolist's economic profit using one of two methods.
	Method 1 Find profit per unit by subtracting the average total cost of the profit-maximizing output from the profit-maximizing price. Then multiply the difference by the profit-maximizing output to determine economic profit (if any).
	Method 2 Find total cost by multiplying the average total cost of the profit-maximizing output by that output. Find total revenue by multiplying the profit-maximizing output by the profit-maximizing price. Then subtract total cost from total revenue to determine economic profit (if any).

📈 **KEY GRAPH**

FIGURE 10-4 Profit Maximization by a Monopolist

The monopolist maximizes profit by producing the MR = MC output, here Q_m = 5 units. Then, as shown by the demand curve, it will charge price P_m = $122. Average total cost will be A = $94, meaning that per-unit profit is $P_m - A$ and total profit is $5 \times (P_m - A)$. Total economic profit is thus represented by the grey rectangle.

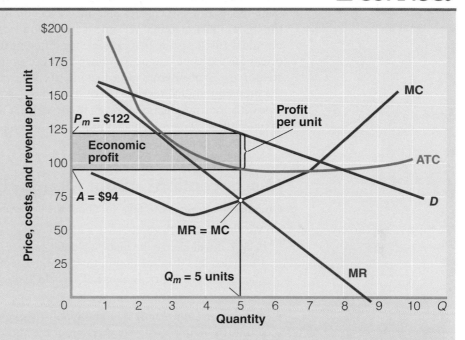

Quick Quiz

1. **The MR curve lies below the demand curve in this figure because**
   a. the demand curve is linear (a straight line).
   b. the demand curve is highly inelastic throughout its full length.
   c. the demand curve is highly elastic throughout its full length.
   d. the gain in revenue from an extra unit of output is less than the price charged for that unit of output.

2. **The area labelled "Economic profit" can be found by multiplying the difference between P and ATC by quantity. It also can be found by**
   a. dividing profit per unit by quantity.
   b. subtracting total cost from total revenue.
   c. multiplying the coefficient of demand elasticity by quantity.
   d. multiplying the difference between P and MC by quantity.

3. **This monopolist**
   a. charges the highest price it can get.
   b. earns only a normal profit in the long run.
   c. restricts output to create an insurmountable entry barrier.
   d. restricts output to increase its price and total economic profit.

4. **At this monopolist's profit-maximizing output**
   a. price equals marginal revenue.
   b. price equals marginal cost.
   c. price exceeds marginal cost.
   d. profit per unit is maximized.

Answers: 1. d; 2. b; 3. d; 4. c

At first glance we would suspect that the monopolist's marginal-cost curve would also be its supply curve, but that is *not* the case. *The monopolist has no supply curve.* Like the competitive firm, the monopolist equates marginal revenue and marginal cost to determine output, but for the monopolist marginal revenue is less than price. Because the monopolist does not equate marginal cost to price, it is possible for different demand conditions to bring about different prices for the same output. To understand this point, refer to Figure 10-4 and pencil in a new, steeper marginal-revenue curve that intersects the marginal-cost curve at the same point as does the present marginal-revenue curve. Then draw in a new demand curve that is roughly consistent with your new marginal-revenue curve. With the new curves, the same MR = MC output of five units now means a higher profit-maximizing price. Conclusion: There is no supply curve for the monopolist.

Misconceptions about Monopoly Pricing

Our analysis exposes two fallacies about the behaviour of a monopolist.

- *Not the Highest Price* Because a monopolist can manipulate output and price, people often believe it will charge the highest price it can get. That is incorrect. Prices above P_m in Figure 10-4 yield less than maximum total profit. The monopolist seeks maximum total profit, not maximum price. Prices above P_m would reduce sales and total revenue by more than a decrease in total cost.

- *Total, Not Unit, Profit* The monopolist seeks maximum total profit, not maximum unit profit. In Figure 10-4 a comparison of the vertical distance between average total cost and price at various possible outputs indicates that per-unit profit is greater at a point slightly to the left of the profit-maximizing output Q_m. This is shown in Table 10-1 where the per-unit profit at four units of output is $32 (= $132 − $100) compared with $28 (= $122 − $94) at the profit-maximizing output of five units. Here the monopolist accepts a lower-than-maximum per-unit profit because additional sales more than compensate for the lower unit profit. A monopolist prefers to sell five units at a profit of $28 per unit (for a total profit of $140) than four units at a profit of $32 per unit (for a total profit of only $128).

Possibility of Losses by Monopolist

The likelihood of economic profit is greater for a monopolist than for a firm in perfect competition; in the long run only a normal profit is possible in a perfectly competitive industry, whereas barriers to entry mean that for the monopolist economic profits can persist. In monopoly there are no new entrants to increase supply, drive down price, and eliminate economic profit.

But monopoly does not *guarantee* profit. The monopolist is not immune to changes in tastes that reduce the demand for its product. Nor is it immune to upward-shifting cost curves caused by escalating prices of factors of production. If the demand and cost situation faced by the monopolist is far less favourable than that in Figure 10-4, the monopolist will incur losses in the short run. Despite its dominance in the market, the monopoly enterprise in Figure 10-5 suffers a loss, as shown, because of weak demand and relatively high costs. Yet it will continue to operate because its total loss is less than its fixed cost. More precisely, at output Q_m the monopolist's price P_m exceeds its average variable cost V. Its loss per unit is $A − P_m$, and the total loss is shown by the pink rectangle.

Like a firm in perfect competition, the monopolist will not operate at a loss in the long run. Faced with continuing losses, in the long run the firm's owners will move their resources to other industries that offer better profit opportunities. A monopolist such as the one depicted in Figure 10-5 must obtain a minimum of a normal profit in the long run or it will go out of business.

FIGURE 10-5 · The Loss-Minimizing Position of a Monopolist

If demand D is weak and costs are high, the monopolist may be unable to make a profit. Because P_m exceeds V, the average variable cost at the MR = MC output Q_m, the monopolist will minimize losses in the short run by producing at that output. The loss per unit is $A - P_m$, and the total loss is indicated by the pink rectangle.

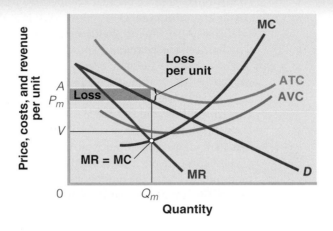

10.3 Economic Effects of Monopoly

Let's now evaluate monopoly from the standpoint of society as a whole. The standard reference for this evaluation is the long-run efficiency in a perfectly competitive market, identified by the triple equality P = MC = minimum ATC.

Price, Output, and Efficiency

Figure 10-6 graphically contrasts the price, output, and efficiency outcomes of monopoly and a perfectly competitive *industry*. Recall that in perfect competition at the equilibrium price–output

FIGURE 10-6 · Inefficiency of Monopoly Relative to a Perfectly Competitive Industry

Panel (a): In a perfectly competitive industry, entry and exit of firms ensures that price (P_c) equals marginal cost (MC) and that the minimum average-total-cost output (Q_c) is produced. Both productive efficiency (P = minimum ATC) and allocative efficiency (P = MC) are obtained. Panel (b): In monopoly, the MR curve lies below the demand curve. The monopolist maximizes profit at output Q_m, where MR = MC, and charges price P_m. Thus, output is lower (Q_m rather than Q_c) and price is higher (P_m rather than P_c) than they would be in a perfectly competitive industry. Monopoly is inefficient, since output is less than that required for achieving minimum ATC (here at Q_c) and because the monopolist's price exceeds MC. Monopoly creates an efficiency loss (here of triangle abc). There is also a transfer of income from consumers to the monopoly (here of rectangle P_cP_mbd).

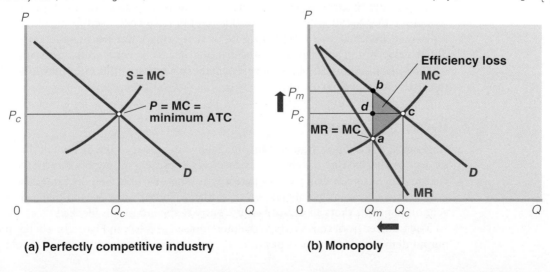

(a) Perfectly competitive industry   **(b) Monopoly**

combination both productive efficiency and allocative efficiency are achieved. *Productive efficiency* is achieved because competitive pressures force firms to operate where average total cost is at a minimum, Q_c. Product price is at the lowest level consistent with minimum average total cost. Also, *allocative efficiency* is achieved because production occurs up to that output at which price (the measure of a product's value or marginal benefit to society) equals marginal cost (the worth of the alternative products forgone by society in producing any given commodity). In short: $P = MC = $ minimum ATC.

Now let's suppose that this industry becomes a monopoly (Figure 10-6b) as a result of one firm acquiring all its competitors. We also assume that no changes in costs or market demand result from this dramatic change in the industry structure. What were formerly thousands of competing firms are now a single monopolist.

The competitive market supply curve S has become the marginal-cost curve (MC) of the monopolist. (Since the monopolist does not have a supply curve as such, we have removed the S label.) The important change, however, is on the demand side. From the viewpoint of each individual competitive firm, demand was perfectly elastic, and marginal revenue was therefore equal to the market equilibrium price P_c. So each firm equated its marginal revenue of P_c dollars per unit with its individual marginal cost curve to maximize profits. But market demand and individual demand are the same to the monopolist. The firm *is* the industry, and thus the monopolist sees the downward-sloping demand curve D shown in Figure 10-6b.

This means that marginal revenue is less than price, and that graphically the MR curve lies below demand curve D. In using the MR = MC rule, the monopolist selects output Q_m and price P_m. A comparison of both graphs in Figure 10-6 reveals that the monopolist finds it profitable to sell a smaller output at a higher price than would prevail in a competitive industry.

Monopoly yields neither productive nor allocative efficiency. The lack of productive efficiency can be understood most directly by noting that the monopolist's output Q_m is less than Q_c, the output at which average total cost is lowest. In addition, the monopoly price P_m is higher than the competitive price P_c that we know in long-run equilibrium in pure competition equals minimum average total cost. Thus, the monopoly price exceeds minimum average total cost, thereby demonstrating in another way that the monopoly will not be productively efficient.

The monopolist's underproduction also implies allocative inefficiency. One way to see this is to note that at the monopoly output level Q_m, the monopoly price P_m that consumers are willing to pay exceeds the marginal cost of production. This means that consumers value additional units of this product more highly than they do the alternative products that could be produced from the resources that would be necessary to make more units of the monopolist's product.

The monopolist's allocative inefficiency can also be understood by noting that for every unit between Q_m and Q_c, marginal benefit exceeds marginal cost because the demand curve lies above the supply curve. By choosing not to produce these units, the monopolist reduces allocative efficiency because the resources that should have been used to make these units will be redirected instead toward producing items that bring lower net benefits to society. The total dollar value of this efficiency loss (or *deadweight loss*) is equal to the area of the blue triangle labelled *abc* in Figure 10-6b. A more detailed explanation of this efficiency loss will be given in the last section of this chapter.

Income Transfer

In general, a monopoly transfers income from consumers to the owners of the monopoly. The income is received by the owners as revenue. Because a monopoly has market power, it can charge a higher price than would a perfectly competitive firm with the same costs. So the monopoly in effect levies a "private tax" on consumers. This private tax can often generate substantial economic profits that can persist because entry to the industry is blocked.

The transfer from consumers to the monopolist is evident in Figure 10-6b. For the Q_m units of output demanded, consumers pay price P_m rather than the price P_c that they would pay to a pure competitor. The total amount of income transferred from consumers to the monopolist is $P_m - P_c$ multiplied by the number of units sold, Q_m. So the total transfer is the dollar amount of rectangle $P_c P_m bd$. What the consumer loses, the monopolist gains. In contrast, the efficiency loss *abc* is a *deadweight* loss—society totally loses the net benefits of the Q_c minus Q_m units that are not produced.

Cost Complications

Our evaluation of monopoly has led us to conclude that, given identical costs, a monopolist will charge a higher price, produce a smaller output, and allocate economic resources less efficiently than a perfectly competitive industry. These inferior results are rooted in the entry barriers characterizing monopoly.

But costs may not be the same for a firm in a perfectly competitive industry and a monopolist. The unit cost incurred by a monopolist may be either larger or smaller than that incurred by a firm in a competitive industry. There are four reasons why costs may differ: (1) economies of scale, (2) a phenomenon called *X-inefficiency,* (3) the need for monopoly-preserving expenditures, and (4) the very long-run perspective, which allows for technological advance.

ECONOMIES OF SCALE ONCE AGAIN

Where economies of scale are extensive, market demand may not be sufficient to support a large number of competing firms, each producing at minimum efficient scale. In such cases, an industry of one or two firms will have a lower average total cost than the same industry made up of numerous competitive firms. At the extreme, only a single firm—a natural monopoly—might be able to achieve the lowest long-run average total cost.

Some firms whose business is in new information technologies—computer software, Internet service, wireless communications—have displayed extensive economies of scale. As these firms have grown, their long-run average total costs have declined. Greater use of specialized inputs, the spreading of product development costs, and learning by doing all have produced economies of scale. Also, *simultaneous consumption* and *network effects* have reduced costs.

simultaneous consumption
A product's ability to satisfy a large number of consumers at the same time.

A product's ability to satisfy a large number of consumers at the same time is called **simultaneous consumption** (or *nonrivalrous consumption*). Dell Computer Corporation needs to produce a personal computer for each customer, but Microsoft needs to produce its Windows program only once. Then, at very low marginal cost, Microsoft delivers its program online or by disc to millions of consumers. Similar low cost of delivering product to additional customers is true for Internet service providers, such as Rogers and Bell Canada, music producers, and wireless communications firms such as Research In Motion and Telus. Because marginal costs are so low, the average total cost of output declines as more customers are added.

network effects
Increases in the value of a product to each user, including existing users, as the total number of users rises.

Increases in the value of a product to each user, including existing users, as the total number of users rises are known as **network effects.** Good examples are computer software, cellphones, and websites like Facebook where the content is provided by users. When others have Internet service and devices to access it, you can conveniently send email messages to them. When they have similar software, you can easily pass around attachments like spreadsheets and photos. The more people are connected to the product, the more its benefits to each person are magnified.

Such network effects may drive a market toward monopoly, because consumers tend to choose standard products that everyone else is using. The focused demand for these products permits their producers to grow rapidly and thus achieve economies of scale. Smaller firms, which have either higher-cost "right" products or "wrong" products, get acquired or go out of business.

Economists generally agree that some new information firms have not yet exhausted their economies of scale, but it is questionable whether such firms are truly natural monopolies. Most firms eventually achieve their minimum efficient scale at less than the full size of the market. That means competition among firms is possible.

FIGURE 10-7 **X-Inefficiency**

The average-total-cost curve (ATC) is assumed to reflect the minimum cost of producing each particular unit of output. Any point above this lowest-cost ATC curve, such as X or X', implies X-inefficiency: operation at greater than lowest cost for a particular level of output.

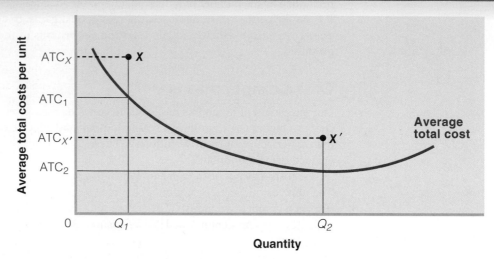

But even if natural monopoly develops, it's unlikely the monopolist will pass cost reductions along to consumers. So, with perhaps a handful of exceptions, economies of scale do not change the general conclusion that monopoly industries are inefficient relative to competitive industries.

X-INEFFICIENCY

ORIGIN OF THE IDEA 10.2
X-Inefficiency

X-inefficiency
The production of output, whatever its level, at higher average (and total) cost than is necessary.

In constructing all the average-total-cost curves used in this book, we have assumed that the firm uses the most efficient technology. This assumption is only natural because firms cannot maximize profits unless they are minimizing costs. **X-inefficiency** occurs when a firm produces output at a higher cost than is necessary to produce it. In Figure 10-7, X-inefficiency is represented by operation at points X and X' above the lowest-cost ATC curve. At these points, per-unit costs are ATC_X (as opposed to ATC_1) for output Q_1 and $ATC_{X'}$ (as opposed to ATC_2) for output Q_2. Producing at any point above the average-total-cost curve in Figure 10-7 reflects inefficiency or bad management by the firm.

Why does X-inefficiency occur if it reduces profits? The answer is that managers of a firm may have goals such as expanding power, an easier work life, avoiding business risk, or giving jobs to incompetent relatives, all which conflict with cost minimization. Or X-inefficiency may arise because a firm's workers are poorly motivated or ineffectively supervised. Or a firm may simply become lethargic and inert, relying on rules of thumb in decision making as opposed to relevant calculations of costs and revenues.

For our purposes the relevant question is whether a monopolist suffers more X-inefficiency than competitive firms do. There is evidence that it does. Firms in competitive industries are continually under pressure from rivals, forcing them to be internally efficient to survive. But monopolists are sheltered from such competitive forces by entry barriers. That lack of pressure may lead to X-inefficiency.

RENT-SEEKING EXPENDITURES

rent-seeking behaviour
The actions by persons, firms, or unions to gain special benefits from government at taxpayers' or someone else's expense.

A **rent-seeking behaviour** is an activity designed to transfer income or wealth to a particular firm or resource supplier at someone else's, or even society's, expense. We have seen that a monopolist can obtain an economic profit even in the long run. Therefore, it is no surprise that a firm may go to great expense to acquire or maintain a monopoly granted by government through legislation or an exclusive licence. Such rent-seeking expenditures add nothing to the firm's output, but they clearly increase its costs. Taken alone, rent seeking implies that monopoly has even higher costs and less efficiency than suggested in Figure 10-6b.

TECHNOLOGICAL ADVANCE

In the very long run, firms can reduce their costs through the discovery and implementation of new technology. If monopolists are more likely than competitive firms to develop more efficient production techniques over time, then the inefficiency of monopoly might be overstated.

The general view of economists is that a monopolist will not be technologically progressive. Although its economic profit provides ample means to finance research and development, it has little incentive to implement new techniques (or products). Because of its sheltered market position, the monopolist can afford to be complacent and lethargic. There simply is no major penalty for not being innovative.

One caveat: Research and technological advance can be a barrier to entry. Thus, the monopolist may continuously seek technological advance to avoid falling prey to new rivals. In this case, technological advance is essential to maintaining monopoly. But it is potential competition—not the monopoly market structure—that drives this technological advance. By assumption, no such competition exists in the monopoly model; entry is completely blocked.

Assessment and Policy Options

Monopoly is of legitimate concern because the monopolist can charge higher-than-competitive prices that result in an underallocation of resources. Monopolists can stifle innovation, foster X-inefficiency, and engage in rent-seeking behaviour. Even when their costs are low because of economies of scale, monopolists are unlikely to charge a price that reflects those low costs. The cost savings may simply accrue to the monopoly as greater economic profit.

Fortunately, however, monopoly is not widespread in the Canadian economy. Barriers to entry are seldom completely successful. Although research and technological advance may strengthen the market position of a monopoly, technology may also undermine monopoly power. Over time, the creation of new technologies may work to destroy monopoly positions. For example, the development of courier delivery, fax machines, and email has eroded the monopoly power of Canada Post Corporation. Similarly, cable television monopolies are now challenged by satellite TV and by new technologies that permit the transmission of audio and video over the Internet.

Patents eventually expire—and even before they do, the development of new and distinct products can undermine existing patent advantages. New sources of monopolized resources can be found, and competition from foreign firms may emerge (see Global Perspective 10.1). Finally,

GLOBAL PERSPECTIVE

10.1

Competition from Foreign Multinational Corporations

Competition from foreign multinational corporations diminishes the market power of firms in Canada. Here are just a few of the hundreds of foreign multinational corporations that compete strongly with Canadian firms in certain Canadian markets.

Company (country)	Main products
Bayer (Germany)	chemicals
BP (United Kingdom)	gasoline
Michelin (France)	tires
NEC (Japan)	computers
Nestlé (Switzerland)	food products
Nokia (Finland)	wireless phones
Royal Dutch/Shell (Netherlands)	gasoline
Royal Philips (Netherlands)	electronics
Sony (Japan)	electronics
Toyota (Japan)	automobiles
Unilever (Netherlands)	food products

Source: Compiled from the Fortune 500 listing of the world's largest firms, www.fortune.com.

if a monopoly is sufficiently fearful of future competition from new products, it may keep its prices relatively low to discourage rivals from developing such products. If so, consumers may pay nearly competitive prices even though present competition is lacking.

So what should a government do about monopoly when it arises in the real world? The government needs to look carefully at monopoly on a case-by-case basis. Three general policy options are available:

1. If the monopoly is achieved and sustained through anticompetitive actions, creates substantial economic inefficiency, and appears to be long lasting, the government can file charges against the monopoly under Canada's anticombines laws. If found guilty of monopoly abuse, the firm can either be prohibited from engaging in certain business activities or be broken into two or more competing firms.

2. If the monopoly is a natural monopoly, it may be allowed to continue expanding. If no competition emerges from new products, the government may then decide to regulate its prices and operations.

3. If the monopoly appears to be unsustainable because of emerging new technology, society can simply choose to ignore it. In such cases, society simply lets the process of creative destruction (discussed in Chapter 9) do its work.

QUICK REVIEW

- The monopolist maximizes profit (or minimizes loss) at the output where MR = MC and charges the price that corresponds to that output on its demand curve.

- The monopolist has no supply curve, since any of several prices can be associated with a specific quantity of output supplied.

- Assuming identical costs, a monopolist will be less efficient than a perfectly competitive industry because it will fail to produce units of output for which marginal benefits exceed marginal costs.

- The inefficiencies of monopoly may be offset or lessened by economies of scale and, less likely, by technological progress, but may be intensified by the presence of X-inefficiency and rent-seeking expenditures.

connect
ORIGIN OF THE IDEA 10.3
Price Discrimination

price discrimination
Selling a product to different buyers at different prices when the price differences are not justified by differences in cost.

10.4 Price Discrimination

We have assumed in this chapter that the monopolist charges a single price to all buyers. But under certain conditions the monopolist can increase its profit by charging different prices to different buyers. In so doing, the monopolist is engaging in **price discrimination,** the practice of selling a product or service at more than one price when the price differences are not justified by cost differences. Price discrimination can take three forms:

- Charging each customer in a single market the maximum price she or he is willing to pay.

- Charging each customer one price for the first set of units purchased and a lower price for subsequent units purchased.

- Charging some customers one price and other customers another price.

Conditions

The opportunity to engage in price discrimination is not readily available to all sellers. Price discrimination is possible when the following conditions are met:

- *Monopoly Power* The seller must be a monopolist with some ability to control output and price.

- *Market Segregation* The seller must be able to segregate buyers into distinct classes, each of which has a different willingness or ability to pay for the product. This separation of buyers is usually based on different price elasticities of demand, as the examples that follow will make clear.

- *No Resale* The original purchaser cannot resell the product or service. If buyers in the low-price segment of the market could easily resell in the high-price segment, the monopolist's price-discrimination strategy would create competition in the high-price segment. This competition would reduce the price in the high-price segment and undermine the monopolist's price-discrimination policy. This suggests that service industries such as transportation or legal and medical services, where resale is impossible, are good candidates for price discrimination.

Examples of Price Discrimination

Price discrimination is widely practised in the Canadian economy. For example, we noted in Chapter 4's The Last Word that airlines, such as Air Canada, charge high fares to travelling executives, whose demand for travel is inelastic, and offer lower highly restricted, nonrefundable fares to attract vacationers and others whose demands are more elastic.

Movie theatres and golf courses vary their charges on the basis of time (higher rates in the evening and on weekends when demand is strong) and age (ability to pay). Railways vary the rate charged per tonne–kilometre of freight according to the market value of the product being shipped; the shipper of 10 tonnes of television sets or costume jewellery is charged more than the shipper of 10 tonnes of gravel or coal.

Issuing discount coupons redeemable at purchase is a form of price discrimination. It enables firms to give price discounts to their most price-sensitive customers who have elastic demand. Less price-sensitive consumers who have less elastic demand are not as likely to take the time to clip and redeem coupons. The firm thus makes a larger profit than if it had used a single-price, no-coupon strategy.

Price discrimination can often occur in international trade. A Russian aluminum producer, for example, might sell aluminum for less in Canada than in Russia. In Canada, this seller faces an elastic demand because several substitute suppliers are available. But in Russia, where the manufacturer dominates the market and trade barriers impede imports, consumers have fewer choices and thus demand is less elastic. (See the *Consider This* box for another example of price discrimination.)

CONSIDER THIS :: Price Discrimination at the Ballpark

A professional baseball team such as the Toronto Blue Jays earns substantial revenues through ticket sales. To maximize profit they offer significantly lower ticket prices for youths (whose demand is elastic) than for adults (whose demand is inelastic). This discount may be as much as 50 percent.

If this type of price discrimination increases revenue and profit, why don't teams also price discriminate at the concession stands? Why don't they offer half-price hot dogs, soft drinks, and peanuts to children?

The answer involves the three requirements for successful price discrimination. All three requirements are met for game tickets: (1) the team has monopoly power; (2) it can segregate ticket buyers by age group, each group having a different elasticity of demand; and (3) youths cannot resell their discounted tickets to adults.

It's a different situation at the concession stands. Specifically, the third condition is *not* met. If the team had dual prices, it could not prevent the exchange or "resale" of the concession goods from youths to adults. Many adults would send youths to buy food and soft drinks for them: "Here's some money, Billy. Go buy *six* hot dogs." In this case, price discrimination would reduce, not increase, team profit. Thus, youths and adults are charged the same high prices at the concession stands. (These prices are high relative to those for the same goods at the local convenience store because the stadium sellers have a captive audience and thus considerable monopoly power.)

FIGURE 10-8   Price Discrimination to Different Groups of Buyers

The price-discriminating monopolist represented here maximizes its total profit by dividing the market into two segments based on differences in elasticity of demand. It then produces and sells the MR = MC output in each market segment. (For visual clarity, average total cost (ATC) is assumed to be constant. Therefore MC equals ATC at all output levels.) Panel (a): The firm charges a higher price (here, P_b) to customers who have a less elastic demand curve and in panel (b) a lower price (here, P_s) to customers with a more elastic demand. The price discriminator's total profit is larger than it would be with no discrimination and therefore a single price.

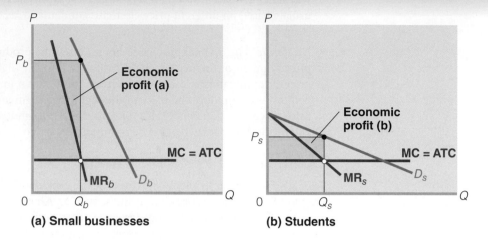

(a) Small businesses

(b) Students

Graphical Analysis

Figure 10-8 demonstrates graphically the most common form of price discrimination—charging different prices to different classes of buyers. The two side-to-side graphs are for a monopolist selling its product—say, software—in two segregated parts of the market. Figure 10-8a illustrates demand for software by small-business customers; Figure 10-8b illustrates demand for software by students. Student versions of the software are identical to the versions sold to businesses but are available (one per person) only to customers with a student ID. Presumably, students have lower ability to pay for the software and are charged a discounted price.

The demand curve D_b, in the graph to the left, indicates a relatively inelastic demand for the product on the part of business customers. The demand curve D_s, located in the right-hand graph, reflects the more elastic demand of students. The marginal revenue curves (MR$_b$ and MR$_s$) lie below their respective demand curves, reflecting the demand–marginal revenue relationship previously described.

For visual clarity we have assumed that average total cost (ATC) is constant. Therefore, marginal cost (MC) equals ATC at all quantities of output. These costs are the same for both versions of the software and therefore appear as the identical straight lines labelled "MC = ATC."

What price will the monopolist charge to each set of customers? Using the MR = MC rule for profit maximization, the firm will offer Q_b units of the software for sale to small businesses. It can sell that profit-maximizing output by charging price P_b. Again using the MR = MC rule, the monopolist will offer Q_s units of software to students. To sell those Q_s units, the firm will charge students the lower price P_s.

Firms engage in price discrimination because it enhances their profit. The numbers (not shown) behind the curves in Figure 10-8 would clearly reveal that the sum of the two profit rectangles shown in colour exceeds the single profit rectangle the firm would obtain from a single monopoly price. How do consumers fare? In this case, students clearly benefit by paying a lower price than they would if the firm charged a single monopoly price; in contrast, the price discrimination results in a higher price for business customers. Therefore, compared to the single-price situation, students buy more of the software and small businesses buy less.

Such price discrimination is widespread in the economy and is illegal only when it is part of a firm's strategy to lessen or eliminate competition. We will discuss illegal price discrimination in Chapter 11 where we discuss anticombines policy.

connect
WORKED PROBLEM 10.2
Price Discrimination

10.5 Regulated Monopoly

THE ROLE OF
GOVERNMENTS

Natural monopolies traditionally have been subject to *rate regulation* (price regulation), although the recent trend has been to deregulate those parts of the industries where competition seems possible. For example, long-distance phone service, natural gas distribution, wireless communication, cable television, and long-distance electricity transmission have been, to one degree or another, deregulated over the past several decades. And regulators in some provinces are beginning to allow new entrants to compete with local telephone and electricity providers. Nevertheless, provincial and local regulatory commissions still regulate the prices that most local natural gas distributors, regional telephone companies, and local electricity suppliers can charge. These locally regulated monopolies are commonly called "public utilities."

Let's consider the regulation of a local natural monopoly. Our example will be a single firm that is the only seller of natural gas in the town of Springfield. Figure 10-9 shows the demand and long-run cost curves facing our firm. Because of extensive economies of scale, the demand curve cuts the natural monopolist's long-run average-total-cost curve at a point where that curve is still falling. It would be inefficient to have several firms in this industry because each firm's lowest average total cost would be substantially higher than that of a single firm. So, efficient, lowest-cost production requires a single seller.

We know by application of the MR = MC rule that Q_m and P_m are the profit-maximizing output and price that an unregulated monopolist would choose. Because price exceeds average total cost at output Q_m, the monopolist enjoys a substantial economic profit. Furthermore, price exceeds marginal cost, indicating an underallocation of resources to this product or service. Can government regulation bring about better results from society's point of view?

Socially Optimal Price: P = MC

One sensible goal for regulators would be to get the monopoly to produce the allocatively efficient output level. For our monopolist in Figure 10-9, this is output level Q_r, determined by where the demand curve D intersects the MC curve. Q_r is the allocatively efficient output level because for each unit of output up to Q_r, the demand curve lies above the MC curve, indicating that for all of these units marginal benefits exceed marginal costs.

But how can the regulatory commission actually motivate the monopoly to produce this output level? The trick is to set the regulated price P_r at a level such that the monopoly will be led by its profit-maximizing rule to voluntarily produce the allocatively efficiently level of output. To see

FIGURE 10-9   Regulated Monopoly

The socially optimal price P_r, found where D and MC intersect, will result in an efficient allocation of resources but may entail losses to the monopoly. The fair-return price P_f will allow the monopolist to break even but will not fully correct the underallocation of resources.

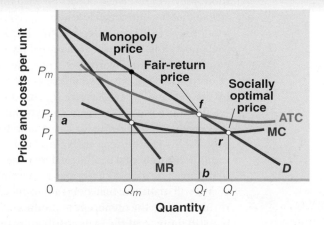

how this works, note that because the monopoly will receive the regulated price P_r for all units that it sells, P_r becomes the monopoly's marginal revenue per unit. Thus, the monopoly's MR curve becomes the horizontal white line moving to the right from price P_r on the vertical axis.

The monopoly will at this point follow its usual rule for maximizing profits or minimizing losses: it will produce where marginal revenue equals marginal cost. As a result, the monopoly will produce where the horizontal white MR ($= P_r$) line intersects the MC curve at point r. That is, the monopoly will end up producing the socially optimal output Q_r not because it is socially minded but because Q_r happens to be the output that either maximizes profits or minimizes losses when the firm is forced by the regulators to sell all units at the regulated price P_r.

The regulated price P_r that achieves allocative efficiency is called the **socially optimal price.** Because it is determined by where the MC curve intersects the demand curve, this type of regulation is often summarized by the equation $P = MC$.

socially optimal price
The price of a product that results in the most efficient allocation of an economy's resources.

Fair-Return Price: $P =$ ATC

The socially optimal price suffers from a potentially fatal problem. P_r may be so low that average total costs are not covered, as is the case in Figure 10-9. In such situations, forcing the socially optimal price on the regulated monopoly would result in short-run losses and long-run exit. In our example, Springfield would be left without a gas company and its citizens without gas.

What can be done to rectify this problem? One option is to provide a public subsidy to cover the loss that the socially optimal price would entail. Another possibility is to condone price discrimination, allow the monopoly to charge some customers prices above P_r, and hope that the additional revenue that the monopoly gains from price discrimination will be enough to permit it to break even.

In practice, regulatory commissions in Canada have often pursued a third option that abandons the goal of producing every unit for which marginal benefits exceed marginal costs but which guarantees that regulated monopolies will be able to break even and continue in operation. Under this third option, regulators set a regulated price that is high enough for monopolists to break even and continue in operation. This price has come to be referred to as a **fair-return price** because the regulatory agencies must permit regulated utility owners to enjoy a "fair return" on their investments.

fair-return price
The price of a product that enables its producer to obtain a normal profit and that is equal to the average cost of producing it.

In practice, a fair return is equal to a normal profit. That is, a fair return is an accounting profit equal in size to what the owners of the monopoly would on average receive if they entered another type of business.

The regulator determines the fair-return price P_f by where the average total cost curve intersects the demand curve at point f. As we will explain, setting the regulated price at this level will cause the monopoly to produce Q_f units while guaranteeing that it will break even and not wish to exit the industry. To see why the monopoly will voluntarily produce Q_f units, note that because the monopoly will receive P_f dollars for each unit it sells, its marginal revenue per unit becomes P_f dollars so that the horizontal line moving rightward from P_f on the vertical axis becomes the regulated monopoly's MR curve. Because this horizontal MR curve is always higher than the monopoly's MC curve, it is obvious that marginal revenues will exceed marginal costs for every possible level of output shown in Figure 10-9. Thus, the monopoly should be willing to supply whatever quantity of output is demanded by consumers at the regulated price P_f. That quantity is of course given by the demand curve. At price P_f, consumers will demand exactly Q_f units. Thus, by setting the regulated price at P_f, the regulator gets the monopoly to voluntarily supply exactly Q_f units.

Even better, the regulator also guarantees that the monopoly firm will earn exactly a normal profit. This can be seen in Figure 10-9 by noting that the rectangle $0afb$ is equal to both the monopoly's total cost and its total revenue. Its economic profit is therefore equal to zero, implying that it must be earning a normal accounting profit for its owners.

We will make one final point about allocative efficiency. By choosing the fair return price P_f, the regulator leads the monopoly to produce Q_f units. This is less than the socially optimal quantity Q_r, but still more than the Q_m units that the monopolist would produce if left unregulated. So while fair-return pricing does not lead to full allocative efficiency, it is still an improvement on what the monopoly would do if left to its own devices.

Dilemma of Regulation

Comparing results of the socially optimal price ($P = \text{MC}$) and the fair-return price ($P = \text{ATC}$) suggests a policy dilemma, sometimes termed the *dilemma of regulation*. When its price is set to achieve the most efficient allocation of resources ($P = \text{MC}$), the regulated monopoly is likely to suffer losses. Survival of the firm would depend on permanent public subsidies from tax revenues. Conversely, although a fair-return price ($P = \text{ATC}$) allows the monopolist to cover costs, it only partially resolves the underallocation of resources that the unregulated monopoly price would foster. Despite this dilemma, regulation can improve on the results of monopoly from the social point of view. Price regulation (even at the fair-return price) can simultaneously reduce price, increase output, and reduce the economic profits of monopolies.

That being said, we need to provide an important caution: "Fair-price" regulation of monopoly looks rather simple in theory but is amazingly complex in practice. In the actual economy, rate regulation is accompanied by large, expensive rate-setting bureaucracies and maze-like sets of procedures. Also, rate decisions require extensive public input via letters and thorough public hearings. Rate decisions are subject to lengthy legal challenges. Further, because regulatory commissions must set prices sufficiently above costs to create fair returns, regulated monopolists have little incentive to minimize average total costs. When these costs creep up, the regulatory commissions must set higher prices.

Regulated firms therefore are noted for higher-than-competitive wages, more managers and staff than necessary, nicer-than-typical office buildings, and other forms of X-inefficiency. These inefficiencies help explain the trend of federal, provincial, and municipal governments to abandon price regulation where the possibility of competition looks promising.

10.6   Monopoly and Deadweight Loss

In Section 10-3 we briefly restated the efficiency of monopoly using consumer surplus and producer surplus. In Figure 10-10 we have once again put a perfectly competitive industry alongside a monopoly to compare them. We have indicated the extent of consumer and producer surplus in each of the market structures. You will recall from Chapter 8 that in a perfectly competitive market structure, equilibrium price P_c (= MC = minimum ATC) will create the maximum amount of consumer surplus and producer surplus, as indicated in Figure 10-10a. We also noted that in perfect competition marginal benefit equals marginal cost (MB = MC) at the equilibrium price and quantity, ensuring allocative efficiency.

In a monopoly, represented in Figure 10-10b, the output is lower than in a perfect competitive market structure, and the profit-maximizing price P_m is above P_c, so consumers pay a price above the firm's (and the industry's) MC. At the lower output Q_m, the sum of consumer surplus and producer surplus has been reduced, compared to the perfect-competition scenario. The net loss of consumer surplus and producer surplus is referred to as **deadweight loss** of monopoly, and is indicated by the area covered by triangles B and C. At output Q_m, marginal benefit is greater than marginal cost (MB > MC), indicating that the monopolist is not producing as much output as consumers would like. Thus, allocative efficiency is not achieved.

Figure 10-10b shows that there has been a redistribution of resources from the consumer to the monopolist. The higher price results in a gain for the monopolist, represented by the grey area A. Consumers lose the consumer surplus represented by areas A and B, while the monopolist loses the producer surplus represented by area C, but gains area A. The monopolist will enjoy a net gain if its gain (area A) is larger than its loss of producer surplus (area C). The monopolist's gain is the difference between the monopoly price (P_m) and the equilibrium price in perfect competition (P_c) multiplied by the quantity sold (Q_m).

deadweight loss
The loss of consumer surplus and producer surplus when output is either above or below its efficient level.

FIGURE 10-10   Monopoly and Deadweight Loss

Panel (a): In perfect competition the long-run equilibrium price (P_c) and quantity (Q_c) maximize the sum of consumer surplus and producer surplus. Panel (b): A monopolist restricts output to Q_m and increases price to P_m. Although the monopolist gains, a deadweight loss is created as a result of the lower consumer surplus brought about by the fall in output and rise in price.

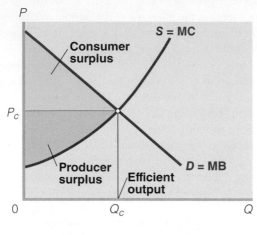

(a) Perfectly competitive industry

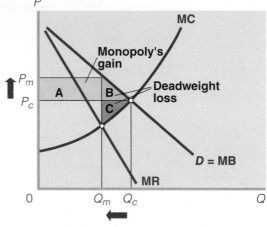

(b) Monopoly

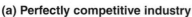

QUICK REVIEW

• Price discrimination occurs when a firm sells a product at different prices that are not based on cost differences.

• The conditions necessary for price discrimination are (1) monopoly power, (2) the ability to segregate buyers based on demand elasticities, and (3) the inability of buyers to resell the product.

• Compared with single pricing by a monopolist, perfect price discrimination results in greater profit and greater output. Many consumers pay higher prices, but other buyers pay prices below the single price.

• Monopoly price can be reduced and output increased through government regulation.

• The socially optimal price (P = MC) achieves allocative efficiency but may result in losses; the fair-return price (P = ATC) yields a normal profit but falls short of allocative efficiency.

• The inefficiency brought about by monopoly is referred to as deadweight loss.

The LAST WORD   De Beers Diamonds: Are Monopolies Forever?

De Beers was one of the world's strongest and most enduring monopolies. But in mid-2000 it announced that it could no longer control the supply of diamonds and thus would abandon its 66-year policy of monopolizing the diamond trade.

De Beers, a Swiss-based cartel controlled by a South African corporation, produces about 45 percent of the world's rough-cut diamonds and purchases for resale a sizable number of the rough-cut diamonds produced by other mines worldwide. As a result, De Beers markets 55 percent of the world's diamonds to a select group of diamond cutters and dealers—but that percentage has declined from 80 percent in the mid-1980s and continues to shrink. Therein lies De Beers' problem.

Classic Monopoly Behaviour De Beers' past monopoly behaviour is a classic example of the unregulated monopoly model illustrated in Figure 10-4. No matter how many diamonds it mined or purchased, De Beers sold only that quantity of diamonds that would yield an appropriate (monopoly) price. That price was well above production costs, and De Beers and its partners earned monopoly profits.

When demand fell, De Beers reduced its sales to maintain price. The excess of production over sales was then reflected in growing diamond stockpiles held by De Beers. It also attempted to bolster demand through advertising ("Diamonds are forever"). When demand was strong, it increased sales by reducing its diamond inventories.

De Beers used several methods to control the production of many mines it did not own. First, it convinced a number of independent producers that *single-channel* or monopoly marketing through De Beers would maximize their profits. Second, mines that circumvented De Beers often found their market suddenly flooded with similar diamonds from De Beers' vast stockpiles. The resulting price

decline and loss of profit often would encourage the "rogue" mine into the De Beers fold. Finally, De Beers simply purchased and stockpiled diamonds produced by independent mines so their added supplies would not undercut the market.

The End of an Era? Several factors have come together to unravel the De Beers monopoly. New diamond discoveries resulted in a growing leakage of diamonds into world markets outside De Beers' control. For example, significant prospecting and trading in Angola occurred. Recent Canadian diamond discoveries in the Northwest Territories pose another threat. Although De Beers is a participant in Canada, a large uncontrolled supply of diamonds is expected to emerge. Another challenge has been technological improvements that now allow chemical firms to manufacture flawless artificial diamonds. To prevent consumers from switching to synthetic

diamonds, De Beers had to launch a costly campaign to promote "mined diamonds" over synthetics.

If that were not enough, Australian diamond producer Argyle opted to withdraw from the De Beers monopoly. Its annual production of mostly low-grade industrial diamonds accounts for about 6 percent of the global $8 billion diamond market. The international media has begun to focus heavily on the role that diamonds play in financing the bloody civil wars in Africa. Fearing a consumer boycott of diamonds, De Beers has pledged not to buy these conflict diamonds or do business with any firm that does. These diamonds, however, continue to find their way into the marketplace, eluding De Beers' control.

In mid-2000 De Beers abandoned its attempt to control the supply of diamonds. It announced that it planned to transform itself from a diamond cartel to a modern firm selling premium diamonds and other luxury goods under the De Beers label. It therefore would gradually reduce its $4 billion stockpile of diamonds and turn its efforts to increasing the overall demand for diamonds through advertising. De Beers proclaimed that it was changing its strategy to being "the diamond supplier of choice."

Diamonds may be forever, but not necessarily so for the De Beers monopoly. Nevertheless, with high market share and ability to control its own production levels, De Beers will continue to wield considerable influence over the price of rough-cut diamonds.

Question

How was De Beers able to control the world price of diamonds even though it produced only 45 percent of the diamonds? What factors ended its monopoly? What is De Beers' new strategy for earning economic profit, rather than just normal profit?

:: CHAPTER SUMMARY

10.1 :: CHARACTERISTICS OF MONOPOLY

- A monopolist is the sole producer of a commodity for which there are no close substitutes.

- The existence of monopoly and other imperfectly competitive market structures is explained by barriers to entry, in the form of (a) economies of scale, (b) patents and licences, (c) ownership or control of essential factors of production, and (d) pricing and other strategic behaviour.

- The monopolist's market situation differs from that of a competitive firm in that the monopolist's demand curve is downsloping, causing the marginal-revenue curve to lie below the demand curve. Like the competitive seller, the monopolist will maximize profit by equating marginal revenue and marginal cost. Barriers to entry may permit a monopolist to acquire economic profit even in the long run. However, (a) the monopolist does not charge the highest price it can get; (b) the price that yields maximum total profit to the monopolist rarely coincides with the price that yields maximum unit profit; (c) high costs and a weak demand may prevent the monopolist from realizing any profit at all; and (d) the monopolist avoids the inelastic region of its demand curve.

10.2 :: OUTPUT AND PRICE DETERMINATION

- With the same costs, the monopolist will find it profitable to restrict output and charge a higher price than would sellers in a purely competitive industry. This restriction of output causes resources to be misallocated, as is shown by the fact that price exceeds marginal cost in monopolized markets.

10.3 :: ECONOMIC EFFECTS OF MONOPOLY

- Monopoly transfers income from consumers to monopolists because a monopolist can charge a higher price than would a perfectly competitive firm with the same costs. So monopolists in effect levy a "private tax" on consumers,

and if demand is strong enough, obtain substantial economic profits.

- The costs monopolists and competitive producers face may not be the same. On the one hand, economies of scale may make lower unit costs available to monopolists but not to competitors, and monopoly may be more likely than perfect competition to reduce costs via technological advance because of the monopolist's ability to realize economic profit, which can be used to finance research. On the other hand, X-inefficiency is more common among monopolists than among competitive firms. Also, monopolists may make costly expenditures to maintain monopoly privileges that are conferred by government. Finally, the blocked entry of rival firms weakens the monopolist's incentive to be technologically progressive.

10.4 :: PRICE DISCRIMINATION

- A monopolist can increase its profit by practising price discrimination, provided (a) it can segregate buyers on the basis of elasticities of demand, and (b) its product or service cannot be readily transferred between the segregated markets.

10.5 :: REGULATED MONOPOLY

- Price regulation can be invoked to wholly or partially eliminate the tendency of monopolists to underallocate resources and to earn economic profits. The socially optimal price is determined where the demand and marginal-cost curves intersect; the fair-return price is determined where the demand and average-total-cost curves intersect.

10.6 :: MONOPOLY AND DEADWEIGHT LOSS

- The inefficiency of monopoly can be measured using the concepts of consumer surplus and producer surplus. The efficiency loss associated with monopoly is called deadweight loss.

:: TERMS AND CONCEPTS

:: QUESTIONS

1. "No firm is completely sheltered from rivals; all firms compete for consumer dollars. If that is so, then monopoly does not exist." Do you agree? Explain. How might you use Chapter 4's concept of cross elasticity of demand to judge whether monopoly exists?   [LO10.1]

2. Discuss the major barriers to entry into an industry. Explain how each barrier can foster either monopoly or oligopoly. Which barriers, if any, do you believe give rise to monopoly that is socially justifiable?   [LO10.1]

3. How does the demand curve faced by a monopolistic seller differ from that confronting a perfectly competitive firm? Why does it differ? Of what significance is the difference? Why is the monopolist's demand curve not perfectly inelastic?   [LO10.1]

4. Use the demand schedule that follows to calculate total revenue and marginal revenue at each quantity. Plot the demand, total-revenue, and marginal-revenue curves, and explain the relationships among them. Explain why the marginal revenue of the fourth unit of output is $3.50, even though its price is $5.00. Use Chapter 4's total-revenue test for price elasticity to designate the elastic and inelastic segments of your graphed demand curve. What generalization can you make about the relationship between marginal revenue and elasticity of demand? Suppose the marginal cost of successive units of output were zero. What output would the profit-seeking firm produce? Finally, use your analysis to explain why a monopolist would never produce in the inelastic region of demand.   [LO10.2]

Price (P)	Quantity demanded (Q)	Price (P)	Quantity demanded (Q)
$7.00	0	$4.50	5
6.50	1	4.00	6
6.00	2	3.50	7
5.50	3	3.00	8
5.00	4	2.50	9

5. Assume that a monopolist and a perfectly competitive firm have the same unit costs. Contrast the two with respect to (a) price, (b) output, (c) profits, (d) allocation of resources, and (e) impact on income transfers. Since both monopolists and competitive firms follow the MC = MR rule in maximizing profits, how do you account for the different results? Why might the costs of a perfectly competitive firm and a monopolist be different? What are the implications of such a cost difference?   [LO10.3]

6. Explain and critically evaluate the following statements: [LO10.3]

   a. Because they can control product price, monopolists are always assured of profitable production by simply charging the highest price consumers will pay.

   b. The monopolist seeks the output that will yield the greatest per-unit profit.

   c. An excess of price over marginal cost is the market's way of signalling the need for more production of a good.

   d. The more profitable a firm, the greater its monopoly power.

   e. The monopolist has a pricing policy; the competitive producer does not.

   f. With respect to resource allocation, the interests of the seller and of society coincide in a perfectly competitive market but conflict in a monopolized market.

7. Assume a monopolistic publisher has agreed to pay an author 10 percent of the total revenue from the sales of a text. Will the author and the publisher want to charge the same price for the text? Explain.   [LO10.3]

8. U.S. pharmaceutical companies charge different prices for prescription drugs to buyers in different nations, including Canada, depending on elasticity of demand and government-imposed price ceilings. Explain why these companies, for profit reasons, oppose laws allowing the re-importation of drugs to the United States.   [LO10.4]

9. Explain in words and graphically how price (rate) regulation may improve the performance of monopolies. In your answer distinguish between (a) socially optimal (marginal-cost) pricing and (b) fair-return (average-total-cost) pricing. What is the "dilemma of regulation"?   [LO10.5]

10. It has been proposed that natural monopolists should be allowed to determine their profit-maximizing outputs and prices and then government should tax their profits away and distribute them to consumers in proportion to their purchases from the monopoly. Is this proposal as socially desirable as requiring monopolists to equate price with marginal cost or average total cost?   [LO10.3]

:: PROBLEMS

1. Suppose a monopolist is faced with the demand schedule shown below and the same cost data as the competitive producer discussed in Problem 4 at the end of Chapter 8. Calculate the missing total-revenue and marginal-revenue amounts, and determine the profit-maximizing price and profit-maximizing output for this monopolist. What is the monopolist's profit? Verify your answer graphically and by comparing total revenue and total cost. [**LO10.2**]

Price	Quantity demanded	Total revenue	Marginal revenue
$115	0	$_____	
			$_____
100	1	_____	
83	2	_____	_____
71	3	_____	_____
63	4	_____	_____
55	5	_____	_____
48	6	_____	_____
42	7	_____	_____
37	8	_____	_____
33	9	_____	_____
29	10	_____	_____

2. Suppose that a price-discriminating monopolist has segregated its market into two groups of buyers. The first group is described by the demand and revenue data that you developed for Problem 1. The demand and revenue data for the second group of buyers is shown in the accompanying table. Assume that MC is $13 in both markets and MC = ATC at all output levels. What price will the firm charge in each market? Based solely on these two prices, which market has the higher price elasticity of demand? What will be this monopolist's total economic profit? [**LO10.4**]

Price	Quantity demanded	Total revenue	Marginal revenue
$71	0	$ 0	
			$63
63	1	63	
			47
55	2	110	
			34
48	3	144	
			24
42	4	168	
			17
37	5	185	
			13
33	6	198	
			5
29	7	203	

3. Assume that the most efficient production technology available for making vitamin pills has the cost structure given in the following table. Note that output is measured as the number of bottles of vitamins produced per day and that costs included a normal profit. [**LO10.4**]

Output	TC	MC
25,000	$100,000	$0.50
50,000	150,000	1.00
75,000	187,500	2.50
100,000	275,500	3.00

a. What is ATC per unit for each level of output listed in the table?

b. Is this a decreasing-cost industry? (Answer yes or no.)

c. Suppose that the market price for a bottle of vitamins is $1.33 and that at that price the total market quantity demanded is 75,000,000 bottles. How many firms will there be in this industry?

d. Suppose that, instead, the market quantity demanded at a price of $1.33 is only 75,000 bottles. How many firms do you expect there to be in this industry?

e. Review your answers to parts (b), (c), and (d). Does the level of demand determine this industry's market structure?

4. A new production technology for making vitamins is invented by a university professor who decides not to patent it. Thus, it is available for anybody to copy and put into use. The TC per bottle for production up to 100,000 bottles per day is given in the following table. [**LO10.4**]

Output	TC
25,000	$50,000
50,000	70,000
75,000	75,000
100,000	80,000

a. What is ATC for each level of output listed in the table?

b. Suppose that for each 25,000 bottle per day increase in production above 100,000 bottles per day, TC increases by $5000 (so that, for instance, 125,000 bottles per day would generate total costs of $85,000 and 150,000 bottles per day would generate total costs of $90,000). Is this a decreasing-cost industry?

c. Suppose that the price of a bottle of vitamins is $1.33 and at that price the total quantity demanded by consumers is 75,000,000 bottles. How many firms will there be in this industry?

d. Suppose that, instead, the market quantity demanded at a price of $1.33 is only 75,000. How many firms do you expect there to be in this industry?

e. Review your answers to parts (b), (c), and (d). Does the level of demand determine this industry's market structure?

f. Compare your answer to part (d) of this question with your answer to part (d) of Problem 3. Do both production technologies show constant returns to scale?

5. Suppose you have been tasked with regulating a single monopoly firm that sells 50-kilogram bags of concrete. The firm has fixed costs of $10 million per year and a variable cost of $1 per bag no matter how many bags are produced. [LO10.5]

a. If this firm kept on increasing its output level, would ATC per bag ever increase? Is this a decreasing-cost industry?

b. If you wished to regulate this monopoly by charging the socially optimal price, what price would you charge? At that price, what would be the size of the firm's profit or loss? Would the firm want to exit the industry?

c. You find out that if you set the price at $2 per bag, consumers will demand 10 million bags. How big will the firm's profit or loss be at that price?

d. If consumers instead demanded 20 million bags at a price of $2 per bag, how big would the firm's profit or loss be?

e. Suppose that demand is perfectly inelastic at 20 million bags, so that consumers demand 20 million bags no matter what the price is. What price should you charge if you want the firm to earn only fair rate of return? Assume as always that TC includes a normal profit.

Mc Graw Hill connect™ Practice and Learn Online with Connect

Connect allows you to practice important concepts at your own pace and on your own schedule, with 24/7 online access to an eBook, algorithmic questions and problems from the textbook, video and logic cases, graphing tutorials, flashcards, Internet exercises, key graphs, and more.

CHAPTER 11

Monopolistic Competition and Oligopoly

AFTER READING THIS CHAPTER, YOU SHOULD BE ABLE TO:

11.1 List the characteristics of monopolistic competition.

11.2 Explain the importance of price and output in monopolistic competition.

11.3 Describe the characteristics of oligopoly.

11.4 Discuss how game theory relates to oligopoly.

11.5 Compare the incentives and obstacles to collusion among oligopolists.

11.6 Contrast the potential positive and potential negative effects of advertising.

A11.1 (Appendix) Utilize additional game theory terminology and applications.

In Canada, most industries have a market structure that falls somewhere between the two poles of perfect competition and monopoly. To begin with, most real-world industries have fewer than the large number of producers required for perfect competition, but more than the single producer that defines monopoly. In addition, most firms in most industries have distinguishable rather than standardized products, as well as some discretion over the prices they charge. As a result, competition often occurs on the basis of price, quality, location, service, and advertising. Finally, entry to most real-world industries ranges from easy to very difficult but rarely is completely blocked.

This chapter examines two models that more closely approximate these widespread industry market structures. You will discover that *monopolistic competition* mixes a small amount of monopoly power with a large amount of competition. *Oligopoly,* in contrast, blends a large amount of monopoly power with both considerable rivalry among existing firms and the threat of increased future competition due to foreign firms and new technologies. (You should quickly review Table 8-1 at this point.)

11.1 Characteristics of Monopolistic Competition

Let's begin by examining **monopolistic competition,** which is characterized by (1) a relatively large number of sellers, (2) differentiated products (often promoted by heavy advertising), and (3) easy entry to, and exit from, the industry. The first and

monopolistic competition
A market structure in which a relatively large number of sellers produce differentiated products.

connect
ORIGIN OF THE IDEA 11.1
Monopolistic Competition

third characteristics provide the "competitive" aspect of monopolistic competition; the second characteristic provides the "monopolistic" aspect. In general, however, monopolistically competitive industries are more competitive than they are monopolistic.

Relatively Large Number of Sellers

Monopolistic competition is characterized by a fairly large number of firms—say, 25, 35, 60, or 70—not by the hundreds or thousands of firms in perfect competition. Consequently, monopolistic competition involves:

- *Small Market Shares* Each firm has a comparatively small percentage of the total market and consequently has limited control over market price.

- *No Collusion* The presence of a relatively large number of firms makes collusion by a group of firms to restrict output and set prices unlikely.

- *Independent Action* With many firms in an industry, there is little interdependence among them; each firm can determine its own pricing policy without considering the possible reactions of rival firms. A single firm may realize a modest increase in sales by cutting its price, but the effect of that action on competitors' sales will be nearly imperceptible and will probably not trigger a response.

Differentiated Products

In contrast to perfect competition, in which there is a standardized product, monopolistic competition is distinguished by **product differentiation**. Firms in monopolistic competition turn out variations of a particular product. They produce products with slightly different physical characteristics, offer varying degrees of customer service, provide varying amounts of location convenience, or proclaim special qualities, real or imagined, for their products.

Let's examine these aspects of product differentiation in more detail.

product differentiation
A strategy in which one firm's product is distinguished from competing products by means of its design, related services, quality, location, or other attribute (except price).

PRODUCT ATTRIBUTES

Product differentiation may take the form of physical or qualitative differences in the products themselves. Real differences in functional features, materials, design, and quality of work are vital aspects of product differentiation. Personal computers, for example, differ in terms of storage capacity, speed, graphic displays, and included software. There are dozens of competing principles of economics textbooks that differ in content, organization, presentation and readability, pedagogical aids, and graphics and design. Most cities have a variety of retail stores selling men's and women's clothing that differ greatly in styling, materials, and quality of work.

SERVICE

Service and the conditions surrounding the sale of a product are also forms of product differentiation. One grocery store may stress the helpfulness of its clerks who bag your groceries and carry them to your car. A warehouse supermarket may leave bagging and carrying to its customers but feature lower prices. Customers may prefer one-day over three-day dry cleaning of equal quality. The prestige appeal of a store, the courteousness and helpfulness of clerks, the firm's reputation for servicing or exchanging its products, and the credit it makes available are all service aspects of product differentiation.

LOCATION

Products may also be differentiated through the location and accessibility of the stores that sell them. Small convenience stores manage to compete with large supermarkets, even though these minimarts have a more limited range of products and charge higher prices. They compete mainly on the basis of location—being close to customers and situated on busy streets. A motel's proximity

Product differentiation may also be created through the use of brand names and trademarks, packaging, and celebrity connections.

to a main highway gives it a locational advantage that may allow it to charge a higher room rate than nearby motels in less convenient locations.

BRAND NAMES AND PACKAGING

Product differentiation may also be created through the use of brand names and trademarks, packaging, and celebrity connections. Most non-steroidal anti-inflammatory drug tablets are very much alike, but many headache sufferers believe that one brand—for example, Advil, Tylenol, or Bayer's Aspirin—is superior and worth a higher price than a generic substitute. A celebrity's name associated with watches, perfume, or athletic shoes may enhance the appeal of those products for some buyers. Many customers prefer one style of ballpoint pen to another. Packaging that touts "natural spring" bottled water may attract additional customers.

SOME CONTROL OVER PRICE

Despite the relatively large number of firms, monopolistic competitors do have some control over their product prices because of product differentiation. If consumers prefer the products of specific sellers, then within limits they will pay more to satisfy their preferences. But the control a firm in monopolistic competition has over price is quite limited, since there are numerous potential substitutes for its product.

Easy Entry and Exit

Entry into industries characterized by a monopolistic competition market structure is relatively easy compared to oligopoly or monopoly. Because firms are typically small, both absolutely and relatively, economies of scale are few and capital requirements are low. However, compared with perfect competition, financial barriers may result from the need to develop and advertise a different product from one's rivals. Some firms may have trade secrets relating to their products or hold trademarks on their brand names, making it difficult and costly for other firms to imitate them.

Exit from industries in monopolistic competition is easier still. Nothing prevents an unprofitable firm from holding a going-out-of-business sale and shutting down.

Advertising

The expense and effort involved in product differentiation would be wasted if consumers were not made aware of product differences. Thus, firms in monopolistic competition advertise their products, often heavily. The goal of product differentiation and advertising—so-called **nonprice competition**—is to make price less of a factor in consumer purchases and make product differences a greater factor. If successful, the firm's demand curve will shift to the right and will become less elastic.

nonprice competition
A selling strategy in which one firm tries to distinguish its product or service from all competing ones based on attributes other than price.

Monopolistically Competitive Industries

Figure 11-1 lists several manufacturing industries that approximate monopolistic competition. Economists measure the degree of industry concentration—the extent to which the largest firms account for the bulk of the industry's output—to identify monopolistic competitive (versus oligopolistic) industries. Two such measures are the four-firm concentration ratio and the Herfindahl index.

A **four-firm concentration ratio,** expressed as a percentage, is the ratio of the output (sales) of the four largest firms in an industry relative to total industry sales.

four-firm concentration ratio
The percentage of total industry sales accounted for by the top four firms in the industry.

$$\text{Four-firm concentration ratio} = \frac{\text{Output of four largest firms}}{\text{Total output in the industry}}$$

Four-firm concentration ratios are very low in perfectly competitive industries in which there are hundreds or even thousands of firms each with a tiny market share. In contrast, four-firm

FIGURE 11-1

Percentage of Output Produced by the Four Largest Firms in Selected Low-Concentration Sectors*

Several Canadian manufacturing industries approximate monopolistic competition, with a relatively large number of sellers producing differentiated products. There is easy entry into the industry and firms often differentiate their products through advertising.

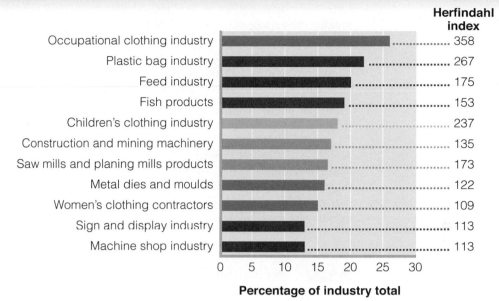

	Herfindahl index
Occupational clothing industry	358
Plastic bag industry	267
Feed industry	175
Fish products	153
Children's clothing industry	237
Construction and mining machinery	135
Saw mills and planing mills products	173
Metal dies and moulds	122
Women's clothing contractors	109
Sign and display industry	113
Machine shop industry	113

Percentage of industry total

Source: Statistics Canada, *Industrial Organization and Concentration in Manufacturing, Mining and Logging Industries,* Catalogue No. 31C0024
*As measured by dollar value of shipments.

ratios are high in oligopoly and monopoly. Industries in which the largest four firms account for 40 percent or more of the market are generally considered to be oligopolies. If the largest four firms account for less than 40 percent, they are likely to be monopolistically competitive. Observe that the concentration ratios in Figure 11-1 range from 13 percent to 27 percent.

Published **concentration ratios** such as those in Figure 11-1 are helpful in categorizing industries, but must be used cautiously because the market shares (percentage of total sales) are national in scope. Some markets with low national concentration ratios are highly localized. For example, the four-firm concentration ratio for ready-mix concrete (not shown) is usually low, suggesting a monopolistically competitive industry. But the sheer bulk of ready-mix concrete and the fact that it sets up as it dries limits the relevant market to a specific town, city, or metropolitan area. In most of these local markets only a few firms compete, not the numerous firms needed for monopolistic competition.

Figure 11-1 lists a second measure of concentration: the **Herfindahl index**. This index is the sum of the squared percentage market shares of all firms in the industry. In equation form:

$$\text{Herfindahl index} = (\%S_1)^2 + (\%S_2)^2 + (\%S_3)^2 + \cdots + (\%S_n)^2$$

where $\%S_1$ is the percentage market share of firm 1, $\%S_2$ is the percentage market share of firm 2, and so on for each firm in the industry. By squaring the percentage market shares of all firms in the industry, the Herfindahl index purposely gives much greater weight to larger, and thus more powerful, firms than to smaller ones. For a perfectly competitive industry, the index would approach zero, since each firm's market share—$\%S$ in the equation—is extremely small. In the case of a single-firm industry, the index would be at its maximum of 10,000 ($= 100^2$), indicating an industry with complete monopoly power.

We will discover later in this chapter that the Herfindahl index is important for assessing oligopolistic industries. But for now, the relevant generalization is that the lower the Herfindahl index, the greater the likelihood an industry is monopolistically competitive rather than oligopolistic. Note that in Figure 11-1 the Herfindahl index values (computed for the top four firms, not

concentration ratio
The percentage of the total sales of an industry produced and sold by an industry's largest firms.

Herfindahl index
The sum of the squared percentage market shares of all firms in the industry.

all the industry firms) are decidedly closer to the bottom limit of the Herfindahl index—0—than to its top limit—10,000.

The numbers in Figure 11-1 are for manufacturing industries. In Canada the least concentrated are machine shops, with a Herfindahl index of only 113. The shops serve manufacturers by making the various parts required for machines—for example, dies, which are then used to stamp metal and plastic forms that are in turn used in a myriad of end products. Many machine shops provide custom service. Windsor, Ontario, where there are major automotive plants, boasts some 60 machine shops. Vancouver has over 100 machine shops, while Halifax has only about 30. In addition, many retail establishments in metropolitan areas fall into the category of monopolistic competition, including grocery stores, gas stations, hair salons, dry cleaners, clothing stores, and restaurants. For example, Canada has some 80,800 commercial food services units. Of this total, about 36,400 are full-service restaurants, and 32,000 are limited-service restaurants. Of the remainder, about 6500 are contract and social caterers, and 6100 are drinking places. While chain restaurants, such as McDonald's, make up 36 percent of Canada's restaurants, the remaining 64 percent are independent brands, meaning small restaurants that serve a local population. Also, many providers of professional services such as legal assistance, real estate sales, and basic bookkeeping are monopolistic competitors.

11.2 Price and Output in Monopolistic Competition ::

How does a firm in monopolistic competition decide on its price and output? To explain, we initially assume that each firm in the industry is producing a specific differentiated product and engaging in a particular amount of advertising. Later we'll see how changes in the product and in the amount of advertising modify our conclusions.

The Firm's Demand Curve

Our explanation is based on **Figure 11-2 (Key Graph)** which shows that the demand curve of each firm is highly, but not perfectly, elastic. It is precisely this feature that distinguishes monopolistic competition from both monopoly and perfect competition. The demand is more elastic than the demand faced by a monopolist because the firm in monopolistic competition has many competitors producing close substitutes. The monopolist has no rivals at all. Yet, there are two reasons why the demand curve of a firm in monopolistic competition is not perfectly elastic, as is the case in perfect competition. First, it has fewer rivals; second, its products are differentiated, so they are not perfect substitutes.

The price elasticity of demand faced by the firm in monopolistic competition depends on the number of rivals and the degree of product differentiation. The larger the number of rivals and the weaker the product differentiation, the greater the price elasticity of each firm's demand, that is, the closer monopolistic competition will be to perfect competition.

The Short Run: Profit or Loss

In the short run, monopolistically competitive firms maximize profit or minimize loss using exactly the same strategy as pure competitors and monopolists: They produce the level of output at which marginal revenue equals marginal cost (MR = MC). Thus, the monopolistically competitive firm in Figure 11-2a produces output Q_1, where MR = MC. As shown by demand curve D_1, the firm then can charge price P_1. It realizes an economic profit, shown by the grey area $[= (P_1 - A_1) \times Q_1]$.

But with less favourable demand or costs, the firm may incur a loss in the short run. This possibility is shown in Figure 11-2b, where the firm's best strategy is to minimize its loss. It does so by producing output Q_2 (where MR = MC) and, as determined by demand curve D_2, by charging

KEY GRAPH

McGraw Hill connect™

FIGURE 11-2   A Monopolistically Competitive Firm: Short Run and Long Run

The firm in monopolistic competition maximizes profit or minimizes loss by producing the output at which MR = MC. The economic profit shown in panel (a) will induce new firms to enter, eventually eliminating economic profit. The loss shown in panel (b) will cause an exit of firms until normal profit is restored. After such entry and exit, the price will settle in panel (c) to where it just equals average total cost at the MR = MC output. At this price P_3 and output Q_3, the firm in monopolistic competition earns only a normal profit, and the industry is in long-run equilibrium.

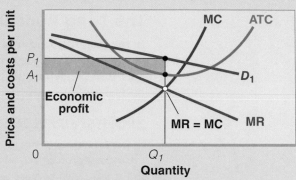

(a) Short-run profits

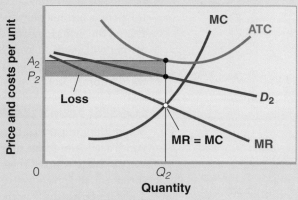

(b) Short-run losses

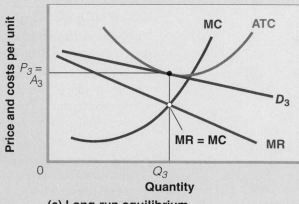

(c) Long-run equilibrium

Quick Quiz

1. **Price exceeds MC in**
   a. graph (a) only.
   b. graph (b) only.
   c. graphs (a) and (b) only.
   d. graphs (a), (b), and (c).

2. **Price exceeds ATC in**
   a. graph (a) only.
   b. graph (b) only.
   c. graphs (a) and (b) only.
   d. graphs (a), (b), and (c).

3. **The firm represented by Figure 11-2c is**
   a. making a normal profit.
   b. incurring a loss, once opportunity costs are considered.
   c. producing at the same level of output as a perfectly competitive firm.
   d. producing a standardized product.

4. **Which of the following pairs are both competition-like elements in monopolistic competition?**
   a. Price exceeds MR; standardized product.
   b. Entry is relatively easy; only a normal profit in the long run.
   c. Price equals MC at the profit-maximizing output; economic profits are likely in the long run.
   d. The firm's demand curve is downward sloping; differentiated products.

Answers: 1. d; 2. a; 3. a; 4. b

price P_2. Because price P_2 is less than average total cost A_2, the firm incurs a per-unit loss of $A_2 - P_2$ and a total loss represented as the pink area $[= (A_2 - P_2) \times Q_2]$.

The Long Run: Only a Normal Profit

In the long run, firms will enter a profitable monopolistically competitive industry and exit an unprofitable one. So, a firm in monopolistic competition will earn only a normal profit in the long run. (Remember that the cost curves include both explicit and implicit costs, including a normal profit.)

PROFITS: FIRMS ENTER

In the case of short-run profit in Figure 11-2a, economic profits attract new rivals because entry to the industry is relatively easy. As new firms enter, the demand curve faced by the typical firm shifts to the left (falls) because each firm has a smaller share of total demand. This decline in the firm's demand reduces its economic profit. When entry of new firms has reduced demand to the extent that the demand curve is tangent to the average-total-cost curve at the profit-maximizing output, the firm is just making a normal profit. This situation is shown in Figure 11-2c, where demand is D_3 and the firm's long-run equilibrium output is Q_3. As Figure 11-2c indicates, any greater or lesser output will entail an average total cost that exceeds product price P_3, meaning a loss for the firm. At the tangency point between the demand curve and ATC, total revenue equals total costs. With the economic profit gone, no further incentive exists for additional firms to enter.

LOSSES: FIRMS LEAVE

When the industry suffers short-run losses, as in Figure 11-2b, some firms will exit in the long run. Faced with fewer substitute products and with an expanded share of total demand, the surviving firms will see their demand curves shift to the right (rise), as to D_3. Their losses will disappear and give way to normal profits, shown in Figure 11-2b. (For simplicity we have assumed constant costs; shifts in the cost curves as firms enter or leave would complicate our discussion slightly but would not alter our conclusions.)

COMPLICATIONS

The representative firm in the monopolistic competition model earns only a normal profit in the long run. That outcome may not always occur for the following reasons:

- Some firms may achieve sufficient product differentiation that other firms cannot duplicate their products, even over time. For example, one hotel in a major city may have the best location for business and tourist activities. Or a firm may have developed a well-known brand name that gives it a slight but very long-lasting advantage over imitators. Such firms may have sufficient monopoly power to realize modest economic profits even in the long run.

- Entry to some monopolistically competitive industries may not be easy. Because of product differentiation, greater financial barriers to entry are likely to exist than if the product were standardized. This suggests some monopoly power, with small economic profits continuing even in the long run.

    With all things considered, however, the outcome that yields only a normal profit—the long-run equilibrium—shown in Figure 11-2c is a reasonable approximation of reality.

Monopolistic Competition and Efficiency

We know from Chapter 9 that economic efficiency requires each firm to produce the amount of output at which $P = MC = $ minimum ATC. The equality of price and minimum average total cost yields *productive efficiency*. The good is being produced in the least costly way, and the price is just sufficient to cover average total cost, including a normal profit. The equality of price and marginal

FIGURE 11-3   The Inefficiency of Monopolistic Competition

In long-run equilibrium a firm in monopolistic competition achieves neither productive nor allocative efficiency. Productive efficiency is not realized because production occurs where the average total cost A_3 exceeds the minimum average total cost A_4. Allocative efficiency is not achieved because the product price P_3 exceeds the marginal cost M_3. The results are an underallocation of resources as well as an efficiency loss and excess production capacity at every firm in the industry. This firm's efficiency loss is area acd and its excess production capacity is $Q_4 - Q_3$.

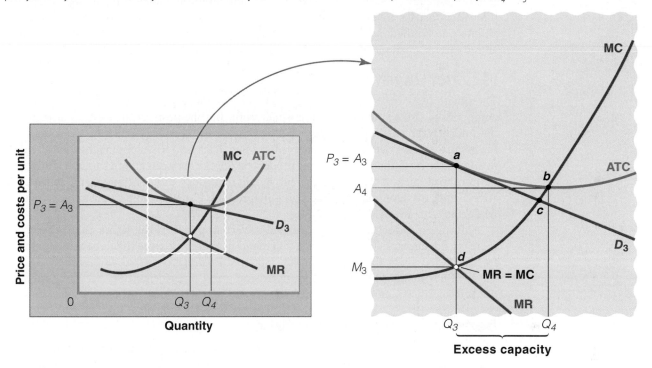

cost also yields *allocative efficiency*. The right amount of output is being produced, and thus the right amount of society's scarce resources is being devoted to this specific use. How efficient is monopolistic competition, as measured against this triple equality? In particular, do monopolistically competitive firms produce the efficient output level associated with $P = MC = $ minimum ATC?

NEITHER PRODUCTIVE NOR ALLOCATIVE EFFICIENCY

In monopolistic competition, neither productive nor allocative efficiency is achieved in long-run equilibrium. Figure 11-3, which includes an enlargement of part of Figure 11-2c, clearly shows this. First note that the profit-maximizing price P_3 slightly exceeds the lowest average total cost, A_4. In producing the profit-maximizing output Q_3, the firm's average total cost therefore is slightly higher than optimal from society's perspective—productive efficiency is not achieved. Also note that the profit-maximizing price P_3 exceeds marginal cost (here M_3), meaning that monopolistic competition causes an underallocation of resources. To measure the size of this inefficiency, note that the allocatively optimal amount of output is determined by point c, where demand curve D intersects the MC curve. So for all units between Q_3 and the level of output associated with point c, marginal benefits exceed marginal costs. Consequently, by producing only Q_3 units, this monopolistic competitor creates an efficiency loss (deadweight loss) equal in size to area acd. The total efficiency loss for the industry as a whole will be the sum of the individual efficiency losses generated by each of the firms in the industry.

excess capacity
Plant or equipment that is underused because the firm is producing less than the minimum-ATC output.

EXCESS CAPACITY

In monopolistic competition, the gap between the minimum-ATC output and the profit-maximizing output identifies **excess capacity:** plant or equipment that is underused because firms are producing less than the minimum-ATC output. This gap is shown as the distance between Q_4 and Q_3 in Figure 11-3. Note in the figure that the minimum ATC is at point b. If each monopolistic competitor could profitably produce at this point on its ATC curve, the lower average total cost would enable a lower price than P_3. More importantly, if each firm produced at b rather than at a, fewer firms would be needed to produce the industry output. But because monopolistically competitive firms produce at a in long-run equilibrium, monopolistically competitive industries are overpopulated with firms, each operating below its optimal capacity. This situation is typified by many kinds of retail establishments. For example, many cities have an abundance of small motels and restaurants that operate well below half capacity.

PRODUCT VARIETY

The situation portrayed in Figures 11-2c and 11-3 is not very satisfying to firms in monopolistic competition, since it allows only a normal profit. But the profit-realizing firm of Figure 11-2a need not stand by and watch new competitors eliminate its profit by imitating its product, matching its customer service, and copying its advertising. Each firm has a product that is distinguishable in some way from those of the other producers. So, the firm can attempt to stay ahead of competitors and sustain its profit through further product differentiation and more effective advertising. By developing or improving its product, it may be able to postpone, at least for a while, the outcome of Figure 11-2c.

Although product differentiation and advertising add to the firm's costs, they can also increase the demand for its product. If demand increases by more than enough to compensate for the added costs, the firm will have improved its profit position. As Figure 11-3 suggests, the firm has little or no prospect of increasing profit by price cutting. So why not engage in nonprice competition?

Benefits of Product Variety

The product variety and product improvement that accompany the drive to maintain above-normal profit in monopolistic competition are a benefit for society—they may offset the cost of the inefficiency associated with monopolistic competition. Consumers have a wide diversity of tastes: Some like hip-hop bands, others like punk bands; some like contemporary furniture, others like traditional furniture. If a product is differentiated, then at any time the consumer will be offered a wide range of types, styles, brands, and quality gradations of that product. Compared with perfect competition, this provides an advantage to the consumer. The range of choice is widened, and producers more fully meet the wide variation in consumer tastes.

In fact, it should be stressed that product differentiation creates a tradeoff between consumer choice and productive efficiency. The stronger the product differentiation, the greater the excess capacity and, therefore, the greater the productive inefficiency. But the greater the product differentiation, the more likely it is that the firms will satisfy the great diversity of consumer tastes. The greater the excess capacity problem, the wider the range of consumer choice.

Further Complexity

Finally, the ability to engage in nonprice competition makes the firm's situation in monopolistic competition more complex than Figure 11-3 indicates. That figure assumes a given (unchanging) product and a given level of advertising expenditures. But we know that, in practice, product attributes and advertising are not fixed. The firm in monopolistic competition juggles three factors—price, product, and advertising—in seeking maximum profit. It must determine what variety of product, selling at what price, and supplemented by what level of advertising will result in the greatest profit. This complex situation is not easily expressed in a simple economic model. At best, we can say that each possible combination of price, product, and advertising poses a different demand and cost (production cost plus advertising cost) situation for the firm, and that only one combination yields the maximum profit. In practice, this optimal combination cannot be readily forecast but must be found by trial and error.

- Monopolistic competition involves a relatively large number of firms operating in a noncollusive way and producing differentiated products, with easy industry entry and exit.

- In the short run, a firm in monopolistic competition will maximize profit or minimize loss by producing that output at which marginal revenue equals marginal cost.

- In the long run, the easy entry and exit of firms in monopolistic competition means they earn only a normal profit.

- The long-run equilibrium output for a firm in monopolistic competition is such that price exceeds the minimum average total cost (implying that consumers do not get the product at the lowest price attainable) and price exceeds marginal cost (indicating that resources are under-allocated to the product).

- The efficiency loss associated with monopolistic competition is greatly muted by the benefits consumers receive from product variety.

11.3 Oligopoly

In terms of competitiveness, the spectrum of market structures reaches from perfect competition to monopolistic competition, to oligopoly, to monopoly (review Table 8-1). We now direct our attention to **oligopoly,** a market structure dominated by a few large producers of a homogeneous or differentiated product. Because of their small number, oligopolists have considerable control over their prices, but each must consider the possible reaction of rivals to its own pricing, output, and advertising decisions.

oligopoly
A market structure in which a few large firms produce homogeneous or differentiated products.

A Few Large Producers

The phrase "a few large producers" is necessarily vague because the market model of oligopoly covers much ground, ranging between monopoly and monopolistic competition. Oligopoly encompasses the Canadian steel industry, in which two firms dominate an entire national market, and the situation in which four or five much smaller auto parts stores enjoy roughly equal shares of the market in a medium-sized town. Generally, however, when you hear a term such as Big Three, Big Four, or Big Six, you can be sure it refers to an oligopolistic industry.

Homogeneous or Differentiated Products

homogeneous oligopoly
An oligopoly in which the firms produce a standardized product.

differentiated oligopoly
An oligopoly in which the firms produce a differentiated product.

An oligopoly may be either a **homogeneous oligopoly** or a **differentiated oligopoly,** depending on whether the firms in the oligopoly produce standardized or differentiated products. Many industrial products (steel, zinc, copper, aluminum, lead, cement, industrial alcohol) are virtually standardized products that are produced in oligopolies. Many consumer goods industries (automobiles, tires, household appliances, electronics equipment, breakfast cereals, cigarettes, sporting goods) are differentiated oligopolies. An example of a differentiated oligopoly in Canada is the media and telecommunications sector. It is dominated by Canwest Global Communications, which owns a daily newspaper in almost every big city in Canada and a variety of television stations, and BCE, which controls Bell Canada and owns satellite broadcaster Bell ExpressVu, television stations, and *The Globe and Mail*. These differentiated oligopolies typically engage in considerable nonprice competition supported by heavy advertising.

Control over Price, but Mutual Interdependence

Because firms are few in oligopolistic industries, each firm is a price-maker; like the monopolist, it can set its price and output levels to maximize its profit. But unlike the monopolist, which has no rivals, the oligopolist must consider how its rivals will react to any change in its price, output,

strategic behaviour
Self-interested behaviour that takes into account the reactions of others.

mutual interdependence
A situation in which a change in strategy (usually price) by one firm will affect the sales and profits of other firms.

product characteristics, or advertising. Oligopoly is thus characterized by *strategic behaviour* and *mutual interdependence*. By **strategic behaviour** we simply mean self-interested behaviour that takes into account the reactions of others. Firms develop and implement price, quality, location, service, and advertising strategies to grow their business and expand their profits. But because rivals are few, there is **mutual interdependence:** a situation in which each firm's profit depends not just on its own price and sales strategies but also on the other firms in its highly concentrated industry. So oligopolistic firms base their decisions on how they think their rivals will react. For example, in deciding whether to increase the price of its cosmetics, L'Oréal will try to predict the response of other major cosmetics producers, such as Estée Lauder. In deciding on its advertising strategy, Burger King will take into consideration how McDonald's might react.

Entry Barriers

The same barriers to entry that create monopoly also contribute to the creation of oligopoly. Economies of scale are important entry barriers in a number of oligopolistic industries, such as the aircraft, rubber, and cement industries. In those industries, three or four firms might each have sufficient sales to achieve economies of scale, but new firms would have such a small market share that they could not do so. They would then be high-cost producers, and as such they could not survive. A closely related barrier is the large expenditure for capital—the cost of obtaining necessary plant and equipment—required for entering certain industries. The automobile, commercial aircraft, and petroleum-refining industries, for example, are all characterized by very high capital requirements. In Canada, the domestic automobile industry is dominated by Ford, General Motors, and Chrysler, whose plants are concentrated in Ontario and Quebec; Quebec's Bombardier is one of the world's largest manufacturers of small short-haul passenger planes, such as the Dash 8; and Suncor Energy is Canada's largest oil refiner, as well as a major international player in the oil and gas sector.

Ownership and control of raw materials helps explain why oligopoly exists in many mining industries, including gold, silver, and copper. In the computer, chemicals, consumer electronics, and pharmaceutical industries, patents have served as entry barriers. Oligopolists can also preclude the entry of new competitors through preemptive and retaliatory pricing and advertising strategies.

Mergers

Some oligopolies have emerged mainly through the growth of the dominant firms in a given industry (breakfast cereals, chewing gum, candy bars). But for other industries the route to oligopoly has been through mergers (examples: steel, in its early history; and, more recently, airlines, banking, and entertainment). The merging, or combining, of two or more competing firms may substantially increase their market share, which in turn may allow the new firm to achieve greater economies of scale.

Oligopolistic Industries

Figure 11-4 lists the Herfindahl index—the percentage of total industry sales accounted for by the four largest firms—for a number of oligopolistic industries. For example, the four largest Canadian producers of tobacco products manufacture more than 90 percent of all cigarettes produced in Canada. (In fact, the domestic tobacco market is largely controlled by the *three* largest Canadian companies: Imperial Tobacco Ltd., owned by Imasco Ltd.; Rothmans, Benson & Hedges Inc.; and JTI-MacDonald Ltd.)

When the largest four firms in an industry control 40 percent or more of the market (as in Figure 11-4), that industry is considered oligopolistic. Using this benchmark, about one-half of all Canadian manufacturing industries are oligopolies. Although concentration ratios help identify oligopoly, they have four shortcomings.

FIGURE 11-4 | Percentage of Output Produced by the Four Largest Firms in Selected High-Concentration Industries*

A concentration ratio reveals the percentage of total output produced and sold by an industry's four largest firms. The Herfindahl index is the sum of the squared percentage market shares of all the firms in the industry. The higher the Herfindahl index, the greater the market power within an industry. The tobacco industry is the most concentrated sector in Canada.

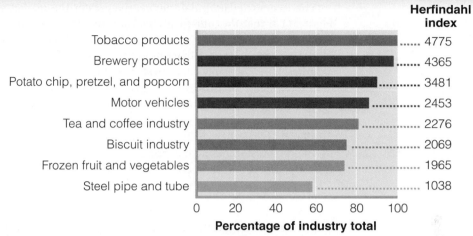

Industry	Herfindahl index
Tobacco products	4775
Brewery products	4365
Potato chip, pretzel, and popcorn	3481
Motor vehicles	2453
Tea and coffee industry	2276
Biscuit industry	2069
Frozen fruit and vegetables	1965
Steel pipe and tube	1038

Percentage of industry total

Source: Statistics Canada, *Industrial Organization and Concentration in Manufacturing, Mining and Logging Industries.* Catalogue No. 31C0024
*As measured by dollar value of shipments

Localized Markets We have already noted that concentration ratios relate to the nation as a whole, whereas the markets for some products are highly localized because of high transportation costs. Local oligopolies can exist even though national concentration ratios are low.

Interindustry Competition Concentration ratios are based on somewhat arbitrary definitions of industries. In some cases, they disguise significant **interindustry competition**—competition between two products associated with different industries. The high concentration ratio for the steel pipe and tube industry shown in Figure 11-4 understates the competition in that industry, because copper and plastic tubing compete with steel tubing in many applications.

interindustry competition
The competition between the products of one industry and the products of another industry.

World Trade The data in Figure 11-4 are for Canadian production only, and may overstate concentration because they do not account for the **import competition** of foreign suppliers. The automobile industry is a good example. Although Figure 11-4 shows that three firms produce almost 90 percent of the domestic output of those goods, it ignores the fact that a large portion of the automobiles and auto tires bought in Canada are imports. Many of the world's largest corporations are foreign, and many of them do business in Canada.

import competition
The competition domestic firms encounter from the products and services of foreign producers.

Dominant Firms The four-firm concentration ratio does not reveal the extent to which one or two firms dominate an industry. Suppose that in industry X one firm produces the entire industry output. In a second industry, Y, four firms compete, each with 25 percent of the market. The concentration ratio is 100 percent for both these industries. But industry X is a pure monopoly, while industry Y is an oligopoly that may be experiencing significant economic rivalry. Most economists would agree that monopoly power (or market power) is substantially greater in industry X than in industry Y, a fact disguised by their identical 100 percent concentration ratios.

The Herfindahl index addresses this problem. Recall from section 11.1 that this index is the sum of the squared percentage market shares of all firms in the industry. Again, in equation form:

$$\text{Herfindahl index} = (\%S_1)^2 + (\%S_2)^2 + (\%S_3)^2 + \cdots + (\%S_n)^2$$

where $\%S_1$ is the percentage market share of firm 1, $\%S_2$ is the percentage market share of firm 2, and so on for each firm in the industry. Also remember that by squaring the percentage market shares of all firms in the industry, the Herfindahl index gives much greater weight to larger, and thus more powerful, firms than to smaller ones. In the case of the single-firm industry X, the index would be at its maximum of 100^2 or 10,000, indicating an industry with complete monopoly power. For our supposed four-firm industry Y, the index would be $25^2 + 25^2 + 25^2 + 25^2$, or 2500, indicating much less market power.

The larger the Herfindahl index, the greater the market power within an industry. Note in Figure 11-4 that the four-firm concentration ratios for the tobacco products industry and the brewery products industry are similar. But the Herfindahl index of 4775 for the tobacco products industry suggests greater market power than the 4365 index for the brewery products industry, although both are highly concentrated. As the Last Word points out, the two largest brewing companies (Anheuser-Busch InBev—maker of Labatt— and Molson-Coors) dominate the Canadian beer market. The automotive industry is dominated by General Motors and Ford, but it has become less concentrated with the establishment of manufacturing plants by the Japanese giants Toyota and Honda. The baked-goods industry in Canada is dominated by Weston Bakeries, owned by George Weston Limited. Among the many products it produces are bread, rolls, cookies, and frozen baked goods. Also, contrast the much larger Herfindahl indexes in Figure 11-4 with those for the low-concentration industries in Figure 11-1.

:: connect
WORKED PROBLEM 11.1
Measures of Industry
Competition

:: connect
**ORIGIN OF THE
IDEA 11.2**
Game Theory

game theory model
A means of analyzing the pricing
behaviour of oligopolists using
the theory of strategy associated
with games such as chess and
bridge.

11.4 Oligopoly Pricing Behaviour: A Game Theory Overview

Oligopoly pricing behaviour has the characteristics of certain games of strategy, such as poker, chess, and bridge. The best way to play such a game depends on the way one's opponent plays. Players (and oligopolists) must plan their actions according to the actions and expected reactions of rivals. The study of how people behave in strategic situations is called *game theory*. We will use a simple **game theory model** to analyze the pricing behaviour of oligopolists. Game theory was first developed in the 1920s, and expanded rapidly during World War II in response to the military need for developing formal ways of thinking about strategy.

Basic Concepts

Any interaction in which individuals or firms must make choices and in which the final outcome depends on what each individual or firm chooses to do is termed a *game*. Games have four basic components: (1) the players, (2) the rules, (3) the possible strategies, and (4) the payoffs. Games may be *cooperative*, meaning players in the game make specific agreements that are binding on the parties, or *noncooperative*, where agreements among the players are not possible.

- *Players* Each participant is referred to as a player. The players may be individuals, as in a chess game; firms, usually in imperfectly competitive markets; or countries, involved for example in a regional conflict. Game theory assumes players can choose among a set of possible actions. The players (decision makers) are rational in that they pursue well-defined objectives. For individuals, the primary objective is utility maximization; for firms, it is profit maximization. Players are assumed to reason strategically, meaning they take into account other players' knowledge and expectations. Games can have any number of players, but for simplicity we will focus on two-player games. We assume that each player chooses a course of action that will yield the greatest benefit for himself or herself.

- *Rules* Games generally have clearly defined rules that players must follow in pursuing their strategies and goals, for example the rules chess players follow as they choose their moves. The rules of a game may also be viewed as *constraints* that players face as they make choices.

- *Strategies* A possible course of action for a player in a game is called a strategy. Usually players can choose among a number of strategies, while considering the likely response from other players in the game. We will focus on possible strategies in cooperative (collusive) and noncooperative (noncollusive) games in a two-firm oligopoly.

- *Payoffs* Players in a game seek the best possible outcomes for themselves. The final returns to each player are called *payoffs*. Payoffs may be large, small, or even negative. In some instances, referred to as *zero-sum games,* one player may gain exactly what the other player loses. *Positive-sum games* offer positive payoffs to all players.

EQUILIBRIUM

Recall from Chapter 3 that competitive markets bring about equilibrium price and quantity for specific products or services. There is no unique equilibrium outcome in game theory. This is because outcomes depend not only on what one player may do, but also on how the other players in the game decide to react to any given initial move by the player making the first move.

Prisoner's Dilemma

prisoner's dilemma
A type of game between two players that shows the difficulty of cooperating when the two cannot communicate with each other, even when it is in their best interests to cooperate.

To illustrate game theory in action, we'll look at the **prisoner's dilemma,** first introduced in the 1940s by Canadian economist A. W. Tucke. The prisoner's dilemma is a type of game between two prisoners that shows the difficulty of cooperating when the two cannot communicate with each other, even when it is in their best interests to cooperate. Let's take a look at an example.

Two individuals, Al and Bill, are caught by police in the act of breaking into a warehouse containing valuable carpets. On the way to headquarters, the police investigators run a check on other crimes in the area and discover that two men closely matching Al's and Bill's physical profiles stole $2 million worth of diamonds just six months earlier, in a robbery for which the police have no leads or witnesses. (Al and Bill had indeed carried out the diamond robbery.) In the hope of getting a confession, the police investigators decide to interrogate Al and Bill in different rooms so they can't communicate with each other. The game has been set in motion.

The police investigators inform Al and Bill that they are now suspects in the diamond robbery. Since they were caught red-handed trying to break into the carpet warehouse, Al and Bill know they each will get the mandatory two-year jail sentence for that crime alone. If both confess to the diamond robbery each will get four years for both crimes. But if one confesses and the other does not, the one who confesses will still receive one year, while the one who does not confess will get 12 years.

What are the options for Al and Bill given the "rules" for this game? Figure 11-5 sets out the *payoff matrix* for Al and Bill. Four combinations are possible, and each of the four combinations

Prisoner's Dilemma Payoff Matrix

Al and Bill each have two possible strategies. Each lettered cell of this four-cell payoff matrix represents the jail terms, in years, that both Al and Bill would receive under various conditions.

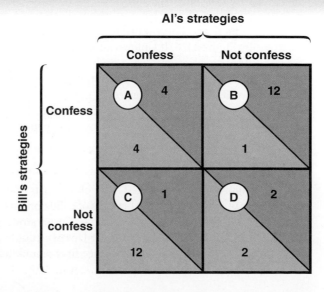

is represented by a lettered cell. If both confess, they each will get four years in jail (cell A). If neither confesses to the diamond robbery, each will get only two years in jail (cell D). If Bill confesses, but Al does not, he gets one year and Al gets 12 years (cell B). Alternatively, if Al confesses, but Bill does not, Al gets one year and Bill goes to the slammer for 12 years (cell C).

Recall that a player in a game will choose a strategy on the basis of what he or she expects the other players will do. If both Al and Bill expect the other to deny they participated in the diamond robbery, then each will not confess. Both Al and Bill know this, but each cannot be sure the other will deny participating in the diamond robbery. If they were allowed to communicate with each other they could cooperate (collude) to minimize their jail sentence. But they can't communicate, which means that they are in a noncooperative game. The dilemma is that Al and Bill should cooperate to minimize jail time, but if one confesses and the other does not, the one who does not confess will face a heavier penalty.

Given the uncertainty of what the other will do, confessing is the best strategy for both Al and Bill in this game. The risk of a much higher jail term is too great for either Al or Bill to consider denying involvement in the diamond robbery. By not confessing, the best that either Al or Bill can hope for is a one-year jail term, but the possibility exists for a 12-year term. If either Al or Bill confesses, his worst-case scenario is a four-year jail sentence. You should be able to see that the *dominant strategy* for both Al and Bill is to confess.

Strategies in a Two-Firm Oligopoly

Let's now apply the game theory model to a two-firm oligopoly, also known as a *duopoly*. We assume a two-firm oligopoly producing athletic shoes. Each firm—let's call them RareAir and Uptown—has a choice of two pricing strategies: price high or price low. The profit each firm earns will depend on the strategy it chooses and the strategy its rival chooses.

Four possible combinations of strategies are possible for the two firms, and a lettered cell in Figure 11-6 represents each combination, also called the payoff matrix. For example, cell C represents a low-price strategy for Uptown along with a high-price strategy for RareAir. Cell C shows that if Uptown adopts a low-price strategy and RareAir a high-price strategy, then Uptown will earn $15 million (green portion) and RareAir will earn $6 million (tan portion).

Mutual Interdependence Revisited

The data in Figure 11-6 are hypothetical, but their relationships are typical of real situations. Recall that oligopolistic firms can increase their profits, and influence their rivals' profits, by changing their pricing strategies. Each firm's profit depends on its own pricing strategy and that of its rivals. This mutual interdependence of oligopolists is the most obvious point demonstrated by Figure 11-6. If Uptown adopts a high-price strategy, its profit will be $12 million, provided that RareAir also employs a high-price strategy (cell A). But if RareAir uses a low-price strategy against Uptown's high-price strategy (cell B), RareAir will increase its market share and boost its profit from $12 million to $15 million. RareAir's higher profit will come at the expense of Uptown, whose profit will fall from $12 million to $6 million. Uptown's high-price strategy is a good strategy only if RareAir also employs a high-price strategy.

Collusion

collusion
A situation in which firms act together and in agreement to fix prices, divide a market, or otherwise restrict competition.

Figure 11-6 also suggests that oligopolists often can benefit from **collusion**—that is, cooperation with rivals. To see the benefits of collusion, first suppose that both firms in Figure 11-6 are acting independently and following high-price strategies. Each realizes a $12 million profit (cell A).

Note that either RareAir or Uptown could increase its profit by switching to a low-price strategy (cell B or C). The low-price firm would increase its profit to $15 million, and the high-price

KEY GRAPH

FIGURE 11-6 Profit Payoff for a Two-Firm Oligopoly (in millions)

Each firm has two possible pricing strategies. RareAir's strategies are shown in the top margin, and Uptown's in the left margin. Each lettered cell of this four-cell payoff matrix represents one combination of a RareAir strategy and an Uptown strategy and shows the profit, in millions of dollars, that combination would earn for each firm.

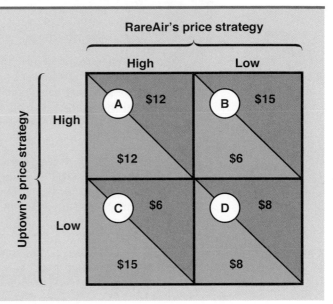

firm's profit would fall to $6 million. The high-price firm would be better off if it, too, adopted a low-price policy. Doing so would increase its profit from $6 million to $8 million (cell D). The effect of all this independent strategy shifting would be to reduce both firms' profits from $12 million (cell A) to $8 million (cell D).

In real situations, too, independent action by oligopolists may lead to mutual competitive low-price strategies: Independent oligopolists compete with respect to price, which leads to lower prices and lower profits. This is clearly beneficial to consumers but not to the oligopolists' profits.

How could oligopolists avoid the low-profit outcome of cell D? The answer is that they could collude, rather than establish prices competitively or independently. In our example, the two firms could agree to establish and maintain a high-price policy. Each firm will increase its profit from $8 million (cell D) to $12 million (cell A).

Incentive to Cheat

The payoff matrix also explains why an oligopolist might be strongly tempted to cheat on a collusive agreement. Suppose Uptown and RareAir agree to maintain high-price policies, with each earning $12 million in profit (cell A). Both are tempted to cheat on this collusive pricing agreement, because either firm can increase its profit to $15 million by lowering its price. For instance, if Uptown secretly cheats and sells at the low price while RareAir keeps on charging the high price, the payoff would move from cell A to cell C so that Uptown's profit would rise to $15 million while RareAir's profit would fall to $6 million. On the other hand, if RareAir cheats and sets a low price while Uptown keeps the agreement and charges the high price, the payoff matrix would move from cell A to cell B so that RareAir would get $15 million while Uptown would get only $6 million. As you can see, cheating is both very lucrative to the cheater and very costly to the firm that gets cheated on. As a result, both firms will probably cheat so that the game will settle back to cell D, with each firm using its low-price strategy. (The appendix to this chapter provides several additional applications of game theory.)

- An oligopoly is made up of relatively few firms producing either homogeneous or differentiated products; these firms are mutually interdependent.

- Barriers to entry such as scale economies, control of patents or strategic resources, or the ability to engage in retaliatory pricing characterize oligopolies. Oligopolies may result from internal growth of firms, mergers, or both.

- The four-firm concentration ratio shows the percentage of an industry's sales accounted for by its four largest firms; the Herfindahl index measures the

degree of market power in an industry by summing the squares of the percentage market shares held by the individual firms in the industry.

- The prisoner's dilemma is a type of game that shows the difficulty of cooperating when the participants cannot communicate with each other.

- Game theory reveals that (1) oligopolies are mutually interdependent in their pricing policies, (2) collusion enhances oligopoly profits, and (3) there is a temptation for oligopolists to cheat on a collusive agreement.

11.5 The Incentives and Obstacles to Collusion: Two Oligopoly Strategies

To gain further insight into oligopolistic pricing and output behaviour, we will examine two distinct pricing strategies: (1) collusive pricing, and (2) price leadership. Why not a simple single model as in our discussions of the other market structures? There are two reasons:

1. *Diversity of Oligopolies* Oligopoly has a greater range and diversity of market situations than other market structures, including the *tight* oligopoly, in which two or three firms dominate an entire market, and the *loose* oligopoly, in which six or seven firms share, say, 70−80 percent of a market while a competitive fringe of firms shares the remainder. Oligopoly includes both differentiated and standardized products. It includes cases in which firms act in collusion and those in which they act independently. The diversity of oligopoly makes it impossible to explain all oligopolistic behaviours with a single market model.

2. *Complications of Interdependence* The mutual interdependence of oligopolistic firms is what complicates matters. Because firms cannot predict the reactions of their rivals with certainty, they cannot estimate their own demand and marginal-revenue data. Without such data, firms cannot determine their profit-maximizing price and output.

Despite these analytical difficulties, two interrelated characteristics of oligopolistic pricing have been observed. First, prices change less frequently under oligopoly than under perfect competition, monopolistic competition, and, in some instances, monopoly. Second, when oligopolists do change prices, firms are likely to change their prices together, suggesting a tendency to act in concert, or collusively, in setting and changing prices (as we mentioned in the preceding section). The diversity of oligopolies and the presence of mutual interdependence are reflected in the models that follow.

Cartels and Other Collusion: Cooperative Strategies

Our game theory model demonstrates that one possible outcome of an oligopoly market structure is collusion. Collusion occurs whenever firms in an industry reach an agreement to fix prices, divide up the market, or otherwise restrict competition among themselves. The danger of noncollusive oligopolies is that a price war may break out, especially during a general business recession. Then each firm finds that, because of unsold goods and excess capacity, it can reduce per-unit

The following story, offered with tongue in cheek, illustrates a localized market that exhibits some characteristics of oligopoly, including strategic behaviour.

Tracy Proudfoot's Native Canadian Arts and Crafts store is located in the centre of a small tourist town that borders on a national park. In the business's early days, Tracy had a mini-monopoly. Business was brisk and prices and profits were high.

But to Tracy's chagrin, two copycat shops opened up right next door, one on either side of her store. Worse yet, the competitors named their shops to take advantage of Tracy's advertising. One was "Native Arts and Crafts," and the other "Indian Arts and Crafts." These new sellers drew business away from Tracy's store, forcing her to lower her prices. The three adjacent stores in the small, isolated town constituted a localized oligopoly for Native Canadian arts and crafts.

Tracy began to think strategically about ways to boost profit. She decided to distinguish her shop from those on either side by offering a greater mix of high-quality, expensive products and fewer inexpensive "souvenir" items. The tactic worked for a while, but the other stores eventually imitated her product mix.

Then, one of the competitors next door escalated the rivalry by hanging up a large sign proclaiming "We Sell for Less!" Shortly thereafter, the other shop put up a large sign stating, "We Won't Be Undersold!"

Not to be outdone, Tracy painted a colourful sign of her own and hung it above her door. It read, "Main Entrance." Clearly, competitive market forces demand creative strategic responses by firms.

costs by increasing market share. The possibility also exists that a new firm may surmount entry barriers and initiate aggressive price cutting to gain a foothold in the market. In addition, the oligopoly's tendency toward rigid prices may adversely affect profits if general inflationary pressures increase costs. But by controlling price through collusion, oligopolists may be able to reduce uncertainty, increase profits, and perhaps even prohibit the entry of new rivals.

PRICE AND OUTPUT

Assume that three oligopolistic firms (Gypsum, Sheetrock, and GSR) produce homogeneous products. All three firms have identical cost curves. Each firm's demand curve is indeterminate unless we know how its rivals will react to any price change. Therefore, we suppose each firm assumes that its two rivals will match either a price cut or a price increase. And, since they have identical cost data, and the same demand and thus marginal-revenue data, we can say that Figure 11-7 represents the position of each of our three oligopolistic firms.

FIGURE 11-7 **Collusion and Joint-Profit Maximization**

If oligopolistic firms face identical or highly similar demand and cost conditions, they may collude to limit their joint output and to set a single, common price. Thus each firm acts as if it were a monopolist, setting output at Q_0 and charging price P_0. This price and output combination maximizes each oligopolist's profit (grey area) and thus their joint profit.

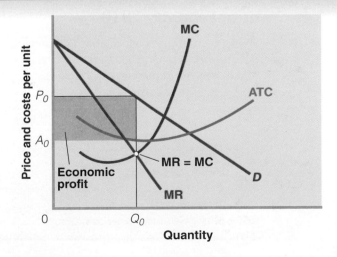

What price and output combination should, say, Gypsum select? If Gypsum were a monopolist, the answer would be clear: Establish output at Q_0, where marginal revenue equals marginal cost, charge the corresponding price P_0, and enjoy the maximum profit attainable. However, Gypsum does have two rivals selling identical products, and if Gypsum's assumption that its rivals will match its price of P_0 proves to be incorrect, the consequences could be disastrous for Gypsum. Specifically, if Sheetrock and GSR actually charge prices below P_0 then Gypsum's demand curve D will shift sharply to the left as its potential customers turn to its rivals, which are now selling the same product at a lower price. Of course, Gypsum can retaliate by cutting its price too, but this will move all three firms down their demand curves, lowering their profits. It may even drive them to a point where average total cost exceeds price and losses are incurred.

So the question becomes, will Sheetrock and GSR want to charge a price below P_0? Under our assumptions, and recognizing that Gypsum has little choice except to match any price they may set below P_0, the answer is no. Faced with the same demand and cost circumstances, Sheetrock and GSR will find it in their interest to produce Q_0 and charge P_0. This is a curious situation; each firm finds it most profitable to charge the same price, P_0, but only if its rivals actually do so! How can the three firms ensure the price P_0 and quantity Q_0 solution in which each is keenly interested? How can they avoid the less profitable outcomes associated with either higher or lower prices?

The answer is evident: They could collude. They could get together, talk it over, and agree to charge the same price, P_0. In addition to reducing the possibility of price wars, this will give each firm the maximum profit. (But it will also subject them to anticombines prosecution if they are caught!) For society, the result will be the same as would occur if the industry were a monopoly composed of three identical plants.

OVERT COLLUSION: THE OPEC CARTEL

cartel
A formal agreement among firms in an industry to set the price of a product and establish the outputs of the individual firms or to divide the market among them.

Collusion may assume a variety of forms. The most comprehensive form of collusion is the **cartel,** a group of producers that typically creates a formal written agreement specifying how much each member will produce and charge. Output must be controlled to maintain the agreed-on price. The collusion is overt, or open to view.

Undoubtedly the most significant international cartel is the Organization of the Petroleum Exporting Countries (OPEC), comprising 12 oil-producing nations (see Global Perspective 11.1).

GLOBAL PERSPECTIVE

11.1

The 12 OPEC Nations, Daily Oil Production Agreement as of February 2010

The OPEC nations produce about 40 percent of the world's oil and 60 percent of the oil sold in the world market.

OPEC country	Barrels of oil
Saudi Arabia	8,165,600
Iran	3,544,000
Kuwait	2,312,100
Venezuela	2,853,600
Iraq	2,358,100
UAE	2,323,800
Nigeria	2,048,300
Angola	1,691,200
Libya	1,486,600
Algeria	1,189,800
Qatar	733,400
Ecuador	476,400

Source: OPEC Secretariat, www.opec.org.

OPEC produces 40 percent of the world's oil and supplies 43 percent of all oil traded internationally. OPEC has in some cases been able to drastically alter oil prices by increasing or decreasing supply. In 1973, for instance, it caused the price of oil to more than triple by getting its members to restrict output. And again, in the late 1990s it caused oil prices to rise from $11 per barrel to $34 per barrel over a 15-month period.

But it should be kept in mind that most increases in the price of oil are not caused by OPEC. Between 2005 and 2008, for example, oil prices went from $40 per barrel to $140 per barrel due to rapidly rising demand from China and supply uncertainties related to armed conflict in the Middle East. But as the recession that began in December 2008 took hold, demand slumped and oil prices collapsed back down to about $40 per barrel. OPEC was largely a non-factor in this rise and fall in the price of oil. But in those cases where OPEC can effectively enforce its production agreements, there is little doubt that it can hold the price of oil substantially above the marginal cost of production.

COVERT COLLUSION: EXAMPLES

Cartels are illegal in Canada, and hence any collusion that exists is covert, or secret. Yet there are examples, found in evidence from anticombines (antimonopoly) cases. One example of covert collusion is the case of four cement firms in the Quebec City region. In 1996, St. Lawrence Cement Inc., Lafarge Canada Inc., Cement Quebec Inc., and Beton Orleans Inc. were fined a total of $5.8 million for price fixing. The conspiracy was discovered by a Quebec City newspaper that reported that the cost of the city's new convention centre was higher than anticipated. The first three of these firms had previously been fined in 1983 for a similar violation of the *Competition Act*. More recently, in 2008 LG Display, Sharp, and Chunghwa Picture Tubes were fined a total of US$585 million by the U.S. Justice Department for conspiring to drive up the price of liquid-crystal display monitors (LCDs), used on most notebook computers, cellphones, and new televisions.

tacit understanding
Any method by competing oligopolists to set prices and outputs that does not involve outright collusion.

In many other instances collusion is even more subtle. An agreement known as a **tacit understanding** (historically called a "gentlemen's agreement") will frequently be made at cocktail parties, on golf courses, through phone calls, or at trade association meetings. In such agreements, competing firms reach a verbal understanding on product price, leaving market shares to be decided by nonprice competition. Although these agreements, too, violate anticombines laws—and can result in severe personal and corporate penalties—the elusive character of tacit understandings makes them difficult to detect.

OBSTACLES TO COLLUSION

Normally, cartels and similar collusive arrangements are difficult to establish and maintain, for several reasons:

- *Demand and Cost Differences* When oligopolists face different costs and demand curves, it is difficult for them to agree on a price. Even with highly standardized products, firms usually have somewhat different market shares and operate with differing degrees of productive efficiency. Thus, it is unlikely that even homogeneous oligopolists would have the same demand and cost curves.

  In either case, differences in costs and demand mean that the profit-maximizing price will differ among firms; no single price will be readily acceptable to all, as we assumed was true in Figure 11-7. So, price collusion depends on compromises and concessions that are not always easy to obtain, and hence they act as obstacles to collusion.

- *Number of Firms* Other things equal, the larger the number of firms, the more difficult it is to create a cartel or other form of price collusion. Agreement on price by three or four producers that control an entire market may be relatively easy to accomplish, but such agreement is more difficult to achieve where there are, say, 10 firms, each with roughly 10 percent of the market, or where the Big Three have 70 percent of the market while a competitive fringe of eight to 10 smaller firms battle for the remainder.

- *Cheating* As the game theory model makes clear, there is a temptation for collusive oligopolists to engage in secret price cutting to increase sales and profit. The difficulty with such cheating is that buyers who are paying a high price for a product may become aware of the lower-priced sales and demand similar treatment. Or buyers receiving a price concession from one producer may use the concession as a wedge to get even larger price concessions from a rival producer. Buyers' attempts to play producers against one another may precipitate price wars among the producers. Although secret price concessions are potentially profitable, they threaten collusive oligopolies over time. Collusion is more likely to succeed when cheating is easy to detect and punish.

- *Recession* Long-lasting recession usually serves as an enemy of collusion, because slumping markets increase average total cost. In technical terms, as the oligopolists' demand and marginal revenue curves shift to the left in Figure 11-7 in response to a recession, each firm moves leftward and upward to a higher operating point on its average-total-cost curve. Firms find they have substantial excess production capacity, sales are down, unit costs are up, and profits are being squeezed. Under such conditions, businesses may feel they can avoid serious profit reductions (or even losses) by cutting price and thus gaining sales at the expense of rivals.

- *Potential Entry* The greater prices and profits that result from collusion may attract new entrants, including foreign firms. Since that would increase market supply and reduce prices and profits, successful collusion requires that colluding oligopolists block the entry of new producers.

- *Legal Obstacles: Competition Policy* Canadian anticombines laws prohibit cartels and price-fixing collusion, so less obvious means of price control have evolved in Canada.

Price Leadership Model: Another Cooperative Strategy

price leadership
An implicit understanding oligopolists use that has the dominant firm initiate price changes and all other firms follow.

One type of implicit understanding by which oligopolists can coordinate prices is called **price leadership**. A practice evolves whereby the "dominant firm" initiates price changes and all other firms more or less automatically follow the leader. Many industries, including cement, newsprint, glass containers, steel, beer, fertilizer, cigarettes, and tin, practise or have recently practised price leadership.

LEADERSHIP STRATEGY

An examination of price leadership in a variety of industries suggests that the price leader is likely to use the following strategies.

- *Infrequent Price Changes* Because price changes always carry the risk that rivals will not follow the lead, price adjustments are made only infrequently, when cost and demand conditions have been altered significantly.

- *Communications* The price leader often communicates impending price adjustments to the industry through speeches by major executives, trade publication interviews, or press releases. By publicizing the need to raise prices, the price leader seeks agreement among its competitors regarding the actual increase.

- *Limit Pricing* The price leader does not always choose the price that maximizes short-run profits for the industry because the industry may want to discourage new firms from entering. To discourage new competitors and to maintain the current oligopolistic structure of the industry, the price leader may keep price below the short-run profit-maximizing level. The strategy of establishing a price that blocks the entry of new firms is called limit pricing.

- *Breakdowns in Price Leadership: Price Wars* Price leadership in oligopoly occasionally breaks down, and sometimes results in a price war. An example of price leadership temporarily breaking down occurred in the breakfast cereal industry, in which Kellogg traditionally had been the price leader. General Mills countered Kellogg's leadership in 1995 by reducing the prices of its cereals by 11 percent. In 1996 Post responded with a 20 percent price cut, which Kellogg then followed. Not to be outdone, Post reduced its prices by another 11 percent.

As another example, in October 2009 with the Christmas shopping season just getting under-way, U.S.–based Walmart, the largest department store in the world, cut its price on 10 highly anticipated new books to just $10 each. Within hours, Amazon.com matched the price cut. Walmart then retaliated by cutting its price for the books to just $9 each. Amazon.com matched that reduction—at which point Walmart went to $8.99! Then, out of nowhere, Target, another large U.S. department store, jumped in at $8.98, a price that Amazon.com and Walmart immediately matched. And that is where the price finally came to rest—at a level so low that each company was losing money on each book it sold.

Most price wars eventually run their course. After a period of low or negative profits, they again cede price leadership to one of the industry's leading firms. That firm then begins to raise prices, and the other firms willingly follow suit.

QUICK REVIEW

- Cartels agree on production limits and set a common price to maximize the joint profit of their members as if each were a unit of a single pure monopoly.

- Collusion among oligopolists is difficult because of (1) demand and cost differences among sellers, (2) the complexity of output coordination among producers, (3) the potential for cheating, (4) a tendency for agreements to break down during recessions, (5) the potential entry of new firms, and (6) competition laws.

- Price leadership involves an informal understanding among oligopolists to match any price change initiated by a designated firm (often the industry's dominant firm).

11.6 Oligopoly and Advertising

We have noted that oligopolists would rather not compete on the basis of price and may become involved in price collusion. Nonetheless, each firm's share of the total market is typically determined through product development and advertising, for two reasons:

1. Product improvements and successful advertising can produce more permanent gains in market share because they cannot be duplicated as quickly and completely as price reductions.

2. Oligopolists have sufficient financial resources to engage in product development and advertising.

In recent years, Canadian advertising has exceeded $6 billion annually, and worldwide advertising, $630 billion. Advertising is prevalent in both monopolistic competition and oligopoly.

Advertising may affect prices, competition, and efficiency both positively and negatively, depending on the circumstances. While our focus here is on advertising by oligopolists, the analysis is equally applicable to advertising by firms in monopolistic competition.

Positive Effects of Advertising

To make rational (efficient) decisions, consumers need information about product characteristics and prices. Media advertising may be a low-cost means for consumers to obtain that information. Suppose you are in the market for a high-quality camera and there is no advertising for such a product in newspapers or magazines or on the Internet. To make a rational choice, you may have to spend several days visiting stores to determine the prices and features of various brands. This search has both direct costs (gasoline, parking fees) and indirect costs (the value of your time). By providing information about the available options, advertising reduces your search time and minimizes these costs.

By providing information about the various competing goods that are available, advertising diminishes monopoly power. In fact, advertising is frequently associated with the introduction of new products designed to compete with existing brands. Could Toyota and Honda have so strongly challenged North American auto producers without advertising? Could FedEx have sliced market share away from UPS and Canada Post without advertising?

Viewed this way, advertising is an efficiency-enhancing activity. It is a relatively inexpensive means of providing useful information to consumers and thus lowering their search costs. By enhancing competition, advertising results in greater economic efficiency. By facilitating the introduction of new products, advertising speeds up technological progress. And by increasing output, advertising can reduce long-run average total cost by enabling firms to obtain economies of scale.

Potential Negative Effects of Advertising

Not all the effects of advertising are positive. Much advertising is designed simply to persuade consumers in favour of the advertiser's product. A television commercial showing that a popular personality drinks a particular brand of soft drink conveys little or no information to consumers about price or quality. Indeed, in some cases advertising may well persuade consumers to pay high prices for much-acclaimed but inferior products, forgoing better but unadvertised products selling at lower prices. For example, *Consumer Reports* recently found that heavily advertised premium motor oils and fancy additives provide no better engine performance and longevity than do cheaper brands.

Firms often establish substantial brand-name loyalty and thus achieve monopoly power via their advertising (see Global Perspective 11.2). As a consequence, they are able to increase their sales, expand their market share, and enjoy greater profits. Larger profit permits still more advertising and further enlargement of the firm's market share and profit. In time, consumers may lose the advantages of competitive markets and face the disadvantages of monopolized markets. Moreover, new entrants to the industry need to incur large advertising costs to establish their products in the marketplace; thus, advertising costs may be a barrier to entry.

Advertising may also be self-cancelling. The advertising campaign of one fast-food hamburger chain may be offset by equally costly campaigns waged by rivals, so each firm's demand actually remains unchanged. Few, if any, extra burgers will be purchased, and each firm's market share will stay the same. But because of the advertising, the cost and hence the price of hamburgers will be higher.

GLOBAL PERSPECTIVE

11.2

The World's Top 10 Brand Names, 2011

Here are the world's top 10 brands, based on three primary criteria: the organization's financial performance, the portion of the decision to purchase that is attributable to brand, and brand strength, which measures the ability of the brand to secure the delivery of expected future earnings.

World's Top 10 Brands

World's Top 10 Brands
Coca-Cola
IBM
Microsoft
Google
General Electric
McDonald's
Intel
Apple
Disney
Hewlett-Packard

Source: Interbrand, www.interbrand.com.

When advertising either leads to increased monopoly power or is self-cancelling, economic inefficiency results.

Oligopoly and Efficiency

Is oligopoly, then, an efficient market structure from society's standpoint? How do the price and output decisions of the oligopolist measure up to the triple equality $P = MC = $ minimum ATC that occurs in perfect competition?

PRODUCTIVE AND ALLOCATIVE EFFICIENCY

Many economists believe that the outcome of some oligopolistic markets is approximately as shown in Figure 11-7. This view is bolstered by evidence that many oligopolists sustain sizable economic profits year after year. In that case, the oligopolist's production occurs where price exceeds marginal cost and average total cost. Moreover, production is below the output at which average total cost is minimized. In this view, neither productive efficiency ($P = $ minimum ATC) nor allocative efficiency ($P = MC$) is likely to occur under oligopoly.

QUALIFICATIONS

A few observers assert that oligopoly is actually less desirable than pure monopoly, because government usually regulates monopoly to guard against abuses of monopoly power. Informal collusion among oligopolists may yield price and output results similar to those under monopoly yet give the outward appearance of competition involving independent firms. We should note, however, three qualifications to this view:

- **Increased Foreign Competition** In recent decades foreign competition has increased rivalry in a number of oligopolistic industries—steel, automobiles, video games, electric shavers, outboard motors, and copy machines, for example. This has helped to break down such cozy arrangements as price leadership and to stimulate much more competitive pricing.

- **Limit Pricing** Recall that some oligopolists may purposely keep prices below the short-run profit-maximizing level in order to bolster entry barriers. In essence, consumers and society may get some of the benefits of competition—prices closer to marginal cost and minimum average total cost—even without the competition that free entry would provide.

- **Technological Advance** Over time, oligopolistic industries may foster more rapid product development and greater improvement of production techniques than would be possible if they were perfectly competitive. Oligopolists have large economic profits from which they can fund expensive research and development (R&D). Moreover, the existence of barriers to entry may give the oligopolist some assurance that it will reap the rewards of successful R&D. Thus, the short-run economic inefficiencies of oligopolists may be partly or wholly offset by the oligopolists' contributions to better products, lower prices, and lower costs over time.

The LAST WORD   Oligopoly in the Beer Industry

The beer industry was once populated by dozens of firms and an even larger number of brands. It is now an oligopoly dominated by a handful of producers.

The brewing industry has undergone profound changes since World War II that have increased the degree of concentration in the industry. In 1945 more than 60 independent brewing companies operated in Canada. By 1967 there were 18, and by 1984 only 11. While the three largest brewers sold only 19 percent of the nation's beer in 1947, the big three brewers (Labatt, Molson, and Carling O'Keefe) sold 97 percent of the nation's domestically produced beer in 1989, the same year Molson and Carling O'Keefe merged. In 1995, Belgium-based Interbrew SA (which later merged with AmBev to become InBev, and subsequently merged with Anheuser-Busch to become Anheuser-Busch InBev) bought Labatt Canada. In 2005, Molson joined forces with U.S.-based Coors, creating Molson-Coors, the fifth largest brewer in the world. Currently, the big two—Labatt (Anheuser-Busch InBev, the largest brewing company in the world) and Molson-Coors (each producing 40 percent)—brew most of the beer in Canada. The industry is clearly an oligopoly.

Changes on the demand side of the market have contributed to the shakeout of small brewers from the industry. First, consumer tastes have generally shifted from the stronger-flavoured beers of the small brewers to the light products of the larger brewers. Second, there has been a shift from the consumption of beer in taverns to consumption in the home. The significance of this change is that taverns were usually supplied with kegs from local brewers to avoid the relatively high cost of shipping cans. But the acceptance of aluminum cans for home consumption made it possible for large, distant brewers to compete with the local brewers, because the former could now ship their products by truck or rail without breakage.

Developments on the supply side of the market have been even more profound. Technological advances have

increased the speed of the bottling and canning lines. Today, large brewers can fill and close 2000 cans per line per minute. Large plants are also able to reduce labour costs through automating brewing and warehousing. Furthermore, plant construction costs per barrel are about one-third less for a 4.0 million-hectolitre plant than for a 1.5 million-barrel plant. As a consequence of these and other factors, the minimum efficient scale in brewing is a plant size of about 4.0 million hectolitres, with multiple plants. Because the construction cost of a modern brewery that size is $330 million, economies of scale may now constitute a significant barrier to entry.

Blind taste tests confirm that most mass-produced Canadian beers taste alike. Undaunted, brewers spend large amounts of money touting the supposed differences between their brands in order to build brand loyalty. Here, Labatt and Molson-Coors, who sell national brands, enjoy major cost advantages over producers that have regional brands (for example, Creemore Springs, Upper Canada, and

Okanagan Spring), because national television advertising is less costly *per viewer* than local spot TV advertising.

Mergers in the brewing industry have been a fundamental cause of the rising concentration. Dominant firms have expanded by heavily advertising their main brands—such as Labatt Blue and Blue Light, and Molson Canadian and Coors Light—sustaining significant product differentiation despite the declining number of major brewers.

But there are problems brewing for Canada's large beer producers. Imported beers such as Beck's, Corona, Foster's, and Guinness constitute about 13 percent of the Canadian market, with individual brands seeming to wax and wane in popularity. Some local or regional microbreweries such as Upper Canada (purchased by Sleeman), which brew specialty beers, and low-cost producers such as Lakeport in Ontario, have whittled into the sales of the major brewers. For example, according to the Brewers Association of Canada, Canadian microbrewery sales rose slightly in the last few years, while mass-produced beer actually declined. Overall, both imports and microbreweries are becoming a threat to the two major brewers in Canada.

Sources: Based on Kenneth G. Elzinga, "Beer," in Walter Adams and James Brock (eds.), *The Structure of American Industry,* 9th ed. (Englewood Cliffs, NJ: Prentice-Hall, 1995), pp. 119–151; Douglas F. Greer, "Beer: Causes of Structural Change," in Larry Duetsch (ed.), *Industry Studies,* 2nd ed. (New York: M. E. Sharpe, 1998), pp. 28–64; authors' updates; the Conference Board of Canada, *The Canadian Brewing Industry: Historical Evolution and Competitive Structure* (Toronto: International Studies and Development Group, 1989).

Question

What firm(s) dominate the beer industry? What demand and supply factors have contributed to the small number of firms in this industry?

:: CHAPTER SUMMARY

11.1 :: CHARACTERISTICS OF MONOPOLISTIC COMPETITION

- The distinguishing features of monopolistic competition are (a) enough firms are in the industry to ensure each firm has only limited control over price, mutual interdependence is absent, and collusion is nearly impossible; (b) products are characterized by real or perceived differences so that economic rivalry entails both price and nonprice competition; and (c) entry to the industry is relatively easy. Many aspects of retailing, and some manufacturing industries in which economies of scale are few, approximate monopolistic competition.

- The four-firm concentration ratio measures the percentage of total industry output accounted for by the largest four firms. The Herfindahl index sums the squares of the market shares of all firms in the industry.

11.2 :: PRICE AND OUTPUT IN MONOPOLISTIC COMPETITION

- Monopolistically competitive firms may earn economic profits or incur losses in the short run. The easy entry and exit of firms results in only normal profits in the long run.

- The long-run equilibrium position of the monopolistically competitive producer is less socially desirable than that of the pure competitor. Under monopolistic competition, price exceeds marginal cost, suggesting an underallocation of resources to the product, and price exceeds minimum average total cost, indicating that consumers do not get the product at the lowest price that cost conditions might allow.

- Nonprice competition provides a means by which monopolistically competitive firms can offset the long-run tendency for economic profit to fall to zero. Through product differentiation, product development, and advertising, a firm may strive to increase the demand for its product more than enough to cover the added cost of such nonprice competition. Consumers benefit from the wide diversity of product choice that monopolistic competition provides.

- In practice, the monopolistic competitor seeks the specific combination of price, product, and advertising that will maximize profit.

11.3 :: OLIGOPOLY

- Oligopolistic industries are characterized by the presence of few firms, each having a significant fraction of the market. Firms thus situated are mutually interdependent: the behaviour of any one firm directly affects, and is affected by, the actions of rivals. Products may be either virtually uniform or significantly differentiated. Various barriers to entry, including economies of scale, underlie and maintain oligopoly.

- High concentration ratios are an indication of oligopoly (monopoly) power. By giving more weight to larger firms, the Herfindahl index is designed to measure market dominance in an industry.

11.4 :: OLIGOPOLY PRICING BEHAVIOUR: A GAME THEORY OVERVIEW

- The prisoner's dilemma is a type of game that shows the difficulty of cooperating when the participants cannot communicate with one another.

- Game theory (a) shows the interdependence of oligopolists' pricing policies, (b) reveals the tendency of oligopolists to collude, and (c) explains the temptation of oligopolists to cheat on collusive arrangements.

11.5 :: THE INCENTIVES AND OBSTACLES TO COLLUSION: TWO OLIGOPOLY STRATEGIES

- The uncertainties inherent in oligopoly promote collusion. Collusive oligopolists such as cartels maximize joint profits— that is, they behave like pure monopolists. Demand and cost differences, a large number of firms, cheating through secret price concessions, recessions, and the anticombines laws are all obstacles to collusive oligopoly.

- Price leadership is an informal means of collusion whereby one firm, usually the largest or most efficient, initiates price changes and the other firms in the industry follow the leader.

- Market shares in oligopolistic industries are usually determined based on product development and advertising. Oligopolists emphasize nonprice competition because (a) advertising and product variations are harder for rivals to match and (b) oligopolists frequently have ample resources to finance nonprice competition.

11.6 :: OLIGOPOLY AND ADVERTISING

- Advertising may affect prices, competition, and efficiency either positively or negatively. Positive effects are that it can provide consumers with low-cost information about competing products, help introduce new competing products into concentrated industries, and generally reduce monopoly power and its attendant inefficiencies. Negative effects include that it can promote monopoly power via persuasion and the creation of entry barriers. Moreover, when used by rivals advertising can be self-cancelling by boosting costs and increasing economic inefficiency while accomplishing little else.

- Neither productive nor allocative efficiency is realized in oligopolistic markets, but oligopoly may be superior to pure competition in promoting research and development and technological progress.

:: TERMS AND CONCEPTS

monopolistic competition, p. 261
product differentiation, p. 261
nonprice competition, p. 262
four-firm concentration ratio, p. 262
concentration ratio, p. 263
Herfindahl index, p. 263
excess capacity, p. 267

oligopoly, p. 269
homogeneous oligopoly, p. 269
differentiated oligopoly, p. 269
strategic behaviour, p. 270
mutual interdependence, p. 270
interindustry competition, p. 271
import competition, p. 271

game theory model, p. 272
prisoner's dilemma, p. 273
collusion, p. 274
cartel, p. 278
tacit understanding, p. 279
price leadership, p. 280

:: QUESTIONS

1. How does monopolistic competition differ from perfect competition in its basic characteristics? From monopoly? Explain fully what product differentiation may involve. Explain how the entry of firms into its industry affects the demand curve facing a monopolistic competitor and how that, in turn, affects its economic profit. [**LO11.1**]

2. Compare the elasticity of a monopolistic competitor's demand with that of a perfectly competitive firm and a monopolist. Assuming identical long-run costs, compare graphically the prices and outputs that would result in the long run under perfect competition and under monopolistic competition. Contrast the two market structures in terms of productive and allocative efficiency. Explain: "Monopolistically competitive industries are characterized by too many firms, each of which produces too little." [**LO11.2**]

3. Explain the following statement: "Monopolistic competition is monopolistic up to the point at which consumers become willing to buy close substitute products and competitive beyond that point." [**LO11.2**]

4. "Competition in quality and service may be just as effective as price competition in giving buyers more for their money." Do you agree? Why? Explain why monopolistically competitive firms frequently prefer nonprice competition to price competition. [**LO11.2**]

5. Critically evaluate and explain the following statements: [**LO11.2**]

   a. In monopolistically competitive industries, economic profits are competed away in the long run; hence, there is no valid reason to criticize the performance and efficiency of such industries.

   b. In the long run, monopolistic competition leads to a monopolistic price but not to monopolistic profits.

6. Why do oligopolies exist? List five or six oligopolists whose products you own or regularly purchase. What distinguishes oligopoly from monopolistic competition? [**LO11.3**]

7. Answer the following questions, which relate to measures of concentration: [**LO11.3**]

   a. What is the meaning of a four-firm concentration ratio of 60 percent? 90 percent? What are the shortcomings

of concentration ratios as measures of monopoly power?

   b. Suppose that the five firms in industry A have annual sales of 30, 30, 20, 10, and 10 percent of total industry sales. For the five firms in industry B the figures are 60, 25, 5, 5, and 5 percent. Calculate the Herfindahl index for each industry and compare their likely competitiveness.

8. Explain the general meaning of the following payoff matrix for oligopolists X and Y. All profit figures are in thousands. [**LO11.4**]

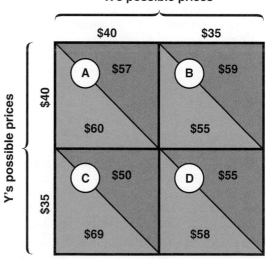

X's possible prices

   a. Use the payoff matrix to explain the mutual interdependence that characterizes oligopolistic industries.

   b. Assuming no collusion between C and D, what is the likely pricing outcome?

   c. In view of your answer to part (b), explain why price collusion is mutually profitable. Why might there be a temptation to cheat on the collusive agreement?

9. Why might price collusion occur in oligopolistic industries? Assess the economic desirability of collusive pricing.

What are the main obstacles to collusion? Speculate why price leadership is legal in Canada, whereas price fixing is not. [LO11.5]

10. Why is there so much advertising in monopolistic competition and oligopoly? How does such advertising help consumers and promote efficiency? Why might it be excessive at times? [LO11.6]

11. **(Advanced Analysis)** Construct a game theory matrix involving two firms and their decisions on high versus low advertising budgets and the effects of each decision on profits. Show a circumstance in which both firms select high advertising budgets even though both would be more profitable with low advertising budgets. Why won't they unilaterally cut their advertising budgets? [LO11.6]

:: PROBLEMS

1. Suppose that a small town has seven burger shops whose respective shares of the local hamburger market are (as percentages of all hamburgers sold): 23, 22, 18, 12, 11, 8, and 6 percent. What is the four-firm concentration ratio of the hamburger industry in this town? What is the Herfindahl index for the hamburger industry in this town? If the top three sellers combined to form a single firm, what would happen to the four-firm concentration ratio and to the Herfindahl index? [LO11.3]

2. Suppose that the most popular car dealer in your area sells 10 percent of all vehicles. If all other car dealers sell either the same number of vehicles or fewer, what is the largest value that the Herfindahl index could possibly take for car dealers in your area? In that same situation,

what would the four-firm concentration ratio be? [LO11.3]

3. Suppose that an oligopolistically competitive restaurant is currently serving 230 meals per day (the output where MR = MC). At that output level, ATC per meal is $10 and consumers are willing to pay $12 per meal. What is the size of this firm's profit or loss? Will there be entry or exit? Will this restaurant's demand curve shift left or right? In long-run equilibrium, suppose that this restaurant charges $11 per meal for 180 meals and that the marginal cost of the 180th meal is $8. What is the size of the firm's profit? Suppose that the allocatively efficient output level in long-run equilibrium is 200 meals. Is the deadweight loss for this firm greater than or less than $60? [LO11.3]

Appendix to Chapter 11

Additional Game Theory Terminology and Applications

We have seen that game theory is helpful in explaining mutual interdependence and strategic behaviour by oligopolists. This appendix provides additional oligopoly-based applications of game theory.

A11.1 A One-Time Game: Strategies and Equilibrium

Consider Figure A11-1, which lists strategies and outcomes for two fictitious producers of the computer memory chips referred to as DRAMs (Dynamic Random Access Memory circuits). Chipco is the single producer of these chips in Canada and Dramco is the only producer in China. Each firm has two alternative strategies: an international strategy in which it competes directly against the other firm in both countries; and a national strategy in which it confines its sales to its home country.

The game and payoff matrix shown in Figure A11-1 is a **one-time game** because the firms select their optimal strategy in a single time period without regard to possible interactions in subsequent time periods. The game is also a **simultaneous game,** because the firms choose their strategies at the same time, and a **positive-sum game**, a game in which the sum of the two firms' outcomes (here, profits) is positive. (In contrast, the net gain in a **zero-sum game** is zero because one firm's gain must equal the other firm's loss, and the net gain in a **negative-sum game** is

negative.) In some positive-sum games, both firms may have positive outcomes. That is the case in Figure A11-1.

To determine optimal strategies, Chipco looks across the two rows in the payoff matrix (green portion of cells in millions of dollars) and Dramco looks down the two columns (tan portion of cells). These payoffs indicate that both firms have a **dominant strategy**—an option that is better than any alternative option *regardless of what the other firm does.* To see this, notice that Chipco's international strategy will give it a higher profit than its national strategy—regardless of whether Dramco chooses to utilize an international or a national strategy. An international strategy will produce an $11 million profit for Chipco (green portion of cell A) if Dramco also uses an international strategy, while a national strategy will result in a $20 million profit for Chipco (green portion of cell B) if Dramco uses a national strategy. Chipco's possible $11 million and $20 million outcomes are clearly better than the $5 million (cell C)

FIGURE A11-1 One-Time Game

In this single-period, positive-sum game, Chipco's international strategy is its dominant strategy—the alternative that is superior to any other strategy regardless of whatever Dramco does. Similarly, Dramco's international strategy is also its dominant strategy. With both firms choosing international strategies, the outcome of the game is cell A, where each firm receives an $11 million profit. Cell A is a Nash equilibrium because neither firm will independently want to move away from it given the other firm's strategy.

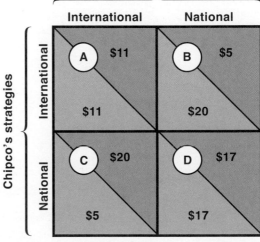

and $17 million (cell D) outcomes it could receive if it chose to pursue a national strategy. Chipco's international strategy is, consequently, its dominant strategy. Using similar logic, Dramco also concludes that its international strategy is its dominant strategy.

In this particular case, the outcome (cell A) of the two dominant strategies is the game's **Nash equilibrium**—an outcome from which neither rival wants to deviate.[1] At the Nash equilibrium, both rivals see their current strategy as optimal *given the other firm's strategic choice.* The Nash equilibrium is the only outcome in the payoff matrix in Figure A11-1 that, once achieved, is stable and therefore will persist.[2]

Credible and Empty Threats

In looking for optimal strategies, Chipco and Dramco both note that they could increase their profit from $11 million to $17 million if they could agree to jointly pursue national strategies (cell D) instead of independently pursuing international strategies (cell A). Presumably the national strategies would leave the firms as pure monopolists in their domestic economies, with each able to set higher prices and obtain greater profits as a result. But if this territorial agreement were put in place, both firms would have an incentive to cheat on the agreement by secretly selling DRAMs in each other's countries. That would temporarily move the game to either cell B or cell C. Once discovered, however, such cheating would undermine the territorial agreement and return the game to the Nash equilibrium (cell A).

Now let's add a new twist—a credible threat—to the game shown in Figure A11-1. A **credible threat** is a statement of coercion (a threat!) that is believable by the other firm. Suppose that Chipco is the low-cost producer of DRAMs because of its superior technology. Also, suppose that Chipco approaches Dramco saying that Chipco intends to use its national strategy and expects Dramco to do the same. If Dramco decides against the national strategy or agrees to the strategy and then later cheats on the agreement, Chipco will immediately drop its price to an ultra-low level equal to its average total cost (ATC). Both firms know that Chipco's ATC price is below Dramco's ATC. Although Chipco will see its economic profit fall to zero, Dramco will suffer an economic loss and possibly go out of business.

If Chipco's threat is credible, the two firms represented in Figure A11-1 will abandon the Nash equilibrium (cell A) to deploy their national strategies and achieve highly profitable cell D. In game theory, credible threats such as this can help establish and maintain collusive agreements. A strong "enforcer" can help prevent cheating and maintain the group discipline needed for cartels, price-fixing conspiracies, and territorial understandings to successfully generate high profits.

But credible threats are difficult to achieve in the actual economy. For example, Dramco might rightly wonder why Chipco had not previously driven it out of business through an ultra-low price strategy. Is Chipco fearful of the Canadian Competition Bureau?

If Dramco does not wish to participate in the proposed scheme, it might counter Chipco's threat with its own: Forget that you ever talked to us and we will not take this illegal "offer" to the Competition Bureau. Dramco can make this threat because strict laws are in place against attempts to restrain trade through price fixing and territorial agreements.

So Dramco may view Chipco's threat as simply an **empty threat**—a statement of coercion that is not believable by the threatened firm. If so, the Nash equilibrium will prevail, with both firms pursuing an international strategy.

Repeated Games and Reciprocity Strategies

The Chipco–Dramco game was a one-time game, but many strategic situations are repeated by the same oligopolists over and over. For example, Coca-Cola and Pepsi face mutual interdependence on pricing, advertising, and product development year after year, decade after decade. The same is true for Boeing and Airbus, Walmart and Target, Toyota and General Motors, Labatt and Molson, Nike and Adidas, and numerous other dominant pairs.

In a **repeated game**—a game that recurs more than once— the optimal strategy may be to cooperate and restrain oneself from competing as hard as possible so long as the other firm reciprocates by also not competing as hard as possible.[3] To see how this works, consider two hypothetical producers of soft drinks: 2Cool and ThirstQ. If 2Cool competes hard with ThirstQ in today's situation, in which ThirstQ would like 2Cool to take things easy, ThirstQ will most like retaliate against 2Cool in any subsequent situation where the circumstances are reversed. In contrast, if ThirstQ cooperates with 2Cool in game 1, ThirstQ can expect 2Cool to reciprocate in game 2 of their repeated interaction. Both firms know full well the negative long-run consequences of ever refusing to cooperate. So the cooperation continues, not only in game 2, but in games 3, 4, 5, and beyond.

Figure A11-2 shows side-by-side payoff matrixes for the two games. In Figure A11-2a, 2Cool and ThirstQ face a situation in which 2Cool is introducing a new cola called Cool

[1] The Nash equilibrium is named for its discoverer, John F. Nash. Nash's life and Nobel Prize are the subject of the motion picture *A Beautiful Mind,* produced by Ron Howard and starring Russell Crowe.

[2] Dominant strategies in games are not required for Nash equilibriums to exist.

[3] We are assuming either an infinitely repeated game or a game of unknown time-horizon. Games with a known ending date undermine reciprocity strategies.

FIGURE A11-2   **A Repeated Game with Reciprocity**

Panel (a): In the payoff matrix to the left, 2Cool introduces its new Cool Cola with a large promotional advertising budget, but its rival ThirstQ maintains its normal advertising budget even though it could counter 2Cool with a large advertising budget of its own and drive the outcome from cell B to cell A. ThirstQ forgoes this $2 million of extra profit because it knows that it will soon be introducing its own new product (Quench It). Panel (b): In the payoff matrix to the right, ThirstQ introduces Quench It with a large promotional advertising budget. Cool2 reciprocates ThirstQ's earlier accommodation by not matching ThirstQ's promotional advertising budget and instead allowing the outcome of the repeated game to be cell C. The profit of both 2Cool and ThirstQ therefore is larger over the two periods than if each firm had aggressively countered the other's single-period strategy.

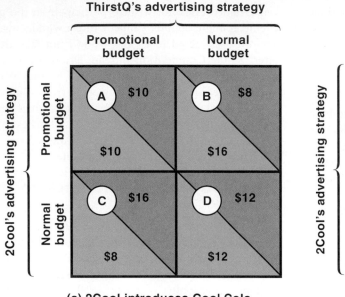

(a) 2Cool introduces Cool Cola

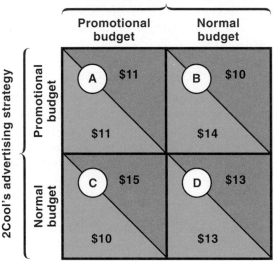

(b) ThirstQ's introduces Quench It

Cola and has two advertising options: a high promotional budget to introduce the new product and a normal advertising budget. ThirstQ has the same two options: a high promotional budget to try to counter 2Cool's product introduction and a normal advertising budget.

The analysis is now familiar to you, so we will speed the pace. The dominant strategies for both firms are their large promotional advertising budgets, and the Nash equilibrium is cell A. Both firms could do better at cell D if each agreed to use normal advertising budgets. But 2Cool could do better still. It could achieve the $16 million of profit in cell B, but only if ThirstQ holds its advertising budget to its normal level during the introduction of Cool Cola.

ThirstQ might voluntarily do just that! It knows that game 2 (Figure A11-2b) is forthcoming, in which it will be introducing its new product, Quench It. By leaving its advertising budget at its normal level during 2Cool's introduction of Cool Cola, and thereby sacrificing profit of $2 million (= $10 million in cell A – $8 million in cell B), it can expect ThirstQ to reciprocate in the subsequent game in which it introduces Quench It. Without formally colluding—and risking antitrust penalties—game 1 ends at cell B and repeated game 2 ends at

cell C. Using reciprocity, 2Cool's total profit of $26 million (= $16 million in game 1 + $10 million in game 2) exceeds the $21 million (= $10 million + $11 million) it would have earned without the reciprocity. ThirstQ similarly benefits. To check your understanding, confirm this fact using the numbers in the two matrixes.

First-Mover Advantages and Preemption of Entry

In the games we have highlighted thus far the two firms simultaneously select their optimal strategies. But in some actual economic circumstances, firms apply strategies sequentially: One firm moves first and commits to a strategy to which a rival firm must subsequently respond. In such a **sequential game**, the final outcome may depend critically upon which firm moves first since the first mover may have the opportunity to establish a Nash equilibrium that works in its favour.

Consider Figure A11-3, which identifies a zero-sum game in which two large retailers—let's call them Big Box and Huge Box—are each considering building a large retail store in a small rural city. As indicated in the figure, each firm has two strategies:

FIGURE A11-3　A First-Mover Advantage and the Preemption of Entry

In this game in which strategies are pursued sequentially, the firm that moves first can take advantage of the particular situation represented in which only a single firm can exist profitably in some geographical market. Here, we suppose that Big Box moves first with its "build" strategy to achieve the $12 million profit outcome in cell C. Huge Box then will find that it will lose money if it also builds in this market because that will result in a $5 million loss, as shown in cell A.

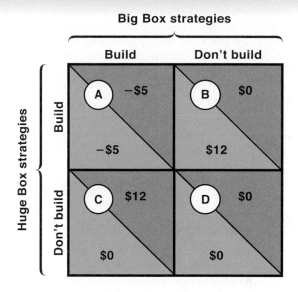

Big Box strategies

	Build	Don't build
Build	A −$5 / −$5	B $0 / $12
Don't build	C $12 / $0	D $0 / $0

Huge Box strategies

"Build" or "Don't build." The payoff matrix reflects that the city is not large enough to support two big box retailers profitably. If both retailers simultaneously build, the outcome will be cell A and each firm will lose $5 million. If neither firm builds the outcome will be cell D with both firms securing zero profit. If only Big Box builds, the outcome will be cell B and Big Box will profit handsomely at $12 million. If Huge Box builds but Big Box stays out, the outcome will be cell C and Huge Box will secure the $12 million profit. Either cell B or cell C is the possible Nash equilibrium. At either cell, both firms will have selected their best option in view of the strategy taken by the other firm.

The payoff matrix in Figure A11-3 clearly reveals that whoever builds first will preempt the other retailer from entering the market. An extremely large **first-mover advantage** exists in this particular game. Suppose that a well-thought-out strategy and adequate financing leave Big Box better prepared than Huge Box to move quickly to build a large retail store in this city. By exploiting its first-mover advantage, Big Box preempts Huge Box's entry to this market.

Many actual firms have used variations of this first-mover strategy to a greater or lesser extent to preempt major rivals, or at least greatly slow their entry. Examples are Canadian Tire, The Bay, Walmart, Home Depot, Costco, Starbucks, and many more. The strategy is highly risky, however, because it requires the commitment of huge amounts of investment funds to saturate the market and preclude entry by other firms. Also, to be the first mover in places that are being transformed from rural land into urban areas, firms may need to build their stores many months prior to the time when the area in question becomes developed enough to provide significant business. That may mean losses until the market grows sufficiently for profitability. Some firms like Walmart have become huge, profitable international enterprises by using a first-mover strategy. Other firms, such as Krispy Kreme Donuts, have lost millions of dollars because their extremely rapid expansion turned out to be unprofitable in many of their outlets when the expected customers never materialized.

APPENDIX　Summary

- Positive-sum games are games in which the payoffs to the firms sum to a positive number; zero-sum games are games in which the payoffs sum to zero; and negative-sum games are games in which the payoffs sum to less than zero. Positive-sum games allow for "win–win" opportunities, whereas zero-sum games always feature "I win/You lose" outcomes. Games can be either one-time games or repeated games. Decisions in games may be made either simultaneously or sequentially.

- When two firms are playing a strategic game, a firm is said to have a dominant strategy if there is an option that leads to better outcomes than all other options regardless of what the other firm does. Not all games have dominant strategies. The Nash equilibrium is an outcome from which neither firm wants to deviate because both firms see their current strategy as optimal given the other firm's chosen strategy. The Nash equilibrium is stable and persistent. Attempts by the firms to rig games to some other outcome are difficult to accomplish and maintain, although credible threats can sometimes work. In contrast, empty threats accomplish nothing and leave the outcome at the Nash equilibrium.

- Reciprocity can improve outcomes for firms participating in repeated games. In such games, one firm avoids taking advantage of the other firm because it knows that the other firm can take advantage of it in subsequent games. Therefore, the profits of the firms are higher over time than they would be without reciprocity.

- Two possible Nash equilibriums can exist in sequential games with first-mover advantages; which one occurs depends on which firm moves first, since that firm can preempt the other firm making it unprofitable for the other to match the move. Several real-world firms have successfully used first-mover advantages to saturate markets and preempt entry by rivals.

APPENDIX Terms and Concepts

one-time game A game in which firms select their optimal strategy in a single time period without regard to possible interactions in subsequent time periods. (p. 288)

simultaneous game A game in which both parties choose their strategies and execute them at the same time. (p. 288)

positive-sum game A game in which the gains (+) and losses (−) add up to more than zero. (p. 288)

zero-sum game A game in which the gains (+) and losses (−) add up to zero. (p. 288)

negative-sum game A game in which the gains (+) and losses (−) add up to some amount less than zero. (p. 288)

dominant strategy In game theory, an option that is better than any alternative option regardless of what the other firm does. (p. 288)

Nash equilibrium In game theory, an outcome from which neither firm wants to deviate; the outcome that once achieved is stable and therefore lasting. (p. 289)

credible threat A statement of harmful intent by one party that the other party views as believable. (p. 289)

empty threat A statement of harmful intent that is easily dismissed by the second party because the threat is not viewed as believable. (p. 289)

repeated game A game that is played again sometime after the previous game ends. (p. 289)

sequential game A game in which the parties make their moves in turn, with one party making the first move, followed by the other party making the next move, and so on. (p. 290)

first-mover advantage In game theory, the benefit obtained by the party that moves first in a sequential game. (p. 291)

APPENDIX Questions

1. Is the game shown in Figure 11-6 a zero-sum game or a positive-sum game? How can you tell? Are there dominant strategies in this game? If so, what are they? What cell represents a Nash equilibrium and why? Explain why it is so difficult for Uptown and RareAir to achieve and maintain a more favourable cell than the Nash equilibrium in this single-period pricing game. **[LOA11.1]**

2. Refer to the payoff matrix in Question 8 at the end of the chapter. First, assume this is a one-time game. Explain how the $60/$57 outcome might be achieved through a credible threat. Next, assume this is a repeated game, not a one-time game, such that the interaction between the two firms occurs indefinitely. Why might collusion with a credible threat not be necessary to achieve the $60/$57 outcome? **[LOA11.1]**

APPENDIX   Problems

1. Consider a "punishment" variation of the two-firm oligopoly situation shown in Figure 11-6 in the chapter (not in this appendix). Suppose that if one firm sets a low price while the other sets a high price, then the firm setting the high price can fine the firm setting the low price. Suppose that whenever a fine is imposed, X dollars are taken from the low-price firm and given to the high-price firm. What is the smallest amount that the fine X can be such that both firms will want to always set the high price?   [**LOA11.1**]

2. Consider whether the promises and threats made toward each other by duopolists and oligopolists are always credible (believable). Look back at Figure 11-3 in the chapter (not in this appendix). Imagine that the two firms will play this game twice in sequence and that each firm claims the following policy. Each says that if both it and the other firm choose the high price in the first game, then it will also choose the high price in the second game

(as a reward to the other firm for cooperating in the first game).   [**LOA11.1**]

   a. As a first step toward thinking about whether this policy is credible, consider the situation facing both firms in the second game. If each firm bases its decision on what to do in the second game entirely on the payouts facing the firms in the second game, which strategy will each firm choose in the second game?

   b. Now move backward in time one step. Imagine that it is the start of the first game and each firm must decide what to do during the first game. Given your answer to part a, is the publicly stated policy credible? (Hint: No matter what happens in the first game, what will both firms do in the second game?)

   c. Given your answers to a and b, what strategy will each firm choose in the first game?

Competition Policy and Regulation

AFTER READING THIS CHAPTER, YOU SHOULD BE ABLE TO:

12.1 Describe what industrial concentration is, and how governments combat it.

12.2 Discuss industrial regulation, and how governments deal with it.

12.3 Discuss the nature of social regulation, and what its goals are.

In this chapter we look at three sets of government policies toward business: competition policy, industrial regulation, and social regulation. Competition policy consists of the laws and government actions designed to prevent monopoly and promote competition. Industrial regulation pertains to government regulation of firms' prices (or rates) within selected industries. Social regulation is government regulation of the conditions under which goods are produced, the physical characteristics of goods, and the impact of the production and consumption of goods on society.

12.1 Industrial Concentration ::

In Chapter 10 we developed and applied a strict definition of monopoly. A *monopoly* is a one-firm industry—a unique product is being produced entirely by a single firm and entry to the industry is totally blocked.

In this chapter we will use the term *industrial concentration* to include monopoly and markets in which much potential monopoly power exists. Industrial concentration occurs whenever a single firm or a small number of firms control the major portion of an industry's output. One, two, or three firms dominate, potentially resulting in higher-than-competitive prices and profits. This definition, which is closer to how the general public understands the monopoly problem, includes many industries we have previously designated as oligopolies.

Industrial concentration in this chapter thus refers to industries in which firms are large in absolute terms and in relation to the total market. Examples in Canada are the wireless mobile communications industry, in which Research In Motion dominates the market; the automobile industry, where General Motors of Canada and Ford of Canada are still dominant (although in recent years Honda and Toyota, both Japanese firms with manufacturing facilities in Ontario, have been catching up); the petro-chemical industry, dominated by Suncor, Imperial Oil (Exxon), and Shell Canada; the aluminum industry, where industrial giant Rio Tinto Alcan reigns supreme; and the steel industry, where the two large producers, Dofasco and U.S. Steel Canada, command the lion's share of the market.

THE ROLE OF GOVERNMENTS

competition policy
The laws and government actions designed to prevent monopoly and promote competition.

Competition Policy

The underlying purpose of **competition policy** is to prevent industrial concentration or monopolization, to promote competition, and to achieve allocative efficiency. Although all economists would agree that these are praiseworthy goals, conflicting opinion exists about the effectiveness of Canadian competition law.

The main economic case against monopoly is familiar to you from Chapter 10. Monopolists produce less output and charge higher prices than if their industries were competitive. With perfect competition, each competitive firm maximizes profit by producing the output level at which $P = MC$. That output level generates allocative efficiency and this equality represents an efficient allocation of resources because P measures the marginal benefit to society of an extra unit of output, while marginal cost MC reflects the cost of an extra unit. When $P = MC$, society cannot gain by producing one more or one fewer unit of the product. In contrast, a monopolist maximizes profit by producing the lower output level at which marginal revenue (rather than price) equals marginal cost. At this MR = MC point, price exceeds marginal cost, meaning that society would obtain more benefit than it would incur cost by producing extra units. There is an underallocation of resources to the monopolized product, and so the economic well-being of society is less than it would be with greater competition.

But an efficiency loss isn't the only consequence of the monopolist's higher-than-competitive price. The higher price also transfers income from consumers to the monopolist. This transfer causes significant resentment because it results purely from the monopolist's ability to restrict output and cannot be justified on the basis of increased production costs. Consumers consequently express their ire to elected officials to "do something about the situation."

Responding to that pressure, government officials concluded in the late 1800s and early 1900s that monopolized industries lacked enough of the beneficial market forces that in competitive industries help to protect consumers, achieve fair competition, and achieve allocative efficiency. So the government instituted two alternative means of control as substitutes for, or supplements to, market forces:

- *Regulatory Agencies* In the few markets where the nature of the product or technology creates a *natural monopoly*, the government established public regulatory agencies to control such firms.

- *Competition Law* In most other markets, government control took the form of laws designed to inhibit or prevent the growth of monopoly.

We will shortly review the anticombines legislation that constitutes the basic law of the land with respect to corporate size and concentration. Before we do, let's examine merger types.

Merger Types

horizontal merger
A merger between two competitors selling similar products in the same market.

Mergers of firms are one of the main causes of industrial concentration. There are three basic types of mergers. A **horizontal merger** occurs between two competitors selling similar products in the same market. Examples of horizontal mergers would be the buyout of Eaton's by Sears, Air Canada's merger with Canadian Airlines, and Best Buy's merger with Future Shop. A

vertical merger
The merger of firms engaged in different stages of the production process of a final product.

conglomerate merger
The merger of a firm in one industry with a firm in another industry or region.

vertical merger occurs between firms at different stages of the production process. Vertical mergers involve firms having buyer–seller relationships. Examples of mergers of this type are PepsiCo's mergers with Pizza Hut, Taco Bell, and Kentucky Fried Chicken; PepsiCo supplies soft drinks to each of these fast-food outlets. A **conglomerate merger** is officially defined as any merger that is not horizontal or vertical; in general, it is the combination of firms in different industries or firms operating in different geographical areas. Conglomerate mergers can extend the line of products sold, or combine totally unrelated companies. An example of a conglomerate is Power Corporation of Canada, headquartered in Montreal. Among its holdings are Great-West Life Co. Inc., a life insurance subsidiary, and Power Broadcast Inc., a subsidiary that owns newspapers and radio stations. In Europe, Power Corporation has investments in major communications, industrial, energy, utility, financial services, and food companies.

Competition Law

The basis of competition policy (sometimes referred to as *anticombines* policy) in Canada is the *Competition Act,* passed in 1986. It replaced the *Combines Investigation Act,* which had been in force in different forms since 1910. The *Competition Act* is administered and enforced by the federal Competition Bureau, which promotes and maintains fair competition in Canada. One of the main innovations of the *Competition Act* was that uncompetitive market structures (monopoly and oligopoly) and mergers, previously adjudicated under criminal law, came under the jurisdiction of civil law, making it easier to prosecute mergers and monopolies not deemed to be in the public interest. Price fixing, however, is still handled by the regular courts, where the standard of evidence is "beyond a reasonable doubt." Those sections of the *Competition Act* now under the jurisdiction of civil law are adjudicated by the federal **Competition Tribunal.** The tribunal is made up of judges of the Federal Court and laypersons, with a judge as chairperson. It must be emphasized that the *Competition Act* does not directly prohibit monopoly: a firm can legally have 100 percent of the market as long as it does not abuse its monopoly position.

Competition Tribunal
A government body adjudicating under a civil law framework that permits the issuing of remedial orders to restore and maintain competition in the market.

Merger Guidelines

The federal government has established merger guidelines based on the concentration ratio. Recall from Chapter 12 that the concentration ratio reveals the percentage of total output produced and sold by an industry's four largest firms (sometimes referred to as the CR4). The Competition Bureau's main concern in the case of a *horizontal merger* is unilateral market power of the new merged entity as well as the combined market power of the four largest firms in the sector. In its assessment of the degree of market power in an industry in which there has been a merger, the Competition Bureau considers such factors as economies of scale created by the new merged firm, the degree of foreign competition, and ease of entry of new firms. Furthermore, horizontal mergers are usually allowed if one of the merging firms is suffering major continuing losses (this is one reason why Air Canada was allowed to acquire Canadian Airlines in 1999). Most *vertical mergers* escape anticombines prosecution because they do not substantially lessen competition in either of the two markets. However, a vertical merger between large firms in a highly concentrated industry may be challenged. *Conglomerate mergers* are generally permitted. If an auto manufacturer acquires a blue jean producer no anticombines action is likely, since neither firm has increased its own market share as a result.

PRICE FIXING

Price fixing among firms is treated strictly. Evidence of price fixing, even by small firms, will bring the action of the Competition Tribunal, as will other collusive activities such as scheming to rig bids on government contracts or dividing up sales in a market. To gain a conviction, the government or other party making the charge need show only that there was a conspiracy to fix prices, rig bids, or divide up markets, not that the conspiracy succeeded or caused serious damage to other parties.

PRICE DISCRIMINATION

Price discrimination is a common business practice that rarely reduces competition and therefore is rarely challenged by the Competition Tribunal. The exception occurs when a firm engages in price discrimination as part of a strategy to block entry or drive out competitors.

TYING CONTRACTS

tying contract
A requirement imposed by a seller that a buyer purchase another (or other) of its products as a condition for buying a desired product.

The Competition Tribunal strictly enforces the prohibition of tying contracts, particularly when practised by dominant firms. A **tying contract** is a requirement imposed by a seller that a buyer purchase another (or other) of its products as a condition for buying a desired product.

RECENT CASES

The *Competition Act* is designed to achieve economic efficiency and to be adaptable to changing market conditions and international trade. Only those mergers resulting in an unacceptable lessening of competition can be prohibited or modified by the competition tribunal. Mergers that result in efficiency gains through capturing economies of scale have generally been allowed. For example, in April 2003, the Competition Bureau reported it would not challenge the merger of certain assets of the coal businesses of Fording Inc., Teck Cominco Ltd., Luscar Ltd., and Consol Energy Inc., in the thermal coal, metallurgical coal, and coal terminal port businesses in Canada.

The Competition Bureau recommended against chartered bank mergers in 1998, when the Royal Bank of Canada and the Bank of Montreal announced their intention to merge. Soon after, the Canadian Imperial Bank of Commerce and the Toronto-Dominion Bank also decided to merge. The banks argued that they needed to merge to capture economies of scale and be able to compete internationally. The Competition Bureau was not convinced by the banks' argument, citing fears that competition would be greatly curtailed in smaller centres for both consumers and small- and medium-sized firms. The Bureau noted that even if more foreign banks were allowed to compete in the Canadian market, the large established network of branches of the Canadian banks provided a large barrier to entry for any new competitor. The Royal Bank of Canada and the Bank of Montreal were, however, successful in merging the processing of their credit card operations.

In May 2005 the Competition Bureau announced that Mitsubishi Corporation, Japan's largest trading company, pleaded guilty to charges of attempting to maintain the international price of graphite electrodes, used mainly in electric arc furnace steel production. Mitsubishi Corporation was fined $1,000,000 by the Federal Court of Canada under the price maintenance provision of the Act. Earlier in 2005 Robert J. Hart and Company, with headquarters in the United Kingdom, was fined $50,000 in the same graphite electrodes price maintenance scheme. In 2008 and 2010 a total of 38 individuals and 14 companies were accused of fixing the price of gas at the pumps in Victoriaville, Thetford Mines, Magog, and Sherbrooke, all in the province of Quebec. Fines totalling almost $3 million were imposed and some of the individuals charged received prison sentences.

The antitrust agency for the European Union (EU) has generally been more aggressive than Canada in prosecuting monopolists. For example, in 2004 the EU fined Microsoft $600 million for monopolization and required it to share its computer coding with other firms that supplied Windows applications (such as media players). The purpose of the code-sharing requirement was to enable competitors to compete on an equal footing against Microsoft's own application software. Microsoft was fined a further $1.3 billion by the EU in 2008 for failing to quickly and fully comply with the 2004 remedy ordering Microsoft to share its computer code.

The U.S. has also prosecuted several international price fixing schemes. For example, between 2008 and 2010, five manufacturers of liquid crystal displays—LG, Sharp, Hitachi, Chi Mei Optoelectronics, and Chunghwa Picture Tubes—were fined a total of over $860 million by the U.S. Justice Department for fixing the prices of the displays they sold to computer maker Dell Inc. In 2009, three international cargo airlines—Cargolux of Luxembourg, Nippon Cargo of Japan, and Asiana Airlines of South Korea—were fined $214 million by the U.S. Justice Department for conspiring to fix international airline cargo rates.

CONSIDER THIS :: Bio-Insecticide and Insect Control and Market Power in Canada

The Competition Bureau began an investigation of two companies—GDG Environnement Ltée and La Société générale de foresterie Sylvico Inc.—in 2007 to determine if these two companies had arranged with competitors to maintain their market share in the supply of bio-insecticides and insect control services by colluding on bids or tenders. The investigation concluded that these two Quebec-based companies lessened competition and frustrated the competitive tendering process. In 2008 the Superior Court of Quebec used the result of the Bureau's investigation as evidence in an order asking the two companies and their CEOs to comply with the conspiracy and bid-rigging provisions of the *Competition Act*. Both firms were made to notify all their employees to comply with the court order to stop efforts to reduce competition in the bidding process, otherwise the employees could be disciplined or even dismissed.

Vigilance by the Competition Bureau and prosecution of lawbreakers prompts firms to think carefully before engaging in anti-competitive activities that lead to higher prices for Canadian consumers.

Source: Adapted from Competition Bureau Canada, http://www.competitionbureau.gc.ca/eic/site/cb-bc.nsf/eng/ 02645.html.

ISSUES OF ENFORCEMENT: TRADEOFFS AMONG GOALS

Promoting competition is only one of society's goals, and strict enforcement of competition laws may sometimes conflict with some other goal.

Occasionally, new technologies combine to create new products and services. A current example is the meshing of computer and communications technologies relating to the Internet. This interactive network has improved the communications capabilities of households, businesses, and governments across the globe.

connect
ORIGIN OF THE IDEA 12.1
Creative Destruction

Should the government strictly enforce competition laws to block some of those mergers, specifically ones that produce dominant firms and threaten to reduce competition? Or should the government temporarily suspend competition rules to encourage the restructuring of industries and speed the expansion of this new technology? Hastening the advance of Internet-related technologies might also increase Canadian exports of electronic services.

Each of these enforcement tradeoffs, by itself, triggers controversy. Some argue that the gains from competition policy must be weighed against the effects of the policy on conflicting objectives. Others contend that selective enforcement of competition laws dangerously interferes with the market process. Obviously, different policymakers and different administrations may view such considerations and tradeoffs differently.

QUICK REVIEW

- Industrial concentration exists where a single firm or a small number of firms control the major portion of an industry's output.

- Three types of mergers can occur: horizontal, vertical, and conglomerate.

- The *Competition Act,* passed in 1986, allows mergers that bring about significant efficiency gains.

12.2 Industrial Regulation

THE ROLE OF GOVERNMENTS

Competition policy assumes that society will benefit if monopoly is prevented from evolving or if it is dissolved where it already exists. We now return to the special situation, first introduced in Chapter 6, in which an economic reason exists for an industry to be a monopoly.

Natural Monopoly

A *natural monopoly* exists when economies of scale are so extensive that a single firm can supply the entire market at a lower unit cost than could a number of competing firms. Clear-cut circumstances of natural monopoly are relatively rare, but such conditions exist for many public utilities, such as local electricity and water. As we discussed in Chapter 10, large-scale operations are necessary in some cases to obtain low unit costs and a low product price. Where natural monopoly exists, competition does not enhance efficiency. If the market were divided among many producers, economies of scale would not be achieved and unit costs and prices would increase.

Two possible alternatives exist for promoting better economic outcomes where natural monopoly occurs. One is public ownership, and the other is public regulation. *Public ownership* or some approximation of it has been established in a few instances, such as Canada Post, water supply systems, and garbage collection at the local level. But *public regulation,* or what economists call industrial regulation, has been the preferred option in Canada. In this type of regulation, government commissions regulate the prices (usually called rates) charged by natural monopolists so as to prevent these from taking advantage of their market power to increase prices not warranted by their costs.

public interest theory of regulation
The theory that industrial regulation is necessary to keep a natural monopoly from charging monopoly prices and thus harming consumers and society.

The economic objective of industrial regulation is reflected in the **public interest theory of regulation,** where industrial regulation is necessary to keep a natural monopoly from charging monopoly prices and thus harming consumers and society. The goal of such regulation is to garner for society at least part of the cost reductions associated with natural monopoly while avoiding the restrictions of output and high prices that come with unregulated monopoly. If competition is impractical, society should allow or even encourage a monopoly but regulate its prices. Regulation should then be structured so that ratepayers benefit from the economies of scale—the lower per-unit costs—that natural monopolists are able to achieve.

In practice, regulators seek to establish rates that will cover production costs and yield a fair return to the enterprise. The goal is to set price equal to average total cost so that the regulated firm receives a normal profit, as described in Chapter 10's section 10.5, Regulated Monopoly. In particular, you should carefully review Figure 10-9.

Problems with Industrial Regulation

There is considerable disagreement on the effectiveness of industrial regulation. Let's examine two criticisms.

COSTS AND INEFFICIENCY

An unregulated firm has a strong incentive to reduce its costs at each level of output, because that will increase its profit. The regulatory commission, however, confines the regulated firm to a normal profit or a fair return on the value of its assets. If a regulated firm lowers its operating costs, the rising profit eventually will lead the regulatory commission to require the firm to lower its rates and return its profits to normal. The regulated firm, therefore, has no incentive to reduce its operating costs.

Worse yet, higher costs do not result in lower profit. Because the regulatory commissions must allow the public utility a fair return, the regulated monopolist can simply pass higher production costs to consumers by charging higher rates. A regulated firm may reason that it might as well have high salaries for its workers, luxurious working conditions for management, and the like, since the return is the same in percentage terms whether costs are minimized or not. So, although a natural monopoly reduces costs through economies of scale, industrial regulation fosters considerable X-inefficiency (refer to Figure 10-7). Because of the absence of competition, the potential cost savings from natural monopoly may never actually materialize.

PERPETUATING MONOPOLY

A second general problem with industrial regulation is that it sometimes perpetuates monopoly long after the conditions of natural monopoly have ended.

Technological change often creates the potential for competition in all or at least some portions of the regulated industry, such as when trucks began competing with railroads, transmission of voice and data by microwave and satellites began competing with transmission over telephone wires, satellite television began competing with cable television, and cellphones began competing with regular phones. But, spurred by the firms they regulate and believing that the regulated firms are natural monopolies, commissions often protect the regulated firms from new competition by either blocking entry or extending regulation to competitors. The rationale usually is that the competitors simply want to "skim the cream" from selected highly profitable portions of the regulated industry but do not want to offer the universal service required of the regulated firm. By losing the highly profitable portion of their business, the regulated firms would have to increase rates for services that do not pay their own way to continue to receive a fair rate of return on their assets.

But spurred by the firms they regulate, commissions often protect the regulated firms from new competition by either blocking entry or extending regulation to competitors. Industrial regulation therefore may perpetuate a monopoly that is no longer a natural monopoly and would otherwise erode. If so, then the regulated prices may be higher than they would be with competition. The beneficiaries of outdated regulations are the regulated firms, their employees, and perhaps consumers of some services. The losers are all other consumers and the potential entrants.

Legal Cartel Theory

legal cartel theory of regulation
The hypothesis that some industries seek regulation or want to maintain regulation so that they may form a legal cartel.

The regulation of potentially competitive industries has produced the **legal cartel theory of regulation.** In place of socially minded officials forcing regulation on natural monopolies to protect consumers, holders of this view see practical politicians as supplying regulation to local, regional, and national firms that fear the impact of competition on their profits or even on their long-term survival. These firms desire regulation because it yields a legal monopoly that can guarantee a profit. Specifically, the regulatory commission performs such functions as blocking entry, or, where there are several firms, the commission divides up the market much like an illegal cartel (for example, before airline deregulation, the federal government assigned routes to specific airlines). The commission may also restrict potential competition by enlarging the "cartel."

Private cartels are illegal, unstable, and often break down, and the special attraction of a government-sponsored cartel under the guise of regulation is that it endures. The legal cartel theory of regulation suggests that regulation results from the rent-seeking activities of private firms and the desire of politicians to be responsive.

Occupational licensing is a labour-market application of the legal cartel theory. Certain occupational groups—dentists, barbers, hairstylists, dietitians, lawyers—demand stringent licensing on the grounds that it protects the public from charlatans and quacks, but skeptics say the real reason may be to limit entry into the occupational group so that practitioners can receive monopoly incomes.

Deregulation

Beginning in the 1970s, the legal cartel theory, evidence of inefficiency in regulated industries, and the contention that the government was regulating potentially competitive industries all contributed to a wave of deregulation. Since then, Parliament and most provincial legislatures have passed legislation that has deregulated in varying degrees the airline, trucking, banking, railroad, natural gas, electricity, and television broadcasting industries. Deregulation has also occurred in the telecommunications industry. Bell Canada now competes with other carriers, such as Rogers Home Phone, in the local and long-distance markets. Bell Canada also competes with cellular companies, such as Telus. Deregulation in the 1970s and 1980s was one of the most extensive experiments in economic policy to take place during the past 50 years.

The overwhelming consensus among economists is that deregulation has produced large net benefits for consumers and society. Most of the gains from deregulation have occurred in three industries: airlines, railroads, and trucking. Airfares (adjusted for inflation) have declined by about one-third, and airline safety has improved. Railroad and trucking freight rates (again, adjusted for inflation) have dropped by about one-half. Significant efficiency gains have occurred in long-distance telecommunications, and slight efficiency gains have been made in cable television, stock brokerage services, and the natural gas industry. Deregulation has unleashed a wave of technological advances that have resulted in such new and improved products and services as fax machines, cellphones, fibre-optic cable, microwave systems in communications, and the Internet.

The success of past deregulation has led to further calls for deregulation. The latest industry to begin the deregulation process is electricity, led by Alberta and Ontario. Deregulation is now occurring at the wholesale level, where firms are free to build generating facilities and sell electricity at market prices.

However, the financial crisis that spread from the U.S. to most economies around the world has many questioning the deregulation of the financial industry in recent decades. As a consequence, in many countries, including Canada, governments and central banks are taking a closer look at their financial sectors to ensure that financial entities do not take on excessive risk and put regulations in place to minimize contagion in the event of financial problems in one of the major economies, such as the U.S. Recent sovereign debt problems in some of the European economies, which has put at risk some large European banks, has further strengthened the view that suitable regulations of the financial sector are needed.

QUICK REVIEW

- Natural monopoly occurs where economies of scale are so extensive that only a single firm can produce the product at minimum average total cost.

- The public interest theory of regulation says that government must regulate natural monopolies to prevent abuses arising from monopoly power. Regulated firms, however, have less incentive than competitive firms to reduce costs; that is, regulated firms tend to be X-inefficient.

- The legal cartel theory of regulation suggests that some firms seek government regulation to reduce price competition and ensure stable profits.

- Deregulation initiated by government in the past three decades has yielded large annual efficiency gains for society.

12.3 Social Regulation

THE ROLE OF GOVERNMENTS

social regulation
Government regulation of the conditions under which goods are produced, the physical characteristics of goods, and the impact of the production on society.

The industrial regulation discussed in the preceding section has focused on the regulation of prices (or rates) in natural monopolies. But in the early 1960s, a new type of regulation began to emerge. A concept known as **social regulation** is concerned with the conditions under which goods and services are produced, the impact of production on society, and the physical qualities of the goods themselves.

Distinguishing Features

Social regulation differs from industrial regulation in several ways. First, social regulation is often applied across the board to all industries and directly affects more producers than does industrial regulation. For instance, while the industrial regulation by the Air Transport Committee of the National Transport Agency of Canada controls only the air transport industry, the rules and regulations of the Canada Labour (Safety) Code and its provincial counterparts apply to every employer.

Second, social regulation intrudes into the day-to-day production process to a greater extent than industrial regulation. While industrial regulation focuses on rates, costs, and profits, social regulation often dictates the design of products, the conditions of employment, and the nature of the production process. For example, rather than specifying safety standards for vehicles, the *Motor Vehicle Safety Act* includes six standards limiting motor vehicle exhaust and noise emission.

Finally, social regulation has expanded rapidly during the same period in which industrial regulation has waned. Under this social regulation, firms must provide reasonable accommodations for qualified workers and job applicants with disabilities. Also, sellers must provide reasonable access for customers with disabilities. As much of our society had achieved a fairly affluent standard of living by the 1960s, attention shifted to improvement in the nonmaterial quality of life. That focus called for safer products, less pollution, improved working conditions, and greater equality of economic opportunity.

The Optimal Level of Social Regulation

While economists agree on the need for social regulation, they disagree on whether the current level of such regulation is optimal. Recall that an activity should be expanded so long as its marginal benefit (MB) exceeds its marginal cost (MC). If the MB of social regulation exceeds its MC, there is too little social regulation; if MC exceeds MB, there is too much social regulation. Unfortunately, the marginal costs and benefits of social regulation are not always easy to measure and therefore may be illusory. So, ideology about the proper size and role of government often drives the debate over social regulation as much as, or perhaps more than, economic cost–benefit analysis.

IN SUPPORT OF SOCIAL REGULATION

Defenders of social regulation say that it has achieved notable successes and, overall, has greatly enhanced society's well-being. They point out that social regulation confronts serious and substantial problems. Hundreds of workers die annually in job-related accidents and many thousands of workers suffer injuries that force them to miss a day or more of work. Air pollution continues to cloud major Canadian cities, imposing large costs in terms of reduced property values and increased health care expense. Numerous children and adults die each year because of poorly designed or manufactured products (for example, car tires) or tainted food (for example, *E. coli* in food products). Discrimination against some ethnic minorities, persons with disabilities, and older workers reduces their earnings and imposes heavy costs on society.

Proponents of social regulation acknowledge that social regulation is costly, but they correctly point out that a high price for something does not necessarily mean that it should not be purchased. They say that the appropriate economic test should be not whether the costs of social regulation are high or low but whether the benefits of social regulation exceed the costs. After decades of neglect, they further assert, society cannot expect to cleanse the environment, enhance the safety of the workplace, and promote economic opportunity for all without incurring substantial costs. So statements about the huge costs of social regulation are irrelevant, say defenders, since the benefits are even greater. The public often underestimates those benefits, since they are more difficult to measure than costs and often become apparent only after some time has passed (for example, the benefits of reducing global warming).

Proponents of social regulation point to its many specific benefits. It is estimated that highway fatalities would be 40 percent greater annually in the absence of auto safety features mandated through regulation. Compliance with child safety-seat and seatbelt laws has significantly reduced the auto fatality rate for small children. The national air quality standards set by law have been reached in nearly all parts of the nation for sulphur dioxide, nitrogen dioxide, and lead. Recent studies clearly link cleaner air, other things equal, with increases in the values of homes. **Employment equity** regulations have increased the labour demand for ethnic minorities and females. The use of childproof lids has resulted in a 90 percent decline in child deaths caused by accidental swallowing of poisonous substances.

Some defenders of social regulation say many areas remain in which greater regulation would generate net benefits to society. For example, some call for greater regulation of the meat, poultry,

employment equity
Policies and programs that establish targets of increased employment and promotion for women and minorities.

and seafood industries to improve food safety. Others say that more regulation is needed to ensure that violent movies, CDs, and video games are not marketed to children.

Advocates of social regulation claim that the benefits of such regulation are well worth the considerable costs. The costs are simply the price we must pay to create a hospitable, sustainable, and just society.

CRITICISMS OF SOCIAL REGULATION

Critics of social regulation contend that, in many instances, it has been expanded to the point where the marginal costs exceed the marginal benefits. In this view, society would achieve net benefits by cutting back on meddlesome social regulation. Critics say that many social regulation laws are poorly written, making regulatory objectives and standards difficult to understand. As a result, regulators pursue goals well beyond the original intent of the legislation. Businesses complain that regulators often press for additional increments of improvement, unmindful of costs.

Also, opponents of social regulation say that the regulatory agencies may attract overzealous workers who are hostile toward the market system and believe too fervently in regulation. For example, some staff members of government agencies may view large corporations as "bad guys" who regularly cause pollution, provide inadequate safety for workers, deceive their customers, and generally abuse their power in the community. Such biases can lead to seemingly never-ending calls for more regulation, rather than objective assessments of the costs and benefits of added regulation.

Two Reminders

The debate over the proper amount of social regulation will surely continue. By helping determine costs and benefits, economic analysis can lead to more informed discussion and to better decisions. In this regard, we leave both ardent supporters and opponents of social regulation with pertinent reminders.

THERE IS NO FREE LUNCH

Fervent supporters of social regulation need to remember that there is no free lunch. Social regulation can produce higher prices, stifle innovation, and reduce competition.

Social regulation raises product prices in two ways. It does so directly because compliance costs normally get passed on to consumers, and it does so indirectly by reducing labour productivity. Resources invested in making workplaces accessible to workers with disabilities, for example, are not available for investment in new machinery designed to increase output per worker. Where the wage rate is fixed, a drop in labour productivity increases the marginal and average total costs of production. In effect, the supply curve for the product shifts leftward, causing the price of the product to rise.

Social regulation may have a negative impact on the rate of innovation. Technological advance may be stifled by, say, the fear that a new plant will not meet Environment Canada's guidelines or that a new medicine will require years of testing before being approved by the federal government.

Social regulation may weaken competition, since it usually places a relatively greater burden on small firms than on large ones. The costs of complying with social regulation are, in effect, fixed costs. Because smaller firms produce less output over which to distribute those costs, their compliance costs per unit of output put them at a competitive disadvantage with their larger rivals. Social regulation is more likely to force smaller firms out of business, thus contributing to the increased concentration of industry.

Less Government Is Not Always Better than More

On the opposite side of the issue, passionate opponents of social regulation need to remember that less government is not always better than more government. Although the market system is a powerful engine for producing goods and services and generating income, it has its flaws.

employment discrimination
Inferior treatment in hiring, promotion, and work assignment for a particular group of employees.

Through appropriate amounts of social regulation, government can clearly increase economic efficiency and thus society's well-being. Ironically, by taking the rough edges off of capitalism, social regulation may be a strong pro-capitalist force. Properly conceived and executed, social regulation helps maintain political support for the market system. Such support could quickly wane if there were a steady stream of reports of unsafe workplaces, unsafe products, discriminatory hiring, choking pollution, deceived loan customers, and the like. Social regulation helps the market system deliver not only goods and services but also a "good society."

QUICK REVIEW

- Social regulation is concerned with the conditions under which goods and services are produced, the effects of production on society, and the physical characteristics of the goods themselves.

- Defenders of social regulation point to the benefits arising from policies that keep dangerous products from the marketplace, reduce workplace injuries and deaths, contribute to clean air and water, and reduce **employment discrimination.**

- Critics of social regulation say uneconomical policy goals, inadequate information, unintended side effects, and overzealous personnel create excessive regulation, for which regulatory costs exceed regulatory benefits.

The LAST WORD | The United States versus Microsoft

The Microsoft antitrust case in the United States is the most significant monopoly case since the break-up of AT&T in the early 1980s, and will have repercussions in Canada.

The Charges In May 1998, the U.S. Justice Department (under President Clinton), 19 individual states, and the District of Columbia (hereafter, "the government") filed antitrust charges against Microsoft under the *Sherman Antitrust Act* (a U.S. anticombines law). The government charged that Microsoft had violated Section 2 of the Act through a series of unlawful actions designed to maintain its Windows monopoly. It also charged that some of that conduct violated Section 1 of the Act.

Microsoft denied the charges, arguing it had achieved its success through product innovation and lawful business practices. Microsoft contended that it should not be penalized for its superior foresight, business acumen, and technological prowess. It also pointed out that its monopoly was highly transitory because of rapid technological advances.

The District Court Findings In June 2000, the District Court ruled that the relevant market was software used to operate Intel-compatible personal computers (PCs). Microsoft's 95 percent share of that market clearly gave it monopoly power. The Court pointed out, however, that being a monopoly is not illegal. The violation of the *Sherman Act* occurred because Microsoft used anticompetitive means to maintain its monopoly power.

According to the Court, Microsoft feared that the success of Netscape's Navigator, which allowed people to browse the Internet, might allow Netscape to expand its software to include a competitive PC operating system—software that would threaten Microsoft's Windows monopoly. It also feared that the Internet applications of Sun's Java programming language might eventually threaten the Windows monopoly.

To counter these and similar threats, Microsoft illegally signed contracts with PC makers that required them to feature Internet Explorer on the PC desktop and penalized companies that promoted software products that competed with Microsoft products. Moreover, it gave friendly companies coding that linked Windows to software applications and withheld it from companies featuring Netscape. Finally, under licence from Sun, Microsoft developed Windows-related Java software that made Sun's own software incompatible with Windows.

The District Court Remedy The District Court ordered Microsoft split into two competing companies, one initially selling the Windows operating system and the other initially selling Microsoft applications and services (such as Word, Hotmail, MSN, PowerPoint, and Internet Explorer). Both companies would be free to develop new products that competed with each other, and both could derive those products from the intellectual property embodied in the common products existing at the time the company was split.

The Appeals Court's Ruling In late 2000 Microsoft appealed the District Court decision to a U.S. Court of Appeals. In 2001 the higher court affirmed that Microsoft illegally maintained its monopoly, but tossed out the District's Court decision to break up Microsoft. It agreed with Microsoft that it was denied due process during the penalty phase of the trial and concluded that the District Court judge had displayed an appearance of bias by holding extensive interviews with the press. The Appeals Court sent the remedial phase of the case to a new District Court judge to determine appropriate remedies. The Appeals Court also raised issues relating to the wisdom of a remedy that involved changing the structure of Microsoft.

The Final Settlement At the urging of the new District Court judge, the federal government (then under President Bush) and Microsoft negotiated a proposed settlement. With minor modification, the settlement became the final court order in 2002. The break-up was overturned and replaced with a remedy that places limits on the company's behaviour. It:

1. prevents Microsoft from retaliating against any firm that develops, sells, or uses software that competes with Microsoft Windows or Internet Explorer or that ships a personal computer that includes both Windows and a non-Microsoft operating system;

2. requires Microsoft to establish uniform royalty and licensing terms for computer manufacturers that want to include Windows on their PCs;

3. requires that manufacturers be allowed to remove Microsoft icons and replace them with other icons on the Windows desktop; and

4. calls for Microsoft to provide technical information to other companies so they can develop programs that work as well with Windows as Microsoft's own products do.

The Microsoft actions and conviction have indirectly resulted in billions of dollars of fines and payouts by Microsoft. Main examples: to AOL Time Warner (Netscape), $750 million; to Sun Microsystems, $1.6 billion; to Novell, $536 million; to Burst.com, $60 million; to Gateway, $150 million; to InterTrust, $440 million; to RealNetworks, $761 million; and to IBM, $850 million. The European Commission of the European Union also brought a case against Microsoft for abuse of its dominant position and eventually levied a $600 million fine against Microsoft.

Sources: *United States v. Microsoft* (District Court Conclusions of Law), April 2000; *United States v. Microsoft* (Court of Appeals), June 2001; *U.S. v. Microsoft* (Final Judgment), November 2002; and Reuters and Associated Press News Services.

Question

Under what law and on what basis did the U.S. federal government find Microsoft guilty of violating U.S. antitrust laws? What was the initial District Court's remedy? How did Microsoft fare with its appeal to the Court of Appeals? Was the final remedy in the case a structural or behavioural remedy?

:: CHAPTER SUMMARY

12.1 :: INDUSTRIAL CONCENTRATION

- Mergers can be of three types: horizontal, vertical, and conglomerate.
- The *Competition Act* was passed in 1986, supplanting the *Combines Investigation Act*.

12.2 :: INDUSTRIAL REGULATION

- The objective of industrial regulation is to protect the public from the market power of natural monopolies by regulating prices and quality of service.

- Critics of industrial regulation contend that it can lead to inefficiency and rising costs and that in many instances it constitutes a legal cartel for the regulated firms. Legislation passed in the late 1970s and the 1980s has brought about varying degrees of deregulation in the airline, trucking, banking, railroad, and television broadcasting industries. Studies indicate that deregulation is producing sizable annual gains to society through lower prices, lower costs, and increased output. The latest Canadian industries to begin the deregulation process are telecommunications, electricity, and natural gas.

12.3 :: SOCIAL REGULATION

- Social regulation is concerned with product safety, working conditions, and the effects of production on society. While industrial regulation is on the wane, social regulation continues to expand. The optimal amount of social regulation occurs where MB = MC.

- People who support social regulation point to its numerous specific successes and assert that it has greatly enhanced society's well-being. Critics of social regulation contend that businesses are excessively regulated to the point where marginal costs exceed marginal benefits. They also say that social regulation often produces unintended and costly side effects.

:: TERMS AND CONCEPTS

competition policy, p. 295
horizontal merger, p. 295
vertical merger, p. 296
conglomerate merger, p. 296

Competition Tribunal, p. 296
tying contract, p. 297
public interest theory
   of regulation, p. 299

legal cartel theory of regulation, p. 300
social regulation, p. 301
employment equity, p. 302
employment discrimination, p. 304

:: QUESTIONS

1. Both competition policy and industrial policy deal with monopoly. What distinguishes their approaches? How does government decide to use one form of remedy rather than the other? **[LO12.1]**

2. Explain how strict enforcement of competition laws might conflict with (a) promoting exports to achieve a balance of trade, and (b) encouraging new technologies. Do you see any dangers in using selective competition enforcement as part of a broader policy to increase exports? **[LO12.1]**

3. How would you expect competition authorities to react to: **[LO12.1]**

   a. a proposed merger of Ford and General Motors.

   b. evidence of secret meetings by contractors to rig bids for highway construction projects.

   c. a proposed merger of a large shoe manufacturer and a chain of retail shoe stores.

   d. a proposed merger of a small life-insurance company and a regional candy manufacturer.

   e. an automobile rental firm that charges higher rates for last-minute rentals than for rentals reserved weeks in advance.

4. Suppose a proposed merger of firms would simultaneously lessen competition and reduce unit costs through economies of scale. Do you think such a merger should be allowed? **[LO12.1]**

5. In the 1980s, PepsiCo Inc., which then had 28 percent of the soft-drink market, proposed to acquire the 7-Up Company. Shortly thereafter the Coca-Cola Company, with 39 percent of the market, indicated it wanted to acquire the Dr. Pepper Company. 7-Up and Dr. Pepper each controlled about 7 percent of the market. In your judgment, was the government's decision to block these mergers appropriate? **[LO12.1]**

6. Read the following statement: "The competition laws serve to penalize efficiently managed firms." Do you agree? Why or why not? **[LO12.2]**

7. Read the following statement: "The social desirability of any particular firm should be judged not on the basis of its market share but on the basis of its conduct and performance." Make a counterargument, referring to the monopoly model in your statement. **[LO12.2]**

8. What types of industry, if any, should be subjected to industrial regulation? What specific problems does industrial regulation entail? **[LO12.2]**

9. In view of the problems involved in regulating natural monopolies, compare socially optimal (marginal-cost) pricing and fair-return pricing by referring again to Figure 10-9. Assuming that a government subsidy might be used to cover any loss resulting from marginal-cost pricing, which pricing policy would you favour? Why? What problems might such a subsidy entail? **[LO12.2]**

10. Use economic analysis to explain why the optimal amount of product safety may be less than the amount that would totally eliminate risks of accidents and deaths. Use automobiles as an example. **[LO12.3]**

11. How does social regulation differ from industrial regulation? What types of benefits and costs are associated with social regulation? **[LO12.3]**

:: PROBLEMS

1. Carrot Computers and its competitors purchase touch screens for their handheld computers from several suppliers. The six makers of touch screens have market shares of 19 percent, 18 percent, 14 percent, 16 percent, 20 percent, and 13 percent. [LO12.2]

   a. What is the Herfindahl index for the touch screen manufacturing industry?

   b. By how much would a proposed merger between the two smallest touch screen makers increase the Herfindahl index? Would the government be likely to challenge that proposed merger?

   c. If Carrot Computers horizontally merges with its competitor Blueberry Handhelds, by how much would the Herfindahl index change for the touch screen industry?

Mc Graw Hill connect™ **Practice and Learn Online with Connect**

Connect allows you to practice important concepts at your own pace and on your own schedule, with 24/7 online access to an eBook, algorithmic questions and problems from the textbook, video and logic cases, graphing tutorials, flashcards, Internet exercises, key graphs, and more.

PART 4 :: MICROECONOMICS OF FACTOR MARKETS

CHAPTER 13 ::

The Demand for Factors of Production

When you finish your education, you will probably be looking for a new job. But why would someone want to hire you? The answer, of course, is that you have much to offer. Employers have a demand for educated, productive workers like you.

We need to learn more about the demand for labour and other factors. So, we now turn from the pricing and production of *goods and services* to the pricing and employment of *resources,* or *factors of production.* Although firms come in various sizes and operate under highly different market conditions, they each have a demand for factors of production. They obtain those resources from households—the owners of land, labour, capital, and entrepreneurial resources. So, referring to the circular flow model (Figure 2-2), we shift our attention from the bottom loop of the diagram (which shows that firms supply products and services that households want) to the top loop (which shows the demand for factors of production that households supply).

This chapter looks at the *demand* for factors of production. Although the discussion concentrates on labour, the principles we develop also apply to land, capital, and entrepreneurial ability. In Chapter 14 we will combine factor (labour) demand with labour *supply* to analyze wage rates. Then in Chapter 15, we will use factor demand and factor supply to examine the prices of, and returns to, other productive factors.

AFTER READING THIS CHAPTER, YOU SHOULD BE ABLE TO:

13.1 Explain how factor prices are determined.

13.2 Discuss what determines the demand for a factor.

13.3 Discuss what determines the elasticity of factor demand.

13.4 Determine how a firm arrives at the optimal combination of factors to use in the production process.

13.1   Factor Pricing and Demand

As you saw in Chapter 2, the circular flow diagram has two main markets: the product market and the factor market. Up to this point, we have concentrated on supply and demand in the product market, where the prices of goods and services are determined. But to produce goods and services, we need factors of production: labour, land, capital, and entrepreneurial resources. As we also noted in Chapter 2, all factors of production are provided by households to firms. We now turn to the determination of supply and demand in the factor market.

Studying factor pricing is important for several reasons:

- *Money-Income Determination* Factor prices are a major determinant of household income. The expenditures that firms make in acquiring factors of production flow as wage, rent, interest, and profit incomes to households.

- *Cost Minimization* To the firm, factor prices are costs, and to realize maximum profit the firm must produce the profit-maximizing output with the most efficient (least costly) combination of resources. Factor prices determine the quantities of land, labour, capital, and entrepreneurial ability that will be combined in producing each good or service.

- *Resource Allocation* Just as product prices allocate finished goods and services to consumers, factor prices allocate inputs among industries and firms. In a dynamic economy, where technology and tastes often change, the efficient allocation of resources over time means a continuous shift of factors of production from one use to another. Changes in factor prices are a major determinant of those shifts.

- *Policy Issues* There are many policy issues surrounding the factor market: To what extent should government redistribute income through taxes and transfers? Should government do anything to discourage "excess" pay to corporate executives? Should it increase the legal minimum wage? Does it make sense to provide subsidies to farmers? Should it encourage or restrict labour unions? The facts and debates relating to these policy questions are based on factor pricing.

Marginal Productivity Theory of Factor Demand

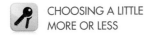

CHOOSING A LITTLE MORE OR LESS

In discussing factor demand, we will first assume that a firm sells its output in a perfectly competitive product market and hires a certain factor in a perfectly competitive factor market. This assumption keeps things simple and is consistent with the model of a competitive factor market that we will develop in Chapter 12. In a competitive *product market* the firm is a price-taker and can dispose of as much output as it chooses at the market price. The firm sells such a negligible fraction of total output that it exerts no influence on product price. Similarly, in the competitive *factor market,* the firm is a wage-taker. It hires such a negligible fraction of the total supply of the factor that it cannot influence its price.

FACTOR DEMAND AS A DERIVED DEMAND

derived demand
The demand for a factor that depends on the products it can be used to produce.

Factor demand is the starting point for any discussion of factor prices. Factor demand is a schedule or a curve showing the amounts of a factor that buyers are willing and able to purchase at various prices over some period of time. Crucially, factor demand is a **derived demand,** meaning that the demand for a factor is derived from the demand for the products that the factor helps to produce. This is true because factors usually do not directly satisfy customer wants but do so indirectly through their use in producing goods and services. No one wants to consume a hectare of land, a tractor, or the labour services of a farmer, but households do want to consume the food products that these factors help produce.

TABLE 13-1 — The Demand for Labour: Perfect Competition in the Sale of the Product

(1) Units of a factor	(2) Total product (output)	(3) Marginal product, MP	(4) Product price	(5) Total revenue, or (2) × (4)	(6) Marginal revenue product, MRP
0	0		$2	$ 0	
		7			$14
1	7		2	14	
		6			12
2	13		2	26	
		5			10
3	18		2	36	
		4			8
4	22		2	44	
		3			6
5	25		2	50	
		2			4
6	27		2	54	
		1			2
7	28		2	56	

MARGINAL REVENUE PRODUCT (MRP)

Because resource demand is derived from product demand, the strength of the demand for any factor of production will depend on (a) the productivity of the factor, and (b) the price of the good it helps to produce.

Other things equal, a factor that is highly productive in turning out a highly valued commodity will be in great demand, while a relatively unproductive factor that is capable of producing only a slightly valued commodity will be in little demand. And no demand whatsoever will exist for a factor of production that is phenomenally efficient in producing something that no one wants to buy.

marginal product (MP)
The extra output produced with one additional unit of a factor.

- *Productivity* Table 13-1 shows the roles of productivity and product price in determining demand for factors of production. Here, we assume that a firm adds a single variable factor, labour, to its fixed plant. Columns 1 and 2 give the number of units of the factor employed and the resulting total product (output). Column 3 shows the **marginal product (MP),** or additional output, from each additional factor unit. Columns 1 through 3 remind us that the law of diminishing returns applies here, causing the marginal product of labour to fall beyond some point. For simplicity, we assume that diminishing marginal returns begin after the first worker hired.

marginal revenue product (MRP)
The change in total revenue from employing one additional unit of a factor.

- *Product Price* The derived demand for a factor depends also on the price of the product it produces. Column 4 in Table 13-1 adds this price information. Product price is constant, in this case at $2, because the product market is competitive. The firm is a price-taker and can sell units of output only at this market price. Multiplying column 2 by column 4 gives us the total-revenue data of column 5. From these total-revenue data we can compute **marginal revenue product (MRP),** the change in total revenue resulting from the use of each additional unit of a factor (labour, in this case). In equation form,

$$\text{Marginal revenue product} = \frac{\text{change in total revenue}}{\text{unit change in factor quantity}}$$

The MRPs are listed in column 6 in Table 13-1.

RULE FOR EMPLOYING FACTORS: MRP = MFC

The demand for factors is derived from the products or services that those factors help produce.

marginal factor cost (MFC)
The amount that each additional unit of a factor adds to the firm's total (factor) cost.

MRP = MFC rule
To maximize economic profit (or minimize losses) a firm should use the quantity of a factor at which its marginal revenue product is equal to its marginal factor cost.

connect
MATH 13.1
MRP = MFC

The MRP schedule, shown as columns 1 and 6, is the firm's demand schedule for labour. To understand why, you must first know the rule that guides a profit-seeking firm in hiring any factor of production: To maximize profit, a firm will hire additional units of a specific factor as long as each successive unit adds more to the firm's total revenue than it adds to total cost.

We have seen that MRP measures how much each successive unit of a factor adds to total revenue. The amount that each additional unit of a factor adds to the firm's total (factor) cost is called its **marginal factor cost (MFC).**

In equation form,

$$\text{Marginal factor cost} = \frac{\text{change in total (factor) cost}}{\text{unit change in factor quantity}}$$

So, we can restate our rule for hiring factors as follows: It will be profitable for a firm to hire additional units of a factor up to the point at which that factor's MRP is equal to its MFC. For example, as the rule applies to labour, if the number of workers a firm is currently hiring is such that the MRP of the last worker exceeds his or her MFC, the firm can increase profit by hiring more workers. But if the number being hired is such that the MFC of the last worker exceeds his or her MRP, the firm is hiring workers who are not paying their way, and it can increase its profit by laying off some workers. You may have recognized that this **MRP = MFC rule** is similar to the MR = MC profit-maximizing rule employed throughout our discussion of price and output determination. The rationale of the two rules is the same, but the point of reference is now *inputs* of a factor of production, not *outputs* of a product.

MRP AS A FACTOR DEMAND SCHEDULE

Let's continue with our focus on labour, knowing that the analysis also applies to other factors. In a perfectly competitive labour market, supply and demand establish the wage rate. Because each firm hires such a small fraction of market supply, it cannot influence the market wage rate; it is a wage-taker, not a wage-maker. This means that for each additional unit of labour hired, each firm's total factor cost increases by exactly the amount of the constant market wage rate. More specifically, the MFC of labour exactly equals the market wage rate. Thus, factor "price" (the market wage rate) and factor "cost" (marginal factor cost) are equal for a firm that hires labour in a competitive labour market. As a result, the MRP = MFC rule tells us that, in perfect competition, the firm will hire workers up to the point at which the market *wage rate* (its MFC) is equal to its MRP.

In terms of the data in columns 1 and 6 in Table 13-1, if the market wage rate is, say, $13.95, the firm will hire only one worker, because only the hiring of the first worker results in an increase in profits. To see this, note that for the first worker MRP (= $14) exceeds MFC (= $13.95). Thus, hiring the first worker is profitable. For each successive worker, however, MFC (= $13.95) exceeds MRP (= $12 or less), indicating that it will not be profitable to hire any of those workers. If the wage rate is $11.95, by the same reasoning we discover that it will pay the firm to hire both the first and second workers. Similarly, if the wage rate is $9.95, three workers will be hired; if $7.95, four; if $5.95, five; and so forth. So here is the key generalization: The MRP schedule constitutes the firm's demand for labour, because each point on this schedule (or curve) indicates the number of workers the firm would hire at each possible wage rate.

In Figure 13-1, we show the $D = MRP$ curve based on the data in Table 13-1. The perfectly competitive firm's factor demand curve identifies an inverse relationship between the wage rate and the quantity of labour demanded, other things equal. The curve slopes downward because of diminishing marginal returns.[1]

---

[1] Note that we plot the points in Figures 13-1 and 13-2 halfway between succeeding numbers of factor units, because MRP is associated with the addition of one more unit. Thus, in Figure 13-2, for example, we plot the MRP of the second unit ($13.00) not at 1 or 2, but rather at 1.5. This smoothing enables us to sketch a continuously downsloping curve rather than one that moves downward in discrete steps as each new unit of labour is hired.

FIGURE 13-1 The Perfectly Competitive Seller's Demand for a Factor

The MRP curve is the factor demand curve; each of its points relates a particular factor price (= MRP when profit is maximized) with a corresponding quantity of the factor demanded. Under perfect competition, product price is constant; therefore, the downslope of the $D = $ MRP curve is due solely to the decline in the factor's marginal product (law of diminishing marginal returns).

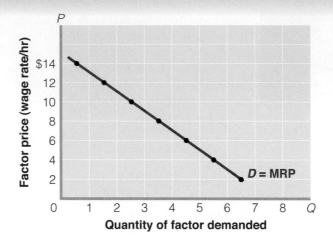

FACTOR DEMAND UNDER IMPERFECT PRODUCT MARKET COMPETITION

Factor demand (here, labour demand) is more complex when the firm is selling its product in an imperfectly competitive market, one in which the firm is a price-maker. That is because imperfect competitors (monopolists, oligopolists, and monopolistic competitors) face downward-sloping product demand curves. As a result, whenever an imperfect competitor's product demand curve is fixed in place, the only way to increase sales is by setting a lower price (and thereby moving down along the fixed demand curve).

The productivity data in Table 13-1 are retained in columns 1 to 3 in Table 13-2. But here in Table 13-2 we show in column 4 that product price must be lowered to sell the marginal product of each successive worker. The MRP of the perfectly competitive seller of Table 13-1 falls for only one reason: marginal product diminishes. The MRP of the imperfectly competitive seller of Table 13-2 falls for two reasons: marginal product diminishes *and* product price falls as output increases.

TABLE 13-2 The Demand for Labour: Imperfect Competition in the Sale of the Product

(1) Units of a factor	(2) Total product (output)	(3) Marginal product, MP	(4) Product price	(5) Total revenue, or (2) × (4)	(6) Marginal revenue product, MRP
0	0		$2.80	$ 0	
		7			$18.20
1	7		2.60	18.20	
		6			13.00
2	13		2.40	31.20	
		5			8.40
3	18		2.20	39.60	
		4			4.40
4	22		2.00	44.00	
		3			2.25
5	25		1.85	46.25	
		2			1.00
6	27		1.75	47.25	
		1			−1.05
7	28		1.65	46.20	

FIGURE 13-2 The Imperfectly Competitive Seller's Demand Curve for a Factor

An imperfectly competitive seller's factor demand curve D (solid) slopes downward because both marginal product and product price fall as factor employment and output rise. This downward slope is greater than that for a perfectly competitive seller (dashed factor demand curve) because the perfect competitor can sell the added output at a constant price.

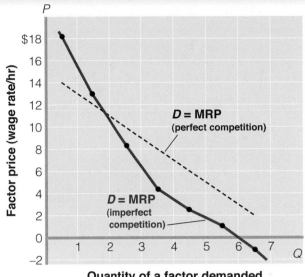

We emphasize that the lower price accompanying each increase in output (total product) applies not only to the marginal product of each successive worker but also to *all prior output*. Note that the second worker's marginal product is six units. These six units can be sold for $2.40 each, or, as a group, for $14.40. But $14.40 is not the MRP of the second worker. To sell these six units, the firm must take a 20-cent price cut on the seven units produced by the first worker—units that otherwise could have been sold for $2.60 each. Thus, the MRP of the second worker is only $13.00 [= $14.40 − (7 × 20 cents)], as shown.

Similarly, the third worker adds five units to total product, and these units are worth $2.20 each, or $11.00 total. But to sell these five units the firm must take a 20-cent price cut on the 13 units produced by the first two workers. So the third worker's MRP is only $8.40 [= $11.00 − (13 × 20 cents)]. The numbers in column 6 reflect such calculations.

In Figure 13-2 we graph the MRP data from Table 13-2 and label it "*D* = MRP (imperfect competition)." The broken-line factor demand curve, in contrast, is that of the perfectly competitive seller represented in Figure 13-1. A comparison of the two curves demonstrates that, other things equal, the factor demand curve of an imperfectly competitive seller is less elastic than that of a perfectly competitive seller. Consider the effects of an identical percentage decline in the wage rate (factor price) from $11 to $6. Comparison of the two curves and a quick mental calculation reveals that the firm in imperfect competition does not expand the quantity of labour by as large a percentage as does the firm in perfect competition.

The result is that the MRP curve—the factor demand curve—of the imperfectly competitive producer is less elastic than that of the perfectly competitive producer. At a wage rate or MRC of $11.95, both the perfectly competitive and the imperfectly competitive seller will hire two workers. But at $9.95 the competitive firm will hire three, and the imperfectly competitive firm only two. You can see this difference in factor demand elasticity when we graph the MRP data in Table 13-2 and compare the graph with Figure 13-1, as we do in Figure 13-2.

It is not surprising that the imperfectly competitive producer is less responsive to factor price cuts than the perfectly competitive producer. When factor prices fall, MC per unit declines for imperfectly competitive firms as well as perfectly competitive firms. Because both types of firms maximize profits by producing where MR = MC, the decline in MC will cause both types of firms to produce more. But the effect will be muted for imperfectly competitive firms because their downward-sloping demand curves cause them also to face downward-sloping MR curves—so that for each additional

---

CONSIDER THIS :: Superstars

In what economist Robert Frank calls "winner-take-all markets," a few highly talented performers have huge earnings relative to the average performers in the market. Because consumers and firms seek out the best performers, small differences in talent or popularity get magnified into huge differences in pay.

In winner-take-all markets, consumer spending gets channelled toward a few performers. The media then hypes these new stars, which further increases the public's awareness of their talents. More consumers then buy the stars' products, and superstars emerge. The high earnings of superstars result from the high revenues they generate from their work. Consider Beyoncé Knowles. If she sold only a few thousand CDs and attracted only a few hundred fans to each concert, the revenue she would produce—her marginal revenue product—would be quite modest. So, too, would be her earnings. But some consumers have anointed Justin Bieber as king of pop culture. The demand for his CDs and concerts is extraordinarily high. He sells millions of CDs, not thousands, and draws thousands to his concerts, not hundreds. His high net earnings derive from his extraordinarily high marginal revenue product.

So it is for the other superstars in winner-take-all markets. Influenced by media hype but coerced by no one, consumers direct their spending toward a select few. The high marginal revenue product that results means strong demand for these stars' services. And because top talent (by definition) is very limited, superstars receive amazingly high earnings.

---

connect

WORKED PROBLEM 13.1
Factor Demand

unit sold, MR declines. By contrast, MR is constant (and equal to the market equilibrium price P) for competitive firms, so that they do not have to worry about MR per unit falling as they produce more units. As a result, competitive firms increase production by a larger amount than imperfectly competitive firms whenever resource prices fall.

MARKET DEMAND FOR A FACTOR

Recall that the total, or market, demand curve for a *product* is found by summing horizontally the demand curves of all individual buyers in the market. The market demand curve for a particular *factor* is derived the same way—by summing horizontally the individual demand or MRP curves for all firms employing that factor (see the *Consider This...Superstars* box for a story about the marginal revenue product of superstars).

QUICK REVIEW

- To maximize profit a firm will purchase or hire a factor of production in an amount at which the factor's marginal revenue product equals its marginal factor cost (MRP = MFC).

- Application of the MRP = MFC rule to a firm's MRP curve demonstrates that the MRP curve is the firm's factor demand curve. In a perfectly competitive factor market, factor price (the wage rate) equals MFC.

- The factor demand curve of a firm in perfect competition is downward sloping solely because the marginal product of the factor diminishes; the factor demand curve of a firm in imperfect competition is downward sloping because marginal product diminishes and product price falls as output is increased.

13.2 Determinants of Factor Demand

What will shift the factor demand curve? The fact that factor demand is derived from *product demand* and depends on *factor productivity* suggests two things that can shift factor demand. Also, our analysis of how changes in the prices of other products can shift a product's demand curve (Chapter 3) suggests another reason: changes in the prices of other *factors of production*.

Changes in Product Demand

Other things equal, an increase in the demand for a product that uses a particular factor will increase the demand for that factor of production, whereas a decrease in product demand will decrease the resource demand.

Let's see how this works. The first thing to recall is that a change in the demand for a product will change its price. In Table 13-1, let's assume that an increase in product demand boosts the product price from $2 to $3. You should calculate the new factor demand schedule (columns 1 and 6), and plot it in Figure 13-1 to verify that the new factor demand curve lies to the right of the old demand curve. Similarly, a decline in the product demand (and price) will shift the factor demand curve to the left.

Example: Assuming no offsetting change in supply, an increase in the demand for new houses will drive up house prices. Those higher prices will increase the MRP of construction workers, and therefore the demand for construction workers will rise. The factor demand curve such as in Figure 13-1 or Figure 13-2 will shift to the right.

Changes in Productivity

Other things equal, an increase in the productivity of a factor of production will increase the demand for that factor. If we doubled the MP data of column 3 in Table 13-1, the MRP data of column 6 would also double, indicating an increase (rightward shift) in the factor demand curve.

The productivity of any factor may be altered over the long run in several ways:

- *Quantities of Other Factors* The marginal productivity of any factor will vary with the quantities of the other factors used with it. The greater the amount of capital and land resources used with, say, labour, the greater will be labour's marginal productivity and, thus, labour demand.

- *Technological Advance* Technological improvements that increase the quality of other factors, such as capital, have the same effect. The better the quality of capital, the greater the productivity of labour used with it. Office workers employed with a specific amount of real capital in the form of computers are more productive than office workers with the same amount of real capital embodied in typewriters and filing cabinets.

- *Quality of the Variable Factor* Improvements in the quality of the variable factor, such as labour, will increase its marginal productivity and therefore its demand.

All these considerations help explain why the average level of (real) wages is higher in industrially advanced nations (for example, Canada, the United States, Germany, Japan, and France) than in developing nations (for example, Nicaragua, Ethiopia, Angola, and Cambodia). Workers in industrially advanced nations are generally healthier, better educated, and better trained than are workers in developing countries. Also, in most industries, workers in industrially advanced nations work with a larger and more efficient stock of capital goods and more abundant natural resources. This increase in productivity creates a strong demand for labour. On the supply side of the market, labour is *relatively* scarce compared with that in most developing nations. A strong demand and a relatively scarce supply of labour result in high wage rates in the industrially advanced nations.

Changes in the Prices of Other Factors

Just as changes in the prices of other products will change the demand for a specific product, changes in the prices of other factors of production will change the demand for a specific factor. Also recall that the effect of a change in the price of product X on the demand for product Y depends on whether X and Y are substitute goods or complementary goods *in consumption*.

Similarly, the effect of a change in the price of factor A on the demand for factor B depends on their complementarity in production.

SUBSTITUTE FACTORS OF PRODUCTION

Suppose the technology in a certain production process is such that labour and capital can be substituted. A firm can produce a specific amount of output using a relatively small amount of labour and a relatively large amount of capital, or vice versa. Now assume that the price of machinery (capital) falls. The effect on the demand for labour will be the net result of two opposed effects: the substitution effect and the output effect.

substitution effect
A firm will purchase more of an input whose relative price has declined and use less of an input whose relative price has increased.

- *Substitution Effect* The decline in the price of machinery prompts the firm to substitute machinery for labour. This substitution allows the firm to produce its output at a lower cost. So, at the fixed wage rate, smaller quantities of labour are now employed. This **substitution effect** decreases the demand for labour. More generally, the substitution effect indicates that a firm will purchase more of an input whose relative price has declined and, conversely, use less of an output whose relative price has increased.

- *Output Effect* Because the price of machinery has fallen, the costs of producing various outputs must also decline. With lower costs, the firm finds it profitable to produce and sell a greater output. The greater output increases the demand for all factors of production, including labour. So, this **output effect** increases the demand for labour. More generally, the output effect means that the firm will purchase more of one particular input when the price of the other input falls and less of that particular input when the price of the other input rises.

output effect
An increase in the price of one input will increase a firm's production costs and reduce its level of output, thus reducing the demand for other inputs (and vice versa).

- *Net Effect* The substitution and output effects are both present when the price of an input changes. The net change in factor demand depends on the relative sizes of the two effects. For example, if the substitution effect outweighs the output effect, a decrease in the price of capital decreases the demand for labour. If the output effect exceeds the substitution effect, a decrease in the price of capital increases the demand for labour.

COMPLEMENTARY FACTORS OF PRODUCTION

Recall from Chapter 3 that certain products, such as computers and software, are complementary goods; they go together and are jointly demanded. Factors of production can also be complementary; an increase in the quantity of one of them used in the production process requires an increase in the amount used of the other as well, and vice versa. Suppose a small design firm does computer-assisted design (CAD) with relatively expensive personal computers as its basic piece of capital equipment. Each computer requires a single design engineer to operate it.

Now assume that a technological advance in the production of these computers substantially reduces their price. No substitution effect can occur, because labour and capital must be used in *fixed proportions,* one person for one machine. Capital cannot be substituted for labour. But there is an output effect. Other things equal, the reduction in the price of capital goods means lower production costs. It will, therefore, be profitable to produce a larger output. In doing so, the firm will use both more capital and more labour. When labour and capital are complementary, a decline in the price of capital increases the demand for labour through the output effect.

We have cast our analysis of substitute factors and complementary factors mainly in terms of a decline in the price of capital. In Table 13-3 we summarize the effects of an *increase* in the price of capital on the demand for labour; study it carefully.

Now that we have discussed the full list of the determinants of labour demand, let's again review their effects. Stated in terms of the labour resource, the demand for labour will increase (the labour demand curve will shift rightward) when

- The demand for the product produced by that labour *increases.*

- The productivity (MP) of labour *increases.*

TABLE 13-3 — The Effect of an Increase in the Price of Capital on the Demand for Labour, D_L

(1) Relationship of inputs	(2) Increase in the price of capital		
	(a) Substitution effect	(b) Output effect	(c) Combined effect
Substitutes in production	Labour substituted for capital	Production costs up, output down, and less of both capital and labour used	D_L increases if the substitution effect exceeds the output effect; D_L decreases if the output effect exceeds the substitution effect
Complements in production	No substitution of labour for capital	Production costs up, output down, and less of both capital and labour used	D_L decreases (since only the output effect applies)

- The price of a substitute input *decreases,* provided the output effect exceeds the substitution effect.
- The price of a substitute input *increases,* provided the substitution effect exceeds the output effect.
- The price of a complementary input *decreases.*

Be sure that you can reverse these effects to explain a *decrease* in labour demand.

Table 13-4 provides several illustrations of the determinants of labour demand, listed by the categories of determinants we have discussed. You will benefit from giving them a close look.

TABLE 13-4 — Determinants of Labour Demand: Factors that Shift the Labour Demand Curve

Determinant	Examples
Changes in product demand	Gambling increases in popularity, increasing the demand for workers at casinos.
	Consumers decrease their demand for leather coats, decreasing the demand for tanners.
	The federal government reduces spending on the military, reducing the demand for military personnel.
Changes in productivity	An increase in the skill levels of physicians increases the demand for their services.
	Computer-assisted graphic design increases the productivity of, and demand for, graphic artists.
Changes in the price of another factor	An increase in the price of electricity increases the cost of producing aluminum and reduces the demand for aluminum workers.
	The price of security equipment used by businesses to protect against illegal entry falls, decreasing the demand for night guards.
	The price of cellphone equipment decreases, reducing the cost of cellphone service, which in turn increases the demand for cellphone assemblers.

13.3   Elasticity of Factor Demand

The employment changes we have just discussed result from shifts of factor demand curves. Such changes in demand must be distinguished from changes in the quantity demanded of a factor of production caused by a change in the price of the specific factor. Such a change is not caused by a shift of the demand curve but rather by a movement from one point to another on a fixed factor demand curve. For example, in Figure 13-1 we note that an increase in the wage rate from $5 to $7 will reduce the quantity of labour demanded from five to four units. This is a change in the *quantity of labour demanded* as distinct from a *change in demand for labour*.

The sensitivity of factor quantity to changes in factor prices along a fixed factor demand curve is measured by the **elasticity of factor demand.** In coefficient form,

$$E_{fd} = \frac{\text{percentage change in factor quantity demanded}}{\text{percentage change in factor price}}$$

When E_{fd} is greater than 1, factor demand is elastic; when E_{fd} is less than 1, factor demand is inelastic; and when E_{fd} equals 1, factor demand is unit-elastic. (Recall from Chapter 4 that demand elasticity has a negative sign, but we use the absolute value.) What determines the elasticity of factor demand? Several determinants are at work.

Ease of Factor Substitutability

The greater the substitutability of other factors, the more elastic is the demand for a particular factor. As an example, the high degree to which computerized voice recognition systems are substitutable for human beings implies that the demand for human beings answering phone calls at call centres is quite elastic. In contrast, there are few good substitutes for physicians, so demand for them is less elastic or even inelastic. If a furniture manufacturer finds that several types of wood are equally satisfactory in making coffee tables, a rise in the price of any one type of wood may cause a sharp drop in the amount demanded as the producer substitutes one of the other woods. At the other extreme, no reasonable substitutes may exist; bauxite is absolutely essential in the production of aluminum ingots. Thus the demand for bauxite by aluminum producers is inelastic.

Time can play a role in the ease of input substitution. For example, a firm's truck drivers may obtain a substantial wage increase with little or no immediate decline in employment. But over time, as the firm's trucks wear out and are replaced, that wage increase may motivate the company to purchase larger trucks and in that way deliver the same total output with fewer drivers.

Elasticity of Product Demand

The elasticity of demand for any factor depends on the elasticity of demand for the product that it helps produce. Other things equal, the greater the elasticity of product demand, the greater the elasticity of factor demand. The derived nature of factor demand leads us to expect this relationship. A small rise in the price of a product with great elasticity of demand will sharply reduce output, bringing about relatively large declines in the amounts of various factors of production demanded; the demand for the factor is elastic.

Ratio of Factor Cost to Total Cost

The larger the proportion of total production costs accounted for by a factor of production, the greater the elasticity of demand for that factor. For example, if labour cost is the only production cost, then a 20 percent increase in wage rates will shift all the firm's cost curves upward by the full 20 percent. If product demand is elastic, this substantial increase in wage costs will cause a relatively large decline in sales and a sharp decline in the amount of labour demanded. So labour demand is highly elastic. Conversely, if labour cost is a small percentage of the same firm's cost, labour demand would be relatively inelastic.

---

elasticity of factor demand
The percentage change in factor quantity divided by the percentage change in factor price.

connect
ORIGIN OF THE IDEA 13.1
Elasticity of Factor Demand

13.4 Optimal Combination of Factors*

CHOOSING A LITTLE MORE OR LESS

So far our main focus has been on one variable input, labour. But in the long run, firms can vary the amounts of all the factors of production they use. That's why we need to consider what combination of factors a firm will choose when *all* its inputs are variable. While our analysis is based on two factors, it can be extended to any number of inputs.

We will consider two interrelated questions: (1) What combination of factors will minimize costs at a specific level of output? (2) What combination of factors will maximize profit?

The Least-Cost Rule

least-cost combination of factors
The quantity of each factor a firm must employ to produce a particular output at the lowest total cost.

A firm is producing a specific output with the **least-cost combination of factors** when the last dollar spent on each factor yields the same marginal product. To see how this rule maximizes profits in a more concrete setting, consider firms that are competitive buyers in resource markets. Because each firm is too small to affect resource prices, each firm's marginal factor costs will equal market factor prices and each firm will be able to hire as many or as few units as it would like of any and all factors at their respective market prices. Thus, if there are just two factors, labour and capital, a competitive firm will minimize its total cost of a specific output when

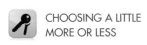
MATH 13.2
The Least-Cost Rule

$$\frac{\text{Marginal Product of Labour } (\text{MP}_L)}{\text{Price of Labour } (P_L)} = \frac{\text{Marginal Product of Capital } (\text{MP}_C)}{\text{Price of Capital } (P_C)} \quad (1)$$

Throughout, we will refer to the marginal products of labour and capital as MP_L and MP_C, respectively, and symbolize the price of labour by P_L and the price of capital by P_C.

A concrete example shows why fulfilling the condition in equation (1) leads to least-cost production. Assume that the price of both capital and labour is $1 per unit, but that Siam Soups is currently employed in such amounts that the marginal product of labour is 10 and the marginal product of capital is 5. Our equation immediately tells us that this is not the least costly combination of resources:

$$\frac{\text{MP}_L = 10}{P_L = \$1} > \frac{\text{MP}_C = 5}{P_C = \$1}$$

---

* *Note to Instructors:* We consider this section optional; it can be skipped without loss of continuity, or deferred until after the discussion of wage determination in the next chapter.

Suppose Siam spends $1 less on capital and shifts that dollar to labour. It loses five units of output produced by the last dollar's worth of capital, but it gains 10 units of output from the extra dollar's worth of labour. Net output increases by 5 (= 10 − 5) units for the same total cost. More such shifting of dollars from capital to labour will push the firm *down* along its MP curve for labour and *up* along its MP curve for capital, increasing output and moving the firm toward a position of equilibrium where equation (1) is fulfilled. At that equilibrium position, the MP per dollar for the last unit of both labour and capital might be, for example, seven. And Siam will be producing a greater output for the same (original) cost.

Whenever the same total resource cost can result in a greater total output, the cost per unit—and therefore the total cost of any specific level of output—can be reduced. The cost of producing any specific output can be reduced as long as equation (1) does not hold. But when dollars have been shifted between capital and labour to the point where equation (1) holds, no additional changes in the use of capital and labour will reduce costs further. Siam is now producing that output using the least-cost combination of capital and labour.

All the long-run cost curves developed in Chapter 7 and used thereafter assume that the least-cost combination of inputs has been realized at each level of output. Any firm that combines factors of production in violation of the least-cost rule will have a higher-than-necessary average total cost at each level of output; that is, it will incur *X-inefficiency*, as shown in Figure 10-7.

The Profit-Maximizing Rule

connect
MATH 13.3
The Profit-Maximizing Rule

Minimizing cost is not sufficient for maximizing profit. A firm can produce any level of output in the least costly way by applying equation (1), but only one unique level of output can maximize profit. Our earlier analysis of product markets showed that this profit-maximizing output occurs where marginal revenue equals marginal cost (MR = MC). Near the beginning of this chapter, we determined that we could write this profit-maximizing condition as MRP = MFC as it relates to factor inputs.

In a perfectly competitive factor market, the marginal factor cost (MFC) is exactly equal to the factor price, P. Thus, for any competitive factor market, we have as our profit-maximizing equation

$$\text{MRP (factor)} = P(\text{factor})$$

profit-maximizing combination of factors
The quantity of each factor a firm must employ to maximize its profits or minimize its losses.

This condition must hold for every variable factor—and in the long run all factors are variable. In competitive markets, a firm will, therefore, achieve its **profit-maximizing combination of factors** when each factor is employed to the point at which its marginal revenue product equals its price. For two factors, labour and capital, we need both $P_L = \text{MRP}_L$ and $P_C = \text{MRP}_C$.

We can combine these conditions by dividing both sides of each equation by their respective prices and equating the results, to get

$$\frac{\text{MRP}_L}{P_L} = \frac{\text{MRP}_C}{P_C} = 1 \qquad (2)$$

Note in equation (2) that it is not sufficient that the MRPs of the two factors be *proportionate* to their prices; the MRPs must be *equal* to their prices and the ratios, therefore, equal to 1. For example, if $\text{MRP}_L = \$15$, $P_L = \$5$, $\text{MRP}_C = \$9$, and $P_C = \$3$, Siam is underemploying both capital and labour even though the ratios of MRP to resource price are identical for both factors. The firm can expand its profit by hiring additional amounts of both capital and labour until it moves down their down-ward sloping MRP curves to the points at which $\text{MRP}_L = \$5$ and $\text{MRP}_C = \$3$. The ratios will then be 5/5 and 3/3 and equal to 1.

connect
WORKED PROBLEM 13.2
Optimal Combination of Factors

The profit-maximizing position in equation (2) includes the cost-minimizing condition of equation (1). That is, if a firm is maximizing profit according to equation (2), then it must be using the least-cost combination of inputs to do so. However, the converse is not true: a firm operating at least cost according to equation (1) may not be operating at the output that maximizes its profit.

TABLE 13-5 — Data for Finding the Least-Cost and Profit-Maximizing Combination of Labour and Capital, Siam's Soup*

LABOUR (PRICE = $8)					CAPITAL (PRICE = $12)				
(1) Quantity	(2) Total product (output)	(3) Marginal product	(4) Total revenue	(5) Marginal revenue product	(1') Quantity	(2') Total product (output)	(3') Marginal product	(4') Total revenue	(5') Marginal revenue product
0	0		$0		0	0		$0	
		12		$24			13		$26
1	12		24		1	13		26	
		10		20			9		18
2	22		44		2	22		44	
		6		12			6		12
3	28		56		3	28		56	
		5		10			4		8
4	33		66		4	32		64	
		4		8			3		6
5	37		74		5	35		70	
		3		6			2		4
6	40		80		6	37		74	
		2		4			1		2
7	42		84		7	38		76	

*To simplify, it is assumed in this table that the productivity of each factor is independent of the quantity of the other. For example, the total and marginal product of labour is assumed not to vary with the quantity of capital employed.

Numerical Illustration

A numerical illustration will help you understand the least-cost and profit-maximizing rules. In columns 2, 3, 2', and 3' in Table 13-5, we show the total products and marginal products for various amounts of labour and capital that are assumed to be the only inputs Siam needs in producing some product, say, key chains. Both inputs are subject to diminishing returns.

We also assume that labour and capital are supplied in competitive factor markets at $8 and $12, respectively, and that Siam's soup sells competitively at $2 per unit. For both labour and capital, we can determine the total revenue associated with each input level by multiplying total product by the $2 product price. These data are shown in columns 4 and 4'. They enable us to calculate the marginal revenue product of each successive input of labour and capital as shown in columns 5 and 5', respectively.

PRODUCING AT LEAST COST

What is the least-cost combination of labour and capital to use in producing, say, 50 units of output? The answer, which we can obtain by trial and error, is three units of labour and two units of capital. Columns 2 and 2' indicate that this combination of labour and capital does, indeed, result in the required 50 (= 28 + 22) units of output. Now, note from columns 3 and 3' that hiring three units of labour gives us $MP_L/P_L = {}^6/_8 = {}^3/_4$, and hiring two units of capital gives us $MP_C/P_C = {}^9/_{12} = {}^3/_4$. So, equation (1) is fulfilled. How can we verify that costs are actually minimized? First, we see that the total cost of employing three units of labour and two of capital is $48 [= (3 × $8) + (2 × $12)].

Other combinations of labour and capital will also yield 50 units of output but at a higher cost than $48. For example, five units of labour and one unit of capital will produce 50 (= 37 + 13) units, but total cost is higher at $52 [= (5 × $8) + (1 × $12)]. This result comes as no surprise, because five units of labour and one unit of capital violate the least-cost rule—$MP_L/P_L = {}^4/_8$, $MP_C/P_C = {}^{13}/_{12}$. Only the combination (three units of labour and two units of capital) that minimizes total cost will satisfy equation (1).

MAXIMIZING PROFIT

Will 50 units of output maximize Siam's profit? No, because the profit-maximizing terms of equation (2) are not satisfied when the firm employs three units of labour and two of capital. To maximize profit, each input should be employed until its price equals its marginal revenue product. But for three units of labour, labour's MRP in column 5 is $12 while its price is only $8; the firm could increase its profit by hiring more labour. Similarly, for two units of capital, we see in column 5' that capital's MRP is $18 and its price is only $12. This result indicates that more capital should also be employed. By producing only 50 units of output (even though they are produced at least cost), labour and capital are being used in less-than-profit-maximizing amounts. The firm needs to expand its employment of labour and capital, thereby increasing its output.

Table 13-5 shows that the MRPs of labour and capital are equal to their prices, so that equation (2) is fulfilled when Siam is employing five units of labour and three units of capital. This is the profit-maximizing combination of inputs.[2] The firm's total cost will be $76, made up of $40 ($= 5 \times \$8$) of labour and $36 ($= 3 \times \$12$) of capital. Total revenue will be $130, found either by multiplying the total output of 65 ($= 37 + 28$) by the $2 product price or by summing the total revenues attributable to labour ($74) and to capital ($56). The difference between total revenue and total cost in this instance is $54 ($= \$130 - \$76$). Experiment with other combinations of labour and capital to demonstrate that they yield an economic profit of less than $54.

Note that the profit-maximizing combination of five units of labour and three units of capital is also a least-cost combination for this particular level of output. Using these factor amounts satisfies the least-cost requirement of equation (1) in that $MP_L/P_L = {}^4/_8 = 1/2$ and $MP_C/P_C = {}^6/_{12} = {}^1/_2$.

Marginal Productivity Theory of Income Distribution

Our discussion of factor pricing is the cornerstone of the controversial view that fairness and economic justice are two of the outcomes of a competitive market economy. Table 13-5 demonstrates, in effect, that workers receive income payments (wages) equal to the marginal contributions they make to their employers' outputs and revenues. In other words, workers are paid according to the value of the labour services that they contribute to production. Similarly, owners of the other factors of production receive income based on the value of the factors they supply in the production process.

In this **marginal productivity theory of income distribution,** income is distributed according to the contribution to society's output. So, if you are willing to accept the proposition "To each according to the values of what he or she creates," income payments based on marginal revenue product provide a fair and equitable distribution of society's income.

This sounds reasonable, but you need to be aware of serious criticisms of this theory of income distribution:

- *Inequality* Critics argue that the distribution of income resulting from payment according to marginal productivity may be highly unequal because productive factors are very unequally distributed in the first place. Aside from their differences in mental and physical attributes, individuals encounter substantially different opportunities to enhance their productivity through education and training. Some people may not be able to participate in production at all because of mental or physical disabilities, and they would obtain no income under a system of distribution based solely on marginal productivity. Ownership of property resources is also highly unequal. Many owners of land and capital resources obtain their property by inheritance rather than through their own productive effort. Hence, income from inherited property resources conflicts with the "To each according to the values of what he or she creates" idea. This reasoning, say critics, calls for progressive taxation and government spending programs that modify the income distributions made strictly according to marginal productivity.

marginal productivity theory of income distribution
The contention that the distribution of income is fair when each unit of each factor receives a money payment equal to its marginal contribution to the firm's revenue (its marginal revenue product).

connect
ORIGIN OF THE IDEA 13.2
Marginal Productivity Theory of Income Distribution

---

[2] Because we are dealing with discrete (non-fractional) units of the two outputs here, the use of four units of labour and two units of capital is equally profitable. The fifth unit of labour's MRP and its price (cost) are equal at $8, so that the fifth labour unit neither adds to nor subtracts from the firm's profit; similarly, the third unit of capital has no effect on profit.

- **Market Imperfections** The marginal productivity theory of income distribution rests on the assumptions of competitive markets. But, as we will see in Chapter 14, not all labour markets are highly competitive. Employers in some labour markets exert their wage-setting power to pay less-than-competitive wages. And some workers, through labour unions, professional associations, and occupational licensing laws, wield wage-setting power to increase their wages in selling their services. In addition, discrimination in the labour market can distort earnings patterns. In short, because of real-world market imperfections, wage rates and other factor prices are not always based solely on contributions to output.

The LAST WORD   Input Substitution: The Case of ABMs

Banks are using more automated banking machines (ABMs) and employing fewer human tellers.

As you have learned from this chapter, a firm achieves its least-cost combination of inputs when the last dollar it spends on each input makes the same contribution to total output. This raises an interesting real-world question: What happens when technological advance makes available a new, highly productive capital good for which MP/P is greater than it is for other inputs, say a particular type of labour? The answer is that the least-cost mix of factors abruptly changes and the firm responds accordingly. If the new capital is a substitute for labour (rather than a complement), the firm replaces the particular type of labour with the new capital. That is exactly what is happening in the banking industry, in which ABMs are replacing human bank tellers.

ABMs made their debut at a bank in London in 1967. Shortly thereafter, U.S. firms Docutel and Diebold each introduced their own models. Today, Diebold and NCR (also a U.S. firm) dominate global sales, with the Japanese firm Fujitsu a distant third. The number of ABMs has exploded, and currently more than 50,000 ABMs are in use in Canada. We rank number one in the world in the number of ABMs per inhabitant: 1631 ABMs per million inhabitants, compared to 1335 for second place U.S. and 1289 for third ranking Belgium.

ABMs are highly productive: A single machine can handle hundreds of transactions daily, thousands weekly, and millions over the course of several years. ABMs not only can handle cash withdrawals, but also can accept deposits and facilitate transfers of funds between various accounts. Although ABMs are expensive for banks to buy and install, they are available 24 hours a day, and their cost per transaction is one-fourth the cost for human tellers. They rarely get held up, and they do not quit their jobs (turnover among human tellers is nearly 50 percent per year). ABMs are highly convenient; unlike human tellers, they are located not only at banks but also at busy street corners, workplaces, colleges and universities, and shopping malls.

The same bank card that enables you to withdraw cash from your local ABM also enables you to withdraw pounds from an ABM in London, yen from an ABM in Tokyo, and even rubles from an ABM in Moscow (assuming, of course, you have money in your account).

In the terminology of this chapter, the more productive, lower-priced ABMs have reduced the demand for a substitute in production—human tellers. Between 1990 and 2000, 8000 human teller positions were eliminated, and more positions may disappear in the coming years. Where will the people holding these jobs go? Some will eventually move to other occupations. Others will be retrained and move to the chartered banks' extensive customer service departments to become investment advisers and wealth-management representatives. Although the lives of some individual tellers are disrupted, society clearly wins. Society gets cheaper, more convenient banking services and more of the other goods that these freed-up labour resources help to produce.

Source: Based partly on Ben Craig, "Where Have All the Tellers Gone?" *Economic Commentary* (Federal Reserve Bank of Cleveland), April 15, 1997; and statistics compiled by the Canadian Bankers Association. These statistics can be found at www.cba.ca/.

Question

Explain the economics of the substitution of ABMs for human tellers. Some banks assess transaction fees when customers use human tellers rather than ABMs. What are these banks trying to accomplish?

:: CHAPTER SUMMARY

13.1 :: FACTOR PRICING AND DEMAND

- Factor prices help determine money incomes, and they simultaneously ration factors of production to various industries and firms.

- The demand for any factor is derived from the product it helps produce. That means the demand for a factor will depend on its productivity and on the market value (price) of the good it is producing.

- Marginal revenue product is the extra revenue a firm obtains when it employs one more unit of a factor. The MRP curve for any factor is the demand curve for that factor, because the firm equates factor price and MRP in determining its profit-maximizing level of factor employment. Thus, each point on the MRP curve indicates how many factor units the firm will hire at a specific factor price.

- The firm's demand curve for a factor slopes downward, because the marginal product of additional units declines in accordance with the law of diminishing returns. When a firm is selling in an imperfectly competitive market, the factor demand curve falls for a second reason: Product price must be reduced for the firm to sell a larger output. We can derive the market demand curve for a factor by summing horizontally the demand curves of all the firms hiring that factor.

13.2 :: DETERMINANTS OF FACTOR DEMAND

- The demand curve for a factor will shift as the result of (a) a change in the demand for, and therefore the price of, the product the factor is producing; (b) changes in the productivity of the factor; and (c) changes in the prices of other factors.

- If factors A and B are substitutable for each other, a decline in the price of A will decrease the demand for B provided the substitution effect is greater than the output effect. But if the output effect *exceeds* the substitution effect, a decline in the price of A will increase the demand for B.

- If factors C and D are complementary or jointly demanded, there is only an output effect; a change in the price of C will change the demand for D in the opposite direction.

13.3 :: ELASTICITY OF FACTOR DEMAND

- The elasticity of demand for a factor measures the responsiveness of producers to a change in the factor's price. The coefficient of the elasticity of factor demand is

$$E_{fd} = \frac{\text{percentage change in factor quantity demanded}}{\text{percentage change in factor price}}$$

When E_{fd} is greater than 1, factor demand is elastic; when E_{fd} is less than 1, factor demand is inelastic; and when E_{fd} equals 1, factor demand is unit elastic.

- The elasticity of demand for a factor will be greater (a) the greater the ease of substituting other resources for labour, (b) the greater the elasticity of demand for the product, and (c) the larger the proportion of total production costs attributable to the factor.

13.4 :: OPTIMAL COMBINATION OF FACTORS

- Any specific level of output will be produced with the least costly combination of variable factors when the marginal product per dollar's worth of each input is the same—that is, when

$$\frac{\text{MP of labour}}{\text{price of labour}} = \frac{\text{MP of capital}}{\text{price of capital}}$$

- A firm is employing the profit-maximizing combination of factors when each factor is used to the point where its marginal revenue product equals its price. In terms of labour and capital, that occurs when the MRP of labour equals the price of labour and the MRP of capital equals the price of capital—that is, when

$$\frac{\text{MRP of labour}}{\text{price of labour}} = \frac{\text{MRP of capital}}{\text{price of capital}} = 1$$

- The marginal productivity theory of income distribution holds that all factors are paid what they are economically worth: their marginal contribution to output. Critics assert that such an income distribution is too unequal and the real-world market imperfections result in pay above and below marginal contributions to output.

:: TERMS AND CONCEPTS

derived demand, p. 309
marginal product (MP), p. 310
marginal revenue product (MRP), p. 310
marginal factor cost (MFC), p. 311
MRP = MFC rule, p. 311

substitution effect, p. 316
output effect, p. 316
elasticity of factor demand, p. 318
least-cost combination of factors, p. 319

profit-maximizing combination
  of factors, p. 320
marginal productivity theory of income
  distribution, p. 322

QUESTIONS

1. What is the significance of factor pricing? Explain how the determinants of factor demand differ from those underlying product demand. Explain the meaning and significance of the fact that the demand for a factor is a derived demand. Why do factor demand curves slope downward? [**LO13.1**]

2. Complete the following labour demand table for a firm that is hiring labour competitively and selling its product in a competitive market. [**LO13.2**]

   a. How many workers will the firm hire if the market wage rate is $27.95? $19.95? Explain why the firm will not hire a larger or smaller number of units of labour at each of these wage rates.

   b. Show in schedule form and graphically the labour demand curve of this firm.

   c. Now redetermine the firm's demand curve for labour, assuming that it is selling in an imperfectly competitive market and that, although it can sell 17 units at $2.20 per unit, it must lower product price by $0.05 to sell the marginal product of each successive labour unit. Compare this demand curve with that derived in part (b). Which curve is more elastic? Explain.

Units of labour	Total product	Marginal product	Product price	Total revenue	Marginal revenue product
0	0		$2	$ ___	
		___			$ ___
1	17		2	___	
		___			___
2	31		2	___	
		___			___
3	43		2	___	
		___			___
4	53		2	___	
		___			___
5	60		2	___	
		___			___
6	65		2	___	

3. In 2009 General Motors (GM) announced that it would reduce employment by 21,000 workers. What does this decision reveal about how it viewed its marginal revenue product (MRP) and marginal factor cost (MFC)? Why didn't GM reduce employment by more than 21,000 workers? By fewer than 21,000 workers? [**LO13.2**]

4. What are the determinants of the elasticity of factor demand? What effect will each of the following have on the elasticity or the location of the demand for factor C, which is being used to produce commodity X? Where there is any uncertainty as to the outcome, specify the causes of that uncertainty. [**LO13.3**]

   a. An increase in the demand for product X.

   b. An increase in the price of substitute factor D.

   c. An increase in the number of factors substitutable for C in producing X.

   d. A technological improvement in the capital equipment with which factor C is combined.

   e. A decline in the price of complementary factor E.

   f. A decline in the elasticity of demand for product X due to a decline in the competitiveness of product market X.

5. Suppose the productivity of capital and labour are as shown in the accompanying table. The output of these factors sells in a perfectly competitive market for $1 per unit. Both capital and labour are hired under perfectly competitive conditions at $3 and $1, respectively. [**LO13.4**]

Units of capital	MP of capital	Units of labour	MP of labour
0		0	
	24		11
1		1	
	21		9
2		2	
	18		8
3		3	
	15		7
4		4	
	9		6
5		5	
	6		4
6		6	
	3		1
7		7	
	1		½
8		8	

   a. What is the least-cost combination of labour and capital the firm should employ in producing 80 units of output? Explain.

   b. What is the profit-maximizing combination of labour and capital the firm should use? Explain. What is the resulting level of output? What is the economic profit? Is this the least costly way of producing the profit-maximizing output?

6. In each of the following four cases, MRP_L and MRP_C refer to the marginal revenue products of labour and capital, respectively, and P_L and P_C refer to their prices. Indicate in each case whether the conditions are consistent with maximum profits for the firm. If not, state which factor(s) should be used in larger amounts and which factor(s) should be used in smaller amounts. [**LO13.4**]

   a. $MRP_L = \$8$; $P_L = \$4$; $MRP_C = \$8$; $P_C = \$4$

   b. $MRP_L = \$10$; $P_L = \$12$; $MRP_C = \$14$; $P_C = \$9$

c. $MRP_L = \$6$; $P_L = \$6$; $MRP_C = \$12$; $P_C = \$12$

d. $MRP_L = \$22$; $P_L = \$26$; $MRP_C = \$16$; $P_C = \$19$

7. Florida citrus growers say that the recent crackdown on illegal immigration is increasing the market wage rates necessary to get their oranges picked. Some are turning to $100,000-to-$300,000 mechanical harvesters known as "trunk, shake, and catch" pickers, which vigorously shake oranges from the trees. If widely adopted, what will be the effect on the demand for human orange pickers? What does that imply about the relative strengths of the substitution and output effects?   [LO13.4]

:: PROBLEMS

1. A delivery company is considering adding another vehicle to its delivery fleet, all the vehicles of which are rented for $100 per day. Assume that the additional vehicle would be capable of delivering 1500 packages per day and that each package that is delivered brings in ten cents ($0.10) in revenue. Also assume that adding the delivery vehicle would not affect any other costs.   [LO13.2]

   a. What is the MRP? What is the MFC? Should the firm add this delivery vehicle?

   b. Now suppose that the cost of renting a vehicle doubles to $200 per day. What are the MRP and MFC? Should the firm add a delivery vehicle under these circumstances?

   c. Next suppose that the cost of renting a vehicle falls back down to $100 per day, but due to extremely congested freeways, an additional vehicle would only be able to deliver 750 packages per day. What are the MRP and MFC in this situation? Would adding a vehicle under these circumstances increase the firm's profits?

2. Suppose that marginal product tripled while product price fell by one-half in Table 13-1. What would be the new MRP values in Table 13-1? What would be the net impact on the location of the factor demand curve in Figure 13-1?   [LO13.2]

3. Suppose that a monopoly firm finds that its MR is $50 for the first unit sold each day, $49 for the second unit sold each day, $48 for the third unit sold each day, and so on. Further suppose that the first worker hired produces 5 units per day, the second 4 units per day, the third 3 units per day, and so on.   [LO13.3]

   a. What is the firm's MRP for each of the first five workers?

   b. Suppose that the monopolist is subjected to rate regulation and the regulator stipulates that it must charge exactly $40 per unit for all units sold. At that price, what is the firm's MRP for each of the first five workers?

   c. If the daily wage paid to workers is $170 per day, how many workers will the unregulated monopoly demand? How many will the regulated monopoly demand? Looking at those figures, will the regulated or the unregulated monopoly demand more workers at that wage?

   d. If the daily wage paid to workers falls to $77 per day, how many workers will the unregulated monopoly demand? How many will the regulated monopoly demand? Looking at those figures, will the regulated or the unregulated monopoly demand more workers at that wage?

   e. Comparing your answers to parts (c) and (d), does regulating a monopoly's output price *always* increase its demand for resources?

4. Consider a small landscaping company run by Mr. Viemeister. He is considering increasing his firm's capacity. If he adds one more worker, the firm's total monthly revenue will increase from $50,000 to $58,000. If he adds one more tractor, monthly revenue will increase from $50,000 to $62,000. Additional workers each cost $4000 per month while an additional tractor would also cost $6000 per month.   [LO13.4]

   a. What is the marginal product of labour? The marginal product of capital?

   b. What is the ratio of the marginal product of labour to the price of labour (MP_L/P_L)? What is the ratio of the marginal product of capital to the price of capital (MP_K/P_K)?

   c. Is the firm using the least costly combination of inputs?

   d. Does adding an additional worker or adding an additional tractor yield a larger increase in total revenue for each dollar spent?

McGraw Hill **connect** **Practice and Learn Online with Connect**

Connect allows you to practice important concepts at your own pace and on your own schedule, with 24/7 online access to an eBook, algorithmic questions and problems from the textbook, video and logic cases, graphing tutorials, flashcards, Internet exercises, key graphs, and more.

CHAPTER 14

Wage Determination

AFTER READING THIS CHAPTER, YOU SHOULD BE ABLE TO:

14.1 Explain the connection between productivity and wages.

14.2 Show how wages are determined in a perfectly competitive labour market.

14.3 Discuss what a monopsony is and its effect on wages.

14.4 Discuss how unions affect wages.

14.5 Explain the pros and cons of a minimum wage.

14.6 List the major causes of wage differentials.

14.7 Explain the principal–agent problem and discuss different compensation schemes designed to avoid it.

Over 16 million Canadians go to work each day. We work at an amazing variety of jobs for thousands of different firms for considerable differences in pay. What determines our hourly wage or annual salary? Why is the salary for, say, a top major league baseball player $18 million a year, whereas the pay for a first-rate schoolteacher is $80,000? Why are starting salaries for university graduates who major in engineering and accounting so much higher than for graduates majoring in journalism and sociology?

Having explored the major factors that underlie labour demand, we now bring *labour supply* into our analysis to help answer these questions. Generally, labour supply and labour demand interact to determine the hourly wage rate or annual salary in each occupation. Collectively, those wages and salaries make up about 75 percent of the national income in Canada.

14.1 Productivity and the General Level of Wages

Economists use the term "labour" broadly to apply to (1) blue-collar and white-collar workers of all varieties; (2) professionals such as lawyers, physicians, dentists, and teachers; and (3) owners of small businesses, including barbers, plumbers, and a host of retailers who provide labour as they operate their own business.

Wages are the price that employers pay for labour. Wages take the form not only of direct money payments such as hourly pay, annual salaries, bonuses, royalties, and commissions, but also fringe benefits, such as paid vacations and dental insurance. We

wage rate
A price paid per unit of labour services.

nominal wage
The amount of money received by a worker per unit of time (hour, day, etc.).

real wage
The amount of goods and services a worker can purchase with a nominal wage.

Wages are the price that employers pay for labour.

will use the term "wages" to mean all such payments and benefits converted to an hourly basis. That will remind us that the **wage rate** is a price paid per unit of labour services, in this case an hour of work. It will also let us distinguish between the wage rate and labour earnings, the latter being determined by multiplying the number of hours worked per week, per month, or per year by the hourly wage or wage rate.

We must also distinguish between nominal wages and real wages. A **nominal wage** is the amount of money received per hour, per day, and so on. A **real wage** is the quantity of goods and services a worker can obtain with nominal wages; real wages reveal the purchasing power of nominal wages.

Your real wage depends on your nominal wage and the prices of the goods and services you purchase. Suppose you receive a 5 percent increase in your nominal wage during a certain year, but in that same year the price level increases by 3 percent. Then your real wage has increased by 2 percent (= 5 percent *minus* 3 percent). Unless otherwise indicated, we will discuss only *real* wages.

Wages differ among nations, regions, occupations, and individuals. Wage rates are much higher in Canada than in China or India. Wages are slightly higher in central Canada and the west than in the east. Plumbers are paid less than NHL hockey players, and lawyer Adam may earn twice as much as lawyer Bharti for the same number of hours of work. The average wages earned by workers also differ by gender, race, and ethnic background.

The general level of wages includes a wide range of different wage rates. It includes the wages of bakers, barbers, brick masons, and brain surgeons. By averaging such wages, we can more easily compare wages among regions and among nations.

As Global Perspective 14.1 suggests, the general level of real wages in Canada, especially in the skilled trades, is relatively high—although not the highest in the world. The explanation for the high real wages in Canada and other industrially advanced economies (referred to hereafter as advanced economies) is that the demand for labour in these nations is relatively large compared to the supply of labour.

GLOBAL PERSPECTIVE

14.1

Hourly Wages of Production Workers, Selected Nations

Worldwide wage differences are pronounced. These data indicate that hourly compensation in Canada is not as high as in some European nations. It is important to note, however, that the prices of goods and services vary greatly among nations, and the process of converting foreign wages into dollars may not accurately reflect such variations.

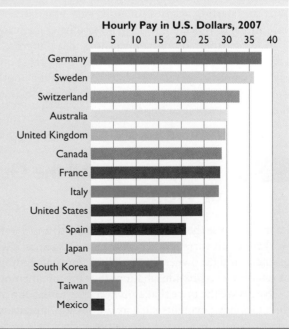

Hourly Pay in U.S. Dollars, 2007

Germany
Sweden
Switzerland
Australia
United Kingdom
Canada
France
Italy
United States
Spain
Japan
South Korea
Taiwan
Mexico

Source: U.S. Bureau of Labor Statistics, www.bls.gov.

The Role of Productivity

We know from the previous chapter that the demand for labour, or for any other factor, depends on its productivity. Generally, the greater the productivity of labour, the greater the demand for it. If the total supply of labour is fixed, then the demand for labour will be stronger, and the average level of real wages will be higher. The demand for labour in Canada and the other major advanced economies is large because labour in these countries is highly productive. There are several reasons for that high productivity:

- *Plentiful Capital* Workers in the advanced economies have access to large amounts of physical capital (machinery and buildings). The total physical capital per worker in Canada is one of the highest in the world.

- *Access to Abundant Natural Resources* In advanced economies, natural resources are abundant in relation to the size of the labour force. Some of those resources are available domestically and others are imported from abroad. Canada, for example, is richly endowed with arable land, mineral resources, and sources of energy for industry.

- *Advanced Technology* The level of technological progress is generally high in advanced economies. Not only do workers in these economies have more capital equipment to work with but that equipment is also technologically superior to the equipment available to the vast majority of workers worldwide. Work methods in the advanced economies are also steadily being improved through scientific study and research.

- *Labour Quality* The health, education, and training of workers in advanced economies are generally superior to those of workers in developing nations. Thus, even with the same quantity and quality of natural and capital resources, workers in advanced economies tend to be more productive than many of their counterparts.

- *Other Factors* Less obvious factors also underlie the high productivity in some of the advanced economies. In Canada, for example, such factors include (1) the efficiency and flexibility of management; (2) business, social, and political environments that emphasize production and productivity; (3) access to a large market, which enables firms to engage in mass production; and (4) increased specialization of production made possible by free trade agreements with other nations.

Real Wages and Productivity

Figure 14-1 shows the close long-run relationship between output per hour of work and real hourly earnings in Canada. Because real income and real output are two ways of viewing the same thing, real income (earnings) per worker can increase only at about the same rate as output per worker. When workers produce more real output per hour, more real income is available to distribute to them for each hour worked.

However, suppliers of land, capital, and entrepreneurial talent also share in the income from production. Real wages, therefore, do not always rise in lockstep with gains in productivity over short spans of time. But over long periods, productivity and real wages tend to rise together.

Long-Run Trend of Real Wages

Basic supply and demand analysis helps explain the long-term trend of real-wage growth in Canada. The nation's labour force has grown significantly over the decades. But, as a result of the productivity-increasing factors we have mentioned, increases in labour demand have outstripped increases in labour supply. Figure 14-2 shows several such increases in labour supply and labour demand. The result has been a long-run increase in wage rates and employment. For example, real hourly compensation in Canada has roughly doubled since 1960. Over that same period, employment has increased by about 11 million workers.

FIGURE 14-1   **Output per Hour and Real Hourly Compensation in Canada**

Over a long time period, output per hour of work and real hourly compensation are closely related.

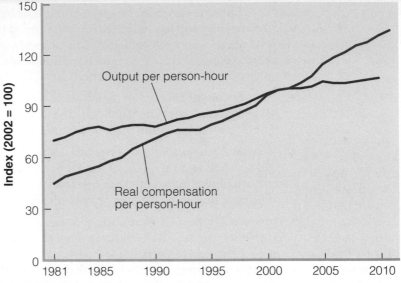

Source: Adapted from Statistics Canada CANSIM database, http://cansim2.statcan.ca, Table 383-0008.

FIGURE 14-2   **The Long-Run Trend of Real Wages in Canada**

The productivity of Canadian labour has increased substantially over the long run, causing the demand for labour, *D*, to shift to the right more rapidly than increases in the supply of labour, *S*. The result has been increases in real wages.

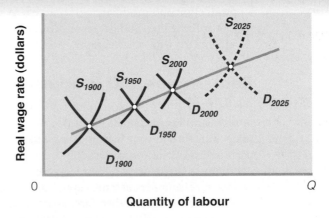

14.2   Wages in a Perfectly Competitive Labour Market

Average levels of wages disguise the great variation of wage rates among and within occupations, however. What determines the wage rate paid for a specific type of labour? Demand and supply

perfectly competitive labour market
A factor market in which a large number of firms demand a particular type of labour supplied by a large number of nonunion workers.

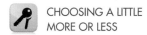 CHOOSING A LITTLE MORE OR LESS

analysis is again revealing. Let's begin by examining labour demand and labour supply in a **perfectly competitive labour market.** In this type of market:

- Numerous firms compete with one another in hiring a specific type of labour.

- Many qualified workers with identical skills supply that type of labour.

- Individual firms and individual workers are wage-takers, since neither can exert any control over the market wage rate.

Market Demand for Labour

Suppose 200 firms demand a particular type of labour, say, carpenters. These firms need not be in the same industry. Thus, firms producing wood-framed furniture, wooden windows and doors, houses and apartment buildings, and wooden cabinets will demand carpenters. To find the total, or market, labour demand curve for a particular labour service, we sum horizontally the labour demand curves (the marginal revenue product curves) of the individual firms, as indicated in **Figure 14-3 (Key Graph)**. The horizontal summing of the 200 labour demand curves like d in Figure 14-3b yields the market labour demand curve D in Figure 14-3a.

Market Supply of Labour

On the supply side of a perfectly competitive labour market, we assume that no union is present and that workers individually compete for available jobs. The supply curve for each type of labour slopes upward, indicating that employers as a group must pay higher wage rates to obtain more workers. They must do this to bid workers away from other industries, occupations, and localities. Within limits, workers have alternative job opportunities. For example, they may work in other industries in the same locality, they may work in their present occupations in different cities or provinces, or they may work in other occupations.

Firms that want to hire these workers (here, carpenters) must pay higher wage rates to attract them away from the alternative job opportunities available to them. They must also pay higher wages to induce people who are not currently in the labour force—perhaps doing household activities or enjoying leisure—to seek employment. In short, assuming that wages are constant in other labour markets, higher wages in a particular labour market entice more workers to offer their labour services in that market—a fact confirmed by the upward-sloping market supply of labour curve S in Figure 14-3a.

Labour Market Equilibrium

The intersection of the market labour demand curve and the market labour supply curve determines the equilibrium wage rate and level of employment in purely competitive labour markets. In Figure 14-3a the equilibrium wage rate is W_c ($10), and the number of workers hired is Q_c (1000). To the individual firm the market wage rate W_c is given. Each of the many firms employs such a small fraction of the total available supply of this type of labour that no single firm can influence the wage rate. As shown by the horizontal line s in Figure 14-3b, the supply of this labour is perfectly elastic to the individual firm.

Each individual firm will find it profitable to hire this type of labour up to the point at which marginal revenue product is equal to marginal factor cost. This is merely an application of the MRP = MFC rule we developed in Chapter 13.

As Table 14-1 indicates, when an individual competitive firm faces the market price for a resource, that resource's marginal factor cost (MFC) is constant and is equal to the market price for each and every unit that the competitive firm may choose to purchase. Note that MFC is constant at $10 and matches the $10 wage rate. Each additional worker hired adds precisely his or her own wage rate ($10 in this case) to the firm's total resource cost. So the firm in a perfectly competitive labour market maximizes its profit by hiring workers to the point at which its wage rate equals MRP. In Figure 14-3b this firm will hire Q_c (five) workers, paying each worker the market

KEY GRAPH

FIGURE 14-3   Labour Supply and Labour Demand in (Panel a) a Perfectly Competitive Labour Market and (Panel b) a Single Competitive Firm

In a perfectly competitive labour market (a) market labour supply S and market labour demand D determine the equilibrium wage rate W_c and the equilibrium number of workers Q_c. Each individual competitive firm (b) takes this competitive wage W_c as given. Thus, the individual firm's labour supply curve $S = MFC$ is perfectly elastic at the going wage rate W_c. Its labour demand curve is its MRP curve (here labelled "mrp"). The firm maximizes its profit by hiring workers up to where MRP = MFC. Area $0abc$ represents both the firm's total revenue and its total cost. The green area is its total wage cost; the blue area is its nonlabour costs, including a normal profit—that is, the firm's payments to the suppliers of land, capital, and entrepreneurship.

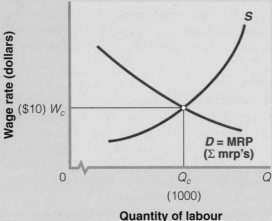

(a) Labour market

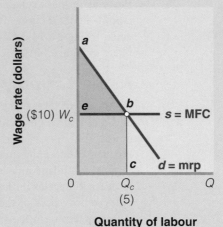

(b) Individual firm

Quick Quiz

1. The supply of labour curve S slopes upward in graph (a) because
   a. the law of diminishing marginal utility applies.
   b. the law of diminishing returns applies.
   c. workers can afford to buy more leisure when their wage rates rise.
   d. higher wages are needed to attract workers away from other labour markets, household activities, and leisure.

2. This firm's labour demand curve d in graph (b) slopes downward because
   a. the law of diminishing marginal utility applies.
   b. the law of diminishing returns applies.
   c. the firm must lower its price to sell additional units of its product.
   d. the firm is a competitive employer, not a monopsonist.

3. In employing five workers, the firm represented in graph (b)
   a. has a total wage cost of $6000.
   b. is adhering to the general principle of undertaking all actions for which the marginal benefit exceeds the marginal cost.
   c. uses less labour than would be ideal from society's perspective.
   d. experiences increasing marginal returns.

4. A rightward shift of the labour supply curve in graph (a) would shift curve
   a. $d = mrp$ leftward in graph (b).
   b. $d = mrp$ rightward in graph (b).
   c. $s = MFC$ upward in graph (b).
   d. $s = MFC$ downward in graph (b).

Answers: 1. d; 2. b; 3. b; 4. d

TABLE 14-1 — The Supply of Labour: Perfect Competition in the Hire of Labour

(1) Units of labour	(2) Wage rate	(3) Total labour cost (wage bill)	(4) Marginal factor (labour) cost
0	$10	$ 0	
			$10
1	10	10	
			10
2	10	20	
			10
3	10	30	
			10
4	10	40	
			10
5	10	50	
			10
6	10	60	

wage rate, W_c ($10). The other 199 firms (not shown) that are hiring workers in this labour market will also each employ 5 workers and pay $10 per hour.

To determine a firm's total revenue from employing a particular number of labour units, we sum the MRPs of those units. For example, if a firm employs three labour units with marginal revenue products of $14, $13, and $12, respectively, then the firm's total revenue is $39 (= $14 + $13 + $12). In Figure 14-3b, where we are not restricted to whole units of labour, total revenue is represented by area $0abc$ under the MRP curve to the left of Q_c. What area represents the firm's total cost, including a normal profit? For Q_c units, the same area—$0abc$. The green rectangle represents the firm's total wage cost ($0Q_c \times 0W_c$). The blue triangle (total revenue minus total wage cost) represents the firm's nonlabour costs—its explicit and implicit payments to land, capital, and entrepreneurship. Thus, in this case, total cost (wages plus other income payments) equals total revenue. This firm and others like it are earning only a normal profit. Figure 14-3b represents a long-run equilibrium for a firm that is selling its product in a perfectly competitive product market and hiring its labour in a perfectly competitive labour market.

14.3 Monopsony Model

monopsony
A market structure in which there is only a single buyer.

In the perfectly competitive labour market described in the preceding section, each employer hires too small an amount of labour to influence the wage rate. The situation is quite different when the labour market is a **monopsony,** a market structure in which there is only a single buyer. Labour market monopsony has the following characteristics:

- There is only a single buyer of a particular type of labour.

- The workers providing this type of labour have few employment options other than working for the monopsony either because they are geographically immobile or because finding alternative employment would mean having to acquire new skills.

- The firm is a wage-maker, because the wage rate it must pay varies directly with the number of workers it employs.

As is true of monopoly power, there are various degrees of monopsony power. In a perfect monopsony such power is at its maximum, because only a single employer exists in the labour market. The best real-world examples are probably the labour markets in some towns that depend almost entirely on one major firm. For example, a copper-mining concern may be almost the only source of employment in a remote British Columbia town, and a textile mill in Quebec's Eastern

When a firm hires most of the available supply of a particular type of labour, its decision to hire more or fewer workers affects the wage rate it pays to those workers.

connect
MATH 14.1
A Monopsonist's MFC
Exceeds the Wage Rate

Townships, a paper mill in Gatineau, or a fish processor in Newfoundland may provide most of the employment in its locale.

In other cases three or four firms may each hire a large portion of the supply of labour in a certain market and, therefore, have some monopsony power. If they tacitly or openly act in concert in hiring labour, they greatly enhance their monopsony power.

Upward-Sloping Labour Supply to a Firm

When a firm hires most of the available supply of a certain type of labour, its decision to employ more or fewer workers affects the wage rate it pays to those workers. If a firm is large in relation to the size of the labour market, it will have to pay a higher wage rate to obtain more labour. Suppose that there is only one employer of a particular type of labour in a certain geographic area. In this monopsony situation, the labour supply curve for the *firm* and the total labour supply curve for the *labour market* are identical. The monopsonist's supply curve—represented by curve S in Figure 14-4—is upward sloping because the firm must pay higher wage rates if it wants to attract and hire additional workers. This same curve is also the monopsonist's average-cost-of-labour curve. Each point on curve S indicates the wage rate (cost) per worker that must be paid to attract the corresponding number of workers.

MFC Higher than the Wage Rate

When a monopsonist pays a higher wage to attract an additional worker, it must pay that higher wage to all the workers it is currently employing at a lower wage. If not, labour morale will deteriorate, and the employer will be plagued with labour unrest because of wage-rate differences for the same job. Paying a uniform wage to all workers means that the cost of an extra worker—the marginal factor (labour) cost (MFC)—is the sum of that worker's wage rate and the amount necessary to bring the wage rate of all current workers up to the new wage level.

Table 14-2 illustrates this point. One worker can be hired at a wage rate of $6, but hiring a second worker forces the firm to pay a higher wage rate of $7. The marginal factor (labour) cost of the second worker is $8—the $7 paid to the second worker plus a $1 raise for the first worker. From another viewpoint, total labour cost is now $14 (= 2 × $7), up from $6 (= 1 × $6). So the MFC of the second worker is $8 (= $14 − $6), not just the $7 wage rate paid to that worker. Similarly, the marginal labour cost of the third worker is $10—the $8 that must be paid to attract this worker from alternative employment, plus $1 raises, from $7 to $8, for the first two workers.

FIGURE 14-4   The Wage Rate and Level of Employment in a Monopsonistic Labour Market

In a monopsonistic labour market, the employer's marginal factor (labour) cost curve (MFC) lies above the labour supply curve, S. Equating MFC with MRP at point b, the monopsonist hires Q_m workers (compared with Q_c under competition). As indicated by point c on S, it pays only wage rate W_m (compared with the competitive wage W_c).

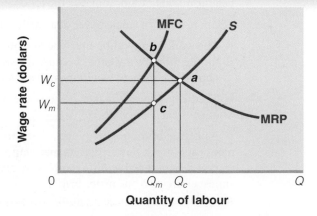

TABLE 14-2	The Supply of Labour: Monopsony in Hiring Labour		
(1) Units of labour	(2) Wage rate	(3) Total labour cost (wage bill)	(4) Marginal factor (labour) cost
0	$ 5	$ 0	
			$ 6
1	6	6	
			8
2	7	14	
			10
3	8	24	
			12
4	9	36	
			14
5	10	50	
			16
6	11	66	

Here is the key point: Because the monopsonist is the only employer in the labour market, its marginal resource (labour) cost exceeds the wage rate. Graphically, the monopsonist's MFC curve lies above the average-cost-of-labour curve, or labour supply curve *S,* as is clearly shown in Figure 14-4.

Equilibrium Wage and Employment

How many units of labour will the monopsonist hire and what wage rate will it pay? To maximize profit, the monopsonist will employ the quantity of labour Q_m in Figure 14-4, because at that quantity MFC and MRP are equal (point *b*).[1] The monopsonist next determines how much it must pay to attract these Q_m workers. From the supply curve *S,* specifically point *c,* it sees that it must pay wage rate W_m. Clearly, it need not pay a wage equal to MRP; it can attract and hire exactly the number of workers it wants (Q_m) with wage rate W_m. And that is the wage rate it will pay.

Contrast these results with those that would prevail in a competitive labour market. With competition in the hiring of labour, the level of employment would be greater (at Q_c) and the wage rate would be higher (at W_c). Other things equal, the monopsonist maximizes its profit by hiring a smaller number of workers and thereby paying a less-than-competitive wage rate. Society obtains a smaller output, and workers receive a wage rate that is less by *bc* than their marginal revenue product. Just as a monopolist finds it profitable to restrict product output to realize an above-competitive price for its goods, the monopsonist finds it profitable to restrict employment to reduce wage rates below those that would occur under competitive conditions.

WORKED PROBLEM 14.1
Labour Markets: Competition and Monopsony

[1] The fact that MFC exceeds factor price when factors are hired or purchased under imperfectly competitive (monopsonistic) conditions calls for adjustments in Chapter 13's least-cost and profit-maximizing rules for hiring factors. (See equations (1) and (2) in section 13.4, "Optimal Combination of Factors.") Specifically, we must substitute MFC for resource price in the denominators of our two equations. That is, with imperfect competition in the hiring of both labour and capital, equation (1) becomes

$$\frac{MP_L}{MFC_L} = \frac{MP_C}{MFC_C} \tag{1'}$$

and equation (2) is restated as

$$\frac{MRP_L}{MFC_L} = \frac{MRP_C}{MFC_C} = 1 \tag{2'}$$

In fact, equations (1) and (2) can be regarded as special cases of (1') and (2') in which firms happen to be hiring under perfectly competitive conditions and factor price is, therefore, equal to, and can be substituted for, marginal factor cost.

Examples of Monopsony Power

Fortunately, monopsonistic labour markets are uncommon in the Canadian economy. In most labour markets, several employers compete for workers, particularly for workers who are occupationally and geographically mobile. Also, in a potential monopsony in a local labour market, unions have often sprung up to counteract that power by forcing firms to negotiate wages. Nevertheless, there is evidence of monopsony power in such diverse labour markets as the markets for nurses, professional athletes, public-school teachers, newspaper employees, and some building trades workers.

14.4 Unions and the Labour Market: Three Models ::

Our assumption thus far has been that workers compete with one another in selling their labour services. But in some labour markets, workers unionize and sell their labour services collectively. When a union is formed in an otherwise competitive labour market, it usually bargains with a relatively large number of employers. It has many goals, the most important of which is to raise wage rates. It can pursue that objective in several ways.

Demand-Enhancement Model

Unions recognize that their ability to influence the demand for labour is limited. But, from the union's viewpoint, increasing the demand for union labour is highly desirable. As Figure 14-5 shows, an increase in the demand for union labour will create a higher union wage along with more jobs. Unions can increase the demand for their labour by increasing the demand for the goods or services they help produce. Political lobby is the main tool for increasing the demand for union-produced goods or services. For example, construction unions lobby for new highways, mass-transit systems, and stadium projects. Teachers' unions and associations push for increased public spending on education. Unions in the steel sector and forest-products sector lobby for tariffs and quotas on imports of steel and lumber, respectively. Such trade restrictions shift the demand for labour away from foreign countries and toward unionized Canadian labour.

Unions can also increase the demand for union labour by altering the price of other inputs. For example, although union members are generally paid significantly more than the minimum wage, unions have strongly supported increases in the minimum wage. The purpose may be to raise the price of low-wage, nonunion labour, which in some cases is substitutable for union labour. A higher minimum wage for nonunion workers will discourage employers from substituting such workers for union workers and thereby increase the demand for union members.

Similarly, unions have sometimes sought to increase the demand for their labour by supporting policy that reduces or holds down the price of complementary factors of production. For example, unions that represent workers who transport fruit and vegetables may support legislation

FIGURE 14-5 Unions and Demand Enhancement

When unions can increase the demand for union labour (say, from D_1 to D_2), they can realize higher wage rates (W_c to W_u) and more jobs (Q_c to Q_u).

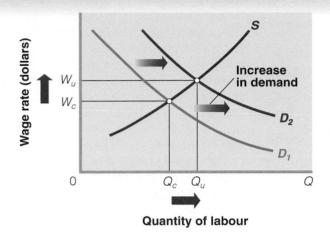

that allows low-wage foreign agricultural workers to work in Canada temporarily. Where union labour and other resources are complementary, a price decrease for the other factors will increase the demand for union labour through Chapter 13's output effect.

Exclusive or Craft Union Model

Unions can also boost wage rates by reducing the supply of labour, and over the years organized labour has favoured policies to do just that. The Canadian Labour Congress, an umbrella organization representing 2.3 million workers, has supported legislation that has (1) restricted permanent immigration, (2) reduced child labour, (3) encouraged compulsory retirement, and (4) enforced a shorter workweek.

Moreover, certain types of workers have adopted techniques designed to restrict the number of workers who can join their union. This is especially true of *craft unions,* whose members possess a particular skill, such as carpenters or brick masons or plumbers. Craft unions have frequently forced employers to agree to hire only union members, thereby gaining virtually complete control of the labour supply. Then, by following restrictive membership policies—for example, long apprenticeships, very high initiation fees, and limits on the number of new members admitted—they artificially restrict labour supply. As indicated in Figure 14-6, such practices result in higher

FIGURE 14-6 Exclusive or Craft Unionism

By reducing the supply of labour (say, from S_1 to S_2) through the use of restrictive membership policies, exclusive unions achieve higher wage rates (W_c to W_u). However, restriction of the labour supply also reduces the number of workers employed (Q_c to Q_u).

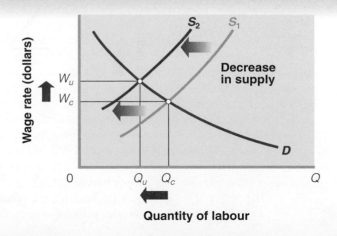

exclusive unionism
The practice of a labour union of restricting the supply of skilled union labour to increase the wages received by union members.

occupational licensing
The laws of provincial or municipal governments that require a worker to satisfy certain specified requirements and obtain a licence from a licensing board before engaging in a particular occupation.

wage rates and constitute what is called **exclusive unionism.** By excluding workers from unions and therefore from the labour supply, craft unions succeed in elevating wage rates.

Another means of restricting the supply of specific kinds of labour is **occupational licensing.** Here a group of workers in a given occupation pressure provincial or municipal governments to pass a law that says that some occupational group (for example, barbers, physicians, plumbers, car mechanics, or pest controllers) can practise their trade only if they meet certain requirements. Those requirements might include level of education, amount of work experience, the passing of an examination, and personal characteristics ("the practitioner must be of good moral character"). Members of the licensed occupation typically dominate the licensing board that administers such laws. The result is self-regulation, which often leads to policies that serve only to restrict entry to the occupation and reduce the labour supply.

The expressed purpose of licensing is to protect consumers from incompetent practitioners—surely a worthy goal. But such licensing also results in above-competitive wages and earnings for those in the licensed occupation (Figure 14-6). Moreover, licensing often includes a residency requirement, which inhibits the interprovincial movement of qualified workers. Some 300 occupations are now licensed in Canada.

Inclusive or Industrial Union Model

Instead of trying to limit their membership, however, most unions seek to organize all available workers. This is especially true of the *industrial unions,* such as the Canadian Auto Workers and the United Steelworkers. Such unions seek as members all available unskilled, semiskilled, and skilled workers in an industry. It makes sense for a union to be exclusive when its members are skilled craft workers for whom the employer has few substitutes. But it does not make sense for a union to be exclusive when trying to organize unskilled and semiskilled workers. To break a strike, employers could then easily substitute unskilled or semiskilled nonunion workers for the unskilled or semiskilled union workers.

By contrast, an industrial union that includes virtually all available workers in its membership can put firms under great pressure to agree to its wage demands. Because of its legal right to strike, such a union can threaten to deprive firms of their entire labour supply; an actual strike can do just that. Further, with virtually all available workers in the union, it will be difficult in the short run for new nonunion firms to emerge and thereby undermine what the union is demanding from existing firms.

inclusive unionism
The practice of a labour union to include as members all workers employed in an industry.

We illustrate such **inclusive unionism** in Figure 14-7. Initially, the competitive equilibrium wage rate is W_c and the level of employment is Q_c. Now suppose an industrial union is formed

---

FIGURE 14-7   **Inclusive or Industrial Unionism**

By organizing virtually all available workers to control the supply of labour, inclusive industrial unions may impose a wage rate, such as W_u, which is above the competitive wage rate W_c. The effect is to change the labour supply curve from S to aeS. At wage rate W_u, employers will cut employment from Q_c to Q_u.

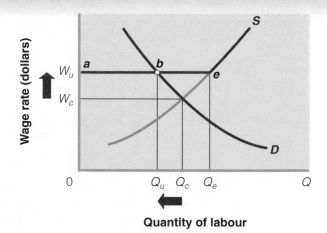

Quantity of labour

that demands a higher, above-equilibrium wage rate of, say, W_u. That wage rate W_u would create a perfectly elastic labour supply over the range *ae* in Figure 14-7. If firms wanted to hire any workers in this range, they would have to pay the union-imposed wage rate. If they decide against meeting this wage demand, the union will supply no labour at all, and the firms will be faced with a strike. If firms decide it is better to pay the higher wage rate than to suffer a strike, they will cut back on employment from Q_c to Q_u.

By agreeing to the union's W_u wage demand, individual employers become wage-takers. Because labour supply is perfectly elastic over range *ae*, the marginal resource (labour) cost is equal to the wage rate W_u over this range. The Q_u level of employment is the result of employers equating this MFC (now equal to the wage rate) with MRP, according to our profit-maximizing rule.

Note from point *e* on labour supply curve *S* that Q_e workers desire employment at wage W_u. But, as indicated by point *b* on labour demand curve *D*, only Q_u workers are employed. The result is a surplus of labour of $Q_e - Q_u$ (also shown by distance *eb*). In a perfectly competitive labour market without the union, the effect of a surplus of unemployed workers would be lower wages. Specifically, the wage rate would fall to the equilibrium level, W_c, where the quantity of labour supplied equals the quantity of labour demanded (each Q_c).

Wage Increases and Job Loss

Have Canadian unions been successful in raising the wages of their members? Evidence suggests that union members on average achieve a 15 percent wage advantage over nonunion workers.

As Figures 14-6 and 14-7 show, the effect of wage-raising actions by both exclusive and inclusive unionism is to reduce employment in unionized firms. A union's success in achieving above-equilibrium wage rates thus tends to be accompanied by a decline in the number of workers employed. That result acts as a restraining influence on union wage demands. A union cannot expect to maintain solidarity within its ranks if it seeks a wage rate so high that 20–30 percent of its members lose their jobs.

Bilateral Monopoly Model

bilateral monopoly
A market in which there is a single seller (monopoly) and a single buyer (monopsony).

Suppose a strong industrial union is formed in a monopsonist labour market rather than a competitive market, creating a combination of the monopsony model and the inclusive unionism model. Economists call the result **bilateral monopoly** because there is a single seller and a single buyer. The union is a monopolistic "seller" of labour that controls labour supply and can influence wage rates, but it faces a monopsonistic "buyer" of labour that can also affect wages by altering its employment. This is not an uncommon case, particularly in less-pure forms in which a single union confronts two, three, or four large employers, such as steel, automobiles, construction equipment, and professional sports.

INDETERMINATE OUTCOME OF BILATERAL MONOPOLY

We show this situation in Figure 14-8, where Figure 14-7 is superimposed onto Figure 14-4. The monopsonistic employer will seek the below-competitive-equilibrium wage rate W_m, and the union will press for some above-competitive-equilibrium wage rate such as W_u. Which will be the outcome? We cannot say with certainty because the bilateral monopoly model does not explain what will happen at the collective bargaining table. We can expect the wage outcome to lie somewhere between W_m and W_u. Beyond that, about all we can say is that the party with the greater bargaining power and the more effective negotiating strategy will probably get a wage closer to the one it seeks.

DESIRABILITY OF BILATERAL MONOPOLY

The wage and employment outcomes in this situation might be more economically desirable than the term "bilateral monopoly" implies. The monopoly on one side of the market might in effect cancel out the monopoly on the other side, yielding competitive or near-competitive results.

FIGURE 14-8   Bilateral Monopoly in the Labour Market

A monopsonist seeks to hire Q_m workers (where MFC = MRP) and pay wage rate W_m corresponding to Q_m labour on labour supply curve S. The inclusive union it faces seeks the above-equilibrium wage rate W_u. The actual outcome cannot be predicted.

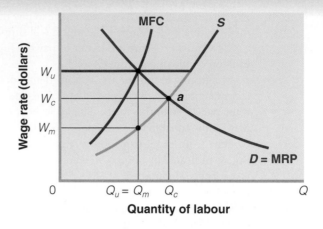

QUICK REVIEW

- In the demand-enhancement union model, a union increases the wage rate by increasing labour demand through actions that increase product demand, or alter the prices of related inputs.

- In the exclusive (craft) union model, a union increases wage rates by artificially restricting labour supply, through, say, long apprenticeships or occupational licensing.

- In the inclusive (industrial) union model, a union raises the wage rate by gaining control over a firm's labour supply and threatening to withhold labour via a strike unless a negotiated wage is obtained.

- Bilateral monopoly occurs in a labour market where a monopsonist bargains with an inclusive, or industrial, union. Wage and employment outcomes are determined by collective bargaining in this situation.

14.5 The Minimum Wage Controversy

minimum wage
The lowest wage employers may legally pay for an hour of work.

In Canada both the federal and provincial governments have enacted **minimum wage** legislation, but it is the provincial laws that cover most workers. The provincial minimum wage ranges from $9.50 per hour in New Brunswick to $10.25 per hour in Ontario. The purpose of the minimum wage is to provide a living wage for less-skilled workers to keep them and their families from poverty.

Case against the Minimum Wage

Critics, reasoning in terms of Figure 14-7, contend that an above-equilibrium minimum wage (say, W_u) will cause employers to hire fewer workers. In other words, increasing the minimum wage leads to a decrease in the number of people employed at that wage. Downward-sloping labour demand curves are a reality. The higher labour costs may even force some firms out of business. Then, some of the poor, low-wage workers whom the minimum wage was designed to help will find themselves out of work. Critics point out that a worker who is *unemployed* at a minimum wage of $6.00 per hour is clearly worse off than if *employed* at a market wage rate of, say, $5.50 per hour.

A second criticism of the minimum wage is that it is "poorly targeted" to reduce household poverty. Critics point out that much of the benefit of the minimum wage accrues to workers, including many teenagers, who do not live in poor households.

Case for the Minimum Wage

Advocates of the minimum wage say that critics analyze its impact in an unrealistic context. Figure 14-7, advocates claim, assumes a competitive, static market. But in a less competitive, low-pay labour market where employers possess some monopsony power (Figure 14-8), the minimum wage can increase wage rates without causing significant unemployment. Indeed, a higher minimum wage may even produce more jobs by eliminating the motive that monopsonistic firms have for restricting employment. For example, a minimum wage floor of W_c in Figure 14-8 would change the firm's labour supply curve to W_caS and prompt the firm to increase its employment from Q_m workers to Q_c workers.

Moreover, even if the labour market is competitive, the higher wage rate might prompt firms to find more productive tasks for low-paid workers, thereby raising their productivity. Alternatively, the minimum wage may reduce *labour turnover* (the rate at which workers voluntarily quit). With fewer low-productive trainees, the *average* productivity of the firm's workers would rise. In either case, the alleged negative employment effects of the minimum wage might not occur.

Evidence and Conclusions

Which view is correct? Unfortunately, there is no clear answer. All economists agree that firms will not hire workers who cost more per hour than the value of their hourly output. So some minimum wage is sufficiently high—say, $20 an hour—that it would severely reduce employment. Consider $30 an hour, as an absurd example. Because the majority of Canadian workers earned less than $20 per hour in 2011, a minimum wage of $30 per hour would render the majority of them unemployable because the minimum wage that they would have to be paid by potential employers would far exceed their marginal revenue products.

It has to be remembered, though, that a minimum wage will only cause unemployment in labour markets where the minimum wage is higher than the equilibrium wage. Because the average provincial minimum wage of $9.50 per hour is much lower than the average hourly wage of about $18.80 that was earned by Canadian workers in 2011, any unemployment caused by the $9.50 per hour minimum wage is most likely to fall on low-skilled workers who earn low wages due to their low productivity. These workers are mostly teenagers, adults who did not complete high school, and immigrants with low levels of education and poor English proficiency. For members of such groups, recent research suggests that a 10 percent increase in the minimum wage will cause a 1–3 percent decline in employment. However, estimates of the employment effect of minimum wage laws vary from study to study so that significant controversy remains.

The overall effect of the minimum wage is thus uncertain. On the one hand, the employment and unemployment effects of the minimum wage do not appear to be as great as many critics fear. On the other hand, because a large part of its effect is dissipated on families not experiencing poverty, the minimum wage is not as strong an antipoverty tool as many supporters contend.

14.6 Wage Differentials

wage differentials
The difference between the wage received by one worker or group of workers and that received by another worker or group of workers.

Hourly wage rates and annual salaries differ greatly among occupations. In Table 14-3 we list average weekly wages for several industries to illustrate such occupational **wage differentials.** For example, observe that construction workers on average earn one-third more than those workers in the health and social service industry. Large wage differentials also exist within some of the occupations listed (not shown). For example, although average wages for retail salespersons are relatively low, some top salespersons selling on commission make several times the average wages for their occupation.

| TABLE 14-3 | Average Weekly Wages in Selected Industries, 2012 |

Industry	Average weekly earnings (including overtime)
All industries	$ 853.19
Mining, and oil and gas extraction	1705.57
Construction	1066.08
Finance, insurance, and real estate	1049.45
Manufacturing	960.43
Logging and forestry	948.38
Transportation and warehousing	883.32
Educational and related services	934.00
Real estate services	818.62
Health and social services	786.27

Source: Adapted from Statistics Canada CANSIM database, http://cansim2.statcan.ca, Table 281-0027, March 2012 .

What explains wage differentials such as these? Once again, the forces of demand and supply are revealing. As we demonstrate in Figure 14-9, wage differentials can arise on either the supply or demand side of labour markets. Figures 14-9a and 14-9b represent labour markets for two occupational groups that have identical *labour supply curves*. The labour market in panel (a) has a relatively high equilibrium wage (W_a) because labour demand is very strong. The labour market in panel (b) has an equilibrium wage that is relatively low (W_b) since labour demand is weak. Clearly, the wage differential between occupations (a) and (b) results solely from differences in the magnitude of labour demand.

Contrast that situation with Figure 14-9c and 14-9d, where the *labour demand curves* are identical. In the labour market in panel (c), the equilibrium wage is relatively high (W_c) because labour supply is low. In the labour market in panel (d) labour supply is highly abundant, so the equilibrium wage (W_d) is relatively low. The wage differential between (c) and (d) results solely from the differences in the magnitude of the labour supply.

Although Figure 14-9 provides a good starting point for understanding wage differentials, we need to know *why* demand and supply conditions differ in various labour markets.

Marginal Revenue Productivity

The strength of labour demand—how far to the right the labour demand curve is located—differs greatly among occupations because of differences in how much various occupational groups contribute to their employers' revenue. This revenue contribution, in turn, depends on the workers' productivity and the strength of the demand for the products they are helping to produce. Where labour is highly productive and product demand is strong, labour demand also is strong and, other things equal, pay is high. Top professional athletes, for example, are highly productive at sports entertainment, for which millions of people are willing to pay billions of dollars over the course of a season. Because the **marginal revenue productivity** of these players is so high, they are in very high demand by sports teams. This high demand leads to their extremely high salaries (as in Figure 14-9a). In contrast, most workers generate much more modest revenue for their employers. This results in much lower demand for their labour and, consequently, much lower wages (as in Figure 14-9b).

marginal revenue productivity
How much workers contribute to their employers' revenue.

FIGURE 14-9 Labour Demand, Labour Supply, and Wage Differentials

The wage differential between labour markets (a) and (b) results solely from differences in labour demand. In labour markets (c) and (d), differences in labour supply cause the wage differential.

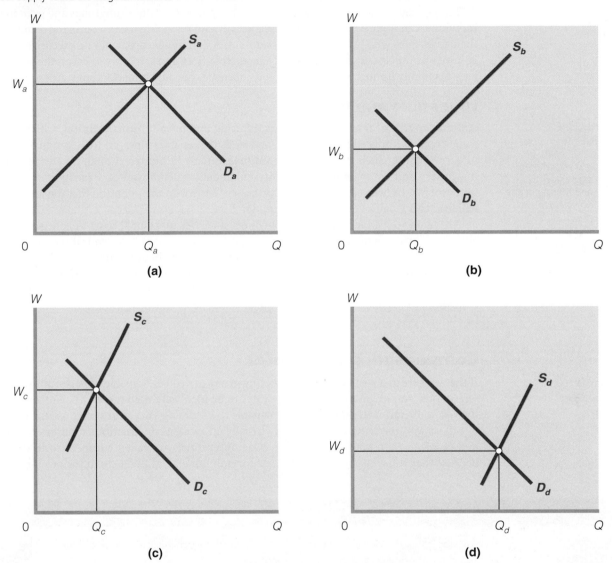

(a)   (b)

(c)   (d)

Noncompeting Groups

noncompeting groups
Collections of workers in the economy who do not compete with each other for employment because the skills and training of the workers in one group are substantially different from those in other groups.

On the supply side of the labour market, workers are not homogeneous; they differ in their mental and physical capabilities and in their education and training. At any given time the labour force is made up of many **noncompeting groups** of workers, each representing several occupations for which the members of a particular group qualify. In some groups qualified workers are relatively few, whereas in others they are highly abundant. Workers in one group do not qualify for the occupations of other groups.

ABILITY

Only a few workers have the ability or physical attributes to be brain surgeons, concert violinists, top fashion models, research scientists, or professional athletes. Because the supply of these particular types of labour is very small in relation to labour demand, their wages are high, as in Figure 14-9c. The members of these and similar groups do not compete with one another or with other skilled or semiskilled workers. The violinist does not compete with the surgeon, nor does the surgeon compete with the professional athlete or the fashion model.

The concept of noncompeting groups can be applied to various subgroups and even to specific individuals in a particular group. An especially skilled violinist can command a higher salary than colleagues who play the same instrument. A handful of top corporate executives earn 10 to 20 times as much as the average chief executive officer. In each of these cases, the supply of top talent is highly limited, since less talented colleagues are only imperfect substitutes.

EDUCATION AND TRAINING

human capital
Any expenditure to improve the education, skills, health, or mobility of workers, with an expectation of greater productivity and thus a positive return on the investment.

Another source of wage differentials is differing amounts of **human capital,** which is the personal stock of knowledge, know-how, and skills that enables a person to be productive and thus to earn income. Such stocks result from investments in human capital. Like expenditures on machinery and equipment, productivity-enhancing expenditures on education or training are investments. In both cases, people incur *present costs* with the intention that those expenditures will lead to a greater flow of *future earnings.*

Although education yields higher incomes, it carries substantial costs. A college or university education involves not only direct costs (tuition, fees, books) but also indirect or opportunity costs (forgone earnings). Does the higher pay received by better-educated workers compensate for these costs? The answer is yes. Rates of return are estimated to be 10–13 percent for investments in secondary education and 8–12 percent for investments in college and university education. One generally accepted estimate is that each year of schooling raises a worker's wage by about 8 percent.

connect
ORIGIN OF THE IDEA 14.2
Human Capital

Compensating Differences

compensating differences
Differences in the wages received by workers in different jobs to compensate for nonmonetary differences in the jobs.

If the workers in a particular noncompeting group are equally capable of performing several different jobs, you might expect the wage rates to be identical for all these jobs. Not so. A group of high-school graduates may be equally capable of becoming sales clerks or construction workers, but these jobs pay different wages. In virtually all locales, construction labourers receive much higher wages than sales clerks. These wage differentials are called **compensating differences,** because they must be paid to compensate for nonmonetary differences in various jobs.

CONSIDER THIS :: My Entire Life

Human capital is the accumulation of outcomes of prior investments in education, training, and other factors that increase productivity and earnings. It is the stock of knowledge, know-how, and skills that enables individuals to be productive and thus earn income. A valuable stock of human capital, together with a strong demand for one's services, can add up to a large capacity to earn income. For some people, high earnings have little to do with actual hours of work and much to do with their tremendous skill,

which reflects their accumulated stock of human capital.

The point is demonstrated in the following story: It is said that a tourist once spotted the famous Spanish artist Pablo Picasso (1881–1973) in a Paris café. The tourist asked Picasso if he would do a sketch of his wife for pay. Picasso sketched the wife in a matter of minutes and said, "That will be 10,000 francs [roughly $2000]." Hearing the high price, the tourist became irritated, saying, "But that took you only a few minutes."

"No," replied Picasso, "it took me my entire life!"

Source: Reunion des Musées Nationaux/Art Resource, NY © Estate of Pablo Picasso/Artisits Right Society (ARS), New York.

The construction job involves dirty working conditions, the hazard of accidents, and irregular employment. The retail sales job means clean clothing, pleasant air-conditioned surroundings, and less fear of injury or layoff. Other things equal, it is easy to see why some workers would rather pick up a credit card than a shovel. So labour supply is less for construction firms, as in Figure 14-9c, than for retail shops, as in Figure 14-9d. Construction firms must pay higher wages than retailers to compensate for the unattractive aspects of construction jobs.

Compensating differences play an important role in allocating society's scarce labour resources. If very few workers want to be garbage collectors, then society must pay high wages to attract garbage collectors. If many more people want to be sales clerks than are needed, then society need not pay them as much as garbage collectors to get those services performed.

Market Imperfections

Differences in marginal revenue productivity, amounts of human capital, and nonmonetary aspects of jobs explain most of the wage differentials in the economy. But other persistent differentials result from various market imperfections that impede workers moving from lower-paying jobs to higher-paying jobs.

- *Lack of Job Information* Workers may simply be unaware of job opportunities and wage rates in other geographic areas and in other jobs for which they qualify. Consequently, the flow of qualified labour from lower-paying to higher-paying jobs may not be sufficient to equalize wages within occupations.

- *Geographic Immobility* Many workers are reluctant to move to new places, to leave friends, relatives, and associates, to force their children to change schools, to sell their houses, or to incur the costs and inconveniences of adjusting to a new job and a new community. As Adam Smith noted more than two centuries ago, "A [person] is of all sorts of luggage the most difficult to be transported." The reluctance of workers to move creates persistent geographic wage differentials within the same occupation. Some economists point out that Canada's employment insurance program contributes to labour immobility.

- *Unions and Government Restraints* Wage differentials may be reinforced by artificial restrictions on mobility imposed by unions and government. We have noted that craft unions keep their wages high by restricting membership. Thus, the low-paid nonunion carpenter of Edmonton, Alberta, may be willing to move to Vancouver in the pursuit of higher wages, but her chances of succeeding are slim. She may be unable to get a union card, and no card means no job. Similarly, an optometrist or lawyer qualified to practise in one province may not meet the licensing requirements of other provinces, so his ability to move is limited. Other artificial barriers involve pension plans and seniority rights that might be jeopardized by moving from one job to another.

- *Discrimination* Despite legislation to the contrary, discrimination results in lower wages being paid to women and visible-minority workers than to white males doing virtually identical work. Also, women and minorities may be crowded into certain low-paying occupations, driving down wages there and raising them elsewhere. If discrimination keeps qualified women and minorities from taking the higher-paying jobs, then differences in pay will persist.

All four considerations—differences in marginal revenue productivity, noncompeting groups, compensating differences, and market imperfections—come into play in explaining actual wage differentials. For example, the differential between the wages of a physician and those of a construction worker can be explained based on marginal revenue productivity and noncompeting groups. Physicians generate considerable revenue because of their high productivity and the strong willingness of consumers (via provincial governments) to pay for health care. Physicians also fall into a noncompeting group where, because of stringent training requirements, only a relatively few persons qualify. So the supply of labour is small in relation to demand.

14.7 Pay for Performance and the Principal–Agent Problem

The models of wage determination we have described in this chapter assume that worker pay is always a standard amount for each hour's work, for example $15 per hour. But pay schemes are often more complex than that in both composition and purpose. For instance, many workers receive annual salaries rather than hourly pay. Many workers also receive fringe benefits: dental insurance, life insurance, paid vacations, paid sick-leave days, pension contributions, and so on. Finally, some pay plans are designed to elicit a desired level of performance from workers. This last aspect of pay plans requires further elaboration.

The Principal–Agent Problem

principal–agent problem
A problem associated with possible differences in the interests of corporate shareholders (principals) and the executives (agents) they hire.

The **principal–agent problem** is usually associated with the possible differences in the interests of corporate shareholders (principals) and the executives (agents) they hire. But this problem extends to all paid employees. Firms hire workers to help produce the goods and services the firms sell for a profit. Workers are the firms' agents; they are hired to advance the interest (profit) of the firms. The principals are the firms; they hire agents to advance their goals. Firms and workers have one interest in common: they both want the firm to survive and thrive. That will ensure profit for the firm and continued employment and wages for the workers.

But the interests of the firm and of the workers are not identical. A principal–agent problem arises when those interests diverge. Workers may seek to increase their utility by shirking on the job, that is, by providing less than the agreed-on effort or by taking unauthorized breaks. The night security guard in a warehouse may leave work early or spend time reading a novel rather than making the assigned rounds. A salaried manager may spend time away from the office visiting friends rather than attending to company business.

≋ connect
ORIGIN OF THE IDEA 14.3
Principal–Agent Problem

Firms (principals) have a profit incentive to reduce or eliminate shirking. One option is to monitor workers, but monitoring is difficult and costly. Hiring another worker to supervise or monitor the security guard might double the cost of maintaining a secure warehouse. Another way of resolving the principal–agent problem is through some sort of **incentive pay plan** that ties worker compensation more closely to output or performance. Such incentive pay schemes include piece rates, commissions and royalties, bonuses and profit sharing, and efficiency wages.

incentive pay plan
A compensation structure, such as piece rates, commissions, royalties, bonuses, stock options, and profit sharing, that ties worker pay directly to performance.

PIECE RATES

Piece rates are compensation paid according to the number of units of output a worker produces. If a principal pays fruit pickers by the bushel or typists by the page, it need not be concerned with shirking or with monitoring costs.

COMMISSIONS OR ROYALTIES

Unlike piece rates, commissions and royalties tie compensation to the value of sales. Employees who sell products or services—including real estate agents, insurance agents, stockbrokers, and retail salespersons—commonly receive *commissions* that are computed as a percentage of the monetary value of their sales. Recording artists and authors are paid *royalties,* computed as a certain percentage of sales revenues from their works. These types of compensation link the financial interests of the salespeople or artists and authors to the profit interest of the firms.

BONUSES, STOCK OPTIONS, AND PROFIT SHARING

Bonuses are payments in addition to one's annual salary that are based on some factor such as the performance of the individual worker, or of a group of workers, or of the firm itself. A professional baseball player may receive a bonus based on a high batting average, the number of home runs hit, or the number of runs batted in. A business manager may receive a bonus based on the profitability of her or his unit. *Stock options* allow workers to buy shares of their employer's stock at a fixed price. If the firm does well and its stock prices rise, the workers' stock holdings rise in value. Such options are part of the compensation packages of top corporate officials, as well as many workers in relatively new high-technology firms. *Profit-sharing plans* allocate a percentage of a firm's profit to its employees. Such plans have in recent years resulted in large annual payments to many Canadian workers.

Addendum: The Negative Side Effects of Pay for Performance

Although pay for performance may help to overcome the principal–agent problem and enhance worker productivity, such plans may have negative side effects and so require careful design. Here are a few examples:

- The rapid production pace that piece rates encourage may result in poor product quality and may compromise the safety of workers. Such outcomes can be costly to the firm over the long run.

- Commissions may cause some salespeople to engage in questionable or even fraudulent sales practices, such as making exaggerated claims about products or recommending unneeded repairs. Such practices may lead to private lawsuits or government legal action.

- Bonuses based on personal performance may disrupt the close cooperation needed for maximum team production. A professional hockey player who receives a bonus for goals scored may be reluctant to pass the puck to teammates.

- Since profit sharing is usually tied to the performance of the entire firm, less energetic workers can free-ride by obtaining their profit share based on the hard work of others.

- Stock options may prompt some unscrupulous executives to manipulate the cost and revenue streams of their firms to create a false appearance of rapidly rising profit. When the firm's stock value rises, the executives exercise their stock options at inflated share prices and reap a personal fortune.

- There may be a downside to the reduced turnover resulting from above-market wages: Firms that pay efficiency wages have fewer opportunities to hire new workers and suffer the loss of the creative energy that new workers often bring to the workplace.

QUICK REVIEW

- Proponents of the minimum wage argue that it is needed to assist the working poor and to counter monopsony where it might exist; critics say that it is poorly targeted to reduce poverty and that it reduces employment.

- Wage differentials are generally attributable to the forces of supply and demand, influenced by differences in workers' marginal revenue productivity, workers' education and skills, and nonmonetary differences in jobs. Several labour market imperfections also play a role.

- As it applies to labour, the principal–agent problem is one of workers pursuing their own interests to the detriment of the employer's profit objective.

- Pay-for-performance plans (piece rates, commissions, royalties, bonuses, stock options, and profit sharing) are designed to improve worker productivity by overcoming the principal–agent problem.

The LAST WORD   Are Top Executives in Canada Overpaid?

The multimillion-dollar pay of major corporate CEOs has drawn considerable criticism.

The Five Highest-Paid Canadian CEOs, 2010*

Name	Company	Total pay (in millions)
1. Frank Stronach	Magna International	$61.8
2. Edward Sampson	Niko Resources	16.5
3. Martin Konig	European Goldfields	14.8
4. Steve Laut	Canadian Natural Resources	13.1
5. Stephen DeFalco	Nordion	13.1

Top executives of Canadian corporations typically receive total annual pay (salary, bonuses, and stock options) in the millions of dollars. As shown in the table, each of the five highest-paid Canadian executives earned more than $10 million in 2010. The highest paid CEO earned over $60 million!

CEO pay in Canada is not only exceptionally high relative to the average pay of Canadian managers and workers, but is also the second highest CEO pay among industrialized countries (surpassed only by the U.S.). Among the highest paid CEOs in the U.S. in 2008, Lawrence J. Ellison of Oracle was paid U.S.$557 million, while Ray Irani of Occidental Petroleum took home U.S.$223 million.

Is high CEO pay simply the outcome of labour supply and labour demand, as is the pay for star athletes and entertainers? Does it reflect marginal revenue productivity—that is, the contributions by CEOs to their company's output and revenue?

Observers who answer affirmatively point out that decisions made by the CEOs of large corporations affect the productivity of every employee in the organization. Good decisions

enhance productivity throughout the organization and increase revenue; bad decisions reduce productivity and revenue. Only executives who have consistently made good business decisions attain the top positions in large corporations. Because the supply of these people is highly limited and their marginal revenue productivity is enormous, top CEOs command huge salaries and performance bonuses.

Also, some economists note that CEO pay in Canada may be like the

prizes professional golfers and tennis players receive for winning tournaments. These valuable prizes are designed to promote the productivity of all those who aspire to achieve them. In corporations the top prizes go to the winners of the "contests" among managers to attain, at least eventually, the CEO positions. Thus high CEO pay does not derive solely from the CEO's direct productivity. Instead, it may exist because the high pay creates incentives that raise the productivity of scores of other corporate executives who seek to achieve the top position. In this view, high CEO pay is still based on high productivity.

Critics of existing CEO pay acknowledge that CEOs deserve substantially higher salaries than ordinary workers or typical managers, but they question pay packages that run into the millions of dollars. They reject the "tournament pay" idea on the grounds that corporations require co-operative team effort by managers and executives, not the type of high-stakes competition promoted by "winner-take-most" pay. They believe that corporations, although owned by their shareholders, are controlled by corporate boards and professional executives. Because many board members are present or past CEOs of other corporations, they often exaggerate CEO importance and, consequently, overpay their own CEOs. These overpayments are at the expense of the firm's shareholders.

In summary, defenders of CEO pay say that high pay is justified by the direct or indirect marginal revenue contribution of CEOs. Like it or not, CEO pay is market-determined pay. In contrast, critics say that multimillion-dollar CEO pay bears little relationship to marginal revenue productivity and is unfair to ordinary shareholders. It is clear from our discussion that these issues remain unsettled.

*Source for salary data: Canadian Centre for Policy Alternatives, "Canada's CEO Elite 100, http://www.policyalternatives.ca/sites/default/files/uploads/publications/National%20Office/2012/01/Canadas%20CEO%20Elite%20100FINAL.pdf Accessed March 21, 2012.

Question

Do you think exceptionally high pay to CEOs is economically justified? Why or why not?

:: CHAPTER SUMMARY

14.1 :: PRODUCTIVITY AND THE GENERAL LEVEL OF WAGES

- The term "labour" encompasses all people who work for pay. The wage rate is the price paid per unit of time for labour. Labour earnings comprise total pay and are found by multiplying the number of hours worked by the hourly wage rate. The nominal wage rate is the amount of money received per unit of time; the real wage rate is the purchasing power of the nominal wage.

- The long-run growth of real hourly earnings—the average real wage—roughly matches that of productivity, with both increasing over the long run.

- Global comparisons suggest that real wages in Canada are relatively high, but not the highest internationally. High real wages in the advanced industrial countries stem largely from high labour productivity.

14.2 :: WAGES IN A PERFECTLY COMPETITIVE LABOUR MARKET

- Specific wage rates depend on the structure of the particular labour market. In a competitive labour market, the equilibrium wage rate and level of employment are determined at the intersection of the labour supply curve and labour demand curve. For the individual firm, the market wage rate establishes a horizontal labour supply curve, meaning that the wage rate equals the firm's constant marginal resource cost. The firm hires workers to the point where its MRP equals this MFC.

14.3 :: MONOPSONY MODEL

- Under monopsony the MFC curve lies above the factor supply curve because the monopsonist must bid up the wage rate to hire extra workers and must pay that higher wage rate to all workers. The monopsonist hires fewer workers than are hired under competitive conditions, pays less-than-competitive wage rates (has lower labour costs), and thus obtains greater profit.

14.4 :: UNIONS AND THE LABOUR MARKET: THREE MODELS

- A union may raise competitive wage rates by (a) increasing the derived demand for labour, (b) restricting the supply of labour through exclusive unionism, or (c) directly enforcing an above-equilibrium wage rate through inclusive unionism.

- In many industries the labour market takes the form of bilateral monopoly, in which a strong union sells labour to a monopsonistic employer. The wage-rate outcome of this labour market model depends on union and employer bargaining power.

- On average, unionized workers realize wage rates 15 percent higher than those of comparable nonunion workers.

14.5 :: THE MINIMUM WAGE CONTROVERSY

- Economists disagree about the desirability of the minimum wage as an antipoverty mechanism. While it causes unemployment for some low-income workers, it raises the incomes of those who retain their jobs.

14.6 :: WAGE DIFFERENTIALS

- Wage differentials are largely explainable in terms of (a) marginal revenue productivity of various groups of workers; (b) noncompeting groups arising from differences in the capacities and education of different groups of workers; (c) compensating differences, that is, wage differences that must be paid to offset nonmonetary differences in jobs; and (d) market imperfections in the form of lack of job information, geographical immobility, union and government restraints, and discrimination.

14.7 :: PAY FOR PERFORMANCE AND THE PRINCIPAL–AGENT PROBLEM

- As it applies to labour, the principal–agent problem arises when workers provide less-than-expected effort. Firms may combat this by monitoring workers or by creating incentive pay schemes that link worker compensation to performance.

:: TERMS AND CONCEPTS

wage rate, p. 328
nominal wage, p. 328
real wage, p. 328
perfectly competitive labour
  market, p. 331
monopsony, p. 333

exclusive unionism, p. 338
occupational licensing, p. 338
inclusive unionism, p. 338
bilateral monopoly, p. 339
minimum wage, p. 340
wage differentials, p. 341

marginal revenue productivity, p. 342
noncompeting groups, p. 343
human capital, p. 344
compensating differences, p. 344
principal–agent problem, p. 346
incentive pay plan, p. 346

:: QUESTIONS

1. Explain why the general level of wages is high in Canada and other industrially advanced countries. What is the single most important factor underlying the long-run increase in average real-wage rates in Canada?   [**LO14.1**]

2. Why is a firm in a perfectly competitive labour market a wage-taker? What would happen if that firm decided to pay less than the going market wage rate?   [**LO14.2**]

3. Describe wage determination in a labour market in which workers are unorganized and many firms actively compete for the services of labour. Show this situation graphically, using W_1 to indicate the equilibrium wage rate and Q_1 to show the number of workers hired by the firms as a group. Show the labour supply curve of the individual firm and compare it with that of the total market. Why are there differences? In the diagram representing the firm, identify total revenue, total wage cost, and revenue available for the payment of nonlabour resources.   [**LO14.2**]

4. Suppose the formerly competing firms in Question 3 form an employers' association that hires labour as a monopsonist would. Describe verbally the effect on wage rates and employment. Adjust the graph you drew for Question 3, showing the monopsonistic wage rate and employment level as W_2 and Q_2, respectively. Using this monopsony model, explain why hospital administrators sometimes complain about a shortage of nurses. How might such a shortage be corrected?   [**LO14.3**]

5. Assume a monopsonistic employer is paying a wage rate of W_m and hiring Q_m workers, as indicated in Figure 14-8. Now suppose an industrial union is formed that forces the employer to accept a wage rate of W_c. Explain verbally and graphically why in this instance the higher wage rate will be accompanied by an increase in the number of workers hired.   [**LO14.4**]

6. Have you ever worked for the minimum wage? If so, for how long? Would you favour increasing the minimum wage by a dollar? By two dollars? By five dollars? Explain your reasoning.   [**LO14.5**]

7. "Many of the lowest-paid people in society—for example, short-order cooks—also have relatively poor working conditions. Hence, the notion of compensating wage differentials is disproved." Do you agree? Explain. [**LO14.6**]

8. What is meant by investment in human capital? Use this concept to explain (a) wage differentials, and (b) the long-run rise of real wage rates in Canada.   [**LO14.6**]

9. What is the principal–agent problem? Have you ever worked in a setting where this problem arose? If so, do you think increased monitoring would have eliminated the problem? Why don't firms simply hire more supervisors to eliminate shirking?   [**LO14.7**]

:: PROBLEMS

1. Workers are compensated by firms with "benefits" in addition to wages and salaries. The most prominent benefit offered by many firms is health insurance. Suppose that, in 2000, workers at one steel plant were paid $20 per hour and in addition received health benefits at the rate of $4 per hour. Also suppose that, by 2010, workers at that plant were paid $21 per hour but received $9 in health insurance benefits.   [**LO14.7**]

   a. By what percentage did total compensation (wages plus benefits) change at this plant from 2000 to 2010? What was the approximate average annual percentage change in total compensation?

   b. By what percentage did wages change at this plant from 2000 to 2010? What was the approximate average annual percentage change in wages?

   c. If workers value a dollar of health benefits as much as they value a dollar of wages, by what total percentage will they feel that their incomes have risen over this time period? What if they only consider wages when calculating their incomes?

   d. Is it possible for workers to feel as though their wages are stagnating even if total compensation is rising?

2. Complete the following labour supply table for a firm hiring labour competitively: [LO14.2]

Units of labour	Wage rate	Total labour cost	Marginal factor (labour) cost
0	$14	$ ___	
			$ ___
1	14	___	
2	14	___	___
3	14	___	___
4	14	___	___
5	14	___	___
6	14	___	___

a. Show graphically the labour supply and marginal factor (labour) cost curves for this firm. Are the curves the same or different? If they are different, which one is higher?

b. Plot the labour demand data of Question 2 in Chapter 13 on the graph used in part (a) above. What are the equilibrium wage rate and level of employment?

3. Assume a firm is a monopsonist that can hire its first worker for $6 but must increase the wage rate by $3 to attract each successive worker (so that the second worker must be paid $9, the third $12, and so on).   [LO14.3]

a. Draw the firm's labour supply and marginal resource cost curves. Are the curves the same or different? If they are different, which one is higher?

b. On the same graph, plot the labour demand data of Question 2 in Chapter 13. What are the equilibrium wage rate and level of employment?

c. Compare these answers with those you found in Problem 2. By how much does the monoposonist reduce wages below the competitive wage? By how much does the monopsonist reduce employment below the competitive level?

4. Suppose that low-skill workers employed in clearing woodland can each clear one hectare per month if they are each equipped with a shovel, a machete, and a chainsaw.

Clearing one hectare brings in $1000 in revenue. Each worker's equipment costs the worker's employer $150 per month to rent and each worker toils 40 hours per week for four weeks each month.   [LO14.4]

a. What is the marginal revenue product of hiring one low-skill worker to clear woodland for one month?

b. How much revenue per hour does each worker bring in?

c. If the minimum wage were $6.20, would the revenue per hour in part (b) exceed the minimum wage? If so, by how much per hour?

d. Now consider the employer's total costs. These include the equipment costs as well as a normal profit of $50 per acre. If the firm pays workers the minimum wage of $6.20 per hour, what will the firm's economic profit or loss be per acre?

e. At what value would the minimum wage have to be set so that the firm would make zero economic profit from employing an additional low-skilled worker to clear woodland?

5. Suppose that a car dealership wishes to see if efficiency wages will help improve its salespeople's productivity. Currently, each salesperson sells an average of one car per day while being paid $20 per hour for an eight-hour day.   [LO14.6]

a. What is the current labour cost per car sold?

b. Suppose when the dealer raises the price of labour to $30 per hour the average number of cars sold by a salesperson increases to two per day. What is now the labour cost per car sold? By how much is it higher or lower than it was before? Has the efficiency of labour expenditures by the firm (cars sold per dollar of wages paid to salespeople) increased or decreased?

c. Suppose that if the wage is raised a second time to $40 per hour the number of cars sold rises to an average of 2.5 per day. What is now the labour cost per car sold?

d. If the firm's goal is to maximize the efficiency of its labour expenditures, which of the three hourly salary rates should it use: $20 per hour, $30 per hour, or $40 per hour?

e. By contrast, which salary maximizes the productivity of the car dealer's workers (cars sold per worker per day)?

Rent, Interest, and Profit

AFTER READING THIS CHAPTER,
YOU SHOULD BE ABLE TO:

15.1 Explain the nature of economic rent and how it is determined.

15.2 Describe how the interest rate is determined.

15.3 Relate why economic profits occur, and how profits, along with losses, allocate resources among alternative uses.

In Chapter 14, we focused on the wages and salaries paid by firms to obtain labour. Here our attention is focused on the rent, interest, and profit paid by firms to obtain, respectively, land, capital, and entrepreneurship. Our analysis will provide answers to numerous practical questions, including:

- How do *land prices* and *land rents* get established, and why do they differ from property to property? For example, why can a hectare of land in the middle of Toronto or Vancouver sell for more than $100 million, while a hectare in northern Manitoba may fetch no more than $500?

- What determines *interest rates* and causes them to change? For instance, why were interest rates on three-month guaranteed investment certificates (GICs) 1.3 percent in January 2003, 5.4 percent in June 2006, and less than 1 percent in November 2011? How does interest compound over time, and how does that compounding relate to the so-called present value and future value of a particular sum of money?

- What are the sources of *profits* and *losses* and why do they vary? For example, why did Research In Motion earn net income of $1.89 billion in 2009 while General Motors went bankrupt and needed a government bailout after losing nearly $75 billion over the previous two years?

15.1 Economic Rent

To most people, "rent" means the money they must pay for the use of an apartment or a room. To the business executive, "rent" is a payment made for the use of a factory building, machine, or warehouse facility owned by others. Such definitions of rent can be confusing and ambiguous, however. On-campus residence rent, for example, may include other payments as well: interest on money the university borrowed to finance the residence, wages for maintenance services, utility payments, and so on.

economic rent
The price paid for the use of land and other natural resources, the supply of which is fixed (perfectly inelastic).

Economists use "rent" in a much narrower sense. What we call **economic rent** is the price paid for the use of land and other natural resources that are completely fixed in total supply. As you will see, this fixed overall supply distinguishes rent payments from wage, interest, and profit payments.

Let's examine this idea and some of its implications through supply and demand analysis. We first assume that all land is of the same quality, meaning that each arable (tillable) hectare of land is as productive as every other hectare. We assume, too, that all land has a single use, for example, producing wheat. And we suppose that land is leased in a competitive market in which many producers are demanding land and many landowners are offering land in the market.

In Figure 15-1, curve S represents the supply of arable land available in the economy as a whole, and curve D_2 represents the demand of producers for use of that land. As with all economic resources, the demand for land is a derived demand, meaning that the demand for land is derived from the demand for the products that land helps to produce. Demand curves such as D_2 reflect the marginal revenue product (MRP = MP $\times$ P) of land. The curve slopes downward because of diminishing returns (MP declines) and because, for producers as a group, additional units of land result in greater output and lower output prices (P is less).

Perfectly Inelastic Supply

The unique feature of our analysis is on the supply side. For all practical purposes the supply of land is perfectly inelastic (in both the short run and long run), as reflected in supply curve S. Land has no production cost; it is a "free and non-reproducible gift of nature." The economy has only so much land, and that's that. Of course, within limits any parcel of land can be made more usable by clearing, drainage, and irrigation, but these are capital improvements and not changes in the amount of land itself.

Equilibrium Rent and Changes in Demand

Since the supply of land is fixed, demand is the only determinant of land rent. In this case, supply is passive. And what determines the demand for land? The factors we discussed in Chapter 14 do: the price of the products produced on the land, the productivity of land (which depends in part on the quantity and quality of the factors of production with which land is combined), and the prices of the other factors that are combined with land.

If demand is D_2, as we have suggested, the equilibrium rent will be R_2. The quantity of land L_0 that producers wish to rent will equal the quantity of land available (also L_0). But if the demand for land in Figure 15-1 increased from D_2 to D_1, land rent would rise from R_2 to R_1. If the demand for land declined from D_2 to D_3, land rent would fall from R_2 to R_3. Finally, if the demand for land were only D_4, land rent would be zero. In this situation, land would be a *free good*—a good for which demand is so low relative to supply that there is an excess supply of it even if the market price is zero. In Figure 15-1, we show this excess supply as distance $b - a$ at a rent of zero. This essentially was the situation in the free-land era of Canadian history.

The ideas underlying Figure 15-1 help answer one of our chapter-opening questions. Land prices and rents are so high in central Toronto and Vancouver because the demand for that land is tremendous; it is capable of producing exceptionally high revenue from offices, hotel lodging, and entertainment. In contrast, the demand for isolated land in northern Manitoba is highly limited because very little revenue can be generated from its use. (It is an entirely different matter, of course, if gold can be mined from the land!)

Productivity Differences and Rent Differences

So far, we have assumed that all land is equally productive. That assumption is unrealistic because land varies widely in terms of productivity. As an example, differences in rainfall, soil quality,

FIGURE 15-1   The Determination of Land Rent

Because the supply S of land (and other natural resources) is perfectly inelastic, demand is the sole active determinant of land rent. An increase in demand from D_2 to D_1 or a decrease in demand from D_2 to D_3 will cause a considerable change in rent: from R_2 to R_1 in the first instance and from R_2 to R_3 in the second. But the amount of land supplied will remain at L_0. If demand is very low (D_4) relative to supply, land will be a free good, commanding no rent.

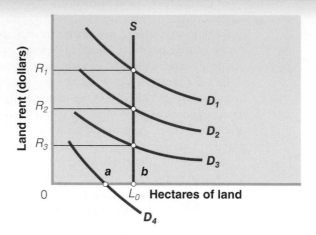

and other factors imply that while land in Manitoba is excellently suited to wheat production, the plains of British Columbia are much less well suited and those of the Yukon are practically useless. Such productivity differences are reflected in resource demands and economic rents. Competitive bidding by producers will establish a high rent for highly productive Manitoba land; less productive British Columbia land will command a lower rent; and the tundra of the Northwest Territories will command no rent at all.

This process whereby differences in productivity lead to differences in rents can be understood graphically if we look at Figure 15-1 from a slightly different perspective. As before, assume that land can only be used for wheat production. But this time assume that there are four different plots of land. Each plot is of the same size L_0 but differs in productivity so that different marginal revenue products emerge when each plot of land is combined with identical amounts of labour, capital, and entrepreneurial talent.

These differences in marginal revenue products lead to four different demand curves: D_1, D_2, D_3, and D_4. D_1 is the highest demand curve because plot 1 has the highest productivity. D_4 is the lowest demand curve because plot 4 has the lowest productivity. When combined with supply curve S, the different demand curves yield different equilibrium rents: R_1, R_2, R_3, and R_4. The differences in rents mirror the differences in productivity so that plot 1 commands the highest rent while plot 4 is so poor in quality that, given supply S, farmers won't pay anything to use it. It will be a free good, because it is not sufficiently scarce in relation to demand for it to command a price above zero.

As a final point, be aware that location itself can affect productivity and rent. Other things equal, renters will pay more for a unit of land that is strategically located with respect to materials, transportation, labour, and customers than they will for a unit of land whose location is remote from these things. Examples include the enormously high land prices near major ski resorts and the high price of land that contains oil beneath it.

perfectly inelastic supply
Product or resource supply in which price can be of any amount at a particular quantity of the product or resource demanded; quantity supplied does not respond to a change in price; graphs as a vertical supply curve.

Land Rent: A Surplus Payment

The supply of land is perfectly inelastic both in total and with respect to individual parcels of land. Whether land prices rise or fall, a nation will have the same total area to work with and individual plots of land will stay the same size.

The **perfectly inelastic supply** of land must be contrasted with the relatively elastic supply of non-land resources. Consider capital, which includes apartment buildings, fibre optic networks, and machinery. When the prices of these and other capital goods rise, entrepreneurs respond by increasing the production of capital goods. Conversely, a decline in capital goods prices results in reduced production of capital goods. As a result, the supply curves of non-land resources are normally upward sloping, so that the prices paid to such resources provide an **incentive function of price.** A high price provides an incentive to offer more of the resource, whereas a low price prompts resource suppliers to offer less.

incentive function of price
The inducement that an increase in the price of a commodity gives to sellers to make more of it available.

Not so with unimproved land. Rent serves no incentive function because both the total area of land in a nation as well as the sizes of individual plots of land will always stay exactly the same no matter what land prices are. As a result, economists consider land rents to be *surplus payments* that are not necessary to ensure that land is made available for economic use. From this perspective, the sum of all the land rents paid across a nation constitutes a giant surplus payment because it has no effect on the total supply of land in the nation. And in the same way, the individual land rents paid on particular plots of land are also surplus payments because they likewise have no effect on the sizes of those individual plots.

Land Ownership: Fairness vs. Allocative Efficiency

If land is a gift of nature, costs nothing to produce, and would be available even without rental payments, why should rent be paid to those who just happen to be landowners? Socialists have long argued that all land rents are unearned incomes because the act of owning land and renting it out to others produces nothing of value in and of itself. They urge that land should be nationalized (owned by the state) so that any payment for its use can be put to work by the government to further the well-being of the entire population.

Opponents of land nationalization argue that private land ownership allows Adam Smith's invisible hand to work its magic in terms of allocating scarce land resources to their best possible uses. In a nation where land is privately owned and rents are charged for the use of land, individuals and firms are forced to consider opportunity costs when deciding whether to secure the use of a particular piece of land. This gives them an incentive to allocate each piece of land to its highest-value use. In particular, renters will only allocate land to uses that generate enough revenue to both pay the rent and cover all other costs, including a normal profit.

Private land ownership and having to pay market-determined land rents also aids economic growth and development because as consumer tastes change and as new technologies are developed, the best uses to which particular pieces of land can be put also change. These changing opportunity costs are reflected in land rents, whose changing values help to reallocate land from lower-value uses to higher-value uses as the economy evolves. Thus, the often-heard remark, "The land was just too valuable for its previous use."

By contrast, if land were nationalized, government planners would have a very difficult time assigning each piece of land to its best possible use and adjusting its use with changing circumstances without the guidance about opportunity costs provided by market-determined rents.

Along those lines, it is important to be clear that while economic rents are surplus payments when viewed from the perspective of society as a whole, they are most definitely costs to individual people and individual firms. To see why this is true, recall that because land is a free gift of nature, there is no cost to society as a whole for obtaining the current supply of land. Thus, economic rents are, from the perspective of society, surplus payments because they have no effect on land supply. But individuals must pay economic rents because such rents determine how society's fixed supply of land is allocated among competing potential uses. Those who are willing and able to pay the market rent get to use the land, while those who are unwilling or unable to pay the market rent do not. Put slightly differently: Economic rents do not cause land to be supplied—they cause land to be directed.

- Rent is the price paid for unimproved land whose supply is perfectly inelastic.

- Rent is socially useful because it puts an opportunity cost on land parcels, thereby

helping to allocate each parcel of land to its best possible use.

15.2   Interest

Interest is the price paid for the use of money. It can be thought of as the amount of money that a borrower must pay a lender for the use of the lender's money over some period of time. As an example, a borrower might be required to pay $100 of interest for the use of $1000 for one year.

Because borrowers pay for loans of money with money, interest can be stated as a percentage of the amount of money borrowed rather than as a dollar amount. This is very useful because it is far less clumsy to say that interest is "12 percent annually" than to say that interest is "$120 per year per $1000."

Stating interest as a percentage also makes it much easier to compare the interest paid on loans involving different amounts of money. By expressing interest as a percentage, we can immediately compare an interest payment of, say, $432 per year per $2880 with one of $1800 per year per $12,000. Both interest payments are 15 percent per year, which is not obvious from the actual dollar figures.

And to make things even simpler, an interest payment of 15 percent per year can also be referred to as a 15 percent interest rate.

Money Is Not a Resource

When considering why borrowers are willing to pay interest for the right to use borrowed money, it is very important to remember that money is not itself an economic resource. Whether money comes in the form of coins, paper currency, or chequing accounts, you cannot directly produce any goods and services with it.

Thus, borrowers do not value money for its own sake. Rather, they value money because of what it can purchase. Individuals and households are willing to pay interest to borrow for consumption spending because they would prefer to consume certain goods and services sooner rather than later. And businesses are willing to pay interest because they can use the money they borrow to expand their businesses and increase their profits. In particular, borrowed money can be used to fund the acquisition of capital goods such as computers, machinery, and warehouses.

Interest Rates and Interest Income

The interest rate on money loans determines the *interest income* earned by households for providing capital to firms. This is true because firms have the choice of either leasing capital from households or purchasing their own capital. Because businesses have this option, households wishing to lease their capital to businesses cannot charge more for the use of their capital than what businesses would have to pay in terms of interest payments to borrow the money needed to purchase their own capital. As an example, consider a custom T-shirt shop that needs a $10,000 embroidering machine to expand production. If the owners of the shop can borrow the money to buy such a machine at an interest rate of 8 percent per year, then anyone wishing to lease them an identical machine could charge them no more than $800 per year for it (since $800 is how much per year the shop would have to pay in interest to borrow $10,000 at an 8 percent interest rate).

Range of Interest Rates

For convenience, economists often speak in terms of a single interest rate. However, there are actually a number of interest rates in the economy. Table 15-1 lists several interest rates often referred to in the media. In April 2012, these rates ranged from 0.90 percent to 19.99 percent. Why the differences?

- *Risk* Loans to different borrowers for different purposes carry varying degrees of risk. The greater the chance that a borrower will not repay his loan, the higher the interest rate the lender will charge to compensate for that risk.

- *Maturity* The time length of a loan or its *maturity* (when it needs to be paid back) also affects the interest rate. Other things equal, longer-term loans usually command higher interest rates than shorter-term loans. This is true because one function of interest rates is to compensate lenders for the inconvenience and potential financial sacrifices involved with forgoing alternative uses of their money until their loans are repaid. Longer-term loans must offer higher interest rates to compensate lenders for having to forgo alternative opportunities for longer periods of time.

- *Loan Size* If there are two loans of equal maturity and risk, the interest rate on the smaller of the two loans usually will be higher. The administrative costs of issuing a large loan and a small loan are about the same in dollars, but the cost is greater *as a percentage* of the smaller loan.

Pure Rate of Interest

When economists and financial specialists talk of "the" interest rate, they typically have in mind the **pure rate of interest.** This is the hypothetical interest rate that would serve purely and solely to compensate lenders for their willingness to patiently forgo alternative consumption and investment opportunities until their money is repaid. The pure rate of interest is best approximated by the interest rates of long-term, virtually riskless securities such as the 30-year Treasury bonds issued by the federal government. The interest paid by such bonds can be thought of as being made purely and solely for the use of money over an extended time period because such **bonds** involve minimal risk and negligible administrative costs. In October 2011 the pure rate of interest in Canada was 2.9 percent.

pure rate of interest
The hypothetical interest rate that would serve purely and solely to compensate lenders for their willingness to patiently forgo alternative consumption and investment opportunities until their money is repaid.

bond
A financial device through which a borrower (a firm or a government) is obligated to pay the principal and interest on a loan at a specific date in the future.

TABLE 15-1	Selected Interest Rates, April 2012
Type of interest rate	**Annual percentage**
10-year Government of Canada bond	2.20
5-year Government of Canada bond	1.70
3-year Government of Canada bond	1.40
91-day Treasury Bill (Government of Canada)	0.90
5-year closed mortgage	5.25
Prime rate (rate charged by banks to their best corporate customers)	3.00
Overnight lending rate	1.00
Visa interest rate	19.99

Source: Bank of Canada.

The following story told by economist Irving Fisher (1867–1947) helps illustrate the time value of money.*

In the process of a massage, a masseur informed Fisher that he was a Socialist who believed that "interest is the basis of capitalism, and is robbery." Following the massage, Fisher asked, "How much do I owe you?"

The masseur replied, "Thirty dollars."

"Very well," said Fisher, "I will give you a note payable a hundred years hence. I suppose you have no objections to taking this note without any interest. At the end of that time, you, or perhaps your grandchildren, can redeem it."

"But I cannot afford to wait that long," said the masseur.

"I thought you said that interest was robbery. If interest is robbery, you ought to be willing to wait indefinitely for the money. If you are willing to wait ten years, how much would you require?"

"Well, I would have to get more than thirty dollars."

His point now made, Fisher replied, "That is interest."

*Irving Fisher, as quoted in Irving Norton Fisher, *My Father Irving Fisher* (New York: Comet, 1956), p. 77.

Loanable Funds Theory of Interest

Because macroeconomics deals with the entire economy, it typically focuses on the pure rate of interest and assumes that it is determined by the total supply and demand for money in the economy. But because our present focus is on microeconomics, we will concentrate on a more micro-based theory of interest rates. By doing so, we will be able to explain why the interest rates on different types of loans vary so greatly, as in Table 15-1.

loanable funds theory of interest
The concept that the supply of and demand for loanable funds determines the equilibrium rate of interest.

The **loanable funds theory of interest** explains the interest rate on any particular type of loan in terms of the supply of and demand for *funds available for lending* in the loanable funds market that exists for that particular type of loan. As Figure 15-2 shows, the equilibrium interest rate (here, 8 percent) on a particular type of loan is the rate at which the quantities of loanable funds supplied and demanded are equal for that type of loan.

To gain a deeper understanding of the loanable funds theory of interest, let's focus on a simplified lending market. First, assume that, for a particular type of loan, households or consumers are the sole suppliers of loanable funds while businesses are the sole demanders of loanable funds. Also assume that lending occurs directly between households and businesses so that there are no financial institutions acting as intermediaries.

SUPPLY OF LOANABLE FUNDS

The supply of loanable funds in our simplified lending market is represented by curve *S* in Figure 15-2. Its upward slope indicates that households will make available a larger quantity of funds at high interest rates than at low interest rates. Most people prefer to use their income to purchase desirable goods and services *today,* rather than to delay purchases to sometime in the *future.* For people to delay consumption and increase their saving, they must be compensated by an interest payment. The larger the amount of that payment, the greater the deferral of household consumption and thus the greater the amount of money made available for loans.

DEMAND FOR LOANABLE FUNDS

Businesses borrow loanable funds primarily to add to their stocks of capital goods, such as new plants or warehouses, machinery, and equipment. Assume that a firm wants to buy a machine that will increase output and sales such that the firm's total revenue will rise by $110 for the year.

 **KEY GRAPH**

FIGURE 15-2   The Market for Loanable Funds

The upsloping supply curve *S* for loanable funds reflects the idea that at higher interest rates, households will defer more of their present consumption (save more), making more funds available for lending. The downsloping demand curve *D* for loanable funds indicates that businesses will borrow more at lower interest rates than at higher interest rates. At the equilibrium interest rate (here, 8 percent), the quantities of loanable funds loaned and borrowed are equal (here, F_0 each).

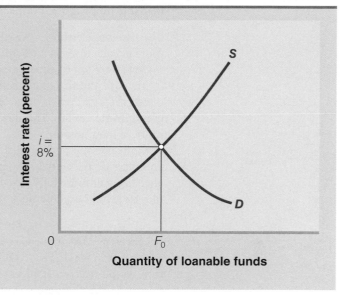

expected rate of return curve
The increase in profit a firm anticipates it will obtain by investing in R&D.

connect
ORIGIN OF THE IDEA 15.1
Interest Rates

Also assume that the machine costs $100 and has a useful life of just one year. Comparing the $10 earned with the $100 cost of the machine, we find that the **expected rate of return** on this investment is 10 percent (= $10/$100) for one year.

To determine whether the investment would be profitable and whether it should be made, the firm must compare the interest rate—the price of loanable funds—with the 10 percent expected rate of return. If funds can be borrowed at some rate less than the rate of return, say, at 8 percent, as in Figure 15-2, then the investment is profitable and should be made. But if funds can be borrowed only at an interest rate above the 10 percent rate of return, say, at 14 percent, the investment is unprofitable and should not be made.

Why is the demand for loanable funds downsloping, as in Figure 15-2? At higher interest rates, fewer investment projects will be profitable and therefore a smaller quantity of loanable funds will be demanded. At lower interest rates, more investment projects will be profitable and, therefore, more loanable funds will be demanded. Indeed, as we have just seen, it is profitable to purchase the $100 machine if funds can be borrowed at 8 percent but not if the firm must borrow at 14 percent.

Extending the Model

There is a loanable funds market for nearly every type of loan in the economy. The best known are the markets for corporate and government bonds. But there are also loanable funds markets for student loans, home mortgages, and car loans. Each type of loan ends up with its own equilibrium interest rate determined by the demand for and supply of loanable funds in its particular market.

We now extend the simple loanable funds model to make it more realistic and better able to capture the diversity of these many lending markets.

FINANCIAL INSTITUTIONS

Households rarely directly lend their savings to the businesses that are borrowing funds for investment. Instead, they place their savings in chartered banks (and other financial institutions). The banks pay interest to savers to attract loanable funds and in turn lend those funds to businesses. Businesses borrow the funds from the banks, paying them interest for the use of the money. Financial institutions profit by charging borrowers higher interest rates than the interest rates they pay savers. Both interest rates, however, are based on the supply of and demand for loanable funds in their respective markets.

Changes in Supply   Anything that causes households to be thriftier will prompt them to save more at each interest rate, shifting the supply curve rightward. For example, if interest earned on savings were to be suddenly exempt from taxation, we would expect the supply of loanable funds to increase and the equilibrium interest rate to decrease. In 2009 the federal government introduced the Tax Free Savings Account (TFSA), which exempts up to $5000 a year in a savings account from taxation. This new policy will undoubtedly give many Canadians an incentive to save more of their income.

Conversely, a decline in thriftiness would shift the supply-of-loanable-funds curve leftward and increase the equilibrium interest rate. For example, if the government expanded social insurance to cover more fully the costs of hospitalization, prescription drugs, and retirement living, the incentive of households to save might diminish.

Changes in Demand   On the demand side, anything that increases the rate of return on potential investments will increase the demand for loanable funds. Let's return to our earlier example, where a firm would receive additional revenue of $110 by purchasing a $100 machine and, therefore, would realize a 10 percent return on investment. What factors might increase or decrease the rate of return? Suppose a technological advance raised the productivity of the machine so that the firm's total revenue increased by $120 rather than $110. The rate of return would then be 20 percent, not 10 percent. Before the technological advance, the firm would have demanded zero loanable funds at, say, an interest rate of 14 percent, but now it will demand $100 of loanable funds at that interest rate, meaning that the demand curve for loanable funds has shifted to the right.

Similarly, an increase in consumer demand for the firm's product will increase the price of its product. So even though the productivity of the machine is unchanged, its potential revenue will rise from $110 to perhaps $120, increasing the firm's rate of return from 10 to 20 percent. Again, the firm will be willing to borrow more than previously at our presumed 8 or 14 percent interest rate, implying that the demand curve for loanable funds has shifted rightward. This shift in demand increases the equilibrium interest rate.

Conversely, a decline in the productivity or in the price of the firm's product would shift the demand curve for loanable funds leftward, reducing the equilibrium interest rate.

Other Participants   We must recognize that participation in many loanable funds markets may go well beyond our simplification of households as suppliers of funds and businesses as demanders of funds. For example, while households are suppliers of loanable funds, many are also demanders of such funds. Households borrow to finance expensive purchases such as housing, automobiles, furniture, and household appliances. Governments also are on the demand side of a loanable funds market when they borrow to finance budgetary deficits. And businesses that have revenues in excess of their current expenditures may offer some of those revenues in various loanable funds markets. Thus, like households, businesses operate on both the supply and the demand sides of the various loanable funds markets.

Finally, in addition to gathering and making available the savings of households, banks and other financial institutions also increase funds through the lending process and decrease funds when the money that is used to pay off loans is retained by the banks rather than being loaned out again to other borrowers. The Bank of Canada (the nation's central bank) controls the amount of this bank activity and thus influences a wide variety of interest rates.

This fact helps answer one of our chapter-opening questions: Why did the interest rate on a one-year GIC drop from 5.08 percent in March 2000 to 1.0 percent in October 2011? There are two reasons: (1) the demand for loanable funds decreased because businesses did not need to purchase more capital goods; and (2) the Bank of Canada, in an effort to stimulate aggregate expenditures, took monetary actions that increased the supply of loanable funds.

Time Value of Money

time value of money
The idea that a specific amount of money is more valuable to a person the sooner it is received because the money can be placed in a financial account or investment and earn compound interest over time.

Interest is central to understanding the **time value of money**—the idea that a specific amount of money is more valuable to a person the sooner it is obtained. To see where money's time value comes from, suppose that you could choose between being paid $1000 today or $1000 in a year. The fact that $1000 received today can be invested at interest and grow into more than $1000 in a year implies that it is better to receive $1000 today than $1000 in a year. By how much is it better? By the amount of interest that can be gained over the course of the year. The higher the interest rate, the greater the time value of money.

In addition to giving money its time value, the fact that money can be invested to earn interest also implies a way in which a given amount of money today can be thought of as being equivalent to a larger amount of money in the future and how a future amount of money can be thought of as being equivalent to a smaller amount of money today. We explore this idea next.

COMPOUND INTEREST

compound interest
The total interest that cumulates over time on money placed into an interest-bearing account.

The total interest that cumulates over time on money placed into an interest-bearing account is called **compound interest.** Table 15-2 helps explain compound interest, as well as the related ideas of future value and present value. Suppose that Max places $1000 in an interest-bearing account at 10 percent interest intending to let the principal (the initial deposit) and interest compound for three years. The first row of each column shows the beginning period sum; the second column shows the yearly computation as to how that sum grows, given a particular interest rate. That growth is found by multiplying the dollar amount by $1 + i$, where i is the interest rate expressed as a decimal.

In year 1 the 10 percent interest rate increases the money in the account from $1000 to $1100 (= $1000 × 1.10). So, as shown in column 3, total interest is $100. Column 4 again lists the $1100, but reinforces that it consists of the original principal plus total interest. Similarly, in year 2, the $1100 now in the account grows to $1210 (= $1100 × 1.10) because $110 of new interest accrues on the $1100. At the end of year 2, the principal remains $1000, but the total interest is $210, and the total amount in the account is $1210. Interest in year 3 is $121 and total interest rises to $331. After this $331 of total interest is added to the $1000 principal, the accumulation is $1331. As shown in Column 3, compound interest builds and builds over time.

FUTURE VALUE AND PRESENT VALUE

future value
The amount to which some current amount of money will grow if the interest earned on the amount is left to compound over time.

Now note from Table 15-2 that we can look at the time value of money in two distinct ways. The **future value** is the amount to which some current amount of money will grow as interest compounds over time. In our table, the future value (FV) of $1000 today at 10 percent interest is $1331 three years from now. Future value is always forward looking.

TABLE 15-2

Compound Interest, Future Value, and Present Value, 10 Percent Interest Rate

(1) Beginning Period Value	(2) Computation	(3) Total Interest	(4) End Period Value
$1000 (Year 1)	$1000 × 1.10 = $1100	$100	$1100 (= $1000 + $100)
$1100 (Year 2)	$1100 × 1.10 = $1210	$210 (= $100 + $110)	$1210 (= $1000 + $210)
$1210 (Year 2)	$1210 × 1.10 = $1331	$331 (= $100 +$110 +$121)	$1331 (= $1000 + $331)

present value
Today's value of some amount of
money that is to be received
sometime in the future.

But we can just as easily look backward from the end value of $1331 and ask how much that amount is worth today, given the 10 percent interest rate. The **present value** is today's value of some amount of money to be received in the future. In terms of the table, the present value (PV) of $1331 is $1000. Here, FV is "discounted" by three years at 10 percent to remove all interest compounding and that way obtain PV. (We explain the discounting procedure in our chapter on financial economics in *Macroeconomics,* but for readers interested in the mathematics, see footnote 1, below.)[1]

With any positive real interest rate, a person would prefer to receive $1000 today rather than $1000 at some time in the future. The higher the interest rate, the greater is the *future value* of a specific amount of money today. To confirm, substitute a 20 percent interest rate for the 10 percent rate in Table 15-2 and rework the analysis. Finally, you should know that the analysis presented in the table is extendable to any number of years.

The time value of money is an important concept. For example, we will use it in the chapter on natural resource economics that follows. Also, we will discuss present discounted value in much more detail in our chapter on financial economics in *Macroeconomics.* Our simple goal in this chapter is to stress that *money has time value because of the potential for compound interest.*

Role of Interest Rates

We have already explained that interest rates on money loans determine the interest incomes earned by the owners of capital goods. This fact implies that interest rates are the crucial prices determining both the *level* and *composition* of new investments in capital goods as well as the amount of research and development (R&D) spending in the economy.

INTEREST AND TOTAL OUTPUT

Lower equilibrium interest rates encourage businesses to borrow more for investment, other things equal. As a result, total spending in the economy rises and, if the economy has unused resources, so does total output. Conversely, higher equilibrium interest rates discourage businesses from borrowing for investment, reducing investment and total spending. Such a decrease in spending may be desirable if an economy is experiencing inflation.

Central banks often manage interest rates to try to expand investment and output on the one hand, or to reduce investment and inflation on the other. Central banks affect the interest rates by changing the supply of money. Increases in the money supply increase the supply of loanable funds, causing the equilibrium interest rate to fall. This boosts investment spending and expands the economy. In contrast, decreases in the money supply decrease the supply of loanable funds, boosting the equilibrium interest rate. As a result, investment is constrained and so is the economy.

INTEREST AND THE ALLOCATION OF CAPITAL

Prices are rationing devices. Interest rates are prices. Thus, when it comes to allocating capital in the economy, the interest rates charged on investment loans ration the available supply of loanable investment funds to investment projects that have expected rates of return at or above the interest rate cost of the borrowed funds.

If, say, the computer industry expects to earn a return of 12 percent on the money it invests in physical capital and it can secure the required funds at an interest rate of 8 percent, it can borrow and expand its physical capital. If the expected rate of return on additional capital in the steel industry is only 6 percent, that industry will find it unprofitable to expand its capital stock at 8 percent interest. The interest rate allocates money, and ultimately physical capital, to those industries in which it will be most productive and, therefore, most profitable. Such an allocation of capital goods benefits society.

---

[1] $FV = PV(1 + i)^t$ and $PV = FV/(1 + i)^t$ where i is the interest rate and t is time, here the number of years of compounding.

INTEREST AND R&D SPENDING

The decision on how much to spend on R&D depends on the cost of borrowing funds in relationship to the expected rate of return. Other things equal, the lower the interest rate, and thus the lower the cost of borrowing funds for R&D, the greater the amount of R&D spending that is profitable. The higher the interest rate, the lower the amount of R&D spending.

Also, the interest rate allocates R&D funds to those firms and industries for which the expected rate of return on R&D is the greatest. Ace Microcircuits may have an expected rate of return of 16 percent on an R&D project, while Glow Paints has only a 2 percent expected rate of return on an R&D project. With the interest rate at 8 percent, loanable funds will flow to Ace, not to Glow. Society will benefit by having R&D spending allocated to projects that have sufficiently high expected rates of return to justify using scarce resources for R&D rather than for other purposes.

NOMINAL AND REAL INTEREST RATES

nominal interest rate
The interest rate expressed in terms of annual amounts currently charged for interest and not adjusted for inflation.

real interest rate
The interest rate expressed in dollars of constant value (adjusted for inflation); equal to the nominal interest rate less the expected rate of inflation.

This discussion of the role of interest in investment decisions and in R&D decisions assumes that there is no inflation. If inflation exists, we must distinguish between nominal and real interest rates, just as we needed to distinguish between nominal and real wages in Chapter 12. The **nominal interest rate** is the rate of interest expressed in dollars of current value. The **real interest rate** is the rate of interest expressed in purchasing power—dollars of inflation-adjusted value. (For a comparison of nominal interest rates on bank loans in selected countries, see Global Perspective 15.1.)

For example, suppose the nominal interest rate and the rate of inflation are both 10 percent. If you borrow $100, you must pay back $110 a year from now. However, because of 10 percent inflation, each of these 110 dollars will be worth 10 percent less. Thus, the real value or purchasing power of your $110 at the end of the year is only $100. In inflation-adjusted dollars you are borrowing $100 and at year's end you are paying back $100. While the nominal interest rate is 10 percent, the real interest rate is zero. We determine this by subtracting the 10 percent inflation rate from the 10 percent nominal interest rate. It is the real interest rate, not the nominal rate, that affects investment and R&D decisions.

GLOBAL PERSPECTIVE

15.1

Short-Term Nominal Interest Rates, Selected Nations

These data show the short-term nominal interest rates (those on three-month loans) in various countries in 2012. Because these are nominal rates, much of the variation reflects differences in rates of inflation, but differences in central bank monetary policies and default risk also influence the variation.

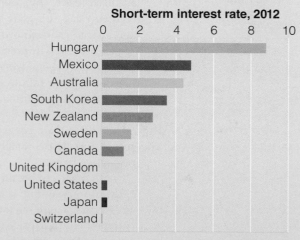

Short-term interest rate, 2012

Source: OECD (2010), "Producer and Consumer Support Estimates: Total Support Estimate OECD 2010", OECD Agriculture Statistics (database). http://dx.doi.org/10.1787data-00501-en.

- Interest is the price paid for the use of money and determines the interest income earned by households for providing capital to firms.

- The range of interest rates is influenced by risk, maturity, and loan size.

- In the loanable funds model, the equilibrium interest rate is determined by the demand for and supply of loanable funds.

- The time value of money is the idea that $1 can be converted into more than $1 of future value through compound interest, therefore $1 to be received sometime in the future has less than $1 of present value.

- Interest rates on investment loans affect the total level of investment and, therefore, the levels of total spending and total output; they also affect allocation of money and real capital to specific industries and firms. Similarly, interest rates also affect the level and composition of R&D spending.

15.3 Economic Profit

Recall from previous chapters that economists define profit narrowly. To accountants, profit is what remains of a firm's total revenue after it has paid individuals and other firms for the materials, capital, and labour they have supplied to the firm. To the economist, these "accounting profits" overstate profit. The reason is that the accountant's view of profit considers only **explicit costs:** payments made by the firm to outsiders. It ignores **implicit costs:** the monetary income the firm sacrifices when it uses resources that it owns, rather than supplying those resources to the market. The economist considers implicit costs to be opportunity costs that must be accounted for in determining profit. The **economic (pure) profit** is what remains after all costs—both explicit and implicit, the latter including a normal profit—have been subtracted from a firm's total revenue. Economic profit may be either positive or negative (a loss).

explicit costs
The monetary payments a firm must make to an outsider to obtain a resource.

implicit costs
The monetary incomes a firm sacrifices when it uses a resource it owns rather than supplying the resource to the market.

economic (pure) profit
The total revenue of a firm less its economic costs (which includes both explicit costs and implicit costs); also called *above normal profit.*

Entrepreneurship and Profit

Economic profit flows to individuals to motivate them to provide the economic resource known as entrepreneurship. For illustration, let's suppose that two entrepreneurs establish a start-up company called Upside and that they are the only owners. They do not incorporate or borrow and instead use their own funds to finance the firm.

As discussed in previous chapters, the resource that these entrepreneurs provide is clearly not labour. Typical workers simply complete assigned tasks and engage in routine activities. For their labour inputs, they are compensated with wages and salaries. Entrepreneurs, by contrast, make non-routine decisions that involve substantial financial risk. Among other things, they (1) decide their firm's strategy for combining land, labour, and capital to produce a good or service; (2) decide whether and how to develop new products and new production processes; and (3) personally bear the financial risks associated with the success or failure of their respective firms.

With regard to bearing those financial risks, it is crucial to understand that a firm's entrepreneurs are its *residual claimants*, meaning that they only receive whatever residual revenue—if any—remains after all the other factors of production have been paid. As residual claimants, the entrepreneurs at Upside receive whatever accounting profit or accounting loss the firm generates. Thus, the financial risks of running the firm are borne by its two entrepreneurs. If Upside loses money, it loses *their* money.

Insurable and Uninsurable Risks

As residual claimants, entrepreneurs face financial risks. These fall into two categories: **insurable risks** are those risks for which it is possible to buy insurance from an insurance company, while **uninsurable risks** are those risks for which it is not possible to buy insurance from an insurance company.

Individuals and firms who purchase insurance policies (contracts) from an insurance company are referred to as policyholders. In exchange for an annual premium (fee), the policyholders obtain the insurance company's guarantee to reimburse them for any financial losses caused by any of the risks covered under the insurance contract. In order to be able to keep that promise, the insurance company must be able to collect enough in premiums from its policyholders in the present to be able to fully reimburse the ones who eventually suffer losses in the future. This is only possible with risks like fire, flood, theft, accident, and death whose frequencies of occurrence can be predicted with relative accuracy. Risks whose frequencies of occurrence cannot be predicted with accuracy are uninsurable.

Sources of Uninsurable Risks

Because insurance is available for insurable risks, entrepreneurs only have to deal with uninsurable risks whose frequency of occurrence cannot be predicted with any accuracy. In practice, these are the result of uncontrollable and unpredictable changes in demand and supply that either reduce revenues or increase costs. These uninsurable risks fall into four main categories:

- *Changes in the General Economic Environment* An economy-wide downturn in business (a recession), can lead to greatly reduced demand, sales, and revenues, and thus to business losses. An otherwise prosperous firm may experience substantial losses through no fault of its own.

- *Changes in the Structure of the Economy* Consumer tastes, technology, resource availability, and prices change unpredictably in the real world, bringing changes in production costs and revenues. For example, Air Canada may earn an economic profit one year, but may sustain substantial losses the next year as the result of a significant increase in the price of jet fuel.

- *Changes in Government Policy* A newly instituted regulation, the removal of a tariff, or a change in national defense policy may significantly alter the cost and revenue data of the affected industry and firms.

- *New Products or Production Methods Pioneered by Rivals* Any firm can suddenly find itself losing sales and revenue to popular new products brought out by rivals. Similarly, a firm may suddenly find itself having to sell its product at a loss if rival firms cut their prices after figuring out a lower-cost way to make the same product.

Profit as Compensation for Bearing Uninsurable Risks

Economists list entrepreneurship as its own economic resource—separate from land, labour, and capital—because it is not possible to run a business without somebody being willing to undertake and live with uninsurable risks. Entrepreneurs are rewarded with profit precisely to compensate them for personally taking on the uninsurable risks of running a business. Indeed, their willingness to bear those uninsurable risks means that the providers of the firm's other resource inputs (of land, labour, and capital) can almost completely ignore those risks.

To see why this is true, again consider our start-up company, Upside, and suppose that its two entrepreneurs used $100,000 of their own money to fund the firm. If revenues ever run below costs, the entrepreneurs will use that pile of money to cover the losses and make sure that the firm's workers and other resource suppliers get paid on time and in full. The resource suppliers are shielded from the losses because the entrepreneurs have taken it upon themselves to bear the firm's uninsurable financial risks. In such situations, no bill is sent to the workers or other resource suppliers asking them to help make up the firm's losses. The entrepreneurs, who took on the firm's uninsurable risks, are "on the hook."

The entrepreneurs' compensation for providing entrepreneurship and shielding the other resource suppliers from uninsurable risk is the opportunity to run the business and keep the firm's profits if things go well. Thus, entrepreneurship boils down to a simple bargain: In exchange for making sure that everyone else gets paid if things go wrong, the entrepreneur gets to receive the firm's profits if things go right.

Sources of Economic Profit

For bearing a firm's uninsurable risks, its entrepreneurs receive control of the firm. This allows them to try to make as much profit as possible in exchange for taking on those risks. Along those lines, there are three main ways in which entrepreneurs can generate economic profits (that is, accounting profits which exceed normal profits):

- *Create Popular New Products* If an entrepreneur can develop a popular new product at a sufficiently low cost, his firm will be able to generate economic profits until competitors bring out competing products.

- *Reduce Production Costs Below Rivals' Costs* Entrepreneurs who implement more-efficient production methods for existing products can generate economic profits until their efficiency gains are matched or exceeded by competitors.

- *Create and Maintain a Profitable Monopoly* Entrepreneurs who possess a monopoly for their product may be able to generate economic rent by restricting their outputs and raising their prices. And such economic profits may persist if entry to the industry is blocked. But remember from Chapter 10 that having a monopoly does not guarantee that a monopoly will be profitable. If demand is weak relative to production costs, monopolies can and will go bankrupt.

By reallocating resources toward the production of popular new products that consumers prefer to old products, entrepreneurs improve allocative efficiency. By reducing production costs, they improve productive efficiency. Thus, with the important exception of monopoly, the entrepreneur's pursuit of profit clearly benefits society.

With monopolies, though, things are very different because a monopoly's profit cannot be justified as rewarding its entrepreneurs for personally taking on a firm's financial risks or for making perceptive business decisions that enhance productive or allocative efficiency. As a result, governments use anticombines laws to impede monopolies from forming, or if they arise, break them up or restrict their business behaviours. In some instances, governments also regulate away their excessive profits.

Profit Rations Entrepreneurship

Even if a firm is making an accounting profit, its entrepreneurs may decide to quit and go into another line of business. This is because they will want their accounting profit to be at least as large as the typical accounting profit that their risk taking and decision making could on average be expected to earn in other business ventures. This typical accounting profit is known as their **normal profit.**

normal profit
The payment made by a firm to obtain and retain entrepreneurial ability.

Because entrepreneurs will be comparing their current accounting profit with the normal profit that they could be making elsewhere, profit can be thought of as the "price" that allocates the scarce resource of entrepreneurship toward different possible economic activities. Just as wages must be paid to attract and retain labour, profits must be paid to attract and retain entrepreneurial talent. And just as higher wages attract workers, higher profits attract entrepreneurs.

Entrepreneurs, Profits, and Corporate Stockholders

In the actual economy, economic profits are distributed widely beyond the entrepreneurs who first start new businesses. The corporate structure of business enterprise has allowed millions of individuals to purchase ownership shares in corporations and therefore to share in the risks and rewards of ownership.

Some of these people participate in the for-profit economy by purchasing the stock of individual firms or by investing in mutual funds which in turn buy **corporate stock.** Millions of additional people share in the profits of corporations through the financial investments of their pension funds. But at their core, all of the profits that are shared with these direct and indirect corporate shareholders are made possible in the first place by the activities of entrepreneurs. For instance, without Mike Lazaridis and Jim Balsillie, there would have been no Research In Motion (RIM) corporation—and, consequently, no RIM profits (dividends) to distribute to the millions of owners of RIM stock in the past. (In recent years RIM has lost much of its lustre as it lost market share to rivals.)

Many millions of people wish to own corporate stock and thereby share in the risks and rewards of business, which reflects the fact that economic profit is the main energizer of the market economy. It influences both the level of economic output and the allocation of resources among alternative uses. The expectation of economic profit motivates firms to innovate. Innovation stimulates new investment, increasing total output and employment.

Profit also helps to allocate resources among alternative lines of production. Entrepreneurs seek profit and avoid losses. Economic profit in an industry is a signal that society wants that particular industry to expand. It attracts factors of production from industries that are not profitable. But the rewards of profit are more than an inducement for an industry to expand; they also attract the financing needed for expansion. In contrast, continuing losses penalize firms or industries that fail to adjust their productive efforts to match wants. Such losses signal society's desire for the afflicted industries to contract.

Innovation, one dynamic feature of a market economy, occurs at the initiative of the entrepreneur.

stock [corporate]
A share in the ownership of a corporation.

CONSIDER THIS :: Apple CEO Steve Jobs

Entrepreneur Steve Jobs made billions of dollars in economic profit at the two major companies he headed, Apple Inc. and Pixar Animation Studios.

He made these economic profits by creating wildly popular versions of existing products. Pixar, for example, was not the first animation studio. But it was the first to develop popular digitally animated movies, starting with *Toy Story* in 1995.

In the same way, Apple did not invent the personal computer, the MP3 music player, the Internet-capable mobile phone, or the touch-screen computer. But its iMac personal computer, iPod music player, Internet-capable iPhone, and iPad touch-screen computer were all major hits, generating billions of dollars of profits.

Jobs was able to achieve these successes largely because he defied conventional wisdom. His key decision was that

Apple should develop its own software as well as its own hardware. By contrast, computer-making rivals like Dell and IBM only made hardware while leaving the production of software up to other firms such as Microsoft. By building both its own hardware *and* its own software, Apple could create products in which the hardware and software were fully integrated and worked nearly flawlessly together.

The result was a string of hit products that rival firms could not easily duplicate because they were in nearly all cases either hardware makers *or* software makers but not both. Thus, another source of Apple's large profits has been a mild amount of monopoly power resulting from the inability of rivals to easily mimic Apple's strategy of producing both software and hardware.

The **LAST WORD**   Determining the Price of Credit

A variety of lending practices may cause the effective interest rate to be quite different from what it appears to be.

Borrowing and lending—receiving and granting credit—are a way of life. Individuals receive credit when they negotiate a mortgage loan and when they use their credit cards. Individuals make loans when they open a savings account in a chartered bank or buy a bond.

It is sometimes difficult to determine exactly how much interest we pay and receive when we borrow and lend. Let's suppose that you borrow $10,000, which you agree to repay with $1,000 of interest at the end of one year. In this instance, the interest rate is 10 percent per year. To determine the interest rate i, we compare the interest paid with the amount borrowed:

$$i = \frac{\$1,000}{\$10,000} = 10\%$$

But in some cases a lender—say, a bank—will discount the interest payment from the loan amount at the time the loan is made. Thus, instead of giving the borrower $10,000, the bank

discounts the $1,000 interest payment in advance, giving the borrower only $9,000. This increases the interest rate:

$$i = \frac{\$1,000}{\$9,000} = 11\%$$

While the absolute amount of interest paid is the same, in this second case the borrower has only $9,000 available for the year.

An even more subtle point is that, to simplify their calculations, some financial institutions assume a 360-day year (twelve 30-day months), which means the borrower has the use of the lender's funds for five fewer days than

the normal year. This use of a short year also increases the actual interest rate paid by the borrower.

The interest rate paid may change dramatically if a loan is repaid in installments. Suppose a bank lends you $10,000 and charges interest in the amount of $1,000 to be paid at the end of the year. But the loan contract requires that you repay the $10,000 loan in 12 equal monthly installments. As a result, the average amount of the loan outstanding during the year is only $5000. Therefore:

$$i = \frac{\$1,000}{\$5,000} = 20\%$$

Here interest is paid on the total amount of the loan ($10,000) rather than on the outstanding balance (which averages $5,000 for the year), making for a much higher interest rate.

Another factor that influences the effective interest rate is whether interest is compounded. Suppose you deposit $10,000 in a savings account that pays a 10 percent interest rate compounded semiannually. In other words, interest is paid on your loan to the bank twice a year. At the end of the first six months, $500 of interest (10 percent of $10,000 for half a year) is added to your account. At the end of the year, interest is calculated on $10,500 so that the second interest payment is $525 (10 percent of $10,500 for half a year). Thus:

$$i = \frac{\$1,025}{\$10,000} = 10.25\%$$

This 10.25 percent return means that a bank offering a 10 percent interest rate compounded semi-annually would pay more interest to its customers than a competitor offering a simple (non-compounded) rate of, say, 10.2 percent.

Similarly, late-payment fees on credit card accounts can boost the actual interest rate paid on credit card balances to extremely high levels. Furthermore, low "teaser" rates designed to attract new customers often contain fine print that raises the interest rate to 16 percent, or even 28 percent, if there is a late payment on the account.

"Let the borrower (or depositor) beware" remains a fitting motto in the world of credit.

Question

Assume that you borrow $5,000 and pay back the $5,000 plus $250 in interest at the end of the year. Assuming no inflation, what is the real interest rate? What would the interest rate be if the $250 of interest had been discounted at the time the loan was made? What would the interest rate be if you were required to repay the loan in 12 equal monthly installments?

:: CHAPTER SUMMARY

15.1 :: ECONOMIC RENT

- Economic rent is the price paid for the use of land and other natural resources whose total supplies are fixed.

- Differences in land rent result from differences in demand, often stemming from differences in the fertility and climactic features of the land or differences in location. Rent is a surplus payment that is socially unnecessary since land would be available to the economy even without rental payments.

- Although land rent is a surplus payment rather than a cost to the economy as a whole, to individual firms and industries rental payments are correctly regarded as costs. The payment of land rents by individuals and firms is socially useful because it puts an opportunity cost on the use of land so that people have the incentive to put each piece of land to its best possible use.

15.2 :: INTEREST

- Interest is the price paid for the use of money. Because money is not itself an economic resource, people do not value money for its own sake; they value it for its purchasing power.

- Interest rates vary in size because loans differ as to risk, maturity, and amount.

- The pure rate of interest is the hypothetical interest rate that would serve purely and solely to compensate lenders for their willingness to patiently forgo alternative consumption

and investment opportunities until their money is repaid. The pure rate of interest is the interest rate on virtually risk-free long-term Government of Canada bonds.

- In the loanable funds theory, the equilibrium interest rate is determined by the demand for and supply of loanable funds. Other things equal, an increase in the supply of loanable funds reduces the equilibrium interest rate, whereas a decrease in supply increases it; increases in the demand for loanable funds raise the equilibrium interest rate, whereas decreases in demand reduce it.

- The time value of money is the idea that $1 today has more value than $1 sometime in the future because the $1 today can be placed in an interest-bearing account and earn compound interest over time. Future value is the amount to which a current amount of money will grow through interest compounding. Present value is the current value of some money payment to be received in the future.

- The equilibrium interest rate influences the level of investment and helps ration financial and physical capital to specific firms and industries. Similarly, this rate influences the size and composition of R&D spending. The real interest rate, not the nominal rate, is critical to investment and R&D decisions.

15.3 :: ECONOMIC PROFIT

- As residual claimants, entrepreneurs receive a firm's accounting profits (total revenue minus explicit costs) in exchange for assuming the uninsurable risks associated with running a business. An entrepreneur can earn an economic profit (total revenue minus both explicit and implicit costs, including a normal profit) if his firm's accounting profit exceeds the normal profit that his entrepreneurship could on average earn in other business ventures.

- The corporate form of business organization has allowed the millions who own corporate stock to share in the financial

risks and economic profits engendered by entrepreneurship. Profits are the key energizer of business firms within the capitalist system. Profit expectations influence innovation and investment activities and, therefore, the economy's levels of employment and economic growth. The basic function of profits and losses, however, is to allocate resources in accordance with consumers' preferences.

TERMS AND CONCEPTS

economic rent, p. 353
incentive function of price, p. 355
perfectly inelastic supply, p. 354
bond, p. 357
pure rate of interest, p. 357
loanable funds theory of interest, p. 358
expected rate of return curve, p. 359

time value of money, p. 361
compound interest, p. 361
future value, p. 361
present value, p. 362
nominal interest rate, p. 363
real interest rate, p. 363
explicit costs, p. 364

implicit costs, p. 364
economic (pure) profit, p. 364
insurable risks, p. 365
uninsurable risks, p. 365
normal profit, p. 366
stock [corporate], p. 367

QUESTIONS

1. How does the economist's use of the term "rent" differ from everyday usage? Explain the following statement: "Though rent need not be paid by society to make land available, rental payments are very useful in guiding land into the most productive uses."   [LO15.1]

2. Explain why economic rent is a surplus payment when viewed by the economy as a whole, but is a cost of production from the standpoint of individual firms and industries. Explain: "Land rent performs no 'incentive function' in the economy."   [LO15.1]

3. In the 1980s, land prices in Japan surged upward in a "speculative bubble." Land prices then fell for 11 straight years between 1990 and 2001. What can we safely assume happened to land *rent* in Japan over those 11 years? Use graphical analysis to illustrate your answer.   [LO15.1]

4. If money is not an economic resource, why is interest paid and received for its use? What considerations account for the fact that interest rates differ greatly on various types of loans? Use those considerations to explain the relative sizes of the interest rates on the following: [LO15.2]

   a. A 10-year $1000 government bond

   b. A $20 pawnshop loan

   c. A 30-year mortgage loan on a $175,000 house

   d. A 24-month $12,000 bank loan to finance the purchase of an automobile

   e. A 60-day $100 loan from a personal finance company

5. Why is the supply of loanable funds upsloping? Why is the demand for loanable funds downsloping? Explain the equilibrium interest rate. List some factors that might cause it to change.   [LO15.2]

6. Here is the deal: You can pay your college or university tuition at the beginning of the academic year or the same

amount at the end of the academic year. You either already have the money in an interest-bearing account or will have to borrow it. Which situation would you choose? Explain your financial reasoning. Relate your answer to the time value of money, present value, and future value.   [LO15.2]

7. What are the major economic functions of the interest rate? How might the fact that many businesses finance their investment activities internally affect the efficiency with which the interest rate performs its functions?   [LO15.2]

8. Distinguish between nominal and real interest rates. Which is more relevant in making investment and R&D decisions? If the nominal interest rate is 12 percent and the inflation rate is 8 percent, what is the real rate of interest?   [LO15.2]

9. How do accounting profit and economic profit differ? Why is economic profit smaller than accounting profit? What are the three basic sources of economic profit? Classify each of the following according to those sources: [LO15.3]

   a. A firm's profit from developing and patenting a new medication that greatly reduces cholesterol and thus diminishes the likelihood of heart disease and stroke

   b. A restaurant's profit that results from construction of a new highway past its door

   c. The profit received by a firm due to an unanticipated change in consumer tastes

10. Why is the distinction between insurable and uninsurable risks significant for the theory of profit? Carefully evaluate the following statement: "All economic profit can be traced to either uncertainty or the desire to avoid it." What are the major functions of economic profit?   [LO15.3]

PROBLEMS

1. Suppose that you own a 10-hectare plot of land that you would like to rent out to wheat farmers. For them, bringing in a harvest involves $30 per hectare for seed, $80 per hectare for fertilizer, and $70 per hectare for equipment rentals and labour. With these inputs, the land will yield 40 bushels of wheat per hectare. If the price at which wheat can be sold is $5 per bushel and if farmers want to earn a normal profit of $10 per hectare, what is the most that any farmer would pay to rent your 10 hectares? What if the price of wheat rose to $6 per bushel?   [LO15.1]

2. Suppose that the demand for loanable funds for car loans in the Vancouver area is $10 million per month at an interest rate of 10 percent per year, $11 million at an interest rate of 9 percent per year, $12 million at an interest rate of 8 percent per year, and so on. If the supply of loanable funds is fixed at $15 million, what will be the equilibrium interest rate? If the government imposes a usury law and says that car loans cannot exceed 3 percent per year, how big will the monthly shortage (or excess demand) for car loans be? What if the usury limit is raised to 7 percent per year?   [LO15.2]

3. To fund its wars against Napoleon, the British government sold consol bonds. They were referred to as "perpetuities" because they would pay £3 every year in perpetuity (forever). If a citizen could purchase a consol for £25, what would its annual interest rate be? What if the price were £50? £100? Bonds are known as "fixed income" securities because the future payments that they will make to investors are fixed by the bond agreement in advance. Do the interest rates bonds and other investments that offer fixed future payments vary directly or inversely with their current prices?   [LO15.2]

4. Suppose that the interest rate is 4 percent. What is the future value of $100 four years from now? How much of the future value is total interest? By how much would total interest be greater at a 6 percent interest rate than at a 4 percent interest rate?   [LO15.2]

5. You are currently a worker earning $60,000 per year but are considering becoming an entrepreneur. You will not switch unless you can expect to earn an accounting profit that is, on average, at least as great as your current salary. You look into opening a small grocery store. Suppose that the store has annual costs of $150,000 for labour, $40,000 for rent, and $30,000 for equipment. There is a 50 percent probability that revenues will be $200,000 and a 50 percent probability that revenues will be $400,000.   [LO15.3]

   a. In the low-revenue situation, what will your accounting profit or loss be? In the high-revenue situation?

   b. On average, how much do you expect your revenue to be? Your accounting profit? Your economic profit? Will you quit your job and try your hand at being an entrepreneur?

   c. Suppose the government imposes a 25 percent tax on accounting profits. This tax is only levied if a firm is earning positive accounting profits. What will your after-tax accounting profit be in the low-revenue case? In the high-revenue case? What will your average after-tax accounting profit be? What about your average after-tax economic profit? Will you now want to quit your job and try your hand at being an entrepreneur?

   d. Other things equal, does the imposition of the 25 percent profit tax increase or decrease the supply of entrepreneurship in the economy?

McGraw Hill **connect**™ **Practice and Learn Online with Connect**

Connect allows you to practice important concepts at your own pace and on your own schedule, with 24/7 online access to an eBook, algorithmic questions and problems from the textbook, video and logic cases, graphing tutorials, flashcards, Internet exercises, key graphs, and more.

CHAPTER 16

Natural Resource and Energy Economics

People like to consume goods and services. But to produce those goods and services, natural resources must be used up. Some natural resources—solar energy, forests, fisheries—are renewable and can potentially be exploited indefinitely. Other resources such as oil and coal are in fixed supply and can be used only once.

This chapter explores two issues in relation to our supplies of resources and energy. The first is whether we are likely to run out of resources in the near or even distant future and thereby face the possibility of either a drastic reduction in living standards or even, perhaps, the collapse of civilization as we know it. The second is how best to utilize and manage our resources so that we can maximize the benefits we receive from them both now and in the future. We begin the chapter by addressing the issue of whether we are about to run out of resources. We then turn to energy economics and natural resource economics, focusing on the incentive structures that help to promote conservation and sustainability.

16.1 Resource Supplies: Doom or Boom? ::

Since the beginning of the Industrial Revolution in the late 18th century, a historically unprecedented increase has occurred in both population and living standards. The world's population has increased from 1 billion people in 1800 to about 7 billion today, and the average person living in Canada enjoys a standard of living at least 12 times

AFTER READING THIS CHAPTER, YOU SHOULD BE ABLE TO:

16.1 Explain why falling birth rates mean that we are not likely to run out of natural resources.

16.2 Describe why using a mix of energy sources is efficient, even if some of them are quite costly.

16.3 Show how the profit motive can encourage resource conservation.

16.4 Relate how property rights help to prevent deforestation and species extinction.

higher than that of the average Canadian living in 1800. Stated slightly differently, there are many more people alive today as well as much higher levels of consumption per person. These two factors mean that human beings are now consuming vastly more resources than before the Industrial Revolution, both in absolute terms and in per capita terms. This fact has led many observers to wonder whether our current economic system and its high living standards are sustainable. In particular, will the availability of natural resources be sufficient to meet the growing demand for them?

A sensible response clearly involves looking at *both* resource demand and resource supply. We begin by examining human population growth, because larger populations mean greater demand for resources.

Population Growth

We can trace the debate over the sustainability of resources back to 1798, when an Anglican minister in England named Thomas Malthus published *An Essay on the Principle of Population*. In that essay, Malthus argued that human living standards could rise above subsistence levels only temporarily. Any temporary increase in living standards would cause people to have more children and thereby increase the population. With so many more people to feed, per capita living standards would be driven back down to subsistence levels.

Unfortunately for Malthus's theory—but fortunately for society—higher living standards have *not* produced higher birth rates. In fact, just the opposite has happened. Higher standards of living are associated with *lower* birth rates. Such rates are falling rapidly throughout the world, and the majority of the world's population is now living in countries that have birth rates lower than the **replacement rate** necessary to keep their respective populations from falling over time.

Table 16-1 lists the total fertility rates for 12 selected nations including Canada. The **total fertility rate** is the average number of children a woman is expected to have during her lifetime. Taking into account infant and child mortality, a total fertility rate of about 2.1 births per woman per lifetime is necessary to keep the population constant—1 child to replace the mother, 1 child to replace the father, and 0.1 extra children that can be expected to die before they are old enough to reproduce.

As you can see from Table 16-1, total fertility rates in many nations are well below the 2.1 rate necessary to keep the population stable over time. As a result, populations are expected to fall rapidly

replacement rate
The birth rate necessary to keep the size of a population constant without relying on immigration.

total fertility rate
The average total number of children that a woman is expected to have during her lifetime.

TABLE 16-1   Total Fertility Rates for Selected Countries, 2012

Country	Total fertility rate
Australia	1.77
Canada	1.59
China	1.55
France	2.08
Germany	1.41
Hong Kong	1.09
Italy	1.40
Japan	1.39
Russia	1.43
South Korea	1.23
Sweden	1.67
United States	2.06

Source: *The CIA World Factbook*, www.cia.gov. Data are 2012 estimates.

demographers
Scientists who study trends in
human populations.

in many countries over the next few decades, with, for instance, the population of Russia expected to fall by about one-third from its current level of 140 million people to fewer than 100 million in 2050. And Russia is not alone. Thirty countries are expected to see their populations fall by at least 10 percent by 2050, and of these 13 are expected to experience a decline of at least 20 percent.

Worldwide, the precipitous fall of birth rates means that many **demographers** (scientists who study human populations) now expect the world's population to reach a peak of 9 billion people or fewer sometime around the middle of this century before beginning to fall, perhaps quite rapidly. For instance, if the worldwide total fertility rate declines to 1 birth per woman per lifetime (which is near Hong Kong's current rate of 1.09 per woman per lifetime) then each generation will be only half as large as the previous one because there will be only one child on average for every two parents. And even a rate of 1.3 births per woman per lifetime will reduce a country's population by half in just under 45 years.

The world's population increased so rapidly from 1800 to the present day because the higher living standards that arrive when a country begins to modernize bring with them much lower death rates. Before modernization happens, death rates are typically so high that women have to give birth to more than six children per lifetime just to ensure that, on average, two will survive to adulthood. But once living standards begin to rise and modern medical care becomes available, death rates plummet so that nearly all children survive to adulthood. This causes a temporary population explosion because parents—initially unaware that such a revolutionary change in death rates has taken place—for a while keep having six or more children. The impression persists that they must have several children to ensure that at least two or more will survive to adulthood. The result is one or two generations of very rapid population growth until parents adjust to the new situation and reduce the number of children that they choose to have.

The overall world population is still increasing because many countries such as India and Indonesia began modernizing only relatively recently and are still in the transition phase where death rates have fallen but birth rates are still relatively high. Nevertheless, birth rates are falling rapidly nearly everywhere, which means the end of rapid population growth is at hand. Furthermore, because fertility rates tend to fall below the replacement rate as countries modernize, we can also expect total world population to begin to decline during the 21st century. This is a crucial fact to remember when considering whether we are likely ever to face a resource crisis: fewer people means fewer demands placed on society's scarce resources.

Demographers have been surprised, however, at just how low fertility rates have fallen and why they have fallen so far below the replacement rate in so many countries. The decline of fertility rates to such low levels is especially surprising given the fact that couples typically tell demographers they would like to have *at least* two children. Because this implies that most couples would prefer higher total fertility rates than we actually observe, it seems probable that there are social or economic factors constraining couples to have fewer children than they desire and causing total fertility rates to fall so low. Demographers have not yet reached an agreement on which factors are most important, but possibilities include changing attitudes toward religion, the many and varied career opportunities available to women in modern economies, and the fact that raising children has become very costly in modern societies. Indeed, children have been transformed from economic assets that could be put to work at an early age in agricultural societies into economic liabilities that are very costly to raise in modern societies where child labour is illegal and where children must attend school until adulthood. The Consider This box discusses current government efforts to raise birth rates by offering financial incentives to parents.

Resource Consumption per Person

Thomas Malthus's tradition of predicting a collapse in living standards has been carried on to this day by various individuals and groups. One well-reported prediction was made by Stanford University butterfly expert Paul Ehrlich. In his 1968 book *The Population Bomb,* he made the Malthusian prediction that the population would soon outstrip resources so that, "In the 1970s and 1980s hundreds of millions of people will starve to death in spite of any crash programs

CONSIDER THIS :: Can Governments Raise Birth Rates?

Low birth rates pose major problems for countries experiencing very slow population growth or actual population decline. The fact that fewer children are being born today means that fewer workers will be available in coming decades to pay the taxes necessary for governments to keep their current promises regarding old-age pension programs. Too few young workers will be supporting too many elderly retirees.

Another potential problem is a lack of soldiers. With Russia's population expected to fall by one-third by mid-century, it will be much harder for the country to defend its borders. As a response, Russian president Vladimir Putin announced a new policy in 2006 that would pay any Russian woman who chooses to have a second child a bounty worth 250,000 rubles ($9280). In addition, the Russian government promised to double monthly child benefits in an effort to make having children less financially burdensome for parents. Many other countries have

experimented with similar policies. In 2004, France began offering its mothers a payment of 800 euros ($1040) for each child born, and Italy began offering a 1000 euro ($1300) payment for second children.

As far as demographers can tell, however, these and other policies aimed at raising birth rates (offering maternity leave, free day care, or other subsidies to mothers or their children) have not been able to generate any substantial increases in fertility levels in any country in which they have been attempted. For example, Australia's policy of paying mothers a AU$5000 (C$4500) incentive for each child increased the number births by less than 4 percent. It therefore appears that the incentives to have more babies provided by these government plans are being swamped by the broader social and economic forces that are leading to declining overall fertility rates.

embarked upon now." Contrary to this prediction, no famines approaching these magnitudes materialized then and none appear likely today.

One reason why Ehrlich's pessimism was not borne out was that the population growth rate slowed dramatically as living standards around the world rose. Another reason is that the supply of productive resources available to be made into goods and services has been increasing more quickly than the demand for those resources for at least 150 years. This is best seen by looking at Figure 16-1, which tracks *The Economist* magazine's commodity price index for the years 1850 to 2009. The index currently contains 25 important commodities including aluminum, copper, corn, rice, wheat, coffee, rubber, sugar, and soybeans. In earlier days, it included commodities such as candle wax, silk, and indigo, which were important at the time. The index also adjusts for inflation so that one can see how the real cost of commodities has evolved over time, and it is standardized so that the real price of commodities during the years 1845 to 1850 is given a value of 100.

As Figure 16-1 demonstrates, a dramatic long-run decline in real commodity prices has occurred. With the current value of the index at about 30, the real cost of buying commodities today is roughly 70 percent lower than it was in the initial 1845–1850 period. This means that commodity supplies have increased more rapidly than commodity demands, since the only way that commodity prices could have fallen so much in the face of increasing demand is if the supply curve for commodities shifted outward and to the right more quickly than the demand curve.

A key point is that the long-run fall of commodity prices implies that commodity supplies have grown more rapidly than the sum total of the two pressures that have acted over this time to increase commodity demands:

1. The huge rise in the total number of people alive and therefore consuming resources (since 1850, the world's population has risen from 1.25 billion to 7 billion).

2. The huge rise in the amount of consumption *per person*. That is, more people are alive today than in 1850, and each person alive today is on average consuming several times more than was consumed by the average person alive in 1850.

FIGURE 16-1   *The Economist* Magazine's Commodity Price Index, 1850–2009

The Economist magazine's commodity price index attempts to keep track of the prices of the commodities most common in international trade. It is adjusted for inflation and scaled so that commodity prices in the years 1845–1850 are set to an index value of 100. The figure shows that real commodity prices are volatile (vary considerably from year to year) but are now 60 percent lower than they were in the mid-19th century. This implies that commodity supplies have increased faster than commodity demands.

Source: *The Economist* magazine, www.economist.com. © The Economist Newspaper Limited, London (2009) Inflation adjustments made using the GDP deflator for the United States calculated by the Bureau of Economic Analysis, www.bea.gov.

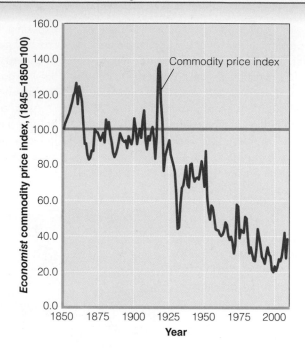

Still, the long-run fall in commodities prices confirms that supplies have managed to grow quickly enough to overcome both of these demand-increasing pressures.

But will supplies be able to overcome these two pressures in the future? Prospects seem positive. First, the rapid and continuing decline in birth rates means that the huge population increases that occurred during the 19th and 20th centuries are not likely to recur in the future. Indeed, we have seen that population decline has begun in several countries and it now seems likely that overall world population will begin to decline within this century. This trend will moderate future increases in the total demand for goods and services. Second, it is also the case that resource consumption *per person* (as distinct from goods and services consumption per person) in the past decade or so has either levelled off or declined in the richest countries such as Canada and the United States, which together currently consume the largest fraction of the world's resources.

That being said, there will very likely be substantial increases in resource demand for the next few decades as large parts of the world modernize and begin to consume as much per capita as the citizens of rich countries do today. One of the world's great economic challenges over the coming decades will be to supply the resources that will be demanded as living standards in poorer countries rise to rich-country levels. But because population growth rates are slowing and because per capita resource uses in rich countries have levelled off, we can now foresee a maximum total demand for resources even if living standards all over the world rise to rich-country levels.

However, significant challenges are still likely to appear in those places where local supplies of certain resources are extremely limited. Water, for instance, is a rare and precious commodity in many places including the Middle East and the American Southwest. Governments will have to work hard to ensure that the limited supplies of water in such areas are used efficiently and that disputes over water rights are settled peacefully. Along the same lines, resources are often produced in certain areas but consumed in others—with, for instance, one-quarter of the world's oil being produced in the Middle East but most of the demand for oil coming from Europe, North America, and East Asia. In such cases, institutions must be developed that can move such resources from the areas in which they originate to the areas in which they are used.

- Thomas Malthus and others have worried that increases in our demand for resources will outpace the supply of resources, but commodity prices have been falling for more than a century, indicating that supply has increased more rapidly than demand.

- Because total fertility rates are very low and falling, population growth for the world will soon turn negative and thereby reduce the demand for natural resources.

- Per capita consumption of resources such as water, energy, and solids has either

fallen or remained constant. If per capita consumption continues to stay the same or decrease while populations fall, total resource demand will fall—meaning that there is little chance that the demand for resources will threaten to use up the available supply of resources.

- Significant increases in resource demands are likely over the next few decades, however, as living standards in poorer countries rise toward those in richer countries

16.2 Energy Economics

Energy economics studies how people deal with energy scarcity. This involves both supply and demand. In terms of energy supply, people are interested in attempting to find and exploit low-cost energy sources. But since energy is only one input into a production process, it is paradoxically often the case that the best energy source to use in a given situation is actually rather expensive—but still the best choice when other costs are taken into account. The economy therefore develops and exploits many different energy sources, from fossil fuels to nuclear power.

In terms of energy demand, the most interesting fact is that per capita energy usage has levelled off in recent years in developed countries. This fact implies that our economy has become increasingly efficient at using energy to produce goods and services.

Efficient Energy Use

Canada has grown increasingly efficient at using energy, and the same is true for other developed countries. An interesting fact about energy efficiency, however, is that it often involves using a mix of energy inputs, some of which are much more expensive than others. The best way to see why this is true is to examine electric power generation.

A typical electric plant has to serve tens of thousands of homes and businesses and is expected to deliver an uninterrupted supply of electricity 24 hours a day, seven days a week. This task is not easy. The problem is that massive changes in energy demand occur over the course of a day. Demand is low at night when people are sleeping, begins to rise rapidly in the morning as people wake up and turn on their lights, rises even more when they are at work, falls a bit as they commute home, rises back up a bit in the evening when they turn on their lights to deal with the darkness and their televisions to deal with their boredom, and finally collapses as they turn out their lights and go to sleep.

The problem for electric companies as they try to minimize the costs of providing for such large variations in demand is that the power plants with the lowest operating costs also have the highest fixed costs in terms of construction. For instance, large coal-fired plants can produce energy at a cost of about 4 cents per kilowatt hour, but they can do this only if they are built large enough to exploit economies of scale and then operated at full capacity. To see why this can be a problem, imagine that such a plant has a maximum generating capacity of 20 megawatts per hour but that its customers' peak afternoon demand for electricity is 25 megawatts per hour. One solution would be to build two 20-megawatt coal-fired plants. But that would be very wasteful given that such plants cost hundreds of millions of dollars to build, since while one was operating at full capacity (and hence minimum cost) the other would be producing only 5 megawatts of its 20-megawatt capacity.

The solution that electric companies employ is to use a mix of different types of generation technology. This turns out to be optimal because even though some electricity generation plants are very expensive in terms of operating costs, they have low fixed costs (that is, they are very inexpensive to build). Thus, the power company in our example might build one large coal-fired plant to generate 20 of the required 25 megawatts of energy at 4 cents per kilowatt hour, but would then build a small 5-megawatt natural gas generator to supply the rest. Such plants produce electricity at the much higher cost of 15 cents per kilowatt hour, but they are relatively inexpensive to build. As a result, this solution would save the electric company from having to build a second very expensive coal-fired plant that would wastefully operate well below its full capacity.

Running Out of Energy?

Some observers worry that we may soon run out of the energy needed to power our economy. Their fears are based largely on the possibility that the world may run out of oil sometime in the next century. It is the case, however, that there is no likelihood of running out of energy. If anything, running out of oil would not mean running out of energy—just running out of *cheap* energy.

Consider Table 16-2, which compares oil prices with the prices at which other energy sources become economically viable. For instance, biodiesel, a type of diesel fuel made from decomposed plant wastes, is so expensive to produce that it becomes economically viable (that is, less costly to produce than oil) only if oil costs $80 or more per barrel. On the other hand, ethanol made from corn costs less to produce and would be an economically viable alternative to oil even if the price of oil were only $60 per barrel.

The key point to gather from this table, however, is that even if we were to run out of oil, alternatives would quickly become available. At a price of $40 per barrel of oil, vast reserves of energy derived from tar sands in Alberta, the conversion of natural gas and coal to liquid petroleum, and even ethanol derived from cheap Brazilian sugar cane become economically viable alternatives. At $50 per barrel, shale oil becomes a viable alternative. At $60 per barrel, corn-based ethanol becomes viable, and at $80 per barrel, so does biodiesel.

TABLE 16-2 **Oil Prices at Which Alternative Energy Sources Become Economically Viable**

Our economy is not totally dependent on oil because alternative fuels do exist. They are, however, more costly to produce than oil, which costs only about $20 per barrel to produce profitably. This table lists the oil price per barrel at which various more costly alternatives become economically viable.

Oil price ($U.S.) per barrel at which alternative is economically viable	Alternative fuel
$80	Biodiesel
60	Corn-based ethanol*
50	Shale oil
40	Tar sands; Brazilian sugar cane-based ethanol; gas-to-liquids**; coal-to-liquids***
20	Conventional oil

Sources: Cambridge Energy Research Associates, www.cera.com; *The Economist,* April 22, 2006, www.economist.com.

* Excludes tax credits.
**Gas-to-liquid is economically viable at $40 if natural gas price is $2.50 or less per million BTUs.
***Coal-to-liquid is economically viable at $40 if coal price is $15 per tonne or less.

In fact, these prices can be thought of as a giant supply curve for energy, with rising energy prices leading to increased energy production. The result is that even if the supply of oil begins to wane and oil prices consequently rise, other energy supplies will quickly be brought on line to fill the energy gap created by the decline in the amount of oil available. Also, the alternative prices listed in Table 16-2 are *current* alternative prices. As technologies improve, the costs of producing these alternatives are likely to fall and, as a result, the potential costs of replacing oil if it runs out will be even lower than suggested by the figures in the table. As a result, economists do not worry about running out of oil or, more generally, running out of energy. There is plenty of energy—the only question is price, and the impact of potentially increasing energy prices on the standard of living.

Finally, we need to acknowledge that energy sources differ not only in their prices but also in the extent of negative externalities they may generate. Negative externalities are costs—such as those associated with air pollution—that are transferred to society during the production process and therefore not reflected in product price. Such externalities need to be accounted for. Some energy sources are relatively "clean," creating little pollution or other externalities. Other sources currently are more problematic. For example, burning coal generates substantial particulate and carbon dioxide emissions that can contribute to health problems and global warming. But a caution is needed here: At sufficiently high electricity prices, burning coal can be both economical and clean. This is true because at sufficiently high electricity prices, the companies that burn coal to generate electricity are able to afford extensive expenditures on pollution reduction. Scrubbers can reduce soot from emissions and new technologies can capture and sequester carbon dioxide in underground storage. At sufficiently high energy prices, clean methods of producing energy are not confined to wind, solar, and other so-called alternative energy sources.

CONSIDER THIS :: Developing Alternative Fuel Sources Is Both Risky and Costly

As Table 16-2 makes clear, conventional oil is much cheaper than alternative energy sources, at least with current technologies. As a result, many billions of dollars are currently being spent by the government and by private businesses in various attempts to improve alternative energy production methods so as to make alternative fuels much less expensive and, therefore, competitive with oil.

These attempts carry heavy financial risks. Consider Changing World Technologies. In 2005, it opened a factory in the United States that could convert 270 tons per day of discarded turkey parts into 500 barrels of fuel oil that could be used immediately to fuel electric generators or further refined into either gasoline or diesel. But while the company originally believed that it could produce its fuel oil at a cost of $10 per gallon, the actual cost turned out to be over $80 per gallon despite the firm's best efforts at reducing costs. As a result, the company went bankrupt in early 2009.

A similar fate has befallen dozens of companies that convert the sugars found in corn into the gasoline substitute

ethanol. Their production costs were so high that many went bankrupt in rapid succession during 2008 and 2009 despite a $50 per barrel U.S. government subsidy for ethanol. In failing, they lost billions of dollars invested by both private individuals and the government.

Currently, a second wave of ethanol producers in the U.S. with a different technology is receiving billions of dollars in government subsidies as they attempt to convert the cellulose that comprises the majority of plant matter into ethanol. While some are hopeful that this new technology may succeed, many others are expecting even more bankruptcies. They are afraid that even with massive government subsidies so-called "cellulosic ethanol" will never be remotely as inexpensive as the gasoline that it hopes to replace.

Critics of the Ontario government's renewable energy policy have also pointed out at the very high cost of generating electrical power from wind and solar panels compared to the traditional methods of hydro and nuclear facilities.

- Energy efficiency has consistently improved so that more output can be produced for every unit of energy used by the economy.

- After taking the different fixed costs of different electricity generating plants into account, utility companies find it efficient to use a variety of energy sources (coal, natural gas, nuclear) to deal with the large daily variations in energy demand.

- Even if we run out of oil, we will not run out of energy because there are many alternative sources of energy available. These alternatives are, however, more costly than oil so that if we were to run out of oil energy costs in the economy would most likely increase.

16.3 Natural Resource Economics

net benefits
The total benefits of some activity or policy less the total costs of that activity or policy.

renewable natural resources
Resources that are capable of renewing themselves if they are harvested at moderate rates.

nonrenewable natural resources
Resources that either are in actual fixed supply or that renew so slowly as to be in virtual fixed supply when viewed from a human time perspective.

The major focus of natural resource economics is to design policies for extracting or harvesting a natural resource that will maximize the **net benefits** from doing so. The net benefits are simply the total dollar value of all benefits minus the total dollar value of all costs, so that a project's net benefit is equal to the dollar value of the gains or losses to be made. A key feature of such policies is that they take into account the fact that present and future decisions about how fast to extract or harvest a resource typically cannot be made independently. Other things equal, taking more today means having less in the future and having more in the future is possible only by taking less today.

In applying this general rule, however, there are large differences between renewable natural resources and nonrenewable natural resources. Some **renewable natural resources** include forests and wildlife that are capable of growing back, or renewing themselves, if they are harvested at moderate rates. This leaves open the possibility of enjoying their benefits in perpetuity. Solar energy, the atmosphere, the oceans, and aquifers are also considered renewable natural resources either because they will continue providing us with their benefits no matter what we do (as is the case with solar energy), or because if we manage them well we can continue to enjoy their benefits in perpetuity (as is the case with the atmosphere, the oceans, and aquifers). Some examples of **nonrenewable natural resources** include oil, coal, and metals that are either in actual fixed supply (like the metals found in the Earth's crust) or that are renewed so slowly as to be in virtual fixed supply when viewed from a human time perspective (as is the case with fossil fuels like oil and coal, which take millions of years to form out of decaying plants and animals).

The key to optimally managing both renewable and nonrenewable resources is designing incentive structures that prompt decision makers to consider not only the present net benefits from *using* the resources under their control, but also the future net benefits from *conserving* the resources under their control now so as to use more of them in the future. Once these incentive structures are in place, decision makers can weigh the costs and benefits of present use against the costs and benefits of future use to determine the optimal allocation of the resource. The key concept used in weighing these alternatives is present value, which allows decision makers to sensibly compare the net benefits of potential present uses with the net benefits of potential future uses.

Using Present Values to Evaluate Future Possibilities

Natural resource economics studies the optimal use of our limited supplies of resources. It is the case, however, that decisions about optimal resource use typically involve choosing how resources will be exploited over time. For instance, suppose a poor country has just discovered that it possesses a small oil field. Should the country pump this oil today, when it can make a profit of $50 per barrel, or should it wait five years given that the profit is then expected to be $60 per barrel due to lower production costs?

Answering this question requires consideration of the time value of money, discussed in Chapter 13. We need a way to compare $60 worth of money in five years with $50 worth of money today. Economists make this comparison by converting the future quantity of money (in this case, $60) into a present-day equivalent measured in present-day money. By making this conversion, it is possible to compare both quantities of money using the same unit of measurement, present-day dollars.

present value
Today's value of some amount of money that is to be received sometime in the future.

The formula for calculating the **present value** of any future sum of money (in this case, $60 in five years) is described in detail in Chapter 16 of *Macroeconomics,* but the intuition is simple. Suppose the current market rate of interest is 5 percent per year. How much money would a person have to save and invest today at 5 percent interest to end up with exactly $60 in five years? The correct answer turns out to be $47.01: If $47.01 is invested at an interest rate of 5 percent per year, it will grow into precisely $60 in five years. Stated slightly differently, $47.01 today can be thought of as being equivalent to $60 in five years because it is possible to transform $47.01 today into $60 in five years by simply investing it at the market rate of interest.

This fact is very important because it allows for a direct comparison of the benefits from the country's two possible courses of action. If it pumps its oil today, it will get $50 per barrel's worth of present-day dollars. But if it pumps its oil in five years and gets $60 per barrel at that time, it will get only $47.01 per barrel's worth of present-day dollars since the present value of $60 in five years is precisely $47.01 today. By measuring both possibilities in present-day dollars, it becomes obvious that the better choice of action would be for the country to pump its oil today since $50 worth of present-day money is obviously greater than $47.01 worth of present-day money.

The ability to calculate present values also allows decision makers to use cost–benefit analysis in situations where the costs and benefits happen at different points in time. For instance, suppose a forestry company is considering spending $1000 per hectare to plant seedlings that it hopes will grow into trees it will be able to harvest in 100 years. It expects the wood from the trees will be worth $125,000 per hectare in 100 years. Should it undertake this investment? No—at the current market interest rate of 5 percent per year, the present value of $125,000 in 100 years is only $950.56, which is less than the $1000 per hectare the firm would have to invest today to plant the seedlings. When both the benefits and costs of the project are measured in the same units (present-day dollars), it is clear that the project is a money loser and should be avoided.

More generally, the ability of policymakers to calculate present values and put present-day dollar values on future possibilities is vitally important because it helps to ensure that resources are allocated to their best possible uses over time. By making it possible for a decision maker to compare the costs and benefits of present use with the costs and benefits of future use, present-value calculations help to ensure that a resource will be used at whatever point in time it will be most valuable.

This is especially important when it comes to conservation, because there is always a temptation to use up a resource as quickly as possible in the present instead of conserving some or all of it for future use. By putting a present-day dollar value on the net benefits to be gained through conservation and future use, present-value calculations provide a financial incentive to make sure resources will be conserved for future use whenever doing so will generate higher net benefits than using them in the present. Indeed, a large part of natural resource economics focuses on nothing more than ensuring the net benefits that can be gained from conservation and future use are accounted for by the governments, companies, and individuals in charge of deciding when and how to use our limited supply of resources. When these future net benefits are properly accounted for, resource use tends to be conservative and sustainable; when they are not properly accounted for, environmental devastation tends to take place, including—as we will discuss in detail below—deforestation and the collapse of fisheries.

Nonrenewable Resources

Nonrenewable resources like oil, coal, and metals must be mined or pumped from the ground before they can be used. Oil companies and mining companies specialize in the extraction of nonrenewable resources and attempt to profit from extracting and then selling the resources they mine or pump out of the ground. But because extraction is costly and because their products' market price is uncertain, profits are not guaranteed and such companies must plan their operations carefully if they hope to realize a profit.

We must note, however, that because an oil field or a mineral deposit is typically very large and will take many years to fully extract, an extraction company's goal of "maximizing profits" actually involves attempting to choose an extraction strategy that will maximize a *stream* of profits—both potential profits today and potential profits in the future. There is, of course, a trade-off. If the company extracts more today, its revenues today will be larger since it will have more product to sell today. On the other hand, more extraction today means less of the resource left in the ground for future extraction and, consequently, smaller future revenues since future extraction will necessarily be reduced. Indeed, every bit of resource that is extracted and sold today comes at the cost of not being able to extract it and sell it in the future. Natural resource economists refer to this cost as the **user cost** of extraction because the user of a resource always faces the opportunity cost of reduced future extraction when choosing to extract a resource now rather than in the future.

user cost
The cost to the user of extracting a resource; current extraction and use means lower future extraction and use.

Present Use versus Future Use

The concept of user cost is very helpful in showing how a resource extraction firm interested in maximizing its flow of profits over time will decide how much to extract in the present as opposed to the future. To give a simple example, consider the case of a coal-mining company called Black Rock, which will have to shut down in two years when the company's mine lease expires. Because the mine will close in two years, the mine's production can be thought of as taking place either during the current year or next year. Black Rock's problem is to figure out how much to mine this year so that it can maximize its stream of profits.

To see how Black Rock's managers might think about the problem, look at Figure 16-2, which shows the situation facing the company during the first year. Begin by noticing P, the market price at which Black Rock can sell each and every tonne of coal that it extracts. The firm's managers will obviously want to take this price into consideration when deciding how much output to produce.

Next, consider the company's production costs, which we will call **extraction costs,** or EC, since this is an extraction company. The extraction costs include all costs associated with running

extraction costs
All costs associated with extracting a natural resource and readying it for sale.

FIGURE 16-2   **Choosing the Optimal Extraction Level**

A firm that takes account only of current extraction costs, EC, will produce Q_0 units of output in the current period—that is, all units for which the market price P exceeds extraction costs, EC. If it also takes account of user cost (UC) and the fact that current output reduces future output, it will produce only Q_1 units of output—that is, only those units for which price exceeds the sum of extraction costs and user cost.

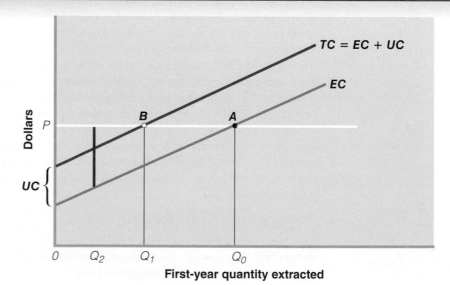

First-year quantity extracted

the mine, digging out the coal, and preparing the coal for sale. Notice that the *EC* curve that represents extraction costs in Figure 16-2 is upsloping because the company's marginal extraction costs increase the more the company extracts, since faster extraction involves having to rent or buy more equipment and to hire more workers or pay overtime to existing workers. Rapid extraction is costly, and the *EC* curve slopes upward to reflect this fact.

Next, consider how much output the firm's managers will choose to produce if they fail to take user cost into account. If the firm's managers ignore user cost, then they will choose to extract and sell Q_0 tonnes of coal (shown where the horizontal *P* line crosses the upsloping *EC* line at point *A*). They will do this because for each and every tonne of coal that is extracted up to Q_0, the market price at which it can be sold exceeds its extraction cost—making each of those tonnes of coal profitable to produce.

But this analysis considers only potential first-year profits. None of those tonnes of coal *has* to be mined this year. Each could be left in the ground and mined during the second year. The question that Black Rock's managers have to ask is whether the company's total stream of profits would be increased by leaving some or all of those tonnes of coal in the ground this year and instead mining and selling them next year.

This question can be answered by taking account of user cost. Specifically, the company's managers can put a dollar amount on how much future profits are reduced by current extraction and then take that dollar amount into account when determining the optimal amount to extract this year. This process is best understood by looking once again at Figure 16-2. There, each tonne of coal extracted this year is assumed to have a user cost of *UC* dollars per tonne that is set equal to the present value of the profits the firm would earn if the extraction and sale of each tonne of coal were delayed until the second year. Taking this user cost into account results in a total cost curve, or *TC*, that is exactly *UC* dollars higher than the extraction cost curve at every extraction level. This parallel upward shift reflects the fact that once the company takes user cost into account, its total costs must be equal to the sum of extraction costs and user cost. That is, $TC = EC + UC$.

If the firm's managers take user cost into account in this fashion, then they will choose to produce less output. In fact, they will choose to extract only Q_1 units of coal (given by where the horizontal *P* line crosses the upward sloping *TC* line at point *B*). They will produce exactly this much coal because for each and every tonne of coal that is extracted up to Q_1, the market price at which it can be sold exceeds its total cost—including not only the current extraction cost but also the cost of forgone future profits, *UC*.

Another way to understand why Black Rock will limit its production to only Q_1 tonnes of coal is to realize that for every tonne of coal up to Q_1, it is more profitable to extract during the current year than during the second year. This is best seen by looking at a particular tonne of coal like Q_2. The profit that the firm can get by extracting Q_2 this year is equal to the difference between Q_2's extraction cost and the market price that it can fetch when it is sold. In terms of the figure, this first-year profit is equal to the length of the vertical red line that runs between the point on the *EC* curve above output level Q_2 and the horizontal *P* line.

Notice that the red line is longer than the vertical distance between the *EC* curve and the *TC* curve. This means that the first-year profit is greater than the present value of the second-year profit because the vertical distance between the *EC* curve and the *TC* curve is equal to *UC*, which is by definition the present value of the amount of profit the company would get if it delayed producing Q_2 until the second year. It is therefore clear that if the firm wants to maximize its profit, it should produce Q_2 during the first year rather than during the second year since the profit to be made by current production exceeds the present value of the profit to be made by second-year production.

This is not true for the tonnes of coal between output levels Q_1 and Q_0. For these tonnes of coal, the first-year profit—which is, as before, equal to the vertical distance between the *EC* curve and the horizontal *P* line—is less than *UC*, the present value of the second-year profit that can be obtained by delaying production until the second year. Consequently, the extraction of these units should be delayed until the second year.

FIGURE 16-3   An Increase in Expected Future Profits Leads to Less Current Extraction

An increase in future profitability increases user cost from UC_0 to UC_1, thereby raising the total cost curve from TC_0 to TC_1. The firm responds by reducing current production from Q_0 to Q_1 so that it can extract more of the resource in the future and take advantage of the increase in future profitability.

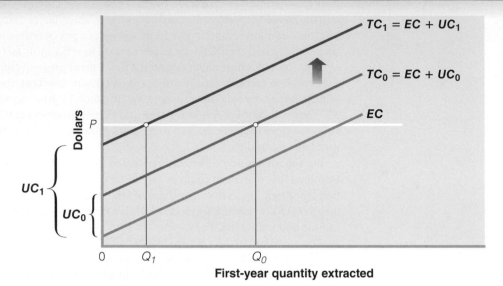

The model presented in Figure 16-2 demonstrates that the goal of profit-maximizing extraction firms is not to simply mine coal or pump oil as fast as possible. Instead, they are interested in extracting resources at whatever rate will maximize their streams of profit over time. This incentive structure is very useful to society because it means that our limited supplies of nonrenewable resources will be conserved for future extraction and use if extraction firms expect that demand (and hence profits) in the future will be higher than they are today. This can be seen in Figure 16-3, where user cost has increased in the current period from UC_0 to UC_1 to reflect an increase in expected future profits. This increase in user cost causes Black Rock's total cost curve to shift up from $TC_0 = EC + UC_0$ to $TC_1 = EC + UC_1$. This shift, in turn, reduces the optimal amount of current extraction from Q_0 tonnes of coal to only Q_1 tonnes of coal.

More generally speaking, Black Rock's behaviour in this case demonstrates that under the right institutional structure, profit-maximizing firms will extract resources efficiently over time, meaning that each unit will tend to be extracted when the net benefits from extraction are the greatest.

Incomplete Property Rights Lead to Excessive Present Use

We have just demonstrated that profit-maximizing extraction companies are very happy to decrease current extraction if they can benefit financially from doing so. In particular, they are willing to reduce current extraction if they have the ability to profit from the future extraction and sale of their product. Indeed, this type of financial situation gives them the incentive to conserve any and all resources that would be more profitably extracted in the future.

This pleasant result breaks down completely if there are market failures such as weak or uncertain property rights that do not allow extraction companies to profit from conserving resources for future use. For instance, look back at Figure 16-2 and consider how much Black Rock would produce if it were suddenly told that its lease would expire at the end of this year rather than at the end of next year. This would be the equivalent of having a user cost equal to zero because there would be no way for the company to profit in the future by reducing current extraction. As a result, the firm will ignore user cost and take into account only current extraction costs, EC. The result will be that it will extract and sell Q_0 tonnes of coal, more than the Q_1 tonnes that it would extract if it could profit from conservation.

- Nonrenewable resources are finite, so it is very important to allocate their limited supply efficiently between present and future uses.

- If resource extraction companies can benefit from both present and future extraction, they will limit current extraction to only those units that are more profitable to extract in the present rather than

in the future. This conserves resources for future use.

- If resource users do not have any way of benefiting from the conservation of a resource, they will use too much of it in the present and not save enough of it for future use—even if future use would be more beneficial than present use.

16.4 Renewable Resources

We just saw that under the right circumstances, extraction companies have a strong profit incentive to moderate their current extraction rates and conserve nonrenewable resources for future use. A similar incentive can also hold true for companies and individuals dealing with renewable resources like forests and wildlife. If property rights are structured properly, then decision makers will have an incentive to preserve resources and manage them on a sustainable basis, meaning they will harvest the resources slowly enough that the resources can always replenish themselves. This section discusses the economics of renewable resources as well as policies that promote the sustainable use of renewable resources. To keep things concrete, we provide a quick example of overhunting and then turn our attention to forests and fisheries.

Forest Management

Forests provide many benefits including wildlife habitat, erosion prevention, oxygen production, recreation, and, of course, wood. In 2005, just under 4 billion hectares, or about 30 percent of the world's land area, was forested and about 225 million hectares, or about 20 percent of Canada's land area, was forested. The amount of land covered by forests is, however, growing in some places but declining in others. This fact is apparent in Global Perspective 16.1, which gives the average annual percentage change over the years 2000 to 2005 in the amount of forest-covered land in 12 selected countries as well as in the entire world.

Economists believe that the large variation in growth rates seen in Global Perspective 16.1 is largely the result of differences in property rights. In certain areas including North America and Western Europe, forests are either private property or strictly regulated government property. In either case, individuals or institutions have an incentive to harvest their forests on a sustainable basis because they can benefit not just from cutting down the trees currently alive but also from managing their forests to reap future benefits.

By contrast, deforestation is proceeding rapidly in countries where property rights over forests are poorly enforced or nonexistent. Consider the situation facing competing loggers if nobody owns the property rights to a given forest: whoever chops down the forest first will be able to reap economic benefits. While nobody can have ownership or control over a living tree, anybody can establish a property right to it by chopping it down and bringing it to market. In such a situation, everybody has an incentive to chop down as many trees as they can to get to them before anyone else. Sadly, nobody has an incentive to preserve trees for future use, because without enforceable property rights there is no way for person A to prevent person B from chopping down the trees that person A would like to preserve.

To reduce and ideally to eliminate nonsustainable logging, governments and international agencies have been taking increasingly strong measures to define and enforce property rights over forests. One major result is that in areas such as Canada, the United States, and Europe, where

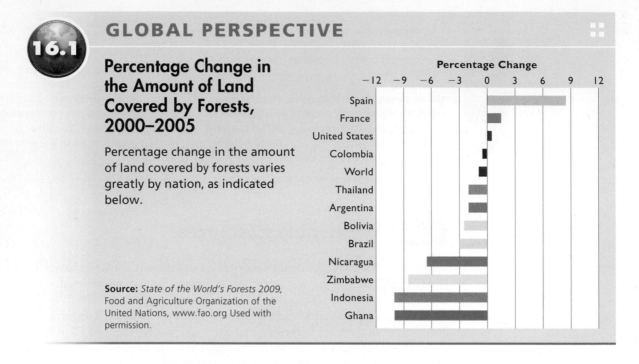

GLOBAL PERSPECTIVE

16.1

Percentage Change in the Amount of Land Covered by Forests, 2000–2005

Percentage change in the amount of land covered by forests varies greatly by nation, as indicated below.

Source: *State of the World's Forests 2009,* Food and Agriculture Organization of the United Nations, www.fao.org Used with permission.

strong property rights over forests have been established, virtually all wood production is generated by commercially run forestry companies. These companies buy up large tracts of land on which they plant and harvest trees. Whenever a harvest takes place and the trees in a given area are chopped down, seedlings are planted to replace the felled trees, thereby replenishing the stock of trees. These companies are deeply concerned about the long-term sustainability of their operations and often plant trees in the expectation that it may be more than a century before they are harvested.

Optimal Forest Harvesting

In cases where the property rights to a forest are clear and enforceable (as they are in Canada), forest owners have a strong incentive to manage their forests on a sustainable basis because they can reap the long-term benefits that derive from current acts of conservation. A key part of their long-term planning is deciding how often to harvest and then replant their trees.

This is an interesting problem because a commercial forestry company that grows trees for lumber or paper production must take into consideration the fact that trees grow at different rates over the course of their lifetimes. Indeed, if the company plants an acre of land with seedlings and lets those seedlings grow into mature trees, the amount of wood contained in the trees at first increases rather slowly as the seedlings turn into saplings, then grows quite quickly as the saplings mature into adult trees, and then tapers off as the adult trees reach their maximum size.

This growth pattern leads forestry companies to think very carefully about when to harvest their trees. If they harvest and replant the acre of land when the trees are only 50 years old, they will miss out on the most rapid years of growth. On the other hand, there is not much point in letting the trees reach much more than 100 years old before harvesting and replanting since at that age there is very little growth left in them. The result is that the forestry company will choose to harvest the trees and replant the land when the trees reach an age of somewhere between 50 and 100 years old. The precise age will be chosen to maximize firm profits and will be affected not only by the growth rate of trees but also by other factors including the cost of harvesting the trees and, of course, the market price of wood and how it is expected to vary over time.

The key point to keep in mind, however, is that forestry companies that have secure property rights over their trees do not harvest them as soon as possible. Instead, they shepherd their resource and harvest their trees only when it finally becomes more profitable to replace older, slow-growing trees with younger, fast-growing trees.

Optimal Fisheries Management

fishery
A stock of fish or another marine animal that is composed of a distinct group, for example Newfoundland cod, Pacific tuna, or Alaska crab.

A **fishery** is a stock of fish or other marine animals that can be thought of as a logically distinct group. A fishery is typically identified by location and species—for example, Newfoundland cod or Pacific salmon. The key difficulty with fishery management is that the only way to establish property rights over a fish swimming in the open ocean is to catch it and kill it. As long as the fish is alive and swimming in the open ocean, it belongs to nobody. But as soon as it is caught, it belongs to whoever catches it. This property rights system means that the only way to benefit economically from a fish is to catch it and thereby turn it into a private good. This creates an incentive for fishers to be very aggressive and try to out-fish each other since the only way for them to benefit from a particular fish is to catch it before someone else does. The calamitous result of this perverse incentive has been tremendous overfishing that has caused many fisheries to collapse and threatens many others with collapse as well. A **fishery collapse** happens when a fishery's population is sent into a rapid decline because fish are being harvested faster than they can reproduce. The speed of the decline depends on how much faster harvesting is than reproduction. In Atlantic Canada, for example, the landings of cod decreased by over 80 percent between 1992 and 2007 because the rapid declining cod population.

fishery collapse
A rapid decline in a fishery's population because the fish are being harvested more quickly than they can reproduce.

Overfishing and fishery collapse are now extremely common, so much so that worldwide stocks of large predatory fish like tuna, halibut, swordfish, and cod are believed to be 90 percent smaller than they were just 50 years ago. In addition, just 3 percent of world fisheries in 2003 were estimated to be underexploited while 76 percent were categorized as either fully exploited, overexploited, depleted, or (it is hoped) recovering from depletion.

POLICIES TO LIMIT CATCH SIZES

Governments have tried several different policies to limit the amount of fish caught each year to try to prevent fisheries from collapsing and to lower annual catch sizes down to sustainable levels where the size of the catch does not exceed the fishery's ability to regenerate. Unfortunately, many of these policies not only fail to reduce catch sizes but also create perverse incentives that raise fishing costs because they do not stop the fishing free-for-all in which each fisher tries to catch as many fish as possible as fast as possible before anyone else can get to them.

total allowable catch (TAC)
A limit on the total number or tonnage of fish that fishers, collectively, can harvest during a particular time period.

A policy that does work to reduce catch size is called the **total allowable catch (TAC).** Under this system, biologists determine the TAC for a given fishery, for instance 100,000 tonnes per year. Fishers can then fish until a total of 100,000 tonnes have been brought to shore. At that point, fishing is halted for the year.

This policy has the benefit of actually limiting the size of the catch to sustainable levels. But it still encourages a race among the fishers to catch as many fish as possible before the TAC limit is reached. The result is that even under TACs, fishing costs rise because fishers buy bigger, faster boats as each one tries to fulfill as much of the overall TAC limit as possible.

individual transferable quota (ITQ)
A limit on the total number or tonnage of fish that individual fishers can harvest during a particular time period.

The catch-limiting system that economists prefer not only limits the total catch size but also eliminates the race among fishers that drives up costs. The system is based on the issuance of **individual transferable quotas (ITQ),** which are individual catch size limits that specify that the holder of an ITQ has the right to harvest a given quantity of a given species during a given time period.

The individual catch sizes of all the ITQs that are issued for a given fishery during a given year add up to the fishery's overall TAC for the year so that they put a sustainable limit on the overall catch size. This preserves the fishery from overexploitation. But the fact that the ITQ quotas are *individual* also eliminates the need for a race. Because each fisher has unlimited time to catch the individual quota, there is no need for a super-expensive, technologically sophisticated boat that is capable of hauling in massive amounts of fish in only a few days to beat competitors to the punch.

This move toward smaller boats and more leisurely fishing greatly reduces fishing costs. But ITQs offer one more cost-saving benefit: They encourage all of the fishing to be done by the lowest-cost, most-efficient fishing vessels. This is true because ITQs are *tradable* fishing quotas, meaning that they can be sold and thereby traded to other fishers. As we will explain, market pressures will cause them to be sold to the fishers who can catch fish most efficiently, at the lowest possible cost.

To see how this works, imagine a situation in which the market price of tuna is $10 per tonne but in which a fisherman named Sven can barely make a profit because his old, slow boat is so expensive that it costs him $9 per tonne to catch tuna. At that cost, if he does his own fishing and uses his ITQ quota of 1000 tonnes himself, he will make a profit of only $1000 (= $1 per tonne × 1000 tonnes). At the same time, one of his neighbours, Tammy, has just bought a new, super-efficient ship that can harvest fish at the very low cost of $6 per tonne. This difference in costs means that Sven and Tammy will both find it advantageous to negotiate the sale of Sven's ITQ to Tammy. Sven, for his part, would be happy to accept any price higher than $1000 since $1000 is the most that he can make if he does his own fishing. Suppose they agree on a price of $2 per tonne or $2000 total. In such a case, both are better off. Sven is happy because he gets $2000 rather than the $1000 he would have earned if he had done his own fishing. Tammy is happy because she is about to make a tidy profit. The 1000 tonnes of tuna that she can catch with Sven's ITQ will bring $10,000 in revenues when sold at $10 per tonne, while her costs of bringing in that catch will only be $8000 since it costs $6000 in fishing costs at $6 per tonne to bring in the catch plus the $2000 she pays to Sven for the right to use his 1000-tonne ITQ.

It remains to be seen, however, whether ITQs and other catch-reduction policies will be enough to save the world's fisheries. Since current international law allows countries to enforce ITQs and other conservation measures only within 200 miles of their shores, most of the world's oceans are a fishing free-for-all. Unless this changes and incentive structures are put in place to limit catch sizes in these areas, economic theory suggests that the fisheries in these areas will continue to decline as fishers compete to catch as many fish as possible as fast as possible before anyone else can get to them.

The **LAST WORD**   Is Economic Growth Bad for the Environment?

Measures of environmental quality are higher in richer countries.

Many people are deeply concerned that environmental degradation is an inevitable consequence of economic growth. Their concern is supported by sensational media events like oil and chemical spills and by the indisputable fact that modern chemistry and industry have created and released into the environment many toxic chemicals and substances that human beings did not even know how to make a couple of centuries ago.

Economists, however, tend to be rather positive about economic growth and its consequences for the environment. They feel this way because there is significant evidence that richer

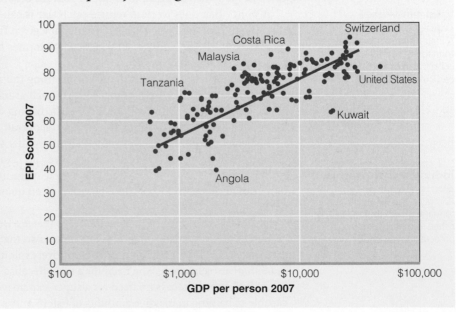

societies spend much more money on keeping their respective environments healthy than do poorer societies. Viewed from this perspective, economic growth and rising living standards are good for the environment because as societies get richer, they tend to spend more on things like reducing emissions from smokestacks, preventing the dumping of toxic chemicals, and insisting that sewage be purified before its water is returned to the environment. They also tend to institute better protections for sensitive ecosystems and engage in greater amounts of habitat preservation for endangered species.

But are these increasing expenditures on environmentally beneficial goods and services enough to overcome the massive increases in environmental harm that seem likely to accompany the enormous amounts of production and consumption in which rich societies engage? The empirical record suggests the answer is yes. The best evidence for this is given by the accompanying figure, in which each of 149 countries is represented by a point that indicates both its GDP per capita (measured on the horizontal axis using a logarithmic scale) and its year 2007 score on the Environmental Performance Index, or EPI.

This index is produced by researchers at Yale University and compares countries based on how well they are

doing in terms of 16 environmental indicators, including atmospheric carbon emissions, measures of air and water quality, the degree of wilderness protection, energy efficiency, and measures of whether or not a country's fisheries and forests are being over-exploited. Out of a maximum possible EPI score of 100, New Zealand and Sweden received the highest scores of, respectively, 95.5 and 93.1. Canada was ranked 37th with a score of 58.4, while the lowest ranked country, Niger, received a score of 39.1.

When EPI scores are combined with measures of GDP per person in the figure, an extremely strong pattern emerges: richer countries have higher EPI scores. In fact, the relationship between the two variables is so strong that 70 percent of the differences between countries in terms of EPI scores are explained by their differences in GDP per person. In addition, the logarithmic scale used on the horizontal axis allows us to look at the best-fit

line drawn through the data and concluded that a tenfold increase in GDP per capita (from, for instance, $1000 to $10,000) is associated with a 20-point increase in EPI. The figure is therefore clear confirmation not only that economic growth and a healthy environment can go together, but that economic growth actually promotes a healthy environment by making people rich enough to pay for pollution-reduction technologies that people living in poorer countries cannot afford.

Looking to the future, many economists are hopeful that economic growth and rising living standards will pay for the invention and implementation of new technologies that could make for an even cleaner environment. If the current pattern continues to hold, increased standards of living will lead to better environmental outcomes.

Note: The horizontal axis is measured using a logarithmic scale, so that each successive horizontal unit represents a tenfold increase in GDP per person. This is useful because in the relationship between EPI and GDP per person, a tenfold increase in GDP per person is associated with a 20-point increase in EPI. Graphing the data using a logarithmic scale makes this relationship obvious.

Source: The EPI data as well as the purchasing-power-parity-adjusted per-person GDP data are from the Yale Center for Environmental Law and Policy (YCELP) and Center for International Earth Science Information Network (CIESIN), http://epi.yale.edu.

Question

The figure in "The Last Word" section shows that a tenfold increase in a country's GDP per person is associated with about a 20-point increase in EPI. Do you think that this pattern can be extrapolated into the future? That is, could Canada (which currently has an EPI of 58.4) gain another 20 points if it increased its GDP per person by a factor of 10 from its current level?

:: CHAPTER SUMMARY

16.1 :: RESOURCE SUPPLIES: DOOM OR BOOM?

- An increase in living standards has entailed using more resources to produce the larger amounts of goods and services currently consumed. This increase can be attributed to two factors: more resource use per person, and more people alive and consuming resources.

- The large increase in total resource use has led to a spirited debate about whether our high and rising living standards are sustainable. In particular, will our demand for resources soon outstrip the supply of resources? A proper answer to this question involves examining both the demand for resources and the supply of resources.

- A good way to examine the demand for resources is to think of total resource demand as being the amount of resources used per person multiplied by the number of people alive; this makes it clear that we should be interested in both the total worldwide population and how much each person is consuming.

- World population growth is not only slowing but is actually turning negative in many countries, which may lead to less demand for resources in the future.

- In Canada and other rich countries resource use per person has either fallen or levelled off during the past several decades; the total demand for resources is likely to reach a peak in the next 50 years before falling over time as populations decline.

- Resource supplies are likely to grow more rapidly than resource demands in the future.

16.2 :: ENERGY ECONOMICS

- Living standards can continue to rise without consuming more energy thanks to more efficient productive technologies that can produce more output using the same amount of energy input.

- Differences in fixed costs mean that a wide variety of energy sources are used in the economy despite the fact that some of these energy sources are much more costly than others.

16.3 :: NATURAL RESOURCE ECONOMICS

- Renewable natural resources like forests and fisheries as well as nonrenewable natural resources like oil and coal tend to be overused in the present unless institutions are created that provide resource users with a way to benefit from conservation.

16.4 :: RENEWABLE RESOURCES

- A lack of property rights leads to severe overfishing and an eventual collapse of the fishery. Governments can define property rights within their sovereign waters and impose limits on fishing. The best system involves combining total allowable catch (TAC) limits for a given fishery with individual transferable quotas (ITQs) for individual fishers.

:: TERMS AND CONCEPTS

replacement rate, p. 373
total fertility rate, p. 373
demographers, p. 374
net benefits, p. 380
renewable natural resources, p. 380

nonrenewable natural resources, p. 380
present value, p. 381
user cost, p. 382
extraction costs, p. 382
fishery, p. 387

fishery collapse, p. 387
total allowable catch (TAC), p. 387
individual transferable quota (ITQ), p. 387

:: QUESTIONS

1. Describe Thomas Malthus' theory of human reproduction. Does it make sense for some species—say, bacteria or rabbits? What do you think makes humans different? **[LO16.1]**

2. Demographers have been very surprised that total fertility rates have fallen below 2.0, especially because most people in most countries tell pollsters that they would like to have at least two children. Can you think of any possible economic factors that may be causing women in many countries to average fewer than two children per lifetime? What about other social or political changes? **[LO16.1]**

3. Resource consumption per person in Canada is either flat or falling, depending on the resource. Yet living standards are rising due to improvements in technology that allow more output to be produced for every unit of input used in production. What does this say about the likelihood of our running out of resources? Could we possibly

maintain or improve our living standards even if the population were expected to rise in the future rather than fall? [**LO16.1**]

4. Suppose you hear two people arguing about energy. The first person says that we are running out of energy. The other counters that we are running out of *cheap* energy. Which person is correct, and why? [**LO16.2**]

5. A community has a nighttime energy demand of 50 megawatts, but a peak daytime demand of 75 megawatts. It has the chance to build a 90 megawatt coal-fired plant that could easily supply all of its energy uses even at peak daytime demand. Should it proceed? Could there be lower-cost options? Explain. [**LO16.2**]

6. Recall the model of nonrenewable resource extraction presented in Figure 16-2. Suppose a technological breakthrough means that extraction costs will fall in the future (but not in the present). What will this do to future profits and, therefore, to current user cost? Will current extraction increase or decrease? Compare this to a situation where future extraction costs remain unchanged but current extraction costs fall. In this situation, does current extraction increase or decrease? Does the firm's behaviour make sense in both situations? That is, does its response to the changes in production costs in each case maximize the firm's stream of profits over time? [**LO16.3**]

7. If the current market price rises, does current extraction increase or decrease? What if the future market price rises? Do these changes in current extraction help to ensure the resource is extracted and used when it is most valuable? [**LO16.3**]

8. **ADVANCED ANALYSIS** Suppose a government wants to reduce its economy's dependence on coal and decides as a result to tax coal-mining companies $1 per tonne for every tonne of coal they mine. Assuming that coal-mining companies treat this tax as an increase in extraction costs this year, what effect will the tax have on current extraction in the model used in Figure 16-2? Now, think one step ahead. Suppose that the tax will be in place forever, so that it will also affect extraction costs in the future. Will the tax increase or decrease user cost? Does this effect increase or decrease the change in current extraction caused by the shift of the *EC* curve? Given your finding, should environmental taxes be temporary? [**LO16.3**]

9. **ADVANCED ANALYSIS** User cost is equal to the present value of future profits in the model presented in Figure 16-2. Will the optimal quantity to mine in the present year increase or decrease if the market rate of interest rises? Does your result make any intuitive sense? (*Hint:* If interest rates are up, would you want to have more or less money right now to invest at the market rate of interest?) [**LO16.3**]

10. Various cultures have come up with their own methods to limit catch size and prevent fishery collapse. In old Hawaii, certain fishing grounds near shore could be used only by certain individuals. And among lobster fishers in Maine, strict territorial rights are handed out so that only certain people can harvest lobsters in certain waters. Discuss specifically how these systems provide incentives for conservation. Then think about the enforcement of these property rights. Do you think similar systems could be successfully enforced for deep sea fishing, far off shore? [**LO16.4**]

11. Aquaculture is the growing of fish, shrimp, and other marine species in enclosed cages or ponds. The cages and ponds not only keep the creatures from swimming away but also provide aquaculturalists with strong property rights over their animals. Does this provide a good incentive for low-cost production as compared with fishing in the open seas where there are few if any property rights? [**LO16.4**]

:: PROBLEMS

1. Suppose that the current (first) generation consists of 1 million people, half of whom are women. If the total fertility rate is 1.3 and the only way people die is of old age, how big will the fourth generation (the great-grandchildren) be? How much smaller (in percentage terms) is each generation than the previous generation? How much smaller (in percentage terms) is the fourth generation than the first generation? Are you surprised by how quickly the population declines? [**LO16.1**]

2. A coal-fired power plant can produce electricity at a variable cost of 4 cents per kilowatt hour when running at its full capacity of 30 megawatts per hour, 16 cents per kilowatt hour when running at 20 megawatts per hour, and 24 cents per kilowatt hour when running at 10 megawatts per hour. A gas-fired power plant can produce electricity at a variable cost of 12 cents per kilowatt-hour at any capacity from 1 megawatt per hour to its full capacity of 5 megawatts per hour. The cost of constructing a coal-fired plant is $50 million but it only costs $10 million to build a gas-fired plant. [**LO16.2**]

   a. Consider a city that has a peak afternoon demand of 80 megawatts of electricity. If it wants all plants to operate at full capacity, what combination of coal-fired plants and gas-fired plants would minimize construction costs?

   b. How much will the city spend on building that combination of plants?

   c. What will the average cost per kilowatt-hour be if you average over all 80 megawatts that are produced by that combination of plants? (*Hint:* A kilowatt is one thousand watts, while a megawatt is one million watts.)

d. What would the average cost per kilowatt-hour be if the city had instead built three coal-fired plants?

3. Suppose that Sea Shell Oil Company (SS) is pumping oil at a field off the coast of Nigeria. At this site, it has an extraction cost of $30 per barrel for the first 10 million barrels it pumps each year and then $60 per barrel for all subsequent barrels that it pumps each year, up to the site's maximum capacity of 90 million barrels per year. [LO16.4]

a. Suppose the user cost is $50 per barrel for all barrels and that the current market price for oil is $90 per barrel. How many barrels will SS pump this year? What is the total accounting profit on the total amount of oil it pumps? What is the total economic profit on those barrels of oil?

b. What if the current market price for oil rises to $120 per barrel while the user cost remains at $50 per barrel? How many barrels will SS pump and what will be its accounting profit and its economic profit?

c. If the current market price remains at $120 per barrel but the user cost rises to $95 per barrel, how many barrels will SS pump this year and what will be its accounting profit and its economic profit?

4. Eric and Kyle are fishers with different equipment and, as a result, different costs for catching fish. Eric's costs for catching fish are $1000 per tonne for the first 5 tonnes

and then $2500 per tonne for any additional tonnes. Kyle can harvest fish at a cost of $3000 for the first 15 tonnes and then $1400 for any additional tonnes. [LO16.4]

a. If society wants 30 tonnes of fish and for some reason will only allow one of the two fishers to do all the fishing, which fisher should society choose if it wants to minimize the cost of catching those 30 tonnes of fish? What will be the total cost of catching the fish? What will be the average cost per tonne for the 30 tonnes?

b. If society wants 30 tonnes of fish and wants them for the least cost regardless of who is catching them, how much should Eric and Kyle each catch? What will be the total cost of catching 30 tonnes? What will be the average cost per tonne for the 30 tonnes?

c. Suppose that Eric and Kyle can both sell whatever amount of fish they catch for $3000 per tonne. Also suppose that Eric is initially given ITQs for 30 tonnes of fish while Kyle is given ITQs for zero tonnes of fish. Suppose that Kyle is willing to pay Eric $550 per tonne for as many tonnes of ITQs as Eric is willing to sell to Kyle. How much profit would Eric make if he used all the ITQs himself? What if Eric sold 25 tonnes of his ITQs to Kyle while using the other 5 tonnes of ITQs to fish for himself?

d. What price per tonne can Kyle offer to pay Eric for 25 tonnes of ITQs such that Eric would make exactly as much money from that deal (in which he sells 25 tonnes' worth of his ITQs to Kyle while using the rest to fish for himself) as he would by using 30 tonnes of ITQs for himself?

Mc Graw Hill connect™ **Practice and Learn Online with Connect**

Connect allows you to practice important concepts at your own pace and on your own schedule, with 24/7 online access to an eBook, algorithmic questions and problems from the textbook, video and logic cases, graphing tutorials, flashcards, Internet exercises, key graphs, and more.

CHAPTER 17 ::

Asymmetric Information and Public Choice Theory

AFTER READING THIS CHAPTER, YOU SHOULD BE ABLE TO:

17.1 Describe how information failures may justify government intervention in some markets.

17.2 Explain the peculiarities of the health care market.

17.3 Explain the difficulties of conveying economic preferences through majority voting.

17.4 Discuss "government failure" and explain why it happens.

Governments in market economies perform several economic tasks. As discussed in various places in the book, these include promoting production and trade by defining property rights, enforcing contracts, and settling disputes; enforcing laws designed to maintain competition; redistributing income via taxes and transfers; reallocating resources by producing public goods and intervening to correct negative and positive externalities; and promoting economic growth and full employment.

In this chapter, we deepen our understanding of government's role in the market economy. We begin by examining a type of market failure known as *asymmetric information* to see how it can justify government intervention in certain markets. Then we examine some of the difficulties that democratic governments face when making specific laws related to the economy.

We will find that governments sometimes pursue policies for which costs outweigh benefits. These inefficient outcomes happen often enough that we need to be just as vigilant in looking for instances of *government failure* as we are in looking for instances of *market failure*.

17.1 Information Failures   ::

As discussed in Chapter 5, *market failures* occur when private markets fail to bring about the allocation of resources that best satisfies society's wants. Chapter 5 also discussed the two most common types of market failure: public goods and externalities.

asymmetric information
A situation in which one party to a market transaction has much more information about a product or service than the other does.

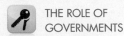 THE ROLE OF GOVERNMENTS

 connect
ORIGIN OF THE IDEA 17.1
Information Failures

But there is also another, subtler, type of market failure. This one results when either buyers or sellers have incomplete or inaccurate information and their cost of obtaining better information is prohibitive. Technically stated, this market failure is the result of **asymmetric information**—information unequally available to buyers and sellers about price, quality, or some other aspect of the good or service.

Sufficient market information is normally available to ensure that goods and services are produced and purchased efficiently. But in some cases, inadequate information makes it difficult to distinguish trustworthy from untrustworthy sellers or buyers (see the Consider This box). In these markets, society's scarce resources may not be used efficiently, implying that the government should intervene by increasing the information available to the market participants. Under rare circumstances the government may itself supply a good for which information problems have prohibited efficient production.

Inadequate Buyer Information about Sellers

Inadequate information among buyers about sellers and their products can cause market failure in the form of underallocation of resources. Examining the market for the services of surgeons will show us how this comes about.

EXAMPLE: LICENSING OF SURGEONS

Suppose that anyone could hang out a shingle and claim to be a surgeon, much as anyone can become a house painter. The market would eventually sort out the true surgeons from those who were learning by doing or were fly-by-night operators. As people died from unsuccessful surgery, lawsuits for malpractice eventually would identify and eliminate most of the medical impostors. People needing surgery for themselves or their loved ones could obtain information from newspaper reports or from people who had undergone similar operations. But this process of obtaining information for those needing surgery would take considerable time and would impose unacceptably high human and economic costs. There is a fundamental difference between getting an amateurish paint job on one's house and being on the receiving end of heart surgery by a bogus physician! The marginal cost of obtaining information about surgeons would be excessively high. The risk of proceeding without good information would result in much less surgery than is desirable—an underallocation of resources to surgery.

The government has remedied this market failure through a system of qualifying tests and licensing. The licensing provides consumers with inexpensive information about a service they buy infrequently. The government has taken a similar role in several other areas of the economy. For example, it approves new medicines, regulates the securities industry, and requires warnings on containers of potentially hazardous substances. It also requires warning labels on cigarette packages and disseminates information about communicable diseases. And it issues warnings about unsafe toys and inspects restaurants for health-related violations.

Inadequate Seller Information about Buyers

Just as inadequate information about sellers can keep markets from achieving economic efficiency, so can inadequate information about buyers. The buyers may be consumers who buy products, or firms that buy resources.

MORAL HAZARD PROBLEM

moral hazard problem
The possibility that individuals will change their behaviour as the result of a contract or agreement.

Private markets may underallocate resources to a particular good or service for which there is a severe **moral hazard problem.** The moral hazard problem is the tendency of one party to a contract to alter her or his behaviour after the contract is signed in ways that could be costly to the other party.

Suppose a firm offers an insurance policy that pays a set amount of money per month to couples that divorce. The attractiveness of such insurance is that it would pool the economic risk of divorce among thousands of people and, in particular, would protect spouses and children from the economic hardship that divorce often brings. Unfortunately, the moral hazard problem reduces the likelihood that insurance companies can profitably provide this type of insurance. After taking out such insurance, married couples would have less incentive to get along and to iron out marital difficulties. Some couples might be motivated to obtain a divorce, collect the insurance, and then continue to live together. Such insurance could even promote more divorces, the very outcome it is intended to protect against. The moral hazard problem would force the insurer to charge such high premiums for this insurance that few policies would be bought. If the insurer could identify in advance those people most prone to altering their behaviour, the firm could exclude them from buying it. But the firm's marginal cost of getting such information is too high compared with the marginal benefit. Thus, this market would fail. Although divorce insurance is not available in the marketplace, society recognizes the benefits of insuring against the hardships of divorce. It has corrected for this underallocation of hardship insurance through child-support laws that dictate payments to the spouse who retains the children, when the economic circumstances warrant such payments. Alimony laws also play a role.

The moral hazard problem is also illustrated in the following statements:

- Drivers may be less cautious because they have car insurance.

- Medical malpractice insurance may increase the amount of malpractice.

- Guaranteed contracts for professional athletes may reduce the quality of their performance.

- Employment compensation insurance may lead some workers to shirk.

- Government insurance on bank deposits may encourage banks to make risky loans.

ADVERSE SELECTION PROBLEM

adverse selection problem
A problem arising when information known to one party to a contract is not known to the other party, causing the latter to incur major costs.

Another problem resulting from inadequate information about buyers is the **adverse selection problem.** This problem arises when information known by the first party to a contract is not known by the second and, as a result, the second party incurs major costs. Unlike the moral hazard problem, which arises after a person signs a contract, the adverse selection problem arises at the time a person signs a contract.

In insurance, the adverse selection problem is that people who are most likely to need insurance payouts are those who buy insurance. For example, those in poorest health are more likely to buy the most generous health insurance policies. Or, at the extreme, a person planning to hire an arsonist to torch his failing business has an incentive to buy fire insurance.

The adverse selection problem thus tends to eliminate the pooling of low and high risks, which is the basis of profitable insurance. Insurance rates then must be so high that few people would want to (or be able to) buy such insurance.

Where private firms underprovide insurance because of information problems, the government often establishes some type of social insurance. It can require everyone in a particular group to take the insurance and thereby can overcome the adverse selection problem. For example, in Canada every citizen is covered by publicly funded health care insurance. The national health care program requires universal participation: People who are most likely to need the health care benefits are automatically participants in the program. So, too, are those not likely to need the benefits. Consequently, no adverse selection problem emerges.

Advocates of our publicly funded health care system point out that we need such a system because private markets would make it impossible for many Canadians who are seriously ill, or are at high risk of serious diseases, to get adequate health insurance. Private insurers would be unwilling to take on clients at high risk for developing serious diseases because of the very high costs this would entail for the insurer. Thus advocates of our present health care system claim that private markets would underallocate resources to health care. Such underallocation of resources in private markets is a powerful argument for a fully publicly funded health care system.

CONSIDER THIS :: "Lemons"

A new car loses substantial market value when it is purchased, even though the same new car can sit on the dealer's lot for weeks, or even months, and retain its market value. One plausible explanation of this paradox is based on the idea of *asymmetric information* and adverse selection.*

Used-car owners (potential sellers) have much better information about the mechanical condition of their cars than do potential buyers. Because of this asymmetric information, an adverse selection problem occurs. Owners of defective cars—so-called "lemons"—have an incentive to sell them to unsuspecting buyers, whereas owners of perfectly operating cars have an incentive to retain their cars. Although both good and bad used cars are offered for sale, the *average* quality of the used cars offered on the market is poorer than the same makes and models that are *not* for sale. The typical consumer finds it difficult to identify the poorer quality used cars simply by looking at them or taking them for a test drive. Anticipating repair costs, the customer is willing to pay only a price that reflects the lower quality.**

So we have a solution to the paradox. When purchased, the market values of new cars drop quickly to the average market value established in the used-car market. This is true even though many used cars may be in perfect operating condition. Adverse selection, asymmetric information, and the resulting risk of "buying someone else's problem" drop the value of used cars relative to new cars still on the lot.

* This explanation is based on the work of economist George Akerlof.
** Transferable warranties reduce, but do not eliminate, the potential repair costs of used cars. Consumers lose time in arranging repairs and forgo the use of their cars when the repairs are being done.

Qualification

Households and businesses have found ingenious ways to overcome information difficulties without government intervention. For example, many firms offer product warranties to overcome the lack of information about themselves and their products. Franchising also helps overcome this problem. When you visit a McDonald's or a Holiday Inn, you know precisely what you are going to get, unlike when you stop at Slim's Hamburger Shop or the Ghost Buster Motel.

Also, some private firms and organizations specialize in providing information to buyers and sellers. Credit reports provide information about credit histories and past bankruptcies to lending institutions and insurance companies. Brokers, bonding agencies, and intermediaries also provide information to clients.

Economists agree, however, that the private sector cannot remedy all information problems. In some situations, government intervention is desirable to promote an efficient allocation of society's scarce resources.

QUICK REVIEW

- Asymmetric information is a source of potential market failure, causing society's scarce resources to be allocated inefficiently.
- Inadequate information about sellers and their products may lead to an underallocation of resources to those products.
- The moral hazard problem is the tendency of one party to a contract to alter its behaviour in ways that are costly to the other party; for example, a person who buys insurance may willingly incur added risk.
- The adverse selection problem arises when one party to a contract has less information than the other party and incurs a cost because of that asymmetrical information. For example, an insurance company offering "no-medical-exam-required" life insurance policies may attract customers who have life-threatening diseases.

17.2 The Economics of Health Care

There is a major debate over the funding, delivery, and cost of health care in Canada. The Canadian health care system provides universal access for covered services. There are no user fees across Canada for basic health services, including hospital and physician services. The Canadian health care system is in essence an insurance program funded by both provincial and federal governments, with zero deductibility. To the individual consumer, health services are "free," even if in reality these services are paid by Canadian taxpayers. The heated debate has arisen because some Canadians are concerned about declining standards and increasing waiting time to see specialists and have surgery.

We noted in Chapter 3 that competitive markets will eliminate surpluses or shortages of a particular product or service. If markets clear, why are there "shortages" in the current Canadian health care system as manifested through longer waiting times for needed health service?

Peculiarities of the Health Care Market

Competitive markets bring about both allocative and productive efficiency: The most desired products and services are produced in the least costly manner. But the health care sector in Canada is not a competitive market industry. Indeed, a competitive market system in health care may not be desirable or attainable because of the unique properties of health care. Here, we discuss some of the unique properties of the health care market.

- *Ethical and Equity Considerations* Ethical questions inevitably intervene in markets when decisions involve the quality of life or, literally, life or death. Although we might not consider it immoral if a person cannot buy a Mercedes or a personal computer, Canadians regard the denial of basic health care as unjust. Generally, Canadians look upon health care as an entitlement or a right and are reluctant to ration it on the basis of price and income.

- *Asymmetric Information* Health care buyers typically have little or no understanding of the complex diagnostic and treatment procedures, while the physicians who are the health care sellers of those procedures possess detailed information. This creates the unusual situation in which the doctor (supplier) as the agent of the patient (consumer) tells the patient what health care services he or she should consume. For example, if a physician tells a patient she needs a follow-up visit in a few weeks, few health care consumers would be informed enough to know whether such a visit was actually needed.

- *The Moral Hazard Problem* The moral hazard problem is the tendency of one party to an agreement to alter her or his behaviour in a way that is costly to the other party. Health care insurance can change behaviour in two ways. First, some insured people might be less careful about their health, taking fewer steps to prevent accident or illness. Second, insured individuals have greater incentives to use health care more intensively than they would if they did not have insurance.

- *The Adverse Selection Problem* The adverse selection problem arises when information known to the first party to a contract is not known by the second, and, as a result, the second party incurs major costs. In health insurance, the adverse selection problem is that people who are most likely to need insurance payouts are those who buy insurance. Those with the poorest health will seek to buy the most generous health insurance policies. Private insurers, knowing this, will try to attract those clients least likely to get sick. Thus, in a competitive health care industry, people either already sick or at a high risk of serious illness will find it difficult to get health insurance except at very high premiums. Those who cannot afford the high premiums will not be covered if they get sick. In the present Canadian system, government insurance covers every citizen, no matter what their state of health.

- *Positive Externalities* The medical care market generates positive externalities (spillover benefits). For example, an immunization against polio, smallpox, or measles benefits the

FIGURE 17-1   **Insurance and the Overallocation of Resources to Health Care**

Panel (a): Without health insurance, the optimal amount of health care consumed is Q_u, where the marginal benefit and marginal cost of health care are equal. Panel (b): The availability of private and public insurance reduces the direct price of health care from P_u to P_i, resulting in its overconsumption (Q_i rather than Q_u) and an overallocation of resources to the health care industry. The area *abc* represents the efficiency loss from that overallocation.

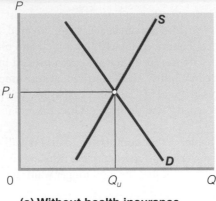

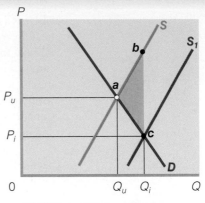

(a) **Without health insurance**   (b) **With health insurance**

immediate purchaser, but it also benefits society because it reduces the risk that other members of society will be infected with highly contagious diseases. Similarly, a healthy labour force is more productive, contributing to the general prosperity and well-being of society. Freely functioning markets underallocate resources to products and services that generate positive externalities. Thus, a competitive health care sector may not deliver as much output as society deems desirable.

Third-Party Payments: Insurance

In Canada, most essential health care expenses are paid primarily through public insurance.

In Canada, essential health care expenses are paid primarily through public insurance. Health care consumers do not pay out-of-pocket the prices they would otherwise. The zero prices are distortions that result in excess consumption of health care services.

GRAPHICAL PORTRAYAL

A simple demand and supply model illustrates the effect of health insurance on the health care market. Figure 17-1a depicts a competitive market for health care services; curve D shows the demand for health care services if all consumers are uninsured, and S represents the supply of health care services. At market price P_u the equilibrium quantity of health care is Q_u. The market clears, and there is no excess demand or supply.

What happens when we introduce private or government health insurance that covers, say, one-half of all health care costs? In Figure 17-1b, with health insurance paying half the price, the consumer is confronted with price P_i ($= 1/2\, P_u$). The health care consumer reacts by purchasing Q_i units rather than Q_u. An excess demand for health care services has been created. If the health care consumer does not pay any portion of health care costs, as is the case in Canada, the shortage would become more acute.

Possible Solutions to Excess Demand

Solutions to the existing excess demand for health care services in Canada come down to either increasing the supply by diverting more tax revenues to health care, or instituting user fees to reduce quantity demanded of health care services. An infusion of more resources is depicted by a rightward shift of the supply curve to S_1 in Figure 17-1b. Although increased resources for health care services will resolve the excess demand, there is as yet no consensus as to whether this is the way Canadians want to move.

In Chapter 1 we discussed the necessary tradeoffs that face any society with limited resources. The federal and provincial governments must either divert tax revenues from other government programs or increase taxes to properly fund the health care needs of Canadians. Neither option is pleasant, but more importantly it is not clear which option the majority of Canadians prefer. Critics argue that even if more resources are made available to the Canadian health care system it will not solve the current shortage problem. They point out that the demand for health care rises with income and the age of its citizens. Both will rise in the future, particularly the number of older Canadians, who generally require more health care services. Critics also point out that there is little competition for the delivery of health care services in Canada, which has created what they see as "inefficiencies" that waste scarce resources.

Proponents of the national health care system in Canada emphasize that, compared to the system in the United States, our system is efficient. Administrative costs of health care delivery are lower in Canada, and the Canadian system costs less than the American system. Canada spends just under 10 percent of gross domestic product (GDP) on health care, while the U.S. health care system consumes almost 16 percent of GDP. The advocates of the existing national health care system in Canada say that even if we have to divert more resources to health care, knowing every Canadian will have the health care he or she needs is a comfort well worth paying for.

17.3 Public Choice Theory

You have now studied several market failures including public goods, externalities, monopolies, and information failures. Each impedes economic efficiency and justifies government intervention in the economy. But the government's response to market failures is not without its own problems and pitfalls. In fact, government can sometimes fail as badly as or even worse than markets in terms of delivering economic efficiency and directing resources to the uses where they will bring the largest net benefits.

public choice theory
The economic analysis of government decision-making, politics, and elections.

That is why it is important to study **public choice theory**—the economic analysis of government decision-making, politics, and elections. Just as the study of *market failure* helps us to understand how regulating markets may help to improve the allocation of resources, the study of *government failure* can help us to understand how changes in the way government functions might help it to operate more efficiently.

As we will discuss shortly, many instances of government failure can be traced to incentive structures that lead political representatives to pursue policies that go against the preferences of the people that they are representing. But an even more fundamental problem exists: The majority voting systems that we rely upon may make it difficult or even impossible to discern voter preferences correctly. In such cases, it is not surprising that government fails to deliver what the voters actually want.

Revealing Preferences through Majority Voting

Through some manner, society must decide which public goods and services it wants and in what amounts. It also must determine the extent to which it wants government to intervene in private markets to correct externalities. Decisions needed to be made about how much regulation of business is necessary, the amount of income redistribution that is desirable, what policies the government might enact to mitigate asymmetric information problems, and more. Furthermore, society must determine the set of taxes it thinks is best for financing government. How should the total tax burden be apportioned (divided) among the public?

Decisions such as these are made collectively in Canada through a democratic process that relies heavily on majority voting. Candidates for office offer alternative policy packages, and citizens elect the people they think will make the best decisions on their collective behalf. Voters retire officials who do not adequately represent their collective wishes. Citizens also periodically

FIGURE 17-2 **Inefficient Voting Outcomes**

Majority voting can produce inefficient decisions. Panel (a): Majority voting leads to rejection of a public good that has greater total benefit than total cost. Panel (b): Majority voting results in acceptance of a public good that has a higher total cost than total benefit.

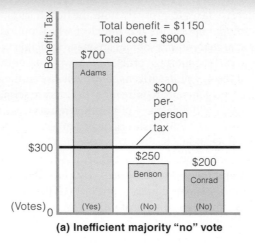

(a) Inefficient majority "no" vote

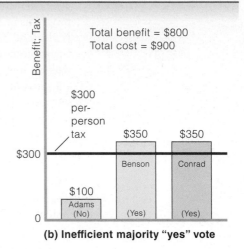

(b) Inefficient majority "yes" vote

have opportunities at the provincial and municipal levels to vote directly on public expenditures or new legislation.

Although the democratic process does a reasonably good job of revealing society's preferences, it is imperfect. Public choice theory demonstrates that majority voting can produce inefficiencies and inconsistencies.

[connect logo]
ORIGIN OF THE
IDEA 17.2
Public Choice Theory

Inefficient Voting Outcomes

Society's well-being is enhanced when government provides a public good whose total benefit exceeds its total cost. Unfortunately, majority voting does not always deliver that outcome.

ILLUSTRATION: INEFFICIENT "NO" VOTE

Assume that the government can provide a public good, say, national defence, at a total expense of $900. Assume there are only three individuals—Adams, Benson, and Conrad—in the society and that they will share the $900 tax expense equally, with each being taxed $300 if the proposed public good is provided. And assume, as Figure 17-2a illustrates, that Adams would receive $700 worth of benefits from having this public good; Benson, $250; and Conrad, $200.

What will be the result if a majority vote determines whether this public good is provided? Although people do not always vote strictly according to their own economic interest, it is likely that Benson and Conrad will vote "no" because they will incur tax costs of $300 each while gaining benefits of only $250 and $200, respectively. Adams will vote "yes." So the majority vote will defeat the proposal even though the total benefit of $1150 (= $700 for Adams + $250 for Benson + $200 for Conrad) exceeds the total cost of $900.

ILLUSTRATION: INEFFICIENT "YES" VOTE

Now consider a situation in which the majority favours a public good even though its total cost *exceeds* its total benefit. Figure 17-2b shows the details. Again, Adams, Benson, and Conrad will equally share the $900 cost of the public good; they will each be taxed $300. But since Adams's benefit now is only $100 from the public good, she will vote against it. Meanwhile, Benson and Conrad will benefit by $350 each. They will vote for the public good because that benefit ($350) exceeds their tax payments ($300). The majority vote will provide a public good costing $900 that produces total benefits of only $800 (= $100 for Adams + $350 for Benson + $350 for

Conrad). Society's resources will be inefficiently allocated to this public good, and there will be too much of it.

IMPLICATIONS

The point is that an inefficient outcome may occur as either an overproduction or an underproduction of a specific public good and, therefore, as an overallocation or underallocation of resources for that particular use. In Chapter 5 we saw that government can improve economic efficiency by providing public goods that the market system will not make available. Now we have extended that analysis to reveal that government might fail to provide some public goods whose production is economically justifiable while providing other goods that are not economically warranted.

In our examples, each person has only a single vote, no matter how much he or she might gain or lose from a public good. In the first example (inefficient "no" vote), Adams would be willing to purchase a vote from either Benson or Conrad if buying votes were legal. That way Adams could be assured of obtaining the national defence she so highly values. But since buying votes is illegal, many people with strong preferences for certain public goods may have to go without them.

When individual consumers have a strong preference for a specific *private good,* they usually can find that good in the marketplace even though it may be unpopular with the majority of consumers. But a person cannot easily buy a *public good* such as national defence once the majority has decided against it.

Conversely, a consumer in the marketplace can decide against buying a particular product, even a popular one. But although you may not want national defence, you must "buy" it through your tax payments when it is favoured by the majority.

Conclusion: Because majority voting fails to incorporate the *strength* of the preferences of the individual voter, it may produce economically inefficient outcomes.

Interest Groups and Logrolling

Some, but not all, of the inefficiencies of majority voting get resolved through the political process. Two examples follow.

INTEREST GROUPS

Those who have a strong preference for a public good may band together into an interest group and use advertisements, mailings, and direct persuasion to convince others of the merits of that public good. Adams might try to persuade Benson and Conrad that it is in their best interest to vote for national defence—that national defence is much more valuable to them than their $250 and $200 valuations. Such appeals are common in democratic politics. Sometimes they are successful; sometimes they are not.

POLITICAL LOGROLLING

logrolling
The trading of votes by legislators to secure favourable outcomes on decisions concerning the provision of public goods and quasipublic goods.

Perhaps surprisingly, **logrolling**—the trading of votes to secure favourable outcomes—can also turn an inefficient outcome into an efficient one. In our first example (Figure 17-1a), perhaps Benson has a strong preference for a different public good—for example, a new road—which Adams and Conrad do not think is worth the tax expense. That would provide an opportunity for Adams and Benson to trade votes to ensure provision of both national defence and the new road. That is, Adams and Benson would each vote "yes" on both measures. Adams would get the national defence and Benson would get the road. Without the logrolling, both public goods would have been rejected. Logrolling will add to society's well-being if, as was true for national defence, the road creates a greater overall benefit than cost.

Logrolling need not increase economic efficiency. Even if national defence and the road each cost more than the total benefit they produced, both might still be provided because of the vote trading.

TABLE 17-1	Paradox of Voting

	PREFERENCES		
Public Good	**Adams**	**Benson**	**Conrad**
National defence	1st choice	3rd choice	2nd choice
Road	2nd choice	1st choice	3rd choice
Weather warning system	3rd choice	2nd choice	1st choice

Election	**Voting Outcomes: Winner**
1. National defence vs. road	National defence (preferred by Adams and Conrad)
2. Road vs. weather warning system	Road (preferred by Adams and Benson)
3. National defence vs. weather warning system	Weather warning system (preferred by Benson and Conrad)

connect
ORIGIN OF THE IDEA 17.3
Paradox of Voting

paradox of voting
A situation in which paired-choice majority voting fails to provide a consistent ranking of society's preferences for public goods or services.

Paradox of Voting

Another difficulty with majority voting is the **paradox of voting,** a situation in which society may not be able to rank its preferences consistently through paired-choice majority voting.

PREFERENCES

Consider Table 17-1, in which we again assume a community of three voters: Adams, Benson, and Conrad. Suppose the community has three alternative public goods from which to choose: national defence, a road, and a weather warning system. We expect that each member of the community prefers the three alternatives in a certain order. For example, one person might prefer national defence to a road, and a road to a weather warning system. We can attempt to determine the preferences of the community through paired-choice majority voting. Specifically, a vote can be held between any two of the public goods, and the winner of that vote can then be matched against the third public good in another vote.

The three goods and the assumed individual preferences of the three voters are listed in the top part of Table 17-1. The data indicate that Adams prefers national defence to the road and the road to the weather warning system. This implies also that Adams prefers national defence to the weather warning system. Benson values the road more than the weather warning system and the weather warning system more than national defence. Conrad's order of preference is weather warning system, national defence, and road.

VOTING OUTCOMES

The lower part of Table 17-1 shows the outcomes of three hypothetical decisions of the majority vote. In the first, national defence wins against the road because a majority of voters (Adams and Conrad) prefer national defence to the road. In the second election to see whether this community wants a road or a weather warning system, a majority of voters (Adams and Benson) prefer the road. We have determined that the majority of people in this community prefer national defence to a road and prefer a road to a weather warning system. It seems logical to conclude that the community prefers national defence to a weather warning system, but the community does not!

To demonstrate this conclusion, we hold a direct election between national defence and the weather warning system. Row (3) shows that a majority of voters (Benson and Conrad) prefer the weather warning system to national defence. As listed in Table 17-1, then, the three paired-choice majority votes imply that this community is irrational: it seems to prefer national defence to a road and a road to a weather warning system, but would rather have a weather warning system than national defence.

The problem is not irrational community preferences but rather a flawed procedure for determining those preferences. We see that the outcome from paired-choice majority voting may depend on the order in which the votes are taken. Different sequences of majority votes can lead to different outcomes, many of which may fail to reflect the electorate's underlying preferences. As a consequence, government may find it difficult to provide the "correct" public goods by acting in accordance with majority voting. One important note: this critique is not meant to suggest that some better procedure exists. Majority voting is much more likely to reflect community preferences than decisions made by, say, a dictator or a group of self-appointed leaders.

Median-Voter Model

median-voter model
The theory that under majority rule the median (middle) voter will be in the dominant position to determine the outcome of an election.

One other aspect of majority voting reveals further insights into real-world phenomena. The **median-voter model** suggests that, under majority rule and consistent voting preferences, the median voter will in a sense determine the outcomes of elections. The median voter is the person holding the middle position on an issue: half the other voters have stronger preferences for a public good, amount of taxation, or degree of government regulation, while half have weaker or negative preferences. The extreme voters on each side of an issue prefer the median choice rather than the other extreme position, so the median voter's choice predominates.

EXAMPLE

Suppose a society composed of Adams, Benson, and Conrad has reached agreement that as a society it needs a weather warning system. Independently each is to submit a total dollar amount he or she thinks should be spent on the weather warning system, assuming each will be taxed one-third of that amount. An election will determine the size of the system. Because each person can be expected to vote for his or her own proposal, no majority will occur if all the proposals are placed on the ballot at the same time. Thus, the group decides on a paired-choice vote: they will first vote between two of the proposals and then match the winner of that vote against the remaining proposal.

The three proposals are as follows: Adams desires a $400 system; Benson wants an $800 system; Conrad opts for a $300 system. Which proposal will win? The median-voter model suggests it will be the $400 proposal submitted by the median voter, Adams. Half the other voters favour a more costly system; half favour a less costly system. To understand why the $400 system will be the outcome, let's conduct the two elections.

First, suppose that the $400 proposal is matched against the $800 proposal. Adams naturally votes for her $400 proposal, and Benson votes for his own $800 proposal. Conrad, who proposed the $300 expenditure for the weather warning system, votes for the $400 proposal because it is closer to his own. So Adams's $400 proposal is selected by a 2-to-1 majority vote.

Next, we match the $400 proposal against the $300 proposal. Again the $400 proposal wins. It gets a vote from Adams and one from Benson, who proposed the $800 expenditure and for that reason prefers a $400 expenditure to a $300 one. Adams, the median voter in this case, is in a sense the person who has decided the level of expenditure on a weather warning system for this society.

REAL-WORLD APPLICABILITY

Although our illustration is simple, it explains a great deal. We do note a tendency for public choices to match the median view most closely. Political candidates, for example, take one set of positions to win the nomination of their political parties; in so doing, they tend to appeal to the median voter within their party to get the nomination. They then shift their views more closely to the political centre when they square off against opponents from the opposite political party. In effect, they redirect their appeal toward the median voter within the total population. They also try to label their opponents as being too liberal, or too conservative, and out of touch with mainstream Canada. They then conduct polls and adjust their positions on issues accordingly.

IMPLICATIONS

The median-voter model has two important implications:

1. At any point in time, many people will be dissatisfied by the extent of government involvement in the economy. The size of government will largely be determined by the median preference, leaving many people desiring a much larger, or a much smaller, public sector. In the marketplace you can buy no zucchinis, two zucchinis, or 200 zucchinis, depending on how much you enjoy them. In the public sector you will tend to get the public health funding that the median voter prefers.

2. Some people may "vote with their feet" by moving into political jurisdictions where the median voter's preferences are closer to their own. They may move from one province to another where the level of government services, and therefore taxes, is lower. Or they may move into an area known for its excellent but expensive school system. Some may move to other provinces; a few may even move to other countries.

For these reasons, and because our personal preferences for publicly provided goods and services are not static, the median preference shifts over time. Moreover, information about people's preferences is imperfect, leaving much room for politicians to misjudge the true median position. When they misjudge, they may have a difficult time getting elected or re-elected.

17.4 Government Failure

government failure
Inefficiencies in resource allocation caused by problems in the operation of the public sector (government).

The term **government failure** refers to economically inefficient outcomes caused by shortcomings in the public sector. One cause of government failure is the voting problems that we have just discussed. But government failures caused by voting problems are somewhat unique in that they are driven by a lack of information about voter preferences. By contrast, most instances of government failure happen *despite* government officials knowing what voters prefer.

In these other situations, government failures occur because the incentive structures facing government officials lead them either to put their own interests ahead of voter interests or to put the interests of a minority of voters ahead of those of a majority of voters. Let's examine what public interest theory has to say about these situations.

Representative Democracy and the Principal–Agent Problem

Our system of representative democracy has the advantage of allowing us to elect full-time representatives who can specialize in understanding the pros and cons of different potential laws and who have more time to digest their details than the average citizen. But the system also suffers from principal–agent problems.

principal–agent problems
Conflicts that arise when tasks are delegated by one group of people (principals) to another group of people (agents).

Conflicts known as **principal–agent problems** arise when tasks are delegated by one group of people (principals) to another group of people (agents). The conflicts arise because the interests of the agents may not be the same as the interests of the principals, so that the agents may end up taking actions that are opposed by the principals whom they are supposed to be representing.

In the business world, principal–agent problems often arise when the managers of a company (the agents) take actions that are not in the best interests of the company's shareholders (the principals). Examples include the managers' spending huge amounts of company money on executive jets and lavish offices or holding meetings at expensive resorts. These luxuries are obviously very enjoyable to managers but are, of course, not in the best interests of shareholders because the money spent on them could either be reinvested back into the firm to increase future profits or be paid out to shareholders immediately as dividends. But to the extent that managers are free to follow their own interests rather than those of their shareholders, they may indeed take these and other actions that are not in the better interests of their shareholders. Hence the conflicts.

In a representative democracy, principal–agent problems often arise because politicians have goals such as re-election that may be inconsistent with pursuing the best interests of their constituents. Indeed, casual reflection suggests that "sound economics" and "good politics" often differ. Sound economics calls for the public sector to pursue various programs as long as marginal benefits exceed marginal costs. Good politics, however, suggests that politicians support programs and policies that will maximize their chances of getting re-elected and staying in office. The result may be that the government will promote the goals of groups of voters that have special interests to the detriment of the larger public.

SPECIAL-INTEREST EFFECT

special-interest effect
Any result of government promotion of the interests (goals) of a small group at the expense of a much larger group.

Efficient public decision-making is often impaired by the **special-interest effect**. This is any outcome of the political process where a small number of people obtain a government program or policy that gives them large gains at the expense of a much greater number of persons who individually suffer small losses.

The small group of potential beneficiaries is well informed and highly vocal on the issue in question, and they press politicians for approval. The large number of people facing very small individual losses, however, are generally uninformed on the issue. Politicians feel they will lose the campaign contributions and votes of the small special-interest group that backs the issue if they legislate against it but will not lose the support of the large group of uninformed voters, who are likely to evaluate the politicians on other issues of greater importance to them.

The special-interest effect is also evident in so-called *pork-barrel politics*, a means of securing a government project that yields benefits mainly to a single political district and its political representative. In this case, the special-interest group comprises local constituents, while the larger group consists of relatively uninformed taxpayers scattered across a much larger geographic area. Politicians clearly have a strong incentive to secure public goods ("pork") for their local constituents.

Finally, a politician's inclination to support the smaller group of special beneficiaries is enhanced because special-interest groups are often quite willing to help finance the campaigns of rightminded politicians and politicians who "bring home the bacon." The result is that politicians may support special-interest programs and projects that cannot be justified on economic grounds.

RENT-SEEKING BEHAVIOUR

rent seeking
The actions by persons, firms, or unions to gain special benefits from government at the taxpayers' or someone else's expense.

The appeal to government for special benefits at taxpayers' or someone else's expense is called **rent seeking.** The term "rent" in "rent seeking" is used loosely to refer to any payment in excess of the minimum amount that would be needed to keep a resource employed in its current use. Those engaged in "rent seeking" are attempting to use government influence to get themselves into a situation in which they will get paid more for providing a good or service than the minimum amount you would actually have to pay them to provide that good or service. (These excess, or surplus, payments are akin to *land rent*, which is also a surplus payment.)

Rent seeking goes beyond the usual profit seeking through which firms try to increase their profits by adjusting their output levels, improving their products, and incorporating cost-saving technologies. Rent seeking looks to obtain extra profit or income by influencing government policies. Corporations, trade associations, labour unions, and professional organizations employ vast resources to secure favourable government policies that result in rent—higher profit or income than would otherwise occur. The government is able to dispense such rent directly or indirectly through laws, rules, hiring, and purchases. Elected officials are willing to provide such rent because they want to be responsive to key constituents, who in turn help them remain in office.

Here are some examples of "rent-providing" legislation or policies: tariffs on foreign products that limit competition and raise prices to consumers, tax breaks that benefit specific corporations, government construction projects that create union jobs but cost more than the benefits they yield, occupational licensing that goes beyond what is needed to protect consumers, and large subsidies to farmers by taxpayers. None of these is justified by economic efficiency.

Clear Benefits, Hidden Costs

Some critics say that vote-seeking politicians will ignore economic rationality by failing to weigh costs and benefits objectively when deciding which programs to support. Because political office-holders must seek voter support every few years, they favour programs that have immediate and clear-cut benefits and vague or deferred costs.

Such biases may lead politicians to reject economically justifiable programs and to accept programs that are economically irrational. For example, a proposal to construct or expand mass-transit systems in large metropolitan areas may be economically rational on the basis of benefit–cost analysis, but if (1) the program is to be financed by immediate increases in highly visible income or sales taxes and (2) benefits will occur only years from now when the project is completed, then the vote-seeking politician may oppose the program.

Another example of possible political bias is the distribution of health care expenditures by both the federal and provincial governments in Canada. Certain government health care expenditures on a relatively small number of Canadians may lead to much media attention, but may not be the most efficient expenditures of health care resources from society's standpoint. But it is this kind of positive and visible front-page coverage that politicians desire in their attempts to get re-elected.

Limited and Bundled Choice

Public choice theorists point out that the political process forces citizens and their elected representatives to be less selective in choosing public goods and services than they are in choosing private goods and services.

In the marketplace, the citizen as a consumer can exactly satisfy personal preferences by buying certain goods and not buying others. However, in the public sector the citizen as a voter is confronted with, say, only two or three candidates for an office, each representing a different bundle of programs (public goods and services). None of these bundles of public goods is likely to fit exactly the preferences of any particular voter, yet the voter must choose one of them. The candidate who comes closest to voter Smith's preference may endorse national health insurance, increases in Old Age Security benefits, subsidies to tobacco farmers, and tariffs on imported goods. Smith is likely to vote for that candidate even though Smith strongly opposes tobacco subsidies.

Parliament is confronted with a similar limited-choice, bundled-goods problem. Appropriations legislation combines hundreds, even thousands, of spending items into a single bill. Many of these spending items may be completely unrelated to the main purpose of the legislation, yet members of Parliament must vote the entire package—"yea" or "nay." Unlike consumers in the marketplace, they cannot be selective.

Bureaucracy and Inefficiency

Some economists contend that public agencies are generally less efficient than private businesses. The reason is that the market system creates incentives and pressures for internal efficiency that are absent from the public sector. The market system imposes a very obvious test of performance on private firms: the test of profit and loss. An efficient firm is profitable and therefore successful; it survives, prospers, and grows. An inefficient firm is unprofitable and unsuccessful; it declines and in time goes bankrupt and ceases to exist. But no similar, clear-cut test exists with which to assess the efficiency or inefficiency of public agencies.

Furthermore, economists assert that government employees, together with the special-interest groups they serve, often gain sufficient political clout to block attempts to pare down or eliminate their agencies. Politicians who attempt to reduce the size of huge federal bureaucracies such as those relating to agriculture, education, and health and welfare incur sizable political risk because bureaucrats and special-interest groups will team up to defeat them.

Finally, critics point out that there is a tendency for government bureaucrats to justify their continued employment by looking for and eventually finding new "problems" to solve. It is not surprising that social problems, as defined by government, tend to persist or even expand.

Corruption

political corruption
When government officials abuse their power for personal gain.

The unlawful misdirection of governmental resources or actions that occurs when government officials abuse their entrusted powers for personal gain is called **political corruption.** For instance, a police supervisor engages in political corruption if she accepts a bribe in exchange for illegally freeing a thief who had been lawfully arrested by another officer. Similarly, a government bureaucrat engages in political corruption if he refuses to issue a building permit to a homebuilder who is in full compliance with the law unless the homebuilder makes a "voluntary contribution" to the bureaucrat's favorite charity.

While relatively uncommon in Canada, political corruption is a daily reality in many parts of the world, as can be seen in Global Perspective 17.1, which gives the percentages of survey respondents in 15 countries who reported that they or someone else in their household had paid a bribe during the previous 12 months.

Political corruption comes in two basic forms. In the first, a government official must be bribed to do what he should be doing for free as part of his job—as with the bureaucrat in our earlier example who demands a bribe to issue a permit to a homebuilder who is in full compliance with the law. In the second, a government official demands a bribe to do something that she is not legally entitled to do—as with the police supervisor in our earlier example who illegally freed a thief.

If a candidate accepts campaign contributions from a special interest group and then shows subsequent support for that group's legislative goals, has a subtle form of political corruption taken place? While there are strong opinions on both sides of the issue, it is often hard to tell in any particular case whether a special interest's campaign contribution amounts to a bribe. On the one hand, the special interest may indeed be trying to influence the politician's vote. On the other hand, the special interest may simply be trying to support and get elected a person who already sees things their way and who would vote the way they wanted no matter what anyone did.

That being said, the impression of impropriety lingers and so laws have been passed in Canada limiting the amount of money that individuals can donate to specific candidates and making it illegal for certain groups such as companies to donate money directly to individual politicians (as distinct from directing funds toward supporting specific issues or advocacy groups—which is both legal and unrestricted). Proponents of these laws hope that the limitations strike a good balance—allowing contributions to be large enough that individuals and groups can meaningfully support candidates they agree with but keeping contributions small enough that no one individual or group can singlehandedly donate enough money to sway a politician's vote.

Imperfect Institutions

Such criticisms of public-sector inefficiency shatter the concept of a benevolent government that responds with precision and efficiency to the wants of its citizens. The market system of the private sector is far from perfectly efficient, and government's economic function is mainly to

GLOBAL PERSPECTIVE

17.1

Percentage of Households Paying a Bribe in the Past Year

The Global Corruption Barometer is an international survey that asks individuals about their personal experiences with government corruption. The 2009 survey of 73,132 people in 69 countries included a question that asked participants whether they or anyone in their respective households had paid a bribe in any form during the previous 12 months. Here are the results for 16 selected countries.

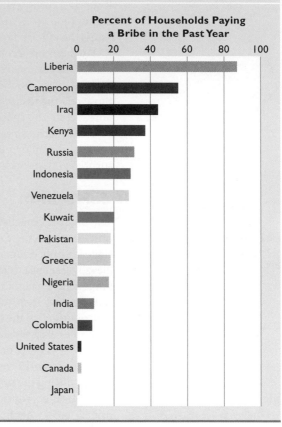

Percent of Households Paying a Bribe in the Past Year

Source: Adapted from Global Corruption Barometer. Copyright 2009 Transparency International: the global coalition against corruption. Used with permission. For more information, visit www.transparency.org.

correct that system's shortcomings. But the public sector, too, is subject to deficiencies in fulfilling its economic function.

Because the market system and public agencies are both imperfect, it is sometimes difficult to determine whether a particular activity can be performed with greater success in the private sector or the public sector. It is easy to reach agreement on opposite extremes: national defence must lie with the public sector, while automobile production can best be accomplished by the private sector. But what about health insurance? Parks and recreation areas? Fire protection? Garbage collection? Housing? Education? It is hard to say absolutely that it should be assigned to either the public sector or the private sector. After all, the goods and services just mentioned are provided in part by *both* private enterprises and public agencies.

QUICK REVIEW

- Principal–agent problems are conflicts that occur when the agents who are supposed to be acting in the best interests of their principals instead take actions that help themselves but hurt their principals.

- Because larger groups are more difficult to organize and motivate than smaller groups, special interests can often obtain what they want politically even when what they want is opposed by a majority of voters.

- Government failure allegedly occurs as a result of voting problems, rent seeking, pressure by special-interest groups, short-sighted political behaviour, limited and bundled choices, bureaucratic inefficiency, and political corruption.

The LAST WORD   Singapore's Efficient and Effective Health Care System

How does Singapore deliver some of the best health care in the world while spending less per person than Canada?

In every health-quality category monitored by the World Health Organization, the small island nation of Singapore is either number one in the world or near the top of the list. Among other achievements, Singapore has the world's lowest rate of infant mortality and the world's fourth highest life expectancy.

One might expect that achieving these exceptional outcomes would be extremely expensive. But Singapore is also number one in another category: It spends less per person on health care than any other developed nation. In 2010 Canada spent about 10 percent of its GDP on health care. Singapore spent just 3.8 percent.

How does Singapore deliver world-class health care while spending less than any other developed nation? The answer is a unique combination of government mandates to encourage competition, high out-of-pocket costs for consumers, and laws requiring people to save for future health expenditures.

Competition is encouraged by forcing hospitals to post prices for each of their services. Armed with this information, patients can shop around for the best deal. The government also

publishes the track record of each hospital on each service so that consumers can make informed decisions about quality as well as price. With consumers choosing on the basis of cost and quality, local hospitals compete to reduce costs and improve quality.

Singapore also insists upon high out-of-pocket costs in order to avoid the overconsumption and high prices that result when insurance policies pick up most of the price for medical procedures. Indeed, out-of-pocket spending represents about 92 percent of all non-government health-care spending in Singapore compared to just less than 10 percent in Canada.

Having to pay for most medical spending out of pocket, however, means that Singapore's citizens are faced with having to pay for most of their health care themselves. How can this be done without bankrupting the average citizen? The answer is mandatory health savings accounts.

Singapore's citizens are required to save about 6 percent of their incomes into "MediSave" accounts. MediSave deposits are private property so that people have an incentive to spend the money in their accounts wisely. In addition, the citizens of Singapore also know that they won't be left helpless if the money in their MediSave accounts runs out. The government subsidizes the health care of those who have exhausted their MediSave accounts as well as the health care of the poor and others who have not been able to accumulate much money in their MediSave accounts.

Given the present universal health care system in Canada, which according to most Canadians functions quite well, it is unlikely that they would opt for a Singapore-style "MediSave" system.

Question

What are the three major cost-reducing features of the Singapore health care system? Which one do you think has the largest effect on holding down the price of medical care in Singapore? How difficult do you think it would be to implement the missing elements in Canada? Explain.

:: CHAPTER SUMMARY

17.1 :: INFORMATION FAILURES

- Asymmetric information between sellers and buyers can cause markets to fail. The moral hazard problem occurs when people alter their behaviour after they sign a contract or reach an agreement, imposing costs on the other party. The adverse selection problem occurs when one party to a contract or agreement takes advantage of the other party's inadequate information, resulting in an unanticipated loss to the latter party.

17.2 :: THE ECONOMICS OF HEALTH CARE

- Special characteristics of the health care market include (a) ethical and equity considerations; (b) an imbalance of information between consumers and suppliers; (c) the moral hazard problem; (d) the adverse selection problem; (e) the presence of positive externalities, (f) the payment of most health care expenses by public insurance.

17.3 :: PUBLIC CHOICE THEORY

- Public choice theory suggests that governments may sometimes suffer from government failures, situations in which governments fail to allocate resources efficiently either because majority voting fails to correctly indicate voter preferences or because principal–agent problems cause government officials to pursue private goals to the detriment of their constituents.

- Majority voting creates a possibility of (a) an underallocation or an overallocation of resources to a particular public good, and (b) inconsistent voting outcomes.

- The median-voter model predicts that, under majority rule, the person holding the middle position on an issue will determine the outcome of an election involving that issue.

- Special interests can succeed in perpetuating policies that are opposed by the majority of voters because the costs of organizing and motivating groups to take political action increase with group size. This collective action problem implies that special interests can perpetuate unpopular policies as long as the costs of organizing an opposition exceed the costs that the general public is currently suffering as a result of those policies.

17.4 :: GOVERNMENT FAILURE

- Public choice theorists cite several reasons for government inefficiency in providing public goods and services: (a) There are powerful incentives for politicians to support rent seeking and support special-interest legislation; (b) Politicians may be biased in favour of programs with immediate and clear-cut benefits and difficult-to-identify costs, and against programs with immediate and easily identified costs and vague or deferred benefits; (c) Citizens as voters and governmental representatives face limited and bundled choices as to public goods and services, whereas consumers in the private sector can be highly selective in their choices; (d) Government bureaucracies have less incentive to operate efficiently than do private businesses; (e) Political corruption may cause governmental resources or actions to be misdirected

:: TERMS AND CONCEPTS

:: QUESTIONS

1. Because medical records are private, an individual applying for private health insurance in Canada will know more about his own health conditions than will the insurance companies to which he is applying for medical services not covered by our national health care system. Is this likely to increase or decrease the insurance premium that he will be offered? Why?   [LO17.1 and 17.2]

2. Why is it in the interest of new homebuyers and builders of new homes to have government building codes and building inspectors?   [LO17.1]

3. Place an "M" beside the items in the following list that describe a moral hazard problem and an "A" beside those that describe an adverse selection problem: [LO17.1]

    a. A person with a terminal illness buys several life insurance policies through the mail.

    b. A person drives carelessly because he or she has automobile insurance.

    c. A person who intends to "torch" his warehouse takes out a large fire insurance policy.

d. A professional athlete who has a guaranteed contract fails to stay in shape during the off-season.

e. A woman who anticipates having a large family takes a job with a firm that offers exceptional child care benefits.

4. Explain how affirmative and negative majority votes can sometimes lead to inefficient allocations of resources to public goods. Is this problem likely to be greater under a benefits-received or an ability-to-pay tax system? Use the information in Figure 17-2 to show how society might be better off if Adams were allowed to buy votes. [LO17.3]

5. Explain the paradox of voting through reference to the accompanying table, which shows the ranking of three public goods by voters Jay, Dave, and Conan: [LO17.3]

| Public good | RANKINGS | | |
	Jay	Dave	Conan
Courthouse	2nd choice	1st choice	3rd choice
School	3rd choice	2nd choice	1st choice
Park	1st choice	3rd choice	2nd choice

6. Suppose there are only five people in a society and each favours one of the five highway construction options listed in Table 5-4 ("No new construction" is one of the five options) Explain which of these highway options will be selected using a majority paired-choice vote. Will this option be the optimal size of the project from an economic perspective? [LO17.3]

7. Jean Baptiste Colbert was the Minister of Finance under King Louis XIV of France. He famously observed that "The art of taxation consists in so plucking the goose as to obtain the largest possible amount of feathers with the smallest possible amount of hissing." How does his comment relate to special interests and the collective action problem? [LO17.3]

8. What is rent seeking and how does it differ from the kinds of profit maximization and profit seeking that we discussed in previous chapters? Provide an actual or a hypothetical example of rent seeking by: firms in an industry, a union, and a professional association (for example, physicians, school teachers, or lawyers). Why do elected officials often accommodate rent-seeking behaviour, particularly by firms, unions, and professional groups located in their home ridings? [LO17.4]

9. How does the problem of limited and bundled choice in the public sector relate to economic efficiency? Why are public bureaucracies possibly less efficient than business firms [LO17.4]

10. Explain the reasoning behind the following statement: "Politicians would make more rational economic decisions if they weren't running for re-election every few years." [LO17.4]

:: PROBLEMS

1. Consider a used car market with asymmetric information. Owners of used cars know what their vehicles are worth but have no way of credibly demonstrating those values to potential buyers. Thus, potential buyers must always worry that the used car they are being offered may be a low-quality "lemon." [LO17.1]

a. Suppose that there are equal numbers of good and bad used cars in the market and that good used cars are worth $13,000 while bad used cars are worth $5,000. What is the average value of a used car?

b. By how much does the average value exceed the value of a bad used car? By how much does the value of a good used car exceed the average value?

c. Would a potential seller of a good used car be willing to accept the average value as payment for her vehicle?

d. If a buyer negotiates with a seller to purchase the seller's used car for a price equal to the average value, is the car more likely to be good or bad?

e. Will the used car market come to feature mostly—if not exclusively—lemons? How much will used cars end up costing if all the good cars are withdrawn?

Credits

Glossary

accounting profit The total revenue of a firm less its explicit costs.

adverse selection problem A problem arising when information known to one party to a contract is not known to the other party, causing the latter to incur major costs.

aggregate A collection of specific economic units treated as if they were one unit.

allocative efficiency The distribution of resources among firms and industries to produce the goods most wanted by society.

anchoring The idea that irrelevant information can unconsciously influence people's feelings about the *status quo*.

asymmetric information A situation in which one party to a market transaction has much more information about a product or service than the other does.

average fixed cost (AFC) A firm's total fixed cost divided by output.

average product (AP) The total output divided by the quantity of that employed resource.

average revenue Total revenue from the sale of a product divided by the quantity of the product sold.

average total cost (ATC) A firm's total cost divided by output.

average variable cost (AVC) A firm's total variable cost divided by output.

barriers to entry Anything that artificially prevents the entry of firms into an industry.

barter The exchange of one good or service for another good or service.

behavioural economics The branch of economics that combines insights from economics, psychology, and neuroscience to better understand those situations in which actual choice behaviour deviates from the predictions made by earlier theories.

bilateral monopoly A market in which there is a single seller (monopoly) and a single buyer (monopsony).

bond A financial device through which a borrower (a firm or government) is obligated to pay the principal and interest on a loan at a specific date in the future.

break-even point An output at which a firm makes a normal profit but not an economic profit.

budget constraint The limit that a consumer's income (and the prices that must be paid for goods and services) imposes on the ability of that consumer to obtain goods and services.

budget line A schedule or curve that shows various combinations of two products a consumer can purchase with a specific money income.

businesses Economic entities (firms) that purchase factors of production and provide goods and services to the economy.

capital Human-made resources (buildings, machinery, and equipment) used to produce goods and services.

capital goods Goods that do not directly satisfy human wants.

cartel A formal agreement among firms in an industry to set the price of a product and establish the outputs of the individual firms or to divide the market among them.

change in demand A change in the quantity demanded of a good or service at every price; a shift of the entire demand curve to the right (an increase in demand) or to the left (a decrease in demand).

change in quantity demanded A movement from one point to another on a fixed demand curve.

change in quantity supplied A movement from one point to another on a fixed supply curve.

change in supply A change in the quantity supplied of a good or service at every price; a shift of the supply curve to the left or right.

circular flow diagram The flow of resources from households to firms and of products from firms to households. These flows are accompanied by reverse flows of money from firms to households and from households to firms.

Coase theorem Under the right conditions, private individuals can often negotiate their own mutually agreeable solutions to externality problems through individual bargaining with no need of government intervention.

collusion A situation in which firms act together and in agreement to fix prices, divide a market, or otherwise restrict competition.

command system An economic system in which most property resources are owned by the government and economic decisions are made by a central government body.

compensating differences Differences in the wages received by workers in different jobs to compensate for nonmonetary differences in the jobs.

competition The presence in a market of a large number of independent buyers and sellers competing with one another and the freedom of buyers and sellers to enter and leave the market.

competition policy The laws and government actions designed to prevent monopoly and promote competition.

Competition Tribunal A government body adjudicating under a civil law framework that permits the issuing of remedial orders to restore and maintain competition in the market.

complementary goods Products and services that are used together.

compound interest The total interest that cumulates over time on money placed into an interest-bearing account.

concentration ratio The percentage of the total sales of an industry produced and sold by an industry's largest firms.

conglomerate merger The merger of a firm in one industry with a firm in another industry or region.

constant-cost industry An industry in which the entry of new firms has no effect on resource prices and thus no effect on production costs.

constant opportunity cost An opportunity cost that remains the same for each additional unit as a consumer (or society) shifts purchases (production) from one product to another along a straight-line budget line (production possibilities curve).

constant returns to scale The range of output between the points where economies of scale end and diseconomies of scale begin.

consumer goods Products and services that satisfy human wants directly.

consumer sovereignty Determination by consumers of the types and quantities of goods and services that will be produced with the scarce resources of the economy.

consumer surplus The difference between the maximum price consumers are willing to pay for a product and the actual price.

corporation A legal entity chartered by the federal or provincial government that operates as a body distinct and separate from the individuals who own it.

cost–benefit analysis Comparing the marginal costs with the marginal benefits to decide whether to employ more or less resources in that project.

creative destruction The hypothesis that the creation of new products and production methods simultaneously destroys the market power of firms that are wedded to existing products and older ways of doing business.

credible threat A statement of harmful intent by one party that the other party views as believable.

cross elasticity of demand The ratio of the percentage change in quantity demanded of one good to the percentage change in price of some other good.

deadweight loss The loss of consumer surplus and producer surplus when output is either above or below its efficient level.

decreasing-cost industry An industry in which the entry of firms lowers resource prices and thus decreases production costs.

demand A schedule or curve that shows the various amounts of a product that consumers are willing and able to purchase at each of a series of possible prices during a specified period of time.

demand curve A curve illustrating the inverse (negative) relationship between the quantity demanded of a good or service and its price, other things equal.

demand-side market failure When demand curves fail to reflect consumers' full willingness to pay for goods or services.

demographers Scientists who study trends in human populations.

dependent variable A variable that changes as a consequence of a change in some other (independent) variable; the "effect" or outcome.

derived demand The demand for a factor that depends on the products it can be used to produce.

determinants of demand Factors other than price that determine the quantities demanded of a good or service.

determinants of supply Causes other than price that determine the quantities supplied of a good or service.

differentiated oligopoly An oligopoly in which the firms produce a differentiated product.

diminishing marginal utility As a consumer increases the consumption of a good or service, the marginal utility obtained from each additional unit of the good or service decreases.

direct relationship The (positive) relationship between two variables that change in the same direction, for example, product price and quantity supplied.

diseconomies of scale Increases in the average total cost of producing a product as the firm increases plant size (output) in the long run.

division of labour Dividing the work required to produce a product into a number of different tasks that are performed by different workers.

dollar votes The "votes" that consumers and entrepreneurs cast for the production of consumer and capital goods, respectively, when they purchase them in product and resource markets.

dominant strategy In game theory, an option that is better than any alternative option regardless of what the other firm does.

economic cost A value equal to the quantity of other products that cannot be produced when resources are instead used to make a particular product.

economic growth An outward shift in the production possibilities curve that results from an increase in factor supplies or quality or an improvement in technology.

economic model A simplified picture of economic reality; an abstract generalization.

economic perspective A viewpoint that envisions individuals and institutions making rational decisions by comparing the marginal benefits and marginal costs associated with their actions.

economic principle A statement about economic behaviour or the economy that enables prediction of the probable effects of certain actions.

economic problem The need to make choices because society's material wants for goods and services are unlimited but the resources available to satisfy these wants are limited (scarce).

economic profit A firm's total revenue less its economic costs (both explicit costs and implicit costs).

economic (pure) profit The total revenue of a firm less its economic costs (which includes both explicit costs and implicit costs); also called above normal profit.

economic rent The price paid for the use of land and other natural resources, the supply of which is fixed (perfectly inelastic).

economic resources The land, labour, capital, and entrepreneurial ability that are used in the production of goods and services.

economic system A particular set of institutional arrangements and a coordinating mechanism for producing goods and services.

economics The social science concerned with how individuals, institutions, and society make optimal (best) choices under conditions of scarcity.

economies of scale Reductions in the average total cost of producing a product as the firm increases plant size (output) in the long run.

efficiency loss of a tax The loss of net benefits to society because a tax reduces the production and consumption of a taxed good below the level of allocative efficiency.

efficiency losses (or deadweight losses) Reductions of combined consumer and producer surplus associated with underproduction or overproduction of a product.

elastic demand Product or resource demand with a price elasticity coefficient that is greater than 1.

elasticity of factor demand The percentage change in factor quantity divided by the percentage change in factor price.

employment equity Policies and programs that establish targets of increased employment and promotion for women and minorities.

empty threat A statement of harmful intent that is easily dismissed by the second party because the threat is not viewed as believable.

endowment effect The tendency that people have to put a higher valuation on anything that they currently possess (are endowed with) than on identical items that they do not.

entrepreneurial ability The human talents that combine the other resources to produce a product, make non-routine decisions, innovate, and bear risks.

equilibrium position The combination of products that yields the greatest satisfaction or utility.

equilibrium price The price in a competitive market at which the quantity demanded and the quantity supplied are equal.

equilibrium quantity The quantity demanded and supplied at the equilibrium price in a competitive market.

excess capacity Plant or equipment that is underused because the firm is producing less than the minimum-ATC output.

exchange rate The rate of exchange of one nation's currency for another nation's currency.

excludability A situation in which sellers can keep people who do not pay for a product from obtaining its benefits.

exclusive unionism The practice of a labour union of restricting the supply of skilled union labour to increase the wages received by union members.

expected-rate-of-return curve The increase in profit a firm anticipates it will obtain by investing in R&D.

explicit costs The monetary payments a firm must make to an outsider to obtain a resource.

externality Benefits or costs from production or consumption accruing without compensation to nonbuyers and nonsellers of the product.

extraction costs All costs associated with extracting a natural resource and readying it for sale.

factor market A market in which households sell and firms buy factors of production.

factors of production Economic resources: land, labour, capital, and entrepreneurial ability.

fair-return price The price of a product that enables its producer to obtain a normal profit and that is equal to the average cost of producing it.

first-mover advantage In game theory, the benefit obtained by the party that moves first in a sequential game.

fishery A stock of fish or other marine animals that is composed of a distinct group, for example Newfoundland cod, Pacific tuna, or Alaska crab.

fishery collapse A rapid decline in a fishery's population because the fish are being harvested more quickly than they can reproduce.

fixed costs Costs that in total do not change when the firm changes its output.

foreign exchange market A market in which the money (currency) of one nation can be used to purchase (can be exchanged for) the money of another nation.

four-firm concentration ratio The percentage of total industry sales accounted for by the top four firms in the industry.

framing effects Changes in people's preferences that are caused by new information that alters the frame used to define whether situations are gains or losses.

freedom of choice The freedom of owners of property resources to employ or dispose of them as they see fit, and of consumers to spend their incomes in a manner that they think is appropriate.

freedom of enterprise The freedom of firms to obtain economic resources, to use these resources to produce products of the firm's own choosing, and to sell their products in markets of their choice.

free-rider problem The inability of potential providers of an economically desirable but indivisible good or service to obtain payment from those who benefit, because the exclusion principle is not applicable.

future value The amount to which some current amount of money will grow if the interest earned on the amount is left to compound over time.

game theory model A means of analyzing the pricing behaviour of oligopolists using the theory of strategy associated with games such as chess and bridge.

generalizations Statements of the nature of the relation between two or more sets of facts.

government failure Inefficiencies in resource allocation caused by problems in the operation of the public sector (government).

guiding function of prices The ability of price changes to bring about changes in the quantities of products and resources demanded and supplied.

Herfindahl index The sum of the squared percentage market shares of all firms in the industry.

homogeneous oligopoly An oligopoly in which the firms produce a standardized product.

horizontal axis The "left–right" or "west–east" axis on a graph or grid.

horizontal merger A merger between two competitors selling similar products in the same market.

household One or more persons occupying a housing unit, who buy businesses' goods and services in the product market using income derived from selling resources in the factor market.

human capital Any expenditure to improve the education, skills, health, or mobility of workers, with an expectation of greater productivity and thus a positive return on the investment.

imperfect competition The market models of monopoly, monopolistic competition, and oligopoly considered as a group.

implicit costs The monetary income a firm sacrifices when it uses a resource it owns rather than supplying the resource in the market; equals what the resource could have earned in the best-paying alternative employment (including a normal profit).

import competition The competition domestic firms encounter from the products and services of foreign producers.

incentive function of price The inducement that an increase in the price of a commodity gives to sellers to make more of it available.

incentive pay plan A compensation structure, such as piece rates, commissions, royalties, bonuses, stock options, and profit sharing, that ties worker pay directly to performance.

inclusive unionism The practice of a labour union including as members all workers employed in an industry.

income effect A change in the price of a product changes a consumer's real income (purchasing power) and thus the quantity of the product purchased.

income elasticity of demand Measures the responsiveness of consumer purchases to income changes.

increasing-cost industry An industry in which the entry of new firms raises resource prices and thus increases production costs.

independent variable The variable causing a change in some other (dependent) variable.

indifference curve A curve showing the different combinations of two products that yield the same satisfaction or utility to a consumer.

indifference map A series of indifference curves, each of which represents a different level of total utility and together show the preferences of the consumer.

individual transferable quota (ITQ) A limit on the total number or tonnage of fish that individual fishers can harvest during a particular time period.

inelastic demand Product or resource demand with a price elasticity coefficient that is less than 1.

inferior goods Goods or services whose consumption falls when income increases and rises when income decreases, price remaining constant.

innovation The first successful commercial introduction of a new product, the first use of a new method of production, or the creation of a new form of business organization.

insurable risks Those risks for which it is possible to buy insurance.

interindustry competition The competition between the products of one industry and the products of another industry.

inverse relationship The (negative) relationship between two variables that change in opposite directions, for example, product price and quantity demanded.

investment Spending for the production and accumulation of capital.

invisible hand The tendency of firms and resource suppliers seeking to further their own self-interests in competitive markets to also promote the interest of society as a whole.

labour The physical and mental talents of individuals used in producing goods and services.

land Natural resources used to produce goods and services.

law of demand Other things equal, as price falls the quantity demanded rises, and vice versa.

law of diminishing marginal utility As a consumer increases consumption of a good or service, the marginal utility obtained from each additional unit of the good or service decreases.

law of diminishing returns As successive increments of a variable factor are added to a fixed factor, the marginal product of the variable factor will eventually decrease.

law of increasing opportunity costs As the production of a good increases, the opportunity cost of producing an additional unit rises.

law of supply The principle that, other things equal, an increase in the price of a product will increase the quantity of it supplied, and conversely for a price decrease.

least-cost combination of factors The quantity of each factor a firm must employ to produce a particular output at the lowest total cost.

legal cartel theory of regulation The hypothesis that some industries seek regulation or want to maintain regulation so that they may form a legal cartel.

limited liability Restriction of the maximum loss to a predetermined amount for the owners (stockholders) of a corporation, the maximum loss is the amount they paid for their shares of stock.

loanable funds theory of interest The concept that the supply of and demand for loanable funds determines the equilibrium rate of interest.

logrolling The trading of votes by legislators to secure favourable outcomes on decisions concerning the provision of public goods and quasi-public goods.

long run A period of time long enough to enable producers to change the quantities of all the resources they employ.

long-run supply curve A curve that shows the prices at which a purely competitive industry will make various quantities of the product available in the long run.

loss averse A characteristic that makes losses feel more intense than the pleasure generated by gains.

macroeconomics The part of economics concerned with the economy as a whole.

marginal analysis The comparison of marginal ("extra" or "additional") benefits and marginal costs, usually for decision making.

marginal cost (MC) The additional cost of producing one more unit of output.

marginal cost = marginal benefit rule For a government project, marginal benefit should equal marginal cost to produce maximum benefit to society.

marginal factor cost (MFC) The amount that each additional unit of a factor adds to the firm's total (factor) cost.

marginal product (MP) The extra output associated with adding a unit of a variable factor to the production process.

marginal productivity theory of income distribution The contention that the distribution of income is fair when each unit of each factor receives a money payment equal to its marginal contribution to the firm's revenue (its marginal revenue product).

marginal rate of substitution (MRS) The rate at which a consumer is prepared to substitute one good for another (from a given combination of goods) and remain equally satisfied (have the same total utility).

marginal revenue The change in total revenue that results from selling one more unit of a firm's product.

marginal revenue product (MRP) The change in total revenue from employing one additional unit of a factor.

marginal revenue productivity How much workers contribute to their employers' revenue.

marginal utility The extra utility a consumer obtains from the consumption of one additional unit of a product.

market Any institution or mechanism that brings together buyers and sellers of particular goods, services, or resources for the purpose of exchange.

market failures When markets fail to function properly, whether by overproducing, underproducing, or failing to produce economically desirable goods.

market period A period in which producers are unable to change the quantity of a product they produce in response to a change in its price.

market system An economic system in which property resources are privately owned and markets and prices are used to direct and coordinate economic activities.

MC = MB rule For a government project, marginal benefit should equal marginal cost to produce maximum benefit to society.

median-voter model The theory that under majority rule the median (middle) voter will be in the dominant position to determine the outcome of an election.

medium of exchange Items sellers generally accept and buyers generally use to pay for a good or service.

mental accounting The idea that people sometimes look at consumption options in isolation, thereby irrationally failing to look at all of their options simultaneously.

microeconomics The part of economics concerned with such individual units as industries, firms, and households.

midpoint formula A method for calculating price elasticity of demand or price elasticity of supply that averages the two prices and two quantities as the reference points for competing percentages.

minimum efficient scale (MES) The lowest level of output at which a firm can minimize long-run average costs.

minimum wage The lowest wage employers may legally pay for an hour of work.

money Any item that is generally acceptable to sellers in exchange for goods and services.

monopolistic competition A market structure in which a relatively large number of sellers produce differentiated products.

monopoly An industry in which one firm is the sole producer or seller of a product or service for which no close substitutes exist.

monopsony A market structure in which there is only a single buyer.

moral hazard problem The possibility that individuals will change their behaviour as the result of a contract or agreement.

MR = MC rule A method of determining the total output at which economic profit is at a maximum (or losses are at a minimum).

MRP = MFC rule To maximize economic profit (or minimize losses) a firm should use the quantity of a factor at which its marginal revenue product is equal to its marginal factor cost.

mutual interdependence A situation in which a change in strategy (usually price) by one firm will affect the sales and profits of other firms.

Nash equilibrium An outcome in a non-cooperative game in which players choose their best strategy given the present strategies the others have chosen.

natural monopoly An industry in which economies of scale are so great that a single firm can produce the product at a lower average total cost than if more than one firm produced the product.

negative externality A cost imposed without compensation on third parties by the production or consumption of sellers or buyers. Example: A manufacturer dumps toxic chemicals into a river, killing the fish sought by sport fishers. An external cost or a spillover cost.

negative-sum game A game in which the gains (+) and losses (−) add up to some amount less than zero.

net benefits The total benefits of some activity or policy less the total costs of that activity or policy.

network effects Increases in the value of a product to each user, including existing users, as the total number of users rises.

nominal interest rate The interest rate expressed in terms of annual amounts currently charged for interest and not adjusted for inflation.

nominal wage The amount of money received by a worker per unit of time (hour, day, etc.).

noncompeting groups Collections of workers in the economy who do not compete with each other for employment because the skills and training of the workers in one group are substantially different from those in other groups.

non-excludability When there is no effective way of excluding individuals from the benefit of the good once it has been created.

nonprice competition A selling strategy in which one firm tries to distinguish its product or service from all competing ones based on attributes other than price.

nonrenewable natural resources Resources that either are in actual fixed supply or that renew so slowly as to be in virtual fixed supply when viewed from a human time perspective.

nonrivalry When the consumption of a good by one person does not preclude consumption of the good by others.

normal goods Goods or services whose consumption rises when income increases and falls when income decreases, price remaining constant.

normal profit The payment made by a firm to obtain and retain entrepreneurial ability.

normative economics The part of economics involving value judgments about what the economy should be like.

occupational licensing The laws of provincial or municipal governments that require a worker to satisfy certain specified requirements and obtain a licence from a licensing board before engaging in a particular occupation.

oligopoly A market structure in which a few large firms produce homogeneous or differentiated products.

one-time game A game in which firms select their optimal strategy in a single time period without regard to possible interactions in subsequent time periods.

opportunity cost The amount of other products that must be forgone or sacrificed to produce a unit of a product.

optimal reduction of an externality The point at which society's marginal cost and marginal benefit of reducing that externality are equal.

other-things-equal assumption The assumption that factors other than those being considered are held constant.

output effect An increase in the price of one input will increase a firm's production costs and reduce its level of output, thus reducing the demand for other inputs (and vice versa).

paradox of voting A situation in which paired-choice majority voting fails to provide a consistent ranking of society's preferences for public goods or services.

partnership An unincorporated firm owned and operated by two or more people.

perfect competition A market structure in which a very large number of firms produce a standardized product.

perfectly competitive labour market A factor market in which a large number of firms demand a particular type of labour supplied by a large number of nonunion workers.

perfectly elastic demand Quantity demanded can be any amount at a particular price.

perfectly inelastic demand Quantity demanded does not respond to a change in price.

perfectly inelastic supply Product or resource supply in which price can be of any amount at a particular quantity of the product or resource demanded; quantity supplied does not respond to a change in price; graphs as a vertical supply curve.

political corruption The unlawful misdirection of governmental resources or actions that occurs when government officials abuse their entrusted powers for personal gain.

positive economics The analysis of facts to establish cause-and-effect relationships.

positive externality A benefit obtained without compensation by third parties from the production or consumption of sellers or buyers.

Example: A beekeeper benefits when a neighbouring farmer plants clover. An external benefit or spillover benefit.

positive-sum game A game in which the gains (+) and losses (−) add up to more than zero.

post hoc, ergo propter hoc **fallacy** Incorrectly reasoning that when one event precedes another the first event must have caused the second event.

present value Today's value of some amount of money that is to be received sometime in the future.

price ceiling A legally established maximum price for a good or service.

price discrimination Selling a product to different buyers at different prices when the price differences are not justified by differences in cost.

price elasticity of demand A measure of the responsiveness of buyers to a change in the price of a product or resource.

price elasticity of supply The ratio of the percentage change in quantity supplied of a product to the percentage change in its price.

price floor A legally established minimum price.

price leadership An implicit understanding oligopolists use that has the dominant firm initiate price changes and all other firms follow.

price-taker A firm in a purely competitive market that cannot change market price, but can only adjust to it.

principal–agent problem A problem associated with possible differences in the interests of corporate shareholders (principals) and the executives (agents) they hire.

prisoner's dilemma A type of game between two players that shows the difficulty of cooperating when the two cannot communicate with each other, even when it is in their best interests to cooperate.

private goods Goods or services that are individually consumed and that can be profitably provided by privately owned firms because they can exclude nonpayers from receiving the benefits.

private property The right of private persons and firms to obtain,

own, control, employ, dispose of, and bequeath land, capital, and other property.

producer surplus The difference between the actual price producers are willing to accept and the minimum acceptable price.

product differentiation A strategy in which one firm's product is distinguished from competing products by means of its design, related services, quality, location, or other attribute (except price).

product market A market in which products are sold by firms and bought by households.

production possibilities curve A curve showing the different combinations of goods or services that can be produced in a full-employment, full-production economy where the available supplies of resources and technology are fixed.

production possibilities table A table showing the different combinations of two products that can be used produced with a specific set of resources in a full-employment, full-production economy.

productive efficiency The production of a good in the least costly way.

profit-maximizing combination of factors The quantity of each factor a firm must employ to maximize its profits or minimize its losses.

prospect theory An explanation of how consumers plan for and deal with life's ups and downs, as well as of why they often appear narrow minded and fail to "see the big picture."

public choice theory The economic analysis of government decision-making, politics, and elections.

public goods Goods or services that can be simultaneously consumed by everyone, and from which no one can be excluded, even if they don't pay for them.

public interest theory of regulation The theory that industrial regulation is necessary to keep a natural monopoly from charging monopoly prices and thus harming consumers and society.

pure rate of interest The hypothetical interest rate that would serve purely and solely to compensate lenders for their willingness to patiently forgo alternative consumption and investment opportunities until their money is repaid.

quasi-public goods Goods provided by the government that fit the economist's definition of a public good but can be produced in such a way that exclusion would be possible.

rational behaviour Human behaviour that seeks to maximize total utility.

rationing function of prices The ability of the competitive forces of supply and demand to establish a price at which selling and buying decisions are consistent.

real interest rate The interest rate expressed in dollars of constant value (adjusted for inflation); equal to the nominal interest rate less the expected rate of inflation.

real wage The amount of goods and services a worker can purchase with a nominal wage.

renewable natural resources Resources that are capable of renewing themselves if they are harvested at moderate rates.

rent seeking The actions by persons, firms, or unions to gain special benefits from government at the taxpayers' or someone else's expense.

rent-seeking behaviour The actions by persons, firms, or unions to gain special benefits from government at taxpayers' or someone else's expense.

repeated game A game that is played again sometime after the previous game ends.

replacement rate The birth rate necessary to keep the size of a population constant without relying on immigration.

rivalry A situation in which when one person buys and consumes a product, it is not available for another person to buy and consume.

scientific method The systematic pursuit of knowledge through observing a problem collecting data, and formulating and testing hypotheses to obtain theories, principles, and laws.

self-interest That which each firm, property owner, worker, and consumer believes is best for itself.

sequential game A game in which the parties make their moves in turn, with one party making the first move, followed by the other party making the next move, and so on.

shortage The amount by which the quantity demanded of a product exceeds the quantity supplied at a specific (below-equilibrium) price.

short run A period of time in which producers are able to change the quantities of some but not all of the resources they employ.

short-run supply curve A curve that shows the quantities of the product a firm in a purely competitive industry will offer to sell at various prices in the short run.

shutdown case The circumstance in which a firm would experience a loss greater than its total fixed cost if it were to produce any output greater than zero; alternatively, a situation in which a firm would cease to operate when the price at which it can sell its product is less than its average variable cost.

simultaneous consumption A product's ability to satisfy a large number of consumers at the same time.

simultaneous game A game in which both parties choose their strategies and execute them at the same time.

slope of a straight line The ratio of the vertical change (the rise or fall) to the horizontal change (the run) between any two points on a line. The slope of an up sloping line is positive, reflecting a direct relationship between two variables; the slope of a down sloping line is negative, reflecting an inverse relationship between two variables.

socially optimal price The price of a product that results in the most efficient allocation of an economy's resources.

social regulation Government regulation of the conditions under which goods are produced, the physical characteristics of goods, and the impact of the production on society.

sole proprietorship An unincorporated firm owned and operated by one person.

special-interest effect Any result of government promotion of the interests (goals) of a small group at the expense of a much larger group.

specialization The use of the resources of an individual, a firm, a region, or a nation to produce one or a few goods and services.

static economy An economy in which factor supplies, technological knowledge, and consumer tastes are constant and unchanging.

status quo The current situation from which gains and losses are calculated.

strategic behaviour Self-interested behaviour that takes into account the reactions of others.

substitute goods Products or services that can be used in place of each other.

substitution effect A firm will purchase more of an input whose relative price has declined and use less of an input whose relative price has increased.

supply A schedule or curve that shows the amounts of a product that producers are willing and able to make available for sale at each of a series of possible prices during a specific period.

supply curve A curve illustrating the positive (direct) relationship between the quantity supplied of a good or service and its price, other things equal.

supply-side market failure When supply curves fail to reflect the full cost of producing a good or service.

surplus The amount by which the quantity supplied of a product exceeds the quantity demanded at a specific (above-equilibrium) price.

tacit understanding Any method by competing oligopolists to set prices and outputs that does not involve outright collusion.

technological advance New and better goods and services and new and better ways of producing or distributing them.

theoretical economics The process of deriving and applying economic theories and principles.

time value of money The idea that a specific amount of money is more valuable to a person the sooner it is received because the money can be placed in a financial account or investment and earn compound interest over time.

total allowable catch (TAC) A limit on the total number or tonnage of fish that fishers, collectively, can harvest during a particular time period.

total cost The sum of fixed cost and variable cost.

total fertility rate The average total number of children that a woman is expected to have during her lifetime.

total product (TP) The total output of a particular good or service produced by a firm.

total revenue (TR) The total amount a seller receives from the sale of a product in a particular time period.

total-revenue test A test to determine elasticity of demand between any two prices, by noting what happens to total revenue when price changes.

total surplus The surplus created by combining the consumer and producer surpluses.

total utility The total amount of satisfaction derived from the consumption of a single product or a combination of products.

tradeoff The sacrifice of some or all of one economic goal, good, or service to achieve some other goal, good, or service.

tying contract A requirement imposed by a seller that a buyer purchase another (or other) of its products as a condition for buying a desired product.

uninsurable risks Those risks for which it is impossible to buy insurance.

unit elasticity Demand or supply with a price elasticity coefficient that is equal to 1.

user cost The cost to the user of extracting a resource; current extraction and use means lower future extraction and use.

utility The want-satisfying power of a good or service; the satisfaction a person gets from consuming a good or service.

utility-maximizing rule To obtain the greatest utility, the consumer should allocate money income so that the last dollar spent on each good or service yields the same marginal utility.

variable costs Costs that increase or decrease with a firm's output.

vertical axis The "up–down" or "north–south" axis on a graph or grid.

vertical intercept The point at which a line meets the vertical axis of a graph.

vertical merger The merger of firms engaged in different stages of the production process of a final product.

wage differentials The difference between the wage received by one worker or group of workers and that received by another worker or group of workers.

wage rate A price paid per unit of labour services.

X-inefficiency The production of output, whatever its level, at higher average (and total) cost than is necessary.

zero-sum game A game in which the gains (+) and losses (−) add up to zero.

Index